Services Marketing

Integrating Customer Focus Across the Firm

Seventh Edition

Valarie A. Zeithaml
University of North Carolina at Chapel Hill

Mary Jo Bitner
Arizona State University

Dwayne D. Gremler
Bowling Green State University

McGraw Hill Education

SERVICES MARKETING: INTEGRATING CUSTOMER FOCUS ACROSS THE FIRM, SEVENTH EDITION

Published by McGraw-Hill Education, 2 Penn Plaza, New York, NY 10121. Copyright © 2018 by McGraw-Hill Education. All rights reserved. Printed in the United States of America. Previous editions © 2013, 2009, and 2006. No part of this publication may be reproduced or distributed in any form or by any means, or stored in a database or retrieval system, without the prior written consent of McGraw-Hill Education, including, but not limited to, in any network or other electronic storage or transmission, or broadcast for distance learning.

Some ancillaries, including electronic and print components, may not be available to customers outside the United States.

This book is printed on acid-free paper.

4 5 6 7 8 9 QVS 22 21 20 19 18

ISBN 978-0-07-811210-2
MHID 0-07-811210-9

Chief Product Officer, SVP Products & Markets: *G. Scott Virkler*
Vice President, General Manager, Products & Markets: *Michael Ryan*
Vice President, Content Design & Delivery: *Betsy Whalen*
Managing Director: *Susan Gouijnstook*
Director, Product Development: *Meghan Campbell*
Product Developer: *Laura Hurst Spell*
Marketing Manager: *Elizabeth Schonagen*
Director, Content Design & Delivery: *Terri Schiesl*
Program Manager: *Mary Conzachi*
Content Project Managers: *Kelly Hart, Danielle Clement, Karen Jozefowicz*
Buyer: *Susan K. Culbertson*
Cover Design: *Studio Montage, St. Louis, MO*
Content Licensing Specialists: *Melissa Homer, Melisa Seegmiller*
Cover Image: *Peter Bernik/Shutterstock.com, Monkey Business Images Ltd/Getty Images*
Compositor: *MPS Limited*
Printer: *Quad/Graphics*

All credits appearing on page or at the end of the book are considered to be an extension of the copyright page.

Library of Congress Cataloging-in-Publication Data

Zeithaml, Valarie A., author. | Bitner, Mary Jo, author. | Gremler, Dwayne D., author.
  Services marketing : integrating customer focus across the firm/Valarie A. Zeithaml,
  Mary Jo Bitner, Dwayne D. Gremler.
  Seventh edition. | Dubuque : McGraw-Hill Education, 2017. |
  Revised edition of the authors' Services marketing, c2013.
  LCCN 2016059704 | ISBN 9780078112102 (hardback)
  LCSH: Service industries—Marketing. | Customer services. |
  Marketing. | BISAC: BUSINESS & ECONOMICS/Marketing/Multilevel.
  LCC HD9980.5 .Z45 2017 | DDC 658.8—dc23
  LC record available at https://lccn.loc.gov/2016059704

mheducation.com/highered

Aan mijn alleriefste, Jan Benedict Steenkamp—soul mate, inspiration, and biggest supporter. And to the three sparkling lights in my life: Jaiman, Milan, and Leela.

—V.A.Z.S.

To my husband, Rich, for his unending love and support.

—M.J.B.

To my wife, Candy, and daughters, Samantha and Mallory, for their many years of love, support, and encouragement.

—D.D.G.

About the Authors

Mary Jo Bitner (left), Dwayne Gremler,
and Valarie Zeithaml

Valarie A. Zeithaml *University of North Carolina–Chapel Hill*

VALARIE ZEITHAML is the David S. Van Pelt Family Professor of Marketing at the Kenan-Flagler Business School of the University of North Carolina at Chapel Hill. Since receiving her MBA and PhD in marketing from the Robert H. Smith School of Business at the University of Maryland, Dr. Zeithaml has devoted her career to researching and teaching the topics of service quality and services management. She is the co-author of *Delivering Quality Service: Balancing Customer Perceptions and Expectations* (The Free Press, 1990), now in its 20th printing, and *Driving Customer Equity: How Customer Lifetime Value Is Reshaping Corporate Strategy* (The Free Press, 2000). In 2002, *Driving Customer Equity* won the first Berry–American Marketing Association Book Prize for the best marketing book of the past three years. In 2014, she published *Profiting from Services and Solutions: What Product Companies Need to Know* with Mary Jo Bitner, Stephen Brown, and Jim Salas.

In 2008, Dr. Zeithaml won the Paul D. Converse Award from the American Marketing Association. The Converse Award, granted every four years to one or more persons, acknowledges enduring contributions to marketing through one or more journal articles, books, or a body of work. This work created the Gaps Model of Service Quality on which this textbook is based. In 2009, she received the American Marketing Association/Irwin/McGraw-Hill Distinguished Marketing Educator Award for lifetime leadership in marketing education and extensive contributions to the field of marketing. She won the 2012 Bullard Research Impact Award in recognition of the broad impact of research on the field, industry, and society, and was appointed an American Marketing Association Lifetime Fellow in 2015. The 2014 List of Thomson Reuters included her in the "2014 World's Most Influential Scientific Minds," reflecting citation data over the last 11 years that identified those scholars who published the highest impact work.

Dr. Zeithaml has won five teaching awards, including the Gerald Barrett Faculty Award from the University of North Carolina and the Fuqua School Outstanding MBA Teaching Award from Duke University. She is also the recipient of numerous research awards, including the Robert Ferber Consumer Research Award from the

Journal of Consumer Research; the Harold H. Maynard Award from the *Journal of Marketing;* the MSI Paul Root Award from the *Journal of Marketing;* the Jagdish Sheth Award from the *Journal of the Academy of Marketing Science;* and the William F. O'Dell Award from the *Journal of Marketing Research.* She has consulted with more than 60 service and product companies. Dr. Zeithaml served on the Board of Directors of the American Marketing Association from 2000 to 2003 and was an Academic Trustee of the Marketing Science Institute between 2000 and 2006. She is currently Chairperson of the Board of the American Marketing Association.

Mary Jo Bitner   *Arizona State University*

MARY JO BITNER is the co-executive director of the Center for Services Leadership, Edward M. Carson Chair in Service Marketing, and professor of marketing at the W. P. Carey School of Business, Arizona State University (ASU). In her career as a professor and researcher, Dr. Bitner has been recognized as one of the founders and pioneers in the field of service marketing and management worldwide. At ASU she was a founding faculty member of the Center for Services Leadership and has been a leader in its emergence as the premier university-based center for the study of services marketing and management. Her professional leadership in the discipline includes serving on the Board of the American Marketing Association from 2011–2014, and serving as Editor in Chief of the *Journal of Service Research* from 2013–2017.

Dr. Bitner led the development of the W. P. Carey MBA marketing and service leadership specialization, a unique full-year focus within the nationally ranked W. P. Carey MBA. The degree specialization has existed for nearly 20 years, and alumni now work in companies worldwide, leading the implementation of service and customer-focused strategies.

Dr. Bitner has received several teaching awards and research recognition for her contributions to the discipline. Dr. Bitner was awarded the Career Contributions to the Service Discipline Award presented by the American Marketing Association. She was also named an IBM Faculty Fellow and received the inaugural International Society for Service Industry Professionals (ISSIP) Fellow Award for Lifetime Achievement in Service Science in 2013, and the Marketing Innovator Award from the Marketing Management Association in 2014. At ASU, Dr. Bitner has received the W. P. Carey School of Business Graduate Teaching Excellence Award and the award for Outstanding Professor, PhD Programs. She served as a Distinguished Faculty member at Fudan University, Shanghai, China and taught for many years in ASU's EMBA program in China.

Dr. Bitner has taught and consulted with numerous service and manufacturing businesses who seek to excel and compete through service. Her current research is concerned with service infusion strategies in goods-dominant companies and the strategic roles of technology and contact employees in determining customer satisfaction with services. In 2014 Dr. Bitner published a trade-oriented book entitled *Profiting from Services and Solutions: What Product Companies Need to Know*, with co-authors Valarie Zeithaml, Stephen Brown, and Jim Salas. She has published articles relevant to service marketing and management in the *Journal of Marketing, Journal of Service Research, Journal of Marketing Research, Journal of Retailing, Journal of Service Management, Journal of the Academy of Marketing Science, Sloan Management Review,* the *Academy of Management Executive,* and others.

Dwayne D. Gremler   *Bowling Green State University*

DWAYNE D. GREMLER is professor of Marketing at Bowling Green State University (BGSU). He received his MBA and PhD degrees from the W. P. Carey School of Business at Arizona State University. Throughout his academic career, Dr. Gremler has been a passionate advocate for the research and instruction of services marketing issues. He has served as chair of the American Marketing Association's Services Marketing Special Interest Group and has helped organize services marketing conferences in Australia, The Netherlands, France, Portugal, Finland, and the United States. Dr. Gremler has been invited to conduct seminars and present research on services marketing issues in several countries. Dr. Gremler's research addresses customer loyalty in service businesses, customer–employee interactions in service delivery, service guarantees, and word-of-mouth communication.

Dr. Gremler has been invited to conduct seminars and present research on service marketing issues in more than a dozen countries. He has published over 40 peer-reviewed journal articles and book chapters. His articles have appeared in the *Journal of Marketing, Journal of the Academy of Marketing Science, Journal of Service Research, Journal of Retailing, Journal of Business Research, Journal of Service Management,* and *Journal of Marketing Education.* Seven of Dr. Gremler's articles have won awards, including the Best Service Research Paper published in 2011 (awarded by AMA's SERVSIG) for an article published in the *Journal of Marketing* and Outstanding Research Paper Award for the best article published in the *Journal of Service Research* in 2002. In 2014 he received the Christopher Lovelock Career Contributions Award from the American Marketing Association's SERVSIG. Dr. Gremler is a former Fulbright Scholar, having received a grant from the U.S. government to teach service marketing courses at the University of Maastricht, Netherlands, in spring 2006. Dr. Gremler's recent research has been concerned with customer-employee interactions in service delivery, service guarantees, servicescapes, word-of-mouth communication, and customer loyalty in service businesses.

Dr. Gremler has been teaching Service Marketing courses for 20 years, and has been identified as having taught more undergraduate classes on this subject during this time than anyone in the United States. He is the recipient of several teaching awards, including the *Academy of Marketing Science* Outstanding Marketing Teacher Award (2009), the Alumni Undergraduate Teaching Award from the College of Business at Bowling Green State University (2010), the Hormel Teaching Excellence Award from the *Marketing Management Association* (2011), and the College of Business Teaching Excellence Award from BGSU (2015). In 2015 Dr. Gremler was appointed *Distinguished Teaching Professor* by the Bowling Green State University Board of Trustees.

Preface

This text is for students and businesspeople who recognize the vital role that services play in the economy and its future. The advanced economies of the world are now dominated by services, and virtually all companies view service as critical to retaining their customers today and in the future. Manufacturing and product-dominant companies that, in the past, have depended on their physical products for their livelihood now recognize that service provides one of their few sustainable competitive advantages.

We wrote this book in recognition of the ever-growing importance of services and the unique challenges faced by service managers.

WHY A SERVICE MARKETING TEXT?

Since the beginning of our academic careers in marketing, we have devoted our research and teaching efforts to topics in service marketing. We strongly believe that service marketing is different from goods marketing in significant ways and that it requires strategies and tactics that traditional marketing texts do not fully reflect. This text is unique in both content and structure, and we hope that you will learn as much from it as we have in writing and revising it now for over 20 years. Over this time period we have incorporated major changes and developments in the field, keeping the book up to date with new knowledge, changes in management practice, and the global economic trend toward services.

Content Overview

The foundation of the text is the recognition that services present special challenges that must be identified and addressed. Issues commonly encountered in service organizations—the inability to inventory, difficulty in synchronizing demand and supply, challenges in controlling the performance quality of human interactions, and customer participation as cocreators of value—need to be articulated and tackled by managers. Many of the strategies include information and approaches that are new to managers across industries. We wrote the text to help students and managers understand and address these special challenges of service marketing.

The development of strong customer relationships through quality service (and services) are at the heart of the book's content. The topics covered are equally applicable to organizations whose core product is service (such as banks, transportation companies, hotels, hospitals, educational institutions, professional services, telecommunication) and to organizations that depend on service excellence for competitive advantage (high-technology manufacturers, automotive and industrial products, information-intensive technology firms, and so on). The topics covered also apply equally to large, well-established companies, and to smaller entrepreneurial ventures. Rarely do we repeat material from marketing principles or marketing strategy texts. Instead, we adjust, when necessary, standard content on topics such as distribution, pricing, and promotion to account for service characteristics.

The book's content focuses on knowledge needed to implement service strategies for competitive advantage across industries. Included are frameworks for customer-focused management and strategies for increasing customer satisfaction and retention through service. In addition to standard marketing topics (such as pricing), this text introduces students to entirely new topics that include management and measurement of service quality, service recovery, the linking of customer measurement to performance measurement, service blueprinting, current ideas related to "value in use," and the cocreation of value by customers. Each of these topics represents pivotal content for tomorrow's businesses as they structure around process rather than task, engage in one-to-one marketing, mass customize their offerings, cocreate value with their customers, and attempt to build strong relationships with their customers. The cross-functional treatment of issues through integration of marketing with disciplines such as operations information systems, and human resources is a constant underlying theme.

New Features

This seventh edition of the text includes the following new features:

1. New or updated chapter openers in all chapters.
2. New research references and examples in every chapter with greater coverage of new business model examples such as Airbnb, Uber, OpenTable, Mint/Intuit, and others.
3. Greater emphasis on technology and how it is transforming service businesses; for example, the book includes examples from application services ("apps"), the "Gig" economy, the sharing economy, and the Internet of Things as a service.
4. Inclusion of current theories and best practices on customer satisfaction, loyalty, and the wallet allocation rule.
5. Increased coverage of the two current logics of marketing: service dominant logic and service logic, both of which focus on customers as creators and cocreators of value and value in use.
6. Focus on digital and social marketing in the communication chapter as well as greater coverage and examples of these topics throughout the book.
7. Increased coverage of Big Data as a source of customer information and data analytics as a service.
8. More discussion and examples of strategic service initiatives and service business models in business-to-business firms, including the trend toward service infusion in goods-dominant companies.
9. New or improved global, technology, and strategic service features in nearly every chapter and updated data in key charts and examples throughout the text.

Distinguishing Structure and Content Features

The text features a structure completely different from the standard 4P (marketing mix) structure of most marketing texts. The text is organized around the gaps model of service quality, which is described fully in Chapter 2. Beginning with Chapter 3, the text is organized into parts around the gaps model. For example, Chapters 3 and 4 each deal with an aspect of the customer gap—customer expectations and perceptions, respectively—to form the focus for service marketing strategies. The managerial content in the rest of the chapters is framed by the gaps model using part openers that build the model gap by gap. Each part of the book includes multiple chapters with strategies for understanding and closing these critical gaps. Specific distinguishing content features of the book include:

1. The only services marketing textbook based on the Gaps Model of Service Quality framework, which departs significantly from other marketing and services marketing textbooks.
2. Greater emphasis on the topic of service quality than existing marketing and service marketing texts.
3. Introduction of three service Ps to the traditional marketing mix and increased focus on customer relationships and relationship marketing strategies.
4. Significant focus on customer expectations and perceptions and what they imply for marketers.
5. A feature called "Strategy Insight" in each chapter—a feature that focuses on emerging or existing strategic initiatives involving services.
6. Increased coverage of business-to-business service applications.
7. Coverage of the increasing influence of technology in services, including a current Technology Spotlight in every chapter.
8. A chapter on service recovery that includes a conceptual framework for understanding the topic.
9. A chapter on the financial and economic impact of service quality.
10. A chapter on customer-defined service standards.
11. Cross-functional treatment of issues through integration of marketing with other disciplines such as operations and human resource management.
12. Consumer-based pricing and value pricing strategies.
13. Description of a set of tools that must be added to basic marketing techniques when dealing with services rather than goods.
14. An entire chapter that recognizes human resource challenges and human resource strategies for delivering customer-focused services.
15. A full chapter on service innovation and design with a detailed and complete introduction to service blueprinting—a technique for describing, designing, and positioning services.
16. An entire chapter on customers' roles in service that recognizes the central role that customers play in creating and cocreating value.
17. A chapter on the role of physical evidence, particularly the physical environment, or "servicescape."
18. "Global Feature" boxes in each chapter and expanded examples of global services marketing.

Conceptual and Research Foundations

We synthesized research and conceptual material from many talented academics and practitioners to create this text. We rely on the work of researchers and businesspeople from diverse disciplines such as marketing, human resources, operations, information systems, and management. Because the field of services marketing is international in its roots, we also have drawn from work originating around the globe. We have continued this strong conceptual grounding in the seventh edition by integrating new research into every chapter. The framework of the book is managerially focused, with every chapter presenting company examples and strategies for addressing issues in the chapter.

WHAT COURSES AND STUDENTS CAN USE THE TEXT?

In our years of experience teaching services marketing, we have found that a broad cross section of students is drawn to learning about services marketing. Students with career interests in service industries as well as goods industries with high service components (such as industrial products, high-tech products, and durable products) want and need to understand these topics. Students with an interest or background in software, technology-based businesses, online applications, and "data as a service" are also drawn to the course since each of these new business models is a form of service, demanding understanding of service concepts and tools. Students who wish to become consultants and entrepreneurs want to learn the strategic view of marketing, which involves not just physical goods but also the myriad services that envelop and add value to these goods. Virtually all students—even those who will work for packaged goods firms—will face employers needing to understand the basics of service marketing and management.

Although service marketing courses are usually designated as marketing electives, a large number of enrollees in our classes have been finance students seeking to broaden their knowledge and career opportunities. Business students with human resource, information technology, accounting, and operations majors also enroll, as do nonbusiness students from such diverse disciplines as health administration, recreation and tourism, public and nonprofit administration, law, sports management, and library science.

Students need only a basic marketing course as a prerequisite for a service marketing course and this text. The primary target audience for the text is service marketing classes at the undergraduate (junior or senior elective courses), graduate (both masters and doctoral courses), and executive student levels. Other target audiences are (1) service management classes at both the undergraduate and graduate levels and (2) marketing management classes at the graduate level in which a professor wishes to provide more comprehensive teaching of services than is possible with a standard marketing management text. A subset of chapters would also provide a concise text for use in a quarter-length or mini-semester course. A further reduced set of chapters may be used to supplement undergraduate and graduate basic marketing courses to enhance the treatment of services.

HOW MANY PARTS AND CHAPTERS ARE INCLUDED IN THE BOOK, AND WHAT DO THEY COVER?

The text material includes 16 chapters divided into seven parts. Part 1 includes an introduction in Chapter 1 and an overview of the gaps model in Chapter 2. Part 2 considers the customer gap by examining customer expectations and perceptions. Part 3 focuses on listening to customer requirements, including chapters covering marketing research for services, building customer relationships, and service recovery. Part 4 involves aligning service strategy through design and standards and includes chapters on service innovation and design, customer-defined service standards, and physical evidence and the servicescape. Part 5 concerns the delivery and performance of service and has chapters on employees' and customers' roles in service delivery, as well as managing demand and capacity. Part 6 focuses on managing services promises and includes chapters on integrated services marketing communications and pricing of services. Finally, Part 7 examines the financial and economic effect of service quality.

WHAT DO WE PROVIDE EDUCATORS WHO TEACH SERVICES MARKETING?

As a team, we have accumulated more than 80 years of experience teaching the subject of services marketing. We set out to create a text that represents the approaches we have found most effective. We incorporated all that we have learned in our many years of teaching services marketing—teaching materials, student exercises, case analyses, research, and PowerPoint slides, which you can find online at connect.mheducation.com, along with a comprehensive instructor's manual and test bank.

McGraw-Hill Connect®: connect.mheducation.com

Continually evolving, McGraw-Hill Connect® has been redesigned to provide the only true adaptive learning experience delivered within a simple and easy-to-navigate environment, placing students at the very center.

- Performance Analytics – Now available for both instructors and students, easy-to-decipher data illuminates course performance. Students always know how they're doing in class, while instructors can view student and section performance at a glance.
- Personalized Learning – Squeezing the most out of study time, the adaptive engine within Connect creates a highly personalized learning path for each student by identifying areas of weakness and providing learning resources to assist in the moment of need.

This seamless integration of reading, practice, and assessment ensures that the focus is on the most important content for that individual.

Instructor Library

The Connect Management Instructor Library is your repository for additional resources to improve student engagement in and out of class. You can select and use any asset that enhances your lecture.

The Library for the seventh edition includes the following resources:

- **Instructor's Manual:** The *Instructor's Manual* includes sample syllabi, suggestions for in-class exercises and projects, teaching notes for each of the cases included in the text, and answers to end-of-chapter discussion questions and exercises. The *Instructor's Manual* uses the "active learning" educational paradigm, which involves students in constructing their own learning experiences and exposes them to the collegial patterns present in work situations. Active learning offers an educational underpinning for the pivotal workforce skills required in business, among them oral and written communication skills, listening skills, and critical thinking and problem solving.
- **PowerPoint:** We have provided PowerPoint slides online for each chapter and case, including figures and tables from the text that are useful for instructors in class. The

full-color PowerPoint slides were created to present a coordinated look for course presentation.

LearnSmart®

The Seventh Edition of Services Marketing is available with LearnSmart, the most widely used adaptive learning resource, which is proven to improve grades. To improve your understanding of this subject and improve your grades, go to McGraw-Hill Connect® connect.mheducation.com, and find out more about LearnSmart. By helping students focus on the most important information they need to learn, LearnSmart personalizes the learning experience so they can study as efficiently as possible.

SmartBook®

An extension of LearnSmart, SmartBook is an adaptive eBook that helps students focus their study time more effectively. As students read, SmartBook assesses comprehension and dynamically highlights where they need to study more.

ACKNOWLEDGMENTS

We owe a great deal to the pioneering service researchers and scholars who developed the field of services marketing. They include John Bateson, Leonard Berry, the late Bernard Booms, David Bowen, Stephen W. Brown, Larry Crosby, John Czepiel, Ray Fisk, William George, Christian Gronroos, Steve Grove, Evert Gummesson, Chuck Lamb, the late Christopher Lovelock, Parsu Parasuraman, Ben Schneider, Lynn Shostack, and Carol Surprenant. We also owe gratitude to the second generation of service researchers who broadened and enriched the services marketing field. When we attempted to compile a list of those researchers, we realized that it was too extensive to include here. The length of that list is testament to the influence of the early pioneers and to the importance that service marketing has achieved both in academia and in practice.

We remain indebted to Parsu Parasuraman and Len Berry, who have been research partners of Dr. Zeithaml's since 1982. The gaps model around which the text is structured was developed in collaboration with them, as was the model of customer expectations used in Chapter 3. Much of the research and measurement content in this text was shaped by what the team found in a 15-year program of research on service quality.

Dr. Zeithaml is particularly indebted to her long-time colleague A. "Parsu" Parasuraman, who has been her continuing collaborator over the 30 years she has been in academia. An inspiring and creative talent, Parsu has always been willing to work with her—and many other colleagues—as a mentor and partner. He is also her treasured friend. She also thanks the W. P. Carey School of Business at Arizona State University and the Center for Services Leadership, from which she has benefited from interactions with her colleagues there. She also thanks her colleagues, Phd and MBA students at the University of North Carolina. The students' interest in the topic of service marketing, their creativity in approaching the papers and assignments, and their continuing contact are appreciated. As always, she credits the Marketing Science Institute (MSI), of which she was a researcher and an academic trustee, for the support and ongoing inspiration from its many executive members, conferences, and working papers. She is especially indebted to David Reibstein and Leigh McAllister, both of whom served as MSI academic directors, for their leadership and talent in bridging the gap between academia and practice.

Dr. Bitner expresses special thanks to the W. P. Carey School of Business at Arizona State University, in particular to Professor Emeritus Stephen W. Brown and the Center for Services Leadership staff and faculty. Their support and encouragement have been invaluable throughout the multiple editions of this book. Dr. Bitner also acknowledges the many ideas and examples provided by the approximately 50 member companies of the Center for Services Leadership that are committed to service excellence and from which she has the opportunity to continually learn. She also acknowledges and thanks the approximately 80 Faculty Network members of the Center for Services Leadership from around the world, whose ideas, energy, and creativity keep the discipline vital in many ways. For this edition, Dr. Bitner wants to again acknowledge the leadership of the IBM Corporation through its research divisions, in particular Dr. James Spohrer, for inspiring academics, government employees, and businesspeople around the world to begin focusing on the science of service. She is also grateful to Buck Pei, Associate Dean at the W. P. Carey School, for providing the opportunity to teach a course on service excellence in ASU's China EMBA. The experience has enriched this book and provided tremendous learning. She also acknowledges and thanks her colleague Amy Ostrom for her support and invaluable assistance in sharing examples, new research, and creative teaching innovations. Finally, Dr. Bitner is grateful to the fine group of Arizona State services doctoral students she has worked with, who have shaped her thinking and supported the text: Lois Mohr, Bill Faranda, Amy Rodie, Kevin Gwinner, Matt Meuter, Steve Tax, Dwayne Gremler, Lance Bettencourt, Susan Cadwallader, Felicia Morgan, Thomas Hollmann, Andrew Gallan, Martin Mende, Mei Li, Shruti Saxena, Nancy Sirianni, Helen Si Wang, and Kathryn Eaton.

Dr. Gremler expresses thanks to several people, beginning with his mentor, Steve Brown, for his advice and encouragement. He thanks other Arizona State University faculty who served as role models and encouragers, including John Schlacter, Michael Mokwa, and David Altheide. Dr. Gremler acknowledges the support of fellow doctoral student colleagues from Arizona State University who have gone on to successful careers and who continue to serve as role models and encouragers, including Kevin Gwinner, Mark Houston, John Eaton, and Lance Bettencourt. Dr. Gremler also expresses thanks to colleagues at various universities who have invited him to speak in their countries in recent years and who have provided insight into services marketing issues internationally, including Jos Lemmink, Ko de Ruyter, Hans Kasper, Chiara Orsingher, Stefan Michel, Thorsten Hennig-Thurau, Silke Michalski, Brigitte Auriacombe, David Martin Ruiz, Caroline Wiertz, Vince Mitchell, Sina Fichtel, Nina Specht, Kathy Tyler, Bo Edvardsson, Patrik Larsson, Tor Andreassen, Jens Hogreve, Andreas Eggert, Andreas Bausch, Javier Reynoso, Thorsten Gruber, Lia Patrício, Lisa Brüggen, Jeroen Bleijerveld, Marcel van Birgelen, Josée Bloemer, Cécile Delcourt, Christof Backhaus, Sabine (Mueller) Benoit, Chatura Ranaweera, Tillmann Wagner, Bart Larivière, Wafa Hammedi, Ina Garnefeld, Mirella Kleijnen, Michael Paul, Gaby Odekerken-Schöder, Jill Sweeney, and Dominique Greer. Finally, a special thanks to Candy Gremler for her unending willingness to serve as copy editor, encourager, wife, and friend.

All three authors want to thank Dr. Kathryn K. Eaton for her excellent editorial and consulting assistance on this edition of the book. Dr. Eaton teaches service marketing at the W. P. Carey School of Business at Arizona State University and thus has the knowledge and teaching experience to assist with elements of the revision. She provided us with excellent updates, editing, rewriting of some sections and features, and locating of timely examples throughout the book.

The panel of academics who helped us by completing a survey to evaluate the previous edition of the book include Janet Turner Parish, Texas A&M University; Joseph Fielding, Troy University, Dothan Campus; Troy Allen Festervand, Middle Tenessee State University; and David Mark Andrus, Kansas State University.

Finally, we would like to acknowledge the professional efforts of the McGraw-Hill Higher Education staff. Susan Gouijnstook, Laura Hurst Spell, Elizabeth Schonagen, Kelly Hart, Melisa Seegmiller, and Melissa Homer.

Valarie A. Zeithaml

Mary Jo Bitner

Dwayne D. Gremler

Brief Contents

About the Authors   iv

Preface   vii

PART 1
Foundations for Service Marketing   1

1   Introduction to Services   2

2   Conceptual Framework of the Book: The Gaps Model of Service Quality   33

PART 2
Focus on the Customer   49

3   Customer Expectations of Service   50

4   Customer Perceptions of Service   76

PART 3
Understanding Customer Requirements   111

5   Listening to Customers through Research   113

6   Building Customer Relationships   144

7   Service Recovery   178

PART 4
Aligning Service Design and Standards   217

8   Service Innovation and Design   218

9   Customer-Defined Service Standards   254

10   Physical Evidence and the Servicescape   281

PART 5
Delivering and Performing Service   313

11   Employees' Roles in Service   315

12   Customers' Roles in Service   349

13   Managing Demand and Capacity   382

PART 6
Managing Service Promises   415

14   Integrated Service Marketing Communications   417

15   Pricing of Services   446

PART 7
Service and the Bottom Line   473

16   The Financial and Economic Impact of Service   474

INDEX   498

Detailed Contents

About the Authors   iv

Preface   vii

PART 1
FOUNDATIONS FOR SERVICE MARKETING   1

Chapter 1
Introduction to Services   2

What are Services?   4
Service Industries, Service as a Product, Customer Service, and Derived Service   4
Tangibility Spectrum   6
Trends in the Service Sector   6
Why Service Marketing?   8
Service-Based Economies   8
Service as a Business Imperative in Goods-Focused Businesses   9
Deregulated Industries and Professional Service Needs   10
Service Marketing Is Different   10
Service Equals Profits   10
Exhibit 1.1: Is the Marketing of Services Different? A Historical Perspective   11
But "Service Stinks"   12
Strategy Insight: Competing Strategically through Service   13
Service and Technology   14
Technology-Based Service Offerings   14
New Ways to Deliver Service   15
Technology Spotlight: The Changing Face of Customer Service   16
Enabling Both Customers and Employees   16
Extending the Global Reach of Services   16
The Internet Is a Service   17
Global Feature: The Migration of Service Jobs   18
The Paradoxes and Dark Side of Technology and Service   19
Characteristics of Services   19
Intangibility   20
Heterogeneity   21

Simultaneous Production and Consumption   21
Perishability   22
Search, Experience, and Credence Qualities   23
Challenges and Questions for Service Marketers   24
Service Marketing Mix   24
Traditional Marketing Mix   25
Expanded Mix for Services   26
Staying Focused on the Customer   27
Exhibit 1.2: Southwest Airlines: Aligning People, Processes, and Physical Evidence   28
Summary   29
Discussion Questions   29
Exercises   29
Notes   30

Chapter 2
Conceptual Framework of the Book: The Gaps Model of Service Quality   33

The Customer Gap   35
The Provider Gaps   36
Provider Gap 1: the Listening Gap   36
Provider Gap 2: the Service Design and Standards Gap   37
Global Feature: An International Retailer Puts Customers in the Wish Mode to Begin Closing the Gaps   38
Provider Gap 3: the Service Performance Gap   40
Technology Spotlight: Technology's Critical Impact on the Gaps Model of Service Quality   42
Provider Gap 4: the Communication Gap   44
Putting It All Together: Closing the Gaps   45
Strategy Insight: Using the Gaps Model to Assess an Organization's Service Strategy   46
Summary   48
Discussion Questions   48
Exercises   48
Notes   48

PART 2
FOCUS ON THE CUSTOMER   49

Chapter 3
Customer Expectations of Service   50

Service Expectations   52
   Types of Expectations   53
      Global Feature: Global Outsourcing of
      Personal Services: What Are Customers'
      Expectations?   54
   The Zone of Tolerance   54
Factors that Influence Customer Expectations
of Service   57
   Sources of Desired Service Expectations   57
      Technology Spotlight: Customer
      Expectations of Airport Services Using
      Technology   58
   Sources of Adequate Service Expectations   60
   Sources of Both Desired and Predicted Service
   Expectations   63
      Strategy Insight: How Service Marketers
      Can Influence Customers' Expectations   65
Issues Involving Customers' Service
Expectations   66
   What Does a Service Marketer Do if Customer
   Expectations Are "Unrealistic"?   66
      Exhibit 3.1: Service Customers Want the
      Basics   67
   Should a Company Try to Delight the
   Customer?   68
   How Does a Company Exceed Customer
   Service Expectations?   69
   Do Customers' Service Expectations
   Continually Escalate?   71
   How Does a Service Company Stay Ahead
   of Competition in Meeting Customer
   Expectations?   71
Summary   72
Discussion Questions   72
Exercises   73
Notes   73

Chapter 4
Customer Perceptions of Service   76

Customer Perceptions   78
   Satisfaction versus Service Quality   79
   Transaction versus Cumulative
   Perceptions   79

Customer Satisfaction   80
   What Is Customer Satisfaction?   80
   What Determines Customer Satisfaction?   81
   National Customer Satisfaction Indexes   83
   The American Customer Satisfaction Index   83
   Outcomes of Customer Satisfaction   85
Service Quality   87
   Outcome, Interaction, and Physical
   Environment Quality   87
   Service Quality Dimensions   87
      Global Feature: Differences in Service
      Quality Perceptions and Customer Rage
      Across Cultures   88
   E-Service Quality   91
   Customer Effort   93
Service Encounters: The Building Blocks for
Customer Perceptions   93
      Strategy Insight: Customer Satisfaction and
      the Bottom Line   94
   Service Encounters or Moments of Truth   94
   The Importance of Encounters   96
      Exhibit 4.1: One Critical Encounter Destroys
      a 30-Year Relationship   97
   Types of Service Encounters   98
   Sources of Pleasure and Displeasure in Service
   Encounters   98
      Technology Spotlight: Customers Love
      Amazon   100
   Technology-Based Service Encounters   102
Summary   104
Discussion Questions   104
Exercises   105
Notes   105

PART 3
UNDERSTANDING CUSTOMER
REQUIREMENTS   111

Chapter 5
Listening to Customers through
Research   113

Using Customer Research to Understand Customer
Expectations   115
   Research Objectives for Services   115
   Criteria for an Effective Service Research
   Program   116
      Exhibit 5.1: Elements in an Effective
      Customer Research Program for
      Services   118

Elements in an Effective Service Marketing
Research Program   121
    Complaint Solicitation   121
      Technology Spotlight: Conducting Customer
      Research on the Web   122
    Critical Incident Studies   124
    Requirements Research   124
    Relationship and SERVQUAL Surveys   125
      Exhibit 5.2: SERVQUAL: A
      Multidimensional Scale to Capture
      Customer Perceptions and Expectations
      of Service Quality   126
    Trailer Calls or Posttransaction
    Surveys   128
    Service Expectation Meetings and
    Reviews   129
    Process Checkpoint Evaluations   130
    Market-Oriented Ethnography   130
    Mystery Shopping   131
    Customer Panels   131
    Lost Customer Research   132
    Future Expectations Research   132
Analyzing and Interpreting Customer Research
Findings   132
      Strategy Insight: Big Data Provides New
      Tools to Research Consumers   133
      Global Feature: Conducting Customer
      Research in Emerging Markets   134
    Customer Journey and Experience Maps   134
    Importance/Performance Matrices   136
Using Marketing Research Information   137
Upward Communication   137
    Objectives for Upward Communication   137
      Exhibit 5.3: Elements in an Effective
      Program of Upward Communication   138
    Research for Upward Communication   138
      Exhibit 5.4: Employees Provide
      Upward Communication at Cabela's,
      "World's Foremost Outfitter"   140
    Benefits of Upward Communication   140
Summary   141
Discussion Questions   141
Exercises   142
Notes   142

Chapter 6
Building Customer Relationships   144

Relationship Marketing   146
    The Evolution of Customer Relationships   147
      Exhibit 6.1: A Typology of Exchange
      Relationships   148
    The Goal of Relationship Marketing   149
      Technology Spotlight: Customer
      Information Systems Help Enhance the
      Customer Relationship   150
    Benefits for Customers and Firms   150
Relationship Value of Customers   154
      Exhibit 6.2: Calculating the Relationship
      Value of an Intuit Customer   155
Customer Profitability Segments   157
    Profitability Tiers—the Customer Pyramid   157
    The Customer's View of Profitability
    Tiers   158
    Making Business Decisions Using Profitability
    Tiers   158
Relationship Development Strategies   159
    Core Service Provision   160
    Switching Barriers   160
    Relationship Bonds   161
      Global Feature: Developing Loyal
      Customers at Airbnb   164
Relationship Challenges   166
    The Customer Is Not *Always Right   166*
      Strategy Insight: "The Customer Is Always
      Right": Rethinking an Old Tenet   168
    Ending Business Relationships   170
Summary   171
Discussion Questions   172
Exercises   172
Notes   172

Chapter 7
Service Recovery   178

The Impact of Service Failure and Recovery   179
    Service Recovery Effects   180
      Exhibit 7.1: The Service Recovery
      Paradox   182
How Customers Respond to Service Failures   183
    Why People Do (and Do Not) Complain   183
      Exhibit 7.2: The Internet Spreads the Story
      of Poor Service Recovery: "United Breaks
      Guitars"   184
    Types of Customer Complaint Actions   186
    Types of Complainers   186
Service Recovery Strategies: Fixing the
Customer   187
    Respond Quickly   188
      Exhibit 7.3: Service Hero Stories   189

Provide Appropriate Communication 190
    Technology Spotlight: Cisco Systems—
    Customers Recover for Themselves 192
Treat Customers Fairly 192
    Exhibit 7.4: Fairness Themes in Service
    Recovery 194
    Global Feature: Service Recovery across
    Cultures 196
Cultivate Relationships with Customers 198
Service Recovery Strategies: Fixing the
Problem 198
Encourage and Track Complaints 198
Learn from Recovery Experiences 199
    Strategy Insight: Eliciting Complaints and
    Reports of Service Failure 200
Learn from Lost Customers 200
*Make the Service Fail-Safe—Do It Right the
First Time! 201*
Service Guarantees 202
Characteristics of Effective Guarantees 203
Types of Service Guarantees 204
Benefits of Service Guarantees 205
When to Use (or Not Use) a Guarantee 205
    Exhibit 7.5: Questions to Consider in
    Implementing a Service Guarantee 206
Switching Versus Staying Following Service
Recovery 207
Summary 209
Discussion Questions 209
Exercises 210
Notes 210

PART 4
**ALIGNING SERVICE DESIGN
AND STANDARDS 217**

Chapter 8
Service Innovation and Design 218

Challenges of Service Innovation and
Design 220
Important Considerations for Service
Innovation 221
Involve Customers and Employees 221
    Global Feature: The Global Service
    Innovation Imperative 222
*Employ Service Design Thinking and
Techniques 222*
    Technology Spotlight: Facebook: A Radical
    Service Innovation 224

Types of Service Innovation 225
Service Offering Innovation 226
Innovating around Customer Roles 227
Innovation through Service Solutions 227
*Service Innovation through Interconnected
Products 228*
    Exhibit 8.1: Pills with Sensors Track Drug
    Usage by Patients 229
Stages in Service Innovation and Development 229
Front-End Planning 231
    Strategy Insight: Strategic Growth through
    Services 232
Implementation 235
    Exhibit 8.2: Service Innovation at the Mayo
    Clinic 236
Service Blueprinting: A Technique for Service
Innovation and Design 238
What Is a Service Blueprint? 238
Blueprint Components 239
Service Blueprint Examples 240
*Blueprints for Technology-Delivered
Self-Service 242*
Reading and Using Service Blueprints 243
Building a Blueprint 244
    Exhibit 8.3: Blueprinting in Action at
    ARAMARK Parks and Destinations 246
    Exhibit 8.4: Frequently Asked Questions
    about Service Blueprinting 248
Summary 248
Discussion Questions 249
Exercises 249
Notes 250

Chapter 9
Customer-Defined Service Standards 254

Factors Necessary for Appropriate Service
Standards 256
*Standardization of Service Behaviors and
Actions 256*
Formal Service Targets and Goals 257
    Strategy Insight: Using Big Data to Define
    Service Standards and Improve Customer
    Experience 258
*Customer-, Not Company-, Defined
Standards 259*
Types of Customer-Defined Service Standards 260
Hard Customer-Defined Standards 260
    Exhibit 9.1: Examples of Hard Customer-
    Defined Standards 261

Soft Customer-Defined Standards 262
One-Time Fixes 263
　　Global Feature: Adjusting Service Standards
　　around the Globe 264
　　Exhibit 9.2: Examples of Soft Customer-
　　Defined Standards 266
Development of Customer-Defined Service
Standards 266
　*Turning Customer Requirements into Specific
　Behaviors and Actions 266*
　　Exhibit 9.3: Hard and Soft Standards for
　　Service at Ford Motor Company 267
　　Exhibit 9.4: Expected Behaviors for Service
　　Encounters at John Robert's Spa 270
　　Technology Spotlight The Power of Good
　　Responsiveness Standards 276
　Developing Service Performance Indexes 278
Summary 278
Discussion Questions 278
Exercises 279
Notes 279

Chapter 10
Physical Evidence and the
Servicescape 281

Physical Evidence 283
　What Is Physical Evidence? 283
　　Technology Spotlight: Virtual
　　Servicescapes: Experiencing Services
　　through the Internet 284
　*How Does Physical Evidence Affect the
　Customer Experience? 284*
Types of Servicescapes 287
　Servicescape Usage 287
　Servicescape Complexity 288
Strategic Roles of the Servicescape 289
　Package 289
　Facilitator 289
　　Strategy Insight: Strategic Positioning
　　through Architectural Design 290
　Socializer 292
　Differentiator 292
Framework for Understanding Servicescape Effects
on Behavior 293
　The Underlying Framework 293
　Behaviors in the Servicescape 293
　　Exhibit 10.1: Servicescapes and Well-Being
　　in Health Care 294

　　Exhibit 10.2: Social Support in
　　"Third Places" 297
　Internal Responses to the Servicescape 298
　*Environmental Dimensions of the
　Servicescape 300*
　　Exhibit 10.3: Designing the Mayo Clinic
　　Hospital 302
　　Global Feature: McDonald's Adapts
　　Servicescapes to Fit the Culture 304
Guidelines for Physical Evidence Strategy 304
　*Recognize the Strategic Impact of Physical
　Evidence 305*
　Blueprint the Physical Evidence of Service 306
　*Clarify Strategic Roles of the
　Servicescape 306*
　*Assess and Identify Physical Evidence
　Opportunities 306*
　Update and Modernize the Evidence 307
　Work Cross-Functionally 307
Summary 307
Discussion Questions 308
Exercises 308
Notes 309

PART 5
DELIVERING AND PERFORMING
SERVICE 313

Chapter 11
Employees' Roles in Service 315

Service Culture 316
　Exhibiting Service Leadership 317
　Developing a Service Culture 317
　　Global Feature: How Well Does a
　　Company's Service Culture Travel? 318
　Transporting a Service Culture 318
The Critical Role of Service Employees 320
　The Service Triangle 321
　*Employee Satisfaction, Customer Satisfaction,
　and Profits 322*
　*The Effect of Employee Behaviors on Service
　Quality Dimensions 323*
Boundary-Spanning Roles 323
　Emotional Labor 324
　Sources of Conflict 325
　　Strategy Insight: Strategies for Managing
　　Emotional Labor 326
　Quality/Productivity Trade-Offs 328

Strategies for Delivering Service Quality
Through People   328
  Hire the Right People   329
    Technology Spotlight: How Technology Is
    Helping Employees Serve Customers More
    Effectively and Efficiently   330
    Exhibit 11.1: Google Quickly Becomes a
    Preferred Employer in Its Industry   332
  *Develop People to Deliver Service
  Quality   334*
    Exhibit 11.2: Potential Benefits and Costs
    of Empowerment   336
  Provide Needed Support Systems   337
  Retain the Best People   338
Customer-Oriented Service Delivery   340
Summary   342
Discussion Questions   342
Exercises   343
Notes   343

Chapter 12
Customers' Roles in Service   349

The Importance of Customers in Service
Cocreation   351
  Customers Themselves   351
    Strategy Insight: Customer Cocreation
    of Value: An Important Strategy
    Frontier   352
  Fellow Customers   354
    Exhibit 12.1: Client Cocreation of Value in
    Business-to-Business Services   356
Customers' Roles   356
  Customers as Productive Resources   356
  *Customers as Contributors to Quality,
  Satisfaction, and Value   358*
    Exhibit 12.2: Which Customer (A or B)
    Will Be Most Satisfied?   359
    Global Feature: At Sweden's IKEA,
    Customers around the World Cocreate
    Customized Value   360
  Customers as Competitors   361
Self-Service Technologies—The Ultimate in
Customer Participation   363
  A Proliferation of New SSTs   363
  Customer Usage of SSTs   364
  Success with SSTs   365
Strategies for Enhancing Customer
Participation   365

  Define Customers' Roles   365
    Technology Spotlight: Technology Facilitates
    Customer Participation in Health Care   368
  *Recruit, Educate, and Reward
  Customers   370*
    Exhibit 12.3: Working Together, U.S.
    Utility Companies and Customers Conserve
    Energy   371
    Exhibit 12.4: Weight Watchers Educates and
    Orients New Members   372
  Manage the Customer Mix   373
Summary   375
Discussion Questions   375
Exercises   376
Notes   376

Chapter 13
Managing Demand and Capacity   382

The Underlying Issue: Lack of Inventory
Capability   384
Capacity Constraints   386
  Time, Labor, Equipment, and Facilities   387
  *Optimal versus Maximum Use of
  Capacity   387*
Demand Patterns   388
  The Charting of Demand Patterns   388
  Predictable Cycles   389
  Random Demand Fluctuations   389
  Demand Patterns by Market Segment   390
Strategies for Matching Capacity and
Demand   390
  Shifting Demand to Match Capacity   390
    Global Feature: Cemex Creatively Manages
    Chaotic Demand for Its Services   391
  Adjusting Capacity to Meet Demand   394
  *Combining Demand and Capacity
  Strategies   397*
    Strategy Insight: Combining Demand
    (Marketing) and Capacity (Operations)
    Strategies to Increase Profits   398
Yield Management: Balancing Capacity Utilization,
Pricing, Market Segmentation, and Financial
Return   398
  *Implementing a Yield Management
  System   400*
    Exhibit 13.1: Simple Yield Calculations:
    Examples from Hotel and Legal
    Services   401

Technology Spotlight: Information and
Technology Drive Yield Management
Systems   402

*Challenges and Risks in Using Yield
Management   402*

Waiting Line Strategies: When Demand and
Capacity Cannot be Matched   404

Employ Operational Logic   404

Exhibit 13.2: Overflow in the ED: Managing
Capacity Constraints and Excess Demand in
Hospital Emergency Departments   405

Establish a Reservation Process   407

Differentiate Waiting Customers   408

Make Waiting More Pleasurable   408

Summary   411

Discussion Questions   411

Exercises   412

Notes   412

PART 6
MANAGING SERVICE PROMISES   415

Chapter 14
**Integrated Service Marketing
Communications   417**

The Need for Coordination in Marketing
Communication   419

Key Service Communication Challenges   421

Service Intangibility   421

Management of Service Promises   422

Management of Customer Expectations   422

Customer Education   423

Internal Marketing Communication   423

Five Categories of Strategies to Match Service
Promises with Delivery   424

Address Service Intangibility   424

Strategy Insight: Mobile Advertising—The
Key to the Future of Digital   428

Exhibit 14.1: Service Advertising
Strategies Matched with Properties of
Intangibility   429

Manage Service Promises   430

Global Feature: Virgin Atlantic Airways   433

Technology Spotlight: Internet Expert Mary
Meeker Predicts What Companies Most
Need to Know   435

Manage Customer Expectations   436

Manage Customer Education   437

*Manage Internal Marketing
Communication   439*

Summary   442

Discussion Questions   443

Exercises   443

Notes   443

Chapter 15
Pricing of Services   446

Three Key Ways that Service Prices are Different
for Customers   448

Customer Knowledge of Service Prices   448

Exhibit 15.1: What Do You Know about the
Prices of Services?   449

The Role of Nonmonetary Costs   451

Price as an Indicator of Service Quality   453

Approaches to Pricing Services   453

Cost-Based Pricing   453

Competition-Based Pricing   455

Strategy Insight: Pricing Variation in
Airlines Offers Strategic Opportunities   456

Demand-Based Pricing   456

Global Feature: Unique Tipping and Pricing
Practices around the World   457

Technology Spotlight: Dynamic Pricing on
the Internet Allows Price Adjustments Based
on Supply and Demand   460

Pricing Strategies That Link to the Four Value
Definitions   461

Exhibit 15.2: Pricing for Customer-
Perceived Value with Modular Service
Pricing and Service Tiering   462

*Pricing Strategies When the Customer Means
"Value Is Low Price"   463*

*Pricing Strategies When the Customer Means
"Value Is Everything I Want in a Service"   464*

*Pricing Strategies When the Customer Means
"Value Is the Quality I Get for the Price I
Pay"   465*

*Pricing Strategies When the Customer Means
"Value Is All That I Get for All That
I Give"   466*

Summary   469

Discussion Questions   469

Exercises   470

Notes   470

PART 7
SERVICE AND THE BOTTOM LINE   473

Chapter 16
The Financial and Economic Impact of Service   474

Service and Profitability: The Direct Relationship   476
  Exhibit 16.1: Customer Satisfaction, Service Quality, and Firm Performance   478
Offensive Marketing Effects of Service: Attracting More and Better Customers   480
Defensive Marketing Effects of Service: Customer Retention   480
  Lower Costs   *481*
  Volume of Purchases   *482*
  Price Premium   *482*
  Word-of-Mouth Communication   *482*
    Exhibit 16.2: Word-of-Mouth Communication and Customer Measurement: The Net Promoter Score   483
Customer Perceptions of Service Quality and Purchase Intentions   484

Exhibit 16.3: Questions That Managers Want Answered about Defensive Marketing   485
Exhibit 16.4: Service Quality and the Economic Worth of Customers: Businesses Still Need to Know More   486
The Key Drivers of Service Quality, Customer Retention, and Profits   488
  Effective Nonfinancial Performance Measurements   *489*
    Strategy Insight: Customer Equity and Return on Marketing: Metrics to Match a Strategic Customer-Centered View of the Firm   490
    Technology Spotlight: Cost-Effective Service Excellence through Technology   493
    Global Feature: Measurement of Customer Satisfaction Worldwide   494
Summary   494
Discussion Questions   495
Exercises   495
Notes   495

Index   498

List of Boxes

PART 1
Foundations for Service Marketing 1

Chapter 1
Introduction to Services 2

Exhibit 1.1
Is the Marketing of Services Different? A Historical Perspective 11

Strategy Insight
Competing Strategically through Service 13

Technology Spotlight
The Changing Face of Customer Service 16

Global Feature
The Migration of Service Jobs 18

Exhibit 1.2
Southwest Airlines: Aligning People, Processes, and Physical Evidence 28

Chapter 2
Conceptual Framework of the Book: The Gaps Model of Service Quality 33

Global Feature
An International Retailer Puts Customers in the Wish Mode to Begin Closing the Gaps 38

Technology Spotlight
Technology's Critical Impact on the Gaps Model of Service Quality 42

Strategy Insight
Using the Gaps Model to Assess an Organization's Service Strategy 46

PART 2
Focus on the Customer 49

Chapter 3
Customer Expectations of Service 50

Global Feature
Global Outsourcing of Personal Services: What Are Customers' Expectations? 54

Technology Spotlight
Customer Expectations of Airport Services Using Technology 58

Strategy Insight
How Service Marketers Can Influence Customers' Expectations 65

Exhibit 3.1
Service Customers Want the Basics 67

Chapter 4
Customer Perceptions of Service 76

Global Feature
Differences in Service Quality Perceptions and Customer Rage Across Cultures 88

Strategy Insight
Customer Satisfaction and the Bottom Line 94

Exhibit 4.1
One Critical Encounter Destroys a 30-Year Relationship 97

Technology Spotlight
Customers Love Amazon 100

PART 3
Understanding Customer Requirements 111

Chapter 5
Listening to Customers through Research 113

Exhibit 5.1
Elements in an Effective Customer Research Program for Services 118

Technology Spotlight
Conducting Customer Research on the Web   122

Exhibit 5.2
SERVQUAL: A Multidimensional Scale to Capture Customer Perceptions and Expectations of Service Quality   126

Strategy Insight
Big Data Provides New Tools to Research Consumers 133

Global Feature
Conducting Customer Research in Emerging Markets   134

Exhibit 5.3
Elements in an Effective Program of Upward Communication   138

Exhibit 5.4
Employees Provide Upward Communication at Cabela's, "World's Foremost Outfitter"   140

Chapter 6
Building Customer Relationships   144

Exhibit 6.1
A Typology of Exchange Relationships   148

Technology Spotlight
Customer Information Systems Help Enhance the Customer Relationship   150

Exhibit 6.2
Calculating the Relationship Value of an Intuit Customer   155

Global Feature
Developing Loyal Customers at Airbnb   164

Strategy Insight
"The Customer Is Always Right": Rethinking an Old Tenet   168

Chapter 7
Service Recovery   178

Exhibit 7.1
The Service Recovery Paradox   182

Exhibit 7.2
The Internet Spreads the Story of Poor Service Recovery: "United Breaks Guitars"   184

Exhibit 7.3
Service Hero Stories   189

Technology Spotlight
Cisco Systems—Customers Recover for Themselves   192

Exhibit 7.4
Fairness Themes in Service Recovery   194

Global Feature
Service Recovery across Cultures   196

Strategy Insight
Eliciting Complaints and Reports of Service Failure   200

Exhibit 7.5
Questions to Consider in Implementing a Service Guarantee   206

PART 4
Aligning Service Design and Standards   217

Chapter 8
Service Innovation and Design   218

Global Feature
The Global Service Innovation Imperative   222

Technology Spotlight
Facebook: A Radical Service Innovation   224

Exhibit 8.1
Pills with Sensors Track Drug Usage by Patients   229

Strategy Insight
Strategic Growth through Services   232

Exhibit 8.2
Service Innovation at the Mayo Clinic   236

Exhibit 8.3
Blueprinting in Action at ARAMARK Parks and
Destinations   246

Exhibit 8.4
Frequently Asked Questions about Service
Blueprinting   248

Chapter 9
**Customer-Defined Service
Standards   254**

Strategy Insight
Using Big Data to Define Service Standards
and Improve Customer Experience   258

Exhibit 9.1
Examples of Hard Customer-Defined
Standards   261

Global Feature
Adjusting Service Standards around the Globe   264

Exhibit 9.2
Examples of Soft Customer-Defined
Standards   266

Exhibit 9.3
Hard and Soft Standards for Service at Ford Motor
Company   267

Exhibit 9.4
Expected Behaviors for Service Encounters at John
Robert's Spa   270

Technology Spotlight
The Power of Good Responsiveness
Standards   276

Chapter 10
**Physical Evidence and the
Servicescape   281**

Technology Spotlight
Virtual Servicescapes: Experiencing Services
through the Internet   284

Strategy Insight
Strategic Positioning through Architectural
Design   290

Exhibit 10.1
Servicescapes and Well-being in Health Care   294

Exhibit 10.2
Social Support in "Third Places"   297

Exhibit 10.3
Designing the Mayo Clinic Hospital   302

Global Feature
McDonald's Adapts Servicescapes to Fit the
Culture   304

PART 5
Delivering and Performing Service   313

Chapter 11
Employees' Roles in Service   315

Global Feature
How Well Does a Company's Service Culture
Travel?   318

Strategy Insight
Strategies for Managing Emotional Labor   326

Technology Spotlight
How Technology Is Helping Employees Serve
Customers More Effectively and Efficiently   330

Exhibit 11.1
Google Quickly Becomes a Preferred Employer in
Its Industry   332

Exhibit 11.2
Potential Benefits and Costs of Empowerment   336

Chapter 12
Customers' Roles in Service   349

Strategy Insight
Customer Cocreation of Value: An Important
Strategy Frontier   352

Exhibit 12.1
Client Cocreation of Value in Business-to-Business Services   356

Exhibit 12.2
Which Customer (A or B) Will Be Most Satisfied?   359

Global Feature
At Sweden's IKEA, Customers around the World Cocreate Customized Value   360

Technology Spotlight
Technology Facilitates Customer Participation in Health Care   368

Exhibit 12.3
Working Together, U.S. Utility Companies and Customers Conserve Energy   371

Exhibit 12.4
Weight Watchers Educates and Orients New Members   372

Chapter 13
Managing Demand and Capacity   382

Global Feature
Cemex Creatively Manages Chaotic Demand for Its Services   391

Strategy Insight
Combining Demand (Marketing) and Capacity (Operations) Strategies to Increase Profits   398

Exhibit 13.1
Simple Yield Calculations: Examples from Hotel and Legal Services   401

Technology Spotlight
Information and Technology Drive Yield Management Systems   402

Exhibit 13.2
Overflow in the ED: Managing Capacity Constraints and Excess Demand in Hospital Emergency Departments   405

PART 6
Managing Service Promises   415

Chapter 14
Integrated Service Marketing Communications   417

Strategy Insight
Mobile Advertising—The Key to the Future of Digital 428

Exhibit 14.1
Service Advertising Strategies Matched with Properties of Intangibility   429

Global Feature
Virgin Atlantic Airways   433

Technology Spotlight
Internet Expert Mary Meeker Predicts What Companies Most Need to Know   435

Chapter 15
Pricing of Services   446

Exhibit 15.1
What Do You Know about the Prices of Services?   449

Strategy Insight
Pricing Variation in Airlines Offers Strategic Opportunities 456

Global Feature
Unique Tipping and Pricing Practices around the World   457

Technology Spotlight
Dynamic Pricing on the Internet Allows Price Adjustments Based on Supply and Demand   460

Exhibit 15.2
Pricing for Customer-Perceived Value with Modular Service Pricing and Service Tiering   462

PART 7
Service and the Bottom Line   473

Chapter 16
The Financial and Economic Impact of Service   474

Exhibit 16.1
Customer Satisfaction, Service Quality, and Firm Performance   478

Exhibit 16.2
Word-of-Mouth Communication and Customer Measurement: The Net Promoter Score   483

Exhibit 16.3
Questions That Managers Want Answered about Defensive Marketing   485

Exhibit 16.4
Service Quality and the Economic Worth of Customers: Businesses Still Need to Know More   486

Strategy Insight
Customer Equity and Return on Marketing: Metrics to Match a Strategic Customer-Centered View of the Firm   490

Technology Spotlight
Cost-Effective Service Excellence through Technology   493

Global Feature
Measurement of Customer Satisfaction Worldwide   494

Foundations for Service Marketing

Chapter 1 Introduction to Services

Chapter 2 Conceptual Framework of the Book: The Gaps Model of Service Quality

This first part of the text provides you with the foundations needed to begin your study of services marketing. The first chapter identifies up-to-date trends, issues, and opportunities in service as a backdrop for the strategies addressed in remaining chapters. The second chapter introduces the gaps model of service quality, the framework that provides the structure for the text. The remaining parts of the book include information and strategies to address specific gaps, giving you the tools and knowledge to become a service marketing leader.

Introduction to Services

This chapter's objectives are to

1. Explain what services are and identify important trends in services.
2. Explain the need for special service marketing concepts and practices and why the need has developed and is accelerating.
3. Explore the profound impact of technology on service.
4. Outline the basic differences between goods and services and the resulting challenges and opportunities for service businesses.
5. Introduce the expanded marketing mix for services and the philosophy of customer focus as powerful frameworks and themes that are fundamental to the rest of the text.

All Businesses are Service Businesses[1]

It is frequently said that "everything is a service" and "all businesses are service businesses." Clearly no one would argue that brand icons like Disney, Marriott, and Starbucks are service companies—service is the core of their business and service excellence is a key to their success. Companies like Siemens, IBM, Cardinal Health, and General Electric are also service providers. They compete effectively in their industries by providing essential services like training, repair, and distribution associated with their products, but also more sophisticated services like consulting, data and technology services, and business process outsourcing in their areas of expertise. Even consumer product companies like Apple and Samsung are service providers. For these companies, services are embedded in the products themselves, with smart phones and tablets providing essential services and solutions that many of us find critical to our daily lives—even though smart phones have existed for a very short time, and we obviously managed without them before. Finally, most of the new business models that are popping up are service models, many based in technology. Some, like Uber and Airbnb, are disrupting entire service industries.

These examples illustrate the diversity of service companies that we will feature in the text and the kinds of businesses you will learn about.

Marriott

Marriott is always a leader in lists of "best service companies" in the United States and the company is also high overall on Fortune's Most Admired Company lists. One reason for these high rankings is Marriott's focus on commitment to its employees and customers. At Marriott, people come first, and their first core value is "take good care of your people, they will take good care of the customers and the customers will come back." This value has translated into a worldwide well-known brand name that is the parent to 19 distinct brands of hotels. Being excellent at service—both for customers and employees—has been one of the keys to Marriott's success for decades.

General Electric

Many traditional manufacturers and high-technology companies have evolved over several decades to become service providers, and now a number of them are evolving further into data-driven service businesses. General Electric (GE) is prime example of a company that is transitioning its core growth strategies to focus on digital services and services built around data spun off from its products. Just as Jack Welch, former CEO, transformed the company into a service giant, its current CEO Jeff Immelt is focused on a digital transformation of the company to make it a top 10 software and digital services company by 2020. A popular GE ad campaign featuring a young man named Owen demonstrates the company's commitment to digital transformation of industries and its desire to hire people like Owen to move it forward.

Apple

In many industries, products are becoming a vehicle for service provision. Nowhere is this more obvious than in consumer electronics. Every app that you have on your smart phone promises to provide you with information, entertainment, purchasing opportunities, or unique solutions for your everyday life—all of these are services. The phone itself is really just a "container" for the services it provides. Apple's status as a service business was recognized when the company was ranked third for service among all companies by *24/7 Wall Street*. Apple continues to stay on the forefront of technology and product design, but it is always geared to providing customers with the innovative services and solutions they have come to expect and depend on from the company.

Uber

Technology, collaboration, and the sharing economy are giving rise to many new services today. Some are short-lived, while others seem to have real staying power. Uber's rapid rise as a prominent, disruptive business model in the personal transportation industry is one of the best known examples. Technology has made Uber's business model possible, and consumer willingness to collaborate underlies its success. Through technology Uber is able to link individual drivers, driving their own personal cars, with customers who are seeking a ride. The technology tracks locations, availability, payment, and evaluations of both drivers and riders, making the service extremely efficient and yet customized. Although it is facing challenges from regulated taxis and others, Uber's rapid expansion globally is a testament to the robustness of the service model.

As the chapter opener suggests, services are prevalent across industries, service strategies can be very profitable, and technology and digital transformation of companies and industries is driving growth and innovation in services. Yet, the University of Michigan's American Customer Satisfaction Index has consistently shown lower scores for services when compared to other products.[2] Given the economic growth in services, their profit and competitive advantage potential, and the overall lower levels of customer satisfaction for services, it seems that the potential and opportunities for companies that can excel in service marketing, management, and delivery have never been greater.

This text will give you a lens with which to approach the marketing and management of services. What you learn can be applied in a company like GE with a traditional manufacturing history or in pure service businesses. You will learn tools, strategies, and approaches for developing and delivering profitable services that can provide competitive advantage to firms. At the base of service marketing and management you will find a strong customer focus that extends across all functions of the firm—thus the subtitle of this book, "integrating customer focus across the firm."

WHAT ARE SERVICES?

Put in the most simple terms, *services are deeds, processes, and performances* provided, coproduced, or cocreated by one entity or person for and/or with another entity or person. Our chapter opener and the four company examples illustrate the range of meanings and types of companies that offer services today. Although we will rely on the simple, broad definition of *services,* you should be aware that over time *services* and the *service sector of the economy* have been defined in subtly different ways. The variety of definitions can often explain the confusion or disagreements people have when discussing services and when describing industries that constitute the service sector of the economy. Compatible with our simple, broad definition is one that defines services to include "all economic activities whose output is not a physical product or construction, is generally consumed at the time it is produced, and provides added value in forms (such as convenience, amusement, timeliness, comfort, or health) that are essentially intangible concerns of its first purchaser."[3] The breadth of industries making up the service sector of the U.S. economy is illustrated in Figure 1.1.

Service Industries, Service as a Product, Customer Service, and Derived Service

As we begin our discussion of service marketing and management, it is important to draw distinctions between *service industries and companies, service as a product, customer service,* and *derived service.* The tools and strategies you will learn in this text can be applied to any of these categories.

Service industries and companies include those industries and companies typically classified within the service sector where the core product is a service. All of the following companies can be considered pure service companies: Marriott International (lodging), American Airlines (transportation), Charles Schwab (financial services), and Mayo Clinic (health care). The total services sector comprises a wide range

FIGURE 1.1
Contributions of Service Industries to U.S. Gross Domestic Product, 2016

Source: *Survey of Current Business,* Online, April 2016.

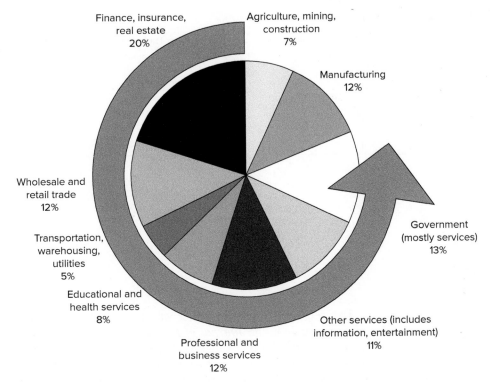

Finance, insurance, real estate
20%

Agriculture, mining, construction
7%

Manufacturing
12%

Government (mostly services)
13%

Other services (includes information, entertainment)
11%

Professional and business services
12%

Educational and health services
8%

Transportation, warehousing, utilities
5%

Wholesale and retail trade
12%

of service industries, as suggested by Figure 1.1. Companies in these industries sell services as their core offering.

Service as a product represents a wide range of intangible product offerings that customers value and pay for in the marketplace. Service products are sold by service companies and by nonservice companies such as manufacturers and technology companies. For example, IBM and Hewlett-Packard offer information technology consulting services to the marketplace, competing with firms such as Accenture, a traditional pure service firm. Other industry examples include department stores like Macy's that sell services such as gift wrapping and shipping, pet stores like PetSmart that sell pet grooming and training services, and distributors like VWR who offer services such as instrument calibration, equipment maintenance, and inventory management to their research lab customers.

Customer service is also a critical aspect of what we mean by "service." Customer service is the service provided in support of a company's core products. Companies typically do not charge for customer service. Customer service can occur on-site (as when a retail employee helps a customer find a desired item or answers a question), or it can occur over the phone or via the Internet through chat in real time. Many companies operate customer service call centers, often staffed around the clock. In other cases, customer service is provided remotely, through machine-to-machine communication without any human interaction. Regardless of the method, quality customer service is essential to building customer relationships. It should not, however, be confused with the services provided for sale by the company.

FIGURE 1.2 **Tangibility Spectrum**

Source: L. G. Shostack, "Breaking Free from Product Marketing," *Journal of Marketing* 41 (April, 1977), pp. 73–80, American Marketing Association.

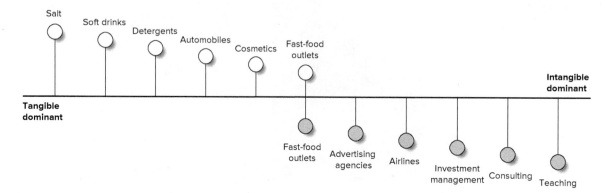

Derived service is yet another way to look at what service means. In an award-winning article in the *Journal of Marketing,* Steve Vargo and Bob Lusch argue for a logic for marketing that suggests that all products and physical goods are valued for the services they provide.[4] Drawing on the work of respected economists, marketers, and philosophers, they suggest that the value derived from physical goods is really the service provided by the good, not the good itself. For example, they suggest that a pharmaceutical drug provides medical service, a razor provides barbering service, and computers provide information and data manipulation service. Although this view is somewhat abstract, it suggests an even broader, more inclusive, view of the meaning of *service.*

Tangibility Spectrum

The broad definition of service implies that intangibility is a key determinant of whether an offering is a service. Although this is true, it is also true that very few products are purely intangible or totally tangible. Instead, services tend to be *more intangible* than manufactured products, and manufactured products tend to be *more tangible* than services. For example, the fast-food industry, while classified as a service, also has many tangible components such as the food, the packaging, and so on. Automobiles, while classified within the manufacturing sector, also supply many intangibles, such as transportation and navigation services. The tangibility spectrum shown in Figure 1.2 captures this idea. Throughout this text, when we refer to services we will be assuming the broad definition of services and acknowledging that there are very few "pure services" or "pure goods." The issues and approaches we discuss are directed toward those offerings that lie on the right side, the intangible side, of the spectrum shown in Figure 1.2.

Trends in the Service Sector

Although you often hear and read that many modern economies are dominated by services, the United States and other countries did not become service economies overnight. As early as 1929, 55 percent of the working population was employed in the service sector in the United States, and approximately 54 percent of the gross national

**FIGURE 1.3
Percentage of U.S.
Labor Force by
Industry**

Sources: Bureau of Labor
Statistics, Online, December
2015; *Survey of Current
Business,* Online, March
2011; *Survey of Current
Business,* February 2001,
Table B.8, July 1988, Table
6.6B, and July 1992, Table
6.4C; E. Ginzberg and G. J.
Vojta, "The Service Sector of
the U.S. Economy," *Scientific
American* 244 (1981),
pp. 31–39.

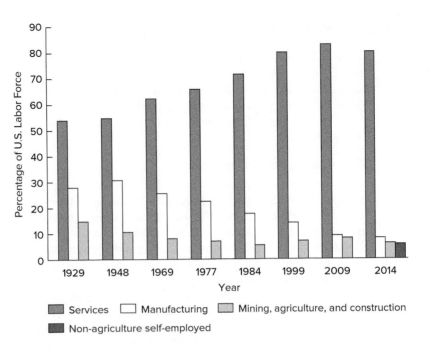

**FIGURE 1.4
Percentage of U.S.
Gross Domestic
Product by Industry**

Sources: Survey of Current
Business, Online, April 2016;
Survey of Current Business,
Online, March 2011; *Survey
of Current Business,* Febru-
ary 2001, Table B.3, and
August 1996, Table 11;
E. Ginzberg and G. J. Vojta,
"The Service Sector of the
U.S. Economy," *Scientific
American* 244 (1981),
pp. 31–39.

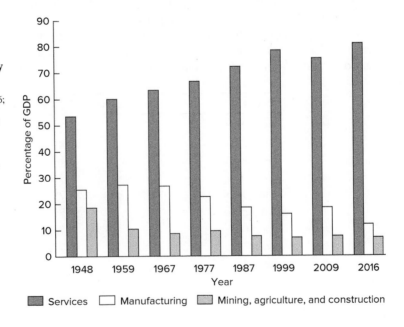

product was generated by services in 1948. The data in Figures 1.3 and 1.4 show that
the trend toward services has continued, until in 2016 services represented 81 percent
of the gross domestic product (GDP), and in 2014, 80 percent of employment. Note
also that these data do not include services provided by manufacturing companies. The
number of employees and value of the services they produce would be classified as
manufacturing sector data.

WHY SERVICE MARKETING?

Why is it important to learn about service marketing, service quality, and service management? What are the differences in services versus manufactured-goods marketing that have led to the demand for books and courses on services? Many forces have led to the growth of services marketing, and many industries, companies, and individuals have defined the scope of the concepts, frameworks, and strategies that define the field.

Service-Based Economies

First, service marketing concepts and strategies have developed in response to the tremendous growth of service industries, resulting in their increased importance to the U.S. and world economies. As was noted, the service sector represented more than 80 percent of total employment in 2014 and 81 percent of gross domestic product of the United States in 2016. Almost all the absolute growth in numbers of jobs and the fastest growth rates in job formation are in service industries, particularly health care and IT professional services.

Another indicator of the economic importance of services is that trade in services is growing worldwide. In fact, while the U.S. balance of trade in goods remains in the red, exports of services have jumped 84 percent since 2000 and there was a $227 billion trade surplus in services in 2015. In fact, the U.S. ranks number one in the world in sales of services abroad.[5,6]

There is a growing market for services and increasing dominance of services in economies worldwide (see the accompanying table). This growth is apparent in established economies as well as emerging economies such as China, where the central government has placed a priority on service sector growth. The growth of the service sector has drawn increasing attention to the challenges of service sector industries worldwide.

Country	Services GDP as of 2015
Hong Kong	93
UK	80
Netherlands	80
France	79
United States	78
Singapore	76
Japan	72
Brazil	72
Canada	71
Germany	69
New Zealand	69
Australia	67
Sweden	65
Mexico	62
India	54
China	48

Source: *The CIA World Fact Book*, 2015.

Service as a Business Imperative in Goods-Focused Businesses

Early in the development of the field of service marketing and management, most of the impetus came from service industries such as banking, transportation, hospitality, and health care. As these traditional service industries have evolved and become even more competitive, the need for effective service management and marketing strategies has continued. Now, however, companies across industries have discovered the value of service innovation and service growth strategies.[7] Manufacturers (e.g., GE, Caterpillar), technology companies (e.g., Avnet, Xerox, IBM), retailers (e.g., PetSmart), and even packaged goods companies (e.g., Procter & Gamble) have begun to discover the potential for service-led growth. (See Chapter 8 and the Strategy Insight in that chapter.) All of these companies have realized that an excellent product alone is not a guarantee for long-term success.

For example Xerox now provides a document management service, whereby it can take over the management of all documents (digital and paper) within an organization. This type of service lies far beyond its traditional printer repair and maintenance service business. In a different industry, PetSmart, a very large pet retailer, attributes nearly all of its growth in recent years to its services, including pet hotels, grooming, and training. Procter & Gamble has also begun a push into services tied to a few of its renowned brands, including Mr. Clean Car Wash, a franchise model for Tide Dry Cleaners, and a new laundry service called "Tide Spin." Knowing the tremendous value of these brands, Procter & Gamble has been very meticulous and careful in its extension of these brands into services. To expand their service business expertise, many technology companies have partnered with or purchased service businesses. IBM purchased PricewaterhouseCoopers, Hewlett-Packard purchased EDS, and Dell acquired Perot Systems, to name just a few.

Why are all these companies choosing to focus on services? There are a number of reasons. First, the commoditization of products in many industries has resulted in price and margin pressures on many physical goods. Services can help firms to customize their offerings, adding value for customers. Second, customers are demanding services and solutions, especially in business-to-business markets. In many situations, customers demand a solution to their problem or challenge that involves multiple products and services. They look to their providers to create and deliver these product-service solutions. Third, services often have higher profit margins than products and can thus provide platforms for firm profitability. As you will learn in later chapters, customer loyalty and customer satisfaction are driven in large part by service quality and service offerings. Again, this knowledge provides firms with another reason to develop services and cement customer loyalty through high-quality service. Finally, many industries are highly competitive today and service can be a differentiator in a crowded market.

As firms transition into services, they often encounter serious challenges in terms of culture change, sales and channel issues, and a need for expertise in designing and delivering services. These companies are typically engineering, technology, science, or operations driven. Their expertise is anchored in what they produce. As these companies transition and seek to grow through service, they find they need a new service logic, and the special concepts and approaches for managing and marketing services become increasingly apparent.[8]

Deregulated Industries and Professional Service Needs

Specific demand for service marketing concepts has come from deregulated industries and professional services as both these groups have gone through rapid changes in the ways they do business. In the past several decades many very large service industries, including airlines, banking, telecommunications, and trucking, have been deregulated by the U.S. government. Similar deregulatory moves have taken place in many other countries as well. As a result, marketing decisions that used to be tightly controlled by the government are now partially, and in some cases totally, within the control of individual firms.[9] For example, historically all airline fares, routes, and commissions paid to travel agents were determined and monitored by the government. All of that changed with deregulation, and airlines have been free to set their own pricing structures and determine which routes they will fly. Deregulation created turmoil in the airline industry, accelerating the need for more sophisticated, customer-based, and competition-sensitive marketing.

Providers of professional services (such as physicians, lawyers, accountants, engineers, and architects) have also demanded new concepts and approaches for their businesses as these industries have become increasingly competitive and as professional standards have been modified to allow advertising. Whereas traditionally the professions avoided even using the word *marketing,* they now seek better ways to understand and segment their customers, to ensure the delivery of quality services, and to strengthen their positions amid a growing number of competitors.

Service Marketing Is Different

As the previously mentioned forces coincided and evolved, businesspeople realized that marketing and managing services presented issues and challenges not faced in manufacturing and packaged goods companies. These differences and challenges were captured in a series of interviews by management consultant Gary Knisely (see Exhibit 1.1). For example, when a firm's core offering is a deed performed by an employee (such as engineering consulting), how can the firm ensure consistent product quality to the marketplace? As service businesses began to turn to marketing and decided to hire marketing people, they naturally recruited from the best marketers in the world—Procter & Gamble, General Foods, Kodak (at the time). People who moved from marketing in packaged goods industries to marketing in health care, banking, and other service industries found that their skills and experiences were not directly transferable. They faced issues and dilemmas in marketing services that their experiences in packaged goods and manufacturing had not prepared them for. These people realized the need for new concepts and approaches for marketing and managing service businesses.

Service marketers responded to these forces and began to work across disciplines and with academics and business practitioners from around the world to develop and document marketing practices for services. As the field evolved, it expanded to address the concerns and needs of *any* business in which service is an integral part of the offering.

Service Equals Profits

In the final decades of the 20th century, many firms jumped on the service bandwagon, investing in service initiatives and promoting service quality as ways to differentiate themselves and create competitive advantage. Many of these investments were based on faith and intuition by managers who believed in serving customers well and who believed in their hearts that quality service made good business sense. Indeed, a dedication to quality service has been the foundation for success for many

In 1979 Gary Knisely, a principal of the consulting firm Johnson Smith & Knisely, asked the title question to practicing service marketers. Specifically, Knisely interviewed several high-ranking marketing executives who had all gone to work in consumer services after extensive experience in the consumer packaged goods industry (known for its marketing prowess).

These executives found differences, all right. Their discoveries came from attempts to apply (with mixed success, it turned out) consumer goods marketing practices directly to services. James L. Schorr of Holiday Inns Inc., formerly with Procter & Gamble, found that he could not overlay a consumer goods firm's marketing system onto a service firm. He, and the other executives interviewed, expressed certain recurring themes. First, more variables exist in the marketing mix for services than for consumer goods. Schorr claimed that in a service business, marketing and operations are more closely linked than in a manufacturing business; thus, the service production process is part of the marketing process. Second, customer interface is a major difference between goods marketing and services marketing. Executives from packaged goods companies never had to think in terms of a direct dialogue with their customers. For Schorr, the marketing of hotel rooms boiled down to a "people-on-people" sale. Robert L. Catlin, in relating his experience in the airline industry, stated, "Your people are as much of your product in the consumer's mind as any other attribute of the service." People buy products because they believe they work. But with services, people deal with people they like and they tend to buy services because they believe they will like them. This thought process makes the customer–employee interface a critical component of marketing.

The executives also commented on how the marketing mix variables common to both goods and services have vastly different implications for marketing strategy in the two contexts. In the distribution and selling of services, the firm cannot rely on well-stocked shelves past which the consumer can push a cart and make selections. Consumers' exposure to the full range of need-fulfilling service products may be limited by the salesperson's "mental inventory" of services and how he or she prioritizes them. You could say that the service product manager is competing for the "mental shelf space" of the firm's sales personnel. For Rodney Woods, group marketing officer at United States Trust Co., pricing was the most critical factor in the marketing of services versus products. For Woods, determining the costs associated with service production and delivery proved very difficult, much more of a challenge than he had faced in his earlier career working with such large packaged goods companies as Pillsbury, Procter & Gamble, and Bristol-Myers. Also, the benefits of using price as a promotional weapon were not as apparent. Promotional price cuts tended to erode hard-fought positioning and image.

While scholars debated early on the issue of whether marketing management differs for goods versus services, for top managers with experience in both areas the differences were pronounced in 1979. They still are today. The differences that these early service marketers noted were the impetus for many of the ideas, concepts, and strategies practiced today.

Source: This discussion is based on interviews conducted by Gary Knisely that appeared in *Advertising Age* on January 15, 1979; February 19, 1979; March 19, 1979; and May 14, 1979.

firms, across industries. In his book *Discovering the Soul of Service,* Leonard Berry describes in detail 14 such companies.[10] The companies featured in his book had been in business an average of 31 years when the book was written. These companies had been profitable in all but five of their combined 407 years of existence. Berry discovered through his research that these successful businesses share devotion to nine common service themes, among them values-driven leadership, commitment to investments in employee success, and trust-based relationships with customers and other partners at the foundation of the organization.

Since the mid-1990s firms have demanded hard evidence of the bottom-line effectiveness of service strategies. And researchers have built a convincing case that service strategies, implemented appropriately, can be very profitable. Work sponsored by the Marketing Science Institute suggests that corporate strategies focused on customer satisfaction, revenue generation, and service quality may actually be more profitable than strategies focused on cost cutting or strategies that attempt to do both simultaneously.[11]

Research out of the Harvard Business School built a case for the "service–profit chain," linking internal service and employee satisfaction to customer value and ultimately to profits.[12] And considerable research shows linkages from customer satisfaction (often driven by service outcomes) to customer loyalty and to profits.[13] From the University of Michigan American Customer Satisfaction Index (ACSI) come data suggesting that customer satisfaction is directly linked to shareholder value. Firms in the top 25 percent of the ACSI rankings show significantly higher shareholder value than do firms in the bottom 25 percent. Research based on ACSI data also shows that the top 20 percent of ACSI firms outperform the Standard & Poor's 500, NASDAQ, and Dow Jones Industrial Average.[14]

An important key to these successes is that the right strategies are chosen and that these strategies are implemented appropriately and well. Three service pioneers, James L. Heskett, W. Earl Sasser Jr., and Leonard A. Schlesinger recently captured much of what has been learned about service success and failures in their new book, *What Great Service Leaders Know and Do*.[15] Much of what you learn from this text will guide you in making correct service strategy decisions and in providing superior implementation. Throughout the text we will point out the profit implications and tradeoffs to be made with service strategies. See this chapter's Strategy Insight for four ways that firms successfully and profitably compete through service. In Chapter 16 we will come back to this topic by providing integrated coverage of the financial and profit impact of service.

But "Service Stinks"

Despite the importance of service and the bottom-line profit potential for service, consumers perceive that overall the quality of service is not great in many companies and industries.[16] We see *BusinessWeek* magazine blatantly condemning service in its cover story "Why Service Stinks" and a *Wall Street Journal* editorial questioning service quality and value that is entitled "We Pay Them to Be Rude to Us."[17] And although there are exceptions in every industry, American Customer Satisfaction Index scores for service industries are on average lower than the scores for durable and nondurable products.[18]

This critique of service is troubling when, at some level, service has never been better. For example, think of just one industry—health care. The ability to prevent and treat diseases has never been greater, resulting in an ever-increasing life expectancy in the United States and in most other industrialized countries. Or take the communications industries—communicating quickly, effectively, and cheaply with people all over the world has never been easier. Access to vast quantities of information, entertainment, and music is unbelievable compared to what people had just 10 years ago. So clearly, in some ways and in many industries, service is better than ever.

Despite these obvious improvements, there is hard evidence that consumers are not satisfied with the services they receive from many companies and industries today. There are many plausible explanations for why this is the case, including:

- With more companies offering tiered service based on the calculated profitability of different market segments, many customers are, in fact, getting less service than they have in the past.
- Increasing use by companies of self-service and technology-based service is perceived as less service because no human interaction or human personalization is provided.

Strategy Insight Competing Strategically through Service

Firms can compete profitably through services in a variety of ways. Through our work with companies across industries and through benchmarking other companies, we see four strategic themes emerge as the primary ways that firms can compete through service. Although firms tend to emphasize one or two of these strategic choices at a given time, it may be possible to do more.

EXEMPLARY OUT-OF-THE-BOX CUSTOMER SERVICE

There are some organizations whose competitive advantage is their reputation for out-of-the-box customer service. Southwest Airlines, Mayo Clinic, Zappos (an online shoe and clothing retailer), and Zanes Cycles (a small bicycle shop in Connecticut) are just a few examples. These organizations focus on going out of their way for customers and providing customer service in unique ways. Special services that these companies provide include:

- At Southwest Airlines, a distinctive sense of humor among employees as well as in-flight games and jokes.
- At Mayo Clinic, a grand piano in the lobby and doctors who sit physically close to patients, look them in the eye, and truly believe that "the best interest of the patient is the only interest to be considered."
- At Zappos.com, nine views and videos of every shoe for sale.
- At Zanes Cycles, a "flat tire club."

INNOVATIVE, CUTTING-EDGE SERVICES

Other organizations compete through providing innovative and cutting-edge services—being the first and/or best in their industry or being on the forefront of new inventions, technology, or science. Examples here include Amazon.com, the first company to introduce really effective and innovative online retailing. Mayo Clinic falls into this category as well. It is on the leading edge of medicine in the United States and typically sees patients who have hard-to-diagnose or complex problems. The clinic's research-based, team-oriented, consultative model of medicine keeps it on the forefront.

Technology helps firms to expand the possibilities in service and create offerings that become an integral part of customers' lives. For example, the Amazon Echo is an Internet-connected device that can play music, give weather updates, order products to be shipped to the home, and control a vast array of other Internet-connected products, such as thermostats and smart light bulbs—all at the sound of the user's voice.

VALUE-ADDED, REVENUE-PRODUCING SERVICES

A major trend in manufacturing, information technology, and other nonservice industries in recent years is the introduction of value-added, revenue-producing services. Firms in these industries have recognized that they cannot compete on the sales and margins produced by their manufactured products alone. Many firms, such as IBM, Hewlett-Packard, Siemens, and General Electric, have integrated services into their mix of offerings.

This focus on revenue-producing services also extends to retailers. For example, PetSmart, the largest pet retailer in the United States, has introduced a host of new services in recent years as a way to compete effectively in this relatively low-margin industry. The company targets "pet parents" in its advertising, and its special services include pet training, grooming, and overnight care.

A SERVICE CULTURE THAT DIFFERENTIATES

Finally, a firm can compete by nurturing a service culture that attracts the very best workers in the industry. In attracting the best workers, the company has an advantage over the competition in terms of providing the very best services and thus becoming both the "employer of choice" and the "provider of choice" in its industry. This approach is used, for example, by Southwest Airlines, Mayo Clinic, Disney, and Marriott Hotels. At Marriott, the underlying company philosophy is "take care of your employees and they will take care of your guests." This philosophy permeates all the Marriott brands, from Fairfield Inns to the Ritz Carlton, giving Marriott a worldwide competitive advantage in its industry.

Source: Center for Services Leadership, W. P. Carey School of Business, Arizona State University (www.wpcarey.asu.edu/csl).

- Customer expectations are higher in all industries because of the excellent service they receive from some companies. Thus, they expect the same from all and are frequently disappointed.
- Organizations have cut costs to the extent that they are too lean and too understaffed to provide quality service.
- The competitive job market results in less-skilled people working in frontline service jobs; talented workers soon get promoted or leave for better opportunities.
- Many companies give lip service to customer focus and service quality, but they fail to provide the training, compensation, and support of employees needed to actually deliver quality service.

These explanations can be debated. But for managers, students, and teachers of service marketing and management, the message is clear: there is plenty of work to be done. In this text we will provide many examples of best practices—companies that understand how to get it right and are succeeding with service. We will also delineate many tools, concepts, and strategies that can help to reverse the "service stinks" mind-set.

SERVICE AND TECHNOLOGY

The preceding sections examined the roots of service marketing and the reasons the field and business function exist. Another major trend—technology, specifically information technology—is shaping the field and profoundly influencing the practice of service marketing. According to researchers Roland T. Rust and Ming-Hui Huang, information technology is causing a "service revolution," resulting in an expansion of the service sector and increased importance of service in all categories of the economy.[19] In this section we explore trends in technology (positive *and* negative) to set the stage for topics that will be discussed throughout this text. In each chapter you will find a Technology Spotlight box that highlights the influence of technology on issues related to the particular chapter. Together with globalization, the influence of technology is the most profound trend affecting service marketing today.

Technology-Based Service Offerings

Looking to the past, it is apparent how technology was the basic force behind service innovations now taken for granted. Automated voice mail, interactive voice response systems, cell phones, automated teller machines (ATMs), and other common services were possible only because of new technologies. Just think how dramatically different your world would be without these basic technology services.

More recently, people have seen the explosion of the Internet, resulting in a host of new services. Internet-based companies like Amazon and Google/Alphabet offer services previously unheard of and smart phones now offer innumerable service applications that were not even imaginable in the recent past. Even established companies and industries find that the Internet provides a way to offer new services as well.[20] For example, *The Wall Street Journal* offers an interactive edition that allows customers to organize the newspaper's content to suit their individual preferences and needs. And, universities are now offering entire degree programs online, providing access to education for many who would not have it otherwise.

Many new technology services are on the evolving as we write this book, and they will continue to explode on the scene at an increasingly rapid rate.[21] For example, the "connected car" allows people to access all kinds of existing and new services while on the road. In-car systems provide recommendations for shopping by informing drivers when they are within a certain number of miles of their preferred retailer. On a road trip, the system may provide weather forecasts and warnings, and when it is time to stop for the night, the car's system can book a room at a nearby hotel, recommend a restaurant, and make dinner reservations.

Other technological advances are making it possible for medical professionals to monitor patients' conditions remotely and even to provide medical diagnoses, treatment, and surgery guidance via technology interfaces. Similarly, large equipment manufacturers like John Deere, Caterpillar, and General Electric can now remotely monitor and service equipment, as well as provide sophisticated information and data to their clients via the Internet. These sophisticated services that depend on data being transmitted from machines are part of what is known as the Internet of Things, or IOT. In addition to generating masses of data, IOT is generating a plethora of new service opportunities.[22]

New Ways to Deliver Service

In addition to providing opportunities for new service offerings, technology is providing approaches for delivering existing services in more accessible, convenient, productive ways. Technology facilitates basic customer service functions (bill paying, questions, checking account records, order tracking), transactions (both retail and business-to-business), and learning or information seeking. Our Technology Spotlight traces how, through history, evolving technologies have changed one aspect of service, namely, customer service, forever. Companies have moved from face-to-face service to telephone-based service to widespread use of interactive voice response systems to Internet-based customer service and now to wireless service. Interestingly, many companies are coming full circle and now offer human contact as the ultimate form of customer service!

Technology also facilitates transactions by offering a direct vehicle for making purchases and conducting business. In the financial services field, Charles Schwab transformed itself from a traditional broker to an online financial services company that currently conducts more than 70 percent of its customer transactions online. Technology company Intuit offers technology-based services designed to make customers' financial lives easier, including TurboTax, and QuickBooks. Their free Mint app allows customers to pull all their accounts, cards, and investments into one place to track spending, create a budget, and receive bill reminders. Technology has also transformed service delivery and transactions for many business-to business firms. For example, technology giant Cisco Systems offers virtually all its customer service and ordering functions to its business customers via technology.

Finally, technology, specifically the Internet, provides an easy way for customers to learn, do research, and collaborate with each other. Access to information has never been easier. For example, more than 20,000 websites currently offer health-related information. Many provide answers to specific disease, drug, and treatment questions. In a study of online health care information usage, the Pew organization found that, among Americans with Internet access, 80 percent had looked for health or medical information on the Web.[23] Technology also facilitates easy and direct communication from companies and individual providers to customers, resulting in new shared services such as Airbnb, Uber, and Fiverr. Collectively these types of services make up the growing "shared economy," sometimes called the Gig Economy.[24]

Technology Spotlight The Changing Face of Customer Service

Excellent customer service—the daily, ongoing support of a company's offerings—is critical in creating brand identity and ultimate success. It includes answering questions, taking orders, dealing with billing issues, handling complaints, scheduling appointments, and similar activities. These essential functions can make or break an organization's relationships with its customers. The quality of customer care can significantly impact brand identity for service, manufacturing, and consumer products companies. Because of its importance in creating impressions and sustaining customer relationships, customer service has sometimes been called the "front door" of the organization or its "face."

So how has the "face" of customer service changed with the influx of technology? Long ago all customer service was provided face-to-face through direct personal interaction between employees and customers. To get service you had to visit stores or service providers in person. The telephone changed this, allowing customers to call companies and speak directly with employees, typically Monday–Friday,

8:00 a.m.–5:00 p.m. Customer service became less personal, but without a doubt more efficient, through use of the telephone. With the evolution of computer technology, customer service representatives (CSRs) became even more efficient. Through computer information systems and customer data files, CSRs are able to call up customer records at their workstations to answer questions on the spot.

Over time, because communication and computer technologies allowed it, large organizations began to centralize their customer service functions, consolidating into a few large call centers that could be located anywhere in the country or the world, with calls handled 24 hours per day. But still, in these types of call centers, customer service is, for the most part, an interpersonal event, with customers talking directly, one-on-one with an employee.

The advent and rapid proliferation of the efficient, but much maligned, automated voice response systems changed personal customer service in many organizations into menu-driven, automated exchanges. In almost every

Enabling Both Customers and Employees

Technology enables both customers and employees to be more effective in getting and providing service.[25] Through self-service technologies, customers can serve themselves more effectively. Via online banking, customers can access their accounts, check balances, apply for loans, shift money among accounts, and take care of just about any banking need they might have—all without the assistance of the bank's employees. Online shopping and hundreds of service applications available via the Internet and smart phones have transformed the lives of consumers forever. Through social media, individuals and companies can communicate and collaborate with each other as well.

For employees, technology can provide tremendous support in making them more effective and efficient in delivering service. Customer relationship management and sales support software are broad categories of technology that can aid frontline employees in providing better service. By having immediate access to information about their product and service offerings as well as about particular customers, employees are better able to serve them. This type of information allows employees to customize services to fit the customer's needs. They can also be much more efficient and timely than in the old days when most customer and product information was in paper files or in the heads of sales and customer service representatives.

Extending the Global Reach of Services

Technology infusion results in the potential for reaching out to customers around the globe in ways not possible before. The Internet itself knows no boundaries, and therefore information, customer service, and transactions can move across countries and industry and any business context, consumers encounter these types of systems, and many are quite frustrating—for example, when a system has a long, confusing set of menu options or when no menu option seems to fit the purpose of the call. Similarly, customers become angered when they cannot get out of the automated system easily or when there is no option to speak to a live person.

Beyond automated telecom systems, the explosion of the Internet has also dramatically changed customer service for many companies. Service can now be provided on the Internet via e-mails, website robots, FAQs, and online chats. In these cases there is no direct human interaction, and customers actually perform their own service. In other cases, there is no human involvement at all in customer service. For example, many manufacturers in business-to-businesses provide remote monitoring of equipment and automated machine-to-machine service without customer or employee intervention.

With the relentless proliferation of technology solutions, firms are finding that expectations for customer service have changed. Customers are demanding choices in how they get customer service, whether it be via phone, automated voice system, e-mail, Internet self-service, or remote machine-to-machine service. Although customers often enjoy technology-based service and even demand it in many cases, they dislike it when it does not work reliably, when it does not seem to have any advantages over the interpersonal service alternatives, and when there are no systems in place to recover from failures. Interestingly, when things do not work as they are supposed to on an Internet site or through an automated response system, customers are quick to look for more traditional interpersonal (in person or via telephone) options, coming full circle to where they started.

Sources: J. A. Nickell, "To Voice Mail Hell and Back," *Business 2.0,* July 10, 2001, pp. 49–53; M. L. Meuter, A. L. Ostrom, R. I. Roundtree, and M. J. Bitner, "Self-Service Technologies: Understanding Customer Satisfaction with Technology-Based Service Encounters," *Journal of Marketing* 64 (July 2000), pp. 50–64; S. Ali, "If you want to Scream, Press . . . ," *The Wall Street Journal,* October 30, 2006, p. R4; J. Light, "With Customer Service, Real Person Trumps Text," *The Wall Street Journal,* April 25, 2011, p. B7.

across continents, reaching any customer who has access to the Internet. Technology also allows employees of international companies to stay in touch easily—to share information, to ask questions, to serve on virtual teams together. All this technology facilitates the global reach as well as the effectiveness of service businesses. Our Global Feature focuses on the migration of service jobs around the world and the ability to produce services almost anywhere.

The Internet *Is* a Service

An interesting way to look at the influence of technology is to realize that the Internet is just "one big service." All businesses and organizations that operate on the Internet are essentially providing services—whether they are giving information, performing basic customer service functions, facilitating transactions, or promoting social interactions among individuals. Even mobile-to-mobile or IOT offerings are all services at their core. Thus, all the tools, concepts, and strategies you learn in studying service marketing and management have direct application in an Internet or e-business world. Although technology and the Internet have profoundly changed how people do business and what offerings are possible, it is clear that customers still want basic service. They want what they have always wanted: dependable outcomes, easy access, responsive systems, flexibility, apologies, and compensation when things go wrong. But now they expect these outcomes from technology-based businesses and from e-commerce solutions.[26] With hindsight it is obvious that many dot-com start-ups suffered and even failed because of lack of basic customer knowledge and failure of implementation, logistics, and service follow-up.[27]

With the ever-growing sophistication of information technology, the global reach of organizations is increasing at a spectacular rate. Activities that used to require close proximity and personal contact can now often be accomplished via the Internet, video, and telecommunication technologies. This advancement means that the jobs that produce and support these activities can be done almost anywhere in the world. The result has been referred to as a "migration of service jobs" out of countries such as the United States and the United Kingdom to countries such as India, Pakistan, the Philippines, Eastern European countries, and, more recently, China, Columbia and Brazil.

This globalization of services is in many ways inevitable, but it comes with considerable controversy. One clear concern is that some of the highest-paying service jobs are being "lost" to lower-wage countries, and this concern is very real for the individuals whose jobs are lost. However, the numbers are not as large as perhaps imagined. Forrester Research in Cambridge, Massachusetts, estimates that, by the year 2015, 3.3 million high-tech and service jobs will have moved overseas from the United States. Others estimate the number to be much higher. On the other side of this concern are arguments that offshore jobs will spur innovation, job creation in other areas, and increases in productivity that will benefit the consumer and keep companies competitive in the global marketplace. In fact, the Bureau of Labor Statistics estimated that, between 2000 and 2010, 22 million new U.S. jobs (mostly in business services, health care, social services, transportation, and communications) would be created. Although the specific outcomes of service job migration are not totally known, it is safe to say that the globalization of services will continue, resulting in further shrinking of the boundaries among people and countries.

Service job migration involves not just call centers and IT help lines but also services that span industries and levels of skills. Software development, IT consulting, chip design, financial analysis, industrial engineering, analytics, and drug research are just a few examples of services performed in India for global firms. Even medical diagnoses and reading of medical records can be done remotely via video, Internet, and scanning technologies.

In addition to off-shore service work for major corporations, other work is being done more piecemeal and through contracts with individual workers. Sometimes referred to as the "Human Cloud" or the "Gig Economy," workers sell their skills and time on the open online market or through specific online platforms that cross geographic and language boundaries. Through this online economy, white collar jobs (some highly skilled and others requiring minimal skills) are performed and paid for in individual negotiations among buyers and sellers. For example, online platforms such as Upwork, Freelancer, and People Per Hour

© David pearson/Alamy Stock Photo

Deloitte US India, Hyderabad, India.

feature tasks such as copywriting, IT, design work, and legal and administrative work to be done, and individuals "bid" on the tasks and get paid for work performed.

Why is service job migration happening now? The root of the acceleration is the rapid development and accessibility of sophisticated information technologies. Services are information intensive, and information can now be shared readily without direct personal contact. For example, at the John F. Welch Technology Center in Bangalore, over 4,000 Indian researchers, engineers, and scientists engage in research for General Electric's divisions. Projects span such diverse areas as developing materials for use in DVDs, boosting the productivity of GE plants, and tweaking the designs of turbine engine blades. The design work can be done in India (perhaps even teaming with engineers elsewhere), and the results can be sent instantaneously wherever they are needed. Another global giant, Deloitte, employs close to 27,000 people in 11 modern office towers in its Deloitte US India operations in Hyderabad, India. Administrative work, audits, research on mergers and acquisitions, and project-based consulting work are examples of the types of things workers do there for Deloitte itself and for its global clients. In all of these cases, *where* the work is done is not important or meaningful to the client as long as it is done well and on time.

U. Karmarkar, "Will You Survive the Services Revolution?" *Harvard Business Review,* 82 (June 2004), pp. 100–107; M. N. Baily and D. Farrell, "Exploding the Myths of Offshoring," *The McKinsey Quarterly,* online at www.mckinseyquarterly.com, July 2004; A. Vashistha and A. Vashistha, *The Offshore Nation* (New York: McGraw-Hill, 2006); A. King, "Inside Deloitte's Indian Growth Engine," *The Australian Financial Review,* April 13, 2016, p. 1; S. O'Connor, "Cloud Atlas: The New World of Work," *Financial Times,* October 9, 2015, p. 11; A. L. Sussman and J. Zumbrun, "'Gig' Economy Spreads Broadly," *The Wall Street Journal,* March 26–27, 2016, p. A1.

The Paradoxes and Dark Side of Technology and Service

Although there is clearly great potential for technology to support and enhance services, there are potential negative outcomes as well. David Mick and Susan Fournier, well-regarded consumer researchers, have pointed out the many paradoxes of technology products and services for consumers.[28] For example, they note that technology can facilitate a sense of freedom and independence for individuals, but it can also be constraining or restrictive if it is perceived as inflexible. It can facilitate social interaction and closeness among people, but it can also isolate or separate them. This section highlights some of the general concerns.

Customer concerns about privacy and confidentiality raise major issues for firms as they seek to learn about and interact directly with customers through the Internet. These types of concerns are what have stymied and precluded many efforts to advance technology applications in the health care industry, for example. Nor are all customers equally interested in using technology as a means of interacting with companies. Research exploring "customer technology readiness" suggests that some customers are simply not interested in using or ready to use technology.[29] Employees can also be reluctant to accept and integrate technology into their work lives—especially when they perceive, rightly or wrongly, that the technology will substitute for human labor and perhaps eliminate their jobs.

With technology infusion comes a loss of human contact, which many people believe is detrimental purely from a quality of life and human relationships perspective. Parents may lament that their children spend hours in front of computer and smart phone screens, interacting with games, seeking information, and relating to their friends only through instant messaging, Twitter, and Facebook without any face-to-face human contact. And workers in organizations become more and more reliant on communicating through technology—even communicating via e-mail or online chat sessions with the person in the next office or with someone riding in the same car! The unintentional consequences and pros and cons of technology infusion into everyday life are the subjects of current research programs at Stanford University, cutting across disciplines from psychiatry and medicine and communications, to computer science and engineering.[30]

Finally, the payback in technology investments is often uncertain. It may take a long time for an investment to result in productivity or customer satisfaction gains. Sometimes it never happens. For example, McKinsey & Company reports that a firm projected a $40 million savings from moving its billing and service calls to the Internet. Instead, it suffered a $16 million loss as a result of lower usage by customers than projected, unanticipated follow-up calls and e-mails to the call center from those who had used the Internet application initially, and loss of revenue from lack of cross-selling opportunities.[31]

CHARACTERISTICS OF SERVICES

There is general agreement that differences between goods and services exist and that the distinctive characteristics discussed in this section result in challenges (as well as advantages) for managers of services.[32] It is also important to realize that each of these characteristics could be arranged on a continuum similar to the tangibility spectrum shown in Figure 1.1. That is, services tend to be more heterogeneous, more intangible, and more difficult to evaluate than goods, but the differences between goods and services are not black and white by any means.[33]

Table 1.1 summarizes the differences between goods and services and the implications of these characteristics. Many of the strategies, tools, and frameworks in this text were developed to address these characteristics, which had been largely ignored by

TABLE 1.1 **Comparing Goods and Services**

Source: A. Parasuraman, V. A. Zeithaml, and L. L. Berry, "A Conceptual Model of Service Quality and Its Implications for Future Research." *Journal of Marketing* 49 (Fall 1985), pp. 41–50.

Goods	Services	Resulting Implications
Tangible	Intangible	Services cannot be inventoried.
		Services cannot be easily patented.
		Services cannot be readily displayed or communicated.
		Pricing is difficult.
Standardized	Heterogeneous	Service delivery and customer satisfaction depend on employee and customer actions.
		Service quality depends on many uncontrollable factors.
		There is no sure knowledge that the service delivered matches what was planned and promoted.
Production separate from consumption	Simultaneous production and consumption	Customers participate in and affect the transaction.
		Customers affect each other.
		Employees affect the service outcome.
		Decentralization may be essential.
		Mass production is difficult.
Nonperishable	Perishable	It is difficult to synchronize supply and demand with services.
		Services cannot be returned or resold.
		Services for any given time-period cannot be sold or delivered at a later date.

marketers. Recently it has been suggested that these distinctive characteristics should not be viewed as unique to services but that they are also relevant to goods, that "all products are services," and that "economic exchange is fundamentally about service provision."[34] This view suggests that all types of organizations may be able to gain valuable insights from service marketing frameworks, tools, and strategies.

Intangibility

The most basic distinguishing characteristic of services is intangibility. Because services are performances or actions rather than objects, they cannot be seen, felt, tasted, or touched in the same manner that you can sense tangible goods. For example, health care services are actions (such as surgery, diagnosis, examination, and treatment) performed by providers and directed toward patients and their families. These services cannot be seen or touched by the patient, although the patient may be able to see and touch certain tangible components of the service (like the equipment or hospital room). In fact, many services such as health care are difficult to grasp even mentally. Even after a diagnosis or surgery has been completed the patient may not fully comprehend the service performed, although tangible evidence of the service (e.g., incision, bandaging, pain) may be apparent.

Resulting Marketing Implications Intangibility presents several marketing challenges. Many services cannot be inventoried due to capacity constraints, and therefore fluctuations in demand are often difficult to manage. For example, there is tremendous demand for resort accommodations in Phoenix in February but little demand in July. Yet resort owners have the same number of rooms to sell year-round.

Services cannot be easily patented, and new service concepts can therefore easily be copied by competitors. Services cannot be readily displayed or easily communicated to customers, so quality may be difficult for consumers to assess. Decisions about what to include in advertising and other promotional materials are challenging, as is pricing. The actual costs of a "unit of service" are hard to determine, and the price–quality relationship is complex.

Heterogeneity

Because services are performances, frequently produced, consumed, and often cocreated by humans, no two services will be precisely alike. The employees delivering the service frequently are the service in the customer's eyes, and people may differ in their performance from day to day or even hour to hour. Heterogeneity also results because no two customers are precisely alike; each will have unique demands or experience the service in a unique way. Because services are often coproduced and cocreated with customers, customer behaviors will also introduce variability and uncertainties, resulting in heterogeneity of outcomes. Thus, the heterogeneity connected with services is largely the result of human interaction (between and among employees and customers) and human behaviors, as well as all of the vagaries that accompany them. For example, a tax accountant may provide a different service experience to two different customers on the same day depending on their individual needs and personalities and on whether the accountant is interviewing them when he or she is fresh in the morning or tired at the end of a long day of meetings.

Resulting Marketing Implications   Because services are heterogeneous across time, organizations, and people, ensuring consistent service quality is challenging. Quality actually depends on many factors that cannot be fully controlled by the service supplier, such as the ability of the customer to articulate his or her needs, the ability and willingness of personnel to satisfy those needs, the presence (or absence) of other customers, and the level of demand for the service. Because of these complicating factors, the service manager cannot always know for sure that the service is being delivered in a manner consistent with what was originally planned and promoted. Sometimes services are provided by a third party, further increasing the potential heterogeneity of the offering.

Simultaneous Production and Consumption

Whereas most goods are produced first, then sold and consumed, many services are sold first and then produced and consumed simultaneously. For example, an automobile can be manufactured in Detroit, shipped to San Francisco, sold two months later, and consumed over a period of years. But restaurant services cannot be provided until they have been sold, and the dining experience is essentially produced and consumed at the same time. Frequently in service situations like the restaurant this also means that customers are present while the service is being produced and thus view and may even take part in the production process as coproducers or cocreators of the service. Simultaneity also means that customers will frequently interact with each other during the service production process and thus may affect each others' experiences. For example, strangers seated next to each other in an airplane may well affect the nature of the service experience for each other. That passengers understand this fact is clearly apparent in the way business travelers will often go to great lengths to be sure they are not seated next to families with small children. Another outcome of simultaneous production and consumption is that service producers find themselves playing a role as

Students in a university class cocreate the service experience with each other and the professor.

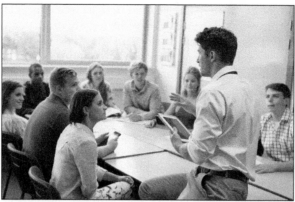

© Monkey Business Images/Shutterstock

part of the product itself and as an essential ingredient in the service experience for the consumer. Interestingly, with the advent of technology, many services can now be produced and consumed at different points in time, resulting in fewer challenges related to this characteristic for some providers.[35] For example, the development of online education allows asynchronous delivery of class lectures and information.

Resulting Marketing Implications Because services often (although not always) are produced and consumed at the same time, mass production is difficult. The quality of service and customer satisfaction will be highly dependent on what happens in "real time," including actions of employees, the interactions between employees and customers, and interactions among customers themselves. Clearly the real-time nature of services also results in advantages in terms of opportunities to customize offerings for individual consumers. Simultaneous production and consumption also means that it is not usually possible to gain significant economies of scale through centralization. Often, operations need to be relatively decentralized, so that the service can be delivered directly to the customer in convenient locations, although the growth of technology-delivered services is changing this requirement for many services. Also because of simultaneous production and consumption, the customer is involved in and observes the production process and thus may affect (positively or negatively) the outcome of the service transaction.

Perishability

Perishability refers to the fact that services cannot be saved, stored, resold, or returned. A seat on an airplane or in a restaurant, an hour of a lawyer's time, or space in a shipping container not used or purchased cannot be reclaimed and used or resold at a later time. Perishability is in contrast to goods that can be stored in inventory or resold another day, or even returned if the consumer is unhappy. Would it not be nice if a bad haircut could be returned or resold to another customer? Perishability makes this action an unlikely possibility for most services.

Resulting Marketing Implications A primary issue that marketers face in relation to service perishability is the inability to inventory. Demand forecasting and creative planning for capacity utilization are therefore important and challenging decision areas. The fact that services cannot typically be returned or resold also implies a need for strong recovery strategies when things do go wrong. For example, although a bad haircut cannot be returned, the hairdresser can and should have strategies for recovering the customer's goodwill if and when such a problem occurs.

Search, Experience, and Credence Qualities

One framework for isolating differences in evaluation processes between goods and services is a classification of properties of offerings proposed by economists.[36] Economists first distinguished between two categories of properties of products: *search qualities*, attributes that a customer can determine before purchasing a product, and *experience qualities*, attributes that can be discerned only after purchase or during consumption. Search qualities include color, style, price, fit, feel, hardness, and smell; experience qualities include taste, wearability, and comfort. Products such as automobiles, clothing, furniture, and jewelry are high in search qualities because their attributes can be almost completely determined and evaluated before purchase. Products such as vacations and restaurant meals are high in experience qualities because their attributes cannot be fully known or assessed until they have been purchased and are being consumed. A third category, *credence qualities,* includes characteristics that the consumer may find impossible to evaluate even after purchase and consumption.[37] Examples of offerings high in credence qualities are appendix operations, brake relinings on a car, and computer software updates. Few consumers possess medical, mechanical, or technical skills sufficient to evaluate whether these services are necessary or are performed properly, even after they have been prescribed and produced by the provider.

Figure 1.5 arrays products that are high in search, experience, or credence qualities along a continuum of evaluation ranging from easy to evaluate to difficult to evaluate. Products high in search qualities are the easiest to evaluate (left end of the continuum). Products high in experience qualities are more difficult to evaluate because they must be purchased and consumed before assessment is possible (center of the continuum). Products high in credence qualities are the most difficult to evaluate because the customer may be unaware of or may lack sufficient knowledge to appraise whether the offerings satisfy given wants or needs even after usage and/or consumption (right end of the continuum). Most goods fall to the left of the

FIGURE 1.5
Continuum of Evaluation for Different Types of Products

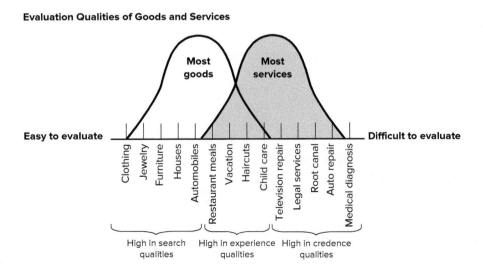

Evaluation Qualities of Goods and Services

continuum, whereas most services fall to the right because of the characteristics of services just described. These characteristics make services more difficult to evaluate than goods, particularly in advance of purchase. Difficulty in evaluation, in turn, forces consumers to rely on different cues and processes when deciding upon and assessing services.

Challenges and Questions for Service Marketers

Because of the basic characteristics of services, marketers of services face some very distinctive challenges. Answers to questions such as the ones listed here still elude managers of services:

How can service quality be defined and improved when the product is intangible and nonstandardized?

How can new services be designed and tested effectively when the service is essentially an intangible process and one that is frequently cocreated with customers and networks of providers?

How can the firm be certain it is communicating a consistent and relevant image when so many elements of the marketing mix communicate to customers and some of these elements are the service providers themselves?

How does the firm accommodate fluctuating demand when capacity is fixed and the service itself is perishable?

How can the firm best motivate and select service employees who, because the service is delivered in real time, become a critical part of the product itself?

How should prices be set when it is difficult to determine actual costs of production and price may be inextricably intertwined with perceptions of quality?

How should the firm be organized so that good strategic and tactical decisions are made when a decision in any of the functional areas of marketing, operations, and human resources may have significant impact on the other two areas?

How can the balance between standardization and personalization be determined to maximize both the efficiency of the organization and the satisfaction of its customers?

How can the organization protect new service concepts from competitors when service processes cannot be readily patented?

How does the firm communicate quality and value to customers when the offering is intangible and cannot be readily tried or displayed prior to the purchase decision?

How can the organization ensure the delivery and cocreation of consistent quality service when both the organization's employees and the customers themselves can affect the service outcome?

SERVICE MARKETING MIX

The preceding questions are some of the many raised by managers and marketers of services that will be addressed throughout the text through a variety of tools and strategies. Sometimes these tools are adaptations of traditional marketing tools, as with the service marketing mix presented here. Other times they are new, as in the case of service blueprinting presented in Chapter 8.

Traditional Marketing Mix

One of the most basic concepts in marketing is the *marketing mix,* defined as the elements an organization controls that can be used to satisfy or communicate with customers. The traditional marketing mix is composed of the four Ps: *product, place* (distribution), *promotion,* and *price*. These elements appear as core decision variables in any marketing text or marketing plan. The notion of a mix implies that all the variables are interrelated and depend on each other to some extent. Further, the marketing mix philosophy implies an optimal mix of the four factors for a given market segment at a given point in time.

Key strategy decision areas for each of the four Ps are captured in the top four groups in Table 1.2. Careful management of product, place, promotion, and price will clearly also be essential to the successful marketing of services. However, the strategies for the four Ps require some modifications when applied to services. For example, traditionally promotion is thought of as involving decisions related to sales, advertising, sales promotions, and publicity. In services these factors are also important, but because many services are produced and consumed simultaneously, service delivery people (such as clerks, ticket takers, nurses, and phone personnel) are involved in real-time promotion of the service even if their jobs are typically defined in terms of the operational functions they perform.

TABLE 1.2
Expanded Marketing Mix for Services

Product	Place	Promotion	Price
Physical good features	Channel type(s)	Promotion blend	Flexibility
Quality level	Exposure	Salespeople	Price level
Accessories	Intermediaries	Selection	Terms
Packaging	Outlet locations	Training	Differentiation
Warranties	Transportation	Incentives	Discounts
Product lines	Storage	Advertising	Allowances
Branding	Managing channels	Media types	
Product-support services		Types of ads	
		Sales promotion	
		Publicity	
		Internet/Web strategy	

People	Physical Evidence	Process
Employees	Facility design	Flow of activities
Recruiting	Equipment	Standardized
Training	Signage	Customized
Motivation	Employee dress	Number of steps
Rewards	Web pages	Simple
Teamwork	Other tangibles	Complex
Customers	Reports	Customer involvement
Education	Business cards	
Training	Statements	
	Guarantees	

Expanded Mix for Services

Because services are usually produced and consumed simultaneously, customers are often present in the firm's factory, interact directly with the firm's personnel, and are actually part of the service production process. Also, because services are intangible, customers will often be looking for any tangible cue to help them understand the nature of the service experience. For example, in the hotel industry the design and decor of the hotel as well as the appearance and attitudes of its employees will influence customer perceptions and experiences.

Acknowledgment of the importance of these additional variables has led service marketers to adopt the concept of an *expanded marketing mix* for services shown in the three remaining groups in Table 1.2.[38] In addition to the traditional four Ps, the services marketing mix includes *people, physical evidence,* and *process.*

> **People** All human actors who play a part in service delivery and thus influence the buyer's perceptions: namely, the firm's personnel, the customer, and other customers in the service environment.

All the human actors participating in the delivery of a service provide cues to the customer regarding the nature of the service itself. Their attitudes and behaviors, how these people are dressed, and their personal appearance all influence the customer's perceptions of the service. In fact, for some services, such as consulting, counseling, teaching, and other professional relationship–based services, the provider *is* the service. In other cases the contact person may play what appears to be a relatively small part in service delivery—for instance, a cable service installer, an airline baggage handler, or an equipment delivery dispatcher. Yet research suggests that even these providers may be the focal point of service encounters that can prove critical for the organization.

In many service situations, customers themselves can also influence service delivery, thus affecting service quality and their own satisfaction. For example, a client of a consulting company can influence the quality of service received by providing needed and timely information and by implementing recommendations provided by the consultant. Similarly, health care patients greatly affect the quality of service they receive when they either comply or do not comply with health regimens prescribed by the provider.

Customers not only influence their own service outcomes, but they can influence other customers as well. In a theater, at a ballgame, in a classroom, or online, customers can influence the quality of service received by others—either enhancing or detracting from other customers' experiences.

> **Physical evidence** The environment in which the service is delivered and where the firm and customer interact, as well as any tangible components that facilitate performance or communication of the service.

The physical evidence of service includes all the tangible representations of the service such as brochures, letterhead, business cards, reports, signage, equipment, and web pages. In some cases it includes the physical facility where the service is offered—the "servicescape"—for example, a retail bank branch facility. In other cases, such as telecommunication services, the physical facility is irrelevant. In this case other tangibles such as billing statements and appearance of the service vehicle and installer may be important indicators of quality. Especially when consumers have little on which to judge the actual quality of service, they will rely on these cues, just as they rely on the cues provided by the people and the service process. Physical evidence cues provide excellent opportunities for the firm to send consistent and strong messages regarding the organization's purpose, the intended market segments, and the nature of the service.

> **Process**   The procedures, mechanisms, and flow of activities by which the service is delivered, consumed, and cocreated—the service delivery and operating systems.

The delivery steps that the customer experiences, or the operational flow of the service, also give customers evidence on which to judge the service. Some services are very complex, requiring the customer to follow a complicated and extensive series of actions to complete the process. Highly bureaucratized services frequently follow this pattern, and the logic of the steps involved often escapes the customer. Another distinguishing characteristic of the process that can provide evidence to the customer is whether the service follows a production-line/standardized approach or whether the process is an empowered/customized one. None of these characteristics of the service is inherently better or worse than another. Rather, the point is that these process characteristics are another form of evidence used by the customer to judge service. For example, two successful airline companies, Southwest and Singapore Airlines, follow extremely different process models. Southwest is a no-frills (no food, no assigned seats), low-priced airline that offers frequent, relatively short domestic flights. All the evidence it provides is consistent with its vision and market position, as illustrated in Exhibit 1.2. Singapore Airlines, on the other hand, focuses on the business traveler and is concerned with meeting individual traveler needs. Thus, its process is highly customized to the individual, and employees are empowered to provide nonstandard service when needed. Both airlines have been very successful.

The three new marketing mix elements (people, physical evidence, and process) are included in the marketing mix as separate elements because they are particularly salient for services, they are within the control of the firm, and any or all of them may influence the customer's initial decision to purchase a service as well as the customer's level of satisfaction and repurchase decisions. The traditional elements as well as the new marketing mix elements will be explored in depth in future chapters.

STAYING FOCUSED ON THE CUSTOMER

Consistent with contemporary views of marketing that place the customer at the center of strategy, a critical theme running throughout the text is *customer focus*.[39] In fact, the subtitle of the book is "integrating customer focus across the firm." From the firm's point of view, this means that all strategies are developed with an eye on the customer, and all implementations are carried out with an understanding of their impact on the customer. From a practical perspective, decisions regarding new services and communication plans will integrate the customer's point of view; operations and human resource decisions will be considered in terms of their impact on customers. All the tools, strategies, and frameworks included in this text have customers at their foundation. The service marketing mix just described is clearly an important tool that addresses the uniqueness of services, keeping the customer at the center.

In this text, we also view customers as assets to be valued, developed, and retained. The strategies and tools we offer thus focus on customer relationship building and loyalty as opposed to a more transactional focus in which customers are viewed as one-time revenue producers. This text looks at customer relationship management not as a software program but as an entire architecture or business philosophy. Every chapter in the text can be considered a component needed to build a complete customer relationship management approach.

Southwest Airlines occupies a solid position in the minds of U.S. air travelers as a reliable, convenient, fun, low-fare, no-frills airline. Translated, this position means high value—a position reinforced by all elements of Southwest's service marketing mix. It has maintained this position consistently for more than 40 years while making money every year; no other U.S. airline comes close to this record.

Success has come for a number of reasons. One is the airline's low cost structure. It flies only one type of plane (Boeing 737s), which lowers costs because of the fuel efficiency of the aircraft itself combined with the ability to standardize maintenance and operational procedures. The airline also keeps its costs down by not serving meals, having no preassigned seats, and keeping employee turnover very low. Herb Kelleher (president of Southwest from its inception until 2001, and subsequently serving as chairman and chairman emeritus) was famous for his belief that employees come first, not customers. The Dallas-based carrier has managed to be the low-cost provider and a preferred employer while enjoying high levels of customer satisfaction and strong customer loyalty. Southwest's insistence that it will not charge for checked baggage—unlike almost every other airline—is another of its popular strategies that has won them customers from other airlines. Southwest Airlines has the best customer service record in the airline industry and has won the industry's "Triple Crown" for best baggage handling, best on-time performance, and best customer complaint statistics many times.

Observing Southwest Airlines's success, it is clear that all of its marketing mix elements are aligned around its highly successful market position. The three traditional service marketing mix elements all strongly reinforce the value image of the airline:

- **People** Southwest uses its people and customers very effectively to communicate its position. Employees are unionized, yet they are trained to have fun, are allowed to define what "fun" means, and are given authority to do what it takes to make flights lighthearted and enjoyable. People are hired at Southwest for their attitudes; technical skills can be and are trained. And they are the most productive workforce in the U.S. airline industry. Customers also are included in the atmosphere of fun, and many get into the act by joking with the crew and each other and by flooding the airline with letters expressing their satisfaction.

- **Process** The service delivery process at Southwest also reinforces its position. There are no assigned seats on the aircraft, so passengers line up and are "herded"

Southwest Airlines employees.

©Southwest Airlines/Stephen M. Keller

by assigned groups and numbers onto the plane, where they jockey for seats. With very few exceptions, the airline does not transfer baggage to connecting flights on other airlines. Food is not served in flight. In all, the process is very efficient, standardized, and low-cost, allowing for quick turnaround and low fares. Customers are very much part of the service process, taking on their roles willingly.

- **Physical evidence** All the tangibles associated with Southwest further reinforce the market position. Employees dress casually, wearing shorts in the summer to reinforce the "fun" and further emphasize the airline's commitment to its employees' comfort. No in-flight meal service confirms the low-price image through the absence of tangibles—no food. Because many people joke about airline food, its absence for many is not viewed as a value detractor. Southwest's simple, easy-to-use website is yet another form of consistent, tangible evidence that supports the airline's strong positioning and reinforces its image.

The consistent positioning using the service marketing mix reinforces the unique image in the customer's mind, giving Southwest Airlines its high-value position.

Source: K. Freiberg and J. Freiberg, *Nuts! Southwest Airlines' Crazy Recipe for Business and Personal Success* (Austin, TX: Bard Press, 1996); K. Labich, "Is Herb Kelleher America's Best CEO?" *Fortune,* May 2, 1994; H. Kelleher and K. Brooker, "The Chairman of the Board Looks Back," *Fortune,* May 28, 2001, pp. 62–76; J. H. Gitell, *The Southwest Airlines Way* (New York: McGraw-Hill, 2003); M. Unnikrishnan, "Southwest Remains Firmly Opposed to Baggage Fees," *Aviation Daily,* October 12, 2015, pp. 1–2.

Summary

This chapter has set the stage for further learning about service marketing by presenting information on changes in the world economy and business practice that have driven the focus on service: the fact that services dominate the modern economies of the world; the focus on service as a competitive business imperative; specific needs of the deregulated and professional service industries; the role of new service concepts growing from technological advances; and the realization that the characteristics of services result in unique challenges and opportunities. The chapter presented a broad definition of services as deeds, processes, and performances, and it drew distinctions among pure service, value-added service, customer service, and derived service.

Building on this fundamental understanding of the service economy, the chapter presents the key characteristics of services that underlie the need for distinct strategies and concepts for managing service businesses. These basic characteristics are that services are intangible, heterogeneous, produced and consumed simultaneously, and perishable. Because of these characteristics, service managers face a number of challenges in marketing, including the complex problem of how to deliver quality services consistently.

The chapter ended by describing two themes that provide the foundation for future chapters: the expanded marketing mix for services and customer focus as a unifying theme. The remainder of the text focuses on exploring the unique opportunities and challenges faced by organizations that sell and deliver services and on developing solutions that will help you become an effective service champion and manager.

Discussion Questions

1. What distinguishes service offerings from customer service? Provide specific examples.
2. How is technology changing the nature of customer service and service offerings?
3. What are the basic characteristics of services compared with goods? What are the implications of these characteristics for Airbnb, GE, Southwest Airlines, or the company you work for?
4. One of the underlying frameworks for the text is the expanded marketing mix for services. Discuss why each of the three new mix elements (process, people, and physical evidence) is included. How might each of these communicate with or help to satisfy an organization's customers?
5. Think of a service job you have had or currently have. How effective, in your opinion, was or is the organization in managing the elements of the service marketing mix?
6. Again, think of a service job you have had or currently have. How did or does the organization handle relevant challenges listed in Table 1.1?
7. How can quality service be used in a manufacturing context for competitive advantage? Think of your answer to this question in the context of automobiles, computers, or some other manufactured product you have purchased.

Exercises

1. Roughly estimate your spending for an average month. What percentage of your spending goes for services versus goods? Do the services you purchase have value? In what sense? If you had to cut back on your expenses, what would you cut out?

2. Visit two local retail service providers that you believe are positioned very differently (such as Target and Nordstrom, or Burger King and a fine restaurant). From your own observations, compare their strategies on the elements of the service marketing mix.

3. Try a service you have never tried before on the Internet or on your smart phone. Analyze the benefits of this service. Was enough information provided to make the service easy to use? How would you compare this service to other methods of obtaining the same benefits?

Notes

1. Sources for Chapter Opener: S. L. Vargo and R. R. Lusch, "Evolving to a New Dominant Logic for Marketing," *Journal of Marketing* 68 (January 2004), pp. 1–17; www.sdlogic.net; M. B. Sauter, T. C. Frohlich, and S. Stebbins, "2015's Customer Service Hall of Fame," *24/7 Wall Street as Reported in USA Today,* http://www.usatoday.com/story/money/business/2015/07/24/24-7-wall-st-customer-service-hallfame/30599943/; D. Leonard and R. Clough, "Move Fast and Break Things," *Bloomberg Businessweek,* March 21–27, 2016, pp. 54–59; Fortune Magazine's World's Most Admired Companies, 2016; D. MacMillan, "Saudis Back Uber as Market Heats Up," *The Wall Street Journal,* June 2, 2016, p. A1.

2. www.theacsi.org, accessed, May 2016.

3. J. B. Quinn, J. J. Baruch, and P. C. Paquette, "Technology in Services," *Scientific American* 257 (December 1987), pp. 50–58.

4. Vargo and Lusch, "Evolving to a New Dominant Logic for Marketing," pp. 1–17; R. F. Lusch and S. L. Vargo (eds.), *The Service-Dominant Logic of Marketing: Dialog, Debate, and Directions* (New York: M. E. Sharpe, 2006); *Journal of the Academy of Marketing Science,* Special Issue or the Service-Dominant Logic, Winter 2008.

5. W. M. Cox, "An Order of Prosperity to Go," *The New York Times,* February 17, 2010.

6. United States Census Bureau, "U.S. International Trade in Goods and Services, December 2015," www.census.gov, accessed May 10, 2016.

7. M. Sawhney, S. Balasubramanian, and V. V. Krishnan, "Creating Growth with Services," *Sloan Management Review* 45 (Winter 2004), pp. 34–43.

8. For research on the topic of goods firms transitioning to services, see: V. A. Zeithaml, S. W. Brown, M. J. Bitner, and J. Salas, *Profiting from Services and Solutions: What Product-Centric Firms Need to Know* (New York, NY, Business Expert Press, 2014). R. Oliva and R. Kallenberg, "Managing the Transition from Products to Services," *International Journal of Service Industry Management* 14 (2003), pp. 160–172; W. A. Neu and S. W. Brown, "Forming Successful Business-to-Business Services in Goods-Dominant Firms," *Journal of Service Research* 8 (August 2005), pp. 3–17; W. Reinartz and W. Ulaga, "How to Sell Services More Profitably," *Harvard Business Review* 86 (May 2008), pp. 90–96; A. Gustafsson, S. Brax, and L. Witell (eds), "Service Infusion in Manufacturing Industries," special issue of the *Journal of Service Management* 21 (2010).

9. R. H. K. Vietor, *Contrived Competition* (Cambridge, MA: Harvard University Press, 1994).

10. L. Berry, *Discovering the Soul of Service* (New York: The Free Press, 1999).

11. R. T. Rust, C. Moorman, and P. R. Dickson, "Getting Return on Quality: Revenue Expansion, Cost Reduction, or Both?" *Journal of Marketing* 66 (October 2002), pp. 7–24.

12. J. L. Heskett, T. O. Jones, G. W. Loveman, W. E. Sasser Jr., and L. A. Schlesinger, "Putting the Service–Profit Chain to Work," *Harvard Business Review* 72 (March–April 1994), pp. 164–174.

13. E. W. Anderson and V. Mittal, "Strengthening the Satisfaction–Profit Chain," *Journal of Service Research* 3 (November 2000), pp. 107–120; S. Gupta and V. A. Zeithaml, "Customer Metrics and Their Impact on Financial Performance," *Marketing Science* 25 (December 2006), pp. 718–739.

14. C. Fornell, S. Mithias, F. V. Morgeson III, and M. S. Krishnan, "Customer Satisfaction and Stock Prices; High Returns, Low Risk," *Journal of Marketing* 70 (January 2006), pp. 3–14; "Economic Indicator," www.theacsi.org, accessed May 11, 2016.

15. J. L. Heskett, W. E. Sasser Jr., and L. A. Schlesinger, *What Great Service Leaders Know and Do* (Oakland, CA: Berrett-Koehler Publishers, Inc., 2015).

16. C. Fishman, "But Wait, You Promised...," *Fast Company,* April 2001, pp. 116–127.

17. D. Brady, "Why Service Stinks," *BusinessWeek,* October 23, 2000, pp. 116–128; P. Noonan, "We Pay Them to Be Rude to Us," *The Wall Street Journal,* August 14–15, 2010, p. A11.

18. www.theacsi.org, accessed May 10, 2016.

19. R. T. Rust and M-H Huang, "The Service Revolution and the Transformation of Marketing Science," *Marketing Science* 33 (March/April 2014), pp. 206–221.

20. L. P. Willcocks and R. Plant, "Getting from Bricks to Clicks," *Sloan Management Review* 42 (Spring 2001), pp. 50–59.

21. I. C. L. Ng, *Creating New Markets in the Digital Economy* (Cambridge, UK: Cambridge University Press, 2014).

22. M. E. Porter and J. E. Heppelmann, "How Smart Connected Products are Transforming Companies," *Harvard Business Review* 92 (October 2015), pp. 64–88.

23. "The Social Life of Health Information, 2011," *Pew Internet and American Life Project,* www.pewinternet.org, accessed, July 7, 2011.

24. K. Steinmatz, "Exclusive: See How Big the Gig Economy Really Is," *Time,* January 6, 2016, http://time.com/4169532/sharing-economy-poll/.

25. M. J. Bitner, S. W. Brown, and M. L. Meuter, "Technology Infusion in Service Encounters," *Journal of the Academy of Marketing Science* 28 (Winter 2000), pp. 138–149.

26. M. J. Bitner, "Self-Service Technologies: What Do Customers Expect?" *Marketing Management* 10 (Spring 2001), pp. 10–11.

27. R. Hallowell, "Service in E-Commerce: Findings from Exploratory Research," *Harvard Business School,* Module Note, N9-800-418, May 31, 2000.

28. D. G. Mick and S. Fournier, "Paradoxes of Technology: Consumer Cognizance, Emotions, and Coping Strategies," *Journal of Consumer Research* 25 (September 1998), pp. 123–147.

29. A. Parasuraman and C. L. Colby, *Techno-Ready Marketing: How and Why Your Customers Adopt Technology* (New York: The Free Press, 2001); A. Parasuraman and C. L. Colby, "An Updated and Streamlined Technology Readiness Index: TRI 2.0," *Journal of Service Research* 18 (February 2015), pp. 59–74.

30. J. O. C. Hamilton, "Separation Anxiety," *Stanford Magazine*, January–February 2011, pp. 55–59.

31. "Customer Care in a New World," McKinsey & Company, 2001.

32. Discussion of these issues is found in many services marketing publications. The discussion here is based on V. A. Zeithaml, A. Parasuraman, and L. L. Berry, "Problems and Strategies in Services Marketing," *Journal of Marketing* 49 (Spring 1985), pp. 33–46. For another viewpoint on the subject of goods vs. services, see: C. Lovelock and E. Gummesson, "Whither Services Marketing? In Search of a New Paradigm and Fresh Perspectives," *Journal of Service Research* 7 (August 2004), pp. 20–41. See also: K. Hellen and J. Gummerus, "Re-Investigating the Nature of Tangibility/Intangibility and Its Influence on Consumer Experiences," *Journal of Service Management* 24 (2013), pp. 130–150.

33. For research supporting the idea of goods–services continua, see D. Iacobucci, "An Empirical Examination of Some Basic Tenets in Services: Goods–Services Continua," in *Advances in Services Marketing and Management,* eds. T. A. Swartz, D. E. Bowen, and S. W. Brown (Greenwich, CT: JAI Press, 1992), vol. 1, pp. 23–52.

34. S. L. Vargo and R. F. Lusch, "The Four Service Marketing Myths," *Journal of Service Research* 6 (May 2004), pp. 324–335.

35. H. T. Keh and J. Pang, "Customer Reactions to Service Separation," *Journal of Marketing* 74 (March 2010), pp. 55–70.

36. P. Nelson, "Information and Consumer Behavior," *Journal of Political Economy* 78 (1970), pp. 311–329.

37. M. R. Darby and E. Karni, "Free Competition and the Optimal Amount of Fraud," *Journal of Law and Economics* 16 (April 1973), pp. 67–86.

38. B. H. Booms and M. J. Bitner, "Marketing Strategies and Organizational Structures for Service Firms," in *Marketing of Services,* eds. J. H. Donnelly and W. R. George (Chicago: American Marketing Association, 1981), pp. 47–51.

39. See: G. S. Day and C. Moorman, *Strategy from the Outside In: Profiting from Customer Value* (New York: McGraw-Hill, 2010); J. Bliss, *Chief Customer Officer 2.0: How to Build Your Customer-Driven Growth Engine* (Hoboken, NJ: John Wiley & Sons, Inc., 2015).

Conceptual Framework of the Book: The Gaps Model of Service Quality

This chapter's objectives are to

1. Introduce the framework, called the gaps model of service quality, used to organize this textbook.
2. Demonstrate that the gaps model is a useful framework for understanding service quality in an organization.
3. Demonstrate that the most critical service quality gap to close is the customer gap, the difference between customer expectations and perceptions.
4. Show that four gaps that occur in companies, which we call provider gaps, are collectively responsible for the customer gap.
5. Identify the factors responsible for each of the four provider gaps.

Service Quality at Trader Joe's: The Specialty Store with Spirit

If you seek a matchless customer experience in grocery shopping, look no further than Trader Joe's, the whimsical privately-held chain of specialty food stores. Selling 80 percent private-label goods and featuring exclusive product favorites such as Speculoos cookie butter, dark chocolate peanut butter cups, $2.99 Charles Shaw label wine known as "Two-Buck Chuck" and white cheddar corn puffs, Trader Joe's also features its own brand of service excellence unlike any other grocery store.

From the moment you walk in, you feel the distinction. Stores are relatively small with a carefully selected set of only 4,000 SKUs versus the typical 50,000 SKUs. The employees—all of them wearing Hawaiian shirts—are virtually all engaged in and having fun doing their jobs. If a customer asks about a product, the employee never points but instead walks the customer over to the location, offering to tear open a package to let the customer sample the product. Walls are decked with cedar planks, signs are hand written, and the flavor of the South Seas pervades all aspects of the stores. Sampling trendy products is happening in most aisles. Bells are ringing rather than intercoms buzzing. And the shelves are packed with innovative, hard-to-find, tasty foods under the "Trader Joe's" name. As Beth Kowitt commented in *Fortune* magazine, ". . . Trader Joe's is no ordinary grocery chain. It's an offbeat, fun discovery zone that elevates food shopping from a chore to a cultural experience."[1]

Not only is the experience outstanding, but the company provides it all to the customer at low prices. Value is the philosophy on which the company bases its positioning—great everyday prices on all of its excellent products. It does this by buying direct from suppliers whenever possible, bargaining hard to get the best price, purchasing in volume, contracting early to get the best prices, eliminating products that do not satisfy customers, and keeping costs in the stores low. All of these approaches result in savings to the customer.

Trader Joe's listens closely to customers using informal, qualitative research. This research is not done through focus groups or contact centers, and the company has neither a toll-free number nor a customer care e-mail address. It finds out what customers want by talking to them—managers ("Captains") spend most of the day on the floor, where there are always multiple product samplings taking place, and anyone on the sales staff ("Crew Members") can directly e-mail a buyer to tell them what people are liking or not.

Besides being small, the interior of Trader Joe's is unique. Registers do not have conveyor belts and perishables are sold by unit instead of weight, which speeds up checkout. Product placement decisions are made based not on sales or profits but instead on what is best for the shopper. The Crew all wear Hawaiian shirts to evoke the image of the South Seas. The company webpage claims that they wear Hawaiian shirts because they are "traders on the culinary seas, searching the world over for cool items to bring home to [their] customers."[2] The bells are a specialty of Trader Joe's and are a simple system to communicate in the maritime tradition. One bell signals the need to open another register. Two bells indicates that there are additional questions needing to be answered at the checkout. Three bells call over a manager-type person.

How does the company get such engagement from its employees? Trader Joe's views employees as assets to be maximized and this results both in better operational efficiency and customer service, both of which result in better sales. Supervisory crew members ("Merchants" and "Mates") can start at $45,000–$75,000 per year and store managers ("Captains") can earn in the low six figures. The company also contributes 15.4 percent of employees' gross income to tax-deferred retirement accounts.[3] (www.traderjoes.com, accessed October 15, 2016). But compensation is not the whole story. A team atmosphere pervades the Crew. All employees, including Captains, work all aspects of the store, cooperating on a myriad of jobs. Besides offering customers free samples, they hand stickers out to your fidgeting children, and refund your money if you are unhappy with a purchase.

The company is known for not spending much money on marketing and advertising and does not even have an official Facebook or Twitter page. Most people hear about Trader Joe's through word of mouth. Virtually all the promotion comes through its zealous fan base acting as brand promoters who feature favorite snacks and experiences in their own social media. The one form of promotion is Trader Joe's Fearless Flyer comic-book-like newsletter, a quirky bulletin with amusing stories and product information.

How does Trader Joe's provide such service excellence and value? We will provide a framework for examining this question in this chapter, which specifies a conceptual framework of the book and—with it—a framework for offering service excellence to customers.

Effective service marketing is a complex undertaking that involves many different strategies, skills, and tasks. Executives of service organizations have long been confused about how to approach this complicated topic in an organized manner. This textbook is designed around one approach: viewing services in a structured, integrated way called the *gaps model of service quality*.[4] This model positions the key concepts, strategies, and decisions in services marketing and will be used to guide the structure of the rest of this book; sections of the book are tied to each of the gaps described in this chapter.

THE CUSTOMER GAP

The *customer gap* is the difference between customer expectations and perceptions (see Figure 2.1). Customer expectations are standards or reference points that customers bring into the service experience, whereas customer perceptions are subjective assessments of actual service experiences. Customer expectations often consist of what a customer believes should or will happen. For example, when you visit an expensive restaurant, you expect a high level of service, one that is considerably superior to the level you would expect in a fast-food restaurant. Closing the gap between what customers expect and what they perceive is critical to delivering quality service; it forms the basis for the gaps model.

Because customer satisfaction and customer focus are so critical to the competitiveness of firms, any company interested in delivering quality service must begin with a clear understanding of its customers. For this reason, we will devote the first part of the textbook to describing the relevant customer concepts, so that the focus of everything can relate back to these concepts. Considerable evidence exists that consumer evaluation processes differ for goods and services and that these differences affect the way service providers market their organizations. Unfortunately, much of what is known and written about consumer evaluation processes pertains specifically to goods.

The sources of customer expectations are marketer-controlled factors (such as pricing, advertising, and sales promises) as well as factors that the marketer has limited ability to affect (innate personal needs, word-of-mouth communications, and competitive offerings). In a perfect world, expectations and perceptions would be identical: customers would perceive that they have received what they thought they would and should. In practice these concepts are often separated by some distance. Broadly, it is the goal of service marketing to bridge this distance, and we will devote virtually the

FIGURE 2.1
The Customer Gap

entire textbook to describing strategies and practices designed to close this customer gap. We will describe customer expectations in detail in Chapter 3 and customer perceptions in Chapter 4.

THE PROVIDER GAPS

To close the all-important customer gap, the gaps model suggests that four other gaps—the *provider gaps*—need to be closed. These gaps occur within the organization providing the service (hence the term *provider gaps*) and include

Gap 1: The listening gap
Gap 2: The service design and standards gap
Gap 3: The service performance gap
Gap 4: The communication gap

The rest of this chapter is devoted to a description of the full gaps model.

Provider Gap 1: the Listening Gap

Provider gap 1, the *listening gap,* is the difference between customer expectations of service and company understanding of those expectations. The primary reason that many firms do not meet customers' expectations is that the firms lack an accurate understanding of exactly what those expectations are. Many reasons exist for managers not being aware of what customers expect: they may not interact directly with customers, they may be unwilling to ask about expectations, or they may be unprepared to address them. When people with the authority to set priorities and the responsibility to do so do not fully understand customers' service expectations, they may trigger a chain of bad decisions and suboptimal resource allocations that result in perceptions of poor service quality. In this text, we broaden the responsibility for the first provider gap from managers alone to any employee in the organization with the authority to change or influence service policies and procedures. In today's changing organizations, the authority to make adjustments in service delivery is often delegated to empowered teams and frontline people. In business-to-business situations, in particular, account teams make their own decisions about how to address their clients' unique expectations.

Figure 2.2 shows the key factors responsible for provider gap 1, the listening gap. An inadequate *customer research orientation* is one of the critical factors. When management or empowered employees do not acquire accurate information about customers' expectations, this gap is large. Formal and informal methods to capture information about customer expectations must be developed through customer research. Techniques involving a variety of traditional research approaches—among them customer interviews, survey research, complaint systems, and customer panels—must be used to stay close to the customer. More innovative techniques, such as structured brainstorming and monitoring online comments, are often needed.

Another key factor that is related to the listening gap is lack of *upward communication.* Frontline employees often know a great deal about customers; if management is not in contact with frontline employees and does not understand what they know, the gap widens.

Also related to the listening gap is a lack of company strategies to retain customers and strengthen relationships with them, an approach called *relationship marketing.* When organizations have strong relationships with existing customers, provider gap 1 is less likely to occur. Relationship marketing is distinct from transactional marketing, which is a more conventional emphasis on acquiring new customers rather than on

FIGURE 2.2
Key Factors Leading
to Provider Gap l:
the Listening Gap

Customer expectations

- *Inadequate customer research orientation*
  Insufficient customer research
  Research not focused on service quality
  Inadequate use of market research
- *Lack of upward communication*
  Lack of interaction between management and customers
  Insufficient communication between contact employees and managers
  Too many layers between contact personnel and top management
- *Insufficient relationship focus*
  Lack of market segmentation
  Focus on transactions rather than relationships
  Focus on new customers rather than relationship customers
- *Inadequate service recovery*
  Lack of encouragement to listen to customer complaints
  Failure to make amends when things go wrong
  No appropriate recovery mechanisms in place for service failures

Company perceptions of customer expectations

retaining them. Relationship marketing has always been a practice of wise business-to-business firms (such as IBM and General Electric) that recognize that clients have the potential to spend more with them if they provide excellent service. Other business-to-business firms, and many companies that sell to end customers, often take a short-term view and see each sale as a transaction. When companies focus too much on attracting new customers, they may fail to understand the changing needs and expectations of their current customers. Technology affords companies the ability to acquire and integrate vast quantities of customer data, which can be used to build relationships. Frequent flyer travel programs conducted by airlines, car rental companies, credit card companies, and hotels are among the most familiar programs of this type.

The final key factor associated with provider gap 1 is lack of *service recovery*. Even the strongest companies, with the best of intentions and clear understanding of their customers' expectations, sometimes fail. It is critical for an organization to understand the importance of service recovery—why people complain, what they expect when they complain, and how to develop effective service recovery strategies for dealing with inevitable service failures. Such strategies might involve a well-defined complaint-handling procedure and an emphasis on empowering employees to react on the spot, in real time, to fix the failure; other times it involves a service guarantee or ways to compensate the customer for the unfulfilled promise.

To address the factors in the listening gap, this text will cover topics that include how to understand customers through multiple research strategies (Chapter 5), how to build strong relationships and understand customer needs over time (Chapter 6), and how to implement recovery strategies when things go wrong (Chapter 7). Through these strategies, this first gap can be minimized.

Provider Gap 2: the Service Design and Standards Gap

Accurate perceptions of customers' expectations are necessary, but not sufficient, for delivering superior service. Another prerequisite is the presence of service designs and performance standards that reflect those accurate perceptions. A recurring theme in service companies is the difficulty experienced in translating customer expectations

Finding out what customers expect is the first step in closing all the gaps in an organization to provide service excellence. In Chapter 5 we will talk about many ways that companies determine customer perceptions, including customer surveys and complaints, but understanding what customers expect can often be more challenging. Putting customers in the "wish mode" is an innovative approach to closing gap 1 that proved successful for IKEA, the world's largest furniture retailer, when it opened its Chicago retail outlet. In this approach, nine groups of a dozen customers each were asked to dream up their ideal IKEA shopping experience. They were told to pretend that all IKEA stores had been destroyed and that new ones had to be designed from scratch. How would the store look? What would the shopping experience be like? Jason Magidson, who helped IKEA create the process, reported that customers responded with statements like the following:

© Volodymyr Kyrylyuk/Shutterstock

> "I never feel disoriented because I always know exactly where I am in relation to every department."
>
> "If I am buying one item, all of the other items that go with it are nearby."
>
> "Shopping is a pleasant, relaxing experience."

Even though they were not technical experts, customers were asked to actually draw up a design for a store that would satisfy their needs.

What is significant about IKEA's approach is not just that the company asked customers what they expected but that it subsequently incorporated these expectations into the service design for the store. Designers created a multistory octagonal building with an atrium in the center that formed a home base for shoppers, addressing their concern about being able to find items easily. In keeping with another customer expectation, items were grouped together with related products. When shoppers were tired or hungry, they could go to the cafeteria-style restaurant on the upper floor that served Swedish food. IKEA's customers were so satisfied with the store (85 percent rated it as "excellent" or "very good") that they returned more and spent about an hour longer than they did in other IKEA stores. These actions close gap 2 because service design was based on customer expectations.

IKEA has done an excellent job of closing all four provider gaps. The company's supplier network is carefully chosen and managed to ensure quality and consistency. Despite the fact that the company has stores in more than 30 countries, it keeps standards, designs, and approaches very consistent everywhere, thereby reducing the service design and standards gap. The company also makes important changes to standards when necessary. In 2006, the company took a major step to address a customer need to reduce long wait times. When company managers realized that wait times were so long that customers were leaving the stores without paying for their items because of congestion at checkout, they implemented a "line busting" initiative using handheld technology. In peak times, extra retail associates now roam the checkout area and invite credit card customers to step out of line and pay with a handheld unit and get a receipt from a mobile printer.

Servicescapes—the indoor and outdoor physical environments—are unique and customer focused, further closing gap 2. IKEA is also well known for its strong employee culture and careful hiring and training—factors that help reduce gap 3. In Chapter 12, we will tell you about another way the company closes gap 3: its innovative service concept that involves customers in the delivery, assembly, and creation of its products. To accomplish this service, the company educates its customers thoroughly with its scriptlike catalogs, thereby helping to close gap 4.

Sources: J. Magidson and G. Brandyberry, "Putting Customers in the 'Wish Mode,'" *Harvard Business Review* 79 (September 2001), pp. 26–28. "Who You Gonna Call?" *Chain Store Age* (January 2006), p. 8.

into service quality specifications that employees can understand and execute. These problems are reflected in provider gap 2, the difference between company understanding of customer expectations and the development of customer-driven service designs and standards. Customer-driven standards are different from the conventional performance standards that companies establish for service in that they are based on pivotal customer requirements that are visible to and measured by customers. They are operations standards set to correspond to customer expectations and priorities rather than to company concerns such as productivity or efficiency.

As shown in Figure 2.3, provider gap 2—which we call the *service design and standards gap*—exists in service organizations for a variety of reasons. Those people responsible for setting standards, typically management, sometimes believe that customer expectations are unreasonable or unrealistic. They may also believe that the degree of variability inherent in service defies standardization and therefore that setting standards will not achieve the desired goal. Although some of these assumptions are valid in some situations, they are often only rationalizations of management's reluctance to tackle head-on the difficult challenges of creating service standards to deliver excellent service. Technology changes and improvements are particularly helpful in closing this gap, as the Technology Spotlight in this chapter describes.

Because services are intangible, they are difficult to describe and communicate. This difficulty becomes especially evident when new services are being developed. It is critical that all people involved (managers, frontline employees, and behind-the-scenes support staff) work with the same concepts of the new service, based on customer needs and expectations. For a service that already exists, any attempt to improve it will also suffer unless everyone has the same vision of the service and associated issues. One of the most important ways to avoid provider gap 2 is to clearly design services without oversimplification, incompleteness, subjectivity, and bias. To do so, tools are needed to ensure that new and existing services are developed and improved in as careful a manner as possible. Chapter 8 describes the tools that are most effective in *service development and design,* including service blueprinting, a unique tool for services.

The quality of service delivered by customer contact personnel is critically influenced by the standards against which they are evaluated and compensated. Standards signal to contact personnel what management priorities are and which types of performance

FIGURE 2.3
Key Factors Leading to Provider Gap 2: the Service Design and Standards Gap

Gap 2

Customer-driven service designs and standards

• *Poor service design*
  Unsystematic new service development process
  Vague, undefined service designs
  Failure to connect service design to service positioning
• *Absence of customer-driven standards*
  Lack of customer-driven service standards
  Absence of process management to focus on customer requirements
  Absence of formal process for setting service quality goals
• *Inappropriate physical evidence and servicescape*
  Failure to develop tangibles in line with customer expectations
  Servicescape design that does not meet customer and employee needs
  Inadequate maintenance and updating of the servicescape

Management perceptions of customer expectations

really count. When service standards are absent or when the standards in place do not reflect customers' expectations, quality of service as perceived by customers is likely to suffer. When standards do reflect what customers expect, perceptions of the quality of service they receive are likely to be enhanced. Chapter 9 discusses the topic of *customer-defined service standards* and shows that if they are developed appropriately they can have a powerful positive impact on closing both provider gap 2 and the customer gap.

In Chapter 10 we focus on the roles of physical evidence in service design and in meeting customer expectations. By *physical evidence,* we mean everything from business cards to reports, signage, Internet presence, equipment, and facilities used to deliver the service. The *servicescape,* the physical setting where the service is delivered, is a particular focus of Chapter 10. Think of a restaurant, a hotel, a theme park, a health club, a hospital, or a school. The servicescape—the physical facility—is critical in these industries in terms of communicating about the service and making the entire experience pleasurable. In these cases the servicescape plays a variety of roles, from serving as a visual metaphor of what the company stands for to actually facilitating the activities of both consumers and employees. In Chapter 10 we explore the importance of physical evidence, the variety of roles it plays, and strategies for effectively designing physical evidence and the servicescape to meet customer expectations.

Provider Gap 3: the Service Performance Gap

Once service designs and standards are in place, it would seem that the firm is well on its way to delivering high-quality service. This assumption is true but is still not enough to deliver excellent service. The firm must have systems, processes, and people in place to ensure that service delivery actually matches (or is even better than) the designs and standards in place.

Provider gap 3—the *service performance gap*—is the discrepancy between the development of customer-driven service standards and actual service performance by company employees. Even when guidelines exist for performing services well and treating customers correctly, high-quality service performance is not a certainty. Standards must be backed by appropriate resources (people, systems, and technology) and must be enforced to be effective—that is, employees must be measured and compensated on the basis of performance along those standards. Thus, even when standards accurately reflect customers' expectations, if the company fails to provide support for those standards—if it does not facilitate, encourage, and require their achievement—standards do no good. When the level of service delivery falls short of the standards, it falls short of what customers expect as well. Narrowing the performance gap—by ensuring that all the resources needed to achieve the standards are in place—reduces the customer gap.

Research has identified many of the critical inhibitors to closing the *service performance gap* (see Figure 2.4). These factors include *employees* who do not clearly understand the roles they are to play in the company, employees who experience conflict between customers and company management, poor employee selection, inadequate technology, inappropriate compensation and recognition, and lack of empowerment and teamwork. These factors all relate to the company's human resource function and involve internal practices such as recruitment, training, feedback, job design, motivation, and organizational structure. To deliver better service performance, these issues must be addressed across functions (such as marketing and human resources).

Another important variable in provider gap 3 is the *customer.* Even if contact employees and intermediaries are 100 percent consistent in their service delivery, the uncontrollable behaviors of the customer can introduce variability in service delivery. If customers do not perform their roles appropriately—if, for example, they fail to provide all the information necessary to the provider or neglect to read and follow

FIGURE 2.4
**Key Factors
Leading to Provider
Gap 3: the Service
Performance Gap**

Customer-driven service
designs and standards

Gap
3

- *Deficiencies in human resource policies*
    Ineffective recruitment
    Role ambiguity and role conflict
    Poor employee–technology job fit
    Inappropriate evaluation and compensation systems
    Lack of empowerment, perceived control, and teamwork
- *Customers not fulfilling roles*
    Customers lack knowledge of their roles and responsibilities
    Customers negatively impact each other
- *Problems with service intermediaries*
    Channel conflict over objectives and performance
    Channel conflict over costs and rewards
    Difficulty controlling quality and consistency
    Tension between empowerment and control
- *Failure to match supply and demand*
    Failure to smooth peaks and valleys of demand
    Inappropriate customer mix
    Overreliance on price to smooth demand

Service delivery

instructions—service quality is jeopardized. Customers can also negatively influence the quality of service received by others if they are disruptive or take more than their share of a service provider's time. Understanding customer roles and how customers themselves can influence service delivery and outcomes is critical.

A third difficulty associated with provider gap 3 involves the challenge in delivering service through such *intermediaries* as retailers, franchisees, agents, and brokers. Because quality in service occurs in the human interaction between customers and service providers, company control over the service encounter is crucial, yet it rarely is fully possible. Most service (and many manufacturing) companies face an even more formidable task: attaining service excellence and consistency in the presence of intermediaries who represent them and interact with their customers yet are not under their direct control. Franchisers of services depend on their franchisees to execute service delivery as they have specified it. And it is that execution by the franchisee which the customer uses to evaluate the service quality of the company. With franchises and other types of intermediaries, someone other than the producer is responsible for the fulfillment of quality service. For this reason, a firm must develop ways to either control these intermediaries or motivate them to meet company goals.

Another issue in the service performance gap is the need in service firms to *synchronize demand and capacity*. Because services are perishable and cannot be inventoried, service companies frequently face situations of over- or underdemand. Lacking inventories to handle overdemand, companies lose sales when capacity is inadequate to handle customer needs. On the other hand, capacity is frequently underutilized in slow periods. Most service companies rely on operations strategies such as cross-training employees or varying the size of the employee pool to synchronize supply and demand. Marketing strategies for managing demand—such as price changes, advertising, promotion, and alternative service offerings—can supplement approaches for managing supply.

Technology Spotlight   Technology's Critical Impact on the Gaps Model of Service Quality

An early hallmark of services was the fact that they could not be provided remotely, that service was a local function provided in the intimate setting of a provider–customer relationship. Technology has relaxed this fundamental interpersonal, real-time requirement, resulting in increasing accessibility and globalization of services that can now be delivered and consumed anytime, anywhere. Many of these changes were not anticipated or reflected in the initial development of the gaps model.

Technology, in particular information technology, has dramatically influenced the nature of services themselves, how they are delivered, and the practice of service innovation and service management. Technology has had an impact on each of the gaps in the gaps model, as we will demonstrate.

TECHNOLOGY'S INFLUENCE ON THE CUSTOMER GAP

Technology advances have significantly influenced the customer gap. First, the nature of services themselves have changed. Now, many services are delivered by technology rather than in person by employees. Consider the personal photography industry. Not long ago, personal photos were taken by individuals, the film was processed by a service provider, and additional prints could be ordered and shared among friends and family. Putting together albums of photos and sharing photos with others was a labor-intensive process, often involving significant time, expense, and the linking together of many different service providers. Now, individuals use digital cameras to take as many photos as they wish, and they can print, manage, and share their photos online. This is just one small example of the proliferation of self-service technologies that have changed consumers' lives.

Technology has also dramatically changed how customers learn about services. Customers' ability to search the web and view photos of service locations, compare prices, and even experience services through virtual tours has dramatically changed the amount and type of information customers have prior to purchasing services. The availability of this information has influenced their expectations and ability to compare and judge services. In earlier days, customers found it difficult to gather this type of information and lacked the ability to compare services as easily as they could tangible goods that were displayed side-by-side in a retail store. To some extent the Internet now provides this same type of comparability for services.

TECHNOLOGY'S INFLUENCE ON PROVIDER GAP 1

The primary way technology has influenced provider gap 1 is in allowing firms to know their customers in ways not imagined in the past. One of the most powerful facilitators of these influences is marketing research conducted through social media such as Twitter, Facebook, and Google. On Twitter, when companies take time to respond to customers' specific tweets, particularly when they mention a problem or issue, customers feel special and that you have listened to them. One of the most important approaches is for companies to provide honest information, whether it is advice customers seek and especially if it is for a specific problem.

If you are on Facebook, you know the incredible ability of the platform to target services directly and individually to you. One of the authors of this book is a member of Plated, a company that configures and sends pre-packaged raw meals for customers to cook. In her feed, she gets ads for all of Plated's competitors (for example, Blue Apron and Hello Fresh). She is also a Nordstrom shopper, and gets regular ads for the retailer, even though she never made a Plated or Nordstrom purchase from Facebook. Facebook and Google have followed Amazon in creating mathematical models that track customer desires and input effectively.

Even more cutting-edge are freezer cases and shelves in retailing that have the ability to gather critical information about who you are and how you react to their products. At the National Retail Federation's Big Show, vendors demonstrated a freezer case with two amazing technology features. First, the glass is a touchscreen, catching a consumer's attention with animations and other promotions, that allows customers to learn more about what is inside without opening the door. Second, there is a camera at the top that analyzes shoppers' faces to record their facial expressions when looking at the products.

TECHNOLOGY'S IMPACT ON PROVIDER GAP 2

The focus of the Design and Standards Gap was on designing interpersonal services and real-time operational processes to meet customer expectations. The variability inherent in interpersonal services made designing and standardizing them quite difficult. There is now increasing focus on technology-enabled services and processes to close provider gap 2. Increasingly, customer expectations can be met through technology-enabled, highly standardized services provided on the Web. For example, take book sales and services provided online by Amazon (just one of its many product lines). Through its highly sophisticated technology infrastructure, the company is able to provide standardized ordering, payment, tracking, and recommendation services at the individual consumer level. Attempting to provide this level of service in a traditional book sales context to masses of people would be very idiosyncratic, inconsistent, and costly if it were done at the level Amazon performs online.

Technology has been the basic force behind service innovations now taken for granted such as Uber, Airbnb, and various smart services—for example the "connected car," smart meters for monitoring energy consumption, and remote health monitoring services. And established companies have developed brand new services based on information technology. Advances in information technology are also making it possible for whole suites of services in what is now termed the "Internet of things."

Technology has also facilitated the development of brand new services to meet needs and expectations that weren't even conceived of in prior decades. In health care, the ability to monitor patient conditions remotely and to train physicians in simulated surgical techniques via video technology are just two additional examples of technologybased services that meet customer expectations in very new and innovative ways.

TECHNOLOGY'S IMPACT ON PROVIDER GAP 3

Technology advances have allowed customer-contact employees to become more efficient and effective in serving customers. For example, today's technology allows Symantec customer service representatives to have several online "chats" with many customers simultaneously. Such capability allows employees to resolve problems much faster, increasing employee efficiency and generally creating a more satisfying customer experience. Thus, many firms today often explore ways that technology can be used to empower employees and close the service performance gap.

Technology has also empowered customers. Through technology customers can be more involved in co-creating and even adding value to their service experience. Self-service technologies—services produced entirely by the customer without any direct involvement or interaction with the firm's employees—have also changed the way companies think about closing provider gap 3. These technologies have proliferated as companies see the potential cost savings and efficiencies that can be achieved: potential sales growth, increased customer satisfaction, and competitive advantage. Medical websites allow patients access to information about particular diseases, drugs and drug interactions, and

specific doctors and hospitals; in this case technology enables patients to make more informed health-care decisions. As these examples illustrate, such technological advances have facilitated customer participation in service delivery—changing the way that provider gap 3 is conceptualized and the thinking of how it can be closed.

TECHNOLOGY'S IMPACT ON PROVIDER GAP 4

Traditional communication channels have been affected by technology infusion. There are a number of new channels that service firms can use for communicating with their customers, including blogs, targeted e-mails, customer communities, and employee chat. The number of channels and modes of communication that must be integrated effectively has exploded, exacerbating the challenge of providing consistent messages across all of them. These new channels are not simply options that service firms can consider—more and more they are becoming *expected* by customers as means of communication.

Online brand communities and easy/quick mass communication via the Internet are new channels that, whether provider or customer-controlled, can influence customer expectations for service firms. While it is well known that word-of-mouth (WOM) communication has always been especially important for services (whether business-to-business [B2B] or business-to-consumer [B2C]), these new avenues of peer-to-peer and customer-to-customer communication make WOM an even more important influence in setting expectations for services today. Technology also results in the potential for reaching out to customers around the globe in ways not possible when, in the not-so-distant past, services were limited to local provision. The Internet itself knows no boundaries, and therefore information, customer service, and transactions can move across countries and across continents, reaching any customer who has access to the Web.

This Technology Spotlight illustrates the profound impact of technology in recent decades on strategies associated with closing each of the provider gaps. We covered some of the examples of how technology advances and how these innovations have influenced these strategies.

Source: L. Northrup, January 19, 2016 at https://consumerist.com/2016/01/19/this-freezer-case-knows-when-youre-frowning-atthe-bagel-bites/; J. Boitnott, pulled June 17 at http://www.inc.com/john-boitnott/howto-learn-more-about-your-customers-through-twitter.html; M. J. Bitner, V. A. Zeithaml, and D. D. Gremler, "Technology's Critical Impact on the Gaps Model of Service Quality," in *The Handbook of Service Science,* ed. P. Maglio, J. Spohrer, and C. Kieliszewski (Springer, Berlin, Heidelberg, Germany, 2009).

We will discuss strategies to deal with the roles of employees in Chapter 11, customers in Chapter 12, and demand and capacity in Chapter 13.

Provider Gap 4: the Communication Gap

Provider gap 4, the *communication gap,* illustrates the difference between service delivery and the service provider's external communications. Promises made by a service company through its media advertising, sales force, and other communications may raise customer expectations, the standards against which customers assess service quality. The discrepancy between actual and promised services, therefore, can widen the customer gap. Broken promises can occur for many reasons: overpromising in advertising or personal selling, inadequate coordination between operations and marketing, and differences in policies and procedures across service outlets. Figure 2.5 shows the key factors that lead to the communication gap.

In addition to unduly elevating expectations through exaggerated claims, there are other, less obvious ways in which external communications influence customers' service quality assessments. Service companies frequently fail to capitalize on opportunities to educate customers to use services appropriately. They also neglect to manage customer expectations of what will be delivered in service transactions and relationships.

One of the major difficulties associated with provider gap 4 is that communications to consumers involve issues that cross organizational boundaries. Because service advertising promises what people do, and because what people do cannot be controlled the way machines that produce physical goods can be controlled, this type of communication involves functions other than the marketing department. This type of marketing is what we call *interactive marketing*—the marketing between contact people and customers—and it must be coordinated with the conventional types of *external marketing* used in product and service firms. When employees who promote the service do not fully understand the reality of service delivery, they are likely to

FIGURE 2.5
Key Factors Leading to Provider Gap 4: the Communication Gap

make exaggerated promises or fail to communicate to customers aspects of the service intended to serve them well. The result is poor service quality perceptions. Effectively coordinating actual service delivery with external communications, therefore, narrows the communications gap and favorably affects the customer gap.

Another issue in provider gap 4 is associated with the pricing of services. In packaged goods (and even in durable goods), customers possess enough price knowledge before purchase to be able to judge whether a price is fair or in line with competition. With services, customers often have no internal reference points for prices before purchase and consumption. Pricing strategies such as discounting, "everyday prices," and couponing obviously need to be different in service situations in which the customer has no initial sense of prices. Techniques for developing prices for services are more complicated than those for pricing tangible goods.

In summary, external communications—whether from marketing communications or pricing—can create a larger customer gap by raising expectations about service delivery. In addition to improving service delivery, companies must also manage all communications to customers, so that inflated promises do not lead to higher expectations. Chapter 14 will discuss integrated services marketing communications, and Chapter 15 will cover pricing to accomplish these objectives.

PUTTING IT ALL TOGETHER: CLOSING THE GAPS

The full conceptual model, shown in Figure 2.6, conveys a clear message to managers wishing to improve their quality of service: the key to closing the customer gap is to close provider gaps 1 through 4 and keep them closed. To the extent that one or more of provider gaps 1 through 4 exist, customers perceive service quality shortfalls. The gaps model of service quality serves as a framework for service organizations attempting to improve quality service and services marketing. The Strategy Insight provides a *service quality gaps audit* based on the model.

The model begins where the process of improving service quality begins: with an understanding of the nature and extent of the customer gap. Given the service organization's need to focus on the customer and to use knowledge about the customer to drive business strategy, this foundation of emphasis is warranted.

FIGURE 2.6
Gaps Model of Service Quality

Strategy Insight Using the Gaps Model to Assess an Organization's Service Strategy

The gaps model featured in this chapter and used as a framework for this textbook is a useful way to audit the service performance and capabilities of an organization. The model has been used by many companies as an assessment or service audit tool because it is comprehensive and offers a way for companies to examine all the factors that influence service quality. To use the tool, a company documents what it knows about each gap and the factors that affect the size of the gap. Although you will learn much more about each of these gaps throughout the book, we provide here a basic gaps audit. In Exercise 1 at the end of the chapter, we propose that you use this audit with a company to determine its service quality gaps. As practice, you could evaluate Trader Joe's, the company featured in the opening vignette, to see how its approaches work to close each of the gaps.

Service Quality Gaps Model Audit

For each of the following factors in the gaps, indicate the effectiveness of the organization on that factor. Use a 1 to 10 scale where 1 is "poor" and 10 is "excellent."

Customer Gap	1 = Poor 10 = Excellent
1. How well does the company understand customer expectations of service quality? 2. How well does the company understand customer perceptions of service?	
Provider Gap 1, the Listening Gap	
1. Market Research Orientation • Are the amount and type of market research adequate to understand customer expectations of service? • Does the company use this information in decisions about service provision? **2. Upward Communication** • Do managers and customers interact enough for management to know what customers expect? • Do contact people tell management what customers expect? **3. Relationship Focus** • To what extent does the company understand the expectations of different customer segments? • To what extent does the company focus on relationships with customers rather than transactions? **4. Service Recovery** • How effective are the service recovery efforts of the organization? • How well does the organization plan for service failures? **Score for Provider Gap 1**	
Provider Gap 2, the Service Design and Standards Gap	
5. Systematic Service Design • How effective is the company's service development process? • How well are new services defined for customers and employees? **6. Presence of Customer-Defined Standards** • How effective are the company's service standards? • Are they defined to correspond to customer expectations? • How effective is the process for setting and tracking service quality goals?	

	1 = Poor 10 = Excellent
7. Appropriate Physical Evidence and Servicescape • Are the company's physical facilities, equipment, and other tangibles appropriate to the service offering? • Are the company's physical facilities, equipment, and other tangibles attractive and effective? **Score for Provider Gap 2**	
Provider Gap 3, the Service Performance Gap **8. Effective Human Resource Policies** • How effectively does the company recruit, hire, train, compensate, and empower employees? • Is service quality delivery consistent across employees, teams, units, and branches? **9. Effective Role Fulfillment by Customers** • Do customers understand their roles and responsibilities? • Does the company manage customers to fulfill their roles, especially frequent customers that are incompatible? **10. Effective Alignment with Service Intermediaries** • How well are service intermediaries aligned with the company? • Is there conflict over objectives and performance, costs and rewards? • Is service quality delivery consistent across the outlets? **11. Alignment of Demand and Capacity** • How well is the company able to match supply with demand fluctuations? **Score for Provider Gap 3**	
Provider Gap 4, the Communication Gap **12. Integrated Service Marketing Communications** • How well do all company communications—including the interactions between company employees and customers—express the same message and level of service quality? • How well does the company communicate to customers about what will be provided to them? • Does the company avoid overpromising and overselling? • How well do different parts of the organization communicate with each other, so that service quality equals what is promised? **13. Pricing** • Is the company careful not to price so high that customer expectations are raised? • Does the company price in line with customer perceptions of value? **Score for Provider Gap 4**	

The score for each gap should be compared to the maximum score possible. Are particular gaps weaker than others? Which areas in each gap need attention?

As you go through the rest of the book, we will provide more detail about how to improve the factors in each of the gaps.

Summary

This chapter presented the integrated gaps model of service quality (shown in Figure 2.6), a framework for understanding and improving service delivery. The entire text will be organized around this model of service quality, which focuses on five pivotal gaps in delivering and marketing service:

The customer gap: Difference between customer expectations and perceptions
Provider gap l: the listening gap
Provider gap 2: the service design and standards gap
Provider gap 3: the service performance gap
Provider gap 4: the communication gap

The gaps model positions the key concepts, strategies, and decisions in service marketing in a manner that begins with the customer and builds the organization's tasks around what is needed to close the gap between customer expectations and perceptions. The final chapter in the book, Chapter 16, discusses the financial implications of service quality, reviewing the research and company data that indicates linkages between service quality and financial performance.

Discussion Questions

1. Think about a service you receive. Is there a gap between your expectations and perceptions of that service? What do you expect that you do not receive?
2. Consider the "wish mode" discussion about IKEA. Think about a service that you receive regularly and put yourself in the wish mode. How would you change the service and the way it is provided?
3. If you were the manager of a service organization and wanted to apply the gaps model to improve service, which gap would you start with? Why? In what order would you proceed to close the gaps?
4. Can provider gap 4, the communication gap, be closed prior to closing any of the other three provider gaps? How?
5. Which of the four provider gaps do you believe is hardest to close? Why?

Exercises

1. Choose an organization to interview, and use the integrated gaps model of service quality as a framework. Ask the manager whether the organization suffers from any of the factors listed in the figures in this chapter. Which factor in each of Figures 2.2 through 2.5 does the manager consider the most troublesome? What does the company do to try to address the problems?
2. Use the Internet to locate the website of Disney, Marriott, Ritz-Carlton, or any other well-known, high-quality service organization. Which provider gaps has the company closed? How can you tell?
3. Interview a nonprofit or public sector organization in your area (it could be some part of your school if it is a state school). Find out if the integrated gaps model of service quality framework makes sense in the context of its organization.

Notes

1. B. Kowitt, *Fortune Magazine,* September 6, 2010, p. 87.
2. Trader Joe's webpage www.traderjoes.com, pulled March 29, 2016.
3. Emily Co, www.popsugar.com, February 1, 2016, accessed March 29, 2016.
4. The gaps model of service quality that provides the structure for this text was developed by and is fully presented in V. A. Zeithaml, A. Parasuraman, and L. L. Berry, *Delivering Quality Service: Balancing Customer Perceptions and Expectations* (New York: The Free Press, 1990).

Focus on the Customer

Chapter 3 Customer Expectations of Service

Chapter 4 Customer Perceptions of Service

THE CUSTOMER GAP

The figure shows a pair of boxes from the gaps model of service quality that correspond to two concepts—*customer expectations* and *customer perceptions*—that play a major role in services marketing. Customer expectations are the standards of performance or reference points for performance against which service experiences are compared, and they are often formulated in terms of what a customer believes should or will happen. Customer perceptions are subjective assessments of actual service experiences.

The Customer Gap

We devote the second part of the textbook to describing this gap and other relevant customer concepts because excellent service marketing requires a focus on the customer. We detail what is known about customer expectations in Chapter 3, and customer perceptions in Chapter 4. Knowing what customers want and how they assess what they receive is the foundation for designing effective services.

Customer Expectations of Service

This chapter's objectives are to

1. Recognize that customers hold different types of expectations for service performance.
2. Discuss several sources of customer expectations of service.
3. Acknowledge that the types and sources of expectations are similar for end consumers and business customers, for pure service and product-related service, for experienced customers and inexperienced customers.
4. Delineate some important issues surrounding customer expectations.

Undoubtedly, the greatest gap between customer expectations and service delivery exists when customers travel from one country to another. For example, in Japan the customer is supreme. At the morning opening of large department stores in Tokyo, sales personnel line up to welcome patrons and bow as they enter! When one of us—who could speak no Japanese—visited Tokyo a few years ago, as many as eight salespeople willingly tried to help find a calligraphy pen. Although the pen was a very low-priced item, several attendants rushed from counter to counter to find someone to translate, several others spread out to find pens that might serve as the perfect gift, and still others searched for maps to other stores where the perfect pen could be found.

Because of the wonderful treatment Japanese customers are used to in their home country, they often have service expectations that exceed service delivery even when shopping in "civilized" countries such as Great Britain. One Japanese tourist was puzzled and annoyed as he stood in a London department

© YOSHIKAZU TSUNO/AFP/Getty Images

Tokyo sales personnel provide excellent customer service.

store while two shop assistants conversed instead of serving him. He left without buying anything.[1] His annoyance is understandable when you realize the standard of service treatment in Japan.

Expectations of hotel service may also differ from one country to another. In the United States, a "two-star" designation for a hotel is generally interpreted to mean customers can expect guest rooms to be clean; beds to be comfortable; rooms to be sparsely decorated and equipped with some modern conveniences such as a microwave oven, refrigerator, color television, sofa bed, telephone, and coffee maker; and the hotel to provide daily maid service. For such hotels the customer is not expecting (and does not want to pay for) luxury, extra service, beautiful, spacious lobbies, or room service availability but still wants to have a fairly decent, clean, and safe place to stay. The hotel might also include a work desk, voicemail, and high-speed Internet access in the room. However, experienced travelers to Great Britain would be very surprised to find this level of service at a two-star hotel in London.

In fact, another one of us had firsthand experience with differing customer expectations with hotel service in London. In particular, a four-night hotel stay was booked for a family of four (including two children) at what was promised by a travel agent to be a two-star hotel. However, this London hotel did not meet expectations of a two-star hotel. Instead, the hotel had rooms for a maximum of two people, slanting floors (and, therefore, beds), 24-inch-wide showers stalls, room entry doors that did not fully latch, hallways with no lights, and a huge hole in the wall behind one toilet with insects coming and going as they pleased. In addition, the daily "maid service" consisted of simply emptying the trash cans in the rooms and leaving the door to one of the rooms unlatched. No new towels or sheets were provided, and no cleaning of any kind was done in the room. Clearly the level of service did not match expectations, although seasoned European travelers were not surprised when we described our service experience. Obviously, not all two-star London hotels have such "features." However, we were surprised to find that many of our European friends did not find our service experience to be extremely unusual for a two-star hotel in a large, expensive city like London. Their expectations of service are quite different from ours.

Customer expectations are beliefs about service delivery that serve as standards or reference points against which performance is judged. Because customers compare their perceptions of performance with these reference points when evaluating service quality, thorough knowledge about customer expectations is critical to service marketers. Knowing what the customer expects is the first and possibly most critical step in delivering quality service. Being wrong about what customers want can mean losing a customer's business when another company hits the target exactly. Being wrong can also mean expending money, time, and other resources on things that do not count to the customer. Being wrong can even mean not surviving in a fiercely competitive market.

Among the aspects of expectations that need to be explored and understood for successful service marketing are the following: What types of expectations do customers hold about service? What factors most influence the formation of these expectations? What role do these factors play in changing expectations? How can a service company meet or exceed customer expectations?

In this chapter we provide a framework for thinking about customer expectations.[2] The chapter is divided into three main sections: (1) the meaning and types of expected service, (2) factors that influence customer expectations of service, and (3) issues involving customers' service expectations.

SERVICE EXPECTATIONS

To say that expectations are reference points against which service delivery is compared is only a beginning. The level of expectation can vary widely depending on the reference point the customer holds. Although most everyone has an intuitive sense of what expectations are, service marketers need a far more thorough and clear definition of expectations to comprehend, measure, and manage them.

Imagine that you are planning to go to a restaurant. Figure 3.1 displays a continuum of possible service expectations. On the left of the continuum are different types or levels of expectations, ranging from high (top) to low (bottom). At each point we give a name to the type of expectation and illustrate on the right side of the figure what it might mean in terms of a restaurant you are considering. Note how important the expectation you hold will be to your eventual assessment of the restaurant's performance. Suppose you went into a restaurant for which you hold the minimum tolerable expectation, paid very little money, and were served immediately with good food. Alternatively, suppose that you went to a restaurant for which you had the highest (ideal) expectations, paid a lot of money, and were served good (but not fantastic) food. Which restaurant experience would you judge to be best? The answer is likely to depend on the reference point that you brought to the experience.

Because the idea of customer expectations is so critical to evaluation of service, we start this chapter by talking about the types of expectations.

FIGURE 3.1
Possible Levels of Customer Expectations

The ideas presented in this figure are based upon R. K. Teas, "Expectations, Performance Evaluation, and Consumers' Perceptions of Quality," *Journal of Marketing* (October 1993), pp. 18–34.

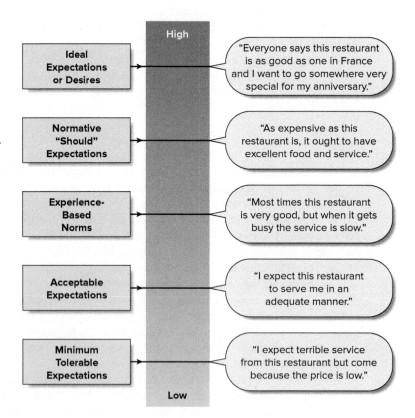

Types of Expectations

As we show in Figure 3.1, customers hold different types of expectations about service. For purposes of our discussion in the rest of this chapter, we focus on two types. The highest expectations can be termed *desired service*: the level of service the customer hopes to receive—the "wished for" level of performance. Desired service is a blend of what the customer believes "can be" and "should be."[3] For example, consumers who sign up for an online dating service expect to find compatible, attractive, interesting people to date and perhaps even someone to marry. This expectation reflects the hopes and wishes of these consumers. In a similar way, you are likely to engage the services of your college's placement office when you are ready to graduate. What are your expectations of the service? In all likelihood you want the office to help find you a job—the right job in the right place for the right salary—because that is what you hope and wish for.

However, you probably also see that the economy may constrain the availability of ideal job openings in companies. And not all companies you may be interested in have a relationship with your university's placement office. In this situation and in general, customers hope to achieve their service desires but recognize this is not always possible. We call the threshold level of acceptable service *adequate service*—the minimum level of service the customer will accept.[4] Sometimes when there is a slowdown in the economy, many college graduates who have trained for high-skilled jobs accept entry-level positions at fast-food restaurants or internships for no pay. Their hopes and desires are still high, but they recognize that they cannot attain those desires in the market that exists at the time. Their standard of adequate service from the placement office was much lower than their desired service. Some graduates accept any job for which they can earn a salary, and others agree to nonpaying, short-term positions as interns to gain experience. Adequate service expectations represents the "minimum tolerable expectation,"[5] the bottom level of performance acceptable to the customer.

Figure 3.2 shows these two expectation standards as the upper and lower boundaries for customer expectations. This figure portrays the idea that customers assess service performance on the basis of two standard boundaries: what they desire and what they deem acceptable. This chapter's Global Feature illustrates some of the challenges firms face in understanding what customers' expectations are, particularly when delivering service to customers in another country.

FIGURE 3.2
Dual Customer Expectation Levels

The characteristics of services often make it difficult for customers to know what to expect from a service provider. Imagine the difficulty of knowing what to expect if you were to "outsource" many of the day-to-day tasks you perform to someone whom you never meet in person and who lives in a foreign country. Many families face this situation when they select a service provider located overseas.

OFFSHORING OF PERSONAL CONSUMER SERVICES

As indicated in Chapter 1, many U.S. companies are involved in offshore outsourcing of services. More than $20 billion is spent annually on services provided outside of the United States. A growing percentage of U.S. families are now using service providers in foreign countries to complete personal tasks for them. Thanks to the technology available to many households today, including instant messaging, computer scanners, and e-mail attachments, services that can be completed without requiring face-to-face interaction have the potential to be done overseas. Some of the services that can be outsourced to foreign countries include interior design, word processing, legal services, mural painting, wedding planning, personal website design, and landscape design. To illustrate,

- One customer wanted to create a short, but professional-looking, video to show at his sister's wedding. He found a graphic artist in Romania, who created a two-minute video with a space theme set to the music of *Star Wars* that was a hit at the wedding. The cost for everything? Only $59.
- A man was looking for a graphic artist to illustrate a children's book his mother had written for her grandchildren about her early childhood experiences in New York City. Rather than search for a graphic artist through a local telephone directory, he described his project on the Guru.com website. Within a week he received 80 bids from artists in countries like Malaysia, Ukraine, and Lebanon.

He ended up hiring a woman from the Philippines who offered to do 25 drawings for $300.

- One family hired an online tutor for their daughter. After obtaining quotes around $40/hour for local tutoring services, they found an online tutor from India who charged $99/month for two-hour, five-day-per-week sessions. The lessons simply required the family to have a digital tablet, instant messaging, and a headset for communication.
- The website Fiverr.com allows customers to purchase a variety of services which are often provided by overseas sellers. The offerings include such services as logo design, personal assistance, editorial work, résumé creation, or white board animation. Fiverr considers their global team of service providers to be their greatest asset—an executive in California can send out a task or project before bedtime, and wake up the next morning to feedback and fresh ideas from a variety of cultural perspectives.

EXPECTATIONS OF SERVICE

Outsourcing services at the consumer level raises some issues. As discussed in this chapter, desired service expectations are influenced by explicit service promises, implicit service promises, word-of-mouth communication, and past experience. However, when outsourcing personal services in the manner listed earlier, many of these factors may not be present. For example, in many cases communication with such service providers be conducted via e-mail or online chat sessions—providing a limited amount of cues upon which promises are based, word-of-mouth recommendations may be restricted to Internet or social media sources, and customers may have no experience with such services. To further complicate the matter for customers, many have limited exposure to having *any* previous work done for them through the Internet, and most are likely to have never hired a foreign service provider.

In such settings, customers may attempt to communicate their expectations of service, but face obstacles in

The Zone of Tolerance

As we discussed in Chapter 1, services are heterogeneous in that performance may vary across providers, across employees from the same provider, and even with the same service employee. The extent to which customers recognize and are willing to accept this variation is called the *zone of tolerance* and is shown in Figure 3.3. If service drops below adequate service—the minimum level considered acceptable—customers will be frustrated and most likely dissatisfied with the company. If service performance is above the zone of tolerance at the top end—where performance exceeds desired service—customers will be very pleased and probably quite surprised as well. You might consider the zone of tolerance as the range in which customers do not particularly notice service performance. When it falls outside the range (either very low or very high), the service gets doing so. If the service provider's native language is not English, there is a good chance for misunderstanding. For example, one customer had a language issue with an outsourcer based in Egypt. The outsourcer put together a personal website for the customer—but drafts included several misspelled words. Not surprisingly, e-mails with instructions and explanations were labor-intensive or time-consuming because of the language gap. Thus, customers looking to outsource services to foreign providers may anticipate having to put significant energy and effort into communicating expectations.

Wall Street Journal reporter Ellen Gamerman asked an India-based outsourcer to design a change-of-address card for someone who was moving from New York to Arizona. Although he did a good job with the design, there were a couple of communication miscues: (1) he initially put ever-greens in the desert background and (2) he had the car in the card driving west to east initially, not east to west. When the instructions were initially given, she did not spell out exactly what she wanted—she gave him a general idea of the theme of the card, then asked him to be creative. Although he was happy to make changes to correct these issues, the price went up to cover the changes.

Using a foreign service provider may require customers to reset their expectations. One customer decided to use outsourcing for his personal income taxes. After he e-mailed his earnings and scanned receipts, his tax return was completed in two days at a cost of $50—about one-third of what a U.S. firm like H&R Block charges. However, he had to file his return as "self-prepared," since it was not prepared by a U.S. accountant.

Another issue customers may face is one of trust: how willing are customers to entrust a worker thousands of miles away—and in a foreign country—with projects of a personal nature? To provide some information about the quality of service a customer might expect from a service provider, services on many websites, such as the previously mentioned Fiverr.com, provide a ratings system that allows customers to leave feedback that is published on the provider's page. Some vendors post short videos of themselves and their offices on the Internet to help shape customers' expectations and gain their trust.

Some U.S. customers receive tutoring service from providers in India.

Sources: E. Gamerman, "Outsourcing Your Life," *The Wall Street Journal,* June 2, 2007, pp. P1, P4; A. Blinder, "Offshoring: The Next Industrial Revolution?" *Foreign Affairs* 85 (March/April 2006), pp. 113–118; E. Gamerman, e-mail communication, July 30, 2007; A. Ngo, "The Death of the Handshake: Rise of Digital Team," *Fiverr,* www.fiverr.com, accessed July 12, 2016.

the customer's attention in either a positive or negative way. As an example, consider waiting in line to purchase movie tickets. Most customers hold a range of acceptable times for this service encounter—probably somewhere between 5 and 10 minutes. If waiting to purchase the tickets consumes that period of time, customers probably do not pay much attention to the wait. If a customer enters the line and finds a sufficient number of movie theater personnel to serve her in the first two or three minutes, she may notice the service and judge it as excellent. On the other hand, if a customer has to wait in line for 15 minutes, he may begin to grumble and look at his watch. The more the wait falls below the zone of tolerance (10 minutes in this example), the more frustrated he becomes.

Customers' service expectations are characterized by a range of levels (like those shown in Figure 3.3), bounded by desired and adequate service, rather than a single level.

FIGURE 3.3
The Zone of
Tolerance

This tolerance zone, representing the difference between desired service and the level of service considered adequate, can expand and contract for a given customer. An airline customer's zone of tolerance will narrow when she is running late and is concerned about making her plane. A minute's delay for anything that occurs prior to boarding the plane seems much longer, and her adequate service level increases. On the other hand, a customer who arrives at the airport early may have a larger tolerance zone, making the wait in line far less noticeable than when he is pressed for time. This example shows that the marketer must understand not just the size and boundary levels for the zone of tolerance but also when and how the tolerance zone fluctuates for a given customer.

Different Customers Possess Different Zones of Tolerance

Another aspect of variability in the range of reasonable services is that different customers possess different tolerance zones. Some customers have narrow zones of tolerance (often because what they consider to be minimally acceptable is greater), requiring a smaller, but higher, range of service from providers, whereas other customers have a greater range of expectations of service. For example, very busy customers would likely always be pressed for time, desire short wait times in general, and hold a constrained range for the length of acceptable wait times. When it comes to meeting plumbers or appliance repair personnel at their homes, customers who work outside the home have a more restricted window of acceptable time duration for that appointment than do customers who work in their homes or do not work at all. For example, airline companies must fully understand customer views of new service technologies (see Technology Spotlight).

A customer's zone of tolerance increases or decreases depending on a number of factors, including company-controlled factors such as price. When prices increase, customers tend to be less tolerant of poor service. In this case, the zone of tolerance decreases because the adequate service level shifts upward. Later in this chapter we will describe many different factors, some company controlled and others customer controlled, that lead to the narrowing or widening of the tolerance zone.

The fluctuation in a customer's zone of tolerance is more a function of changes in the adequate service level, which moves readily up and down because of situational circumstances, than in the desired service level, which tends to move upward incrementally because of accumulated experiences. Desired service is relatively stable compared with adequate service, which moves up and down and in response to competition and other factors. Fluctuation in the zone of tolerance can be likened to an accordion's movement, but with most of the gyration coming from one side (the adequate service level) rather than the other (the desired service level).

FIGURE 3.4
**Differing Zones
of Tolerance for
Different Service
Dimensions**

Adapted from L. L. Berry,
A. Parasuraman, and
V. A. Zeithaml, "Ten Lessons
for Improving Service
Quality," *Marketing Science
Institute,* Report No. 93–104
(May 1993).

Zones of Tolerance Vary for Service Dimensions

Customers' tolerance zones also vary with different service attributes or dimensions. The more important the factor, the narrower the zone of tolerance is likely to be. In general, customers are likely to be less tolerant about unreliable service (broken promises or service errors) than other service deficiencies, which means that they have higher expectations for this factor. In addition to higher expectations for the most important service dimensions and attributes, customers may relax their expectations for the less important factors, making the zone of tolerance for the most important service dimension smaller and the desired and adequate service levels higher.[6] Figure 3.4 portrays the likely difference in tolerance zones for the most important factor (in this case, reliability) and a factor that might be considered less important (such as empathy) for a given service.[7]

FACTORS THAT INFLUENCE CUSTOMER EXPECTATIONS OF SERVICE

Because expectations play such a critical role in customer evaluation of services, marketers need to understand the factors that shape them. In this section of the chapter we describe some of the key influences on customer expectations.

Sources of Desired Service Expectations

Personal Needs

As shown in Figure 3.5, there are three major influences on desired service level. The first, *personal needs,* are those states or conditions essential to the physical or psychological well-being of the customer and are pivotal factors that shape what customers desire in service. Personal needs can fall into many categories, including physical, social, psychological, and functional. A fan who regularly goes to baseball games right from work, and is therefore thirsty and hungry, hopes and desires that the food and drink vendors will pass by his section frequently, whereas a fan who regularly has dinner elsewhere has a lower level of desired service from the vendors. A customer with high social and dependency needs may have relatively high expectations for a hotel's ancillary services, hoping, for example, that the hotel has a bar with live music and

Technology Spotlight Customer Expectations of Airport Services Using Technology

One of the most difficult tasks that marketers face is understanding what customers expect from services, and nowhere is this problem more evident than when these services involve technology. Customers almost always resist technology initially—perhaps because they do not understand it, perhaps because they fear change—even when the technology leads to improved service. Technology that makes obtaining service easier and faster is springing up all over, even in airports around the country. Customers are accepting some new service technologies and resisting others. Here we discuss two innovations that are meeting different fates.

One service technology that has been accepted by customers is automatic airline check-in: customers walk up to computer screens, slide credit cards, and use touch pads to retrieve their boarding passes and receipts. On most flights, including many international ones, customers can check luggage automatically as well, and an attendant takes their luggage from them before they go to their gates. The service generally takes less time than working with an attendant, and most airlines now have more computers than they previously had lines for attendants, saving customers considerable time. When these computers were first installed, customers were not sure what to expect and did not know how to use them. Airlines that supplied extra employees to stand and help customers use the computers found success in converting customers from the human handling to the technology. More recently, most of the larger airlines have created mobile phone apps that allow customers to check seat assignments (and change them), identify arrival and departure gates, examine itineraries for upcoming trips, and review recent activity on their frequent flier accounts.

Another airport technology that has been accepted more slowly by customers is called Exit Express and is a technology substitute for toll booths as customers leave airport parking areas. It works like this: before customers exit the airport, they use a machine (similar to a subway token machine) to pay their parking fees in advance. They insert their parking ticket, then their credit card or cash, and receive back their stamped parking ticket. When they exit the parking lot, they use one of the many Exit Express lanes, insert their paid ticket, and leave. Airports typically still retain a small number of lanes that use live employees and operate in the traditional way. Surprisingly, many airports are finding that customers do not use Exit Express technology as much as expected.

Why are many customers resisting the Exit Express technology that clearly meets or exceeds their expectations of getting out of the airport quickly? One possible reason is that they do not understand how the system works, even though a loudspeaker in the parking lots trumpets the new system continuously. They also may not clearly see the benefits being provided, possibly because the airport does not communicate them well enough, leading customers to believe that the old system with toll booths is quick enough. Another reason is that most airports have not stationed employees near the

FIGURE 3.5
Factors that Influence Desired Service

© andresr/Getty Images RF

Some airlines allow customers to check in by using a mobile phone.

tickets issued by the airlines, which allowed them to get boarding passes. When "advanced check-in" became available on most domestic U.S. flights, customers grew accustomed to checking in before arriving at the airport (as much as 24 hours in advance of departure) and printing their boarding passes themselves. Now, most airlines can send electronic boarding passes (complete with a bar code) directly to customers' mobile phones—thus removing the requirement for customers to carry a physical (printed) boarding pass altogether. As with Exit Express, some customers have been slow to embrace the use of electronic boarding passes—and for similar reasons: they do not understand how the technology works, they do not understand how to retrieve their electronic boarding pass, they get anxious when having to retrieve it quickly on their phone when other passengers are waiting in line behind them, and they are not sure what to do if the technology fails them during their travels.

If services enhanced by technology are to meet the expectations of customers, they must be trusted, understood, and introduced as valuable to customers. Otherwise, the promise of meeting or exceeding customer expectations will not be realized despite large investments.

Source: M. L. Meuter, M. J. Bitner, A. L. Ostrom, and S. W. Brown, "Choosing among Alternative Service Delivery Modes: An Investigation of Customer Trial of Self-Service Technologies," *Journal of Marketing* 69 (April 2005), pp. 61–83.

technology (i.e., check-out kiosk) to familiarize customers with it and to deal with service failures, as the airlines did with automatic check-in. Customers may also fear that, if something were to go wrong, they would be embarrassed and not know how to resolve the situation. A final compelling reason is that many customers distrust the technology the way they used to distrust automated teller machine (ATM) technology when it was first introduced.

Over the years customers have adapted to changes in various aspects of airline travel brought on by technology. Less than 20 years ago most travelers carried

dancing. The effect of personal needs on desired service is illustrated by the different expectations held by two business insurance customers:

> "I expect [an insurance] broker to do a great deal of my work because I don't have the staff . . . I expect the broker to know a great deal about my business and communicate that knowledge to the underwriter."

> "My expectations are different . . . I do have a staff to do our certificates, etc., and use the broker minimally."[8]

Personal Service Philosophy

A second influence on desired service expectations is *personal service philosophy*—the customer's underlying generic attitude about the meaning of service highest expectations and the proper conduct of service providers. If you have ever been employed as a server in a restaurant, you are likely to have standards for restaurant service that have been shaped by your training and experience in that role. You might, for example, believe that servers should not keep customers waiting longer than 15 minutes to take their orders. Knowing the way a kitchen operates, you may be less tolerant of lukewarm food or errors in the order than customers who have not held the role of server. In general, customers who are themselves in service businesses or have worked for them in the past seem to have especially strong service philosophies.

Derived Service Expectations

Another influence on desired service expectations is called *derived service expectations,* which occur when customer expectations are driven by another person or group of people. A niece from a big family who is planning a 90th birthday party for a favorite aunt is representing the entire family in selecting a restaurant for a successful celebration. Her needs are driven in part by expectations derived from the other family members. A parent choosing a vacation for the family, a spouse selecting a home-cleaning service, an employee choosing an office for the firm—all these customers' individual expectations are intensified because they represent and must answer to other parties who will receive the service. In the context of business-to-business service, customer expectations are driven by the expectations of their own customers. The head of an information technology department in an insurance company, who is the business customer of a large computer vendor, has expectations based on those of the insurance customers she serves: when the computer equipment is down, her customers complain. Her need to keep the system up and running is not just her own desire but is derived from the pressure of her firm's customers.

Sources of Adequate Service Expectations

A different set of determinants affects adequate service, the level of service the customer finds acceptable. In general, these influences are short-term and tend to fluctuate more than the factors that influence desired service. In this section we discuss three factors shown in Figure 3.6, which influence adequate service: perceived service alternatives, situational factors, and predicted service.

Problems with the initial service can also lead to heightened expectations. Performing a service right the first time is very important because customers value service reliability above all other dimensions. If the service fails in the recovery

FIGURE 3.6
Factors that Influence Adequate Service

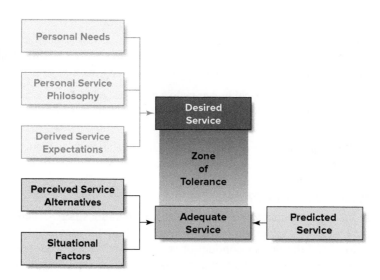

phase, fixing it right the second time (i.e., being reliable in service recovery) is even more critical than it was the first time. Automobile repair service provides a case in point. If a problem with your automobile's brakes sends you to a car repair provider, you expect the company to fix the brakes. If you experience further problems with the brakes after the repair, the level of service you consider to be adequate will increase. In these and other situations where temporary service intensifiers are present, the level of adequate service will increase and the zone of tolerance will narrow.

Perceived Service Alternatives

Perceived service alternatives are other providers from whom customers can, or perceive they can, obtain service. If customers believe they have multiple service providers to choose from, or if they can provide the service for themselves (such as lawn care or personal grooming), their levels of adequate service are higher than those of customers who believe it is not possible to get better service elsewhere. An airline customer who lives in a small town with a tiny airport, for example, has a reduced set of options in airline travel. This customer will be more tolerant of the service performance of the carriers in the town because few alternatives exist. She will accept the limited schedule of flights and lower levels of service more than the customer in a big city who has myriad flights and airlines from which to choose. The customer's perception that service alternatives exist raises the level of adequate service and narrows the zone of tolerance.

It is important that service marketers fully understand the complete set of options that customers view as perceived alternatives. In the small town airport example just discussed, the set of alternatives from the customer's point of view is likely to include more than just other airlines: limousine service to a nearby large city, rail service, or driving. In general, service marketers must discover the alternatives that the customer views as comparable rather than those in the company's competitive set.

Situational Factors

Levels of adequate service are also influenced by *situational factors* that are generally considered contemporary in nature. One type is *uncontrollable situational factors,* which include service performance conditions that customers view as beyond the control of the service provider. For example, catastrophes that affect a large number of people at one time (tornadoes or earthquakes) may lower service expectations for insurance customers in other geographic locations because they recognize that insurers are inundated with demands for their services. During the days following the Hurricane Katrina disaster, telephone and Internet service was poor because so many people were trying to get in touch with friends and relatives. Similarly, guests at the Ritz-Carlton, Omni, and Marriott hotels in New Orleans quickly realized that they should not expect the level of service to which they had become accustomed. Customers of all these services were quite forgiving during these days because they understood the source of the problem. Customers who recognize that situational factors are not the fault of the service company may accept lower levels of adequate service, given the context. Situational factors often temporarily lower the level of adequate service, widening the zone of tolerance.

Personal situational factors consist of short-term, individual factors that make a customer more aware of the need for service. Personal emergency situations in which service is urgently needed (such as an accident and the need for automobile insurance or a breakdown in office equipment during a busy period) raise the level

FIGURE 3.7
Factors that Influence Desired and Predicted Service

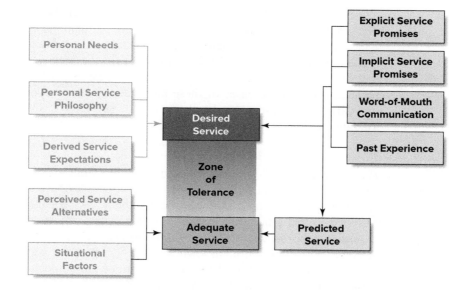

of adequate service expectations, particularly in terms of the level of responsiveness required and considered to be acceptable. An online company that depends on network connectivity to receive customer orders will be more demanding of its Internet service provider during peak demand periods. Any system breakdown will be tolerated less during these intense periods than at other times. The impact of personal situational factors is evident in these comments by two participants in a research study:

> An automobile insurance customer: "The nature of my problem influences my expectations; for example, a broken window versus a DWI accident requiring brain surgery."

> A business equipment repair customer: "I had calibration problems with the X-ray equipment. They should have come out and fixed it in a matter of hours because of the urgency."[9]

Predicted Service

The final factor that influences adequate service is *predicted service* (Figure 3.7), the level of service that customers anticipate they are likely to get. This type of service expectation can be viewed as predictions made by customers about what is likely to happen during an impending transaction or exchange. Predicted service performance implies some objective calculation of the probability of performance or estimate of anticipated service performance level. If customers predict good service, their levels of adequate service are likely to be higher than if they predict poor service. For example, full-time residents in a college town usually predict faster restaurant service during the summer months when students are not on campus. This prediction will probably lead them to have higher standards for adequate service in restaurants during the summer than during school months. On the other hand, customers of cable service providers and utilities in a college town know that installation service from these firms will be difficult to obtain during the first few weeks of school when myriad students are setting up their apartments for the year. In this case, levels of adequate service decrease and zones of tolerance widen.

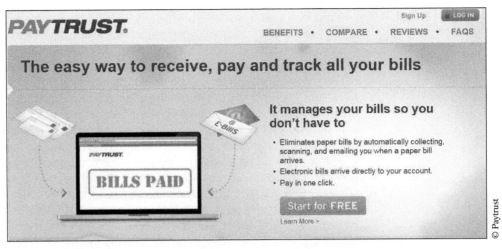

Paytrust's explicit service promises influence expectations of desired service.

Predicted service is typically an estimate or a calculation of the service that a customer will receive in an individual transaction rather than in the overall relationship with a service provider. Whereas desired and adequate service expectations are global assessments comprising many individual service transactions, predicted service is almost always an estimate of what will happen in the next service encounter or transaction that the customer experiences. For this reason, predicted service is viewed in this model as an influencer of adequate service.

Sources of Both Desired and Predicted Service Expectations

When consumers are interested in purchasing services, they are likely to seek or take in information from several different sources. For example, they may call a store, ask a friend, or deliberately track newspaper advertisements to find the needed service at the lowest price. They may also receive service information by watching television, surfing the Internet, or hearing an unsolicited comment from a colleague about a service that was performed well. In addition to these active and passive types of external search for information, consumers may conduct an internal search by reviewing the information held in memory about the service. This section discusses four factors that influence both desired service and predicted service expectations: explicit service promises, implicit service promises, word-of-mouth communication, and past experience.

Explicit Service Promises

Explicit service promises are personal and nonpersonal statements about the service made by the organization to customers. The statements are personal when they are communicated by the firm's salespeople or service personnel; they are nonpersonal when they come from the company's web pages, advertising, brochures, and other written publications. The web page depicted above displays the promises made on the Internet by Paytrust, an online bill-paying service. On this web page Paytrust influences customers' expectations by indicating that *all* bills can be received and paid online. Explicit service promises are one of the few influences on expectations that are completely within the control of the service provider.

Promising exactly what will ultimately be delivered would seem a logical and appropriate way to manage customer expectations and ensure that reality fits the promises. However, companies and the personnel who represent them often deliberately overpromise to obtain business or inadvertently overpromise by stating their best estimates about delivery of a service in the future. In addition to overpromising, company representatives simply do not always know the appropriate promises to make because services are often customized and therefore not easily defined and repeated; the representative may not know when or in what final form the service will be delivered.

All types of explicit service promises have a direct effect on desired service expectation. If a firm's website promises to design an ideal home theater experience for a customer, perform audio and video set-up, and connect all of the customer's various components and home network, the customer's desires for that service (as well as the service of competitors) will be shaped by this promise. A hotel customer describes the impact of explicit promises on expectations: "They get you real pumped up with the beautiful ad. When you go in you expect the bells and whistles to go off. Usually they don't." A business equipment repair customer states, "When you buy a piece of equipment you expect to get a competitive advantage from it. Service is promised with the sale of the equipment." A particularly dangerous promise that many companies today make to their business customers is to provide a "total solution" to their business needs. This promise is very difficult to deliver.

Explicit service promises influence the levels of both desired service and predicted service. They shape what customers desire in general as well as what they predict will happen in the next service encounter from a particular service provider or in a certain service encounter.

A service firm with a "posh" interior is likely to lead to greater customer expectations.

Implicit Service Promises

Implicit service promises are service-related cues, other than explicit promises, that lead to inferences about what the service should and will be like. These quality cues are dominated by price and the tangibles associated with the service. In general, the higher the price and the more impressive the tangibles, the more a customer will expect from the service. Consider a customer who shops for insurance, finding two firms charging radically different prices. She may infer that the firm with the higher price should and will provide higher-quality service and better coverage. Similarly, a customer who stays at a posh hotel with a luxurious lobby is likely to desire and predict a higher standard of service than from a hotel with less impressive facilities.

Word-of-Mouth Communication

The importance of *word-of-mouth communication* in shaping expectations of service is well documented.[10] These statements made by parties other than the organization—such as those found on social networking websites—convey to customers what the service will be like and influence both predicted and desired service.[11] Word-of-mouth communication carries particular weight as an information source because it is perceived as unbiased. Word-of-mouth communication tends to be very important in services that are difficult for customers to evaluate before purchase and before having direct experience of them. Experts (including *Consumer Reports,* friends, and family)

Strategy Insight How Service Marketers Can Influence Customers' Expectations

How might a manager of a service organization use the information we have developed in this chapter to create, improve, or market services? First, managers need to know the pertinent expectation sources and their relative importance for a customer population, a customer segment, and perhaps even a particular customer. They need to know, for instance, the relative weight of word-of-mouth communication, explicit service promises, implicit service promises, and past experience in shaping desired service and predicted service. Some of these sources are more stable and permanent in their influence (such as personal service philosophy and personal needs) than the others, which fluctuate considerably over time (like perceived service alternatives and situational factors). We provide here some ways that customer expectations might be influenced.

Factor	Possible Influence Strategies
Personal needs	• Educate customers on ways the service addresses their needs.
Personal service philosophy	• Use market research to profile personal service philosophies of customers and use this information in designing and delivering services.
Derived service expectations	• Use market research to determine sources of derived service expectations and their requirements. Then, focus advertising and marketing strategy on ways the service allows the focal customer to satisfy the requirements of the influencing customer(s).
Perceived service alternatives	• Be fully aware of competitive offerings and, where possible and appropriate, match them.
Situational factors	• Increase service delivery capacity during peak periods or in emergencies. • Use service guarantees to assure customers about service recovery regardless of the situational factors that occur.
Predicted service	• Tell customers when service provision is higher than what can normally be expected, so that predictions of future service encounters will not be inflated.
Explicit service promises	• Make realistic and accurate promises that reflect the service actually delivered rather than an idealized version of the service. • Ask contact people for feedback on the accuracy of promises made in advertising and personal selling. • Avoid engaging in price or advertising wars with competitors because they take the focus off customers and escalate promises beyond the level at which they can be met. • Formalize service promises through a service guarantee that focuses company employees on the promise and that provides feedback on the number of times promises are not fulfilled.
Implicit service promises	• Ensure that service tangibles are consistent with and accurately reflect the type and level of service provided. • Ensure that price premiums can be justified by higher levels of performance by the company on important service attributes.
Word-of-mouth communications	• Simulate word of mouth in advertising by using testimonials and opinion leaders. • Identify influencers and opinion leaders for the service and concentrate marketing efforts on them. • Use incentives with existing customers to encourage them to say positive things about the service or create positive reviews via social media.
Past experience	• Use marketing research to profile customers' previous experience with similar services.

and social media (such as Facebook and Twitter) are also word-of-mouth sources that can affect the levels of desired and predicted service.

Past Experience

Past experience, the customer's previous exposure to service that is relevant to the focal service, is another force in shaping predictions and desires. For example, you probably compare each stay in a particular hotel with all previous stays in that hotel. But past experience with the focal hotel is likely to be a very limited view of your past experience. You may also compare each stay with your experiences in other hotels and hotel chains. Customers also compare across industries: hospital patients, for example, compare hospital stays against the standard of hotel visits. Cable service customers tend to compare cable service with the standards set by telephone service, one reason cable service is often judged to be poor. Past experience may incorporate previous experience with the focal service provider, typical performance of similar service offerings, and experience with the last service purchased.[12]

The different sources vary in terms of their credibility as well as their potential to be influenced by the marketer. The Strategy Insight shows the breakdown of various factors and how service marketers can influence them. Chapter 14 will detail these and other strategies that service marketers can use to match delivery to promises and thereby better manage customer expectations.

ISSUES INVOLVING CUSTOMERS' SERVICE EXPECTATIONS

The following issues represent topics of particular interest to service marketers concerning customer expectations. In this section we discuss frequently asked questions about customer expectations:

- What does a service marketer do if customer expectations are "unrealistic"?
- Should a company try to delight the customer?
- How does a company exceed customers' service expectations?
- Do customers' service expectations continually escalate?
- How does a service company stay ahead of competition in meeting customer expectations?

What Does a Service Marketer Do if Customer Expectations Are "Unrealistic"?

One inhibitor to learning about customer expectations is management's and employees' fear of asking. This apprehension often stems from the belief that customer expectations will be extravagant and unrealistic and that by asking about them a company will set itself up for even loftier expectation levels (that is, "unrealistic" levels). However, compelling evidence, shown in Exhibit 3.1, suggests that customers' main expectations of service are quite simple and basic: "Simply put, customers expect service companies to do what they are supposed to do. They expect fundamentals, not fanciness; performance, not empty promises."[13] Customers want service to be delivered as promised. They want planes to take off on time, hotel rooms to be clean, food to be hot, and service providers to show up when scheduled. Unfortunately, many service customers are disappointed and let down when companies fail to meet these basic service expectations.

A simple way to learn if customers' expectations are realistic is to ask them. Asking customers about their expectations does not so much raise the levels of the

Expectation	What This Means to the Customer	Illustrative Service Provider Behaviors
Competency	• "I want everything handled correctly the first time." • "I expect them to know how this works."	• *Appliance Repairman*: Fix the broken refrigerator correctly so that it does not break down again a week later. • *Travel Agent*: Inform the traveler of the visa requirements for each country to be visited.
Explanations	• "I want to know what is happening." • "I want to know how this works."	• *Airline Counter Agent*: Provide passengers frequent updates on the delayed flight's status. • *Insurance Agent*: Clearly explain the policy and answer all questions the customer has about what is (or is not) covered.
Respect	• "I want to feel like a valued customer."	• *Hotel Desk Manager*: Listen to the guest's concerns about his room and act accordingly. • *Health Care Clinic Receptionist*: Verbally greet each patient and make eye contact upon entrance into the clinic.
Hygiene	• "I expect the facilities to be clean and well kept." • "I expect my home to be kept clean while they are working."	• *Restaurant Manager*: Walk through the dining area every 15 minutes and sweep the floor as needed. • *Plumber*: Wear protective shoe coverings when walking through the customer's house.
Flexibility	• "I would like them to be able to accommodate my situation." • "I expect them to be able to bend the rules a little."	• *Golf Instructor*: Provide concurrent lessons for the customer and his daughter. • *Credit Card Service Representative*: Examine the customer's payment history and waive the late payment fee if this is not a regular occurrence.
Urgency	• "I expect my situation to be taken seriously and addressed quickly."	• *Forklift Service Manager*: Arrange for replacement parts to be delivered and installed for the client by the end of the day. • *Tax Accountant*: Respond within 4 hours to any inquiries from existing customers, within one business day to potential new customers.
Consistency	• "I expect to receive the same level of service each and every time."	• *Dry Cleaner*: Provide the same level of cleanliness and crease the pants in the same spot each and every time. • *Oil Change Technician*: Check and "top off" all six fluids for the customer automobile on every visit.
Hassle-free	• "I want the process to be simple and easy for me."	• *Lawn Care Technician*: Arrive each quarter without being prompted and provide an automatic payment option once service is completed. • *Computer Remote Support Agent*: Complete laptop computer tune-up and install needed software updates without requiring any additional input from the customer.
Promptness	• "I do not want to wait a long time to be served." • "I expect to receive help quickly."	• *Post Office Clerk*: Request assistance/additional help from staff in the back room when the line of customers grows to more than six. • *Financial advisor*: Respond to all telephone calls within 2 (business) hours and emails within 4 hours.
Competence	• "I want some assurance they know what they are doing."	• *Auto Service Repairman*: Explain what was done to the vehicle and demonstrate what was faulty with the old parts. • *Tailor*: Explain the process involved in resizing and altering the dress while the customer is present in the store.
Fairness	• "I expect to receive the same treatment as other customers."	• *Rental Car Agent*: Honor the customer's reservation by holding the car for her even if she is from out of town or a first-time customer.
Empathy	• "I want them to put themselves in my shoes." • "I expect them to be able to see things from my perspective."	• *Retail Clerk*: Use the phrase "I am sorry you have experienced that" and exert visible effort to try to help the customer. • *Veterinarian*: Assume the pet is very important to its owner and show compassion in explaining the pet's medical condition.

Source: Adapted from "Understanding Customer Expectations of Service" by A. Parasuraman, L.L. Berry, and V.A. Zeithaml, *Sloan Management Review* 32 (Spring 1991), pp. 39–48.

expectations themselves but rather heightens the belief that the company will do something with the information that surfaces. Arguably the worst thing a company can do is show a strong interest in understanding what customers expect and then never act on the information. At a minimum, a company should acknowledge to customers that it has received and heard their input and that it will expend effort trying to address their issues. The company may not be able to—and indeed does not always have to—deliver to expressed expectations. An alternative and appropriate response would be to let customers know the reasons that desired service is not being provided at the present time or describe the efforts planned to deliver such service in the future. Another approach could be to educate customers about ways to use and improve the service they currently receive. Giving customers progress updates as service is improved to address their needs and desires is sensible because it allows the company to get credit for incremental efforts to improve service.

Should a Company Try to Delight the Customer?

Some management consultants urge service companies to "delight" customers to gain a competitive edge. The *delight* they refer to is a profoundly positive emotional state that results from having one's expectations exceeded to a surprising degree.[14] One author describes the type of service that results in delight as "positively outrageous service"— that which is unexpected, random, extraordinary, and disproportionately positive.[15]

A way that managers can conceive of delight, as depicted in Figure 3.8, is to consider product and service features in terms of concentric rings.[16] The innermost bull's-eye refers to attributes central to the basic function of the product or service, called *musts*. Their provision is not particularly noticeable, but their absence would be. Around the musts is a ring called *satisfiers*: features that have the potential to further satisfy beyond the basic function of the product. At the next and final outer level are *delights,* or product features that are unexpected and surprisingly enjoyable. These features are things that consumers would not expect to find and are therefore highly surprised and sometimes excited when they receive them. For example, in your classes the musts consist of professors, rooms, syllabi, and class meetings. Satisfiers might include interesting course lectures, professors who are entertaining or friendly, and good audiovisual aids

FIGURE 3.8
**Musts, Satisfiers,
and Delights**

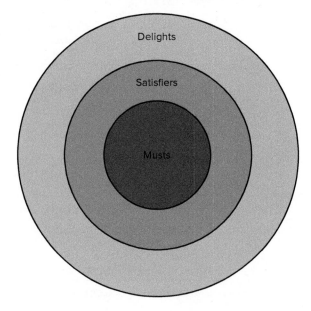

provided in the classroom. Delights might include a free textbook for students signing up for the course or punch and cookies provided for the first day of class.

Delighting customers may seem like a good idea, and can lead to repeat purchasing and customer loyalty,[17] but this level of service provision comes with extra effort and cost to the firm. And, as we discuss in more detail in Chapter 4, delighting customers does not build their loyalty; what has more influence is providing service that requires customers to put in minimal effort to get a satisfactory solution to their service issue.[18] Therefore, the benefits of providing delight must be weighed. Among the considerations are the staying power and competitive implications of delight.

Staying power involves the question of how long a company can expect an experience of delight to maintain the consumer's attention. If it is fleeting and the customer forgets it immediately, it may not be worth the cost. Alternatively, if the customer remembers the delight and adjusts her level of expectation upward accordingly, it will cost the company more just to satisfy, effectively raising the bar for the future. Research indicates that delighting customers does, in fact, raise expectations and make it more difficult for a company to satisfy customers in the future.[19]

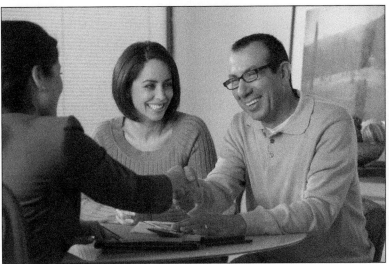

A delighted customer.

The competitive implication of delight relates to its impact on expectations of other firms in the same industry. If a competitor in the same industry is unable to copy the delight strategy, it will be disadvantaged by the consumer's increased expectations. If you were offered that free textbook in one of your classes, you might then expect to receive one in each of your classes. Those classes not offering the free textbook might not have high enrollment levels compared to the delighting class. If a competitor can easily copy the delight strategy, however, neither firm benefits (although the consumer does!), and all firms may be hurt because their costs increase and profits erode. The implication is that, if companies choose to delight, they should do so in areas that cannot be copied by other firms.

How Does a Company Exceed Customer Service Expectations?

Many companies talk about exceeding customer expectations—delighting and surprising them by giving more than they expect. One such example is Pebble Beach Resort, located along the Pacific coast of Northern California. The golf resort not only talks about exceeding customer expectations, it actually prints the following phrase on the back side of employee business cards: "Exceed the expectations of every guest, by providing a once in a lifetime experience, every time." This philosophy raises the question, Should a service provider try simply to meet customer expectations or to exceed them?

First, it is essential to recognize that exceeding customer expectations of the basics is virtually impossible. Honoring promises—having the reserved room available, meeting deadlines, showing up for meetings, delivering the core service—is what the company is supposed to do. Companies are *supposed* to be accurate and dependable and provide the service they promised to provide.[20] As you examine the examples of basic expectations of customers in Exhibit 3.1, ask yourself if a provider's doing any of these things would delight you. The conclusion you should reach is that it is very difficult to surprise or delight customers consistently by delivering reliable service.

How, then, does a company delight its customers and exceed their expectations? In virtually any service, developing a customer relationship is one approach for exceeding service expectations. The United Services Automobile Association (USAA), a provider of insurance to military personnel and their dependents, illustrates how a large company that seldom has face-to-face interactions with its customers can surprise and delight them with its personalization of service and knowledge of the customer. Using a state-of-the-art imaging system, all USAA employees can access any customer's entire information file in seconds, giving them full knowledge of the customer's history and requirements and the status of the customer's recent interactions with the company. Expecting a lower level of personalization from an insurance company and from most any service interaction on the telephone, USAA's customers are surprised and impressed with the care and concern that employees demonstrate.

Using a similar type of information technology, Ritz-Carlton Hotels, a two-time recipient of the Malcolm Baldrige Quality Award, provides highly personalized attention to its customers. The company trains each of its employees to note guest likes and dislikes and to record these into a computerized guest history profile. The company has information on the preferences of several hundred thousand repeat Ritz-Carlton guests, resulting in more personalized service. The aim is not simply to meet expectations of guests but to provide them with a "memorable visit." The company uses the guest history information to exceed customers' expectations of the way they will be treated. When a repeat customer calls the hotel's central reservations number to book accommodations, the reservation agent can call up the individual's preference information. The agent then sends this information electronically to the particular hotel at which the reservation is made. The hotel puts the data in a daily guest recognition and preference report circulated to employees. Employees then greet the repeat guest personally at check-in and ensure that the guest's needs/preferences are anticipated and met.[21]

How well does this approach work? Quite well. According to an independent survey of luxury hotels conducted annually by J. D. Power and Associates, the Ritz-Carlton was the top-rated hotel in terms of customer satisfaction seven times between 2007 and 2015.[22]

Another way to exceed expectations is to deliberately underpromise the service to increase the likelihood of exceeding customer expectations.[23] The strategy is to underpromise and overdeliver. If every service promise is less than what will eventually happen, customers can be delighted frequently. Although this reasoning sounds logical, a firm should weigh two potential problems before using this strategy. First, customers with whom a company interacts regularly are likely to notice the underpromising and adjust their expectations accordingly, negating the desired benefit of delight. Customers will recognize the pattern of underpromising when time after time a firm promises one delivery time ("we cannot get that to you before 5:00 p.m. tomorrow") yet constantly exceeds it (by delivering at noon). Second, underpromising in a sales situation potentially reduces the competitive appeal of an offering and must be tempered by what the competition is offering. When competitive pressures are high, presenting a cohesive and honest portrayal of the service both explicitly (through advertising and personal selling) and implicitly (such as through the appearance of service facilities and the price of the service) may be wiser. Controlling the firm's promises, making them consistent with the deliverable service, may be a better approach.

A final way to exceed expectations without raising them in the future is to position unusual service as unique rather than the standard. On a flight between Raleigh-Durham and Charlotte, North Carolina, one of us experienced an example of this strategy. The flight is extremely short, less than half an hour, and typically too brief for beverage service. On that flight, however, a crew member announced over the intercom that an unusually ambitious crew wanted to try to serve beverages anyway. He warned passengers that the crew may not get to all of us and positioned the service as unique by imploring passengers not to expect beverage service on other flights. In this scenario, passengers seemed delighted but their expectations for regular service were not heightened by the action. (To this day, we have never received beverage service on that route, but are really not expecting it!)

Do Customers' Service Expectations Continually Escalate?

As we illustrated in the beginning of this chapter, customers' service expectations are dynamic. In both the credit card and mobile telephone industries, as in many competitive service industries, battling companies seek to best each other and thereby raise the level of service above that of competing companies. Service expectations—in this case, adequate service expectations—rise as quickly as service delivery or promises rise. In a highly competitive and rapidly changing industry, expectations can thus rise quickly. For this reason companies need to monitor adequate service expectations continually—the more turbulent the industry, the more frequent is the monitoring needed.

Desired service expectations, on the other hand, are far more stable. Because they are driven by more enduring factors, such as personal needs or personal service philosophy, they tend to be high to begin with and remain high.

How Does a Service Company Stay Ahead of Competition in Meeting Customer Expectations?

All else being equal, a company's goal is to meet customer expectations better than its competitors. Given the fact that adequate service expectations change rapidly in a turbulent environment, how can a company ensure that it stays ahead of competition?

The adequate service level reflects the minimum performance level expected by customers after they consider a variety of personal and external factors (Figure 3.7), including the availability of service options from other providers. Companies whose service performance falls short of this level are clearly at a competitive disadvantage, with the disadvantage escalating as the gap widens. These companies' customers may well be "reluctant" customers, ready to take their business elsewhere the moment they perceive an acceptable alternative exists.

If they are to use service quality for competitive advantage, companies must perform above the adequate service level. This level, however, may signal only a temporary advantage. Customers' adequate service levels, which are less stable than desired service levels, will rise rapidly when competitors promise and deliver a higher level of service. If a company's level of service is barely above the adequate service level to begin with, a competitor can quickly erode that advantage. To develop a true customer franchise—immutable customer loyalty—companies must not only consistently exceed the adequate service level but also reach the desired service level. Exceptional service can intensify customers' loyalty to a point at which they are impervious to competitive options.

Firms might also consider how they present their promises to customers relative to the competition. In Chapter 14 we describe various techniques for communicating a firm's promises, but for now consider two options. First, if the salesperson knows that no competitor can meet an inflated sales promise in an industry, he could point that fact out to the customer, thereby refuting the promise made by competitive salespeople. The second option is for the provider to follow a sale with a "reality check" about service delivery. One of us bought a new house from a builder. Typical sales promises were made about the quality of the home, some less than accurate, to make the sale. Before closing on the house, the builder conducted a final check on the house. At the front door, the builder pointed out that each new home has between 3,000 and 5,000 individual elements and that in his experience the typical new home has 100–150 defects. Armed with this reality check, the 32 defects found in the house then seemed to be a relatively small amount.

Summary

Using a conceptual framework of the nature and determinants of customer expectations of service, we showed in this chapter that customers hold two types of service expectations: desired service, which reflects what customers want, and adequate service, or the minimum level of service customers are willing to accept. The desired service level is less subject to change than the adequate service level. A zone of tolerance separates these two levels of expectations. This zone of tolerance varies across customers and can expand or contract for the same customer.

Customer expectations are influenced by a variety of factors. Desired service expectations are influenced by personal needs, personal service philosophy, derived service expectations, explicit service promises, implicit service promises, word-of-mouth communication, and the customer's past experience. Adequate service expectations are influenced by perceived service alternatives and situational factors. These sources of expectations are the same for end consumers and business customers, for pure service and product-related service, and for experienced customers and inexperienced customers.

Discussion Questions

1. What is the difference between desired service and adequate service? Why would a service marketer need to understand both types of service expectations?
2. Consider a recent service purchase that you have made. Which of the factors influencing expectations were the most important in your decision? Why?
3. Why are desired service expectations more stable than adequate service expectations?
4. How do the technology changes discussed in the Technology Spotlight in this chapter influence customer expectations?
5. Describe several instances in which a service company's explicit service promises were inflated and led you to be disappointed with the service outcome.

6. Consider a small business preparing to buy a computer system. Which of the influences on customer expectations do you believe will be pivotal? Which factors will have the most influence? Which factors will have the least importance in this decision?

7. What strategies can you add to the Strategy Insight in this chapter for influencing the factors?

8. Do you believe that any of your service expectations are unrealistic? Which ones? Should a service marketer try to address unrealistic customer expectations?

9. In your opinion, what service companies have effectively built customer franchises (immutable customer loyalty)?

10. Intuitively, it would seem that managers want their customers to have wide tolerance zones for service. But if customers do have these wide zones of tolerance for service, is it more difficult for firms with superior service to earn customer loyalty? Would superior service firms be better off to attempt to narrow customers' tolerance zones to reduce the competitive appeal of mediocre providers?

11. Should service marketers delight their customers?

Exercises

1. What factors influenced your expectations of this course? Which were the most important factors? How would your expectations change if this were a required course? (Alternatively, if this course *is* required, would your expectations change if this were an optional course?)

2. Keep a service journal for a day and document your use of services. Ask yourself before each service encounter to indicate your predicted service of that encounter. After the encounter, note whether your expectations were met or exceeded. How does the answer to this question relate to your desire to do business with that service firm again?

3. List five incidents in which a service company has exceeded your expectations. How did you react to the service? Did these incidents change the way you viewed subsequent interactions with each of the companies? In what way?

Notes

1. "Japanese Put Tourism on a Higher Plane," *International Herald Tribune,* February 3, 1992, p. 8.

2. The model on which this chapter is based is taken from V. A. Zeithaml, L. L. Berry, and A. Parasuraman, "The Nature and Determinants of Customer Expectations of Service," *Journal of the Academy of Marketing Science* 21 (Winter 1993), pp. 1–12.

3. See sources such as C. Gronroos, *Strategic Management and Marketing in the Service Sector* (Helsingfors, Sweden: Swedish School of Economics and Business Administration, 1982); R. K. Teas and T. E. DeCarlo, "An Examination and Extension of the Zone-of-Tolerance Model: A Comparison to Performance-Based Models of Perceived Quality," *Journal of Service Research* 6 (February 2004), pp. 272–286; K. B. Yap and J. C. Sweeney, "Zone-of-Tolerance Moderates the Service Quality-Outcome Relationship," *Journal of Services Marketing* 21 (2007), pp. 137–148.

4. R. B. Woodruff, E. R. Cadotte, and R. L. Jenkins, "Expectations and Norms in Models of Consumer Satisfaction," *Journal of Marketing Research* 24 (August 1987), pp. 305–314.

5. J. A. Miller, "Studying Satisfaction, Modifying Models, Eliciting Expectations, Posing Problems, and Making Meaningful Measurements," in *Conceptualization and Measurement of Consumer Satisfaction and Dissatisfaction,* ed. H. K. Hunt (Bloomington: Indiana University School of Business, 1977), pp. 72–91.

6. A. Parasuraman, L. L. Berry, and V. A. Zeithaml, "Understanding Customer Expectations of Service," *Sloan Management Review* 32 (Spring 1991), p. 42.

7. L. L. Berry, A. Parasuraman, and V. A. Zeithaml, "Ten Lessons for Improving Service Quality," *Marketing Science Institute,* Report No. 93–104 (May 1993).

8. Parasuraman, Berry, and Zeithaml, "Understanding Customer Expectations of Service," p. 7.

9. Ibid., p. 8.

10. D. L. Davis, J. G. Guiltinan, and W. H. Jones, "Service Characteristics, Consumer Research, and the Classification of Retail Services," *Journal of Retailing* 55 (Fall 1979), pp. 3–21; W. R. George and L. L. Berry, "Guidelines for the Advertising of Services," *Business Horizons* 24 (May–June 1981), pp. 52–56; F. v. Wangenheim and T. Bayón, "The Effect of Word-of-Mouth on Services Switching: Measurement and Moderating Variables," *European Journal of Marketing* 38 (2004), pp. 1173–1185; T. J. Brown, T. E. Barry, P. A. Dacin, and R. F. Gunst, "Spreading the Word: Investigating Antecedents of Consumers' Positive Word-of-Mouth Intentions and Behaviors in a Retailing Context," *Journal of the Academy of Marketing Science* 33 (Spring 2005), pp. 123–138. For a meta-analysis of the effect of electronic word-of-mouth communication on services, see A. B. Rosario, F. Sotgiu, K. de Valck, and T. H. A. Bijmolt, "The Effect of Electronic Word of Mouth on Sales: A Meta-Analytic Review of Platform, Product, and Metric Factors," *Journal of Marketing Research* 53 (June 2016), pp. 297–318.

11. M. Trusov, R. E. Bucklin, and K. Pauwels, "Effects of Word-of-Mouth versus Traditional Marketing: Findings from an Internet Social Networking Site," *Journal of Marketing* 73 (September 2009), pp. 90–102.

12. Discussions of the role of past experience in shaping customer expectations of service are included in L. L. Berry, "Cultivating Service Brand Equity," *Journal of the Academy of Marketing Science* 28 (Winter 2000), pp. 128–137; and R. L. Hess Jr., S. Ganesan, and N. M. Klein, "Interactional Service Failures in a Psuedorelationship: The Role of Organizational Attributions," *Journal of Retailing* 83 (January 2007), pp. 79–95.

13. Parasuraman, Berry, and Zeithaml, "Understanding Customer Expectations of Service," p. 40.

14. R. T. Rust and R. L. Oliver, "Should We Delight the Customer?" *Journal of the Academy of Marketing Science* 28 (Winter 2000), pp. 86–94.

15. T. S. Gross, *Positively Outrageous Service* (Chicago: Dearborn Trade Publishing, 2004).

16. J. Clemmer, "The Three Rings of Perceived Value," *Canadian Manager* 15 (Summer 1990), pp. 12–15.

17. T. Keiningham and T. Vavra, *The Customer Delight Principle: Exceeding Customers' Expectations for Bottom-Line Success* (New York: Mcgraw-Hill, 2001); R. Chitturi, R. Raghunathan, and V. Mahajan, "Delight by Design: The Role of Hedonic versus Utilitarian Benefits," *Journal of Marketing* 72 (May 2008), pp. 48–63; D. C. Barnes, M. B. Beauchamp, and C. Webster, "To Delight, or Not

to Delight? This Is the Question Service Firms Must Address," *Journal of Marketing Theory and Practice* 18 (Summer 2010), pp. 275–283.

18. M. Dixon, K. Freeman, and N. Toman, "Stop Trying to Delight Your Customers," *Harvard Business Review* 88 (July–August 2010), pp. 116–122.

19. Rust and Oliver, "Should We Delight the Customer?"

20. Parasuraman, Berry, and Zeithaml, "Understanding Customer Expectations," p. 41.

21. "How the Ritz-Carlton Hotel Company Delivers 'Memorable' Service to Customers," *Executive Report on Customer Satisfaction* 6 (March 15, 1993), pp. 1–4; L. A. Dhir, "Top Ten Things Luxury Guests Absolutely Want," http://www.hospitalitynet.org/news/4060166.html, accessed June 28, 2016.

22. J. D. Power and Associates, http://businesscenter.jdpower.com/, accessed February 15, 2016.

23. W. H. Davidow and B. Uttal, "Service Companies: Focus or Falter," *Harvard Business Review* 67 (July–August, 1989), pp. 77–85; C. Sewell and P. B. Brown, *Customers for Life: How to Turn That One-Time Buyer into a Lifetime Customer* (New York: Random House, 2002).

Chapter **Four**

Customer Perceptions of Service

This chapter's objectives are to

1. Provide a solid basis for understanding what influences customer perceptions of service and the relationships among customer satisfaction, service quality, and individual service encounters.

2. Demonstrate the importance of customer satisfaction—what it is, the factors that influence it, and the significant outcomes resulting from it.

3. Develop critical knowledge of service quality and its five key dimensions: reliability, responsiveness, empathy, assurance, and tangibles.

4. Show that service encounters, or the "moments of truth," are the essential building blocks from which customers form their perceptions.

Zane's Cycles: Service as a Strategic Differentiator

For Zane's Cycles in Branford, Connecticut, service has been the company's key to success and what truly differentiates it from competing bike stores.[1] Chris Zane, its forty-something chief executive officer (CEO), has owned the business since he was 16 years old, when he convinced his grandfather to loan him $20,000 to buy the store from its original owner. As a young man he built the business on basic principles such as "unparalleled service," "one-to-one marketing," "customer relationships," and "employee respect and empowerment." Since then, the business has grown to more than $10 million in annual sales (including retail and corporate sales), and Zane's has eliminated all but a small handful of the original 16 competitors. Moreover, the company has developed highly successful ways to compete with the likes of Walmart and has built a whole new business providing bicycles to corporations for incentive gifts to their employees. So how does Zane's compete? What are some of the things that Chris Zane has done to provide exemplary, out-of-the-box service—service that has driven his competitors out of business? Here are a few examples of the company's exemplary service strategies:

- *Lifetime free service.* Zane's provides "lifetime free service" on the bikes it sells, because it is in the service business, not just the bike business. Of course, lifetime free service (free service for as long as the customer owns the bike) is also a good way to get customers to return to the shop, providing an opportunity to build a lasting relationship.

- *Lifetime parts warranty.* Following the lifetime free service strategy, Zane's soon realized that it should also offer a lifetime warranty on parts as well. He is able to do this by having a small number of vendor partners and holding them accountable for their products.

- *90-day price protection.* To quell possible rumors and beliefs that Zane's is high priced (to cover the lifetime guarantees), the company instituted a 90-day price protection guarantee, so that customers can go back within 90 days to receive a cash rebate, plus 10 percent, if they find the same bike elsewhere for less money. Because Zane's is truly in the relationship business, few customers shop the competitors or meticulously compare prices, so the plan results in very few refunds. And, when they do give a refund, the customer frequently spends the cash right on the spot, in the store!

- *Flat insurance.* For those first-time bike purchasers or less experienced bikers, the idea of a flat tire seems daunting. So Zane's offers "flat insurance" for a nominal annual fee. Although few tires are ever fixed under the policy, those bikers that do go back to the store to use their flat insurance are treated like royalty. Everything stops, the bike is taken to the back, where the tire is changed and the bike is cleaned up—all in record time with much fanfare. Again, the customer (and anyone else in the store) is treated to an unexpected, delightful experience, and relationships are strengthened, all at little cost to Zane's—especially given the amount of the flat insurance that is sold and never used!

- *Less than $1 giveaways.* Another way that Zane's delights customers is by giving away small but essential parts that cost less than $1. He figures these giveaways result in additional purchases (at the same time or on another visit) far beyond the few cents it costs to provide them.

- *Kids' play area.* The kids' play area in Zane's is a popular place for youngsters to play and remain entertained while their parents shop. Some are even able to purchase the infamous "Christmas Bike" right under the noses of their preoccupied children!

- *Coffee and Snapple bar, with free coffee.* To provide a social context and a place for folks to wait when the store is busy, Chris Zane built a mahogany coffee bar, modeled after a similar cozy coffee bar he had seen in a bike shop on a trip to Switzerland. Here, coffee and other drinks are offered, and customers can watch bike repairs going on through a huge glass window. And, because the cost of a cup of coffee is less than $1, of course, there is no charge!

- *Kids, bike upgrades.* One of the most innovative service strategies at Zane's is one that helps them compete head-on with Walmart. This is the trade-in policy that allows parents to buy a child's bike and then trade it in for full price, credited toward a larger bike. Like many of their service plans, this one is retroactive. When they first started it, Zane's sent postcards to everyone who had bought a small bicycle within the past few years, letting them know about the upgrade plan.

You might wonder how all of these seemingly "too good to be true" service offers can be provided without draining profits. The fact is that Zane's is very profitable and financially successful. There is nothing "soft" about this strategy, and Chris Zane is as focused on hard-nosed, quantitative financial analytics as any other excellent CEO. What Zane has figured out, much to the chagrin of his competitors, is that great service can be the key to cementing customer loyalty and that customer loyalty, in the end, is what drives growth and profits. No wonder Zane's was one of *Fast Company* magazine's "Local Heroes" in its Customer First Awards.

Zane's Cycles in Branford, Connecticut, USA.

© Courtesy Zane's Cycles, photograph, Richard House

Quality bikes, excellent service quality, lots of little extras, and the unexpected attention of Zane's team members all add up to customer satisfaction for customers of Zane's Cycles. The same is true for other landmark service companies such as Lands' End, IBM Global Services, Amazon.com, and Ritz-Carlton Hotels. In all of these companies, the quality of the core product and exemplary customer service result in high customer satisfaction ratings.

CUSTOMER PERCEPTIONS

How customers perceive services, how they assess whether they have experienced quality service and whether they are satisfied are the subjects of this chapter. We will be focusing on the *perceived service* box in the gaps model. As we move through this chapter, keep in mind that perceptions are always considered relative to expectations. Because expectations are dynamic, evaluations may also shift over time—from person to person and from culture to culture. What is considered quality service or the things that satisfy customers today may be different tomorrow. Also keep in mind that the entire discussion of quality and satisfaction is based on *customers' perceptions of the service*—not some predetermined objective criteria of what service is or should be.

FIGURE 4.1
Customer Perceptions of Quality and Customer Satisfaction

Satisfaction versus Service Quality

Practitioners and writers in the popular press tend to use the terms *satisfaction* and *quality* interchangeably, but researchers have attempted to be more precise about the meanings and measurement of the two concepts, resulting in considerable debate.[2] Consensus is that the two concepts are fundamentally different in terms of their underlying causes and outcomes.[3] Although they have certain things in common, *satisfaction* is generally viewed as a broader concept, whereas *service quality* focuses specifically on dimensions of service. Based on this view, *perceived service quality* is a component of customer satisfaction. Figure 4.1 graphically illustrates the relationships between the two concepts.

As shown in Figure 4.1, service quality is a focused evaluation that reflects the customer's perception of reliability, assurance, responsiveness, empathy, and tangibles.[4] Satisfaction, on the other hand, is more inclusive: it is influenced by perceptions of service quality, product quality, and price, as well as situational factors and personal factors. For example, service quality of a health club is judged on attributes such as whether equipment is available and in working order when needed, how responsive the staff are to customer needs, how skilled the trainers are, and whether the facility is well maintained. Customer satisfaction with the health club is a broader concept that will certainly be influenced by perceptions of service quality but that will also include perceptions of product quality (such as the quality of products sold in the pro shop), the price of membership,[5] personal factors such as the consumer's emotional state, and even uncontrollable situational factors such as weather conditions and experiences driving to and from the health club.[6]

Transaction versus Cumulative Perceptions

In considering perceptions, it is also important to recognize that customers will have perceptions of single, transaction-specific encounters as well as overall perceptions of a company based on all their experiences.[7] For example, a bank customer will have a perception of how he was treated in a particular encounter with an employee at a branch and will form a perception of that transaction based on elements of the service experienced during that transaction. That perception is at a very micro, transaction-specific level. The same bank customer will also have overall perceptions of the bank based on all his encounters over a period of time. The experiences might include multiple in-person encounters at the bank branch, online banking experiences, and experiences using the bank's ATMs across many cities. At an even more general level, the customer may have perceptions of banking services or the whole banking industry as a result of all his experiences with banks and everything he knows about banking.

Research suggests that it is important to understand all these types of perceptions for different reasons and that the viewpoints are complementary rather than competing.[8] Understanding perceptions at the transaction-specific level is critical for diagnosing service issues and making immediate changes. These isolated encounters are also the building blocks for overall, cumulative experience evaluations, as you will learn later in this chapter. On the other hand, cumulative experience evaluations are likely to be better predictors of overall loyalty to a company. That is, customer loyalty most often results from the customer's assessment of all her experiences, not just one encounter.

CUSTOMER SATISFACTION

What Is Customer Satisfaction?

"Everyone knows what satisfaction is until asked to give a definition. Then, it seems, nobody knows."[9] This quote from the late Richard Oliver, respected expert and long-time writer and researcher on the topic of customer satisfaction, expressed the challenge of defining this most basic of customer concepts. Building from previous definitions, Oliver offered his own formal definition (p. 13):

> Satisfaction is the consumer's fulfillment response. It is a judgment that a product or service feature, or the product or service itself, provides a pleasurable level of consumption-related fulfillment.

In less technical terms, we interpret this definition to mean that *satisfaction* is the customer's evaluation of a product or service in terms of whether that product or service has met the customer's needs and expectations. Failure to meet needs and expectations is assumed to result in *dissatisfaction* with the product or service.

In addition to a sense of *fulfillment* in the knowledge that one's needs have been met, satisfaction can also be related to other types of feelings, depending on the context or type of service.[10] For example, satisfaction can be viewed as *contentment*—more of a passive response that customers may associate with services they do not think a lot about or services that they receive routinely over time. Satisfaction may also be associated with feelings of *pleasure* for services that make the customer feel good or are associated with a sense of happiness. For those services that really surprise the customer in a positive way, satisfaction may mean *delight.* In some situations, where the removal of a negative leads to satisfaction, the customer may associate a sense of *relief* with satisfaction. Finally, satisfaction may be associated with feelings of *ambivalence* when there is a mix of positive and negative experiences associated with the product or service.

Although customer satisfaction tends to be measured at a particular point in time as if it were static, satisfaction is a dynamic target that may evolve over time, influenced by a variety of factors and by the passage of time itself.[11] Particularly when product usage or the service experience takes place over time, satisfaction may be highly variable, depending on which point in the usage or experience cycle one is focusing on. Similarly, in the case of very new services or a service not previously experienced, customer expectations may be barely forming at the point of initial purchase; these expectations will solidify as the process unfolds and the customer begins to form his or her perceptions. Through the service cycle the customer may have a variety of experiences—some good, some not good—and each will ultimately impact satisfaction.

What Determines Customer Satisfaction?

As shown in Figure 4.1, customer satisfaction is influenced by specific product or service features, perceptions of product and service quality, and price. In addition, personal factors such as the customer's mood or emotional state and situational factors such as family member opinions influence satisfaction.

Product and Service Features

Customer satisfaction with a product or service is influenced significantly by the customer's evaluation of product or service features.[12] For a service such as a resort hotel, important features might include the pool area, access to golf facilities, restaurants, room comfort and privacy, the helpfulness and courtesy of staff, room price, and so forth. In conducting satisfaction studies, most firms determine through some means (often focus groups) what the important features and attributes are for their service and then measure perceptions of those features as well as overall service satisfaction. Research has shown that customers of services make trade-offs among different service features (e.g., price level versus quality versus friendliness of personnel versus level of customization), depending on the type of service being evaluated and the criticality of the service.[13]

Customer Emotions

Customers' emotions can also affect their perceptions of satisfaction with products and services.[14] These emotions can be stable, preexisting emotions—for example, mood state or life satisfaction. Think of times when you are at a very happy stage in your life (such as when you are on vacation), and your good, happy mood and positive frame of mind have influenced how you feel about the services you experience. Alternatively, when you are in a bad mood, your negative feelings may carry over into how you respond to services, causing you to overreact or respond negatively to any little problem. The effects of emotions on satisfaction are heightened for "high-emotion services" where customers have strong feelings (positive or negative) even before the service begins. Think, for example, of services associated with birth, marriage, illness, or death. In such situations, customers' emotions are particularly influential.[15]

Specific emotions may also be induced by the consumption experience itself, influencing a customer's satisfaction with the service. Research done in a river-rafting context showed that the river guides had a strong effect on their customers' emotional responses to the trip and that those feelings (both positive and negative) were linked to overall trip satisfaction.[16] Positive emotions such as happiness, pleasure, elation, and a sense of warm-heartedness enhanced customers' satisfaction with the rafting trip. In turn, negative emotions such as sadness, sorrow, regret, and anger led to diminished customer satisfaction. Overall, in the rafting context, positive emotions had a stronger effect than negative ones. (These positive emotions are apparent in the photo shown on page 82.) In a different context, drawing on emotional contagion theory, researchers found that the authenticity of employees' emotional display directly affected customers' emotions in a video retail and consulting service.[17] Similar emotional contagion effects were found in a sequence of multiple emotional displays by employees in the context of restaurant service recovery in China. In this research employees' positive and negative emotions both affected the customer's emotional state and ultimate satisfaction.[18]

River rafters experience many positive emotions, increasing their satisfaction with the service.

© David L. Ryan/The Boston Globe/Getty Images

Attributions for Service Success or Failure

Attributions—the perceived causes of events—influence perceptions of satisfaction as well.[19] When customers have been surprised by an outcome (the service is either much better or much worse than expected), they tend to look for the reasons, and their assessments of the reasons can influence their satisfaction. For example, if a customer of a weight-loss organization fails to lose weight as hoped for, she will likely search for the causes—was it something she did, was the diet plan ineffective, or did circumstances simply not allow her to follow the diet regimen—before determining her level of satisfaction or dissatisfaction with the weight-loss company.[20] For many services, customers take at least partial responsibility for how things turn out.

Even when customers do not take responsibility for the outcome, customer satisfaction may be influenced by other kinds of attributions. For example, research done in a travel agency context found that customers were less dissatisfied with a pricing error made by the agent if they felt that the reason was outside the agent's control or if they felt that it was a rare mistake, unlikely to occur again.[21]

Perceptions of Equity or Fairness

Customer satisfaction is also influenced by perceptions of equity and fairness.[22] Customers ask themselves: Have I been treated fairly compared with other customers? Did other customers get better treatment, better prices, or better-quality service? Did I pay a fair price for the service? Was I treated well in exchange for what I paid and the effort I expended? Notions of fairness are central to customers' perceptions of satisfaction with products and services, particularly in service recovery situations. As you will learn in Chapter 7, satisfaction with a service provider following a service failure is largely determined by perceptions of fair treatment. Sometimes cases of extreme unfairness result in FTC investigations into company practices. For example AT&T settled a case to stop them from "mobile cramming," a practice deemed as unfair, and even unknown, to many consumers. Through this practice, customers had been charged via their mobile phone bills for third-party subscriptions to services they had never ordered or authorized.[23]

Other Customers, Family Members, and Coworkers

In addition to product and service features and one's own feelings and beliefs, customer satisfaction is often influenced by other people.[24] For example, family decisions about a vacation destination and satisfaction with the trip are dynamic phenomena, influenced by the reactions and emotions of individual family members.[25] Later, what family members express in terms of satisfaction or dissatisfaction with the trip will be influenced by stories retold among the family and selective memories of the events. Similarly, the satisfaction of the rafters in the photo is certainly influenced by individual perceptions, but it is also influenced greatly by the experiences, behavior, and views of the other rafters. In a business setting, satisfaction with a new service or technology— for example, a new customer relationship management software service—will be influenced not only by individuals' personal experiences with the software itself but also by what others say about it in the company, how others use it and feel about it, and how widely it is adopted in the organization.

National Customer Satisfaction Indexes

Because of the importance of customer satisfaction to firms and overall quality of life, many countries have a national index that measures and tracks customer satisfaction at a macro level.[26] Many public policymakers believe that these measures could and should be used as tools for evaluating the health of the nation's economy, along with traditional measures of productivity and price. Customer satisfaction indexes begin to get at the *quality* of economic output, whereas more traditional economic indicators tend to focus only on *quantity*. The first such measure was the Swedish Customer Satisfaction Barometer introduced in 1989.[27] Later, similar indexes were introduced in Germany (Deutsche Kundenbarometer, or DK, in 1992), the United States (American Customer Satisfaction Index, ACSI, in 1994), and Switzerland (Swiss Index of Customer Satisfaction, SWICS, in 1998).[28] More recently, other countries, including the United Kingdom, Indonesia, the Dominican Republic, Turkey, Mexico, Colombia, and Singapore, have adopted the ACSI methodology in creating national customer satisfaction indices.[29]

The American Customer Satisfaction Index

The American Customer Satisfaction Index (ACSI),[30] developed by researchers at the National Quality Research Center at the University of Michigan, is a measure of satisfaction with goods and services. The measure tracks, on a quarterly basis, customer perceptions across 200 firms representing all major economic sectors, including government agencies. Within each industry group, major industry segments are included, and within each industry, the largest companies in that industry are selected to participate. For each company approximately 250 interviews are conducted with current customers. Each company receives an ACSI score computed from its customers' perceptions of quality, value, satisfaction, expectations, complaints, and future loyalty.[31]

The 2015 ACSI results by industry are shown in Table 4.1.[32] Interestingly many categories across industries have declined significantly in terms of percentage change

TABLE 4.1
American Customer Satisfaction Index— Ratings by Industry

Source: "American Customer Satisfaction Index—Ratings by Industry," ACSI website, www.theacsi.org.

Industry	2015 ACSI Score	Percent Change in ACSI Score from Previous Year
Full-Service Restaurants	82	0.0
Televisions and Video Players	82	−4.7
Consumer Shipping	81	−1.2
Credit Unions	81	−4.7
Household Appliances	81	1.3
Cooperative Utilities	80	−5.0
Internet Retail	80	−2.4
Automobiles and Light Vehicles	79	−3.7
Property and Casualty Insurance	79	0.0
Soft Drinks	79	−3.7
Athletic Shoes	78	−2.5
Cellular Telephones	78	0.0
Internet Travel Services	78	1.3
Life Insurance	77	−3.8
Limited-Service Restaurants	77	−3.8
Personal Care and Cleaning Products	77	−6.1
Personal Computers	77	−1.3
Specialty Retail Stores	77	−2.5
Ambulatory Care	76	1.3
Apparel	76	−2.6
Banks	76	0.0
Breweries	76	−3.8
Food Manufacturing	76	−3.8
Internet Investment Services	76	−7.3
Internet Search Engines and Information	76	−5.0
Gasoline Stations	75	2.7
Hotels	75	−1.3
Computer Software	74	−2.6
Department and Discount Stores	74	−3.9
Hospitals	74	1.4
Internet Social Media	74	4.2
Investor-Owned Utilities	74	−2.7
Health and Personal Care Stores	73	−5.2
Internet News and Opinion	73	−1.4
Municipal Utilities	73	−6.8
Supermarkets	73	−3.9
Wireless Telephone Service	70	−2.8
Airlines	69	4.3
Fixed-Line Telephone Service	69	−5.5
Health Insurance	69	−1.4
U.S. Postal Service	69	5.8
Internet Service Providers	63	0.0vv
Subscription Television Service	63	−3.1

from the past year. Looking at the table, it is evident that most durable and non-durable goods appear in the top half of the table (above 76) and all of the categories in the bottom half are services with the very lowest being subscription TV and Internet service providers. It is important to point out, however, that these rankings are industry averages. Almost every industry has some strong performers in terms of customer satisfaction. For example, in 2015 scores for airlines ranged from 62 (Spirit) to 80 (JetBlue and Southwest Airlines).

Outcomes of Customer Satisfaction

Why all this attention to customer satisfaction? As mentioned in the previous section, some public policymakers believe that customer satisfaction is an important indicator of national economic health. They believe that it is not enough to track economic efficiency and pricing statistics. Satisfaction, they believe, is also an important indicator of well-being. Further, many believe that customer satisfaction is correlated with other measures of economic health such as corporate earnings and stock value. Through the ACSI data, researchers at the University of Michigan have been able to document a clear relationship between performance of the ACSI stock market portfolio (made up of companies that perform well on the ACSI index) when compared to the S&P 500. This relationship is depicted in Figure 4.2, which shows the ACSI stock portfolio consistently out-performing the S&P 500.[33]

Beyond these macroeconomic implications, however, individual firms have discovered that increasing levels of customer satisfaction can be linked to customer loyalty and profits.[34] Research also shows that firms that invest in service and excel in customer satisfaction offer excess returns to their shareholders. One study found that firms that did better than their competition in terms of satisfying customers (as measured by the ACSI) generated superior returns at a lower systematic risk.[35]

FIGURE 4.2 **Stock Market Performance of ACSI Stock Portfolio**

Source: ACSI website, www.theacsi.org, "National Economic Indicator, Financial Indicator," accessed May 21, 2016.

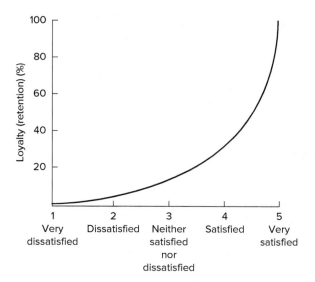

FIGURE 4.3
Relationship between Customer Satisfaction and Loyalty in Competitive Industries

Source: J. L. Heskett, W. E. Sasser Jr., and L. A. Schlesinger, *The Service Profit Chain: How Leading Companies Link Profit and Growth to Loyalty, Satisfaction, and Value* (New York: The Free Press, 1997), p. 83. The Free Press, a Division of Simon & Schuster, Inc.

Another study found that retailer announcements of customer service strategies resulted in a significant abnormal return for these firms and increased market value of 1.09 percent on average.[36] Research has also shown that portfolios of stocks consisting of firms with high levels and positive changes in customer satisfaction outperform other portfolio combinations.[37]

As shown in Figure 4.3, there is an important relationship between customer satisfaction and customer loyalty. This relationship is particularly strong when customers are very satisfied. Thus, firms that simply aim to satisfy customers may not be doing enough to engender loyalty—they must instead aim to more than satisfy or even delight their customers. Xerox Corporation was one of the first, if not the first, companies to pinpoint this relationship. Xerox discovered through its extensive customer research that customers giving Xerox a 5 (very satisfied) on a satisfaction scale were six times more likely to repurchase Xerox equipment than were those giving the company a 4 (somewhat satisfied).[38] Enterprise Rent-A-Car has also learned through its research that customers who give the highest rating to their rental experience are three times more likely to rent again than are those who give the company the second-highest rating.[39] Information provided by TARP Worldwide Inc.—based on data from 10 studies, including 8,000 customers worldwide from across industries—drew similar conclusions. TARP found that 96 percent of those customers who are "very satisfied" say they will "definitely repurchase" from the same company. The number drops precipitously to only 52 percent for those customers who are "somewhat satisfied." Only 7 percent of customers who are "neutral or very dissatisfied" say they will definitely repurchase.[40]

At the opposite end of the satisfaction spectrum, researchers have also found that there is a strong link between dissatisfaction and disloyalty—or defection. Customer loyalty can fall off precipitously when customers reach a particular level of dissatisfaction or when they are dissatisfied with critically important service attributes.[41] We discuss these relationships and the implications for relationship and loyalty marketing in Chapter 6, but suffice it to say that clear linkages have been drawn between customer satisfaction, loyalty, and firm profitability. Thus, many companies are spending significant time and money understanding the underpinnings of customer satisfaction and ways that they can improve.

SERVICE QUALITY

We now turn to *service quality,* a critical element of customer perceptions. In the case of pure services (e.g., health care, financial services, education), service quality will be the dominant element in customers' evaluations. In cases in which customer service or services are offered in combination with a physical product (e.g., IT services, auto services), service quality may also be critical in determining customer satisfaction. Figure 4.1 highlighted these relationships. We will focus here on the left side of Figure 4.1, examining the underlying factors that form perceptions of service quality. First we discuss *what* customers evaluate; then we look specifically at the five dimensions of service that customers rely on in forming their judgments.

Outcome, Interaction, and Physical Environment Quality

What is it that consumers evaluate when judging service quality? Over the years, service researchers have suggested that consumers judge the quality of services based on their perceptions of the technical outcome provided, the process by which that outcome was delivered, and the quality of the physical surroundings where the service is delivered.[42] For example, in the case of a lawsuit, a legal services client will judge the quality of the technical outcome, or how the court case was resolved, as well as the quality of the interaction. Interaction quality includes such factors as the lawyer's timeliness in returning phone calls, his empathy for the client, and his courtesy and listening skills. Similarly, a restaurant customer will judge the service on her perceptions of the meal (technical outcome quality) and on how the meal was served and how the employees interacted with her (interaction quality). The decor and surroundings (physical environment quality) of both the law firm and the restaurant will also affect the customer's perceptions of overall service quality.

Service Quality Dimensions

Research suggests that customers do not perceive quality in a unidimensional way but rather judge quality based on multiple factors relevant to the context. The dimensions of service quality have been identified through the pioneering research of Parsu Parasuraman, Valarie Zeithaml, and Leonard Berry. Their research has identified five dimensions of service quality that apply across a variety of service contexts.[43] The five dimensions defined here are shown in Figure 4.1 as drivers of service quality. These five dimensions appear again in Chapter 5, along with the scale developed to measure them, SERVQUAL.

- *Reliability:* ability to perform the promised service dependably and accurately.
- *Responsiveness:* willingness to help customers and provide prompt service.
- *Assurance:* employees' knowledge and courtesy and their ability to inspire trust and confidence.
- *Empathy:* caring, individualized attention given to customers.
- *Tangibles:* appearance of physical facilities, equipment, personnel, and communication materials.

Customers in different parts of the world perceive, experience, and react to service experiences differently.

SERVICE QUALITY

The development of the service quality dimensions of reliability, responsiveness, assurance, empathy, and tangibles was based on research conducted across multiple contexts within the United States. As a general rule, reliability comes through as the most important dimension of service quality in the United States, with responsiveness also being relatively important when compared with the remaining three dimensions. But what happens when we look across cultures? Are the service quality dimensions still important? Which ones are most important? Answers to these questions can be extremely valuable for companies delivering services across cultures or in multicultural environments.

Researchers have used Geert Hofstede's well-established cultural dimensions to assess whether service quality importance would vary across different cultural orientations. For example, *power distance* refers to the extent to which status differences are expected and accepted within a culture. Research has suggested that most Asian countries are characterized by high power distance, whereas many Western countries score lower on power distance measures. Broadly speaking, *individualism* reflects a self-orientation that is characteristic of Western culture, whereas its opposite, *collectivism,* is more typical of the East. Similar comparisons across cultures have been made for the other dimensions: *masculinity, uncertainty avoidance,* and *long-term orientation.* The question is whether these types of cultural differences affect the importance consumers place on the service quality dimensions.

The figure shown here suggests strong differences in the importance of service quality dimensions across clusters of customers defined by different cultural dimensions. The cultural profile of the clusters is described as

Followers: Large power distance, high collectivism, high masculinity, neutral uncertainty avoidance, and short-term orientation.

Balance seekers: Small power distance, high collectivism, neutral masculinity, high uncertainty avoidance, and medium-term orientation.

Self-confidents: Small power distance, high individualism, medium femininity, low uncertainty avoidance, and long-term orientation.

Sensory seekers: Large power distance, medium individualism, high masculinity, low uncertainty avoidance, and short-term orientation.

Functional analyzers: Small power distance, medium individualism, high femininity, high uncertainty avoidance, and long-term orientation.

From this figure it is clear that the service quality dimensions are relevant across cultures, but their relative importance varies depending on cultural value orientation.

CUSTOMER RAGE

Extremely negative reactions to service experiences are connected with the idea of customer rage. In these situations, customers feel extreme anger and frustration, and often they react by spreading negative word of mouth, ceasing to do business with the company, and even engaging in retaliation or revenge aimed at the company.

These dimensions represent how consumers organize information about service quality in their minds. On the basis of exploratory and quantitative research, these five dimensions were found relevant for banking, insurance, appliance repair and maintenance, securities brokerage, long-distance telephone service, automobile repair service, and others. The dimensions are also applicable to retail and business services, and logic suggests they would be relevant for internal services as well. Sometimes customers use all the dimensions to determine service quality perceptions, at other times not. For example, for an ATM, empathy is not likely to be a relevant dimension. And in a phone encounter to schedule a repair, tangibles will not be relevant.

Research suggests that cultural differences also affect the relative importance placed on the five dimensions, as discussed in our Global Feature. Interesting differences in service quality dimensions themselves also emerge in country-specific studies. For example, research in Pakistan that builds upon the original service quality

Legend:
- Followers
- Balance seekers
- Self-confidents
- Sensory seekers
- Functional analyzers

(y-axis: Relative Importance, from -1.0 to 1.0)
(x-axis: Reliability, Responsiveness, Assurance, Empathy, Tangibles)

(Australia and the United States), finding some surprising differences. The researchers found that customers in Western cultures were more likely to experience rage emotions following a failed service than were their Eastern counterparts, most likely due to higher expectations and lower tolerance. Yet, somewhat surprisingly, customers from Eastern cultures who experienced rage were more likely to report a desire for revenge and to express their rage emotions in overt, sometimes physical, ways. While they might be slower to anger, customers from Eastern cultures express their anger more forcefully and vengefully once they surpass a certain threshold. It is believed to be more acceptable in Eastern cultures to display anger and hostility toward frontline workers, whereas in Western cultures such behavior is frowned upon.

Research conducted every two years has shown that customer rage is on the rise in the United States where, in 2015, 54 percent of customers experienced a serious problem with a product or service in the past year, and of those 66 percent were enraged by the incident. Other researchers have compared rage experiences and reactions in Eastern (China and Thailand) versus Western cultures

Sources: G. Hofstede, *Cultures and Organizations: Software of the Mind* (New York, McGraw-Hill, 1991); O. Furrer, B. Shaw-Ching Liu, and D. Sudharshan, "The Relationships between Culture and Service Quality Perceptions," *Journal of Service Research* 2 (May 2000), pp. 355–371; www.geert-hofstede.com; Customer Rage Study (2015), accessed May 21, 2016, Customer Rage www.wpcarey.asu.edu/csl; P. G. Patterson, M. K. Brady, and J. R. McColl-Kennedy, "Geysers or Bubbling Hot Springs: A Cross-Cultural Examination of Customer Rage from Eastern and Western Perspectives," *Journal of Service Research* 19 (August 2016), pp. 243–259.

dimensions revealed the following dimensions of service quality: tangibles, reliability, assurance, sincerity, personalization, and formality.[44] This study also illustrated that cultural differences may cause the original dimensions to be interpreted slightly differently as well. In Pakistan, "reliability" was not as absolute in its meaning, but rather was interpreted as "promises are mostly kept," "minimum errors are made on reports or statements," and "service is usually available when needed."

In the following pages we expand on each of the five original SERVQUAL dimensions and provide illustrations of how customers judge them.

Reliability: Delivering on Promises

Of the five dimensions, reliability has been consistently shown to be the most important determinant of perceptions of service quality among U.S. customers.[45] *Reliability* is defined as the ability to perform the promised service dependably and accurately. In

© Tim Boyle/Getty Images

The Geek Squad emphasizes the service quality dimension of *responsiveness* in its service positioning.

its broadest sense, reliability means that the company delivers on its promises—promises about delivery, service provision, problem resolution, and pricing. Customers want to do business with companies that keep their promises, particularly their promises about the service outcomes and core service attributes.

One company that has effectively communicated and delivered on the reliability dimension for decades is Federal Express (FedEx). Over many decades, FedEx's service positioning around reliability has been reflected in phrases such as "when it absolutely, positively has to get there," and "the world on time." But even when firms do not choose to position themselves explicitly on reliability, as FedEx historically has done, this dimension is extremely important to consumers. All firms need to be aware of customer expectations of reliability. Firms that do not provide the core service that customers think they are buying fail their customers in the most direct way.

Responsiveness: Being Willing to Help

Responsiveness is the willingness to help customers and to provide prompt service. This dimension emphasizes attentiveness and promptness in dealing with customer requests, questions, complaints, and problems. Responsiveness is communicated to customers by the length of time they have to wait for assistance, answers to questions, or attention to problems.

To excel on the dimension of responsiveness, a company must view the process of service delivery and the handling of requests from the customer's point of view rather than from the company's point of view. Standards for speed and promptness that reflect the company's view of internal process requirements may be very different from the customer's requirements for speed and promptness. To truly distinguish themselves on responsiveness, companies need well-staffed customer service departments as well as responsive frontline people in all contact positions. The Geek Squad's 24-hour, 365-days-per-year technical assistance for computers, tablets, and other related equipment earned it a reputation for responsive, quick service—"because viruses aren't known for keeping business hours" (see photo). Responsiveness perceptions are diminished when customers must wait to get through by telephone, are put through to a complex voice mail system, or have trouble accessing the firm's website.

Assurance: Inspiring Trust and Confidence

Assurance is defined as employees' knowledge and courtesy and the ability of the firm and its employees to inspire customer trust and confidence. This dimension is likely to be particularly important for services that customers perceive as high risk or for services of which they feel uncertain about their ability to evaluate outcomes—for example, banking, insurance, brokerage, medical, and legal services.

Trust and confidence may be embodied in the person who links the customer to the company, such as securities brokers, insurance agents, lawyers, or counselors. In such service contexts the company seeks to build trust and loyalty between key contact people and individual customers. The "personal banker" concept captures this idea: customers are assigned to a banker who will get to know them individually and who will coordinate all their banking services.

In other situations, trust and confidence are embodied in the organization itself. Insurance companies such as Allstate ("You're in good hands with Allstate") and

Prudential ("Own a piece of the rock") illustrate efforts to create trusting relationships between customers and the company as a whole. An ad campaign by FedEx used the tagline "Relax, it's FedEx," going beyond its traditional reliability message to focus on assurance and trust.

Empathy: Treating Customers as Individuals

Empathy is defined as the caring, individualized attention that the firm provides its customers. The essence of empathy is conveying, through personalized service, that customers are unique and special and that their needs are understood. Customers want to feel understood by and important to firms that provide service to them. Personnel at small service firms often know customers by name and build relationships that reflect their personal knowledge of customer requirements and preferences. When such a small firm competes with larger firms, the ability to be empathetic may give the small firm a clear advantage.

In business-to-business services, customers want supplier firms to understand their industries and issues. Many small computer consulting firms successfully compete with large vendors by positioning themselves as specialists in particular industries. Even though larger firms have superior resources, the small firms are perceived as more knowledgeable about customers' specific issues and needs and are able to offer more customized services.

Tangibles: Representing the Service Physically

Tangibles are defined as the appearance of physical facilities, equipment, personnel, and communication materials. Tangibles provide physical representations or images of the service that customers, particularly new customers, will use to evaluate quality. Service industries that emphasize tangibles in their strategies include services in which the customer visits the establishment to receive the service, such as restaurants and hotels, retail stores, and entertainment companies.

Although tangibles are often used by service companies to enhance their image, provide continuity, and signal quality to customers, most companies combine tangibles with another dimension to create a service quality strategy for the firm. For example, Jiffy Lube, a car maintenance and servicing chain in the United States, emphasizes both responsiveness and tangibles—providing fast, efficient service and a comfortable, clean waiting area. In contrast, firms that do not pay attention to the tangibles dimension of the service strategy can confuse and even destroy an otherwise good strategy.

Table 4.2 provides examples of how customers judge each of the five dimensions of service quality across a variety of service contexts, including both consumer and business services.

E-Service Quality

The growth of e-tailing and e-services has led many companies to wonder how consumers evaluate service quality on the Web and whether the criteria are different from those used to judge the quality of non-Internet services.[46] A study sponsored by the Marketing Science Institute was conducted to understand how consumers judge e-service quality.[47] In that study, *E-S-QUAL* is defined as the extent to which a website facilitates efficient and effective shopping, purchasing, and delivery. Through exploratory focus groups and two phases of empirical data collection and analysis, this research identified seven dimensions that are critical for core service evaluation (four dimensions) and service recovery evaluation (three dimensions).

TABLE 4.2 Examples of How Customers Judge the Five Dimensions of Service Quality

Industry	Reliability	Responsiveness	Assurance	Empathy	Tangibles
Car repair (consumer)	Problem fixed the first time and ready when promised	Accessible; no waiting; responds to requests	Knowledgeable mechanics	Acknowledges customer by name; remembers previous problems and preferences	Repair facility; waiting area; uniforms; equipment
Airline (consumer)	Flights to promised destinations depart and arrive on schedule	Prompt and speedy system for ticketing, in-flight baggage handling	Trusted name; good safety record; competent employees	Understands special individual needs; anticipates customer needs	Aircraft; ticketing counters; baggage area; uniforms
Medical care (consumer)	Appointments are kept on schedule; diagnoses prove accurate	Accessible; no waiting; willingness to listen	Knowledge; skills; credentials; reputation	Acknowledges patient as a person; remembers previous problems; listens well; has patience	Waiting room; exam room; equipment; written materials
Architecture (business)	Delivers plans when promised and within budget	Returns phone calls; adapts to changes	Credentials; reputation; name in the community; knowledge and skills	Understands client's industry; acknowledges and adapts to specific client needs; gets to know the client	Office area; reports; plans themselves; billing statements; dress of employees
Information processing (internal)	Provides needed information when requested	Prompt response to requests; not "bureaucratic"; deals with problems promptly	Knowledgeable staff; well trained; credentials	Knows internal customers as individuals; understands individual and departmental needs	Internal reports; office area; dress of employees
Internet brokerage (consumer and business)	Provides correct information and executes customer requests accurately	Quick website with easy access and no downtime	Credible information sources on the site; brand recognition; credentials apparent on-site	Responds with human interaction as needed	Appearance of the website as well as flyers, brochures, and other print materials

The four core dimensions that customers use to judge websites at which they experience no questions or problems are as follows:[48]

Efficiency: The ease and speed of accessing and using the site.

Fulfillment: The extent to which the site's promises about order delivery and item availability are fulfilled.

System availability: The correct technical functioning of the site.

Privacy: The degree to which the site is safe and protects customer information.

The study also revealed three dimensions that customers use to judge recovery service when they have problems or questions:

Responsiveness: The effective handling of problems and returns through the site.

Compensation: The degree to which the site compensates customers for problems.

Contact: The availability of assistance through telephone or online representatives.

CUSTOMER EFFORT

Customer effort is another driver of customer loyalty (distinct from quality or satisfaction) that has attracted considerable attention from businesses. Based on surveys of more than 75,000 business-to-consumer and business-to-business customers about their non-face-to-face service interactions (including live calls, web-based interactions, chat, and email) researchers determined that customer loyalty was based not so much on "delighting" customers or even satisfying them, but rather on minimizing the effort they needed to expend to get their problems solved.[49] They contend that making things difficult (high effort) for customers will drive them away, while delighting them is not as likely to make them stay. In the context of customer service this makes total sense. When customers have a problem that needs to be solved, they want it solved quickly with minimal effort on their part. In this context, the researchers suggest that companies should focus on anticipating and heading off the need for follow-up calls, dealing with the emotional side of interactions, minimizing the need for customers to switch to a different service channel to solve their problem, and truly—not just speedily—solving the customer's problem.

Many companies today are engaged in measuring customer effort as a way to predict loyalty, and it seems to be a good predictor in customer service situations. The concept also seems to be very compatible with the five dimensions of service quality and the dimensions of e-Service quality, all of which are focused on delivery of the basic service rather than delighting or going above and beyond. That said, there are likely many service situations, outside of basic customer service, where customers are seeking to be delighted (e.g., a long-awaited vacation, a special concert, or a first (or fiftieth) anniversary dinner). In other cases, customers may prefer or expect to expend considerable personal effort to cocreate the service for themselves. In other words, they are not looking to minimize their effort. This is often true of such important service experiences as weddings, educational degrees, or health-related services. In these cases, other elements are likely more important in determining their loyalty than is effort. While customers are never looking to waste their effort in any situation, they are not always looking to minimize it either.

SERVICE ENCOUNTERS: THE BUILDING BLOCKS FOR CUSTOMER PERCEPTIONS

We have just finished a discussion of customer perceptions, specifically customer satisfaction and service quality. As discussed in our Strategy Insight, companies today recognize that they can compete more effectively by distinguishing themselves with respect to service quality, satisfaction, and loyalty. Next we turn to what have been termed the building blocks for customer perceptions—service encounters, or "moments of truth." Service encounters are where promises are kept or broken and where the proverbial rubber meets the road—sometimes called

Strategy Insight Customer Satisfaction and the Bottom Line

The relationships among customer satisfaction and strategic corporate goals such as growth, profitability, and market share are complex. On the one hand, long-term growth and profitability are very unlikely for companies that do not satisfy their customers. On the other hand, investments in improving customer satisfaction do not automatically pay off in growth, profitability, or market share. In this chapter we focus on the fundamental, positive relationships between service, satisfaction, loyalty, and company outcomes. Based on an accumulation of studies over many decades, research has clearly established that these relationships exist across a wide range of industries and contexts. A review of this research published by the Marketing Science Institute reconfirms the fundamental, core beliefs in these important relationships. Yet no one would deny that there are important nuances, and managers must be cognizant of these. Simply improving customer satisfaction does not ensure bottom-line outcomes, let alone precisely predict the levels of these outcomes.

The nuances and complexities of these strategic relationships were studied by Timothy Keiningham, Sunil Gupta, Lerzan Aksoy, and Alexander Buoye, and reported in the *MIT Sloan Management Review*. This team of researchers demonstrated that the overall direct relationship between customer satisfaction and customer spending is weak, that the return on investments for customer satisfaction is often very low, and that absolute levels of satisfaction are not what truly matters. Instead, what matters is the level of satisfaction relative to competing alternatives.

The researchers raise some issues to consider when determining whether "satisfaction is worth the cost."

ISSUE 1: MONEY-LOSING DELIGHTERS

Similar to the research on customer effort discussed earlier in this chapter, these researchers found that the benefits of delighting customers are not clear cut. They point to a number of companies whose customers are "extremely satisfied," but the company is not profitable due to the high cost of satisfaction in those cases. In some cases companies may create highly satisfied customers by offering them very low prices, which does not generate profits at all. They point to the e-commerce marketplace Groupon, where six of its top-performing categories in terms of customer satisfaction were actually money-losers. Thus managers need to look carefully at the potential payback for delighting customers, compared to the costs of doing so.

ISSUE 2: SMALLER OFTEN EQUALS HAPPIER

The idea that high customer satisfaction would correlate positively with market share seems to carry with it some logic. Yet these researchers show that customer satisfaction and market share do not go hand in hand. In fact, some of the highest levels of customer satisfaction are experienced by smaller businesses and non-market-share leaders, and conversely, high market share companies do not necessarily have the highest levels of satisfaction. Examples of this

"real-time marketing." It is from these service encounters that customers build their perceptions.

Service Encounters or Moments of Truth

From the customer's point of view, the most vivid impression of service occurs in the *service encounter,* or *moment of truth,* when the customer interacts with the service firm. For example, among the service encounters that a hotel customer experiences are checking into the hotel, being taken to a room by a bellperson, eating a restaurant meal, requesting a wake-up call, and checking out. You could think of the linking of these moments of truth as a service encounter cascade (see Figure 4.4).

phenomenon include McDonald's and Walmart, which are the market-share leaders in their categories, but which do not enjoy the highest levels of satisfaction by any means. The likely explanation is the diverse appeal that these market leaders must have in these broad industry categories. They are serving a diversity of needs and types of customers, resulting in more variability, and lower overall satisfaction. Thus, if market share is a company's primary goal, it must carefully weigh its corresponding customer satisfaction investments.

ISSUE 3: THE IMPORTANCE OF BEING NO. 1

The researchers also found that customer satisfaction is not a good predictor of what a customer will spend with a particular company—that is, their "share of wallet." They show conclusively that customers' share of wallet is related to their relative satisfaction—that is, how do they feel about a particular service brand when compared to others? Absolute satisfaction is therefore not a good predictor of spending or share of wallet. Rather, it is the relative satisfaction that counts.

So What Is a Manager to Do?

First, it is important for all managers to understand that no company will survive very long without satisfied customers. And, having too many truly dissatisfied customers can quickly ruin a business. These are fundamental truths. Yet managers must go into the customer satisfaction business with their eyes open and a clear understanding of their corporate goals, aligning these with their satisfaction strategies.

For example, if the overriding corporate goal is to increase market share and be the market leader, then there needs to be more latitude for customer satisfaction. Often, mass-market brands suffer in terms of customer satisfaction when compared with their smaller, niche, competitors. If the overriding corporate goal is to maximize profits (particularly in the short run), then the costs of investing in customer satisfaction must be carefully considered and balanced with the benefits. Careful segmentation to understand which customers are profitable will also allow for more targeted investments to enhance the satisfaction of the most profitable (or potentially profitable) customers.

The bottom line: think carefully about customer satisfaction and understand how it fits into the total picture of the company's goals. Then measure it and invest in it accordingly. But never ignore it or dismiss it as unimportant!

Sources: V. Mittal and C. Frennea, "Customer Satisfaction: A Strategic Review and Guidelines for Managers," Marketing Science Institute, 2010; S. Gupta and V. Zeithaml, "Customer Metrics and Their Impact on Financial Performance," *Marketing Science* 25 (November-December 2006), pp. 718–739; T. Keiningham, S. Gupta, L. Aksoy, and A. Buoye, "The High Price of Customer Satisfaction," *MIT Sloan Management Review*, 55 (April 2014), pp. 37–46; T. Keiningham, L. Aksoy and L. Williams, *The Wallet Allocation Rule* (Hoboken, NJ: John Wiley & Sons, Inc., 2015).

It is in these encounters that customers receive a snapshot of the organization's service quality, and each encounter contributes to the customer's overall satisfaction and willingness to do business with the organization again. From the organization's point of view, each encounter thus presents an opportunity to prove its potential as a quality service provider and to increase customer loyalty. A sequence of encounters can also be linked to form a customer experience. In the hotel example, all individual encounters would link together to comprise an "end-to-end customer experience," or "customer journey" as described in Chapter 5. Such a customer journey could include many encounters and extend over days—or even weeks, in the case of an extended stay.

FIGURE 4.4
A Service Encounter Cascade for a Hotel Visit

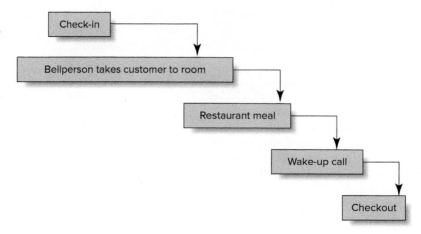

Some services have few service encounters, and others have many. The Disney Corporation estimates that each of its amusement park customers experiences about 74 service encounters and that a negative experience in any one of them can lead to a negative overall evaluation. Mistakes or problems that occur in the early stages of the service cascade may be particularly critical. Marriott Hotels learned this through its extensive customer research to determine what service elements contribute most to customer loyalty. It found that four of the top five factors come into play in the first 10 minutes of the guest's stay.[50]

The Importance of Encounters

Although early events in the encounter cascade are likely to be especially important, *any* encounter can be critical in determining customer satisfaction and loyalty. If a customer is interacting with a firm for the first time, that initial encounter will create a first impression of the organization. In these first encounter situations, the customer frequently has no other basis for judging the organization, and the initial phone contact or face-to-face experience with a representative of the firm can take on significant importance in the customer's perceptions of quality. A customer calling for repair service on a household appliance may well hang up and call a different company if he is treated rudely by a customer service representative, put on hold for a lengthy period, or told that two weeks is the soonest someone can be sent out to make the repair. Even if the technical quality of the firm's repair service is superior, the firm may not get the chance to demonstrate it if the initial telephone encounter drives the customer away.

Even when the customer has had multiple interactions with a firm, each individual encounter is important in creating a composite image of the firm in the customer's memory. In today's technology-mediated world, these encounters can occur online through websites and other Internet-based channels as well as in person or over the phone. Many positive experiences add up to a composite image of high quality, whereas many negative interactions have the opposite effect. On the other hand, a combination of positive and negative interactions leave the customer feeling unsure of the firm's quality, doubtful of its consistency in service delivery, and vulnerable to the appeals of competitors. For example, a large corporate customer of an institutional food provider that provides food service in all its company dining rooms and cafeterias could have a series of positive encounters with the account manager or

Exhibit 4.1 One Critical Encounter Destroys a 30-Year Relationship

"If you have $1 in a bank or $1 million, I think they owe you the courtesy of stamping your parking ticket," said John Barrier. One day Mr. Barrier paid a visit to his bank in Spokane, Washington. He was wearing his usual shabby clothes and pulled up in his pickup truck, parking in the lot next to the bank. After cashing a check, he went outside to drive away and was stopped by a parking attendant who told him there was a 60-cent fee but that he could get his parking slip validated in the bank and park for free. No problem, Barrier thought and he went back into the bank (where, by the way, he had been banking for 30 years). The teller looked him up and down and refused to stamp his slip, telling him that the bank validated parking only for people who have transactions with the bank and that cashing a check wasn't a transaction. Mr. Barrier then asked to see the bank manager, who also looked him up and down, stood back, and "gave me one of those kinds of looks," also refusing to validate the parking bill. Mr. Barrier then said, "Fine. You don't need me, and I don't need you." He withdrew all his money and took it down the street to a competing bank, where the first check he deposited was for $1,000,000.

Source: "Shabby Millionaire Closes Account, Gives Bank Lesson about Snobbery", *The Arizona Republic,* February 21, 1989, p. A3.

salesperson who handles the account. These encounters may occur through multiple channels, including online, through the corporate website, via e-mail, over the phone, or in person. These experiences could be followed by positive encounters with the operations staff who actually set up the food service facilities. However, even with these positive encounters, later negative experiences with the staff who serve the food or the accounting department that administers the billing procedures can result in a mixture of overall quality impressions. This variation in experiences could result in the corporate customer wondering about the quality of the organization and unsure of what to expect in the future. Each encounter with different people and departments representing the food service provider adds to or detracts from the potential for a continuing relationship.

Logic suggests that not all encounters are equally important in building relationships. For every organization, certain encounters are probably key to customer satisfaction. For Marriott Hotels, as noted, the early encounters are most important. In a hospital context, a study of patients revealed that encounters with nursing staff were more important in predicting satisfaction than were encounters with meal service or patient discharge personnel.[51] Research also suggests that service quality will be influenced by the pattern of events in terms of the timing, frequency, and proximity of negative, or failed service encounters, relative to delightful service encounters.[52]

In addition to these key encounters, there are some momentous encounters that, like the proverbial "one bad apple," simply ruin the rest and drive the customer away no matter how many or what type of encounters have occurred in the past. These momentous encounters can occur in connection with very important events (such as the failure to deliver an essential piece of equipment before a critical deadline), or they may seem inconsequential, as in the story of the bank customer described in Exhibit 4.1. Similarly, momentous positive encounters can sometimes bind a customer to an organization for life. Research in a call center context concludes that, although the average quality of the individual events in a service encounter sequence are important, satisfaction can be enhanced by providing a positive peak experience within the sequence.[53] This and other research suggest that "not all events in an experience sequence are created equal" and that, in fact, there are benefits to be gained by creating truly delightful (or "peak") experiences at predetermined points in the sequence.

Types of Service Encounters

A service encounter occurs every time a customer interacts with the service organization. There are three general types of service encounters: *remote encounters, technology-mediated encounters,* and *face-to-face encounters.*[54] A customer may experience any of these types of encounters, or a combination of all three, in his or her interactions with a service firm.

First, encounters can occur without any direct human contact *(remote encounters),* such as when a customer interacts with a bank through the ATM system, with a retailer through its website, or with a mail-order service through automated touch-tone phone ordering. Remote encounters also occur when the firm sends its billing statements or communicates other types of information to customers by regular mail or e-mail. Although there is no direct human contact in these remote encounters, each represents an opportunity for the firm to reinforce or establish quality perceptions in the customer. In remote encounters the tangible evidence of the service and the quality of the technical processes and systems become the primary bases for judging quality. Retail purchases, airline ticketing, repair and maintenance troubleshooting, and package and shipment tracking are just a few examples of services available via the Internet. All these types of service encounters can be considered remote encounters (see our Technology Spotlight).

In many organizations (such as insurance companies, utilities, and telecommunications), the most frequent type of encounter between an end-customer and the firm occurs over the telephone or via simultaneous texting, live chats, or other platforms that allow technology-based communication with a real person in real time *(technology-mediated encounters).* Almost all firms (whether goods manufacturers or service businesses) rely on basic telephone encounters to some extent for customer service, general inquiry, or order-taking functions. The judgment of quality in phone encounters is different than in remote encounters because there is greater potential variability in the interaction.[55] Tone of voice, employee knowledge, and effectiveness/efficiency in handling customer issues become important criteria for judging quality in these encounters. For real time e-mail or text exchanges or live chat encounters, where there is no human voice to rely on for cues, the actual words chosen and tone of the communication will determine perceptions of quality.

A third type of encounter is the one that occurs between an employee and a customer in direct personal contact *(face-to-face encounters).* At Mayo Clinic, face-to-face encounters occur between patients and reception staff, nurses, doctors, lab technicians, food service workers, pharmacy staff, and others. For a company such as IBM, in a business-to-business setting, direct encounters occur between the business customer and salespeople, delivery personnel, maintenance representatives, and professional consultants. Determining and understanding service quality issues in face-to-face contexts is the most complex of all. Both verbal and nonverbal behaviors are important determinants of quality, as are tangible cues such as employee dress and other symbols of service (equipment, informational brochures, physical setting). In face-to-face encounters the customer also plays a role in creating quality service for herself through her own behavior during the interaction.

Sources of Pleasure and Displeasure in Service Encounters

Because of the importance of service encounters in building perceptions, researchers have extensively analyzed service encounters in many contexts to determine the sources of customers' favorable and unfavorable impressions. The research uses the critical incident technique to get customers and employees to provide verbatim stories about satisfying and dissatisfying service encounters they have experienced (see Chapter 5 for a detailed description and references for this research technique.)

On the basis of research that documents thousands of service encounter stories, four common themes—recovery (after failure), adaptability, spontaneity, and coping—have been identified as the sources of customer satisfaction/dissatisfaction in memorable service encounters.[56] The themes encompass service behaviors in encounters spanning a wide variety of industries.

Recovery—Employee Response to Service Delivery System Failures

The first theme includes all incidents in which there has been a failure of the service delivery system and an employee is required to respond in some way to consumer complaints and disappointments. The failure may be, for example, a hotel room that is not available, an airplane flight that is delayed six hours, an incorrect item sent from a mail-order company, or a critical error on an internal document. The content or form of the employee's response is what causes the customer to remember the event either favorably or unfavorably. The nuances of service recovery, including employee behaviors and customer responses, have been studied extensively by researchers and organizations. You will find an entire chapter in this book, Chapter 7, devoted to service recovery research and best practices.

Adaptability—Employee Response to Customer Needs and Requests

A second theme underlying satisfaction/dissatisfaction in service encounters is how adaptable the service delivery system is when the customer has special needs or requests that place demands on the process. In these cases, customers judge service encounter quality in terms of the flexibility of the employees and the system. Incidents categorized within this theme all contain an implicit or explicit request for customization of the service to meet a need. Research has categorized the types of special requests that customers have as resulting from "customer deficiencies," including deficiencies of physical capabilities, knowledge, financial resources, and/or time constraints.[57] Much of what customers see as special needs or requests may actually be rather routine from the employee's point of view; what is important is that the customer perceives that something special is being done for her based on her own individual needs. External customers and internal customers alike are pleased when the service provider puts forth the effort to accommodate and adjust the system to meet their requirements. On the flip side, they are angered and frustrated by an unwillingness to try to accommodate and by promises that are never followed through. Contact employees also see their abilities to adapt the system as being a prominent source of customer satisfaction, and often they are equally frustrated by constraints that keep them from being flexible.

Spontaneity—Unprompted and Unsolicited Employee Actions

Even when there is no system failure and no special request or need, customers can still remember service encounters as being very satisfying or very dissatisfying. Employee spontaneity in delivering memorably good or poor service is the third theme. Satisfying incidents in this group represent very pleasant surprises for the customer (special attention, being treated like royalty, receiving something nice but not requested), whereas dissatisfying incidents in this group represent negative and unacceptable employee behaviors (rudeness, stealing, discrimination, ignoring the customer).

Technology Spotlight Customers Love Amazon

Amazon.com's website states that the company "seeks to be Earth's most customer-centric company, where customers can find and discover anything they might want to buy online." Jeff Bezos, CEO of Amazon, whose company name has become a household word worldwide, has always believed that his customers come first, and in his 2011 letter to shareowners he stated that "the long-term interests of shareowners are perfectly aligned with the interests of customers." Building on this clear focus on customers, relationships, and value, net sales were up 20 percent in 2015, reaching $107 billion for the year. The 2015 American Customer Satisfaction Index reflected a rating of 83 for Amazon—one of the highest ratings of any company in any industry. According to Bezos, "Customers come first. If you focus on what customers want and build a relationship, they will allow you to make money."[58]

In its core business, online book sales, Amazon has taken a historically interpersonally dominated transaction and successfully transformed it into a web-based service experience. Let's take a closer look at what the company is doing in this space and why customers love it so much. Since its inception in July 1995, Amazon has grown to the point where it offers more book titles than any brick-and-mortar bookstore could ever hope to stock, so selection and availability of titles are one key to its popularity with customers. But that is just the beginning. In addition to a wide selection, Amazon has invested significant effort to simulate the feel of a neighborhood bookstore, where a patron can mingle with other customers, discuss books, and get recommendations from bookstore employees.

Over the years, Amazon has incorporated user feedback into product pages and added the "look inside" feature, so that readers can sample books easily. It offers a personalized shopping experience for each customer, along with convenient checkout through its "1-Click®Shopping." Amazon allows customers to find related books on virtually any topic by simply typing key words and initiating a search of its massive database. Its one-to-one marketing system allows the company to track what individual customers buy and let them know of additional titles that might interest them.

In 2007, Amazon introduced the Kindle, a technology device that allows customers to read books and other print materials on a personal electronic reader. But the Kindle is more than a reading device—it also allows owners to shop for books, read reviews, and purchase and download books in seconds via a wireless connection that operates 24 hours per day. Its trademarked Whispersync technology ensures that customers have their reading library with them wherever they go and that they have all of their highlights, notes, and most recently read pages immediately accessible. In only a few years, sales of books on Kindles overtook those of paper books as the most popular format for Amazon book sales.

As with its other innovations and services, Amazon has designed the Kindle from the customer's perspective, enhancing the design and changing features to ensure the loyalty of serious readers, rather than to keep up with the latest available bells and whistles of technology. The technology that powers the Kindle is invisible to the customer, and the enhancements are made to improve the experience. As Bezos has said, "For the vast majority of books, adding video and animation is not going to be helpful. It is distracting rather than enhancing. You are not going to improve Hemingway by adding video snippets."

Few would deny that Amazon is a master of technology and technology-based services for consumers. The rapid growth of Amazon Web Services (AWS) since its launch in 2006 is a testament to this fact. AWS allows companies to offload data storage and computing to Amazon's cloud, and more recently, it has added databases, developer tools, and analytics software to its portfolio of capabilities.

Additionally, in 2015 Amazon expanded into smart home automation technology with its Amazon Echo

Coping—Employee Response to Problem Customers

The incidents categorized in this group came to light when employees were asked to describe service encounter incidents in which customers were either very satisfied or dissatisfied. In addition to describing incidents of the types outlined under the first three themes, employees described many incidents in which customers were the cause of their own dissatisfaction. Such customers were basically uncooperative—that is, unwilling to cooperate with the service provider, other customers, industry

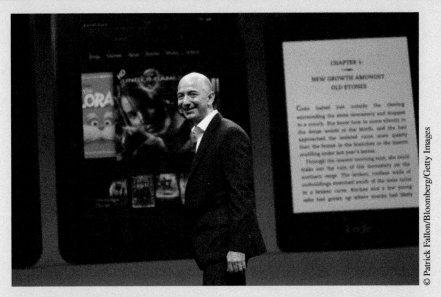

Jeff Bezos, CEO, and the Amazon Kindle.

device. Echo, also known as Alexa, began as a voice-activated speaker that can play music and provide information, such as the latest news, weather, and sports scores. Amazon has continued to build on Echo's capabilities by releasing "skills," which allow the device to communicate with other apps and smart devices in the home, such as Uber, Nest thermostats, Philips Hue lightbulbs, and even Domino's Pizza. By allowing Echo to interact with a wide variety of apps and devices, customers have the flexibility to use the device in a way that best suits their lifestyle. This customer-centricity yields reviews that say things like, "We love Alexa!", "The best money I've ever spent on Amazon," and "Alexa, my love, thou art a nearly perfect spouse."

Lastly, from its humble beginnings as a free two-day shipping program for avid Amazon customers, Amazon Prime has grown to offer music, movies, books, photo storage, and many other perks, all for a yearly fee.

As Amazon stays on the forefront of technology-delivered retail and reading services, few doubters of its long-term success remain. By all accounts, the philosophy of keeping the customer central to the firm's strategy seems to have paid off.

Sources: Amazon.com, www.amazon.com, accessed July 18, 2011; ACSI results at www.theacsi.org, 2015; A. Penenberg, "The Evolution of Amazon," *Fast Company*, July–August 2009, pp. 66–72, 74; J. Authors, "An Amazing 10-year Amazonian Adventure LONG VIEW," *Financial Times*, April 28, 2007, p. 24; G. Fowler, "Kindle to Go 'Mass Market,'" *The Wall Street Journal*, July 29, 2010, p. 6; S. Woo, "Amazon Grows—at a High Price," *The Wall Street Journal*, January 28, 2011, p. B1; "Amazon.com Announces Fourth Quarter Sales Up 22% to $35.7 Billion," Businesswire.com, January 28, 2016, http://www.businesswire.com/news/home/20160128006357/en/Amazon.com-Announces-Fourth-Quarter-Sales-22-35.7; G. A. Fowler, "Amazon's Alexa Listens and Learns," *The Wall Street Journal*, April 14, 2016, p. D1.

regulations, and/or laws. In these cases nothing the employee could do would result in the customer feeling pleased about the encounter. The term *coping* is used to describe these incidents because coping is the behavior generally required of employees to handle problem customer encounters. Rarely are such encounters satisfying from the customer's point of view.[59] Also of interest is that customers themselves did not relate any "problem customer" incidents. That is, customers either do not see, or choose not to remember or retell, stories of the times when they

TABLE 4.3 General Service Behaviors Based on Service Encounter Themes—Dos and Don'ts

Theme	Do	Don't
Recovery	Acknowledge problem Explain causes Apologize Compensate/upgrade Lay out options Take responsibility	Ignore customer Blame customer Leave customer to fend for himself or herself Downgrade Act as if nothing is wrong "Pass the buck"
Adaptability	Recognize the seriousness of the need Acknowledge Anticipate Attempt to accommodate Adjust the system Explain rules/policies Take responsibility	Ignore Promise but fail to follow through Show unwillingness to try Embarrass the customer Laugh at the customer Avoid responsibility "Pass the buck"
Spontaneity	Take time Be attentive Anticipate needs Listen Provide information Show empathy	Exhibit impatience Ignore Yell/laugh/swear Steal from customers Discriminate
Coping	Listen Try to accommodate Explain Let go of the customer	Take customer's dissatisfaction personally Let customer's dissatisfaction affect others

themselves were unreasonable to the point of causing their own dissatisfactory service encounter.

Table 4.3 summarizes the specific employee behaviors that cause satisfaction and dissatisfaction in service encounters according to the four themes just presented: recovery, adaptability, spontaneity, and coping. The left side of the table suggests what employees do that results in positive encounters, whereas the right side summarizes negative behaviors within each theme.

Technology-Based Service Encounters

All the research on service encounters described thus far and the resulting themes underlying service encounter evaluations are based on interpersonal services, including face-to-face or voice-to-voice encounters between customers and employees. Researchers have also examined the sources of satisfaction in technology-based service encounters, whether online, through interactive kiosks, mobile applications, or automated phone systems. The rapidly growing availability of technology service options means that customers have more and more choices every day to get services through technology that they had previously received in person and to experience groundbreaking innovations. While there are many similarities in the drivers of satisfaction across these different types of encounters, there are some differences.[60]

Whether service is delivered through technology or face-to-face, customers still expect the company to *not fail to deliver* on the core promise—they expect the technology to work reliably and to have their needs met quickly and efficiently. For technology-based service encounters failure often comes in the form of technology system failures, process failures in follow-up, poor website or technology design, or errors on the part of the customer. When there is a failure, one of the biggest complaints customers have with technology-delivered service is that there is no effective service recovery in place to solve the problem easily, and they frequently have to call the company—something they were trying to avoid in the first place. More sophisticated use of real-time chat and online help resources are a couple of the ways companies are addressing these challenges.

As with interpersonal encounters, customers also expect *flexibility of the systems* and the ability to be served in a personalized manner that adapts to meet their needs and requests. This aspect of service can at first seem counterintuitive for technology-based services where the goal is often standardization and consistent delivery of the same service over and over. Yet, customers are not interested in standardized service if it does not meet their needs. Thus, technology-based services have developed ways to be adaptive through, for example, asking a series of questions to zero in on the customer's needs (as with automated voice response systems), or by learning about the customer and offering customized choices based on the customer's purchase or search history. For example, Netflix and Amazon Prime both know what individual customers prefer in movies, books, and other categories of purchases and they make sophisticated recommendations for each individual based on personal history. Amazon, featured in our Technology Spotlight, is probably the company most known for these types of adaptive and customized services, provided through technology. Automated assistants like Cortana (Microsoft), Alexa (Amazon), and Siri (Apple) are also increasingly able to personalize and adapt to customers' questions and requests.

Research also shows that customers are happy to use technology-based services if they perceive them to be *better than the alternative*. When compared to the interpersonal, face-to-face, or brick-and-mortar alternative, is the technology-based service easier to use, is it more reliable, does it save time, or perhaps money? Research has shown that perceived convenience of a self-service technology (e.g., can use any time, do not have to leave home to use), when compared with the personal alternative, is a big motivator for customers in choosing the technology option.[61] Yet even when they are more convenient, innovative, and provide other benefits, not all customers are interested in or willing to use technology-based alternatives. Research documents that when it comes to adopting technology services, customers can be grouped into five categories:[62]

- Skeptics (38 percent of consumers)—those who are a bit detached from technology and not extremely positive or negative toward using it.
- Explorers (18 percent)—those who are highly motivated to try new technologies.
- Avoiders (16 percent)—those who are resistant and not motivated to try new technologies.
- Pioneers (16 percent)—those who hold both strong positive and strong negative views about using technology.
- Hesitaters (13 percent)—those who are not very innovative and therefore less likely to use new technologies.

The technology transformation of service industries will continue to march forward, and most customers will use more and more technology-delivered services over time. Even robots are likely to become a service option in some contexts.[63] Yet we predict that however service is delivered, customers will still want encounters that are reliable (and recoverable when there is a failure), personalized, and convenient—just as they always have.

Summary

This chapter described customer perceptions of service by first introducing two critical concepts: customer satisfaction and service quality. These critical customer perceptions were defined and discussed in terms of the factors that influence each of them. Customer satisfaction is a broad perception influenced by features and attributes of the product as well as by customers' emotional responses, their attributions, and their perceptions of fairness. Service quality, the customer's perception of the service component of a product, is also a critical determinant of customer satisfaction. Sometimes, as in the case of a pure service, service quality may be the *most* critical determinant of satisfaction. Perceptions of service quality are based on five dimensions: reliability, assurance, empathy, responsiveness, and tangibles.

Another major purpose of the chapter was to introduce the idea of service encounters, or "moments of truth," as the building blocks for both satisfaction and quality. Every service encounter (whether remote, technology-mediated, or in person) is an opportunity to build customer perceptions of quality and satisfaction. The underlying themes of pleasure and displeasure in service encounters were also described.

Chapters 3 and 4 have provided you with a grounding in customer issues relevant to services. These two chapters are intended to give you a solid understanding of service expectations and perceptions. Through the rest of the book, we illustrate strategies that firms can use to close the gap between customer expectations and perceptions.

Discussion Questions

1. What is customer satisfaction, and why is it so important? Discuss how customer satisfaction can be influenced by each of the following: product attributes and features, customer emotions, attributions for success or failure, perceptions of fairness, and family members or other customers.

2. What is the ACSI? Do you believe that such national indicators of customer satisfaction should be included as benchmarks of national economic well-being similar to gross domestic product (GDP), price indicators, and productivity measures?

3. Why do service companies generally receive lower satisfaction ratings in the ACSI than nondurable and durable product companies?

4. Discuss the differences between perceptions of service quality and customer satisfaction.

5. List and define the five dimensions of service quality. Describe the services provided by a firm you do business with (e.g., your bank, your doctor, your favorite restaurant) on each of the dimensions. In your mind, has this organization distinguished itself from its competitors on any particular service quality dimension?

6. Describe a remote encounter, a technology-mediated encounter (phone, real-time texting, or live chat), and a face-to-face encounter that you have had recently. How did you evaluate the encounter, and what were the most important factors determining your satisfaction/dissatisfaction in each case?

7. Describe an "encounter cascade" for an airplane flight. In your opinion, what are the most important encounters in this cascade for determining your overall impression of the quality of the airline?

8. Why did the gentleman described in Exhibit 4.1 leave his bank after 30 years? What were the underlying causes of his dissatisfaction in that instance, and why would that cause him to leave the bank?

9. Assume that you are a manager of a health club. Discuss general strategies you might use to maximize customers' positive perceptions of your club. How would you know if you were successful?

Exercises

1. Keep a journal of your service encounters with different organizations (at least five) during the week. For each journal entry, ask yourself the following questions: What circumstances led up to this encounter? What did the employee say or do? How did you evaluate this encounter? What exactly made you evaluate the encounter that way? What should the organization have done differently (if anything)? Categorize your encounters according to the four themes of service encounter satisfaction/dissatisfaction (recovery, adaptability, spontaneity, coping).

2. Interview someone with a non-U.S. cultural background. Ask the person about service quality, whether the five dimensions of quality are relevant, and which are most important in determining the quality of banking services (or some other type of service) in the person's country.

3. Interview an employee of a local service business. Ask the person to discuss each of the five dimensions of service quality with you as it relates to the person's company. Which dimensions are most important? Are any dimensions *not* relevant in this context? Which dimensions does the company do best? Why? Which dimensions could benefit from improvement? Why?

4. Interview a manager, an owner, or a president of a business. Discuss with this person the strategies he or she uses to ensure customer satisfaction. How does service quality enter into the strategies, or does it? Find out how this person measures customer satisfaction and/or service quality.

5. Visit Amazon.com's website. Visit a traditional bookstore. How would you compare the two experiences? Compare and contrast the factors that most influenced your satisfaction and perceptions of service quality in the two different situations. When would you choose to use one versus the other?

Notes

1. C. Zane, *Reinventing the Wheel* (Dallas, TX: BenBella Books, 2011); "Creating Lifetime Customers," http://www.Christopherzanecom/media/, accessed July 2011; A. Danigelis, "Local Hero: Zane's Cycles," *Fast Company,* September 2006, p. 60; D. Fenn, *Alpha Dogs: How Your Small Business Can Become a Leader of the Pack* (New York: Collins, 2003); Chris Zane presentation at "Compete through Service" Symposium, November 2010, Center for Services Leadership, Arizona State University. Also see excellent YouTube videos of Chris Zane speaking to business audiences about his strategy, accessed 2016.

2. For more discussion of the debate on the distinctions between quality and satisfaction, see A. Parasuraman, V. A. Zeithaml, and L. L. Berry, "Reassessment of Expectations as a Comparison Standard in Measuring Service Quality: Implications for Future Research," *Journal of Marketing* 58 (January 1994), pp. 111–124; R. L. Oliver, "A Conceptual Model of Service Quality and Service Satisfaction: Compatible Goals, Different Concepts," in *Advances in Services Marketing and Management,* vol. 2, ed. T. A. Swartz, D. E. Bowen, and S. W. Brown (Greenwich, CT: JAI Press, 1994), pp. 65–85; M. J. Bitner and A. R. Hubbert, "Encounter Satisfaction vs. Overall Satisfaction vs. Quality: The Customer's Voice," in *Service Quality: New Directions in Theory and Practice,* ed. R. T. Rust and R. L. Oliver (Newbury Park, CA: Sage, 1993), pp. 71–93; D. Iacobucci, K. A. Grayson, and A. L. Omstrom, "The Calculus of Service Quality and Customer Satisfaction: Theory and Empirical Differentiation and Integration," in *Advances in Services Marketing and Management,* vol. 3, ed. T. A. Swartz, D. E. Bowen, and S. W. Brown (Greenwich, CT: JAI Press, 1994), pp. 1–67; P. A. Dabholkar, C. D. Shepherd, and D. I. Thorpe, "A Comprehensive Framework for Service Quality: An Investigation of Critical Conceptual and Measurement Issues through a Longitudinal Study," *Journal of Retailing* 76 (Summer 2000), pp. 139–173; J. J. Cronin Jr., M. K. Brady, and G. T. M. Hult, "Assessing the Effects of Quality, Value, and Customer Satisfaction on Consumer Behavioral Intentions in Service Environments," *Journal of Retailing* 76 (Summer 2000), pp. 193–218.

3. See, in particular, Parasuraman, Zeithaml, and Berry, "Reassessment of Expectations"; Oliver, "A Conceptual Model of Service Quality"; and M. K. Brady and J. J. Cronin Jr., "Some New Thoughts on Conceptualizing Perceived Service Quality: A Hierarchical Approach," *Journal of Marketing* 65 (July 2001), pp. 34–49.

4. A. Parasuraman, V. A. Zeithaml, and L. L. Berry, "SERVQUAL: A Multiple-Item Scale for Measuring Consumer Perceptions of Service Quality," *Journal of Retailing* 64 (Spring 1988), pp. 12–40.

5. Parasuraman, Zeithaml, and Berry, "Reassessment of Expectations."

6. Oliver, "A Conceptual Model of Service Quality."

7. See V. Mittal, P. Kumar, and M. Tsiros, "Attribute-Level Performance, Satisfaction, and Behavioral Intentions over Time," *Journal of Marketing* 63 (April 1999), pp. 88–101; L. L. Olsen and M. D. Johnson, "Service Equity, Satisfaction, and Loyalty: From Transaction-Specific to Cumulative Evaluations," *Journal of Service Research* 5 (February 2003), pp. 184–195; P. C. Verhoef, G. Antonides, and A. N. De Hoog, "Service Encounters as a Sequence of Events: The Importance of Peak Experiences," *Journal of Service Research* 7 (August 2004), pp. 53–64.

8. Olsen and Johnson, "Service Equity, Satisfaction, and Loyalty."

9. R. L. Oliver, *Satisfaction: A Behavioral Perspective on the Consumer* (New York: McGraw-Hill, 1997).

10. For a more detailed discussion of the different types of satisfaction, see E. Arnould, L. Price, and G. Zinkhan, *Consumers,* 2nd ed. (New York: McGraw-Hill, 2004), pp. 754–796.

11. S. Fournier and D. G. Mick, "Rediscovering Satisfaction," *Journal of Marketing* 63 (October 1999), pp. 5–23; Verhoef, Antonides, and De Hoog, "Service Encounters as a Sequence of Events;" G. Pizzi, G. L. Marzocchi, C. Orsinger, A. Zammit, "The Temporal Construal of Customer Satisfaction," *Journal of Service Research* 18 (November 2015), pp. 484–497.

12. Oliver, *Satisfaction,* chap. 2.

13. A. Ostrom and D. Iacobucci, "Consumer Trade-Offs and the Evaluation of Services," *Journal of Marketing* 59 (January 1995), pp. 17–28.

14. For more on emotions and satisfaction, see Oliver, *Satisfaction,* chap. 11; L. L. Price, E. J. Arnould, and S. L. Deibler, "Consumers' Emotional Responses to Service Encounters," *International Journal of Service Industry Management* 6 (1995), pp. 34–63.

15. L. L. Berry, S. W. Davis, and J. Wilmet, "When the Customer is Stressed," *Harvard Business Review,* October 2015, Vol. 93, No. 10, pp. 86-94.

16. L. L. Price, E. J. Arnould, and P. Tierney, "Going to Extremes: Managing Service Encounters and Assessing Provider Performance," *Journal of Marketing* 59 (April 1995), pp. 83–97.

17. T. Hennig-Thurau, M. Groth, M. Paul, and D. D. Gremler, "Are All Smiles Created Equal? How Emotional Contagion and Emotional Labor Affect Service Relationships," *Journal of Marketing* 70 (July 2006), pp. 58–73.

18. J. Du, X. Fan, and T. Feng, "Multiple Emotional Contagions in Service Encounters," *Journal of the Academy of Marketing Science* 39 (June 2011), pp. 449–466.

19. For more on attributions and satisfaction, see V. S. Folkes, "Recent Attribution Research in Consumer Behavior: A Review and New Directions," *Journal of Consumer Research* 14 (March 1988), pp. 548–565; and Oliver, *Satisfaction,* chap. 10; and Y. Van Vaerenbergh, C. Orsingher, I. Vermeir, and B. Lariviere, "A Meta-Analysis of Relationships Linking Service Failure Attributions to Customer Outcomes," *Journal of Service Research* 17 (November 2014), pp. 381–398.

20. A. R. Hubbert, "Customer Co-Creation of Service Outcomes: Effects of Locus of Causality Attributions," doctoral dissertation, Arizona State University, Tempe, Az, 1995.

21. M. J. Bitner, "Evaluating Service Encounters: The Effects of Physical Surroundings and Employee Responses," *Journal of Marketing* 54 (April 1990), pp. 69–82.

22. For more on fairness and satisfaction, see E. C. Clemmer and B. Schneider, "Fair Service," in *Advances in Services Marketing and Management,* vol. 5, ed. T. A. Swartz, D. E. Bowen, and S. W. Brown (Greenwich, CT: JAI Press, 1996), pp. 109–126; Oliver, *Satisfaction,* chap. 7; Olsen and Johnson, "Service Equity, Satisfaction, and Loyalty;" K. Seiders and L. L. Berry, "Service Fairness: What It Is and Why It Matters," *Academy of Management Executive* 12 (May 1998), pp. 8–20.

23. C. Miranda, "AT&T's $105 Million "Cramming" Settlement Leads to Refunds," Federal Trade Commission Consumer Information, October 8, 2014, https://www.consumer.ftc.gov/blog/atts-105-million-cramming-settlement-leads-refunds.

24. Fournier and Mick, "Rediscovering Satisfaction."

25. A. M. Epp and L. L. Price, "Designing Solutions around Customer Network Identity Goals," *Journal of Marketing* 75 (March 2011), pp. 36–54.

26. C. Fornell, M. D. Johnson, E. W. Anderson, J. Cha, and B. E. Bryant, "The American Customer Satisfaction Index: Nature, Purpose, and Findings," *Journal of Marketing* 60 (October 1996), pp. 7–18; *ACSI 10-Year Report Analysis (1994–2004),* University of Michigan, National Quality Research Center, 2005, www.theacsi.org.

27. E. W. Anderson, C. Fornell, and D. R. Lehmann, "Customer Satisfaction, Market Share, and Profitability: Findings from Sweden," *Journal of Marketing* 58 (July 1994), pp. 53–66.

28. M. Bruhn and M. A. Grund, "Theory, Development and Implementation of National Customer Satisfaction Indices: The Swiss Index of Customer Satisfaction (SWICS)," *Total Quality Management* 11 (2000), pp. S1017–S1028; A. Meyer and F. Dornach, "The German Customer Barometer," http://www.servicebarometer.de.or.

29. See www.theacsi.org and F. V. Morgeson III, S. Mithas, T. L. Keiningham, and L. Aksoy, "An Investigation of the Cross-national Determinants of Customer Satisfaction," *Journal of the Academy of Marketing Science* 39 (April 2011), pp. 198–215.

30. Fornell, Johnson, Anderson, Cha, and Bryant, "The American Customer Satisfaction Index;" *ACSI 10-Year Report Analysis.*

31. For a listing of companies and their scores, go to the ACSI website at www.theacsi.org.

32. ACSI website, www.theacsi.org.

33. Ibid, "National Economic Indicator, Financial Indicator," ACSI website, accessed May 21, 2016, www.theacsi.org.

34. See J. L. Heskett, W. E. Sasser Jr., and L. A. Schlesinger, *The Service Profit Chain* (New York: Free Press, 1997); S. Gupta and V. A. Zeithaml, "Customer Metrics and Their Impact on Financial Performance," *Marketing Science* 25 (November–December 2006), pp. 718–739.

35. C. Fornell, S. Mithas, F. V. Morgeson III, and M.S. Krishnan, "Customer Satisfaction and Stock Prices: High Returns, Low Risk," *Journal of Marketing* 70 (January 2006), pp. 3–14.

36. M. A. Wiles, "The Effect of Customer Service on Retailers' Shareholder Wealth: The Role of Availability and Reputation Cues," *Journal of Retailing,* Special Issue on Service Excellence 83 (January 2007), pp. 19–32.

37. L. Aksoy, B. Cooil, C. Groening, T. L. Keiningham, and A. Yalcin, "The Long-Term Stock Market Valuation of Customer Satisfaction," *Journal of Marketing* 72 (July 2008), pp. 105–122.

38. M. A. J. Menezes and J. Serbin, *Xerox Corporation: The Customer Satisfaction Program,* case no. 591-055 (Boston: Harvard Business School, 1991).

39. F. F. Reichheld, "The One Number You Need to Grow," *Harvard Business Review,* December 2003, pp. 47–54.

40. Information provided by TARP Worldwide, Inc., August 2007.

41. E. W. Anderson and V. Mittal, "Strengthening the Satisfaction–Profit Chain," *Journal of Service Research* 3 (November 2000), pp. 107–120; B. Hindo, "Satisfaction Not Guaranteed," *BusinessWeek,* June 19, 2006, pp. 32–36.

42. Brady and Cronin, "Some New Thoughts on Conceptualizing Perceived Service Quality"; C. Gronroos, "A Service Quality Model and Its Marketing Implications," *European Journal of Marketing* 18 (1984), pp. 36–44; R. T. Rust and R. L. Oliver, "Service Quality Insights and Managerial Implications from the Frontier," in *Service Quality: New Directions in Theory and Practice,* ed. R. T. Rust and R. L. Oliver (Thousand Oaks, CA: Sage, 1994), pp. 1–19; M. J. Bitner, "Managing the Evidence of Service," in *The Service Quality Handbook,* ed. E. E. Scheuing and W. F. Christopher (New York, AMACOM, 1993), pp. 358–370.

43. Parasuraman, Zeithaml, and Berry, "SERVQUAL: A Multiple-Item Scale." Details on the SERVQUAL Scale and the actual items used to assess the dimensions are provided in Chapter 5.

44. N. Raajpoot, "Reconceptualizing Service Encounter Quality in a Non-Western Context," *Journal of Service Research* 7 (Novemer 2004), pp. 181–201.

45. Parasuraman, Zeithaml, and Berry, "SERVQUAL: A Multiple-Item Scale."

46. For more on customer satisfaction and service quality delivery via the Internet and technology see: M. L. Meuter, A. L. Ostrom, R. I. Roundtree, and M. J. Bitner, "Self-Service Technologies: Understanding Customer Satisfaction with Technology-Based Service Encounters," *Journal of Marketing* 64 (July 2000), pp. 50–64; V. A. Zeithaml, A. Parasuraman, and A. Malhotra, "Service Quality Delivery through Web Sites: A Critical Review of Extant Knowledge," *Journal of the Academy of Marketing Science* 30 (Fall 2002), pp. 362–375; M. Wolfinbarger and M. Gilly, "Etailq: Dimensionalizing, Measuring and Predicting Etail Quality," *Journal of Retailing* 79 (2003), pp. 183–198; B. B. Holloway and S. E. Beatty, "Satisfiers and Dissatisfiers in the Online Environment," *Journal of Service Research* 10 (May 2008), pp. 347–364.

47. A. Parasuraman, V. A. Zeithaml, and A. Malhotra, "E-S-QUAL: A Multiple-Item Scale for Assessing Electronic Service Quality," *Journal of Service Research* 7 (February 2005), pp. 213–233.

48. Ibid.

49. M. Dixon, N. Toman, and R. Delisi, *The Effortless Experience: Conquering the New Battleground for Customer Loyalty* (London: Penguin Books, Ltd., 2013); M. Dixon, K. Freeman, and N. Toman, "Stop Trying to Delight Your Customers," *Harvard Business Review,* July–August 2010, pp. 116–122.

50. "How Marriott Makes a Great First Impression," *The Service Edge* 6 (May 1993), p. 5.

51. A. G. Woodside, L. L. Frey, and R. T. Daly, "Linking Service Quality, Customer Satisfaction, and Behavioral Intention," *Journal of Health Care Marketing* 9 (December 1989), pp. 5–17.

52. K. Sivakumar, M. Lei, and B. Dong, "Service Quality: The Impact of Frequency, Timing, Proximity, and Sequence of Failures and Delights," *Journal of Marketing* 78 (January 2014), pp. 41–58.

53. Verhoef, Antonides, and De Hoog, "Service Encounters as a Sequence of Events."

54. G. L. Shostack, "Planning the Service Encounter," in *The Service Encounter,* ed. J. A. Czepiel, M. R. Solomon, and C. F. Surprenant (Lexington, MA: Lexington Books, 1985), pp. 243–254.

55. Ibid.

56. For a complete discussion of the research on which this section is based, see M. J. Bitner, B. H. Booms, and M. S. Tetreault, "The Service Encounter: Diagnosing Favorable and Unfavorable Incidents," *Journal of Marketing* 54 (January 1990), pp. 71–84; M. J. Bitner, B. H. Booms, and L. A. Mohr, "Critical Service Encounters: The Employee's View," *Journal of Marketing* 58 (October 1994), pp. 95–106; D. Gremler and M. J. Bitner, "Classifying Service Encounter Satisfaction across Industries," in *Marketing Theory and Applications,* ed. C. T. Allen et al. (Chicago: American Marketing Association, 1992), pp. 111–118; D. Gremler, M. J. Bitner, and K. R. Evans, "The Internal Service Encounter," *Journal of Service Industry Management* 5 (1994), pp. 34–56.

57. S. E. Beatty, J. Ogilvie, W. M. Northington, M. P. Harrison, B. B. Holloway, and S. Wang, "Frontline Service Employee Compliance with Customer Special Requests," *Journal of Service Research* 19 (May 2016), pp. 158–173.

58. Amazon.com, www.amazon.com, accessed July 18, 2011.

59. Bitner, Booms, and Mohr, "Critical Service Encounters."

60. M. L. Meuter, A. L. Ostrom, R. I. Roundtree, and M. J. Bitner, "Self-Service Technologies: Understanding Customer Satisfaction with Technology-Based Service Encounters," *Journal of Marketing* 64 (July 2000), pp. 50–64; M. J. Bitner, S. W. Brown, and M. L. Meuter, "Technology Infusion in Service Encounters," *Journal of the Academy of Marketing Science* 28 (Winter 2000), pp. 138–149; Parasuraman, Zeithaml, and Malhotra, "E-S-QUAL: A Multiple-Item Scale."

61. J. E. Collier and S. E. Kimes, "Only If It Is Convenient: Understanding How Convenience Influences Self-Service Technology Evaluation," *Journal of Service Research* 16 (February 2013), pp. 39–51.

62. A. Parasuraman and C. L. Colby, "An Updated and Streamlined Technology Readiness Index: TRI 2.0," *Journal of Service Research* 18 (February 2015), pp. 59–74.

63. J. van Doorn, M. Mende, S. M. Noble, J. Hulland, A. L. Ostrom, D. Grewal, and J. A. Peterson, "Domo Arigato Mr. Roboto: Emergence of Automated Social Presence in Organizational Frontlines and Customers' Service Experiences," *Journal of Service Research* 20 (February 2017), forthcoming.

Part Three

Understanding Customer Requirements

Chapter 5 Listening to Customers through Research

Chapter 6 Building Customer Relationships

Chapter 7 Service Recovery

THE LISTENING GAP

Not knowing what customers expect is one of the root causes of not delivering to customer expectations. Provider gap 1, the listening gap, is the difference between customer expectations of service and company understanding of those expectations. Note that in the accompanying figure we created a link between the customer and the company, showing customer expectations above the line that dissects the model and provider perceptions of those expectations below the line. This alignment signifies that what customers expect is not always the same as what companies believe they expect.

Provider Gap 1: The Listening Gap

Part 3 describes three ways to close provider gap 1. In Chapter 5, we detail ways that companies listen to customers through research. Both formal and informal methods of customer research are described, including surveys, critical incident studies, and complaint solicitation. Upward communication from frontline employees to managers, another key factor in listening to customers, is also discussed.

Chapter 6 covers company strategies to retain customers and strengthen relationships with them, an approach called relationship marketing. Relationship marketing is distinct from transactional marketing, the more conventional approach that tends to focus on acquiring new customers rather than retaining them. When organizations have strong relationships with existing customers, opportunities for in-depth listening increase over time, and the listening gap is less likely to occur. A variety of strategies, including the creation of switching barriers and the development of relationship bonds, are suggested as a means of relationship development and, ultimately, the cultivation of customer loyalty.

Chapter 7 describes service recovery, the other major strategy needed to close provider gap 1. Service recovery involves understanding why customers complain, what they expect when they complain, and how to deal with service failures. Firms engaged in service recovery must, along with other approaches, create a complaint-handling procedure, empower employees to react in real time to fix failures, and guarantee service. Excellent service recovery strategies seek to gain insight from service failures, allowing firms to better understand customers and their expectations.

Chapter Five

Listening to Customers through Research

This chapter's objectives are to

1. Present the types of and guidelines for customer research in services.
2. Show how customer research information can and should be used for services.
3. Describe the strategies by which companies can facilitate interaction and communication between management and customers.
4. Present ways that companies can and do facilitate interaction between contact people and management.

Improving Customer Experiences by Researching Customer Journeys

As you will learn in this chapter, many different research approaches are needed to fully understand customer expectations and perceptions. You will also discover that most of the approaches involve either measuring touchpoints—individual encounters between the customer and the company—or overall service quality/customer satisfaction summary assessments at the end of the service. As we will discuss, each of these two major categories has its benefits but each also has its limitations. Measuring customer touchpoints or individual interactions such as a single telephone call, service visit, or a sale helps the company understand the performance in that encounter, allowing for process improvements in the interaction and assessment of how employees are performing in that process.

However, the problem with measuring touchpoints in isolation is that each of them can be optimized (even 95 percent satisfaction or higher) while the customer's overall satisfaction can be significantly lower. Consider a service for which customers must make multiple phone calls (to initiate a service, to begin using the service, to question, to report problems, to report additional problems). If short surveys follow each phone call, customers may rate each of the isolated encounters high but because they had to make so many calls for the service, they will evaluate the overall service as tedious, confusing, and unsatisfactory. A summary score on service at the very end of the provision, on the other hand, limits the ability of the company to pinpoint which encounters are the most critical.

An innovative trend is to research the more encompassing view known as "customer journeys," which contribute to end-to-end experiences. Research experts now know that only by looking at experiences through the customers' own eyes—along the entire experience taken—can companies really learn to improve service excellence. Customer journeys are clusters of integrated touchpoints that happen before, during, and after the experience of using a service. Examples of such clusters are deciding on a service, beginning to use the service, resolving issues, upgrading a service, or renewing a subscription service. Rather than viewing the multiple touchpoints involved in each cluster as single, isolated events, each with its own metric, journeys are groups of events that to the customer are perceived as connected. Therefore, they should be measured as linked clusters rather than as individual touchpoints.

So how does a company change to a journey-focused measurement approach? Let us take an example of a purchase that some of you may be making within the next decade or so: a kitchen remodel. How should a remodeling company such as Lowe's or Home Depot tackle this issue? According to McKinsey Consulting, six actions are critical to managing customer experience journeys. The first is to step back and identify the nature of the journeys customers take—from *their points of view*. The second step is to understand how customers navigate across the touchpoints as they move through the journey. Third, the company must anticipate the customers' needs, expectations, and desires during each part of the journey. The company must develop a research approach to determine these in each *cluster* rather than each touchpoint. Instead of conducting simple focus groups, companies must use techniques to deepen empathy for the customer's pain points using customer diaries or ethnographic observation In these types of approaches, researchers watch or accompany customers in stores, and conduct continual live testing and design iteration with customers during the process.

The fourth step, again according to McKinsey, is to build an understanding of what is working and what is not. Fifth, the company must set priorities for the most important gaps and opportunities to improve the journey. Sixth, they must fix root cause issues.

Customer research has demonstrated that there are huge benefits to examining the total customer experience rather than individual touchpoints. In a recent study, for example, McKinsey found that improving a customer experience from merely average to something that wows the consumer can lead to a 30- to 50-percent increase in behavioral measures such as likelihood to renew purchasing a service or buying the product again.[1]

Despite a genuine interest in meeting customer expectations, many companies miss the mark by thinking inside out—they believe they know what customers *should* want and deliver that, rather than finding out what they *do* want. When this happens, companies provide services that do not match customer expectations: important features are left out, and the levels of performance on features that are provided are inadequate. Because services have few clearly defined and tangible cues, this difficulty may be considerably larger than it is in manufacturing firms. A far better approach involves thinking *outside in*—determining customer expectations and then delivering to them. Thinking outside in uses marketing research to understand customers and their requirements fully. Marketing research, the subject of this chapter, involves far more than conventional surveys. It consists of a portfolio of listening strategies that allows companies to deliver service to customer expectations.

USING CUSTOMER RESEARCH TO UNDERSTAND CUSTOMER EXPECTATIONS

Finding out what customers expect is essential to providing service quality, and customer research is a key vehicle for understanding customer expectations and perceptions of services. In services, as with any offering, a firm that does no customer research at all is unlikely to understand its customers. A firm that does customer research, but not on the topic of customer expectations, may also fail to know what is needed to stay in tune with changing customer requirements. Customer research must focus on service issues such as what features are most important to customers, what levels of these features customers expect, and what customers think the company can and should do when problems occur in service delivery. Even when a service firm is small and has limited resources to conduct research, avenues are open to explore what customers expect.

In this section we discuss the elements of service marketing research programs that help companies identify customer expectations and perceptions. In the sections that follow, we will discuss ways in which the tactics of general customer research may need to be adjusted to maximize its effectiveness in services.

Research Objectives for Services

The first step in designing service marketing research is without doubt the most critical: defining the problem and research objectives. This is where the service marketer poses the questions to be answered or problems to be solved with research. Does the company want to know how customers view the service provided by the company, what customer requirements are, how customers will respond to a new service introduction, or what customers will want from the company five years from now? Each of these research questions requires a different research strategy. Thus, it is essential to devote time and resources to define the problem thoroughly and accurately. In spite of the importance of this first stage, many customer research studies are initiated without adequate attention to objectives.

Research objectives translate into action questions. While many different questions are likely to be part of a customer research program, the following are the most common research objectives in services:

- To discover customer requirements or expectations for service.
- To monitor and track service performance.
- To assess overall company performance compared with that of competition.
- To assess gaps between customer expectations and perceptions.
- To identify dissatisfied customers, so that service recovery can be attempted.
- To gauge the effectiveness of changes in service delivery.

- To appraise the service performance of individuals and teams for evaluation, recognition, and rewards.
- To determine customer expectations for a new service.
- To monitor changing customer expectations in an industry.
- To forecast future expectations of customers.

These research objectives are similar in many ways to the research conducted for physical products: both aim to assess customer requirements, dissatisfaction, and demand. Service research, however, incorporates additional elements that require specific attention.

First, service research must continually monitor and track service performance because performance is subject to human variability and heterogeneity. Conducting performance research at a single point in time, as might be done for a physical product such as an automobile, would be insufficient in services. A major focus of service research involves capturing human performance—at the level of individual employee, team, branch, organization as a whole, and competition. Another focus of service research involves documenting the process by which service is performed. Even when service employees are performing well, a service provider must continue to track performance because the potential for variation in processes associated with service delivery always exists.

A second distinction in service research is the need to consider and monitor the gap between expectations and perceptions. This gap is dynamic because both perceptions and expectations fluctuate. Does the gap exist because performance is declining, because performance varies with demand and supply level, or because expectations are escalating?

Exhibit 5.1 lists a number of service research objectives. Once objectives such as these have been identified, they will point the way to decisions about the most appropriate type of research, methods of data collection, and ways to use the information. The additional columns in this table are described in sections of this chapter.

Criteria for an Effective Service Research Program

A *service research program* can be defined as the portfolio of research studies and types needed to address research objectives and execute an overall measurement strategy. Many types of research could be considered in a research program. Understanding the criteria for an effective service research program (see Figure 5.1) will help a company evaluate different types of research and choose the ones most appropriate for its research objectives. In this section we discuss these criteria.

Includes Qualitative and Quantitative Research

Marketing research is not limited to surveys and statistics. Some forms of research, called *qualitative research,* are exploratory and preliminary and are conducted to clarify problem definition, prepare for more formal research, or gain insight when more formal research is not necessary. Insights gained through customer focus groups, critical incidents research (described more fully later in this chapter), and direct observation of service transactions show the marketer the right questions to ask of consumers. Because the results of qualitative research play a major role in designing quantitative research, it is often the first type of research done. Qualitative

FIGURE 5.1
Criteria for an
Effective Service
Research Program

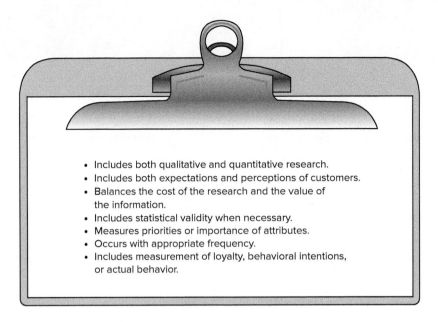

- Includes both qualitative and quantitative research.
- Includes both expectations and perceptions of customers.
- Balances the cost of the research and the value of the information.
- Includes statistical validity when necessary.
- Measures priorities or importance of attributes.
- Occurs with appropriate frequency.
- Includes measurement of loyalty, behavioral intentions, or actual behavior.

research can also be conducted after quantitative research to make the numbers in computer printouts meaningful by giving managers the perspective and sensitivity that are critical in interpreting data and initiating improvement efforts.[2]

One of the most innovative and successful qualitative approaches is called Zaltman Metaphor Elicitation Technique (ZMET), an approach developed by Gerald Zaltman and executed by Olson Zaltman Associates, a cutting-edge research and consulting organization. The approach depends on ZMET interviews, which are intense two-hour discussions with customers who are asked to collect visual images that represent their thoughts and feelings about a research topic beforehand and then discuss them in the interview. This storytelling allows the researcher to delve deep into the metaphors that underlie their beliefs and feelings. There are no numbers in this approach, but it results in insightful findings from which a company can build an advertising or marketing campaign.[3]

Quantitative research in marketing is designed to describe the nature, attitudes, or behaviors of customers empirically and to test specific hypotheses that a service marketer wants to examine. These studies are key for quantifying the customers' satisfaction, the importance of service attributes, the extent of service quality gaps, and perceptions of value. Such studies also provide managers with yardsticks for evaluating competitors. Finally, results from quantitative studies can highlight specific service deficiencies that can be more deeply probed through follow-up qualitative research.

Includes Both Perceptions and Expectations of Customers

As we discussed in Chapter 3, expectations serve as standards or reference points for customers. In evaluating service quality, customers compare what they perceive they get in a service encounter with their expectations of that encounter. For this reason, a measurement program that captures only perceptions of service is missing a critical part of the service quality equation. Companies also need to incorporate measures of customer expectations.

Exhibit 5.1 Elements in an Effective Customer Research Program for Services

Type of Research	Primary Research Objectives	Qualitative/ Quantitative	Costs of Information		
			Monetary	Time	Frequency
Complaint solicitation	To identify/attend to dissatisfied customers	Qualitative	Low	Low	Continuous
	To identify common service failure points				
Critical incident studies	To identify "best practices" at transaction level	Qualitative	Low	Moderate	Periodic
	To identify customer requirements as input for quantitative studies				
	To identify common service failure points				
	To identify systemic strengths and weaknesses in customer-contact services				
Requirements research	To identify customer requirements as input for quantitative research	Qualitative	Moderate	Moderate	Periodic
Relationship surveys and SERVQUAL surveys	To monitor and track service performance	Quantitative	Moderate	Moderate	Annual
	To assess overall company performance compared with that of competition				
	To determine links between satisfaction and behavioral intentions				
	To assess gaps between customer expectations and perceptions				
Trailer calls or posttransaction surveys	To obtain immediate feedback on performance of service transactions	Quantitative	Low	Low	Continuous
	To measure effectiveness of changes in service delivery				
	To assess service performance of individuals and teams				
	To use as input for process improvements				
	To identify common service failure points				
Social media	To identify/attend to dissatisfied customers	Qualitative and quantitative	Low	Moderate	Continuous
	To encourage word of mouth				
	To measure the impact of other advertising				

Measurement of expectations can be included in a research program in multiple ways. First, basic research that relates to customers' requirements—that identifies the service features or attributes that matter to customers—can be considered expectation research. In this form, the *content* of customer expectations is captured, initially

Type of Research	Primary Research Objectives	Qualitative/ Quantitative	Costs of Information		
			Monetary	Time	Frequency
Service expectation meetings and reviews	To create dialogue with important customers	Qualitative	Moderate	Moderate	Annual
	To identify what individual large customers expect and then to ensure that it is delivered				
	To close the loop with important customers				
Process checkpoint evaluations	To determine customer perceptions of long-term professional services during service provision	Quantitative	Moderate	Moderate	Periodic
	To identify service problems and solve them early in the service relationship				
Market-oriented ethnography	To research customers in natural settings	Qualitative	Moderate	High	Periodic
	To study customers from cultures other than America in an unbiased way				
Mystery shopping	To measure individual employee performance for evaluation, recognition, or rewards	Quantitative	Low	Low	Quarterly
	To identify systemic strengths and weaknesses in customer-contact services	Qualitative			
Customer panels	To monitor changing customer expectations	Qualitative	Moderate	Moderate	Continuous
	To provide a forum for customers to suggest and evaluate new service ideas				
Lost customer research	To identify reasons for customer defection	Qualitative	Low	Low	Continuous
	To assess gaps between customer expectations and perceptions				
Future expectations research	To forecast future expectations of customers	Qualitative	High	High	Periodic
	To develop and test new service ideas				
Database customer research	To identify the individual requirements of customers using information technology and database information	Quantitative	High	High	Continuous

in some form of qualitative research such as focus group interviews. Research on the *levels* of customer expectations also is needed. This type of research quantitatively assesses the levels of customer expectations and compares these with perception levels, usually by calculating the gap between expectations and perceptions.

Balances the Cost of the Research and the Value of the Information

An assessment of the cost of research compared with its benefits or value to the company is another key criterion. One cost is monetary, including direct costs to customer research companies, payments to respondents, and internal company costs incurred by employees collecting the information. Time costs are also important, including the time commitment needed internally by employees to administer the research and the interval between data collection and availability for use by the firm. These and other costs must be weighed against the gains to the company in improved decision making, retained customers, and successful new product launches.

Includes Statistical Validity When Necessary

We have already seen that research has multiple and diverse objectives. These objectives determine the appropriate type of research and methodology. To illustrate, some companies use research not so much to measure as to build relationships with customers—to allow contact employees to find out what customers desire, to diagnose the strengths and weaknesses of their and the firm's efforts to address the desires, to prepare a plan to meet requirements, and to confirm after a period of time (usually one year) that the company has executed the plan. The underlying objective of this type of research is to allow contact people to identify specific action items that will gain the maximum return in customer satisfaction for individual customers. This type of research does not need sophisticated quantitative analysis, anonymity of customers, careful control of sampling, or strong statistical controls.

On the other hand, research used to track overall service quality that will be used for bonuses and salary increases of salespeople must be carefully controlled for sampling bias and statistical validity. One of us worked with a company that paid salespeople on the basis of customers' satisfaction scores while allowing the salespeople to control the customers sampled. Obviously, the salespeople quickly learned that they could have surveys sent only to satisfied customers, artificially inflating the scores and—of course—undermining the confidence in the measurement system.

Not all forms of research have statistical validity, and not all forms need it. Most forms of qualitative research, for example, do not possess statistical validity.

Measures Priorities or Importance

Customers have many service requirements, but not all are equally important. One of the most common mistakes managers make in trying to improve service is spending resources on the wrong initiatives, only to become discouraged because customer perceptions of the firm's service do not improve! Measuring the relative importance of service dimensions and attributes helps managers to channel resources effectively; therefore, research must document the priorities of the customer.

Occurs with Appropriate Frequency

Because customer expectations and perceptions are dynamic, companies need to institute a service quality research process, not just do isolated studies. A single study of service provides only a "snapshot" view of one moment in time. For full understanding of the marketplace's acceptance of a company's service, customer research must be ongoing. Without a pattern of studies repeated with appropriate frequency, managers cannot tell whether the firm is moving forward or falling back and which of their service improvement initiatives are working. Just what does "ongoing research" mean in terms of frequency? The answer is specific to the type of service and to the purpose and method of each type of service research a company might do. As we discuss the different types in the following section, you will see the frequency with which each type of research could be conducted.

Includes Measures of Loyalty, Behavioral Intentions, or Behavior

An important trend in service research involves measuring the positive and negative consequences of service quality along with overall satisfaction or service quality scores. Among the most frequently used generic *behavioral intentions* are willingness to recommend the service to others and repurchase intent. These behavioral intentions can be viewed as positive and negative consequences of service quality. Positive behavioral intentions include saying positive things about the company, recommending the company to others, remaining loyal, spending more with the company, and paying a price premium. Negative behavioral intentions include saying negative things to others, doing less business with the company, switching to another company, and complaining to outside organizations such as the Better Business Bureau and to other companies using social media outlets. Other, more specific behaviors differ by service; for example, behaviors related to medical care include following instructions from the doctor, taking medications, and returning for follow-up. Tracking these areas can help a company estimate the relative value of service improvements to the company and can identify customers who are in danger of defecting.

ELEMENTS IN AN EFFECTIVE SERVICE MARKETING RESEARCH PROGRAM

A good service marketing research program includes multiple types of research studies. The composite of studies and types of research will differ by company because the range of uses for service quality research—from employee performance assessment to advertising campaign development to strategic planning—requires a rich, multifaceted flow of information. If a company were to engage in virtually all types of service research, the portfolio would look like Exhibit 5.1, but few companies do all types of research. The particular portfolio for any company will match company resources and address the key areas needed to understand the customers of the business. So that it will be easier for you to identify the appropriate type of research for different research objectives, we list the objectives in column 2 of Exhibit 5.1. In the following sections we describe each major type of research and show the way each type addresses the criteria associated with it. The Technology Spotlight discusses research conducted online.

Complaint Solicitation

You may have complained to employees of service organizations, only to find that nothing happens with your complaint. No one rushes to solve it, and the next time you experience the service the same problem is present. How frustrating! Good service organizations take complaints seriously. Not only do they listen to complaints but they also employ *complaint solicitation* as a way of communicating about what can be done to improve their service and their service employees. Vail Resorts, which owns the Vail, Breckenridge, Heavenly, Keystone, and Beaver Creek resorts, has an innovative way to capture complaints and comments of its customers. The resort hires researchers to ride the lifts with skiers and ask and record into handheld computer devices customers' responses to questions about their perceptions of the resorts. Then the researchers ski down the mountain and ride up again with other customers. At the end of the day, the researchers download the results into a computer at the base. The researchers survey

Technology Spotlight Conducting Customer Research on the Web

One of the most intriguing applications of the Internet is online research, replacing comment cards and intrusive telephone calls with cyber-surveys that are challenging and fun for consumers. The application is growing rapidly. The reasons are obvious—Internet research has many benefits to marketers besides more willing respondents, including the following:

- *Speed.* Rather than the three to four months required to collect data through mail questionnaires, or the six to eight weeks needed to train interviewers and obtain data from telephone questionnaires, online surveys can be prepared and executed quickly. A sample of 300 to 400, large enough for many studies, can be completed in a weekend and the results made available for viewing by clients on a secure website the following week. One market research firm reportedly completed 1,000 customer satisfaction surveys in only two hours.

- *Equivalent quality.* One team of scholars and colleagues found that the quality of the data when using an online method is comparable: "in the context of a large business-to-business service quality assessment, an analysis of the accuracy and completeness of respondent answers to both open and closed questions suggests that online and mail surveys produce equivalent results."[4]

- *Ability to target hard-to-reach populations.* One of the traditional difficulties in research, particularly segmentation research, is to identify and access respondents who fit a particular lifestyle or interest profile. The hard-to-reach, business-to-business market accounts for about a quarter of all customer research studies conducted by U.S. research firms.

Doctors, lawyers, other professionals, and working mothers are all valuable but difficult-to-access groups of customers. These people might read special interest magazines (such as professional or hobby publications) that are expensive to advertise in. They could be reached in surveys only by having the service company purchase at great cost the mailing list of that magazine. However, online sites for special interests are quite simple to identify, access, and insert survey banners in.

- *Ability to target customers with money.* Online research allows service companies to reach customers who have higher incomes, higher education levels, and greater willingness to spend. Consumers with computers who use online services regularly tend to be in these demographic target groups, and they can be effectively surveyed with online research. Compared with the sample that would be obtained from traditional research using all telephone subscribers, the sample of online users is often far better in terms of marketing potential.

- *Opportunity to use multimedia to present video and audio.* Telephone surveys are limited to voice alone, whereas mail surveys are constrained to two-dimensional visuals. In the past, to present the full range of audio and video needed to give respondents the true sense of a service being researched, surveys had to be conducted in person and were, therefore, very expensive ($30 to $150 per person, depending on the topic and sample). Online research offers broader stimuli potential through all multimedia possibilities at a fraction of the cost.

200 skiers per week, looking for patterns of customer comments and complaints. For example, if the researchers receive a number of complaints about certain lift lines or service in one of the restaurants, they will alert managers in those areas so the problems can be resolved quickly. At the end of the week, the data are collected and reported at weekly meetings.

Firms that use complaints as research collect and document them, then use the information to identify dissatisfied customers, correct individual problems where possible, and identify common service failure points. Although this research is used for both goods and services, it has a critical real-time purpose in services—to improve failure points and to improve or correct the performance of contact personnel. Research on complaints is one of the easiest types for firms to conduct, leading many companies to depend solely on complaints to stay in touch with customers. Unfortunately, there is

- *No interviewers—and therefore no interviewer errors or interviewer bias.* Bias occurs when the interviewer is in a bad mood, tired, impatient, or not objective. These problems occur with human interviews but not cyber-interviews.
- *Control over data quality, which can eliminate contradictory or nonsensical answers.* With traditional surveys, researchers need a step called "data cleaning and editing," in which all data are checked for such problems; electronic checks can be built into online surveys that take care of this problem as it occurs.
- *Inexpensive research.* Data collection costs can be the most expensive part of a study, and the most expensive part of data collection can be paying subjects to participate. Online customer research, astonishingly, is 10 to 80 percent less expensive than other approaches. The Internet also eliminates the postage, phone, labor, and printing costs that are typical with other survey approaches. Respondents also seem to complete Web-based surveys in half the time it would take an interviewer to conduct the survey, perhaps contributing to the lack of need for incentives.

One additional, but to date undersubstantiated, benefit is higher response rate—reportedly as high as 70 percent—possibly stemming from the fact that the interactive nature of cyber-research can make answering surveys fun for respondents. While it is getting more difficult to get consumers to answer traditional surveys, the entertainment value of cyber-surveys makes it easier to recruit participants. One study shows that consumers are five times more likely to complete an electronic survey than the same survey with written materials and that researchers obtain the following three additional benefits: (1) consumers "play" an e-survey longer, answering more questions than in a traditional survey; (2) people tend to concentrate more fully on their answers; and (3) the entertainment value of an e-survey actually lowers the respondent's perceived time to complete the survey.

The advantages of online research likely far outnumber the disadvantages. However, marketers need to be aware that there are also drawbacks. Perhaps the major problem is the composition of the sample. Unlike the process used with most telephone and mail surveys, the population of responders is not usually selected but is a matter of convenience, consisting of whomever responds to the survey. This is a particular problem when respondents are recruited from other websites and click through to the survey. In these cases, marketers may not even know who the responders are and whether they are, in fact, the right profile for answering the survey. To address this problem, companies are prequalifying respondents by telephone or e-mail, then asking for enough demographic information to ensure that the respondents meet the desired requirements. They can also ask qualifying questions early in the Web survey to screen respondents.

Sources: R. Kottler, "Eight Tips Offer Best Practices for Online Market Research, *Marketing News,* April 1, 2005; E. Deutskens, K. de Ruyter, and M. Wetzels, "An Assessment of Equivalence Between Online and Mail Surveys in Service Research," *Journal of Service Research* 8 (May 2006), pp. 346–355.

evidence suggesting that customer complaints alone are a woefully inadequate source of information. As discussed in Chapter 7, only a small percentage of customers with problems actually complain to the company; the rest stay dissatisfied, telling other people about their dissatisfaction.

To be effective, complaint solicitation requires rigorous recording of numbers and types of complaints through many channels and then working to eliminate the most frequent problems. Complaint channels include employees at the front line, intermediary organizations like retailers who deliver service, managers, and complaints to third parties such as customer advocate groups. Companies must both solve individual customer problems and identify overall patterns to eliminate failure points. More sophisticated forms of complaint resolution define "complaint" broadly to include all comments—both negative and positive—as well as questions from customers. Firms should build depositories for this information and report results frequently, perhaps weekly or monthly.

Critical Incident Studies

The *critical incident technique (CIT),* is a qualitative interview procedure in which customers are asked to provide verbatim stories about satisfying and dissatisfying service encounters they have experienced. According to a summary of the use of the technique in services, CIT has been used to study satisfaction in hotels, restaurants, airlines, amusement parks, automotive repair, retailing, banking, cable television, public transportation, and education.[5] The studies have explored a wide range of service topics: consumer evaluation of services, service failure and recovery, employees, customer participation in service delivery, and service experience.[6] With this technique, customers (either internal or external) are asked the following questions:

Think of a time when, as a customer, you had a particularly *satisfying* (or *dissatisfying*) interaction.

When did the incident happen?

What specific circumstances led up to this situation?

Exactly what did the employee (or firm member) say or do?

What resulted that made you feel the interaction was *satisfying* (or *dissatisfying*)?

What could or should have been done differently?

Sometimes contact employees are asked to put themselves in the shoes of a customer and answer the same questions: "Put yourself in the shoes of *customers* of your firm. In other words, try to see your firm through your customers' eyes. Now think of a recent time when a customer of your firm had a particularly *satisfying/ unsatisfying* interaction with you or a fellow employee." The stories are then analyzed to determine common themes of satisfaction/dissatisfaction underlying the events. In Chapter 4, we described the four common themes that are sources of pleasure and displeasure in service encounters—recovery (after failure), adaptability, spontaneity, and coping—that have been identified through research. Individual companies conduct these studies to identify sources of satisfaction and dissatisfaction for their firms or industries.

CIT has many benefits. First, data are collected from the respondents' perspective and are usually vivid because they are expressed in consumers' own words and reflect the way they think. Second, the method provides concrete information about the way the company and its employees behave and react, thereby making the research easy to translate into action. Third, like most qualitative methods, the research is particularly useful when the topic or service is new and very little other information exists. Finally, the method is well suited for assessing perceptions of customers from different cultures because it allows respondents to share their perceptions rather than answer researcher-defined questions.[7]

Requirements Research

Requirements research involves identifying the benefits and attributes that customers expect in a service. This type of research is very basic and essential because it determines the type of questions that will be asked in surveys and ultimately the improvements that will be attempted by the firm. Because these studies are so foundational, qualitative techniques are appropriate to begin them. Quantitative techniques may follow, usually during a pretest stage of survey development. Individual companies conduct these studies to identify sources of satisfaction and dissatisfaction for their firms or industries.

An approach to requirements research that has been effective in service industries is to examine existing research about customer requirements in similar service industries. The five dimensions of service quality are generalizable across industries, and sometimes the way these dimensions are manifest is also remarkably similar. Hospital patients and customers of hotels, for example, expect many of the same features when using these two services. Besides expert medical care, patients in hospitals expect comfortable rooms, courteous staff, and food that tastes good—the same features that are salient to hotel customers. In these and other industries that share common customer expectations, managers may find it helpful to seek knowledge from existing research in the related service industry. Because hotels have used marketing and customer research longer than hospitals have, insights into hotel guests' expectations can inform about hospital patients' expectations. Hospital administrators at Albert Einstein Medical Center in Philadelphia, for example, asked a group of nine local hotel executives for advice in understanding and handling patients. Many improvements resulted, including better food, easier-to-read name tags, more prominent information desks, and radios in many rooms.[8]

Relationship and SERVQUAL Surveys

One category of surveys are named *relationship surveys* because they pose questions about all elements in the customer's relationship with the company (including service, product, and price). This comprehensive approach can help a company diagnose its relationship strengths and weaknesses. For example, Federal Express conducts many different customer satisfaction studies to assess satisfaction, identify reasons for dissatisfaction, and monitor satisfaction over time. They conduct 2,400 telephone interviews per quarter, measuring 17 domestic service attributes, 22 export service attributes, 8 drop-box attributes, and 8 service center attributes. They also conduct 10 targeted satisfaction studies on specialized business functions.

Relationship surveys typically monitor and track service performance annually, with an initial survey providing a baseline. Relationship surveys are also effective in comparing company performance with that of competitors, often focusing on the best competitor's performance as a benchmark. When used for this purpose, the sponsor of the survey is not identified, and questions are asked about both the focal company and one or more competitors.

A sound measure of service quality is necessary for identifying the aspects of service needing performance improvement, assessing how much improvement is needed on each aspect, and evaluating the impact of improvement efforts. Unlike goods quality, which can be measured objectively by such indicators as durability and number of defects, service quality is abstract and is best captured by surveys that measure customer evaluations of service. One of the first measures to be developed specifically to measure service quality was the *SERVQUAL survey*.

The SERVQUAL scale involves a survey containing 21 service attributes, grouped into the five service quality dimensions (discussed in Chapter 4) of reliability, responsiveness, assurance, empathy, and tangibles. The survey sometimes asks customers to provide two different ratings on each attribute—one reflecting the level of service they would expect from excellent companies in a sector and the other reflecting their perception of the service delivered by a specific company within that sector. The difference between the expectation and perception ratings constitutes a quantified measure of service quality. Exhibit 5.2 shows the items on the basic SERVQUAL

Exhibit 5.2 SERVQUAL: A Multidimensional Scale to Capture Customer Perceptions and Expectations of Service Quality

The SERVQUAL scale was first published in 1988 and has undergone numerous improvements and revisions since then. The scale contains 21 perception items that are distributed throughout the five service quality dimensions. The scale also contains expectation items. Although many different formats of the SERVQUAL scale are now in use, we show here the basic 21 perception items as well as a sampling of ways the expectation items have been posed.

PERCEPTIONS

Perceptions Statements in the Reliability Dimension

	Strongly Disagree						Strongly Agree
1. When XYZ Company promises to do something by a certain time, it does so.	1	2	3	4	5	6	7
2. XYZ Company performs the service right the first time.	1	2	3	4	5	6	7
3. XYZ Company provides its services at the time it promises to do so.	1	2	3	4	5	6	7
4. XYZ Company insists on error-free records.	1	2	3	4	5	6	7

Statements in the Responsiveness Dimension

1. XYZ Company keeps customers informed about when services will be performed.	1	2	3	4	5	6	7
2. Employees in XYZ Company give you prompt service.	1	2	3	4	5	6	7
3. Employees in XYZ Company are always willing to help you.	1	2	3	4	5	6	7
4. Employees in XYZ Company are never too busy to respond to your request.	1	2	3	4	5	6	7

Statements in the Assurance Dimension

1. The behavior of employees in XYZ Company instills confidence in you.	1	2	3	4	5	6	7
2. You feel safe in your transactions with XYZ Company.	1	2	3	4	5	6	7
3. Employees in XYZ Company are consistently courteous with you.	1	2	3	4	5	6	7
4. Employees in XYZ Company have the knowledge to answer your questions.	1	2	3	4	5	6	7

Statements in the Empathy Dimension

1. XYZ Company gives you individual attention.	1	2	3	4	5	6	7
2. XYZ Company has employees who give you personal attention.	1	2	3	4	5	6	7
3. XYZ Company has your best interests at heart.	1	2	3	4	5	6	7
4. Employees of XYZ Company understand your specific needs.	1	2	3	4	5	6	7
5. XYZ Company has operating hours that are convenient to all its customers.	1	2	3	4	5	6	7

Statements in the Tangibles Dimension

	Strongly Disagree						Strongly Agree
1. XYZ Company has modern-looking equipment.	1	2	3	4	5	6	7
2. XYZ Company's physical facilities are visually appealing.	1	2	3	4	5	6	7
3. XYZ Company's employees appear neat.	1	2	3	4	5	6	7
4. Materials associated with the service (such as pamphlets or statements) are visually appealing at XYZ Company.	1	2	3	4	5	6	7

EXPECTATIONS: Several Formats for Measuring Customer Expectations Using Versions of SERVQUAL

There are a number of different ways that expectations can be asked in surveys. We present four of these types below: (1) matching expectations statements, (2) referent expectations formats, (3) statements that combine both expectations and perceptions, and (4) statements that cover different types of expectations.

Matching Expectations Statements (Paired with the Previous Perception Statements)

	Strongly Disagree						Strongly Agree
When customers have a problem, excellent firms will show a sincere interest in solving it.	1	2	3	4	5	6	7

Referent Expectations Formats

1. Considering a "world-class" company to be a "7," how would you rate XYZ Company's performance on the following service features?

	Low						High
Sincere, interested employees	1	2	3	4	5	6	7
Service delivered right the first time	1	2	3	4	5	6	7

2. Compared with the level of service you expect from an excellent company, how would you rate XYZ Company's performance on the following?

	Low						High
Sincere, interested employees	1	2	3	4	5	6	7
Service delivered right the first time	1	2	3	4	5	6	7

Combined Expectations/Perceptions Statements

For each of the following statements, circle the number that indicates how XYZ Company's service compares with the level you expect:

	Lower Than My Desired Service Level			The Same as My Desired Service Level			Higher Than My Desired Service Level		
1. Prompt service	1	2	3	4	5	6	7	8	9
2. Courteous employees	1	2	3	4	5	6	7	8	9

(continued)

Exhibit 5.2 (concluded)

Expectations Distinguishing between Desired Service and Adequate Service

For each of the following statements, circle the number that indicates how XYZ Company's performance compares with your *minimum service level* and with your *desired service level.*

When it comes to ...	Compared with my *minimum* service level XYZ's service performance is									Compared with my *desired* service level XYZ's service performance is								
	Lower			Same			Higher			Lower			Same			Higher		
1. Prompt service	1	2	3	4	5	6	7	8	9	1	2	3	4	5	6	7	8	9
2. Employees who are consistently courteous	1	2	3	4	5	6	7	8	9	1	2	3	4	5	6	7	8	9

Source: A. Parasuraman, V. A. Zeithaml, and L. L. Berry, "SERVQUAL: A Multiple-Item Scale for Measuring Consumer Perceptions of Service Quality," *Journal of Retailing* 64 (Spring 1988), pp. 12–40.

scale as well as the phrasing of the expectations and perceptions portions of the scale.[9] Data gathered through a SERVQUAL survey can be used for a variety of purposes:

- To determine the average gap score (between customers' perceptions and expectations) for each service attribute.
- To assess a company's service quality along each of the five SERVQUAL dimensions.
- To track customers' expectations and perceptions (on individual service attributes and/or on the SERVQUAL dimensions) over time.
- To compare a company's SERVQUAL scores against those of competitors.
- To identify and examine customer segments that differ significantly in their assessments of a company's service performance.
- To assess internal service quality (that is, the quality of service rendered by one department or division of a company to others within the same company).

This instrument has spawned many studies focusing on service quality assessment and is used all over the world in service industries. Published studies have used SERVQUAL and adaptations of it in a variety of contexts: real estate brokers, physicians in private practice, public recreation programs, dental schools, business school placement centers, tire stores, motor carrier companies, accounting firms, discount and department stores, gas and electric utility companies, hospitals, banking, pest control, dry cleaning, fast food, and higher education.

Trailer Calls or Posttransaction Surveys

Whereas the purpose of SERVQUAL and relationship surveys is usually to gauge the overall relationship with the customer, the purpose of transaction surveys is to capture information about key service encounters with the customer. In this method, customers are asked a short list of questions immediately after a particular transaction (hence the name *trailer calls*) about their satisfaction with the transaction and contact personnel with whom they interacted. Because the surveys are administered continuously to a broad spectrum of customers, they are more effective than complaint solicitation (where the information comes only from dissatisfied customers).

At checkout, immediately after staying at Fairfield Inns, customers are asked to use a computer to answer four or five questions about their stay in the hotel. This approach has obvious benefits over the ubiquitous comment cards left in rooms—the response rate is far higher because the process engages customers and takes only a few minutes. In other companies, transaction surveys are by e-mail (Best Buy, Geek Squad, and Panera Bread). Customers are asked to complete a survey by calling an 800-number or going to a website listed on their receipt. The incentive for completing the survey is a chance to win prizes or coupons from the stores.

A strong benefit of this type of research is that it often appears to customers that the call is following up to ensure that they are satisfied; consequently, the request does double duty as a market research tool and customer service. This type of research is simple and fresh and provides management with continuous information about interactions with customers. Further, the research allows management to associate service quality performance with individual contact personnel, so that high performance can be rewarded and low performance corrected. It also serves as an incentive for employees to provide better service because they understand how and when they are being evaluated. The chapter opener described some limitations of this approach and discussed customer journey measurement as an innovative way to improve upon post-transaction surveys alone.

Service Expectation Meetings and Reviews

In business-to-business situations when large accounts are involved, a form of customer research that is highly effective involves eliciting the expectations of the client at a specified time of the year and then following up later (usually after a year) to determine whether the expectations were fulfilled. Even when the company produces a physical product, the meetings deal almost completely with the service expected and provided by an account or sales team assigned to the client. Unlike other forms of research we have discussed, these meetings are not conducted by unbiased researchers but are instead initiated and facilitated by senior members of the account team, so that they can listen carefully to the client's expectations. You may be surprised to find that such interaction does not come naturally to sales teams who are used to talking *to* clients rather than listening carefully to their needs. Consequently, teams have to be carefully trained not to defend or explain but instead to comprehend. One company found that the only way it could teach its salespeople not to talk on these interviews was to take a marketing researcher along to gently kick the salesperson under the table whenever he or she strayed from the format!

The format, when appropriate, consists of (1) asking clients what they expect in terms of 8 to 10 basic requirements determined from focus group research, (2) inquiring what particular aspects of these requirements the account team performed well in the past as well as what aspects need improvement, and (3) requesting that the client rank the relative importance of the requirements. After getting the input, senior account members go back to their teams and plan their goals for the year around client requirements. The next step is verifying with the client that the account plan will satisfy requirements or, when it will not, managing expectations to let the client know what cannot be accomplished. After executing the plan for the year, the senior account personnel then return to the client, determine whether the plan has been successfully executed and expectations met, and establish a new set of expectations for the coming year.

Process Checkpoint Evaluations

With professional services such as consulting, construction, and architecture, services are provided over a long period, and there are no obvious ways or times to collect customer information. Waiting until the entire project is complete—which could last years—is undesirable because myriad unresolvable problems could have occurred by then. In these situations, the smart service provider defines a process for delivering the services and then structures the feedback around the journey, checking in at frequent points to ensure that the client's expectations are being met. For example, a management consulting firm might establish the following process for delivering its services to clients: (1) collect information, (2) diagnose problems, (3) recommend alternative solutions, (4) select alternatives, and (5) implement solutions. Next, it could agree with the client up-front that it will communicate at major *process checkpoints*—after diagnosing the problem, before selecting the alternative, and so on—to make certain that the job is progressing as planned. These process checkpoints are the key places along the customer journey.

Market-Oriented Ethnography

Structured questionnaires make key assumptions about what people are conscious of or can recall about their behavior and what they are willing to explain to researchers about their opinions. To fully understand how customers assess and use services, it may be necessary and effective to use other approaches, such as *market-oriented ethnography*. The new product/service firm called IDEO is founded on this approach to design research. This set of approaches allows researchers to observe consumption behavior in natural settings. The goal is to enter the consumer's world as much as possible—observing how and when a service is used in an actual home environment or consumption environment, such as watching consumers eat in restaurants or attend concerts. Among the techniques used are observation, interviews, documents, and examination of material possessions such as artifacts. Observation involves entering the experience as a participant observer and watching what occurs rather than asking questions about it. One-on-one interviews, particularly with key informants in the culture rather than consumers themselves, can provide compelling insights into culture-based behavior. Studying existing documents and cultural artifacts can also provide valuable insights, especially about lifestyles and usage patterns.[10] ZMET, a technique described in the chapter opener, is a form of ethnographic research.

Best Western International used this technique to better understand its senior market. Rather than bringing participants into focus group facilities and asking them questions, the company paid 25 over-55 couples to videotape themselves on cross-country journeys. The firm was able to listen to how couples actually made decisions rather than the way they reported them. The insights they gained from this research were decidedly different from what they would have learned otherwise. Most noteworthy was the finding that seniors who talked hotel clerks into better deals on rooms did not need the lower price to afford staying at the hotel—they were simply after the thrill of the deal, as illustrated in this description:

> The 60-ish woman caught on the grainy videotape is sitting on her hotel bed, addressing her husband after a long day spent on the road. "Good job!" she exults. "We beat the s—t out of the front desk and got a terrific room."[11]

These customers then spent their discount money on better dinners elsewhere, contributing nothing to Best Western. "The degree of discount clearly isn't what it used to be in importance—and we got that right out of the research," claimed the manager of programs for Best Western. This finding would be highly unlikely using traditional research and asking customers directly, for few customers would admit to being willing to pay a higher price for a service.

Mystery Shopping

In this form of research, which is unique to services, companies hire outside research organizations to send people into service establishments and experience the service as if they were customers. These *mystery shoppers* are trained in the criteria important to customers of the establishment. They deliver objective assessments about service performance by completing questionnaires about service standards or, in other cases, open-ended questions that have a qualitative feel to them. Questionnaires contain items that represent important quality or service issues to customers. Au Bon Pain, for example, sends mystery shoppers to its stores to buy meals and then complete questionnaires about the servers, the restaurant, and the food. Servers are evaluated on standards that include the following:

Acknowledged within three seconds after reaching first place in line.

Acknowledged pleasantly.

Server suggested additional items.

Server requested payment prior to delivering order.

Received receipt.

Received correct change.

Correct order received.

Au Bon Pain motivates workers to perform to service standards by using the mystery shopper program as a key element in its compensation and reward system. Individual workers who receive positive scores have their names posted on the store's bulletin board and receive letters of congratulations as well as bonuses. Managers whose stores earn high scores can receive on-the-spot bonuses of "Club Excellence" dollars that can be traded like green stamps for items in a company catalog. Perhaps more important, the overall scores received by shift and district managers qualify them for monthly profit-sharing cash bonuses. A score lower than 78 percent removes them from consideration for a bonus, whereas high numbers lead to good bonuses.

Mystery shopping keeps workers on their toes because they know they may be evaluated at any time. They know they are being judged on the company's service standards and therefore carry out the standards more consistently than if they were not going to be judged. Mystery shopping can be a very effective way of reinforcing service standards.

Customer Panels

Customer panels are groups of customers assembled to provide attitudes and perceptions about a service over time. They offer the company regular and timely customer information—virtually a pulse on the market. Firms can use customer panels to represent large segments of end-customers.

Customer panels are used in the entertainment industry to screen movies before they are released to the public. After a rough cut of a film has been created, the movie is viewed by a panel of consumers that matches the demographic target. In the most basic of these panels, consumers participate in postscreening interviews or focus groups in which they report on their responses to the movie. They may be asked questions as general as their reactions to the ending of the movie and as specific as whether they understood different aspects of the plot line. Based on these panels, movies are revised and edited to ensure that they are communicating the desired message and that they will succeed in the marketplace. In extreme situations, entire endings of movies have been changed to be more consistent with customer attitudes.

Lost Customer Research

This type of research involves deliberately seeking customers who have dropped the company's service to inquire about their reasons for leaving. Some *lost customer research* is similar to exit interviews with employees in that it asks open-ended, in-depth questions to expose the reasons for defection and the particular events that led to dissatisfaction. It is also possible to use more standard surveys on lost customers. For example, a midwestern manufacturer used a mail survey to ask former customers about its performance during different stages of the customer–vendor relationship. The survey also sought specific reasons for customers' defections and asked customers to describe problems that triggered their decreases in purchases.

One benefit of this type of research is that it identifies failure points and common problems in the service and can help establish an early-warning system for future defectors. Another benefit is that the research can be used to calculate the cost of lost customers.

Future Expectations Research

Customer expectations are dynamic and can change very rapidly in markets that are highly competitive and volatile. As competition increases, as tastes change, and as consumers become more knowledgeable, companies must continue to update their information and strategies. In dynamic market situations, companies want to understand not just current customer expectations but also future expectations—the service features desired in the future. *Future expectations research* includes different types. First, *features research* involves environmental scanning and querying of customers about desirable features of possible services. *Lead user research* brings in customers who are opinion leaders/innovators and asks them what requirements are not currently being met by existing products or services.

The question of customer involvement in expectation studies is often debated. Designers and developers claim that consumers do not know what they might want, especially in industries or services that are new and rapidly changing. Consumers and marketing researchers, on the other hand, counter that services developed independently of customer input are likely to be targeted at needs that do not exist. To study this question, researchers assessed the contributions made by users compared with professional developers for end-user telecom services. Three groups were studied: users alone, developers alone, and users with a design expert present to provide information on feasibility. Findings showed that users created more original but less producible ideas. However, inviting users to test and explore possibilities once a prototype has been created can produce positive results.[12]

ANALYZING AND INTERPRETING CUSTOMER RESEARCH FINDINGS

One of the biggest challenges facing a customer researcher is converting a complex set of data to a form that can be read and understood quickly by executives, managers, and other employees who will make decisions from the research. For example, "big data" is being adopted as strategic initiative by many firms (see the Strategy Insight box),

Strategy Insight Big Data Provides New Tools to Research Consumers

One of the tools you will hear about frequently as you move into the business world is "big data." According to McKinsey Global Institute, "big data refers to data-sets whose size is beyond the ability of typical database software tools to capture, store, manage, and analyze." It involves accessing the vast new flows of information available to companies to understand and link virtually all the information they need, much of it critical to understanding their customers. However, as we will explain later, big data is only relevant when used to make decisions and influence strategy.

You may be familiar with Amazon's big data and algorithms. Not only can Amazon track what you buy, but also what else you view, how you move through the website, how offers and reviews affect you, and even what you will buy next. As Andrew McAfee and Erik Brynjolfsson describe it, big data possesses three pivotal differences from previous analytical approaches:

- **Volume** Think exabytes, not gigabytes. Because of the Internet, companies can now collect petabytes on its customers. A petabyte is one quadrillion bytes (equal to 20 million filing cabinets of text) and an exabyte is 1,000 times that!

- **Velocity** No longer does it take marketing researchers months or weeks to collect data; data collection can now be done in real time, providing virtually instant insights.

- **Variety** Big data includes information from social networks, mobile phones, images, text, locations, sensor readings, and more.

Skeptics say that big data is just that—data—unless companies have ways to use algorithms to make it useful in decision making. The data may spit out relationships in the data but how valid and valuable are those relationships? An infamous example of the limitations of big data is "Google Flu Trends" which was featured in *Nature,* a top scientific journal, a few years ago. At the time, Google reported a coup: the company was able to track an influenza's spread across the United States more quickly than the Centers for Disease Control (one-day delay for Google, a week or more for the CDC).

Unfortunately, the following year Google was unable to replicate this feat.

As this example shows, big data is helpful only when it allows managers to reliably make decisions and influence strategy. One team of scholars have written a book to address three important objectives in achieving this, rather than just using data for data's sake. First, they show how big data presents many opportunities for companies to create value but to also demonstrate what they call the "dark side" of big data—issues such as over-investment in unproven data and mistaking correlation (x is related to y) for causation (x causes y). Second, they describe the specific analytical approaches that are necessary to get answers from big data. Third, they discuss solutions on how to organize the marketing analytical function within the company to obtain value from the data. Theirs is likely to be among many articles and books to describe this topic.

Another key question is whether data-driven companies are better performers than those who make decisions the "old-fashioned" way, through intuition or structured company databases. The Massachusetts Institute of Technology's Center for Digital Business, along with the Wharton School, found that the more companies characterize themselves as data-driven, the better they performed on financial and operational measures. In fact, they found that companies in the top third of their industry in the use of data-driven decision making were 5 percent more productive and 6 percent more profitable.

Even with the advantages big data provides, leaders' and researchers' insights are still needed. As either W. Edwards Deming or Peter Drucker famously first said, "You can't manage what you don't measure." And you must use those measurements wisely to make good strategic decisions.

Sources: P. Verhoef, E. Kooge, and N. Walk, *Creating Value with Big Data Analytics: Making Smarter Marketing Decisions* (New York: Routlege, 2016); A. McAfee and E. Brynjolfsson, "Big Data: the Management Revolution," *Harvard Business Review* 90 (October 2012), pp. 61–67; McKinsey Global Institute, "Big Data—The Next Frontier for Innovation Competition," www.mckinsey.com, 2011; H. Chen, R. H. L. Chiang, and V. C. Storey, "Business Intelligence and Analytics: From Big Data to Big Impact," *MIS Quarterly* 36 (December 2012), pp. 1165–1188.

but merely having sophisticated data does not ensure that the findings will be useful to managers. Many of the people who use customer research findings have not been trained in statistics and have neither the time nor the expertise to analyze computer printouts and other technical research information. The goal in this stage of the customer research

When conducting customer research in emerging markets—Brazil, Russia, India, and China—U.S.-based marketers need to adapt their practices to be successful. As authors Linda Steinbach and Virginia Weil claim, marketers need important background information before conducting research to be sure they do not make bad decisions based on the wrong information or analysis. These authors, global key account directors from a top international customer research firm called Synovate, offer helpful lists of do's and don'ts for each of the four emerging markets. The following insights are excerpted from the article listed at the end of this Global Feature.

BRAZIL

In doing research in Brazil, a marketer must realize the following:

- Secondary research, including "official" statistics, is not to be fully trusted, in part because of the small number of sources but also because there are discrepancies among the sources.
- Because consumers are concerned about violence, face-to-face interviewers are unlikely to get inside people's homes to interview them. Telephone and Web surveys are better options.
- Personal contacts are very important, so knowing someone who knows someone allows researchers much quicker access. In a similar vein, references are essential. If you have done business with someone a Brazilian knows and respects, that information will be very useful.

- Price is important for both general consumers and business purchasers.

RUSSIA

Steinbach and Weil recommend that, when companies are conducting research in Russia, they should connect with local companies because most Russian managers prefer to speak Russian and deal with Russians. Other facts to know include the following:

- Secondary research is not likely to be accurate due to limited sources and discrepancies among them.
- Face-to-face surveys for B-to-B are greatly preferred over telephone surveys.
- The local postal service takes several weeks to deliver a package or survey, so use another means of distribution.
- While personal contacts are very important, cold calling is also effective.
- Most researchers in Russia have a math background, leading to very specific explanations of solutions when they present findings.
- For each recommendation, companies in Russia must be convinced that it reflects Russian realities, as they strongly believe that Russia is very different from the rest of the world.
- Russia has 11 time zones, and temperatures range from 0 to -40 degrees, so outdoor marketing or research initiatives can be affected.

process is to communicate information clearly to the right people in a timely fashion. Among considerations are the following: Who gets this information? Why do they need it? How will they use it? Does it mean the same thing across cultures? When users feel confident that they understand the data, they are far more likely to apply it appropriately. When managers do not understand how to interpret the data, or when they lack confidence in the research, the investment of time, skill, and effort will be lost.

Depicting marketing research findings graphically is a powerful way to communicate research information. Here are samples of graphic representations of the types of marketing research data we have discussed throughout this chapter.

Customer Journey and Experience Maps

As described in the chapter opener, measuring journeys and clusters is on the cutting edge of measurement. By looking at clusters from the customer point of view, companies can completely redesign the journey to be simpler and superior. Individual service encounters can be positive in a narrow sense—employees in each siloed touchpoint can answer questions or solve issues as they arise. However, underlying problems remain avoidable, root causes are unaddressed, and the aggregate effect on customer experience can persist as negative.

- To be representative of the nation, a survey should cover at least 53 cities across seven regions of total territory.
- Shared responsibility (collectivism), rather than individualism, is a core value.

INDIA

Only 70 percent of adults are literate, and one-third of Indians live on the equivalent of 70 cents per day. Some of these demographics affect research, as do the following:

- Keep consumer research simple. The quality of interviews on complex concepts is likely to be low.
- English is the language of business, but there are 14 "first languages" among consumers and many dialects. For this reason, telephone interviewing for research must be regionalized for language.
- Many people will not want to do in-home interviews because they are sensitive about the poverty of their homes.
- For B-to-B surveys, e-mail is popular and phone interviews possible, but in-person interviews are difficult.
- Corruption in the public sector is common and cash payments to grease the wheels at any level may be requested.
- Gender relations are important. Many women, or their male partners, will be uncomfortable with male interviewers in informal environments.

CHINA

China has 1.3 billion consumers and is therefore a key market for many products. The following are facts to know about research done there:

- Politics, religion, and sex are considered to be too sensitive as topics and can never be included in surveys.
- Because company personnel are spread across large distances, face-to-face B-to-B interviews are difficult to conduct.
- Mandarin is the official language, but local dialects are still strong.
- Online interviews work if the target audience is educated and younger than 40 years old.
- Because China is big, the behavioral styles and sophistication of marketers and researchers can differ by region.
- Most projects require many meetings and involve many people.
- The Chinese have a deep respect for hierarchy and saving face is critical.
- In business, it is important to capture the sense of "Guanzi": personal rather than corporate relationships.

Source: L. Steinbach and V. Weil, "From Tactical to Personal: Synovate's Tips for Conducting Market Research in Emerging Markets," *Marketing News,* April 30, 2011.

Figure 5.2 shows a hypothetical kitchen remodel. The first journey cluster would involve such touchpoints as Internet search, examining magazines, and asking friends or neighbors who have recently made the purchase. This cluster is a particular pain point to customers because of the uncertainty about price and process.

FIGURE 5.2   Customer Journey and Experience Map for Measurement of a Kitchen Remodel

In this type of major purchase, customers typically depend on friends and neighbors. In the second cluster, customers visit stores and look at sample kitchens, talk to salespeople, and try to resolve their issues about price and process. Among the improvements a company could make is to build a CAD computer model of a kitchen with the attributes that the particular customer desires and give an estimate of cost. During the choosing journey cluster, a company can contact the customer with personalized emails showing kitchen ideas with their exact specifications and schedules for delivery of the service. This journey cluster could also include provision of a contract with a price cut to motivate the customer to take immediate action. Delivery and installation would be the next cluster, and follow-up would complete the end-to-end experience.

Measurement of this experience, as shown in Figure 5.2, would involve surveys or other approaches at the end of the *journeys,* shown as small stars. A final measure of the entire customer experience is shown as the large seven-sided star.

Importance/Performance Matrices

One of the most useful forms of analysis in customer research is the *importance/ performance matrix.* This chart combines information about customer perceptions and importance ratings. An example is shown in Figure 5.3. Attribute importance is represented on the vertical axis from high (top) to low (bottom). Performance is shown on the horizontal axis from low (left) to high (right). There are many variations of these matrices: some companies define the horizontal axis as the gap between expectations and perceptions, or as performance relative to competition. The shading on the chart indicates the area of highest leverage for service quality improvements— where importance is high and performance is low. In this quadrant are the attributes that most need to be improved. In the adjacent upper quadrant are attributes to be maintained, ones that a company performs well and that are very important to customers. The lower two quadrants contain attributes that are less important, some of which are performed well and others poorly. Neither of these quadrants merit as much attention in terms of service improvements as the upper quadrants because customers are not as concerned about the attributes that are plotted in them as they are the attributes in the upper quadrants.

FIGURE 5.3
**Importance/
Performance Matrix**

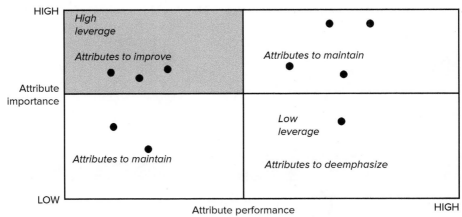

USING MARKETING RESEARCH INFORMATION

Conducting research about customer expectations is only the first part of understanding the customer, even if the research is appropriately designed, executed, and presented. A service firm must also use the research findings in a meaningful way—to drive change or improvement in the way service is delivered. The misuse (or even nonuse) of research data can lead to a large gap in *understanding customer expectations*. When managers do not read research reports because they are too busy dealing with the day-to-day challenges of the business, companies fail to use the resources available to them. And when customers participate in research studies but never see changes in the way the company does business, they feel frustrated and annoyed with the company. Understanding how to make the best use of research—to apply what has been learned to the business—is a key way to close the gap between customer expectations and management perceptions of customer expectations. Managers must learn to turn research information and insights into action and to recognize that the purpose of research is to drive improvement and customer satisfaction.

The research plan should specify the mechanism by which customer data will be used. The research should be actionable: timely, specific, and credible. It can also have a mechanism that allows a company to respond to dissatisfied customers immediately.

UPWARD COMMUNICATION

In some service firms, especially small and localized firms, owners or managers may be in constant contact with customers, thereby gaining firsthand knowledge of customer expectations and perceptions. But in large service organizations, managers do not always get the opportunity to experience firsthand what their customers want.

The larger a company is, the more difficult it is for managers to interact directly with the customer and the less firsthand information they have about customer expectations. Even when they read and digest research reports, managers can lose the reality of the customer if they never get the opportunity to experience delivery of the actual service. A theoretical view of how things are supposed to work cannot provide the richness of the service encounter. To truly understand customer needs, management benefits from hands-on knowledge of what really happens in stores, on customer service telephone lines, in service queues, and in face-to-face service encounters. If the listening gap is to be closed, managers in large firms need some form of customer contact.

Objectives for Upward Communication

Exhibit 5.3 shows the major research objectives for improving upward communication in an organization. These objectives include gaining firsthand knowledge about customers, improving internal service quality, gaining firsthand knowledge of employees, and obtaining ideas for service improvement. These objectives can be met by two types of interactive activities in the organization: one designed to improve the type and effectiveness of communications from customers to management and the other designed to improve communications between employees and management.

Exhibit 5.3 Elements in an Effective Program of Upward Communication

Type of Interaction or Research	Research Objective	Qualitative/ Quantitative	Cost of Information		
			Money	**Time**	**Frequency**
Executive visits to customers	To gain firsthand knowledge about customers	Qualitative	Moderate	Moderate	Continuous
Executive listenings	To gain firsthand knowledge about customers	Qualitative	Low	Low	Continuous
Research on intermediate customers	To gain in-depth information on end-customers	Quantitative	Moderate	Moderate	Annual
Employee internal satisfaction surveys	To improve internal service quality	Quantitative	Moderate	Moderate	Annual
Employee visits or listenings	To gain firsthand knowledge about employees	Qualitative	Moderate	Moderate	Continuous
Employee suggestions	To obtain ideas for service improvements	Qualitative	Low	Low	Continuous

Research for Upward Communication

Executive Visits to Customers

This approach is frequently used in business-to-business service marketing. In some visits, executives of the company make sales or service calls with customer contact personnel (salespeople). In other situations, executives of the selling company arrange meetings with executives at a similar level in client companies.

Executive or Management Listening to Customers

Direct interaction with customers adds clarity and depth to managers' understanding of customer expectations and needs. Many companies require executives to perform entry-level jobs to promote understanding of their customers. One vice president from DaVita Inc., the nation's number 2 dialysis-treatment operator, spent three days helping treat seriously ill patients alongside technicians.[13] A growing number of service companies—including Walt Disney, Continental Airlines, Amazon.com, and Sysco—require that managers spend time on the line, interacting with customers and experiencing service delivery. A formal program for encouraging informal interaction is often the best way to ensure that the contact takes place.

Research on Intermediate Customers

Intermediate customers (such as contact employees, dealers, distributors, agents, and brokers) are people the company serves who serve the end-customer. Researching the needs and expectations of these customers *in serving the end-customer* can be a useful and efficient way to both improve service to and obtain information about end-users. The interaction with intermediate customers provides opportunities for understanding end-customers' expectations and problems. It can also help the company learn about and satisfy the service expectations of intermediate customers, a process critical in their providing quality service to end-customers.

Research on Internal Customers

Employees who perform services are themselves customers of internal services on which they depend heavily to do their jobs well. As discussed in Chapter 11, there is a strong and direct link between the quality of internal service that employees receive and the quality of the service they provide their own customers. For this reason, it is important to conduct employee research that focuses on the service that internal customers give and receive. In many companies this focus requires adapting existing employee opinion research to focus on service satisfaction. Employee research complements customer research when service quality is the issue being investigated. Customer research provides insight into what is occurring, whereas employee research provides insight into why. The two types of research play unique and equally important roles in improving service quality. Companies that focus service quality research exclusively on external customers are missing a rich and vital source of information.

Executive or Management Listening Approaches to Employees

Employees who actually perform the service have the best possible vantage point for observing the service and identifying impediments to its quality. Customer contact personnel are in regular contact with customers and thereby come to understand a great deal about customer expectations and perceptions. If the information they know can be passed on to top management, top managers' understanding of the customer may improve. In fact, it could be said that in many companies top management's understanding of the customer depends largely on the extent and types of communication received from customer contact personnel and from noncompany contact personnel (such as independent insurance agents and retailers) who represent the company and its services. When these channels of communication are closed, management may not get feedback about problems encountered in service delivery and about how customer expectations are changing.

Sam Walton, the late founder of the highly successful discount retailer Walmart, once remarked, "Our best ideas come from delivery and stock boys."[14] To stay in touch with the source of new ideas, Walton spent endless hours in stores, working the floor, helping clerks, or approving personal checks, even showing up at the loading dock with a bag of doughnuts for a surprised crew of workers.[15] He was well known for having his plane drop him next to a wheat field, where he would meet a Walmart truck driver. Giving his pilot instructions to meet him at another landing strip 200 miles down the road, he would make the trip with the Walmart driver, listening to what he had to say about the company.

Employee Suggestions

Most companies have some form of employee suggestion program whereby contact personnel can communicate to management their ideas for improving work. Suggestion systems have come a long way from the traditional suggestion box. Effective suggestion systems are ones in which employees are empowered to see their suggestions through, supervisors can implement proposals immediately, employees participate for continuous improvement in their jobs, supervisors respond quickly to ideas, and coaching is provided in ways to handle suggestions. In today's companies, suggestions from employees are facilitated by self-directed work teams that encourage employees to identify problems and then work to develop solutions to those problems.

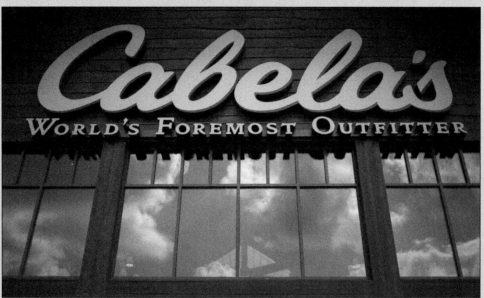

© David L. Ryan/The Boston Globe/Getty Images

Unless you fish, hunt, shoot, camp, or cave, you may not know Cabela's, the largest mail order, Internet, and retail outdoor outfitter in the world. Established in 1961 as a specialty cataloger selling fly fishing lures, the company grew rapidly because of its philosophy that the customer was number 1 and that employees were critical to realizing that philosophy. Because the company was a catalog retailer for the first 30 years of its existence, it relied heavily on employees who were knowledgeable about the outdoors to describe products to consumers.

Its incredibly large (245,000 items) and varied (hunting, archery, shooting, optics, camping, boating, fishing) product mix make Cabela's the ultimate source for outdoor-focused customer needs and wants, but its many items make it difficult to match customers with products. From this challenge was born a novel and creative solution, one that made employees as happy as it made customers. The company decided to loan products to employees so they could learn what the products were like by using them. The extensive loaner program allows employees, who are typically outdoor enthusiasts themselves, to borrow the products for a month and learn to ask the same questions

customers would ask. Employees then become experts both on products and on experiences that customers will have using them.

After using the product, the employee returns and teaches everyone else about the product—both by giving a talk to others and by filling out a form about the product's pros and cons. This information becomes part of a giant product database, called "Item notes," that allows easy access to employees, even call center reps, so that customer questions—even the most esoteric ones—can be answered quickly and accurately. The company also invites a small number of knowledgeable customers to borrow products and contribute information as well.

The upward communication extends to the company's cofounder, Jim Cabela, who intercepts and reads all customer comments as they come in before routing them to the appropriate employee. He likes to keep an eye on what customers want to know, so that he can be sure his employees are staying informed.

Source: M. A. Prospero, "Leading Listener Winner: Cabela's," *Fast Company,* October 2005, p. 47.

Benefits of Upward Communication

Upward communication of this sort provides information to upper-level managers about activities and performances throughout the organization. Specific types of communication that may be relevant are formal (such as reports of problems and exceptions in service delivery) and informal (like discussions between contact personnel and upper-level managers). Managers who stay close to their contact people benefit not only by keeping their employees happy but also by learning more about their customers.[16] These companies encourage, appreciate, and reward upward communication from contact people, as Exhibit 5.4 shows. Through this important channel, management learns about customer expectations from employees in regular contact with customers and can thereby reduce the size of provider gap 1.

Summary	This chapter discussed the role of customer research in understanding customer perceptions and expectations. The chapter began by describing criteria for effective service research that should be incorporated into a service marketing research program. Next, we discussed the elements in an effective service marketing research program and indicated how the approaches satisfied the criteria. In addition to the types and techniques of research (shown in Exhibit 5.1), the boxes in this chapter showed how electronic and other technologies add to the information that managers can collect.

The chapter described key forms of service research, including critical incident studies, mystery shopping, service expectation meetings and reviews, process checkpoint evaluations, and database research. Important topics in researching services—including developing research objectives—were also described. Finally, upward communication, ways in which management obtains and uses information from customers and customer contact personnel, was discussed. These topics combine to help close the listening gap—the gap between customer expectations and company understanding of customer expectations and the first of four provider gaps in the gaps model of service quality.

Discussion Questions	1. Give five reasons research objectives must be established before customer research is conducted.

2. Why are both qualitative and quantitative research methods needed in a service marketing research program?

3. Why does the frequency of research differ across the research methods shown in Exhibit 5.1?

4. Compare and contrast the types of research that help a company identify common failure points (see column 2 in Exhibit 5.1). Which of the types do you think produces better information? Why?

5. In what situations does a service company need requiremènts research?

6. What reasons can you give for companies' lack of use of research information? How might you motivate managers to use the information to a greater extent? How might you motivate frontline workers to use the information?

7. Given a specific customer research budget, what would be your recommendations for the percentage to be spent on customer research versus upward communication? Why?

8. What kinds of information could be gleaned from research on intermediate customers? What would intermediate customers know that service providers might not?

9. For what types of products and services would research on the Internet be preferable to traditional research?

Exercises

1. Choose a local service organization to interview about customer research. Find out what the firm's objectives are and the types of customer research it currently uses. Using the information in this chapter, think about the effectiveness of its customer research. What are the strengths? Weaknesses?

2. Choose one of the services you consume. If you were in charge of creating a survey for that service, what questions would you ask on the survey? Give several examples. What type of survey (relationship versus transaction-based) would be most appropriate for the service? What recommendations would you give to management of the company about making such a survey actionable?

3. If you were the marketing director of your college or university, what types of research (see Exhibit 5.1) would be essential for understanding both external and internal customers? If you could choose only three types of research, which ones would you select? Why?

4. Using the SERVQUAL scale in this chapter, create a questionnaire for a service firm that you use. Give the questionnaire to 10 people, and describe what you learn.

5. To get an idea of the power of the critical incident technique, try it yourself with reference to restaurant service. Think of a time when, as a customer, you had a particularly satisfying interaction with a restaurant. Follow the instructions here, which are identical to the instructions in an actual study, and observe the insights you obtain about your requirements in restaurant service:

   a. When did the incident happen?

   b. What specific circumstances led up to this situation?

   c. Exactly what did the employee (or firm) say or do?

   d. What resulted that made you feel the interaction was satisfying?

   e. What could or should have been done differently?

Notes

1. Sources for the chapter opener include H. Fanderl, K. Neher, and A. Pulido, "Are You Really Listening to What Your Customers are Saying?" *McKinsey Newsletter,* March 2016, pp. 1–6; N. Maechler, K. Neher, and R. Park, "From Touchpoints to Journeys: Seeing the World as Customers Do," *McKinsey Newsletter,* March 2016, pp. 1–10; D. Edelman and M. Singer, "The New Customer Decision Journey," *McKinsey Newsletter,* October 2015, pp. 1–3; X. Lhuer, T. Olanrewaju, and H. Yeon, "What It Takes to Deliver Breakthrough Customer Service," *McKinsey Insights,* November 2015, pp. 1–3.

2. A. Parasuraman, L. L. Berry, and V. A. Zeithaml, "Guidelines for Conducting Service Quality Research," *Marketing Research: A Magazine of Management and Applications,* December 1990, pp. 34–44.

3. "Zaltman Metaphor Elicitation Technique," Olson Zaltman, [insert accessed date here], www.olsonzaltman.com/zmet.

4. J. Neff, "Chasing the Cheaters Who Undermine Online Research," *Advertising Age,* March 31, 2008, p. 12; B. Johnson, "Forget Phone and Mail: Online's the Best Place to Administer Surveys," *Advertising Age,* July 17, 2006, p. 23.

5. This section is based on a comprehensive assessment of the critical incident technique in D. D. Gremler, "The Critical Incident Technique in Service Research," *Journal of Service Research* 7 (August 2004), pp. 65–89.

6. For detailed discussions of the critical incident technique, see J. C. Flanagan, "The Critical Incident Technique," *Psychological Bulletin* 51 (July 1954), pp. 327–358; M. J. Bitner, J. D. Nyquist, and B. H. Booms, "The Critical Incident as a Technique for Analyzing the Service Encounter," in *Services Marketing in a Changing Environment,* ed. T. M. Bloch, G. D. Upah, and V. A. Zeithaml (Chicago: American Marketing Association, 1985), pp. 48–51; S. Wilson-Pessano, "Defining Professional Competence: The Critical Incident Technique 40 Years Later," presentation to the Annual Meeting of the American Educational Research Association, New Orleans, 1988; I. Roos, "Methods of Investigating Critical Incidents," *Journal of Service Research* 4 (February 2002), pp. 193–204; Gremler, "The Critical Incident Technique in Service Research."

7. Ibid.

8. J. Carey, J. Buckley, and J. Smith, "Hospital Hospitality," *Newsweek,* February 11, 1985, p. 78.

9. See V. A. Zeithaml and A. Parasuraman, *Service Quality,* MSI Relevant Knowledge Series (Cambridge, MA: Marketing Science Institute, 2004) for a complete review of this research, including the many publications by the original authors of SERVQUAL and the extensions by other authors.

10. E. Day, "Researchers Must Enter Consumer's World," *Marketing News,* August 17, 1998, p. 17.

11. G. Khermouch, "Consumers in the Mist," *BusinessWeek,* February 26, 2001, pp. 92–93.

12. P. R. Magnusson, J. Mathing, and P. Kristensson, "Managing User Involvement in Service Innovation: Experiments with Innovating End Users," *Journal of Service Research* 6 (November 2003), pp. 111–124.

13. J. S. Lublin, "Top Brass Try Life in the Trenches," *The Wall Street Journal,* June 25, 2007, p. B1.

14. S. Koepp, "Make That Sale, Mr. Sam," *Time,* May 18, 1987.

15. Ibid.

16. Zeithaml, Parasuraman, and Berry, *Delivering Quality Service,* p. 64.

Chapter Six

Building Customer Relationships

This chapter's objectives are to

1. Explain relationship marketing, its goals, and the benefits of long-term relationships for firms and customers.

2. Explain why and how to estimate customer relationship value.

3. Introduce the concept of customer profitability segments as a strategy for focusing relationship marketing efforts.

4. Present relationship development strategies—including quality core service, switching barriers, and relationship bonds.

5. Identify challenges in relationship development, including the somewhat controversial idea that "the customer is not always right."

USAA Focuses on Long-Term Relationships

United Services Automobile Association (USAA) is a preeminent example of an organization focused on building long-term relationships with customers—or what it refers to as members.[1] Member retention has been a core value of USAA since long before customer loyalty became a popular business concept. In business since 1922, USAA provides for the insurance needs of a highly targeted market segment: current and former U.S. military personnel and their families. Headquartered in San Antonio, Texas, USAA owns and manages more than $130 billion in assets. It was ranked in the top 100 of *Fortune*'s annual list of the best companies to work for in America every year from 2010 to 2016. Member retention figures approach 98 percent.[2]

The goal of USAA is to "think about the events in the life of a career officer and then work out ways to help him get through them." USAA is intent on serving its current member base and growing with them. To do this, USAA relies heavily on extensive research through surveys and a member advisory board that meets regularly with executives. USAA also focuses on retaining the best employees and rewarding them for member-oriented objectives such as percentage of member questions or requests handled on the first call with no need for follow-up. USAA believes so strongly in the importance of member retention that a portion of managers' and executives' bonuses are based on this metric. Such emphasis has been rewarded: 92 percent of their members feel so strongly about their relationship with USAA that they plan to stay with the organization for life.[3]

USAA: a regular at the top of many organizations' customer service award lists.

© USAA

USAA: A Consistent Customer Service Award Winner

A striking example of how USAA attempts to listen to its members is illustrated in this excerpt from *BusinessWeek*:

> Many companies give lip service to listening to the "voice of the customer." At USAA, that voice is transformed into what it calls "surround sound"—a comprehensive approach to training its employees to empathize with its members' unique needs. "We want to cover the light moments, the heart-wrenching moments, what it's like to be bored in the field," says Elizabeth D. Conklyn, USAA's [former] executive vice-president for people services. "We try to develop empathy, not only for our members but also for the family side."[4]

> USAA has developed an enhanced military awareness program that requires member service representatives to engage in tasks that allow them to empathize with their members. For example, employees may have to strap on a military helmet, 65-pound backpack, and flak vest; consume a "meal ready to eat" given to soldiers in the field; and read real letters from troops stationed abroad. It is not uncommon for an employee to read a letter, written by a soldier to his mother, from someone who later died in a war.

USAA provides a strong example of an organization that has focused on keeping its customers and building long-term relationships with them. Unlike the USAA example, however, many companies fail to understand customers accurately because they fail to focus on customer relationships. They tend to fixate on acquiring new customers rather than viewing customers as assets that they need to nurture and retain. By concentrating on new customers, firms can easily fall into the traps of short-term promotions, price discounts, or catchy ads that bring customers in but are not enough to bring them back. By adopting a relationship philosophy, on the other hand, companies begin to understand customers over time and in great depth and are better able to meet their changing needs and expectations.

Marketing strategies for understanding customers over time and building long-term relationships are the subjects of this chapter.

RELATIONSHIP MARKETING

Over the past few decades firms have shifted from a transaction focus to a relationship focus in their marketing efforts. Customers have become partners and cocreators as firms have made "long-term commitments to maintaining those relationships with quality, service, and innovation."[5]

A company interested in a committed relationship with its customers will experience long-term benefits.

Relationship marketing essentially represents a paradigm shift within marketing—away from an acquisitions/transaction focus toward a retention/relationship focus.[6] Relationship marketing (or relationship management) is a philosophy of doing business, a strategic orientation, that focuses on *keeping and improving* relationships with current customers rather than on acquiring new customers. This philosophy assumes that many consumers and business customers prefer to have an ongoing relationship with one organization rather than to switch continually among providers in their search for value. Building on this assumption and another that suggests it is usually less expensive to keep a current customer than to attract a new one,[7] successful marketers develop effective strategies for retaining customers. Our opening example shows how USAA has built its business around a relationship philosophy.

It has been suggested that firms frequently focus on attracting customers (the "first act") and then pay little attention to what they should do to keep them (the "second act").[8] Ideas expressed in an interview with James Schorr, then executive vice president of marketing at Holiday Inns, illustrate this point.[9] In the interview he referred to the "bucket theory of marketing." By this he meant that marketing can be thought of as a big bucket: it is what the sales, advertising, and promotion programs do that pours customers into the top of the bucket. As long as these programs are effective, the bucket stays full. However, "There's only one problem," he said, "there are holes in the bucket." When the business is running well and the hotel is delivering on its promises, any holes are small and few customers are leaving. As indicated in Figure 6.1, when the operation is weak and customers are not satisfied with what they are getting—and therefore the relationship is weak—people start falling out of the bucket through the holes faster than they can be poured in through the top.

The bucket theory illustrates why a relationship strategy that focuses on plugging the holes in the bucket makes so much sense. Historically, marketers have been more concerned with acquisition of customers, so a shift to a relationship strategy often represents changes in mind-set, organizational culture, and employee reward systems. For example, the sales incentive systems in many organizations are set up to reward bringing in new customers. There are often fewer (or no) rewards for retaining current accounts. Thus, even when people see the logic of customer retention, the existing organizational systems may not support its implementation.

FIGURE 6.1
Holes in the Bucket: Why Relationship Development Makes Sense

The Evolution of Customer Relationships

Firms' relationships with their customers, like other social relationships, tend to evolve over time. Scholars have suggested that marketing exchange relationships between providers and customers often have the potential to evolve from strangers to acquaintances to friends to partners. Exhibit 6.1 illustrates different issues at each successive level of the relationship.[10]

Customers as Strangers

Strangers are those customers who have not yet had any transactions (interactions) with a firm and may not even be aware of the firm. At the industry level, strangers may be conceptualized as customers who have not yet entered the market; at the firm level, they may include customers of competitors. Clearly the firm has no relationship with the customer at this point. Consequently, the firm's primary goal with these potential customers ("strangers") is to initiate communication with them to *attract* them and *acquire* their business. Thus, the primary marketing efforts directed toward such customers deal with familiarizing those potential customers with the firm's offerings and, subsequently, encouraging them to give the firm a try.

Customers as Acquaintances

Once customer awareness and trial are achieved, familiarity is established and the customer and the firm become *acquaintances,* creating the basis for an exchange relationship. A primary goal for the firm at this stage of the relationship is *satisfying* the customer. In the acquaintance stage, firms are generally concerned about providing a value proposition to customers comparable with that of competitors. For a customer, an acquaintanceship is effective as long as the customer is relatively satisfied and what is being received in the exchange is perceived as fair value. With repetitive interactions, the customer gains experience and becomes more familiar with the firm's offerings. These encounters can help reduce uncertainty about the benefits expected in the exchange and, therefore, increase the attractiveness of the company relative to the competition. Repetitive interactions improve the firm's knowledge of the customer, helping to facilitate marketing, sales, and service efforts. Thus, an acquaintance relationship facilitates transactions primarily through the reduction of the customer's perceived risk and the provider's costs.

Customers as Friends

As a customer continues to make purchases from a firm and to receive value in the exchange relationship, the firm begins to acquire specific knowledge of the customer's needs, allowing it to create an offering that directly addresses the customer's situation. The provision of a unique offering, and thus differential value, transforms the relationship from acquaintance to *friendship*. This transition, particularly in service exchange relationships, requires the development of trust.[11] Because customers may not be able to assess a service outcome prior to purchase and consumption, they may not be able to discern service performance even after experiencing it and, therefore, must trust the provider to do what is promised. As customers become friends they not only become familiar with the company but also come to trust that it provides superior value.

A primary goal for firms at the friendship stage of the relationship is customer *retention.* A firm's potential to develop sustainable competitive advantage through friends should be higher than for acquaintances because the offering is more unique (and more difficult for competition to imitate) and the customer comes to trust that uniqueness.[12]

Exhibit 6.1 A Typology of Exchange Relationships

Customers As . . .	Strangers	Acquaintances	Friends	Partners
Product offering	Attractive relative to competitive offerings or alternative purchases.	Parity product as a form of industry standard.	Differentiated product adapted to specific market segments.	Customized product and dedicated resources adapted to an individual customer or organization.
Source of competitive advantage	Attractiveness	Satisfaction	Satisfaction + trust	Satisfaction + trust + commitment
Buying activity	Interest, exploration, and trial.	Satisfaction facilitates and reinforces buying activity and reduces need to search for market information.	Trust in firm is needed to continue the buying activity.	Commitment in the form of information sharing and idiosyncratic investments is needed to achieve customized product and to adjust product continuously to changing needs and situations.
Focus of selling activities	Awareness of firm's offerings (encouraging trial) facilitates initial selling.	Familiarity and general knowledge of customer (identification) facilitates selling.	Specific knowledge of customer's need and situation facilitates selling.	Specific knowledge of customer's need and situation and idiosyncratic investments facilitates selling.
Relationship time horizon	*None:* Buyer may have had no previous interactions with or knowledge of the firm.	*Short:* Generally short because the buyer can often switch firms without much effort or cost.	*Medium:* Generally longer than acquaintance relationships because trust in a differentiated position takes a longer time to build and imitate.	*Long:* Generally long because it takes time to build (or replace) interconnected activities and to develop a detailed knowledge of a customer's needs and the unique resources of a supplier to commit resources to the relationship.
Sustainability of competitive advantage	*Low:* Generally low, as firm must continually find ways to be attractive, in terms of the value offered, to induce trial.	*Low:* Generally low, but competitors can vary in how they build unique value into selling and serving even if the product is a form of industry standard.	*Medium:* Generally medium, but depends on ability of competitors to understand heterogeneity of customer needs and situations and the ability to transform this knowledge into meaningful, differentiated products.	*High:* Generally high, but depends on how unique and effective the interconnected activities between customer and supplier are organized.
Primary relationship marketing goal	*Acquire* the customer's business.	*Satisfy* the customer's needs and wants.	*Retain* the customer's business.	*Enhance* the relationship with the customer.

Source: Adapted from M. D. Johnson and F. Selnes, "Customer Portfolio Management: Toward a Dynamic Theory of Exchange Relationships," *Journal of Marketing* 68 (April 2004), p. 5.

Customers as Partners

As a customer continues to interact with a firm, the level of trust often deepens and the customer may receive more customized product offerings and interactions. The trust developed in the friendship stage is a necessary but not sufficient condition for a customer–firm *partnership* to develop.[13] That is, the creation of trust leads to (ideally) the creation of commitment—and that is the condition necessary for customers to extend the time perspective of a relationship.[14] The deepening of trust and the establishment of commitment reduce the customer's need to solve problems in the traditional sense of "finding a better alternative." Thus, to move the relationship into a partner relationship, a firm must use customer knowledge and information systems to deliver highly personalized and customized offerings.

At the partnership stage, the firm is concerned with *enhancing* the relationship. Customers are more likely to stay in the relationship if they feel that the company understands their changing needs and is willing to invest in the relationship by constantly improving and evolving its product and service mix. By enhancing these relationships, the firm expects such customers to be less likely to be lured away by competitors and more likely to buy additional products and services from the company over time. These loyal customers not only provide a solid base for the organization, they may represent growth potential. This is certainly true for USAA, our opening example in this chapter, whose members' needs for insurance increase over their lifetimes as well as the lifetimes of their children. Other examples abound. A bank checking account customer becomes a better customer when she sets up a savings account, takes out a loan, and/or uses the financial advising services of the bank. And a corporate account becomes a better customer when it chooses to do 75 percent of its business with a particular provider rather than splitting the business equally among three providers. In recent years, in fact, many companies have aspired to be the "exclusive provider" of a particular product or service for their customers. Over time these enhanced relationships can increase market share and profits for the organization. Our Technology Spotlight features Hilton Hotels and how the company is successfully using information technology to enhance relationships with their customers.

FIGURE 6.2
The Goal of Relationship Marketing:
Moving Customers Up the Ladder

The Goal of Relationship Marketing

The discussion of the evolution of customer relationships demonstrates how a firm's relationship with its customers might be enhanced as customers move further along this relationship continuum. As the relationship value of a customer increases, the provider is more likely to pursue a closer relationship. Thus, the primary goal of relationship marketing is *to build and maintain a base of committed customers who are profitable for the organization.* Figure 6.2 graphically illustrates the goals of relationship marketing. The overriding goal is to move customers up the ladder (i.e., along the relationship continuum) from the point at which they are strangers that need to be attracted through to the point at which they are highly valued, long-term customers whose relationship with the firm has been enhanced. From a customer's problem-solving perspective, the formation of satisfaction, trust, and commitment corresponds to the customer's willingness to more fully engage in an exchange relationship as an acquaintance, friend, and partner, respectively. From a firm's resource-allocation perspective, the delivery of differential, and perhaps customized, value corresponds

Technology Spotlight   Customer Information Systems Help Enhance the Customer Relationship

The potential of today's customer information systems far exceeds any traditional marketing information system that has gone before. The amount of information about individual customers that can now be captured allows the organization to customize to the individual level what previously would have been undifferentiated services.

HILTON'S OnQ SYSTEM

Hilton Hotels has an integrated technology platform called "OnQ" that provides the basis for its customer relationship management (CRM) system. OnQ centralizes all of the personal profile information that guests provide to Hilton—via hotel or central reservations, their websites, or membership in the HHonors loyalty program—to create a "Guest Profile Manager." Profiles are created for any guest who is an HHonors member or simply visits a Hilton hotel at least four times within a year. Such a system requires an extraordinary investment in information technology to capture information from Hilton's over 4,600 hotels and nearly 760,000 rooms in six continents across 100 countries and territories worldwide. The information collected via OnQ is combined with the customer's stay history and any prior complaints made during previous visits. The entire packet of information enables many of Hilton's 300,000 employees to recognize and reward guests with appropriate welcome messages, room upgrades, or information related to previous visits.

USING THE INFORMATION TO DEVELOP RELATIONSHIPS WITH CUSTOMERS

OnQ provides a mechanism for Hilton Hotels to learn—and remember—customer interests and preferences. Tim Harvey, former chief information officer for Hilton, describes it this way:

> It's like when your grandmother comes to your house. You know exactly who she is. You know exactly what she eats for breakfast. You know what kind of pillow she likes. You know whether she can climb the stairs or not so you know what room to put her in. We have the same passion about our hotel business. We want to know who our customers are and we want to take care of those customers every time we have an opportunity to touch them. So the value of OnQ is primarily having that information with that in-depth knowledge about customers.

Collecting information on all of its customers is not an easy task, particularly given the many different hotels in the Hilton family of brands: the company owns, manages, or franchises a hotel portfolio of some of the best known and highly regarded brands, including Hilton, Conrad Hotels & Resorts, Doubletree, Embassy Suites, Hampton Inn, Hilton Garden Inn, Homewood Suites, and the Waldorf-Astoria. OnQ provides a method for capturing and managing information on Hilton customers across a diverse set of properties, differing brands, and various countries with local requirements.

to the extent of its ability and/or desire to create an acquaintance, friend, or partner relationship with the customer. As customers make the transition from satisfaction-based acquaintanceships to trust-based friendships to commitment-based partnerships, increases are required in both the value received and the level of cooperation.

Benefits for Customers and Firms

Both parties in the customer–firm relationship can benefit from customer retention. That is, it is not only in the best interest of the organization to build and maintain a loyal customer base, but customers themselves also benefit from long-term associations.

PROVIDING GUESTS WITH OPTIONS

Over the years a large percentage of customers have contacted Hilton via the Internet, and the percentage of rooms reserved in this manner has steadily increased. However, in spite of the lack of face-to-face contact, OnQ has allowed Hilton to create a personal relationship with these customers. Once a customer identifies him- or herself when using the Internet, Hilton knows if the customer is an HHonors member, the customer's preferred room type, and the customer's preferred in-room amenities. OnQ also provides the capability for customers to check into their hotel via the Internet prior to arriving—just as customers do for an airline seat. Customers can view the hotel floor plan, see all of the rooms available, and then pick the room they want—perhaps on the west side of the building for those who like to sleep in late or one close to the pool.

Hilton also allows organizers of relatively small groups to book their entire group event or meeting from start to finish on the Internet—and receive immediate confirmation of their reservation. Potential customers who represent groups requiring 25 rooms or less—such as family reunions, wedding parties, or those attending a sporting event—can see about room availability across all Hilton brands and locations. Through OnQ amateur event planners, small-business owners or family representatives can find a hotel that best fits their needs based on price, room types, and proximity to local attractions. Organizers can reserve guest rooms, meeting spaces, food and beverages, audio/visual equipment, and more up to one year in advance without a request for proposal or a waiting period.

Additionally, OnQ enables planners to manage their room block, including instant, online access 24/7 to their group reservation details and guest room information. Planners can instantly see who has booked guest rooms for their event or can reserve rooms on behalf of guests, thus keeping track of the total head count at all times.

THE RESULTS

How well has OnQ worked in managing customer relationships? Hilton was ranked the number 1 hotel company in the United States by the American Customer Satisfaction Index in both 2015 and 2016. And, three of the Hilton brands (Hilton Garden Inn, Embassy Suites, and Homewood Suites) regularly receive the top awards for customer satisfaction in their respective hotel segments by independent research conducted by J. D. Power and Associates. Since 2001, these three brands combined to receive the number 1 ranking more than 30 times. Additionally, Harvey estimated that Hilton's "share of wallet" from its best customers increased from 40 percent to 60 percent once OnQ was fully operational. Hilton's relationship with its many customers has certainly been enhanced through OnQ.

Sources: Tim Harvey, Interview on ZDNet.com, http://www.zdnet.com/article/hilton-hotels-tim-harvey-cio/, accessed February 12, 2016; www.hilton.com, accessed July 6, 2016; http://news.hiltonworldwide.com/assets/HWW/docs/brandFactSheets/HWW_Corporate_Fact_Sheet.pdf, accessed July 6, 2016; http://news.hiltonworldwide.com/assets/HWW/docs/brandFactSheets/Diversity_Fact_Sheet.pdf, accessed July 6, 2016.

Benefits for Customers

Assuming they have a choice, customers will remain loyal to a firm when they receive greater value relative to what they expect from competing firms. *Value* represents a trade-off for the consumer between the "give" and the "get" components. (In Chapter 15 we provide an extended discussion of value.) Consumers are more likely to stay in a relationship when the gets (quality, satisfaction, specific benefits) exceed the gives (monetary and nonmonetary costs). When firms can consistently deliver value from the customer's point of view, clearly the customer benefits and has an incentive to stay in the relationship.

Beyond the specific inherent benefits of receiving service value, customers also benefit in other ways from long-term associations with firms. Sometimes these relationship benefits keep customers loyal to a firm more than the attributes of the core service. Research has uncovered specific types of relational benefits that customers experience in long-term service relationships including confidence benefits, social benefits, and special treatment benefits.[15]

Confidence Benefits Confidence benefits comprise feelings of trust or confidence in the provider along with a sense of reduced anxiety and comfort in knowing what to expect. One customer described his confidence that resulted from having developed a relationship with a service provider:

> There is a comfort [in having] a certain level of experience [with the service provider]. In other words, I know that I am going to be treated right because they know me . . . I don't have any anxiety that I will have a less-than-acceptable experience . . . You know it's going to be good in advance, or if something is wrong it will be taken care of.[16]

Across all the services studied in the relational benefits research, confidence benefits were the most important to customers.

Human nature is such that most consumers would prefer not to change service providers, particularly when there is a considerable investment in the relationship. The costs of switching are frequently high in terms of dollar costs of transferring business and the associated psychological and time-related costs. Most consumers (whether individuals or businesses) have many competing demands for their time and money and are continually searching for ways to balance and simplify decision making to improve the quality of their lives. When they develop confidence in—and can maintain a relationship with—a service provider, they free up time for other concerns and priorities.

Social Benefits Over time, customers develop a sense of familiarity and even a social relationship with their service providers. These ties make it less likely that they would consider switching, even if they learn about a competitor that might have better quality or a lower price. This customer's description of her hair stylist in a quote from the research previously cited illustrates the concept of social benefits:

> I like him. . . . He's really funny and always has lots of good jokes. He's kind of like a friend now. . . . It's more fun to deal with somebody that you're used to. You enjoy doing business with them.

In some long-term customer–firm relationships, a service provider may actually become part of the consumer's social support system.[17] Hairdressers, as in the example just cited, often serve as personal confidants. Less common examples include proprietors of local retail stores who become central figures in neighborhood networks, the health club or restaurant manager who knows her customers personally, the private school principal who knows an entire family and its special needs, and the river guide who befriends patrons on a long rafting trip.[18]

These types of personal relationships can develop for business-to-business customers as well as for end-consumers of services. The social support benefits resulting from these relationships are important to the consumer's quality of life (personal and/or work life) above and beyond the technical benefits of the service provided. Many times the close personal and professional relationships that develop between service providers and clients are the basis for the customer's loyalty. The flip side of this customer benefit is the risk to the firm of losing customers when a valued employee leaves the firm and takes customers with him or her.[19]

Special Treatment Benefits   Special treatment includes being given a special deal or price, getting preferential treatment, or perhaps receiving the "benefit of the doubt" from the service provider, as exemplified by the following quotes from the research:

> I think you get special treatment [when you have established a relationship]. My pediatrician allowed me to use the back door to the office so my daughter could avoid contact with other sick children. Other times I have been in a hurry and they take me right back.

> You should get the benefit of the doubt in many situations. For example, I always pay my VISA bill on time, before a service charge is assessed. One time my payment didn't quite arrive on time. When I called them, by looking at my past history, they realized that I always make an early payment. Therefore, they waived the service charge.

Interestingly, in some service industries special treatment benefits, while important, are found to be less important than the other types of benefits received.[20] Although special treatment benefits can clearly be critical for customer loyalty in some industries (think of frequent flyer benefits in the airline industry), they seem to be less important to customers in other industries (such as medical services or legal services).

Benefits for Firms

The benefits to organizations of maintaining and developing a loyal customer base are numerous. In addition to the economic benefits that a firm receives from cultivating close relationships with its customers, a variety of customer behavior benefits and human resource management benefits are also often received.

Economic Benefits   One of the most commonly cited economic benefits of customer retention is *increased purchases* over time; in many industries customers tend to spend more each year with a particular relationship partner.[21] As customers get to know a firm and are satisfied with the quality of its services relative to that of its competitors, they tend to give more of their business to the firm. Research also suggests that highly satisfied customers are *willing to pay more* for a provider's services.[22]

Another economic benefit for the firm is *lower costs*. Some estimates suggest that repeat purchases by established customers require as much as 90 percent less marketing expenditure.[23] Many start-up costs are associated with attracting new customers, including advertising and other promotion costs, the operating costs of setting up new accounts, and time costs of getting to know the customers. Sometimes these initial costs outweigh the revenue expected from the new customers in the short term, so it is to the firm's advantage to cultivate long-term relationships. In Chapter 16 we provide more specifics on the financial impact of customer retention.

Satisfied, loyal customers are likely to provide a service provider with strong word-of-mouth endorsements.

© Yellow Dog Productions/Taxi/Getty Images

Customer Behavior Benefits   The contribution that loyal customers make to a service business can go well beyond their direct financial impact on the firm.[24] Maybe the most easily recognized customer behavior benefit that a firm receives from long-term customers is the free advertising provided through *word-of-mouth communication*. When a product is complex and difficult to evaluate and when risk is involved in the decision to buy it—as is the case with many services—consumers often look to others for advice on which providers to consider. Satisfied, loyal customers are likely to provide a firm with strong word-of-mouth endorsements, both via face-to-face communication and social media. This form of advertising can be more effective than any paid advertising that the firm might use, and it has the added benefit of reducing the costs of attracting new customers.

In addition to word-of-mouth communication, a second customer behavior benefit can be *social support* provided to other customers in the form of friendships or encouragement.[25] At a physical therapy clinic, for example, a patient who is recovering from knee surgery is likely to think more highly of the clinic when fellow patients provide encouragement and emotional support to the patient during the rehabilitation process. Loyal customers may also serve as *mentors* and, because of their experience with the provider, help other customers understand the explicitly or implicitly stated rules of conduct.[26]

Human Resource Management Benefits Loyal customers may also provide a firm with human resource management benefits. First, loyal customers may, because of their experience with and knowledge of the provider, be able to contribute to the coproduction of the service by *assisting in service delivery*; often the more experienced customers can make the service employees' job easier. For example, a regular patient of a medical service provider is likely to know how the system works; she would know to bring her medication with her on a visit, to plan on paying by debit card (having previously learned that the office cannot process personal checks), and to schedule an annual mammogram without waiting for her doctor to prompt her. A second benefit is that customers who are loyal and thus familiar with a firm's processes and procedures are likely to have more realistic expectations of what the firm can achieve for them.[27] A third benefit of customer retention is *employee retention.* It is easier for a firm to retain employees when it has a stable base of satisfied customers. People like to work for companies whose customers are happy and loyal. Their jobs are more satisfying, and they are able to spend more of their time fostering relationships than scrambling to serve new customers. In turn, customers are more satisfied and become even better customers—a positive upward spiral. Because employees stay with the firm longer, service quality improves and costs of turnover are reduced, adding further to profits.

RELATIONSHIP VALUE OF CUSTOMERS

Relationship value of a customer is a concept or calculation that looks at customers from the point of view of their lifetime revenue and/or profitability contributions to a company. This type of calculation is needed when companies start thinking of building long-term relationships with their customers. Just what is the potential financial value of those long-term relationships? Or, to put it another way, what are the financial implications of *losing* a customer? In the next paragraphs we consider some of the factors that influence a customer's relationship value and show some ways it can be estimated. In Chapter 16 we provide more detail on lifetime value financial calculations.

The lifetime or relationship value of a customer is influenced by the length of an average "lifetime," the average revenues generated per relevant time period over the lifetime, sales of additional products and services over time, referrals generated by the customer over time,[28] and costs associated with serving the customer. *Lifetime value* sometimes refers to lifetime revenue stream only; when costs are considered, the more appropriate term to use is *lifetime profitability.* Exhibit 6.2 provides an example of some factors that could be considered when calculating the potential relationship value of a Quicken (personal finance) software customer.

Customers can sign up for Intuit Corporation's personal finance software, Mint, for free. Intuit also offers a bill-paying service, which is also free. However, the relationship value of a Mint customer to Intuit can be substantially more than zero. How can this be?

First, Mint has a "Ways to Save" feature that suggests new checking, savings, or brokerage accounts. When a customer signs up, Mint earns a referral fee. Also consider the additional products available to Intuit customers. Once a customer gets hooked on using the Mint software, there are several other Intuit products she might find appealing. For example, for $50–$100, depending on individual needs, Mint customers can purchase TurboTax, a software product that can automatically use previously created Mint data to help in preparation of federal and state income tax returns.

Intuit also offers QuickBooks—an accounting software product to help self-employed and small business owners keep track of their books—with prices ranging between $10 and $40 per month. Customers can also buy checks with matching envelopes and deposit slips for about $200 (for a pack of 250). Additionally, small business customers may purchase Intuit payroll services for about $30 (plus $2 per employee) per month.

If a customer uses all these services, the revenue generated in just one year would be between $730 and $1,140, and that does not include the referral fees. (Intuit provides several other services, such as more advanced accounting software and a ProAdvisor program, which might be of interest to larger customers. Intuit also offers its business customers a credit card processing service and receives a percentage of the transaction amount plus a small fee per swipe.)

After the first year, a satisfied Intuit customer is quite likely to continue to purchase annual software updates to acquire the latest product features and tax information. Over the course of five years, the revenue generated from this single customer could be between $3,650 and $5,700.

Finally, these satisfied customers are likely to refer new customers to Intuit, thus further enhancing the value of the initial customer relationship. Even one new customer referral per year can increase the relationship value potential of the first customer to several thousand dollars in just a few years!

*Figures in this example are based on 2016 prices as listed on http://www.intuit.com.

If companies knew how much it really costs to lose a customer, they would be able to accurately evaluate investments designed to retain customers. One way of documenting the dollar value of loyal customers is to estimate the increased value or profits that accrue for each additional customer who remains loyal to the company rather than defecting to the competition. Past research has found that when the retention or loyalty rate rises by 5 percentage points the total firm profits can increase from 25 percent to 95 percent.[29]

With sophisticated accounting systems to document actual costs and revenue streams over time, a firm can be quite precise in documenting the dollar value and costs of retaining customers. These systems attempt to estimate the dollar value of *all* the benefits and costs associated with a loyal customer, not just the long-term revenue stream. The value of word-of-mouth advertising, employee retention, and declining account maintenance costs can also enter into the calculation.[30]

For example, Table 6.1 shows how First Data Corporation estimates the lifetime value of an average business customer at its TeleCheck International subsidiary. TeleCheck is a large check acceptance company that provides a range of financial services for business customers related to check guarantees, verifications, and collection services. By including estimates over a five-year lifetime of increased revenues from its core product (QuickResponse), declining per-unit service costs, increasing re-venues from a new product (FastTrack), and profit from referrals, the company estimated that an annual increase in revenue of 20 percent on its base product would result in a 33 percent annual increase in operating profit over a five-year customer life.[31]

TABLE 6.1 Lifetime Value of an Average Business Customer at Telecheck International

Source: J. L. Heskett, W. E. Sasser, L. A. Schlesinger, *The Service Profit Chain: How Leading Companies Link Profit and Growth to Loyalty* (New York: The Free Press, 1997), p. 201.

	Year 0	Year 1	Year 2	Year 3	Year 4	Year 5
Revenue: [a]						
QuickResponse	—	$33,000	$39,600	$47,520	$57,024	$68,429
FastTrack	—	—	5,500	6,600	7,920	9,504
Costs:						
QuickResponse	$6,600	$24,090	$28,908	$34,690	$41,627	$49,953
FastTrack	—	—	4,152	4,983	5,980	7,175
Lifetime customer value:						
QuickResponse profit	($6,600)	$ 8,910	$10,692	$12,830	$15,397	$18,476
FastTrack profit	—	—	1,348	1,617	1,940	2,329
Reduced overhead allocation [b]	—	—	1,155	1,486	1,663	1,995
Profit from referrals [c]	—	—	1,100	1,650	3,300	6,600
Total profit	($6,600)	$ 8,910	$14,295	$17,583	$22,300	$29,400

Note: Product names and data have been disguised. As a result, profit on these products is overstated.
[a]Assuming revenue increases on both products of 20 percent per year.
[b]Declining at the rate of 15 percent per year in relation to revenue, to reflect lower costs of customer relationship associated with both customer and supplier learning curve effects.
[c]Estimated, based on assumptions concerning (1) the importance of referrals to new customers from old customers, (2) the frequency with which satisfied customers refer new customers, (3) the size of customers referred, and (4) the lifetime value calculations for new customers.

CUSTOMER PROFITABILITY SEGMENTS

Companies may want to provide all customers with excellent service, but they generally find that customers differ in their relationship value and that it may be neither practical nor profitable to meet (or to exceed) *all* customers' expectations.[32] FedEx Corporation, for example, once categorized its customers internally as "the good, the bad, and the ugly"—based on their profitability. Rather than treating all its customers the same, the company paid particular attention to enhancing their relationships with the good, moving the bad to the good, and discouraging the ugly.[33] Other companies also try to identify segments—or, more appropriately, tiers of customers—that differ in current and/or future profitability to a firm.[34] This approach goes beyond usage or volume segmentation because it tracks costs and revenues for segments of customers, thereby capturing their financial worth to companies. After identifying profitability bands, the firm offers services and service levels in line with the identified segments. Building a high-loyalty customer base of the right customers increases profits. Research suggests that it is not uncommon for a service firm to see profits increase by more than 60 percent when the retention of the right customers increases by 5 percent.[35]

Profitability Tiers—the Customer Pyramid

Although some people may view the FedEx grouping of customers into "the good, the bad, and the ugly" as negative, descriptive labels of the tiers can be very useful internally. Labels are especially valuable if they help the company keep track of which customers are profitable. Virtually all firms are aware at some level that their customers differ in profitability and that a minority of their customers account for the highest proportion of sales or profit.

One useful approach for thinking of how customers differ in terms of profitability is the four-tier system, shown in Figure 6.3, which includes the following:

1. The *platinum tier* describes the company's most profitable customers, typically those who are heavy users of the product, are not overly price sensitive, are willing to invest in and try new offerings, and are committed customers of the firm.

2. The *gold tier* differs from the platinum tier in that profitability levels are not as high, perhaps because these customers are not as loyal or they want price discounts that limit margins. They may be heavy users who minimize risk by working with multiple providers rather than just the focal company.

FIGURE 6.3
The Customer Pyramid

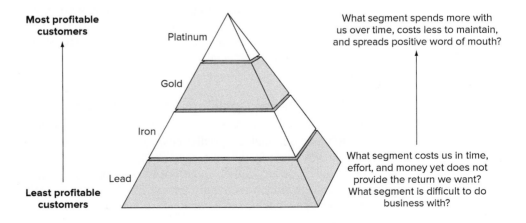

3. The *iron tier* contains essential customers who provide the volume needed to utilize the firm's capacity, but their spending levels, loyalty, and profitability are not substantial enough for special treatment.

4. The *lead tier* consists of customers who are costing the company money. They demand more attention than they are due given their spending and profitability and are sometimes problem customers—complaining about the firm to others and tying up the firm's resources.

Note that this classification is superficially reminiscent of, but very different from, traditional usage segmentation performed by airlines such as American Airlines. Two differences are obvious. First, in the customer pyramid, profitability rather than usage defines all levels. Second, the lower levels actually articulate classes of customers who require a different sort of attention. The firm must work either to change the customers' behavior—to make them more profitable through increases in revenue—or to change the firm's cost structure to make them more profitable through decreases in costs.

Once a system has been established for categorizing customers, the multiple levels can be identified, motivated, served, and expected to deliver differential levels of profit. Companies improve their opportunities for profit when they increase shares of purchases by customers who either have the greatest need for the services or show the greatest loyalty to a single provider. By strengthening relationships with the loyal customers, increasing sales with existing customers, and increasing the profitability on each sale opportunity, companies thereby increase the potential of each customer.

The Customer's View of Profitability Tiers

Whereas profitability tiers make sense from the company's point of view, customers are not always understanding, nor do they appreciate being categorized into a less desirable segment.[36] For example, at some companies (e.g., eTrade), the top clients have their own individual account representative, whom they can contact personally. The next tier of clients may be handled by representatives who each have a limited number (e.g., 100) of clients. Meanwhile, most clients are served by a website, an 800-number, or an automated voice response system. Customers are often aware of this unequal treatment, and many resist and resent it. It makes perfect sense from a business perspective, but customers are often disappointed in the level of service they receive and give firms poor marks for quality as a result. Therefore, it is important that firms communicate with customers so they understand the level of service they can expect and what they would need to do or pay to receive faster or more personalized service.

The ability to segment customers narrowly based on profitability implications also raises questions of privacy for customers. To know who is profitable and who is not, companies must collect large amounts of individualized behavioral and personal data on consumers. Many consumers today resent what they perceive as an intrusion into their lives in this way, especially when it results in differential treatment that they perceive is unfair.

Making Business Decisions Using Profitability Tiers

Prudent business managers are well aware that past customer purchase behavior, although useful in making predictions, can be misleading.[37] What a customer spends today, or has spent in the past, may not necessarily be reflective of what he or she will do (or be worth) in the future. Banks serving college students know this well—a typical college student generally has minimal financial service needs (i.e., a checking account and a debit card) and tends to not have a high level of deposits. However, within a few years that student may embark on a professional career, start a family, and/or purchase a house, and thus require several financial services and become a potentially very profitable customer to the bank. Generally speaking, a firm would like to keep its consistent big spenders and lose the erratic small spenders. But all too often a firm also has two other groups they must consider: erratic big spenders and consistent small spenders. So, in some situations where consistent cash flow is a concern, it may be helpful to a firm to have a portfolio of customers that includes steady customers, even if they have a history of being less profitable.[38]

Some service providers have actually been quite successful in targeting customers who were previously considered to be unworthy of another firm's marketing efforts.[39] Paychex, a payroll processing company, became very successful in serving small businesses that the major companies in this industry did not think were large enough to serve profitably. Similarly, Progressive Insurance became very successful in selling automobile insurance to undesirable customers—young drivers and those with poor driving records—that most of the competition did not feel had a sufficient relationship value. As these examples suggest, firms should think carefully and strategically when applying customer value calculations.

RELATIONSHIP DEVELOPMENT STRATEGIES

To this point in the chapter, we have focused on the rationale for relationship marketing, the benefits (to both firms and customers) of the development of strong exchange relationships, and an understanding of the relationship value of a customer. In this section we examine a variety of factors that influence the development of strong customer relationships, including the customer's overall evaluation of a firm's offering, bonds created with customers by the firm, and barriers that the customer faces in leaving a relationship. These factors, illustrated in Figure 6.4, provide the rationale for specific strategies that firms often use to keep their current customers.

FIGURE 6.4
Relationship Development Model

Sources: Adapted from D. D. Gremler and S. W. Brown, "Service Loyalty: Antecedents, Components, and Outcomes," in 1998 *AMA Winter Educators' Conference: Marketing Theory and Applications,* vol. 9, ed. D. Grewal and C. Pechmann (Chicago, IL: American Marketing Association), pp. 165–166.

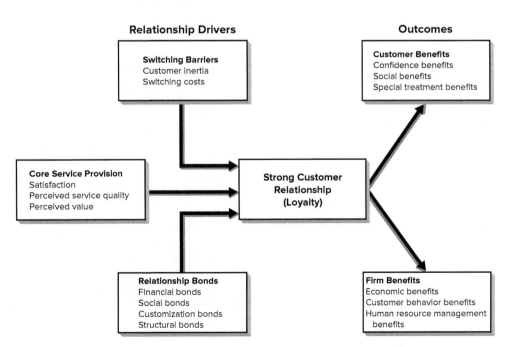

Relationship Drivers

Switching Barriers
Customer inertia
Switching costs

Core Service Provision
Satisfaction
Perceived service quality
Perceived value

Relationship Bonds
Financial bonds
Social bonds
Customization bonds
Structural bonds

Strong Customer Relationship (Loyalty)

Outcomes

Customer Benefits
Confidence benefits
Social benefits
Special treatment benefits

Firm Benefits
Economic benefits
Customer behavior benefits
Human resource management benefits

Core Service Provision

Retention strategies will have little long-term success unless the firm has a solid base of service quality and customer satisfaction on which to build. All the retention strategies that we describe in this section are built on the assumption of competitive quality and value being offered. Clearly, a firm needs to begin the relationship development process by providing a good core service delivery that, at a minimum, meets customer expectations and provides customers with perceived value;[40] it does no good to design relationship strategies for inferior services. Two earlier examples, Intuit and USAA, provide convincing support for the argument that excellence in the core service or product offered is essential to a successful relationship strategy. Both of these companies have benefited tremendously from their loyal customer base; both offer excellent quality; both use relationship strategies to enhance their success.

Switching Barriers

When considering a switch in service providers, a customer may face a number of barriers that make it difficult to leave one service provider and begin a relationship with another. Literature suggests that these *switching barriers* influence consumers' decisions to exit from relationships with firms and, therefore, help to facilitate customer retention.[41]

Customer Inertia

One reason that customers commit to developing relationships with firms is that a certain amount of effort may be required to change firms. Sometimes consumers simplistically state that "it's just not worth it" to switch providers. *Inertia* may even explain why some dissatisfied customers stay with a provider. In discussing why people remain in relationships (in general) that they no longer find satisfying, scholars suggest that people may stay because breaking the relationship would require them to restructure their life—to develop new habits of living, to refashion old friendships, and to find new ones.[42] All would require effort and a change in behavior—and people do not like to change their behavior.

To retain customers, firms might consider increasing the *perceived effort* required on the part of the customer to switch service providers.[43] If a customer believes that a great deal of effort is needed to change companies, the customer is more likely to stay put. For example, automobile repair facilities might keep a complete and detailed maintenance history of a customer's vehicle. These records remove from the customer the burden of having to remember all the services performed on the vehicle and would force the customer to expend considerable effort in providing a complete maintenance history if the vehicle were taken to a new mechanic. Conversely, if a firm is looking to attract a competitor's customers, it might automate the process for switching providers as much as possible to overcome customer inertia.

Switching Costs

In many instances, customers develop loyalty to an organization in part because of costs involved in changing to and purchasing from a different firm. These costs, both real and perceived, monetary and nonmonetary, are termed *switching costs*. Switching costs include investments of time, money, or effort—such as setup costs, learning costs, and contractual costs—that make it challenging for the customer to move to another provider.[44] To illustrate, a patient may incur *setup costs* such as paying for a complete physical when changing doctors or for new X-rays when switching dentists. *Learning costs* are those costs associated with learning the idiosyncrasies of how to use a product or service; in many situations, a customer who wishes to switch firms may need to accumulate new user skills or customer know-how. *Contractual costs* arise when the customer is required to pay a penalty to switch providers (e.g., prepayment charges for customer-initiated switching of mortgage companies or mobile telephone services), making it financially difficult, if not impossible, for the customer to initiate an early termination of the relationship.

To retain customers, firms might consider increasing their switching costs to make it difficult for customers to exit the relationship (or at least create the perception of difficulty). Indeed, many firms explicitly specify such costs in the contracts that they require their customers to sign (e.g., mobile telephone services, health clubs). To attract new customers, a service provider might consider implementing strategies designed to *lower* the switching costs of customers not currently using the provider. To reduce the setup costs involved when switching, providers could complete the paperwork required from the customer. Some banks, for example, attempt to decrease perceived switching costs in their marketing communications and others employ "switch kits" that automatically move a customer's online billing information from a competitor's bank; such kits remove the switching costs surrounding one of the biggest barriers preventing customers from changing banks—transferring online bill payments.[45]

Relationship Bonds

Switching barriers tend to serve as constraints that keep customers in relationships with firms because they "have to."[46] However, firms can engage in activities that encourage customers to remain in the relationship because they "want to"—thus creating relationship bonds. In this section we present a framework which suggests that relationship marketing can occur at different levels and that each successive level of strategy results in ties that bind the customer a little closer to the firm—and thus increase the potential for sustained competitive advantage.[47] Building on the levels of the retention strategy idea, Figure 6.5 illustrates four types of retention strategies. Recall, however, that the most successful retention strategies are built on foundations of core service excellence.

FIGURE 6.5
Levels of Relationship Strategies

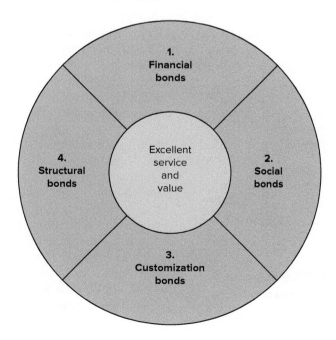

Level 1—Financial Bonds

At level 1, the customer is tied to the firm primarily through financial incentives—lower prices for greater volume purchases or lower prices for customers who have been with the firm a long time. For example, think about the airline industry and related travel service industries like hotels and car rental companies. Frequent-flyer programs provide financial incentives and rewards for travelers who bring more of their business to a particular airline. Hotels and car rental companies do the same. One reason these financial incentive programs flourish is that they are not difficult to initiate and frequently result in at least short-term profit gains. Unfortunately, financial incentives do not generally provide long-term advantages to a firm because, unless combined with another relationship strategy, they do not differentiate the firm in the long run because they are generally not difficult for competitors to imitate.

Other types of retention strategies that depend primarily on financial rewards are focused on bundling and cross-selling of services. Frequent-flyer programs provide a common example. Many airlines link their reward programs with hotel chains, auto rental, and in some cases credit card usage. By linking airline mileage points earned to usage of other firms' services, customers can enjoy even greater financial benefits in exchange for their loyalty.

Although widely and increasingly used as retention tactics, loyalty programs based on financial rewards merit caution.[48] As mentioned earlier, these programs are often easily imitated. Thus, any increased usage or loyalty from customers may be short-lived. And, these strategies are not likely to be successful unless they are structured to truly lead to repeat or increased usage rather than serving as means to attract new customers and potentially causing endless switching among competitors.

Level 2—Social Bonds

Level 2 strategies bind customers to the firm through more than financial incentives. Although price is still assumed to be important, level 2 strategies seek to build long-term relationships through social and interpersonal bonds.[49] Customers are viewed as "clients," not nameless faces, and become individuals whose needs and wants the firm seeks to understand.

Social, interpersonal bonds are common among professional service providers (lawyers, accountants, teachers) and their clients as well as among personal care providers (hairdressers, counselors, health care providers) and their clients.[50] A dentist who takes a few minutes to review her patient's file before going into the exam room is able to jog her memory on personal facts about the patient (occupation, family details, interests, dental health history). By bringing these personal details into the conversation, the dentist reveals her genuine interest in the patient as an individual and builds social bonds.

Interpersonal bonds are also common in business-to-business relationships in which customers develop relationships with salespeople and/or relationship managers working with their firms.[51] Recognizing the value of continuous relationships in building loyalty, Caterpillar Corporation credits its success to its extensive, stable distribution organization worldwide. Caterpillar is the world's largest manufacturer of mining, construction, and

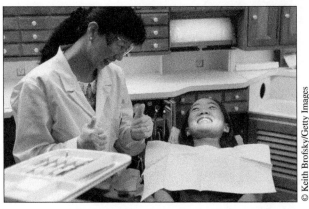

Level 2 strategies create positive social bonds between the client and service provider employees.

© Keith Brofsky/Getty Images

agricultural heavy equipment. Although its engineering and product quality are superior, the company attributes much of its success to its strong dealer network and product support services offered throughout the world. Knowledge of the local market and the close relationships with customers that Caterpillar's dealers provide is invaluable. Caterpillar's dealers tend to be prominent business leaders in their service territories who are deeply involved in community activities; the social bonds formed from these long-term relationships with customers are an important ingredient in the company's success.

Sometimes relationships are formed with the organization because of the social bonds that develop *among customers* rather than between customers and the provider of the service.[52] Such bonds are often formed in health clubs, country clubs, educational settings, and other service environments where customers interact with each other. Over time the social relationships they have with other customers are important factors that keep them from switching to another organization. Our Global Feature illustrates how Airbnb has focused its strategy on cultivating social relationships among its customers.

Social bonds alone may not tie the customer permanently to the firm, but they are much more difficult for competitors to imitate than are price incentives.[53] In the absence of strong reasons to shift to another provider, interpersonal bonds can encourage customers to stay in a relationship.[54] In combination with financial incentives, social bonding strategies may be very effective.

Level 3—Customization Bonds

Level 3 strategies involve more than social ties and financial incentives, although there are common elements of level 1 and 2 strategies encompassed within a customization strategy. A customization approach suggests customer loyalty can be encouraged through intimate knowledge of individual customers—often referred to as *customer intimacy*—and through the development of one-to-one solutions that fit the individual customer's needs.

To illustrate customization bonds, consider Pandora—an Internet-based music discovery service that helps its customers find and enjoy music that they like. Based on a huge database that has categorized about a million songs of more than 10,000 different artists based on unique attributes, it customizes its service offering to play music for customers that has the same characteristics of songs or artists they like. A customer can create up to 100 unique "stations" by identifying favorite songs or artists, and then Pandora's expert system analyzes what they like and provides suggestions based on this analysis. To do this Pandora analyzes each song using about 450 distinct musical characteristics, or "genes," by a trained music analyst. Taken together these genes capture the unique and musical identity of a song—everything from melody, harmony, and rhythm to instrumentation, orchestration, arrangement, lyrics, singing, and vocal harmony. Pandora then uses this information to customize music to each customer's unique tastes and interests. The earlier Technology Spotlight illustrates how Hilton Hotels uses technology to customize services to a large number of individual customers.

Level 4—Structural Bonds

Level 4 strategies are the most difficult to imitate; they can involve structural as well as financial, social, and customization bonds between the customer and the firm. Structural bonds are created by providing services to the client that are designed right into the service delivery system. Often, structural bonds are created by providing customized services to the client that are technology based and make the customer more productive.

CREATING RELATIONSHIPS WITH CUSTOMERS

A key part of Airbnb's global success has been its ability to develop strong relationships with its customers. To cultivate relationships with hosts and guests from so many different countries, Airbnb ensures that all parties have a sense of trust for how things operate. Hosts must agree to ensure their home is clean and that they are there on time to welcome guests and hand over the keys. In turn, guests must agree to keep the house secure and tidy, and Airbnb agrees to facilitate the whole process and act as an intermediary or source of compensation if anything goes wrong. Before being able to make (or accept) a reservation through Airbnb, each customer (whether a host, a guest, or both) must create a thorough (online) profile to cultivate a sense of accountability. Airbnb encourages customers to upload profile photos that clearly show their faces, and to write detailed descriptions that reveal themselves on a personal level. Additionally, customers can create their own Airbnb symbols, and upload a 30-second profile video to further illustrate who they are to the Airbnb community.

To further develop relationships with its customers, Airbnb includes what it calls "Verified ID" as a safety measure as part of its platform, mandating that customers verify their identity through government documents (such as a passport or driver's license), social accounts (such as Facebook or LinkedIn), and contact information before they can host or stay with another guest. Airbnb also assigns each reservation a "trust score," based on the reservation's details, payment, reviews, and the communication between guest and host. Airbnb uses such capabilities in developing customers' trust and confidence in its service.

FACILITATING SOCIAL BONDS AMONG CUSTOMERS

Airbnb attributes part of its success to understanding well that people want to deal with humans. Customers can access Airbnb's services from their laptop, tablet, or mobile phone, and many feel they are instantly connected with people they can trust. To develop strong social relationships among its customers (i.e., between hosts and guests), Airbnb cultivates interpersonal connections

Airbnb relies on the internet to connect guests with hosts.

In less than a decade, Airbnb has become a major player in the global hospitality arena. It began in 2007 when roommates Brian Chesky and Joe Gebbia could not afford the rent for their loft in San Francisco. They made their living room into a bed and breakfast, accommodating three guests on air mattresses and providing them breakfast; thus the company was originally called "Airbed & Breakfast." They eventually shortened the name to "Airbnb" and now serve two types of customers, hosts and guests, by being an intermediary that provides an online database of personal properties to rent. Airbnb *hosts* are customers who list properties—which can be single rooms, a suite of rooms, apartments, houseboats, or entire houses—on the Airbnb website with the intent of renting them. The listing is free and hosts decide how much to charge per night, per week, or per month. Travelers (or *guests*) are customers who search the Airbnb database of available properties to rent by entering details about when and where they would like to travel, considering such issues as location, room type (e.g., private room or shared room), price, size, amenities, and host language.

From Airbnb's humble beginnings the company has developed an incredible global presence. Consider the following facts: as of 2016, Airbnb had more than 60 million users, 640,000 hosts, and 2 million listings, averaged 500,000 stays per night, and was active in 57,000 cities in nearly 200 countries. Airbnb's revenue for 2015 was $900 million and as of 2016 it was valued at $25 billion; this valuation is more than the InterContinental Hotels Group or Hyatt Hotels, making Airbnb the world's largest hospitality brand.

An example of structural bonds can be seen in a business-to-business health care context with Cardinal Health. By working closely with its hospital customers, Cardinal Health has established ways to improve hospital supply ordering, delivery, and billing that have greatly enhanced its value as a supplier. Many of Cardinal Health's hospital customers use their ValueLink® service, a "just-in-time" distribution program through Airbnb groups, promotes communication between hosts and guests, provides post-reservation reviews, and hosts in-person events. This, along with the other safety precautions mentioned earlier, encourages users to not only trust each other, but to trust in Airbnb's brand as a whole.

CULTIVATING LOYALTY

Airbnb does not offer a traditional rewards program for hosts or guests that hotel chains often do. Instead it focuses on building loyalty with hosts by:

- **Identifying "Superhosts."** Just like PowerSellers on eBay or Google's Trusted Stores, hosts who continually provide a great experience for guests are rewarded with stellar reviews and subsequently become part of the Airbnb Superhost program.
- **Providing Perks.** Those who reach Superhost status receive several perks, including a badge they can put on their listings, priority support, and travel coupons. Their places are also profiled in visible spots such as "Airbnb Picks," appear high in property listings, and are featured in the company's quarterly magazine, *Pineapple.*
- **Creating Local Groups.** Airbnb has created a platform for hosts to form local groups that get together and learn from each other. One event entitled "Airbnb Open" brought 1,500 hosts together face-to-face so that Airbnb could share future plans and product news with them.

When it comes to cultivating loyalty with guests, Airbnb periodically sends out inspirational emails and it allows customers to create wish lists of where they would like to go on future trips. It has seen such efforts change people's behavior and actually get them to travel more.

FOCUSING ON THE CORE SERVICE OFFERING

Airbnb believes responsiveness is important to their customers and therefore provides 24/7 coverage in 12 languages around the world, making it highly accessible when customers need assistance. It encourages hosts to respond quickly and has a system through which guests can rate hosts on their responsiveness. To help create a great experience for customers, Airbnb has a team that monitors social media to ensure customer service issues are dealt with quickly.

To facilitate good rental experiences, Airbnb encourages each customer (both hosts and guests) to write a review for the other immediately after each stay. This review system creates a sort of quality control to hold both hosts and guests accountable. Reviews not only provide insights into hosts and guests, they also provide "insider tips" about where to visit, have dinner, or experience things that only "locals" would know about. Airbnb feels that hosts can help guests, particularly international ones, get a view into their lives and how they live—creating a more memorable experience.

In the "sharing" economy people are increasingly trusting direct connections with other people (who are often strangers to each other); however, they tend to rely on the intermediary (i.e., Airbnb) when peer trust fails. For that reason, and to provide additional confidence in their services, Airbnb has a $1 million guarantee to protect their hosts. That is, Airbnb guarantees that every booking on its platform is covered by its "Host Guarantee," which states that Airbnb will reimburse hosts for damage to their property up to $1 million—at no cost to them. Nothing is more important to Airbnb than engendering the trust of its customers. Indeed, convincing hosts to entrust complete strangers with their most valuable possessions (their homes and belongings) is the greatest obstacle in the Airbnb business model.

A SERVICE BASED ON TRUST

Airbnb sees itself as more than just a service; it believes it created a global community built on trust—and that each transaction is an experience, not merely a purchase. Airbnb has been able to compete in the hospitality industry and develop a loyal customer base internationally because it acts as the safety net that people can trust, which then gives them the confidence to host strangers or sleep in others' homes.

Sources: Katerina Jeng, "Trust in the Sharing Economy: 3 Lessons to Learn From Airbnb," https://brandfolder.com/blog/shared-story-3/building-trust/; Brett Lyons, "Customer Loyalty: Lessons from Airbnb," http://www.tlsasalestraining.com/content/customer-loyalty-lessons-airbnb; Rachel Botsman, "Where Does Loyalty Lie in the Collaborative Economy," http://rachelbotsman.com/work/where-does-loyalty-in-lie-in-the-collaborative-economy/.

that eliminates their need to maintain and manage large amounts of inventory. Using sophisticated technology and tracking systems to monitor inventory, ValueLink allows Cardinal Health to deliver ready-to-use quantities of supplies as needed—often several times a day—directly to the floors and departments where they are being used. By linking the hospital through its ValueLink service into a database

Cardinal Health's ValueLink creates structural bonds with its hospital customers.

ordering system and by providing enhanced value in the actual delivery, Cardinal Health has structurally tied itself to its more than 200 acute care hospitals in the United States. In addition to the enhanced service that ValueLink provides, Cardinal Health estimates that the system reduces the average customer's inventory costs by 30 to 60 percent per year and labor costs by 25 to 30 percent per year.[55]

RELATIONSHIP CHALLENGES

Given the many benefits of long-term customer relationships, it would seem that a company would not want to refuse to serve or terminate a relationship with any customer. Yet situations arise in which either the firm, the customer, or both want to end (or have to end) their relationship. This final section of the chapter discusses situations in which the *firm* might actually consider ending the relationship and how that might occur; in the next chapter we discuss situations in which the *customer* might decide to terminate the relationship and switch providers.

The Customer Is *Not* Always Right

The assumption that *all* customers are good customers is very compatible with the belief that "the customer is always right," an almost sacrosanct tenet of business. Yet any service worker can tell you that this statement is *not* always true, and in some cases it may be preferable for the firm to not continue its relationship with a customer. The following discussion presents a view of customer relationships suggesting that all relationships may not be beneficial and that every customer is not right all the time.

The Wrong Segment

A company cannot target its services to all customers; some segments are more appropriate than others. It would not be beneficial to either the company or the customer for a company to establish a relationship with a customer whose needs the company cannot meet. For example, a school offering a lock-step, daytime MBA program would not encourage full-time working people to apply for its program, nor would a law firm specializing in government issues want to establish a relationship with individuals seeking advice on trusts and estates. In both cases, the organization most likely would struggle to deliver services that meet the expectations of these people. Often firms give in to the temptation to make a sale by agreeing to serve a customer who would be better served by someone else.

Similarly, it would not be wise to forge relationships simultaneously with incompatible market segments. In many service businesses (such as restaurants, hotels, tour package operators, entertainment, and education), customers experience the service together and can influence each other's perceptions about value received. Thus, to maximize service to core segments, an organization may choose to turn away marginally profitable segments that would be incompatible. For example, a conference hotel may find that mixing executives in town for a serious educational program with students in town for a regional track meet is not wise. If the executives are deemed to be key long-term customers, the hotel may choose to pass up the sports group in the interest of retaining the executives.

Not Profitable in the Long Term

In the absence of ethical or legal mandates, organizations will prefer *not* to have long-term relationships with unprofitable customers. Some segments of customers will not be profitable for the company even if their needs can be met by the services offered. Some examples of this situation are when there are not enough customers in the segment to make it profitable to serve, when the segment cannot afford to pay the cost of the service, and when the projected revenue flows from the segment would not cover the costs incurred to originate and maintain their business.

At the individual customer level, it may not be profitable for a firm to engage in a relationship with a customer who has bad credit or who is a poor risk for some other reason. Retailers, banks, mortgage companies, and credit card companies routinely refuse to do business with individuals whose credit histories are unreliable. Although the short-term sale may be beneficial, the long-term risk of nonpayment makes the relationship unwise from the company's point of view. Similarly, some car rental companies check into the driving records of customers and reject bad-risk drivers.[56] This practice, while controversial, is logical from the car rental companies' point of view because they can cut back on insurance costs and accident claims (thus reducing rental costs for good drivers) by not doing business with accident-prone drivers.

Beyond the monetary costs associated with serving the wrong customers, there can be substantial time investments in some customers that, if actually computed, would make them unprofitable for the organization. Everyone has had the experience of waiting in a bank, a retail store, or even an educational setting while a particularly demanding customer seems to use more than his share of the service provider's time. The dollar value of the time spent with a specific customer is typically not computed or calculated into the price of the service.

In a business-to-business relationship, the variability in time commitment to customers is even more apparent. Some customers may use considerable resources of a service provider through inordinate numbers of phone calls, excessive requests for information, and other time-consuming activities. In the legal profession, clients are billed for every hour of the firm's time that they use because time is essentially the only resource the firm has. Yet in other service businesses, all clients essentially pay the same regardless of the time demands they place on the organization.

Difficult Customers

Managers have repeated the phrase "the customer is always right" so often that you would expect it to be accepted by every employee in every service organization. So why isn't it? Perhaps because it simply is not true. The customer is not always right. No matter how frequently it is said, repeating that mantra does not make it become reality, and service employees know it.

In many situations, firms have service encounters that fail because of *dysfunctional customers*. Dysfunctional customer behavior consists of the actions by customers who intentionally, or perhaps unintentionally, act in a manner that in some way disrupts otherwise functional service encounters.[57] Such customers have been described as "customers from hell," "problem customers," or "jay customers." One of us was awakened during a hotel stay at 4:00 a.m. by drunk customers who were arguing with each

Some customers may be difficult, if not impossible, to serve.

© Ocean/Corbis RF

Strategy Insight "The Customer Is Always Right": Rethinking an Old Tenet

The old tenet "the customer is always right" has operated as the basic rule in business for so long that for many firms it has become entrenched as an "absolute truth." The practical reality, however, is that sometimes the customer is wrong. When taken to the extreme, the issue for the firm becomes what to do about it. Service managers understand that there are situations when employees should be fired. In some situations, this strategy may need to be applied to customers, too.

SPRINT/NEXTEL FIRES 1,000 CUSTOMERS

On June 29, 2007, Sprint/Nextel sent a letter to about 1,000 of its 53 million customers telling them, in effect, they had been fired from the company. In doing so Sprint was attempting to rid itself of customers who frequented its customer service lines by informing them that it was canceling their service at the end of the next month. In these letters the company stated: "While we have worked to resolve your issues and questions to the best of our ability, the number of inquiries you have made to us during this time has led us to determine that we are unable to meet your current wireless needs."

The customers were told their service agreements were being terminated, they would not owe anything on their final bill, and the company would waive its standard early termination fees. They also were told to switch to another wireless provider by July 30 if they wanted to keep their phone number.

A disgruntled Spint/Nextel customer.

© Mark Lennihan/AP Photo

These 1,000 customers had been calling Sprint's customer service an average of 25 times a month, which is 40 times more frequently than a typical customer. Sprint determined these customers were not generating enough revenue to make up for the high cost of serving them. The company conducted an internal review, lasting more than six months, to determine what types of problems these customers had and what information they were seeking when they contacted the customer service department. The review found that these customers often were calling about the same problems over and over after Sprint officials felt they had resolved the issue. Additionally, some callers were repeatedly asking for information about other customers' accounts, which customer service representatives are not allowed to divulge. Sprint indicated that the amount of time being spent to resolve the same issues again and again was affecting their ability to serve other customers.

The Results

Initially Sprint's move made headlines in the business press, stimulated negative word of mouth from some portion of these 1,000 customers, and may have cost them some new customers in the short run. But it also improved the customer experience for other customers calling customer service. Indeed, customer service improved to the point that just three years later Sprint was named one of the top 40 Customer Service Champions by J. D. Power and Associates.

ZANE'S CYCLES TELLS CUSTOMER: "GET OUT . . . AND TELL ALL YOUR FRIENDS"

A *Business Horizons* article tells the following story of a bicycle store well known for its dedication to customer service—Zane's Cycles in Branford, Connecticut (for more insights into Zane's Cycles, see our Chapter 4 opener):

> A father was picking up a repaired bicycle for his daughter, who, without telling him, had approved the recommended replacement of both tires (a $40 service). Although the employee patiently and repeatedly explained that the purchase was approved and offered to further verify it, the customer made accusatory remarks

and yelled at her angrily, saying at one point, "Either you think I'm stupid or you're stupid. You're trying to rip me off." At that point, Chris Zane, the store's owner, walked up to the customer and said, "I'm Chris Zane, get out of my store, and tell all your friends!" After the customer wordlessly slapped $40 on the counter and stormed out, the besieged employee looked at Zane and asked "'. . . and tell all your friends'?"

Zane explained to her and other employees who had gravitated to the front of the store that he wanted it to be clear that he valued his employee infinitely more than a rude, belligerent customer. "I also explained that this was the first time I had ever thrown a customer out of the store and that I would not tolerate my employees being mistreated by anyone . . . I believe that my employees need to know that I respect them and expect them to respect our customers. Simply, if I am willing to fire an employee for mistreating a customer (and I have) then I must also be willing to fire a customer for mistreating an employee."

The Results
After returning home and thinking about the service encounter, the fired customer phoned the owner to apologize three hours later. He explained that he had argued with his wife prior to visiting the store and was therefore already in a poor mood. Once the customer returned home and verified the accuracy of the store employee's explanation, he realized he had been unreasonable. The customer asked if he could be allowed to shop in the store again. He also commented that he respected the owner for supporting his employee even if it might mean losing a customer. Mr. Zane thanked him for the call, welcomed him back to the store, and indicated that the apology would be conveyed to the employee.

EVENTS PLANNER TELLS MAJOR CLIENT: "NEVER AGAIN"
Capitol Services Inc. (CSI)—an event planning company in Washington, DC—spent considerable time and money attempting to secure a major automobile company's potentially very lucrative business. In the midst of the first-ever event for the client at a museum in Washington,

DC, the person overseeing the event (who was not an employee of the company but working for a third party) became very demanding, degrading, and disrespectful to the CSI staff. Nearly everything the firm did was, in her opinion, not good enough. The entire team, who was in the midst of delivering an event exactly as promised, was being micromanaged. CSI employees felt they were being abused, and for no good reason. David Hainline, company president, approached the client representative and said that CSI would finish the event but would never conduct business again with her—knowing full well this decision might result in the loss of a client with a very high potential relationship value.

The Results
The event was delivered as promised, but the belligerent staff member was not happy. After the event was completed, she demanded that CSI reduce the amount owed for their services—so CSI reduced the amount by $60,000. Months later Hainline had a meeting with the automobile company and began the meeting with an explanation of the situation that had occurred at the Smithsonian. The company understood, and agreed to use CSI to organize future events for them in Washington, DC. And CSI employees felt valued and supported by the management team.

ENDING A CUSTOMER RELATIONSHIP MAY BE THE RIGHT STRATEGIC DECISION
Service providers are not obligated to serve any and all customers, no matter how much revenue they might generate. Although service marketing strategies intended to develop relationships with customers receive much attention—and rightly so—from managers, occasionally selecting a strategy that results in ending a relationship with a customer may be the most prudent approach to take.

Sources: S. Srivastava, "Sprint Drops Clients over Excessive Inquiries," *The Wall Street Journal*, July 7, 2007, p. A3; L. L. Berry and K. Seiders, "Serving Unfair Customers," *Business Horizons* 51 (January/February 2008), pp. 29–37; D. Hainline, President, Capitol Services Inc., Washington, DC, personal interview, August 15, 2007.

other in a room above; management eventually called the police and asked them to escort the customers off the property. An Enterprise Rent-A-Car customer demanded that she not be charged for any of the two weeks that she had a car because, near the end of the rental period, she found a small stain in the back seat.[58] Such behavior is considered dysfunctional from the perspective of the service provider and perhaps fellow customers.

Dysfunctional customer behavior can affect employees, other customers, and the organization. Research suggests that exposure to dysfunctional customer behavior can have psychological, emotional, behavioral, and physical effects on employees.[59] For example, customer-contact employees who are exposed to rude, threatening, obstructive, aggressive, or disruptive behavior by customers often have their mood, motivation, or morale negatively affected. Such customers are difficult to work with and often create stress for employees.[60] (See photo on page 167 for one example.) Dysfunctional customers can also have an impact on other customers: such behavior can spoil the service experience for other customers, and the dysfunctional customer behavior may become contagious for other customers witnessing it. Finally, dysfunctional customer behavior can create both direct costs and indirect costs for the organization. Direct costs of such behavior can include the expense of restoring damaged property, increased insurance premiums, property loss by theft, costs incurred in compensating customers affected by the dysfunctional behavior of others, and costs incurred through illegitimate claims by dysfunctional customers. Additionally, indirect costs might include increased workloads for staff required to deal with dysfunctional behavior as well as increased costs for attracting and retaining appropriate personnel and, perhaps, for absenteeism payments.

Ending Business Relationships

As suggested in the previous section, firms may identify some customers who are not in their targeted segment, who are not profitable in the long run, or who are difficult to work with or dysfunctional. A company may *not* want to continue in a relationship with every customer. For the effective management of service relationships, managers should not only know how to establish a relationship but also how to end one. However, gracefully exiting a relationship may not be easy. Customers may end up feeling disappointed, confused, or hurt if a firm attempts to terminate the relationship. Our Strategy Insight illustrates how three firms chose to end relationships with their customers.

Relationship Endings

Relationships end in different ways—depending on the type of relationship in place.[61] In some situations, a relationship is established for a certain purpose and/or time period and then dissolves when it has served its purpose or the time frame has elapsed. For example, a house painting service may be engaged with the customer for four days while painting the house exterior, but both parties understand that the end of the relationship is predetermined—the end occurs when the house has been painted and the customer has paid for the service. Sometimes a relationship has a natural ending.[62] Piano lessons for children, for example, often cease as the child gets older and develops interests in other musical areas (such as singing or playing the saxophone); in such situations, the need for the relationship has diminished or become obsolete. In other situations, an event may occur that forces the relationship to end; a provider who relocates to the other side of town may force some customers to select a different company. Or an ending may occur because the customer is not fulfilling his obligations. For example, a bank may choose to end the relationship with a customer who regularly has insufficient funds in her checking account. Whatever the reason for ending the relationship, firms should clearly communicate their reasons for wanting (or needing) to terminate it, so that customers understand what is occurring and why.[63]

Should Firms Fire Their Customers?

A logical conclusion to be drawn from the discussion of the challenges firms face in customer relationships is that perhaps firms should seek to get rid of those customers who are not right for the company. Many companies make these types of decisions based on the belief that troublesome customers are usually less profitable and less loyal and that it may be counterproductive to retain their business.[64] Another reason for "firing" a customer is the negative effect that these customers can have on employee quality of life and morale.

Companies today are making it easier to justify firing customers. Service providers such as Uber, Lyft, and Airbnb, for example, allow drivers and hosts to review and rate customers. If a customer receives low scores or has several complaints from enough people, that customer may not be chosen to receive services or, even more, no longer be allowed to use the company's website to schedule services. Similarly, the online restaurant reservation company OpenTable offers a feature to member restaurants where they can make (internal) notes about guests—such as if they frequently send their food back. The website also keeps track of how many reservations a customer misses; those who miss four or more reservations within a year are banned from the site.[65]

Although it may sound like a good idea, firing customers is not that simple and needs to be done in a way that avoids negative publicity or negative word of mouth. Sometimes raising prices or charging for services that previously had been given away for free can move unprofitable customers out of the company. Helping a client find a new provider who can better meet its needs is another way to gracefully exit a nonproductive relationship. If the customer has become too demanding, the relationship may be salvaged by negotiating expectations or finding more efficient ways to serve the client. If not, both parties may need to find an agreeable way to end the relationship.

Summary

In this chapter we focused on the rationale for, benefits of, and strategies for developing long-term relationships with customers. It should be obvious by now that organizations that focus only on acquiring new customers may well fail to understand their current customers; thus, while a company may be bringing customers in through the front door, equal or greater numbers may be exiting. Estimates of lifetime relationship value accentuate the importance of retaining current customers.

The particular strategy that an organization uses to retain its current customers can and should be customized to fit the industry, the culture, and the customer needs of the organization. However, in general, customer relationships are driven by a variety of factors that influence the development of strong customer relationships, including (1) the customer's overall evaluation of the quality of a firm's core service offering, (2) the switching barriers that the customer faces in leaving a relationship, and (3) the relationship bonds the firm has developed with that customer. By developing strong relationships with customers and by focusing on factors that influence customer relationships, the organization will accurately understand customer expectations over time and consequently will narrow service quality gap 1.

The chapter concluded with a discussion of the challenges that firms face in developing relationships with customers. Although long-term customer relationships are critical and can be very profitable, firms should not attempt to build relationships with just any customer. In other words, "the customer is not always right." Indeed, in some situations it may be best for firms to discontinue relationships with some customers—for the sake of the customer, the firm, or both.

Discussion Questions

1. Discuss how relationship marketing or retention marketing is different from the traditional emphasis in marketing.

2. Describe how a firm's relationships with customers may evolve over time. For each level of relationship discussed in the chapter, identify a firm with which you have that level of relationship, and discuss how its marketing efforts differ from those of other firms.

3. Think about a service organization that retains you as a loyal customer. Why are you loyal to this provider? What are the benefits to you of staying loyal and not switching to another provider? What would it take for you to switch?

4. With regard to the same service organization, what are the benefits to the organization of keeping you as a customer? Calculate your "lifetime value" to the organization.

5. Describe the logic behind "customer profitability segmentation" from the company's point of view. Also discuss what customers may think of the practice.

6. Describe the various switching barriers discussed in the text. What switching barriers might you face in switching banks? Cellphone service providers? Universities?

7. Describe the four levels of retention strategies, and give examples of each type. Again, think of a service organization to which you are loyal. Can you describe the reason(s) you are loyal in terms of the different levels? In other words, what ties you to the organization?

8. Have you ever worked as a frontline service employee? Can you remember having to deal with difficult or "problem" customers? Discuss how you handled such situations. As a manager of frontline employees, how would you help your employees deal with difficult customers?

Exercises

1. Interview the manager of a local service organization. Discuss with the manager the target market(s) for the service. Estimate the lifetime value of a customer in one or more of the target segments. To do this estimate, you will need to get as much information from the manager as you can. If the manager cannot answer all of your questions, make some assumptions.

2. In small groups in class, debate the question "Is the customer always right?" In other words, are there times when the customer may be the wrong customer for the organization?

3. Choose a specific company context (your class project company, the company you work for, or a company in an industry you are familiar with). Calculate the lifetime value of a customer for this company. You will need to make assumptions to do this calculation, so make your assumptions clear. Using ideas and concepts from this chapter, describe a relationship marketing strategy to increase the number of lifetime customers for this firm.

Notes

1. USAA is featured in the following two books, and material in this section is drawn from them: L. L. Berry, *Discovering the Soul of Service* (New York: The Free Press, 1999); F. F. Reichheld, *Loyalty Rules!* (Boston: Harvard Business School Press, 2001).

27. P. J. Danaher, D. M. Conroy, and J. R. McColl-Kennedy, "Who Wants a Relationship? Conditions When Consumers Expect a Relationship with Their Service Provider," *Journal of Service Research* 11 (August 2008), pp. 43–62.

28. I. Garnefeld, A. Eggert, S. V. Helm, and S. S. Tax, "Growing Existing Customers' Revenue Streams Through Customer Referral Programs," *Journal of Marketing* 77 (July 2014), pp. 17–32.

29. F. F. Reichheld and P. Schefter, "E-Loyalty: Your Secret Weapon on the Web," *Harvard Business Review* 78 (July/August 2000), pp. 105–113.

30. Additional frameworks for calculating lifetime customer value that include a variety of other variables can be found in W. J. Reinartz and V. Kumar, "The Impact of Customer Relationship Characteristics on Profitable Lifetime Duration," *Journal of Marketing* 67 (January 2003), pp. 77–99; Dhar and Glazer, "Hedging Customers"; H. K. Stahl, K. Matzler, and H. H. Hinterhuber, "Linking Customer Lifetime Value with Shareholder Value," *Industrial Marketing Management* 32 (2003), pp. 267–279.

31. This example is cited in J. L. Heskett, W. E. Sasser Jr., and L. A. Schlesinger, *The Service Profit Chain* (New York: The Free Press, 1997), pp. 200–201.

32. For more on customer profitability segments and related strategies, see V. A. Zeithaml, R. T. Rust, and K. N. Lemon, "The Customer Pyramid: Creating and Serving Profitable Customers," *California Management Review* 43 (Summer 2001), pp. 118–142.

33. R. Brooks, "Alienating Customers Isn't Always a Bad Idea, Many Firms Discover," *The Wall Street Journal,* January 7, 1999, p. A1.

34. C. Homburg, M. Droll, and D. Totzek, "Customer Prioritization: Does It Pay Off, and How Should It Be Implemented?" *Journal of Marketing* 72 (September 2008), pp. 110–130.

35. F. Reichheld, "Loyalty-Based Management," *Harvard Business Review* 71 (March–April 1993), pp. 64–74.

36. D. Brady, "Why Service Stinks," *BusinessWeek,* October 23, 2000, pp. 118–128.

37. Dhar and Glazer, "Hedging Customers."

38. C. O. Tarsi, R. N. Bolton, M. D. Hutt, and B. A. Walker, "Balancing Risk and Return in a Customer Portfolio," *Journal of Marketing* 75 (May 2011), pp. 1–17.

39. D. Rosenblum, D. Tomlinson, and L. Scott, "Bottom-Feeding for Blockbuster Businesses," *Harvard Business Review* 81 (March 2003), pp. 52–59.

40. M. D. Johnson, A. Herrman, and F. Huber, "The Evolution of Loyalty Intentions," *Journal of Marketing* 70 (April 2006), pp. 122–132.

41. See T. A. Burnham, J. K. Frels, and V. Mahajan, "Consumer Switching Costs: A Typology, Antecedents, and Consequences," *Journal of the Academy of Marketing Science* 32 (Spring 2003), pp. 109–126; F. Selnes, "An Examination of the Effect of Product Performance on Brand Reputation, Satisfaction, and Loyalty," *European Journal of Marketing* 27 (2003), 19–35; M. Colgate, V. T.-U. Tong, C. K.-C. Lee, and J. U. Farley, "Back from the Brink: Why Customers Stay," *Journal of Service Research* 9 (February 2007), pp. 211–228.

42. L. White and V. Yanamandram, "Why Customers Stay: Reasons and Consequences of Inertia in Financial Services," *Managing Service Quality* 14 (2004), pp. 183–194. See also Y. F. Kuo, T. L. Hu, and S. C. Yang, "Effects of Inertia and Satisfaction in Female Online Shoppers on Repeat-Purchase Intention: The Mod-

erating Roles of Word-of-Mouth and Alternative Attraction," *Managing Service Quality* 23 (2012), pp. 168–187.

43. Colgate, Tong, Lee, and Farley, "Back from the Brink."

44. See J. P. Guiltinan, "A Classification of Switching Costs with Implications for Relationship Marketing," in *Marketing Theory and Practice,* ed. T. L. Childers, R. P. Bagozzi, and J. P. Peter (Chicago: American Marketing Association, 1989), pp. 216–220; P. G. Patterson and T. Smith, "A Cross-Cultural Study of Switching Barriers and Propensity to Stay with Service Providers," *Journal of Retailing* 79 (Summer 2003), pp. 107–120; M. A. Jones, K. E. Reynolds, D. L. Mothersbaugh, and S. E. Beatty, "The Positive and Negative Effects of Switching Costs on Relational Outcomes," *Journal of Service Research* 9 (May 2007), pp. 335–355.

45. See D. Pick, " 'Switching Is Easy'—Service Firm Communications to Encourage Customer Switching," *Journal of Retailing and Consumer Services* 21 (2014), pp. 502–509; and J. J. Kim, "Banks Push Harder to Get You to Switch—Services Aim to Ease Hassle of Moving Your Accounts," *The Wall Street Journal,* October 12, 2006, p. D1.

46. See Bendapudi and Berry, "Customers' Motivations for Maintaining Relationships with Service Providers"; H. S. Bansal, P. G. Irving, and S. F. Taylor, "A Three-Component Model of Customer Commitment to Service Providers," *Journal of the Academy of Marketing Science* 32 (Summer 2004), pp. 234–250.

47. Figure 6.6 and the discussion of the four levels of relationship strategies is based on Berry and Parasuraman, *Marketing Services,* pp. 136–142.

48. For more information on cautions to be considered in implementing rewards strategies, see H. T. Keh and Y. H. Lee, "Do Reward Programs Build Loyalty for Services? The Moderating Effect of Satisfaction on Type and Timing of Rewards," *Journal of Retailing* 82 (June 2006), pp. 127–136; L. Meyer-Waarden and C. Benavent, "Rewards That Reward," *The Wall Street Journal,* September 17, 2008, p. R5; J. D. Hansen, G. D. Deitz, and R. M. Morgan, "Taxonomy of Service-based Loyalty Program Members," *Journal of Services Marketing* 24 (2010), pp. 271–282; R. Lacey, "Relationship Marketing Tools: Understanding the Value of Loyalty Programs," in *Handbook on Research in Relationship Marketing,* ed. R. M. Morgan, J. Turner Parish, and G. Deitz (Cheltenham, UK: Edward Elgar Publishing, 2015), pp. 104–122.

49. C. K. Yim, D. K. Tse, and K. W. Chan, "Strengthening Customer Loyalty through Intimacy and Passion: Roles of Customer-Firm Affection and Customer-Staff Relationships in Services," *Journal of Marketing Research* 45 (December 2008), pp. 741–756.

50. Colgate, Tong, Lee, and Farley, "Back from the Brink."

51. Bendapudi and Leone, "How to Lose Your Star Performer Without Losing Customers"; E. Anderson and S. D. Jap, "The Dark Side of Close Relationships," *Sloan Management Review* 46 (Spring 2005), pp. 75–82; R. W. Palmatier, R. P. Dant, D. Grewal, and K. R. Evans, "Factors Influencing the Effectiveness of Relationship Marketing: A Meta-Analysis," *Journal of Marketing* 70 (October 2006), pp. 136–153. However, some scholars have recently questioned the use of the relationship metaphor in business-to-business contexts; see L. A. Bettencourt, C. P. Blocker, M. B. Houston, and D. J. Flint, "Rethinking Customer Relationships," *Business Horizons* 58 (2015), pp. 99–108; C. P. Blocker, M. B. Houston, and D. J. Flint, "Unpacking What a 'Relationship' Means to Commercial Buyers: How the Relationship Metaphor Creates Tension and Obscures Experience," *Journal of Consumer Research* 38 (February 2012), pp. 886–908.

52. Rosenbaum and Massiah, "When Customers Receive Support from Other Customers."

53. W. Ulaga and A. Eggert, "Value-Based Differentiation in Business Relationships: Gaining and Sustaining Key Supplier Status," *Journal of Marketing* 70 (January 2006), pp. 119–136.

54. D. D. Gremler and S. W. Brown, "Service Loyalty: Its Nature, Importance, and Implications," in *Advancing Service Quality: A Global Perspective,* ed. B. Edvardsson, S. W. Brown, R. Johnston, and E. E. Scheuing (Jamaica, NY: International Service Quality Association, 1996), pp. 171–180; H. Hansen, K. Sandvik, and F. Selnes, "Direct and Indirect Effects of Commitment to a Service Employee on the Intention to Stay," *Journal of Service Research* 5 (May 2003), pp. 356–368.

55. A. Andersen, *Best Practices: Building Your Business with Customer-Focused Solutions* (New York: Simon & Schuster, 1998), pp. 125–127; http://www.cardinalhealth.com/en/services/acute/logistics-solutions-acute/distribution/valuelink-services.html, accessed July 6, 2016.

56. S. Stellin, "Avoiding Surprises at the Car Rental Counter," *The New York Times*, June 4, 2006, p. TR6.

57. See L. C. Harris and K. L. Reynolds, "The Consequences of Dysfunctional Customer Behavior," *Journal of Service Research* 6 (November 2003), p. 145, for cites; see also, A. A. Grandey, D. N. Dickter, and H. P. Sin, "The Customer Is *Not* Always Right: Customer Aggression and Emotion Regulation of Service Employees," *Journal of Organizational Behavior* 25 (2004), pp. 397–418. Also see R. Fisk, S. Grove, L. C. Harris, D. A. Keeffe, K. L. Daunt, R. Russell-Bennett, and J. Wirtz, "Customers Behaving Badly: A State of the Art Review, Research Agenda, and Implications for Practitioners," *Journal of Services Marketing* 24 (2010), pp. 417–429.

58. K. Ohnezeit, recruiting supervisor for Enterprise Rent-A-Car, personal communication, February 12, 2004.

59. See Harris and Reynolds, "The Consequences of Dysfunctional Customer Behavior."

60. L. L. Berry and K. Seiders, "Serving Unfair Customers," *Business Horizons* 51 (January/February 2008), pp. 29–37.

61. For a detailed discussion on relationship ending, see A. Halinen and J. Tähtinen, "A Process Theory of Relationship Ending," *International Journal of Service Industry Management* 13 (2002), pp. 163–180.

62. H. Åkerlund, "Fading Customer Relationships in Professional Services," *Managing Service Quality* 15 (2005), pp. 156–71.

63. M. Haenlein and A. M. Kaplan, "Unprofitable Customers and Their Management," *Business Horizons* 52 (2009), pp. 89-97; M. Haenlein, A. M. Kaplan, and D. Schoder, "Valuing the Real Option of Abandoning Unprofitable Customers When Calculating Customer Lifetime Value," *Journal of Marketing* 70 (July 2006), pp. 5–20.

64. For additional thoughts on firing customers, see J. Shin, K. Sudhir, and D. H. Yoon, "When to 'Fire' Customers: Customer Cost-Based Pricing," *Management Science* 58 (May 2012), pp. 932–947.

65. J. Weed, "For Uber, Airbnb and Other Companies, Customer Ratings Go Both Ways, @ *New York Times,* December 1, 2014, www.nytimes.com/2014/12/02/business/for-uber-airbnb-and-other-companies-customer-ratings-go-both-ways.html.

Chapter **Seven**

Service Recovery

This chapter's objectives are to

1. Illustrate the importance of recovery from service failures in keeping customers and building loyalty.
2. Discuss the nature of customer complaints and why people do and do not complain.
3. Provide evidence of what customers expect and the kind of responses they want when they do complain.
4. Present strategies for effective service recovery, including ways to "fix the customer" after a service failure and to "fix the problem."
5. Discuss service guarantees—what they are, the benefits of guarantees, and when to use them—as a type of service recovery strategy.

JetBlue and the Valentine's Day Ice Storm at JFK

When JetBlue Airways began flying daily in 2000 from New York City to Fort Lauderdale, Florida, and Buffalo, New York, it promised fares that would be as much as 65 percent lower than their competitors'. At that time JetBlue had 300 employees and provided its customers with comforts like assigned seating, leather upholstery, and satellite TV on individual screens in every seat. The low fares were an immediate hit with passengers, as they found friendly, snappily dressed flight attendants who served animal crackers, Oreo cookies, and blue potato chips on flights very appealing. Indeed, by early 2007 JetBlue had 9,300 employees and 125 jetliners, operating about 575 daily flights to 52 destinations in the United States and the Caribbean. Customers had come to love the airline. It had won many awards for its service and had regularly been ranked near the top of airline satisfaction ratings by J.D. Power and Associates, among others.

JetBlue's reputation for excellent service was challenged on Valentine's Day, February 14, 2007, when a severe storm dumped two inches of ice at New York's JFK Airport. Although the weather created headaches for just about all air carriers in the eastern United States that Wednesday, it was JetBlue who received the most attention. Why? The airline that had developed a reputation for its customer-friendly approach had suffered a startling breakdown. More than 1,000 flights were canceled over the next six days. Passengers were stuck on planes for up to nine hours. Delays averaged nearly 4 hours. It took nearly a week for JetBlue to return operations to normal.

What actually happened? Bad weather and poor management decisions led to full gates and a substantial queue of planes waiting for gates. JetBlue's initial responses to the

© Richard Drew/AP Photo

Some JetBlue customers spent as much as nine hours stuck on planes and in terminals.

weather disruptions on Valentine's Day were not good. While the storm was occurring, and even immediately afterward, JetBlue failed to cancel flights, leaving some passengers stranded on the tarmac for as long as 10 hours. The policy of initially postponing, but not canceling, flights resulted in snowballing cancellations for nearly a week, with long lines at the airport as customers attempted to get on flights.

Unfortunately for JetBlue, this happened in the media capital of the world—thus, its service failures received major attention in the press. Perhaps the most devastating blow of all was delivered by *BusinessWeek*; the magazine described the situation as "one extraordinary stumble" on its March 5 cover touting its first-ever rating of the best firms in customer service. Why did JetBlue receive such attention when airlines such as Delta and American had had similar problems? Customers had come to expect more from JetBlue than from other airlines.

Clearly this service failure received more attention in the press than most failures that customers experience. Customers obviously would prefer to not have experienced such a failure, but even more important in many situations is how a firm responds to such a situation. So how did JetBlue ultimately respond to this service failure? Although their initial response when the ice first hit was not ideal, JetBlue followed many of the suggestions for service recovery we discuss in this chapter by being humble, apologizing publicly and often, and acting quickly. They ultimately created a Customer's Bill of Rights to make explicit promises to their customers to eliminate a great deal of uncertainty and create a strong signal that JetBlue was committed to keeping its promises.

The preceding two chapters have given you a foundation for understanding customers' service expectations through research as well as through knowing them as individuals and developing strong relationships with them. These strategies, matched with effective service design, delivery, and communication—treated in other parts of the text—form the foundations for service success. But in all service contexts—whether customer service, consumer services, or business-to-business services—service failure is inevitable. Failure is inevitable even for the best of firms with the best of intentions, even for those with world-class service systems.

To fully understand and retain their customers, firms must know what customers expect when service failures occur and must implement effective strategies for service recovery. Our chapter-opening vignette illustrates the problems a firm can face when it has a service failure.

THE IMPACT OF SERVICE FAILURE AND RECOVERY

A *service failure* is generally described as service performance that falls below a customer's expectations in such a way that leads to customer dissatisfaction. *Service recovery* refers to the actions taken by an organization in response to a service failure to improve the situation for the customer. Failures occur for all kinds of reasons—the

FIGURE 7.1
Complaining
Customers: The Tip
of the Iceberg

Source: Data from TARP
Worldwide Inc., 2007.

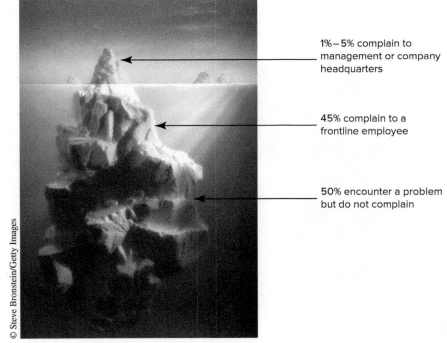

1%–5% complain to
management or company
headquarters

45% complain to a
frontline employee

50% encounter a problem
but do not complain

© Steve Bronstein/Getty Images

service may be unavailable when promised, it may be delivered late or too slowly, the outcome may be incorrect or poorly executed, or employees may be rude or uncaring.[1] Although these types of failures bring about negative feelings from customers, research suggests that only a portion (45 percent) of customers who experience a problem with service delivery actually complain to the employees serving them, and a very small number (1–5 percent) complain to management or the company headquarters.[2] This phenomenon, commonly referred to as the "tip of the iceberg" and demonstrated in Figure 7.1, suggests every complaint that management actually receives represents 20–100 other customers who experienced the problem and did not complain. Service failures left unfixed can result in customers leaving, telling other customers about their negative experiences, and even challenging the organization through consumer rights organizations or legal channels.

Service Recovery Effects

Research has shown that resolving customer problems effectively has a strong impact on customer satisfaction, loyalty, word-of-mouth communication, and bottom-line performance.[3] That is, customers who experience service failures, but who are ultimately satisfied based on recovery efforts by the firm, will be more loyal than those whose problems are not resolved. That loyalty translates into profitability, as you learned in Chapter 6. Data from a recent Customer Rage Study verify this relationship, as shown in Figure 7.2.[4] Among customers from service businesses who complain and have their problems satisfactorily resolved, 41 percent indicate they would definitely purchase again from the same provider—illustrating the power of good service recovery. Occasionally, as described in Exhibit 7.1, firms do so well in their

FIGURE 7.2
Unhappy Customers' Repurchase Intentions

Source: 2015 Customer Rage Study, conducted by Customer Care Measurement and Consulting and the Center for Services Leadership at Arizona State University.

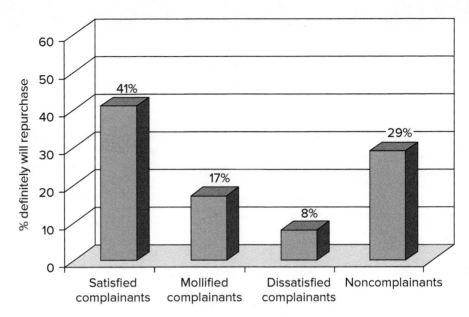

service recovery that customers end up more satisfied than they would have been if the firm had never failed in the first place—a situation referred to as the "service recovery paradox."

A well-designed service recovery strategy also provides information that can be used to improve service as part of a continuous improvement effort. By making adjustments to service processes, systems, and outcomes based on previous service recovery experiences, companies increase the likelihood of "doing it right the first time." In turn, this reduces costs of failures and increases initial customer satisfaction.

Unfortunately, many firms do not employ effective recovery strategies. Studies suggest as much as 63 percent of customers who experience a serious problem receive no response from the firm.[5] There are tremendous downsides to having no service recovery or ineffective service recovery strategies. First, the Customer Rage Study mentioned earlier and other research have found that customers who are dissatisfied with the recovery process after making a complaint are far less likely to repurchase than those who do not complain—suggesting the power of poor service recovery![6] Second, poor recovery following a bad service experience creates, in effect, two poor experiences (often referred to as a "double deviation") and can lead to customers who are so dissatisfied that they actively pursue opportunities to openly criticize the company.[7] When customers experience a service failure, they talk about it to others, no matter what the outcome. Research has found that customers who are satisfied with a firm's recovery efforts tell an average of nine people, whereas those customers who are dissatisfied with the response tell an average of 22 people.[8] With the ability to share such stories on the Internet and social media, the potential reach of such dissatisfied customers is even greater. (See Exhibit 7.2 about a United Airlines customer who was not happy with the company's service recovery efforts.) Third, repeated service failures without an effective recovery strategy in place can aggravate even the best employees. The reduction in employee

Exhibit 7.1 The Service Recovery Paradox

Occasionally some businesses have customers who are initially dissatisfied with a service experience and then experience a high level of excellent service recovery, seemingly leading them to be even more satisfied and more likely to repurchase than if no problem had occurred at all; that is, some customers appear to be more satisfied after they experience a service failure than they otherwise would have been![9] To illustrate, consider a rental car customer who arrives to check in and finds that no automobile is available of the size reserved and the price quoted. In an effort to recover, the car rental agent immediately upgrades this customer to a much better vehicle at the original price. The customer, thrilled with this compensation, reports that she is extremely satisfied with this experience, is even more impressed with the firm than she was before, and vows to be loyal into the future. Although such extreme instances are relatively rare, this idea—that an initially disappointed customer who has experienced good service recovery might be even more satisfied and loyal as a result—has been labeled the *recovery paradox.*

So should a firm "screw up" just a little, so that it can "fix the problem" superbly? If doing so would actually lead to more satisfied customers, is this strategy worth pursuing? The logical, but not very rational, conclusion is that companies should *plan to disappoint customers,* so they can recover well and (hopefully) gain even greater loyalty from them!

What are the problems with such an approach?

- As we indicated earlier in this chapter, a vast majority of customers do not complain when they experience a problem. The possibility of a recovery exists only in situations in which the firm is aware of a problem and is able to recover well; if customers do not make the firm aware of the failure—and most do not—dissatisfaction is most likely to be the result.

- It is expensive to fix mistakes; re-creating or reworking a service may be quite costly to a firm.

- It would appear somewhat ludicrous to encourage service failures—after all, reliability ("doing it right the first time") is the most critical determinant of service quality across most industries.

- Research suggests that even if a customer's satisfaction with the firm increases as a result of the great service recovery, repurchase intentions and image perceptions of the firm do not increase—that is, customers do not necessarily think more highly of the firm in the long run.[10]

- Although the recovery paradox suggests that a customer *may* end up more satisfied after experiencing excellent recovery, there is certainly no guarantee that the customer actually will end up more satisfied.

The recovery paradox is highly dependent on the context and situation; although one customer may find it easy to forgive a restaurant that provides him with a gift certificate for a later date for having lost his dinner reservation, another customer who had planned to propose marriage to his date over dinner may not be all that happy with the same recovery scenario.

The intrigue stimulated by the recovery paradox has led to empirical research specifically on this issue. Although anecdotal evidence provides some support for the recovery paradox, research seems to indicate that this phenomenon is not pervasive. In one study, researchers found that only the very highest levels of customers' service recovery ratings resulted in increased satisfaction and loyalty.[11] This research suggests that customers weigh their most recent experiences heavily in their determination of whether to buy again. If the most recent experience is negative, overall feelings about the company will decrease, and repurchase intentions will diminish significantly. Unless the recovery effort is absolutely superlative, it cannot overcome the negative impression of the initial experience enough to build repurchase intentions beyond the point at which they would be if the service had been provided correctly in the first place. Other studies suggest the conditions under which a service recovery paradox is most likely to occur is when the failure is not considered by the customer to be severe, the customer has not experienced prior failures with the firm, the cause of the failure is viewed as unstable by the customer, or the customer perceives that the company had little control over the cause of the failure.[12] Apparently, conditions must be just right in order for the recovery paradox to be present.

Given the mixed opinions on the extent to which the recovery paradox exists, "doing it right the first time" is still a firm's best and safest strategy in the long run.[13] However, when a failure does occur, then every effort at a superior recovery should be made to mitigate its negative effects. If the failure can be fully overcome, if the failure is less critical, or if the recovery effort is clearly superlative, it may be possible to observe evidence of the recovery paradox.[14]

morale and even the loss of employees can be huge but often overlooked costs of not having an effective service recovery strategy.

HOW CUSTOMERS RESPOND TO SERVICE FAILURES

Customers who experience service failures can respond in a variety of ways, as illustrated in Figure 7.3.[15] It is assumed that, following a failure, dissatisfaction at some level will occur for the customer. In fact, research suggests that a variety of negative emotions can occur following a service failure, including such feelings as anger, discontent, disappointment, self-pity, anxiety, and regret.[16] These initial negative responses will affect how customers evaluate the service recovery effort and presumably their ultimate decision to return to the provider or not.

Many customers are very passive about their dissatisfaction, simply saying or doing nothing. Whether they take action or not, at some point the customers will decide whether to stay with that provider or switch to a competitor. As we already have pointed out, customers who do not complain are not very likely to return. For companies, customer passivity in the face of dissatisfaction is a threat to future success.

Why People Do (and Do Not) Complain

Customers who are unlikely to take any action—the majority of customers in most situations—have many reasons for not doing anything. They often see complaining as a waste of their time and effort.[17] They do not believe anything positive will occur

FIGURE 7.3   **Customer Complaint Actions Following Service Failure**

© 2009 Big Break Enterprises/Dave Carroll

UNITED BREAKS GUITARS

While traveling with United Airlines, musician Dave Carroll's guitar was broken by baggage handlers. After fifteen months of seeking compensation with no resolution from United Airlines, Carroll posted a music video on YouTube about his experience, called "United Breaks Guitars." The video with its catchy song quickly went viral and was picked up by countless news outlets, including the *Los Angeles Times,* CNN, and the CBS Morning Show. In less than a month, the video was viewed more than 4.6 million times, causing United Airlines's stock to tumble and costing shareholders more than $180 million.

The trouble started when Carroll witnessed baggage handlers throwing his guitar on the tarmac while he waited for his flight to take off from Chicago's O'Hare Airport. Carroll immediately reported the problem to flight attendants, who instructed him to take up the issue with the ground crew when they arrived at their destination in Omaha. Unfortunately, when they got there, the ground crew was unavailable, and Carroll was only able to confirm his suspicions that they had broken his $3,500 Taylor guitar. What followed was fifteen months of what Carroll describes in his song as "pass the buck, don't ask me, I'm sorry sir, your claim can go nowhere."

Eventually Carroll and United Airlines reached an impasse, and Carroll informed the airline that he would be writing a series of three songs, along with a video, about his experience. His goal was to have at least one million views of the video within one year. The video was uploaded to YouTube on July 6, 2009, and friends of Carroll posted links to the video on Digg and other social news sites. They also tweeted the link to other disgruntled United Airlines customers and to TV personalities such as Jay Leno, Jimmy Fallon, and Perez Hilton. *Consumerist* and other news outlets then picked up the video, and it spread like wildfire. By July 10, only four days later, the video had been viewed over 1.6 million times.

United Airlines took to Twitter to address the video, tweeting, "This has struck a chord [with] us and we've contacted him directly to make it right." United continued to tweet regularly, reiterating this sentiment. Once United got in touch with Carroll, they offered him the $1,200 it had cost Carroll to repair the guitar, plus an additional $1,200 in flight vouchers. However, to Carroll this was too little, too late. Carroll suggested they give the compensation to another customer in a similar situation, and United ultimately opted to donate $3,000 to a music school. Months later, Carroll met with United Airlines executives,

for them or others based on their actions. Many customers may have no confidence in the complaint process and thus refrain from complaining because they do not think it will do any good. Sometimes customers do not know how to complain—they do not understand the process or may not realize that avenues are open to them to voice their complaints. Sometimes customers believe it is too difficult to report a complaint to a firm and, in some cases, may feel like they are being punished by having to do too much to make a complaint. In some cases noncomplainers may engage in "emotion-focused coping" to deal with their negative experiences. This type of coping involves self-blame, denial, and possibly seeking social support.[18] They may feel that the failure was somehow their fault and that they do not deserve redress.

Some customers are more likely to complain than others for a variety of reasons. These customers believe that positive consequences may occur and that there are social benefits of complaining, and their personal norms support their complaining behavior.

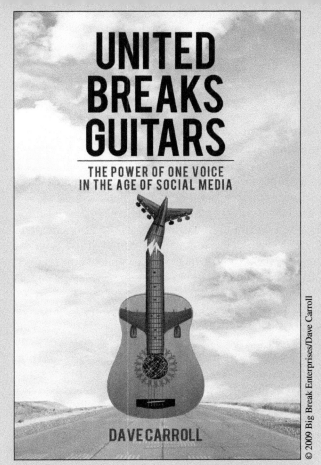

who admitted that Carroll's claim should not have been denied. They now use Carroll's video in customer service training to ensure that a similar incident does not occur again.

Despite United's (delayed) actions, however, the damage was done. In the days following the release of Carroll's video, United Airlines stock fell 10 percent. This single badly handled customer complaint had come with a $180 million price tag. And, the video has since been viewed by more than 16 million people. These consequences are particularly jarring, considering that it would have only cost the airline $1,200 to address the initial complaint.

This incident highlights the importance of careful handling of customer issues and grievances—gone are the days when customer gripes only reach a few close friends and family. Now, thanks to the Internet, complaints have the potential to reach millions of sympathetic ears within a matter of hours!

Sources: J. Deighton and L. Kornfeld, *United Breaks Guitars (Case Study),* Boston: Harvard Business Publishing, 2010; "United Breaks Guitars" YouTube video, 4:36, posted by "sonsofmaxwell," July 6, 2009, https://www.youtube.com/watch?v=5YGc4zOqozo; and R. Sawhney, "Broken Guitar Has United Playing the Blues to the Tune of $180 Million," *FastCompany,* July 30, 2009, http://www.fastcompany.com/1320152/broken-guitar-has-united-playing-blues-tune-180-million.

© 2009 Big Break Enterprises/Dave Carroll

Dave Carroll wrote a book about his experience with United Airlines.

They believe they should and will be provided compensation for the service failure in some form. They believe that fair treatment and good service are their due and that, in cases of service failure, someone should make good. In some cases they feel a social obligation to complain—to help others avoid similar situations or to punish the service provider. A very small number of customers have "complaining" personalities—they just like to complain or cause trouble.

Personal relevance of the failure can also influence whether people complain.[19] If the service failure is really important, if the failure has critical consequences for the customer, or if the customer has much ego involvement in the service experience, then he or she is more likely to complain. The situation at United Airlines, which was described in Exhibit 7.2, illustrates a failure for a service that was considered especially important to one customer. In such situations, when customer emotions are high, customer rage may result.[20]

Customers are more likely to complain about expensive, high-risk, and ego involving services (like vacation packages, airline travel, and medical services) than they are about less expensive, frequently purchased services (fast-food drive-through service, a cab ride, a call to a customer service help line). These latter services are often simply not important enough to warrant the time to complain. Unfortunately, even though the experience may not be important to the customer at the moment, a dissatisfying encounter can still drive him or her to a competitor the next time the service is needed.

Types of Customer Complaint Actions

If customers initiate actions following service failure, the action can be of various types. A dissatisfied customer can choose to complain on the spot to the service provider, giving the company the opportunity to respond immediately. This reaction is often the best-case scenario for the company because it has a second chance right at that moment to satisfy the customer, keep his or her business in the future, and potentially avoid any negative word of mouth. Customers who do not complain immediately may choose to complain later to the provider by phone, in writing, via the Internet, or through social media. Again, the company has a chance to recover. Researchers refer to these proactive types of complaining behavior as *voice* responses or *seeking redress*.

Some customers choose not to complain directly to the provider but rather spread negative word of mouth about the company to friends, relatives, and coworkers. This negative word-of-mouth communication can be extremely detrimental because it can reinforce the customer's feelings of negativism and spread that negative impression to others. Further, the company has no chance to recover unless the negative word of mouth is accompanied by a complaint directly to the company. In recent years, customers have taken to complaining via the Internet or through social media. A variety of websites, including web-based consumer opinion platforms, blogs, and a variety of social media (including Twitter and Facebook),[21] have been created to facilitate customer complaints, and in doing so, provide customers with the possibility of spreading negative word-of-mouth communication to a much broader audience. Some customers become so dissatisfied with a product or service failure that they construct websites targeting the firm's current and prospective customers. On these "gripe sites",[22] angry customers convey their grievances against the firm in ways designed to convince other customers of the firm's incompetence and evil.[23]

Finally, customers may choose to complain to third parties such as the Better Business Bureau, to consumer affairs arms of the government, to a licensing authority, to a professional association, or to a private attorney. No matter the action (or inaction), ultimately the customers determine whether to patronize the service provider again or to switch to another provider.

Types of Complainers

Research suggests that people can be grouped into four categories based on how they respond to failures: *passives, voicers, irates,* and *activists.*[24] Although the proportion of the types of complainers is likely to vary across industries and contexts, it is likely that these four types of complainers will be relatively consistent and that each type can be found in all companies and industries.

© Corbis RF

Irate customers are likely to share their frustrations with others.

Passives

This group of customers is least likely to take any action. They are unlikely to say anything to the provider, less likely than others to spread negative word of mouth, and unlikely to complain to a third party. They often doubt the effectiveness of complaining, thinking that the consequences will not merit the time and effort they will expend. Sometimes their personal values or norms argue against complaining.

Voicers

These customers actively complain to the service provider, but they are less likely to spread negative word of mouth, switch patronage, or go to third parties with their complaints. *These customers should be viewed as the service provider's best friends.* They actively complain and, by doing so, give the company a second chance. They tend to believe complaining has social benefits and therefore do not hesitate to voice their opinions. They believe that the consequences of complaining to the provider can be very positive, and they believe less in other types of complaining such as spreading negative word of mouth or talking to third parties. Their personal norms are consistent with complaining.

Irates

These customers are more likely than others to engage in negative word-of-mouth communication with friends and relatives and to switch providers. They are about average in their propensity to complain to the provider and are unlikely to complain to third parties. As their label suggests, they are quite angry with the provider, although they do believe that complaining to the provider can have social benefits. They are less likely to give the service provider a second chance and instead will switch to a competitor, spreading the word to friends and relatives along the way. Such customers are more likely than the other types to go to the trouble of creating websites, blogs, or YouTube videos to share their frustrations with others.

Activists

These customers are characterized by above-average propensity to complain on all dimensions: they will complain to the provider, they will tell others, and they are more likely than any other group to complain to third parties or express their opinions via social media (such as Twitter). Complaining fits with their personal norms. They have a very optimistic sense of the potential positive consequences of all types of complaining.

SERVICE RECOVERY STRATEGIES: FIXING THE CUSTOMER

Many companies have learned the importance of providing excellent recovery for disappointed customers. In the next two sections we examine their strategies and share examples of benchmark companies and what they are doing. It will become clear that

FIGURE 7.4
Service Recovery
Strategies

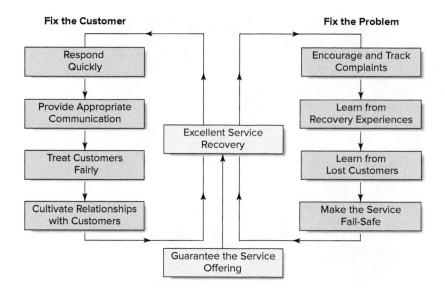

excellent service recovery is really a combination of a variety of strategies, illustrated in Figure 7.4. Generally speaking, service recovery strategies fall into two general types. One type includes the actions taken by the firm to restore the relationship with the customer—that is, to "fix the customer." The second type is the actions taken to correct the problem and, ideally, to prevent it from recurring—that is, to "fix the problem." Clearly both types of actions are important, but in many situations fixing the customer needs to be done before fixing the problem. Thus, we begin by examining strategies that involve fixing the customer.

When they take the time and effort to complain, customers generally have high expectations. They not only expect a response, but also expect the firm to be accountable. They expect to be helped quickly. They expect to be compensated for their grief and for the hassle of being inconvenienced. They expect to be treated nicely in the process. And they expect the issue to be satisfactorily resolved. Exhibit 7.3 epitomizes this kind of service recovery.

Respond Quickly

Complaining customers want quick responses.[25] Thus, when the company has service failures or receives complaints from customers, it must be prepared to act on them quickly. As indicated in Figure 7.5, research conducted on service customers has found that more than one-third of all customers who have problems resolved immediately or within 24 hours are "completely satisfied" with the action taken by the company.[26] Unfortunately, many companies require customers to contact multiple employees (a practice often referred to as "ping-ponging") before getting a problem resolved; one study found that an average of 4.2 contacts is typically needed to resolve a complaint.[27] This study also found that, if a problem can be handled by the first contact, customers are satisfied with the firm's response 35 percent of the time; however, once three or more contacts are needed the percentage of customers who are satisfied with the response drops to 9 percent.[28] And, of those customers who use Twitter, a staggering 81 percent expect a same-day response to the complaints they voice via their tweets.[29] The lesson here? A quick response to a service failure can go a long way in appeasing a dissatisfied customer.

The ability to provide immediate responses requires not only systems and procedures that allow quick action but also empowered employees. That is, to enable them to respond quickly, employees should be trained and empowered to solve problems as they

Exhibit 7.3 Service Hero Stories

TRADER JOE'S DELIVERS FOOD TO MAN IN NEED

An 89-year-old man was snowed in at his home in Pennsylvania just before the Christmas holidays, with the promise of heavier storms on the horizon. His daughter, worried that he would run out of food during the bad weather, called several stores in the area hoping that one would be willing to deliver supplies to her father.

She finally got in touch with someone at Trader Joe's who told her that Trader Joe's normally does not make deliveries, but that the company would be willing to make an exception due to the extreme circumstances. The Trader Joe's associate took the woman's order and even suggested additional items that would work with her father's low-sodium diet, making sure he would have everything he needed should he be stuck at home for an extended period of time.

When it came to paying for the food, the associate told her not to worry—the food and the delivery would be free of charge. The employee concluded the conversation by wishing her a Merry Christmas, and her father received the food less than thirty minutes later.

This example shows that service recovery goes beyond fixing a simple mistake. Authorizing employees to do the right thing for customers, even when the recovery is made necessary because of circumstances outside the firm's control (such as Mother Nature), is how firms can build lasting and meaningful relationships with their customers.

UNITED AIRLINES DELAYS FLIGHT FOR PASSENGER TO SEE DYING MOTHER

Though United Airlines has made a name for itself in the guitar-breaking business (see Exhibit 7.2 earlier in this chapter), there are also examples of when the airline has gone above and beyond for a customer.

Passenger Kerry Drake anxiously boarded a flight in San Francisco on his way to see his dying mother in Lubbock, Texas, who had only hours left to live. Drake knew that if he missed his connecting flight in Houston, he would likely not get to see her before she passed away.

When his first flight to Houston was delayed, Drake realized he would miss his Lubbock connection, preventing him from seeing his mother one last time. He broke down into tears on the plane, unable to contain his grief.

When a flight attendant learned of the circumstances surrounding this situation, she informed the captain, who radioed ahead to the next flight from Houston to Lubbock. The flight crew waiting in Houston, sympathetic to Drake's situation, delayed the flight in order to wait for Drake.

As Drake arrived at the gate for the last leg of his journey, the crew greeted him by name as they welcomed him. As a result of the coordinated efforts of a large set of United Airlines employees, Drake was able to get to the hospital in time to say goodbye to his mother.

This story is remarkable because airlines are often evaluated in terms of their efficiency and the number of on-time flights. However, United Airlines employees were able to see that this situation was more important than a schedule, and they were able to give a passenger a priceless gift—a final moment with his mother.

Sources: G. Ciotti, "10 Stories of Unforgettable Customer Service," *Help Scout*, www.helpscout.net, accessed on June 17, 2016; K. Hetter, "United Airlines Delays Flight for Man to See Dying Mother," *CNN*, March 10, 2013, http://edition.cnn.com/2013/03/06 /travel/united-flight-delay-dying-mother/.

occur. A problem not solved can quickly escalate. As we indicated earlier, customers often experience ping-ponging from employee to employee when service failures occur. Empowerment of employees, a practice discussed in more detail in Chapter 11, can often allow for quick responses, reduce (or eliminate) ping-ponging, and help placate dissatisfied customers. The Ritz-Carlton, for example, insists that the first person to hear a complaint from a customer "owns" that complaint until the employee is sure it is resolved. If a maintenance employee hears a complaint from a customer while the employee is in the middle of fixing a light in the hotel corridor, he owns that complaint and is charged with making sure that the problem is handled appropriately before returning to his work.

Another way that problems or complaints can be handled quickly is by building systems that allow customers to actually solve their own service needs and fix their own problems. Typically, this approach is done through technology. Customers directly interact with the company's technology to perform their own customer service, which provides them with instant answers. FedEx uses this strategy for its package tracking

FIGURE 7.5
Customer Satisfaction with Timeliness of Firm Responses to Service Failures

Source: 2015 Customer Rage Study, conducted by Customer Care Measurement and Consulting and the Center for Services Leadership at Arizona State University.

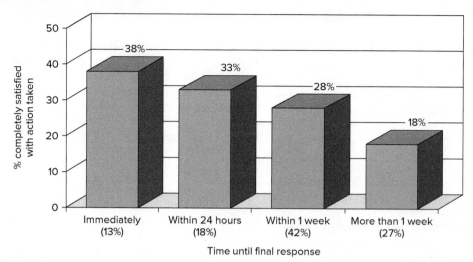

The numbers across the bottom are the percentage of the total sample whose response (by the firm) was received in that time frame. So, for example, 13 percent of the sample received an immediate response. Of that group, 38 percent were completely satisfied with the response.

service, for example, as does Symantec for its Internet security software products. Our Technology Spotlight features a company that is a master at online customer self-service—Cisco Systems.

Provide Appropriate Communication

Display Understanding and Accountability

In many service failure situations, customers are not looking for extreme actions from the firm; however, they are looking to understand what happened and for firms to be accountable for their actions (or inactions).[30] Research by the Customer Care Measurement, depicted in Table 7.1, has identified the twelve most common "remedies" that customers seek when they experience a serious problem;[31] four of these remedies are to have the product repaired or service fixed, to receive their money back, to be reimbursed for the hassle of having experienced a problem, and to receive a free product or service in the future. Interestingly, however, the other eight remedies—including an explanation by the firm as to what happened, assurance that the problem will not be repeated, a thank you for the customer's business, an apology from the firm, being treated with dignity, being talked to in everyday language, for the offending company to put itself in the customer's shoes, and providing an opportunity for the customer to vent his or her frustrations to the firm—cost the firm very little to provide.

These eight nonmonetary remedies consist primarily of providing employees the opportunity to communicate with customers. Understanding and accountability are very important to many customers after a service failure because, if they perceive an injustice has occurred, someone is to blame. Customers expect an apology when things go wrong, and a company that provides one demonstrates courtesy and respect; customers also want to know what the company is going to do to ensure that the problem does not recur.[32] As Table 7.1 suggests, customer discontent can be moderated if firms simply communicate well with customers. Customers clearly value such communication, because these nonmonetary remedies are positively related to satisfaction with the complaint process, continued loyalty, and positive word-of-mouth communication.[33] Of course, firms need to put more effort into their response than

TABLE 7.1
Top 12 Remedies Customers Seek From Firms in Responding to Service Failures

Remedy	% Desired	% Received
To be treated with dignity	93%	32%
Offending company put itself in my shoes	83%	19%
An assurance that my problem would not be repeated	81%	15%
My product repaired/service fixed	80%	25%
An explanation of why the problem occurred	80%	18%
To be talked to in everyday language; not scripted response	79%	29%
A thank you for my business	76%	27%
An apology	75%	28%
Just to express my anger/tell my side of the story	58%	35%
My money back	57%	18%
A free product or service in the future	44%	8%
Financial compensation for my lost time, inconvenience, or injury	42%	5%

Note: Gray shading indicates non-monetary remedy.

Source: 2015 Customer Rage Study, conducted by Customer Care Measurement and Consulting and the Center for Services Leadership at Arizona State University.

simply apologizing well—such as providing appropriate compensation—if they want to fully recover from a severe service failure.[34]

Supply Adequate Explanations

In many service failures, customers try to understand why the failure occurred. Explanations can help to diffuse negative reactions and convey respect for the customer.[35] Research suggests that when the firm's ability to provide an adequate outcome is not successful, further dissatisfaction can be reduced if an adequate explanation is provided to the customer.[36] For an explanation to be perceived as adequate, it must possess two primary characteristics. First, the *content* of the explanation must be appropriate; relevant facts and pertinent information are important in helping the customer understand what occurred. Second, the *style* of the delivery of the explanation, or how the explanation is delivered, can also reduce customer dissatisfaction. Style includes the personal characteristics of the explanation givers, including their credibility and sincerity. Explanations perceived by customers as honest, sincere, and not manipulative are generally the most effective. For example, if a customer were to be kept waiting at the doctor's office for a long time, the customer may start to feel undervalued or disregarded if there is no explanation for the wait. However, if an employee came and apologized for the wait and kindly explained that

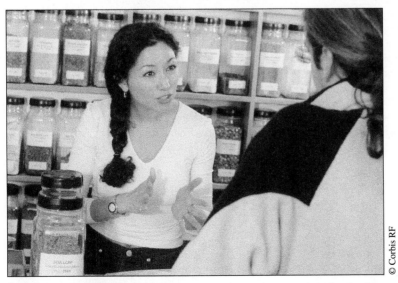

© Corbis RF

Customers who experience a service failure often want an explanation by the firm as to what happened.

Technology Spotlight Cisco Systems—Customers Recover for Themselves

One of the challenges of high growth and increasingly diversified product lines is learning how to handle customers' service needs quickly. This is a challenge continually faced by Cisco, a worldwide leader in enabling people to make powerful connections—whether in business, education, philanthropy, or creativity. Cisco hardware, software, and service offerings are used to create the Internet solutions that make networks possible and provide Cisco clients (and their customers) with easy access to information anywhere, at any time. As networks become mission-critical to Cisco's customers and their business, failures in this environment become extremely costly very quickly. Customers want to know that their problems can be solved immediately, and they want control over the situation and its solution.

To address these issues—high growth coupled with the critical and increasingly complex nature of the business—Cisco has turned to the Internet to build upon its already world-class suite of customer service offerings. The resulting Cisco support website and online communities provide documentation, suggestions, and tools to help troubleshoot and resolve technical issues with Cisco products and technologies. This online offering has set Cisco apart in its industry and helped the company build customer loyalty in a highly competitive environment.

CUSTOMERS USING TECHNOLOGY TO SOLVE PROBLEMS THEMSELVES

Essentially, Cisco has enabled customers to be in charge of much of their own service and support through the company's corporate self-support website and online communities. In most cases, customers can solve their own service problems, with no intervention from Cisco personnel—allowing Cisco staff to focus on complex issues that require hands-on support. Through the Cisco self-support website, access to information is immediate. This is important because speed and immediacy are frequently key concerns for customers in these mission-critical

situations. The Cisco Support Community includes (1) community forums, which provide customers with the ability to ask questions and acquire information on problems they have encountered from fellow Cisco customers from other companies, (2) opportunities to acquire the latest support-related knowledge through a variety of programs and blogs led by Cisco experts, and (3) technical support documents and tutorials published by Cisco experts and partners on such issues as local area networks, network management, security, and data storage.

Over the past decade Cisco has evolved to provide to a unified customer experience that is channel and location agnostic by bringing together all of the previously mentioned modalities of support. Customers can contact Cisco for support through any modality (i.e., communities, self-support, agents) and get all of the right support without having to jump back and forth between various channels. Cisco refers to this approach as Digital Support—which it sees as having three components.

The first component is a *unified customer experience*. Digital Support provides Cisco with the ability to offer a unified support experience for its customers and partners across all the modalities it provides. With Digital Support, all of Cisco's support channels have been coordinated to provide a seamless and consistent experience for its customers.

Although customers can use the telephone to speak to a call center agent, more than ever they are demanding real-time access to information and expertise when they encounter problems and expect to resolve them through a variety of channels. Digital Support provides Cisco customers support at a time that is convenient to them, whether they are "on the road," helping their clients, or troubleshooting on site. One such channel is the Cisco Support Community. The community is continually available and is up-to-date in its understanding of issues and resolutions—even call center agents frequently look to the community to help them diagnose problems. Those

a patient with an emergency had come in, then the customer would be more likely to understand the extenuating circumstances and be more tolerant of the wait.

Treat Customers Fairly

Customers also want justice and fairness in handling their complaints. Service recovery experts Steve Brown and Steve Tax have documented three specific types of justice that customers are looking for following their complaints: *outcome fairness,* in the community who are particularly frequent contributors to helping others are given the title of "Cisco VIP." These people have a "badge" placed next to their user name on the communities; the badge indicates their VIP status and displays the category in which they earned their status. ("Cisco Designated VIPs" are the top contributors and are often invited to advise the communities on community direction, features, and other items.)

The second component of Digital Support is *anytime, anywhere support*. Recognizing customer needs for anytime/anywhere engagement with Cisco expertise and tools, Cisco has expanded its customer support experience into social media and mobile devices. Indeed, customers are increasingly using these tools when troubleshooting problems they encounter while using Cisco products. Often these issues arise when they are away from the office, making it difficult to access Cisco resources from a more traditional personal computer or laptop. A few years ago, Cisco launched applications (apps) for technical support on both the iPhone and the iPad. The ease of use offered by the iPad app has been a hit—particularly among younger customers and those in emerging markets. When they encounter problems, Cisco customers can also participate in discussion forums, get real-time access to Cisco experts, and access technical support resources directly from Facebook, Twitter, LinkedIn, and YouTube.

The third component is proactive and preemptive support provided by Application Programmable Interfaces (APIs) and Support Automation with advanced diagnostics executed on the customer' device. The APIs permit an application within the customer's environment to connect to Cisco and obtain information concerning the health of the device, status of their support contract with Cisco, any security vulnerabilities their devices are susceptible to, and other information important to managing their devices.

Support Automation takes the concept of connectivity between Cisco and the customer to another level by enabling both Cisco technicians and the customer's own support team to connect to the customer's network devices. Once connected, technical procedures are executed by Cisco call center experts to collect relevant device data, diagnose errors, and send the information to Cisco. With the results in hand, the customer and call center engineer can take corrective action to restore interrupted service. This data can also be collected as part of a periodic checkup to maintain optimal health of the customer's environment. The intent is for customers to be thinking about and exposed to issues they may face, so that than can resolve problems before they occur—the ultimate service recovery!

THE RESULTS

The goal of the Digital Support approach is to make Cisco support seamless to all of its customers and allow them to assemble a wealth of knowledge, participate in a stream of forum discussions, and learn from technical experts in the community to resolve whatever problems they face. Through its continual innovation in providing service to its customers on the Internet, Cisco has recognized tremendous benefits. Currently, 85 percent of customer support problems are handled via the Cisco.com self-support site and communities, using intellectual property provided by Cisco experts and self-help tools that allow customers to diagnose and solve their own problems. Customer satisfaction and loyalty have increased with the introduction of Internet-based customer service and support communities, productivity has increased as Cisco Support Community has helped resolve customer issues, and the company saves approximately $300 million per year through case deflection to its communities and self-support site. This is truly a win–win situation for Cisco's bottom line, its employees, and its business customers.

Sources: www.cisco.com/support, accessed June 2016; e-mail communications from Mike Friday, Director of Product Manage ment, Cisco Services, June 2016.

procedural fairness, and *interactional fairness.*[37] Outcome fairness concerns the results that customers receive from their complaints; *procedural fairness* refers to the policies, rules, and timeliness of the complaint process; and interactional fairness focuses on the interpersonal treatment received during the complaint process.[38] Exhibit 7.4 shows examples of each type of fairness taken from Brown and Tax's study of customers who reported on their experiences with complaint resolution. Our Global Feature discusses how customers across cultures view fair service recovery.

Exhibit 7.4   Fairness Themes in Service Recovery

	Fair	Unfair
Outcome fairness: the results that customers receive from complaints	*"The waitress agreed that there was a problem. She took the sandwiches back to the kitchen and had them replaced. We were also given a free drink."* *"When I was checking out I complained at the front desk about being awakened at 3:45 a.m. They apologized, informed me that the fire department had been called because of an issue across the hall, and offered me 2,000 bonus points for the inconvenience."*	*"Their refusal to refund our money or make up for the inconvenience and cold food was inexcusable."* *"Once we were onboard the pilot announced that the plane had equipment problems; later the customer service rep told me that I would not be able to fly out until the next day. Since I would have to spend an extra night, I asked the airline to at least cover my taxi fare to return to my brother's house. They refused."*
Procedural fairness: the policies, rules, and timeliness of the complaint process	*"The hotel manager said that it didn't matter to her who was at fault, she would take responsibility for the problem immediately."* *"The product came with a lifetime guarantee. However, I could not find my original receipt when it stopped working. The customer service rep said I simply needed to take a picture of the defect and send it to them, along with my address, and they would send me a new one—no questions asked."*	*"They should have assisted me with the problem instead of giving me a phone number to call. No one returned my calls, and I never had a chance to speak to a real person."* *"I returned the next day to inform them that they had made a mistake on my order. Rather than deal with the situation on the spot, while I was right there in front of them, the manager asked me if I had gone online to file a complaint. When I said "no" she said that is what I needed to do."*
Interactional fairness: the interpersonal treatment received during the complaint process	*"The loan officer was very courteous, knowledgeable, and considerate—he kept me informed about the progress of the complaint."* *"I was having problems getting my device to sync with my phone. When I called to get help, the telephone rep was very personable, and patiently walked me through the process."*	*"The person who handled my complaint about the faulty air conditioner repair wasn't going to do anything about it and didn't seem to care."* *"I had contacted "Dan" several times over the course of two weeks about this problem. He repeated told me: "Don't worry" and "I will take care of you." However, he quit returning my telephone calls and responding to my email messages. His actions conveyed the message that he really didn't consider my problem to be a big priority."*

Source: Adapted from S. S. Tax and S. W. Brown, "Recovering and Learning from Service Failure," *Sloan Management Review* 40 (Fall 1998), p. 79, Massachusetts Institute of Technology.

Outcome Fairness

In their service recovery efforts firms should provide customers with outcomes, or compensation, that match the level of their dissatisfaction. This compensation can take the form of actual monetary compensation, future free service, reduced charges, repairs, and/or replacements. Customers expect equity in the exchange—that is, they want to feel that the company has "paid" for its mistakes in a manner at least equal to what the customer has suffered. The company's "punishment should fit the crime." Customers expect equality—that is, they want to be compensated in a manner similar to other customers who have experienced the same type of service failure. They also appreciate it when a company gives them choices in terms of compensation. For example, a student whose senior portraits taken by a professional studio are not properly printed could be offered the choice of a refund or a free sitting and package of portraits as compensation for the original portraits not arriving as promised. Outcome fairness is especially important in settings in which customers have particularly negative emotional responses to the service failure; in such situations recovery efforts should focus on improving the outcome from the customer's point of view.[39]

For example, an Amazon customer ordered a brand new PlayStation for Christmas, which was duly delivered to his porch. However, the package was stolen before the customer had a chance to bring it inside. Amazon compensated the customer by rush-delivering a second PlayStation, free of charge, in time for Christmas. This customer considered the final outcome (the timely replacement of the package contents) to be more than adequate, given the stolen package was not Amazon's fault.[40]

On the other hand, customers can be uncomfortable if they are overly compensated. Early in its experience with service guarantees, Domino's Pizza offered not to charge for a pizza if the driver arrived after the 30-minute guaranteed delivery time. Many customers were not comfortable asking for this level of compensation, especially if the driver was only a few minutes late. In this case "the punishment was greater than the crime." For a while Domino's changed the compensation to a more reasonable $3 off for late deliveries. Later the time guarantee was dropped altogether because of problems it caused with employees who were driving too fast to make their deliveries.

Procedural Fairness

In addition to fair compensation, firms should treat customers fairly in terms of policies, rules, and timeliness of the complaint process. Customers want easy access to the complaint process, and they want things handled quickly, preferably by the first person they contact. They appreciate companies that can be adaptable in their procedures, so that the recovery effort can match their individual circumstances. In some cases, particularly in business-to-business services, companies actually ask the customer, "What can we do to compensate you for our failure?" Many times what the customer asks for is actually less than the company might have expected.

Fair procedures are characterized by clarity, speed, and absence of hassles. Unfair procedures are those that customers perceive as slow, prolonged, illogical, and inconvenient. Customers also feel it is unfair if they have to prove their case—when the company's assumption seems to be they are wrong or lying until they can prove otherwise.

A classic story of procedural fairness in the midst of service recovery comes from Club Med–Cancun, a story still being retold nearly three decades later. A group of Club Med vacationers had nothing but trouble getting from New York to their Mexican destination. The flight took off six hours late, made two unexpected stops, and circled 30 minutes before it could land. Because of all the delays and mishaps, the plane was en route for 10 hours more than planned and ran out of food and drinks. It finally arrived at two o'clock in the morning, with a landing so rough that oxygen masks and luggage dropped from overhead. By the time the plane pulled up to the gate, the soured passengers were faint with hunger and convinced that their vacation was ruined before it had even the company and its employees have uncaring attitudes and have done little to try to resolve the problem. This type of behavior on the part of employees may seem strange— why would they treat customers rudely or in an uncaring manner under these circumstances? Often it is due to lack of training and empowerment—a frustrated frontline employee who has no authority to compensate the customer may easily respond in an aloof or uncaring manner, especially if the customer is angry and/or rude.

In the Trader Joe's case in Exhibit 7.3, the Trader Joe's employee was caring and helpful as he suggested additional items for the customer's snowed-in father. The employee even delivered the groceries, though delivery is not normally part of his job description. Finally, by wishing the customer Merry Christmas, the employee gave the experience a personal touch and showed that he cared about the customer.

Cultivate Relationships with Customers

In Chapter 6 we discussed the importance of developing long-term relationships with customers. One additional benefit of relationship marketing is that if the firm fails in service delivery, those customers who have a strong relationship with the firm are often more forgiving of service failures and more open to the firm's service recovery efforts. That is, it may be easier to "fix the customer" if the firm has established a strong relationship with that customer; indeed, research suggests that strong customer–firm relationships can help shield the firm from the negative effects of failures on customer satisfaction.[41] To illustrate, one study demonstrated that the presence of rapport between customers and employees provided several service recovery benefits, including increased postfailure satisfaction, increased loyalty intentions, and decreased negative word-of-mouth communication.[42] Another study found that customers who expect the relationship to continue also tend to have lower service recovery expectations and may demand less immediate compensation for a failure because they consider the balance of equity across a longer time horizon.[43] Thus, cultivation of strong customer relationships can provide an important buffer to service firms when failures occur.[44]

SERVICE RECOVERY STRATEGIES: FIXING THE PROBLEM

Often the most pressing and immediate need in service recovery is to "fix the customer." However, in many situations the actual problem created by the poor service delivery also needs to be fixed. This may require reworking, redoing, or redelivering the service, if possible, to provide what the customer initially expected. And, if the problem is likely to recur for this or other customers, then the service delivery process may need to be fixed, too. This section highlights strategies that can be used to help the firm "fix the problem" both in the short term and in the long term.

Encourage and Track Complaints

Even if an organization aims for 100 percent service quality, failures occur. A critical component of a service recovery strategy is thus to encourage and track complaints. Our Strategy Insight describes several ways in which customer complaints can be encouraged.

Firms can utilize a number of ways to encourage and track complaints. Customer research can be designed specifically for this purpose through satisfaction surveys, critical incident studies, and lost customer research, as discussed in Chapter 5. As an alternative to using toll-free call centers and e-mail, in recent years customers have taken to social media to complain. Firms are using a variety of new technologies to track, analyze, sort, and even respond to customer complaints made online.

For example, Amazon uses artificial intelligence to identify key words in online complaints and then suggests an appropriate response to the complainer. Similarly, British Airways can retrieve from its database information on each customer as well as data regarding what solutions were offered in the past in similar situations to understand how to best satisfy the customer.[45]

In some cases technology can anticipate problems and complaints before they happen, allowing service employees to diagnose problems before the customer recognizes they exist. At companies such as IBM, John Deere, and Caterpillar, "smart" systems have been implemented to anticipate equipment failures and to send out an electronic alert to the local field technician with the nature of the problem as well as which parts and tools will be needed to make the repair—a repair the customer does not yet know is needed.

Learn from Recovery Experiences

Service recovery situations are more than just opportunities to fix flawed services and strengthen ties with customers. They can also provide valuable information for improving service delivery. By tracking service recovery efforts and solutions, managers can often learn about systematic problems in the delivery system that need fixing. By conducting root-cause analysis, firms can identify the sources of the problems and modify processes, sometimes almost eliminating the need for recovery. At Ritz-Carlton Hotels, all employees carry service recovery forms called "instant action forms" with them at all times, so that they can immediately record service failures and suggest actions to address them. Each employee "owns" any complaint that he or she receives and is responsible for seeing that service recovery occurs. In turn, the employees report to management these sources of service failure and the remedies. At Hampton Inn® Hotels, whenever the service guarantee (see Figure 7.6) is invoked, the reason for the customer's dissatisfaction is recorded as part of the process and the information forwarded to management. Such information is then entered into a database and analyzed to identify patterns and systemic service issues that need to be fixed. If common themes are observed across a number of failure situations, changes are made to service processes or attributes. In addition, at the Ritz-Carlton the information is entered into the customer's personal data file, so when that customer stays at

FIGURE 7.6
The 100 Percent Hampton Inn® Hotels Guarantee

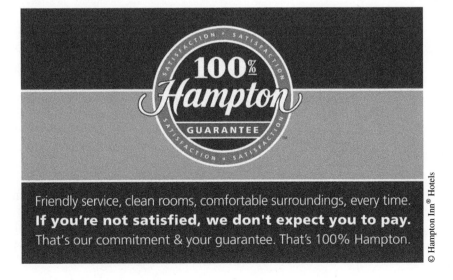

Strategy Insight   Eliciting Complaints and Reports of Service Failure

Service failures can occur in a variety of ways and at numerous times throughout the service delivery process. However, in many cases it is difficult, if not impossible, for the firm to know that a service failure has occurred unless the customer informs the firm accordingly. Unfortunately, a relatively low percentage of customers will actually complain to the firm. Thus, a major challenge facing management is how to get customers to complain when they experience a service failure and/or they are not satisfied with service delivery. What can a firm do to elicit complaints? Here are some issues to consider.

- *Develop the mind-set that complaints are good.* Too often the complaining customer is looked on by employees in the organization as the *enemy*—someone to be conquered and subdued. The more prudent approach is to develop the mind-set that the complaining customer is the firm's *friend*. Complaints provide valuable feedback to the firm, giving it the opportunity not only to address the service failure for the complaining customer but also to identify problems that other (less vocal) customers may also be experiencing (the "tip of the iceberg" phenomenon). One scholar suggests that "complainers ought to be treated with the dignity and respect afforded to the highest-priced analysts and consultants." One company puts all customers who have complained on a VIP list. Accepting complaints is truly reflective of firms who are close to their customers.
- *Make complaining easy.* If the firm truly wants to hear from customers who experience poor service,

it needs to make it easy for them to share their experiences with the firm. Sometimes customers have no idea whom to speak to if they have a complaint, what the process is, or what will be involved. Complaining should be easy—the last thing customers want when they are dissatisfied is to face a complex, difficult-to-access process for complaining. Customers should know where to go and/or whom to talk to when they encounter problems, and they should be made to feel confident that something positive will result from their efforts. Technological advances have made it possible to provide customers with multiple avenues to complain, including toll-free customer call centers, company e-mail addresses, social media, and website feedback forms. Some restaurants have even begun to ask customers to fill out brief surveys on a tabletop point-of-sale system while they wait for their bill to arrive. The firm should regularly communicate to customers that complaining is easy and that it welcomes and appreciates such feedback.

- *Encourage customers to be partners.* Customers may not be aware of the active role they can take in achieving their desired outcome with the firm. By helping customers to view the relationship as a partnership, they will be more likely to complain (as the form of input) throughout the process, giving the firm the opportunity to correct or prevent problems as they arise.
- *Say thank you.* The complaint should be treated as what it is: valuable feedback for the firm that provides an opportunity to fix the problem and make the

---

any Ritz-Carlton again (no matter what hotel), employees can be aware of the previous experience, ensuring that it does not happen again for that customer.

Learn from Lost Customers

Another key component of an effective service recovery strategy is to learn from the customers who defect or decide to leave. Formal marketing research to discover the reasons customers have left can assist in preventing failures in the future. This type of research is difficult, even painful for companies, however. No one really likes to examine their failures. Yet such examination is essential for preventing the same mistakes and losing more customers in the future.[46]

As presented in Chapter 5, lost customer research typically involves in-depth probing of customers to determine their true reasons for leaving. This information is most effectively obtained by depth interviews, administered by skilled interviewers who truly understand the business. It may be best to have this type of research done by senior people in the company, particularly in business-to-business contexts in which service better in the future. Showing gratitude will help customers see that the firm values their input and that the complaint will make a difference, increasing the likelihood that a customer will complain again in the future.

- *Be an active listener.* Employees should be encouraged and trained to actively listen to customers, particularly to see if they can pick up on any cues to suggest less-than-ideal service. A restaurant customer might respond "fine" to the waiter's question "How is your meal?" However, the customer's body language and tone of voice, or the amount of food not eaten, might indicate that all is not fine. Some customers may not be assertive in voicing their displeasure, but they may drop clues to suggest that something is amiss. Employees as well as managers should be consistently listening not only to the customer's actual words but also to what he or she may really be trying or wanting to communicate.

- *Ask customers about specific service issues.* A very simple, informal way to find out about any service failure is simply to ask. Managers at one hotel with a high percentage of business travelers make it a point to be at the front desk between 7:45 and 8:45 a.m. every day, because approximately 80 percent of their business travelers check out at that time. During the checkout process, managers avoid questions that can be answered with a simple "yes," "OK," or "fine" (e.g., "How was your stay?") and instead ask questions that force customers to provide specific feedback (e.g., "How could we have improved the technology accommodations in your room?" or "What needs to be done to improve our recreation center?"). Asking customers very specific questions that cannot be answered with a simple "yes" or "no" may provide customers with an easy way to point out expectations that were not fulfilled.

- *Conduct short, trailer surveys.* A follow-up telephone call to a customer still in the midst of the service experience can help to identify problems in real time and thus enable real-time recovery. Enterprise Rent-A-Car Company, for example, regularly calls customers a day after they have picked up a rental car and asks if everything is okay with the car. Customers who report problems, such as a broken window or a car that smells of smoke, are brought a replacement vehicle that day without any additional questions or hassle. Trailer surveys work especially well in business-to-business services in addressing problems early, before they become major issues.

Sources: S. S. Tax and S. W. Brown, "Recovering and Learning from Service Failure," *Sloan Management Review* 40 (Fall 1998), pp. 75–88; O. Harari, "Thank Heaven for Complainers," *Management Review* 81 (January 1992), p. 59; A. Obston, "Getting Customers to Complain," *Entrepreneur.com,* October 18, 2004, https://www.entrepreneur.com/article/72908; M. Solomon, "Restaurant Customer Service and Technology: Chili's' Tableside (POS) and Mobile Approach," *Forbes.com,* May 29, 2016, http://www.forbes.com/sites/micahsolomon/2016/05/29/restaurant-customer-service-and-technology-how-chilis-does-it-tableside-pos-and-via-mobile/#1dd277c15783.

customers are large and the impact of even one lost customer is great. The type of depth analysis often requires a series of "why" questions or "tell me more about that" questions to get at the actual, core reason for the customer's defection.[47]

In conducting this kind of research, a firm must focus on important or profitable customers who have left—not just everyone who has left the company. An insurance company in Australia once began this type of research to learn about their lost customers, only to find that the customers they were losing tended to be their least profitable customers, anyway. They quickly determined that depth research on how to keep these unprofitable customers would not be a good investment!

Make the Service Fail-Safe—Do It Right the First Time!

The first rule of service quality, and arguably the best service recovery strategy, is to do it right the first time. In this way recovery is unnecessary, customers get what they expect, and the costs of redoing the service and compensating for errors can be avoided. As you have already learned, reliability, or doing it right the first time, is the most important dimension of service quality across industry contexts.[48] Indeed, research suggests that many customers stay in a relationship because they have not experienced a (negative) critical incident.[49]

Dick Chase, noted service operations expert, suggests that services adopt the quality notion of *poka yokes* to improve service reliability.[50] Poka yokes are automatic warnings or controls in place to ensure that mistakes are not made; essentially, they are quality control mechanisms, typically used on assembly lines. Chase suggests that poka yokes can be devised in service settings to "mistakeproof" the service, ensure that essential procedures are followed, and ensure that service steps are carried out in the proper order and in a timely manner. In a hospital setting, numerous poka yokes ensure that procedures are followed to avoid potentially life-threatening mistakes. For example, trays for surgical instruments have indentations for specific instruments, and each instrument is nested in its appropriate spot. In this way surgeons and their staff know that all instruments are in their places prior to closing the patient's incision.[51]

Similarly, poka yokes can be devised to ensure that the tangibles associated with the service are clean and well maintained and that documents are accurate and up-to-date. Poka yokes can also be implemented for employee behaviors (checklists, role-playing and practice, reminder signs) and even for ensuring that customers perform effectively. Many of the strategies we discuss in Parts 4 and 5 of the text ("Aligning Service Design and Standards" and "Delivering and Performing Service") are aimed at ensuring service reliability and can be viewed as applications of the basic fail-safe notion of poka yokes.

Even more fundamentally, it is important for a firm to create a culture of doing it right the first time. Within such a culture, everyone understands the importance of reliability, everyone aims to satisfy every customer and looks for ways to improve service, and everyone fully understands and appreciates the "relationship value of a customer" concept that was presented in Chapter 6. Thus, they are motivated to provide quality service *every time* and to *every customer.*

SERVICE GUARANTEES

A guarantee is a particular type of recovery tool that can be used to both "fix the customer" and "fix the problem." In a business context, a *guarantee* is a pledge or assurance that a product offered by a firm will perform as promised, and if not then some form of reparation will be undertaken by the firm. Although guarantees are relatively common for manufactured products, they have only recently been used for services.[52] Traditionally, many people believed that a service simply could not be guaranteed, given its intangible and variable nature. What would be guaranteed? With a tangible product, the customer is guaranteed that it will perform as promised and, if not, that it can be returned. With a service, it is generally not possible to receive a return or to "undo" what has been performed. The skepticism about service guarantees is being dispelled, however, as more and more companies find they can guarantee their service and that there are tremendous benefits for doing so.

Companies are finding that effective service guarantees can complement the company's service recovery strategy—serving as one tool to help support the service recovery strategies depicted in Figure 7.4. The Hampton Inn® Hotels guarantee shown in Figure 7.6 is an example of such an effective guarantee.

Characteristics of Effective Guarantees

At a minimum, a service guarantee should include a promise regarding the service and appropriate remuneration if the promise is broken. With these two elements in mind, certain characteristics tend to make some guarantees more effective than others. The most effective guarantees tend to have similar characteristics, including having limited restrictions, as well as being meaningful, easy to understand, and easy to invoke.[53]

Limited Restrictions and Exclusions

Effective guarantees should be free of the "if, and, or but" conditions and exclusions associated with many legal documents.[54] Service guarantees with a limited number of restrictions are easier for customers to understand and easier for a firm to communicate than guarantees that have numerous exclusions or conditions. The Hampton Inn® Hotels guarantee (see Figure 7.6) does not impose any conditions. Some guarantees can appear as if they were written by the legal department (and often are), with all kinds of restrictions, proof required, and limitations. Guarantees with a large number of restrictions are generally not effective, and they tend to lose power in direct proportion to the number of conditions they contain.

Meaningful

An effective guarantee should be *meaningful*. Guaranteeing what is obvious or expected is not meaningful to customers. For example, a water delivery company offered a guarantee to deliver water on the day promised or a free jug of water would be provided next time. In that industry, delivery on the day scheduled was an expectation nearly always met by every competitor—thus, the guarantee was not meaningful to the customer. It was a bit like guaranteeing four wheels on an automobile! The payout, if a problem occurs, should also be meaningful. Customers expect to be reimbursed in a manner that fully compensates them for their dissatisfaction, their time, and even for the hassle involved. One of us has offered university students a guarantee in our Service Marketing, classes; compensation for poor service, which includes reimbursement for the cost of the three-credit course, is generally perceived by students as quite meaningful.[55]

Easy to Understand

A firm's guarantee should also be *easy to understand* and communicate to both customers and employees. If the wording is confusing or the language within the guarantee is verbose, neither customers nor employees may be clear as to what is being guaranteed. Bennigan's restaurants guarantee that lunch will be served quickly—within 15 minutes with its Lunch Crunch guarantee. The promise "It's Fast or It's Free" makes it clear to customers that they will not have to spend a lot of time waiting for lunch; the guarantee also makes it clear to employees that lunches should take no longer than 15 minutes to get to customers.

Easy to Invoke

Similarly, an effective guarantee should be *easy to invoke*. California Pizza Kitchen offers a guarantee, presented on page 204, to encourage customers to try new menu items. To invoke the guarantee, customers merely have to inform the waitstaff that they prefer their old "favorite" dish, and it is provided at no additional charge. Requiring customers to write a detailed letter and/or provide documented proof of service failure are common pitfalls that make invoking a guarantee time-consuming and not worth it to the customer, particularly if the dollar value of the service is relatively low.

California Pizza Kitchen service guarantee offer sent out via Twitter.

© California Pizza Kitchen

Types of Service Guarantees

Service guarantees can be *unconditional satisfaction guarantees* or *service attribute guarantees.* For unconditional satisfaction guarantees, any aspect of the service, whether related to the outcome or the delivery process, should be to the customer's liking—there are no limits or conditions. The Hampton Inn® Hotels guarantee is an unconditional satisfaction guarantee. In another context, Inflectra, a company that provides software to a variety of businesses, offers its clients an unconditional guarantee for its services.[56] If clients are unhappy, they can request their money back for the service. Professional Staffing Group offers an unconditional guarantee to any client using its staffing service; if the client organization is unhappy with the person assigned to the client, the client is not billed. Lands' End, a catalog retailer, has abbreviated its guarantee to "Guaranteed. Period."

In other cases, firms offer guarantees focused on particular attributes of the service that are important to customers. FedEx offers a money-back guarantee if a package is not delivered by the delivery commitment agreement. Benjamin Franklin Plumbing promises to arrive on time: "If there's any delay, it's you we pay." If they do not show up to the customer's house in the time frame promised, the billing system automatically subtracts from the final bill five dollars for every minute they are late.[57] The Bennigan's guarantee mentioned earlier ensures customers will not have to wait longer than 15 minutes to receive their lunch. In all these cases, the companies have guaranteed specific elements of the service that they know are important to customers.

Benefits of Service Guarantees

Service organizations are now recognizing that guarantees can serve not only as a marketing tool but also as a means for defining, cultivating, and maintaining quality throughout an organization. The benefits to the company of an effective service guarantee are numerous:[58]

- *A good guarantee forces the company to focus on its customers.* To develop a meaningful guarantee, the company must know what is important to its customers—what they expect and value. In many cases "satisfaction" is guaranteed, but for the guarantee to work effectively, the company must clearly understand what satisfaction means for its customers (what they value and expect).

- *An effective guarantee sets clear standards for the organization.* It prompts the company to clearly define what it expects of its employees and to communicate that expectation to them. The guarantee gives employees service-oriented goals that can quickly align employee behaviors with customer strategies. For example, Pizza Hut's guarantee "If you're not satisfied with your pizza, let our restaurant know. We'll make it right or give you your money back" lets employees know exactly what they should do if a customer complains. It is also clear to employees that making it right for the customer is an important company goal.

- *A good guarantee generates immediate and relevant feedback from customers.* Having a guarantee can provide an incentive for customers to complain and thereby provides more representative feedback to the company than simply relying on a relatively small number of customers to voice their concerns. The guarantee communicates to customers that they have the right to complain.

- *When the guarantee is invoked there is an instant opportunity to recover.* Dissatisfaction can perhaps be controlled, or at least not allowed to grow, if the customer is exposed to instant recovery. A quick recovery can go a long way toward satisfying the customer and helping retain loyalty.

- *Information generated through the guarantee can be tracked and integrated into continuous improvement efforts.* Guarantees can provide a somewhat structured mechanism for listening to the customer, thus helping to close the listening gap. A feedback link between customers and service operations decisions can be strengthened through the guarantee.

- *For customers, the guarantee reduces their sense of risk and builds confidence in the organization.* Because services are intangible and often highly personal or ego-involving, customers seek information and cues that will help reduce their sense of uncertainty. Guarantees have been shown to reduce risk and increase positive evaluation of the service prior to purchase.[59]

The bottom line for the company is that an effective guarantee can affect profitability through building customer awareness and loyalty, through positive word-of-mouth communication, and through reduction in costs as service improvements are made and service recovery expenses are reduced. Indirectly, the guarantee can reduce costs of employee turnover through creating a more positive service culture.

When to Use (or Not Use) a Guarantee

Service guarantees are not appropriate for every company and certainly not in every service situation. Before putting a guarantee strategy in place, a firm needs to address

Exhibit 7.5 Questions to Consider in Implementing a Service Guarantee

DECIDING WHO DECIDES

- Is there a guarantee champion in the company?
- Is senior management committed to a guarantee?
- Is the guarantee design a team effort?
- Are customers providing input?

WHEN DOES A GUARANTEE MAKE SENSE?

- How high are quality standards?
- Can we afford a guarantee?
- How high is customer risk?
- Are competitors offering a guarantee?
- Is the company's culture compatible with a guarantee?

WHAT TYPE OF GUARANTEE SHOULD WE OFFER?

- Should we offer an unconditional guarantee or a specific-outcome one?
- Is our service measurable?
- What should our specific guarantee be about?
- What are the uncontrollables?
- Is the company particularly susceptible to unreasonable triggerings?
- What should the payout be?
- Will a refund send the wrong message?
- Could a full refund make customers feel guilty?
- Is the guarantee easy to invoke?

Source: A. L. Ostrom and C. W. L. Hart, "Service Guarantees: Research and Practice," in *Handbook of Services Marketing and Management*, ed. D. Iacobucci and T. Swartz (Thousand Oaks, CA: Sage Publications, 2000).

a number of important questions (see Exhibit 7.5). A guarantee is probably *not* the right strategy when:

- *Existing service quality in the company is poor.* Before instituting a guarantee, the company should fix any significant quality problems. A guarantee will certainly draw attention to failures and to poor service quality, so the costs of implementing the guarantee could easily outweigh any benefits. These costs include actual monetary payouts to customers for poor service as well as costs associated with customer goodwill.

- *A guarantee does not fit the company's image.* If the company already has a reputation for very high quality, and in fact implicitly guarantees its service, then a formal guarantee is most likely unnecessary and provides limited benefits.[60] For example, if the Four Seasons Hotel were to offer an explicit guarantee, it could confuse customers who already expect the highest of quality, implicitly guaranteed, from this high-end hotel chain. Research suggests that the benefits of offering a guarantee for luxury hotels like the Four Seasons or the Ritz-Carlton may be significantly less than the benefits that a hotel of lesser quality would offer, and the benefits might not be justified by the costs.[61]

- *Service quality is truly uncontrollable.* Service providers can encounter situations in which service quality is truly uncontrollable. To illustrate, it would not be a good practice for a university to guarantee that all MBA students will get the job they want immediately upon graduation—it cannot control what jobs are available in the marketplace. Similarly, an airline flying out of Chicago in the winter would probably not guarantee on-time departure because of the unpredictability and uncontrollability of the weather.

- *Potential exists for customer abuse of the guarantee.* Fear of opportunistic customer behavior, including customer cheating or fraudulent invocation of service guarantees, is a common reason that firms hesitate to offer guarantees.[62] One study found that guarantees are more likely to be abused when offered in situations in which a large percentage of customers are not regular (repeat) customers.[63] However, customer abuse of service guarantees is fairly minimal and not at all widespread.[64] For example, each year Hampton Inn® Hotels refunds less than 0.5 percent of its total room revenue to dissatisfied customers.

- *Costs of the guarantee outweigh the benefits.* As it would with any quality investment, the company will want to carefully calculate expected costs (payouts for failures and costs of making improvements) against anticipated benefits (customer loyalty, quality improvements, attraction of new customers, word-of-mouth advertising).

- *Customers perceive little risk in the service.* Guarantees are usually most effective when customers are uncertain about the company and/or the quality of its services. A service guarantee can allay uncertainties and help reduce risk.[65] If customers perceive little risk, if the service is relatively inexpensive with many potential alternative providers, and if quality is relatively invariable, then a guarantee will likely produce little effectiveness for the company other than perhaps some promotional value.

SWITCHING VERSUS STAYING FOLLOWING SERVICE RECOVERY

Ultimately, how a service failure is handled and the customer's reaction to the recovery effort can influence future decisions to remain loyal to the service provider or to switch to another provider. In a study of airline customers, researchers found that those who were not satisfied with service recovery were four times more likely to believe their relationship with the airline was weakened or broken, and more likely to switch to a different airline, than were those who were happy with how their problems were addressed.[66] Whether customers switch to a new provider following service failure will depend, in addition, on a number of other factors. The magnitude and criticality of the failure will clearly be a factor in future repurchase decisions. The more serious the failure, the more likely the customer is to switch, no matter what the recovery effort.[67]

The nature of the customer's relationship with the firm may also influence whether the customer stays or switches providers. Research suggests that customers who have "true relationships" with their service providers are more forgiving of poorly handled service failures and are less likely to switch than are those who have a "pseudo-relationship" or a "first-time encounter" type of relationship.[68] A true relationship is one in which the customer has had repeated contact over time with the same service provider. A first-time encounter relationship is one in which the customer has had only one contact, on a transaction basis, with the provider. And a pseudo-relationship is one in which the customer has interacted many times with the same company, but with different service providers each time.

Other research reveals that a customer's attitude toward switching strongly influences whether he or she ultimately stays with the provider and that this attitude will be even more influential than basic satisfaction with the service.[69] This research suggests that certain customers will have a greater propensity to switch service providers no matter how their service failure situations are handled. Research in an online service context, for example, shows that demographic factors such as age and income as well as individual factors such as risk aversion influence whether a customer continues to use an online service or switches to another provider.[70] The profile of an "online service switcher" emerged in the research as a person who was influenced to subscribe to the service through positive word-of-mouth communication, who used the service less, who was less satisfied and less involved with the service, who had a lower income and education level, and who had a lower propensity for taking risks.

Finally, the decision to switch to a different service provider may not occur immediately following service failure or poor service recovery but may follow an accumulation of events. That is, service switching can be viewed as a process resulting from a series of decisions and critical service encounters over time rather than one specific moment in time when a decision is made.[71] This process orientation suggests that companies could track customer interactions and predict the likelihood of defection based on a series of events, intervening earlier in the process to head off the customer's decision to switch.

Although customers decide to switch service providers for a variety of reasons, service failure and poor service recovery are often a cause of such behavior. A study of approximately 500 service-switching incidents identified eight broad themes underlying the decision to defect.[72] These themes (pricing, inconvenience, core service failure, service encounter failure, response to service failure, competition, ethical problems, and involuntary switching) are shown in Figure 7.7. In about 200 of the incidents, a single theme was identified as the cause for switching service providers, and the two largest categories were related to service failure. Core service failure was the cause of switching for 25 percent of the respondents, and service encounter failure was the reason for switching services for an additional 20 percent of the sample. In incidents that listed two themes, 29 percent listed core service failure and 18 percent service encounter failure as contributing to their desire to switch providers; poor response to failure was mentioned by an additional 11 percent of the respondents as the cause for switching. As these findings and others suggest, service failure can cause customers to switch companies.[73] To minimize the impact of service failure, excellent service recovery is needed.

FIGURE 7.7
Causes of Service Switching

Source: S. Keaveney, "Customer Switching Behavior in Service Industries: An Exploratory Study," *Journal of Marketing* 59 (April 1995), pp. 71–82, American Marketing Association.

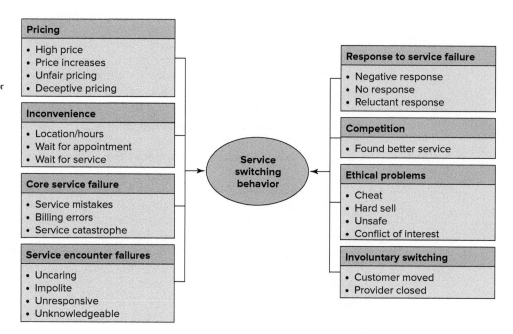

Summary

Part 3 of this text (chapters 5, 6, and 7) focuses on the critical importance of understanding customer expectations as well as many of the strategies firms use to accomplish this goal. Part of understanding customer expectations is being prepared for and knowing what to do when things go wrong or when the service fails. In this chapter we focused on service recovery, the actions taken by an organization in response to a service failure to improve the situation for the customer.

You learned in this chapter the importance of an effective service recovery strategy for retaining customers and increasing positive word-of-mouth communication. Another major benefit of an effective service recovery strategy is that the information it provides can be useful for service improvement. The potential downsides of poor service recovery are tremendous—negative word of mouth, lost customers, and declining business when quality issues are not addressed.

In this chapter you learned how customers respond to service failures and why some complain, while others do not. You learned that customers expect to be treated fairly when they complain—not just in terms of the actual outcome or compensation they receive but also in terms of the procedures used and how they are treated interpersonally. We pointed out in this chapter that there is tremendous room for improvement in service recovery effectiveness across firms and industries.

The second half of the chapter focused on two types of strategies that firms are using for service recovery. To "fix the customer" after a service failure, firms should (1) respond quickly; (2) provide appropriate communication with customers after the service has failed; (3) treat customers fairly throughout the service recovery process; and (4) cultivate relationships with customers to perhaps create a buffer when failures do occur. To "fix the problem" and prevent future recurrences of a service failure, firms should (1) encourage and track complaints; (2) learn from recovery experiences; (3) learn from lost customers; and, ideally, (4) make the service fail-safe by doing it right the first time. The chapter ended with a discussion of service guarantees as a tool used by many firms to facilitate service recovery and to listen to customers—thereby helping to close the listening gap. You learned the elements of a good guarantee, the benefits of service guarantees, and the pros and cons of using guarantees under various circumstances.

Discussion Questions

1. Why is it important for a service firm to have a strong recovery strategy? Think of a time when you received less-than-desired service from a particular service organization. Was any effort made to recover? What did the firm do to "fix the customer"? What was done to "fix the problem"? What should/could have been done differently? Do you still buy service from the organization? Why or why not? Did you tell others about your experience?

2. Discuss the benefits to a company of having an effective service recovery strategy. Describe an instance in which you experienced (or delivered as an employee) an effective service recovery. In what ways did the company benefit in this situation?

3. Explain the recovery paradox, and discuss its implications for a service firm manager.

4. Discuss the types of actions that customers can take in response to a service failure. What type of complainer are you? Why? As a manager, would you want to encourage your customers to be voicers? If so, how?

5. Review Exhibit 7.2. What would you have done if you were on the management team at United Airlines?

6. Explain the logic behind these two quotes: "a complaint is a gift" and "the customer who complains is your friend."

7. Choose a firm you are familiar with. Describe how you would design an ideal service recovery strategy for that organization.

8. What are the benefits to the company of an effective service guarantee? Should every service organization have one?

9. Describe three service guarantees that are currently offered by companies or organizations in addition to the ones already described in the chapter. (Examples are readily available on the Internet.) Are your examples good guarantees or poor guarantees based on the criteria presented in this chapter?

Exercises

1. Write a letter of complaint (or voice your complaint in person) to a service organization from which you have experienced less-than-desired service. What do you expect the organization to do to recover? (Later, report to the class the results of your complaint, whether you were satisfied with the recovery, what could/should have been done differently, and whether you will continue using the service.)

2. Interview five people about their service recovery experiences. What happened, and what did they expect the firm to do? Were they treated fairly based on the definition of recovery fairness presented in the chapter? Will they return to the company in the future?

3. Interview a manager about service recovery strategies used in his or her firm. Use the strategies shown in Figure 7.4 to frame your questions.

4. Reread the Technology Spotlight in this chapter, featuring Cisco Systems. Visit Cisco System's support website (www.cisco.com/support). Review what the company is doing to help its customers solve their own problems. Compare what Cisco is doing with the self-service efforts of another service provider of your choice.

5. Choose a service you are familiar with. Explain the service offered and develop a good service guarantee for it. Discuss why your guarantee is a good one, and list the benefits to the company of implementing it.

Notes

1. For research that shows different types of service failures, see M. J. Bitner, B. H. Booms, and M. S. Tetreault, "The Service Encounter: Diagnosing Favorable and Unfavorable Incidents," *Journal of Marketing* 54 (January 1990), pp. 71–84; S. M. Keaveney, "Customer Switching Behavior in Service Industries: An Exploratory Study," *Journal of Marketing* 59 (April 1995), pp. 71–82.

2. Information provided by TARP Worldwide Inc., based on data from 10 studies (representing responses from more than 8,000 customers) conducted in 2006 and 2007. Companies from the following industries were included: retail (stores, catalog and online), auto financing, and insurance (property/casualty).

3. For research on important outcomes associated with service recovery, see S. S. Tax, S. W. Brown, and M. Chandrashekaran, "Customer Evaluations of Service Complaint Experiences: Implications for Relationship Marketing," *Journal of Marketing* 62 (April 1998), pp. 60–76; S. S. Tax and S. W. Brown, "Recovering and Learning from Service Failure," *Sloan Management Review* 40 (Fall 1998), pp. 75–88; A. K. Smith and R. N. Bolton, "An Experimental Investigation of

Customer Reactions to Service Failure and Recovery Encounters," *Journal of Service Research* 1 (August 1998), pp. 65–81; R. N. Bolton, "A Dynamic Model of the Customer's Relationship with a Continuous Service Provider: The Role of Satisfaction," *Marketing Science* 17 (1998), pp. 45–65; A. K. Smith and R. N. Bolton, "The Effect of Customers' Emotional Responses to Service Failures on Their Recovery Effort Evaluations and Satisfaction Judgments," *Journal of the Academy of Marketing Science* 30 (Winter 2002), pp. 5–23; C. M. Voorhees, M. K. Brady, and D. M. Horowitz, "A Voice from the Silent Masses: An Exploratory and Comparative Analysis of Noncomplainers," *Journal of the Academy of Marketing Science* 34 (Fall 2006), pp. 514–527; C. Orsingher, S. Valentini, and M. de Angelis, "A Meta-Analysis of Satisfaction with Complaint Handling in Services," *Journal of the Academy of Marketing Science* 38 (2010), pp. 169–186.

4. Information included in Figure 7.2 is based on data from the 2015 Customer Rage Study, conducted by Customer Care Measurement and Consulting, Alexandria, Virginia, in collaboration with the Center for Services Leadership at Arizona State University's W. P. Carey School of Business.

5. 2015 and 2013 Customer Rage Studies conducted by Customer Care Measurement and Consulting.

6. Ibid; Voorhees, Brady, and Horowitz, "A Voice from the Silent Masses."

7. Tax and Brown, "Recovering and Learning from Service Failure."

8. 2015 Customer Rage Study, conducted by Customer Care Measurement and Consulting and the Center for Services Leadership at Arizona State University.

9. See C. W. Hart, J. L. Heskett, and W. E. Sasser Jr., "The Profitable Art of Service Recovery," *Harvard Business Review* 68 (July–August 1990), pp. 148–156; M. A. McCollough and S. G. Bharadwaj, "The Recovery Paradox: An Examination of Consumer Satisfaction in Relation to Disconfirmation, Service Quality, and Attribution Based Theories," in *Marketing Theory and Applications,* ed. C. T. Allen et al. (Chicago: American Marketing Association, 1992), p. 119.

10. C. A. de Matos, J. L. Henrique, and C. A. V. Rossi, "Service Recovery Paradox: A Meta-analysis," *Journal of Service Research* 10 (August 2007), pp. 60–77.

11. Smith and Bolton, "An Experimental Investigation of Customer Reactions to Service Failure and Recovery Encounters."

12. V. P. Magnini, J. B. Ford, E. P. Markowski, and E. D. Honeycutt Jr., "The Service Recovery Paradox: Justifiable Theory or Smoldering Myth?" *Journal of Services Marketing* 21 (2007), pp. 213–225; J. G. Maxham III and R. G. Netemeyer, "A Longitudinal Study of Complaining Customers' Evaluations of Multiple Service Failures and Recovery Efforts," *Journal of Marketing* 66 (October 2002), pp. 57–71; M. A. McCullough, L. L. Berry, and M. S. Yadav, "An Empirical Investigation of Customer Satisfaction after Service Failure and Recovery," *Journal of Service Research* 3 (November 2000), pp. 121–137.

13. G. Knox and R. van Oest, "Customer Complaints and Recovery Effectiveness: A Customer Base Approach," *Journal of Marketing* 24 (September 2014), pp. 42–57.

14. S. Michel and M. L. Meuter, "The Service Recovery Paradox: True but Overrated?" *International Journal of Service Industry Management* 19 (2008), pp. 441–457; R. Priluck and V. Lala, "The Impact of the Recovery Paradox on Retailer-Customer Relationships," *Managing Service Quality* 19 (2009), pp. 42–59.

and most reliable predictors of success for new introductions relate to *product/ service characteristics* (product meeting customer needs, product advantage over competing products, technological sophistication), *strategy characteristics* (dedicated human resources to support the initiative, dedicated research and development [R&D] focused on the new product initiative), *process characteristics* (marketing, predevelopment, technological, and launch proficiencies), and *marketplace characteristics* (market potential).[2] Failures, on the other hand, can be traced to a number of causes: no unique benefits offered, insufficient demand, unrealistic goals for the new product/ service, poor fit between the new service and others within the organization's portfolio, poor location, insufficient financial backing, or failure to take the necessary time to develop and introduce the product.[3] Frequently a good service idea fails because of development, design, and specification flaws, topics emphasized in this chapter. As more firms, across industries, move into services as a growth strategy, the challenges of and opportunities for developing and delivering service offerings become even more apparent.

CHALLENGES OF SERVICE INNOVATION AND DESIGN

Because services are largely intangible and process oriented (such as a hospital stay, a golf lesson, an NBA basketball game, or a sophisticated information technology consulting service), they are difficult to describe and communicate. When services are delivered or cocreated with the customer over a long period—a week's resort vacation, a six-month consulting engagement, a multi-year business process outsourcing contract, or 10 weeks on a Weight Watchers program—their complexity increases, and they become even more difficult to define and describe. Further, because services are delivered by employees to customers, and often cocreated *with* customers, they are variable. Rarely are two services alike or experienced in the same way. These fundamental characteristics of service offerings, which we explored in the first chapter of this book, are the heart of the challenge involved in innovating and designing services. Global companies and governments around the world are awakening to these challenges and the recognition that, despite the dominance of services in the world's economies, there is disproportionately less focus on service innovation in companies and in research.[4] Our Global Feature discusses the importance of service innovation as a priority for companies and national economies.

Because service offerings typically cannot be touched, examined, or easily tried out, people have historically resorted to words in their efforts to describe them. Yet, there are a number of risks inherent in attempting to describe services in words alone.[5] The first risk is *oversimplification.* "To say that 'portfolio management' means 'buying and selling stocks' is like describing the space shuttle as 'something that flies.' Some people will picture a bird, some a helicopter, and some an angel."[6] Words are simply inadequate to describe a complex service system such as financial portfolio management. In our modern global economy, service systems have significantly increased in complexity, often involving networks of service firms, customers, and evolution of offerings over time.[7] Within these complex systems, the risks of oversimplification are even more apparent.

The second risk of using words alone is *incompleteness.* In describing services, people (employees, managers, customers) tend to omit details or elements of the service with which they are not familiar. A person might do a fairly credible job of describing how a discount stock brokerage service takes orders from customers. But would that person be able to describe fully how the monthly statements are created, how the interactive computer system works, and how these two elements of the service are integrated into the order-taking process?

The third risk is *subjectivity.* Any one person describing a service in words will be biased by personal experiences and degree of exposure to the service. There is a natural (and mistaken) tendency to assume that, because all people have gone to a fast-food restaurant, they all understand what that service is. Persons working in different functional areas of the same service organization (a marketing person, an operations person, a finance person) are likely to describe the service very differently as well, biased by their own functional blinders.

A final risk of describing services using words alone is *biased interpretation.* No two people will define "responsive," "quick," or "flexible" in exactly the same way. For example, a supervisor or manager may suggest to a frontline service employee that the employee should try to be more flexible or responsive in providing service to the customer. Unless the term "flexibility" is further defined, the employee is likely to interpret the word differently than the manager.

All these risks and challenges become very apparent in the innovation and service development process, when organizations attempt to design complex services never before experienced by customers or when they attempt to change existing services.[8]

IMPORTANT CONSIDERATIONS FOR SERVICE INNOVATION

In this section we highlight some important considerations when innovating or developing new services. Because of the inherent characteristics of services described in detail in Chapter 1, and the challenges of service development and innovation just described, it has become clear to many service managers that service innovation is different from tangible product innovation. Because services are intangible and process based, and because they frequently involve interactions among and between customers and employees, it is important to involve both customers *and* employees at various points in the innovation process. It is also important to use a systems or design mind-set, sometimes referred to as "design thinking," to be sure all elements are considered and integrated. Here we overview these considerations as a backdrop for the tools, techniques, and approaches described in the rest of the chapter.

Involve Customers and Employees

Because services are produced, consumed, and cocreated in real time and often involve interaction between and among employees and customers, it is critical that innovation and new service development processes involve both employees and customers throughout the process.[9] Employees frequently *are* the service, or at least they perform or deliver the service, and thus their involvement in choosing which new services to develop and how these services should be designed and implemented can be very beneficial. Contact employees are psychologically and physically close to customers and research has shown they can be very helpful in identifying customer needs for innovative new services.[10] Involving employees in service innovation and design also increases the likelihood of new service success because employees can identify the organizational issues that need to be addressed to support the delivery of the service to customers.[11]

Innovation, across all economic sectors, is required for the continued growth and competeveness of individual companies, governmental entities, and entire economies. Based on approximately 80 indicators, The Global Innovation Index (GII) is an annual ranking of countries based on their overall capacity and success in innovation (see insert for the top 25 countries for 2015). While the countries comprising the top 25 have not changed a lot over the years, the report identifies "innovation achievers" among middle-income (e.g., China, Vietnam, India) and low-income (e.g., Malawi, Kenya, Cambodia) countries as well as the predictable high-income countries shown in the top-25 rankings. The report also notes that the technology gap between developing and developed countries is narrowing. This index, published annually by Cornell University, INSEAD, and The World Intellectual Property Organization (WIPO), does not distinguish service innovation from innovation generally. Yet, the dominance and/or growth of services in most economies would logically suggest innovation in services is critical.

Focusing specifically on services, a 2015 study on "Service Research Priorities in a Rapidly Changing Context" identified "stimulating service innovation" as one of the top priorities. Seeking to identify priorities for both practice and research, this study was based on input from academics and business practitioners from around the world and across disciplines and functions. Interviews, surveys, and roundtables were conducted with people from 37 countries. The study's findings identify priorities for research as well as knowledge gaps. Among the 12 priorities identified in the study, stimulating service innovation was ranked third in terms of importance and fourth in terms of knowledge gap. The following five sub-topics were seen as specific areas where knowledge is needed to advance service innovation in companies and countries:

- Innovating within complex service systems and value networks.
- Identifying drivers of sustained service innovation.
- Managing customers' and partners' collaboration throughout the service innovation process.
- Innovating services through crowdsourcing and open innovation.
- Understanding the interrelationships among service–product, service–process, and business–model innovation.

Despite the importance of innovation generally and service innovation in particular, a benchmarking review of service innovation policies in Europe reported great diversity in policies and intensity of focus on service innovation across countries. The authors of the report called out a few

Because customers often actively participate in service delivery and/or cocreation, they, too, should be involved in the new service development process. Beyond just providing input on their own needs, customers can help design the service concept and the delivery process, particularly in situations in which the customer personally carries out part of the service process. For example, Bank of America was successful with developing new service innovations in branch banking by relying on results of a series of experiments in its Atlanta branches.[12] The experiments were designed to more rigorously test new service innovations, in real time and with real customers, before launching them more broadly throughout the branch system. Similarly, the Mayo Clinic has established its Center for Innovation in Rochester to experiment with new service innovations by testing them with actual patients and doctors in a prototype setting prior to introducing them (see Exhibit 8.2 later in the chapter).

Employ Service Design Thinking and Techniques

One of the challenges of service innovation and design is that services are processes and they are experiential, taking place over time. In some cases, the time required to deliver the service may translate into just a few minutes, but other times the service experience can encompass hours, days, weeks, and even years, as in the case of a university degree program or a service outsourcing contract. Services often occur as a sequence of interrelated steps and activities and engage a number of people, processes, and tangible elements. For example, employees, customers, subcontractors, countries that are very advanced in service innovation policies and practices—namely, Finland, Sweden, and Ireland. They also mention Austria, Germany, and Denmark as being among other countries that have maintained a policy interest in service innovation.

In the United States, much of the impetus behind the growing awareness of the need for service innovation is attributed to the leadership of IBM. The company catalyzed a global movement to shape the future of service innovation and a potential new discipline called "service science, management and engineering" (SSME) to develop skilled professionals for the service economy. Together with Cisco, Hewlett-Packard and several universities, IBM cofounded ISSIP, the International Society for Service Industry Professionals. The mission of ISSIP is to promote service innovation for the interconnected world and its purpose is to help institutions and individuals to grow and be successful in the global service economy. Although the primary thrust for service innovation in the United States has come from the private sector, government agencies, notably the National Science Foundation (NSF), are beginning to respond. For several years, the NSF has provided Smart Service Systems funding support for specific research proposals through its Partnerships for Innovation: Building Innovation Capacity (PFI/BIC) program.

Top 25, Global Innovation Index Rankings, 2015

1. Switzerland	13. Iceland
2. United Kingdom	14. Korea, Republic of
3. Sweden	15. New Zealand
4. Netherlands	16. Canada
5. United States of America	17. Australia
	18. Austria
6. Finland	19. Japan
7. Singapore	20. Norway
8. Ireland	21. France
9. Luxembourg	22. Israel
10. Denmark	23. Estonia
11. Hong Kong	24. Czech Republic
12. Germany	25. Belgium

Sources: Cornell University, INSEAD, and WIPO, "The Global Innovation Index 2015: Effective Innovation Policies for Development," Ithaca, Fontainebleau, and Geneva, 2015, Creative Commons Attribution; A. L. Ostrom, A. Parasuraman, D. E. Bowen, L. Patricio, and C. A. Voss, "Service Research Priorities in a Rapidly Changing Context," *Journal of Service Research* 18 (May 2015), pp. 127–159; European Commission, ESIC European Service Innovation Centre Discussion Paper, "Service Innovation Policy—A Benchmarking Review," January 2015, www.issip.org.

technology, equipment, and physical spaces are often involved in service and therefore need to be considered in its design. As a result, designing a service offering or service system requires collaboration and coordination across functions, and perhaps even across different organizations.

Recognizing the complexities and requirements of service innovation, the field of "service design" has emerged and is gaining increasing attention from business practitioners, design consultants, service marketers, and a variety of academic disciplines. In a global study to identify the research priorities for the science of service, service design came to the forefront as one of the top 12 research priorities for the future.[13] There are a number of global consultancy firms that focus their efforts on service design. For example design firm IDEO, based in the United States; Engine Service Design in the United Kingdom; and Live/Work, also in the United Kingdom, all have practices devoted to service design.

So what is meant by service design and service design thinking? And what do these service design consultancy firms do to help their clients produce great service innovations? While there is not one shared definition, here are two from noted companies and experts:

"Service design aims to ensure service interfaces are useful, usable, and desirable from the client's point of view and efficient and distinctive from the supplier's point of view." Birgit Mager, professor of service design, University of Cologne, Germany[14] "Service design is focused on bringing service strategy and innovative

Technology Spotlight   Facebook: A Radical Service Innovation

When Facebook was launched in Mark Zuckerberg's dormitory room at Harvard University in 2004, it was not much more than a communication vehicle for Harvard students. According to David Kirkpatrick's authoritative book on the company, Facebook's beginnings can be traced to other Zuckerberg projects during the same year at Harvard—first to Course Match (a way to learn about who was registered for a particular class and what classes your friends were taking) and then to Facemash, whose purpose was to figure out who was the hottest person on campus. In the winter of 2004 Zuckerberg launched Thefacebook.com, borrowing from his previous projects and adding elements that invited individuals to create personal profiles of themselves. The original Facebook concept was limited and innocent enough. Similar to most social networks up to that time, its primary purpose was to help people connect socially, often for dating, and its audience was limited initially to Harvard students. Quickly, other schools asked to join Thefacebook and set up sites for their students. By the end of the 2004 academic year, 34 schools had joined and Thefacebook had about 100,000 users. That was the beginning, but it was only the very beginning.

In a few years, Facebook (the name was changed in 2005) grew to be the powerhouse of social media. In 2010, approximately 143 million Americans were active on Facebook, representing 46.8 percent of the entire population! According to March 2016 Facebook statistics on its website, there were 1.09 billion active daily users worldwide, with over 84 percent of those residing outside the United States and Canada. Including active monthly users, that number jumps to over 1.5 billion. Users spend their time reacting to, commenting on, sharing, and scrolling through status updates, with the average user spending approximately 20 minutes per day on the site. This accounts for almost 20 percent of all time spent online, making Facebook one of the most valuable websites online today. In 2015, Facebook reported year-end revenues of over $17.9 billion.

Clearly, Facebook is a radical service innovation that has shown extraordinary growth and is extremely popular. Nothing like it existed before, and its limits and bounds are unknown. From the original basic social site for Harvard students, the company has evolved into a complex social networking giant. Some claim that entire industries—such as the photo-sharing industry and games—have been transformed through Facebook. Going far beyond its original focus on facilitating individual social connections, Facebook has introduced many new features and mobile phone applications such as "Nearby Friends," which allows smart phone users to see which of their friends is physically nearby, giving

service ideas to life by aligning various internal and external stakeholders around the creation of holistic service experiences for customers, clients, employees, business partners, and/or citizens." Center for Services Leadership, Arizona State University[15]

Given the interdisciplinary and interactional nature of service design and its focus on customer experiences, a set of five principles has been proposed as central to service design thinking:[16]

User-centered: Services should be experienced and designed through the customer's eyes.
Cocreative: All stakeholders should be included in the service design process.
Sequencing: A service should be visualized as a sequence of interrelated actions.
Evidencing: Intangible services should be visualized in terms of physical artifacts.
Holistic: The entire environment of a service should be considered.

Service designers who adhere to these principles are "engaged visualizing, formulating, and choreographing solutions that are not yet available. They watch and interpret needs and behaviors and transform them into potential future services."[17] Designing, innovating, and improving service experiences based on these principles has resulted in a number of new terms, techniques, and methods being developed and applied,

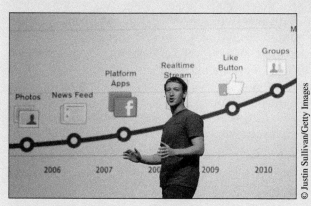

Facebook CEO, Mark Zuckerberg, describes the company's rapid growth.

creation of even more stringent options for users to control access to their personal information. Competition is always a challenge, and Facebook has continued to make strategic acquisitions to stay relevant (some examples include Instagram and WhatsApp). Recently, Facebook also acquired Masquerade (Msqrd), an app that allows users to apply filters to their photos and videos, in a bid to compete with Snapchat, whose CEO declined Facebook's $3 billion purchase offer.

Time will tell who succeeds and who fails in the online social networking world. No matter how it turns out, it is certain that Mark Zuckerberg and Facebook have launched a revolution and service innovation in networking that will affect individuals, companies, governments, and industries well into the future.

users the chance to message each other and meet up if they choose.

It is easy to imagine that the future of Facebook will be bright, given its history and trajectory. It is highly innovative and far-reaching, and it seems to anticipate and understand the ways that people want to interact through technology. Still, the company has its challenges. The issue of user privacy comes up frequently and was addressed recently by Facebook through the

Sources: D. Gelles, "Every Industry Is Going to Be Rethought in a Social Way," *Financial Times*, December 4, 2010, p. 14; D. Kirkpatrick, *The Facebook Effect,* New York: Simon & Schuster Paperbacks, 2010; www.facebook.com, accessed June 2016; Facebook 2015 Annual Report; J. D'Onfro, "Here's How Much Time People Spend on Facebook per Day," *Business Insider*, July 8, 2015, http://www.businessinsider.com/how-much-time-people-spend-on-facebook-per-day-2015-7; I. Lunden, "Facebook Acquires Video Filter App Masqrd to Square Up to Snapchat," *TechCrunch*, March 9, 2016, https://techcrunch.com/2016/03/09/facebook-acquires-video-filter-app-msqrd-to-square-up-to-snapchat/.

specifically for service innovation.[18] For example, terms such as *customer journey, touchpoints, personas, cocreation,* and *service prototypes* are common among service designers. Methodologies include customer journey mapping, storytelling, service safaris, shadowing, storyboard, service role-play, and others. One of the primary techniques for service design is service blueprinting, presented in detail later in this chapter. Exhibit 8.2 (later in the chapter), describing Mayo Clinic's Center for Innovation, provides an example of design thinking in action.

TYPES OF SERVICE INNOVATION

Service innovation has been defined in various ways. Sometimes when people talk about service innovation they are referring to innovation and improvement related to service offerings themselves. For example, McDonald Corporation's significant restaurant redesign and menu changes are examples of offering innovations. In other cases service innovation is associated with new internal service processes that will make an organization more productive and efficient. The introduction of new technology support systems for frontline employees represents this type of service innovation. In other cases service innovation is associated with enhancements in the customer experience or significant changes in the role of the customer. For example, the proliferation of self-service innovations has significantly altered the role of the customer in many industries. Our Technology Spotlight on the preceding two pages, featuring Facebook, provides an example of this type of radical service innovation. The term *service innovation* is also tied to major change initiatives within organizations, such as when a traditional manufacturing or operations-driven company decides to transform its entire go-to-market strategy around service and solutions rather than its products. At an even more macro level, service innovation can be tied to entire industries and service systems. For example, many of IBM's Smarter Planet initiatives are aimed at transforming entire service systems, including health care, education, transportation, and government, through service innovations.

In this section, we cover several meanings and types of service innovations, including service offering innovation, innovating around customer roles, and innovation through service solutions.

Service Offering Innovation

Not all service innovations are "new" to the same degree. New services run the gamut from major or radical introductions to minor style changes, described below.

- *Major or radical innovations* are new services for markets as yet undefined. Past examples include the first broadcast television services and Federal Express's introduction of nationwide, overnight small-package delivery. Many current and future examples of radical innovations will be provided through the Cloud, mobile apps, and the Internet of Things. For example, many of the new services spawned by data being gathered from machines and people (e.g., remote repair service of machines and remote health diagnostics for people) were never even thought of until the data and software existed to support the service innovation. Many innovations now and in the future will evolve from information, computer, and Internet-based technologies. Often these major innovations create brand-new markets.[19]

- *Start-up businesses* consist of new services for a market already served by existing products that meet the same generic needs. Service examples include the creation of health maintenance organizations to provide an alternative form of health care delivery, online banking for financial transactions, and ride sharing services that compete with traditional taxi and limousine services. Many new mobile phone applications fit in this category.

- *New services for the currently served market* represent attempts to offer existing customers of the organization a service not previously available from the company (although it may be available from other companies). Examples include retailers adding a coffee bar or children's play area, a health club offering nutrition classes, and airlines offering phone and Internet services during flights. Sometimes they represent only modest enhancement services, as in these examples. Other times the offering may represent a radically new stand-alone service such as PetSmart's PetsHotels, described in the chapter opener.

- *Service-line extensions* represent augmentations of the existing service line, such as a restaurant adding new menu items, an airline offering new routes, a law firm offering additional legal services, and a university adding new courses or degrees.

- *Service improvements* represent perhaps the most common type of service innovation. Changes in features of services already offered might involve faster execution of an existing service process, extended hours of service, or augmentations such as added amenities in a hotel room (e.g., the addition of wireless Internet connections).

- *Style changes* represent the most modest service innovations, although they are often highly visible and can have significant effects on customer perceptions, emotions, and attitudes. Changing the color scheme of a restaurant, revising the logo for an organization, redesigning a website, or painting aircraft a different color all represent style changes. These innovations do not fundamentally change the service, only its appearance, similar to how packaging changes are used for consumer products.

Innovating around Customer Roles

The types of service innovations described in the preceding section are tied to the offerings themselves, suggesting that innovation occurs when a service offering is altered or expanded in some way—either radically on one extreme or stylistically at the other extreme. It is also possible that service innovations may come about when the customer's usage or cocreation role is redefined. For example, assuming the customer plays the role of user, buyer, or payer in a service context, new services can result when the previous role is redefined.[20] Many radical innovations effectively redefine the customer's role in these ways. For example, Netflix totally redefined the customer's role for movie rentals. While customers used to visit their local Blockbuster store to rent one or more movies for a predetermined period of time and pay for them on a per-movie basis, Netflix's initial innovation was to allow customers to receive movies through the mail, pay for them on a service contract, and return them whenever they were ready to do so. While it is still possible to receive movies via mail, more often now customers stream movies, TV episodes, and other content via the Internet directly to their smart phones, TVs, or other devices. Thus, while movie watching in the home has not changed, the entire service process for acquiring, receiving, paying for, and returning the movies is radically different.

Innovation through Service Solutions

Many organizations realize that customers are not looking for one stand-alone product or service but, rather, innovative solutions to their problems. Traditional thinking has viewed solutions as "bundles of goods and services" that companies offer to customers. However, research by Kapil Tuli, Ajay Kohli, and Sundar Bharadwaj shows that solutions, as defined by customers, are not bundles of products and services at all, but rather they are sets of customer-facing processes. These relational processes comprise (1) customer requirements definition, (2) customization and integration of goods and/or services, (3) deployment of these integrated solutions, and (4) postdeployment customer support.[21] Another researcher, Lance Bettencourt, suggests that service innovation is the result of understanding customers' problems and the jobs they are trying to get done, then developing solutions to help them reach those goals.[22] In Bettencourt's experience, the keys are to figure out what customers are trying to do and to develop services and solutions around that understanding. Yet other researchers focus on "customer activity chains" and the development of services and solutions to enhance these activities.[23] For example, Shutterfly offers all kinds of services online to enhance customers' sharing of memories through photography.

When companies begin to think in terms of solutions for customers, they start to spend more time with customers, listening to and observing their problems and identifying pain points that can be addressed through innovative solutions. In business-to-business

FIGURE 8.1
Service Innovation
and Development
Process

- **Business strategy development or review**

- **New service strategy development**

Front-end planning

- **Idea generation**
  Screen ideas against new service strategy **STOP**

- **Concept development and evaluation**
  Test concept with customers and employees **STOP**

- **Business analysis**
  Test for profitability and feasibility **STOP**

Implementation

- **Service development and testing**
  Conduct service prototype test **STOP**

- **Market testing**
  Test service and other marketing mix elements **STOP**

- **Commercialization**

- **Postintroduction evaluation**

internal processes, and facilities within already-existing systems. Partially because of these challenges, service firms are generally less likely to carry out a structured development process for new innovations than are their manufacturing and consumer-goods counterparts.[30]

An underlying assumption of new product development process models is that new product ideas can be dropped at any stage of the process if they do not satisfy the criteria for success at that stage.[31] Figure 8.1 shows the checkpoints (represented by stop signs) that separate the critical stages of the development process. The checkpoints specify requirements that a new service must meet before it can proceed to the next stage of development.

Despite what Figure 8.1 suggests, however, new service or product development is not always a linear process. Many companies find that some steps can be worked on simultaneously and in some instances a step may even be skipped, particularly for simple products and services. The overlapping of steps and simultaneous development of various pieces of the new service/product development process has been referred to as *flexible product development*. This type of flexible, speedy process is particularly important in technology industries, in which products and services evolve extremely quickly. In these environments, computer technology lets companies monitor customer opinions and needs during development and change the final offering right up until it is launched. Often, the next version of the service is in planning stages at the same time that the current version is being launched. Even if the stages are handled simultaneously, however, the important checkpoints noted in Figure 8.1 should be assessed to maximize chances of success.

The process shown in Figure 8.1 is divided into two sections: front-end planning and implementation. The front end determines what service concepts will be developed, whereas the back end implements the service concept. When asked where the greatest weaknesses in product and service innovation occur, managers typically report problems with the *fuzzy front end.*[32] The front end is called "fuzzy" because of its relative abstractness, which is even more apparent with intangible, complex, and variable services than with manufactured products.

Front-End Planning

Business Strategy Development or Review

One of the first steps in new service development is to review the organization's mission and vision. The new service strategy and specific new service ideas must fit within the larger strategic mission and vision of the organization. For example, PetSmart, the company featured in this chapter's opening vignette, has as its mission to serve "pet parents" through the "lifetime care of pets." This mission has led to the development of a host of new services, such as training, grooming, overnight care, and day care, in addition to traditional food, toys, and accessories offered in its stores. For PetSmart, the company's new services strategy clearly fits the mission of the company.

New Service Strategy Development

Research suggests that a product portfolio strategy and a defined organizational structure for new product or service development are critical—and are the foundations—for success. The types of new services that will be appropriate depend on the organization's goals, vision, capabilities, and growth plans. By defining a new service innovation strategy (possibly in terms of markets, types of services, time horizon for development, profit criteria, or other relevant factors), the organization will be in a better position to begin generating specific ideas. For example, it may focus its growth on new services at a particular level of the described continuum from major innovations to style changes. Or the organization may define its new service strategy even more specifically in terms of particular markets or market segments or in terms of specific profit generation goals.

One way to begin formulating a new service strategy is to use the framework shown in Figure 8.2 for identifying growth opportunities. The framework allows an organization to identify possible directions for growth and can be helpful as a catalyst for creative ideas. The framework may also later serve as an initial idea screen if, for example, the organization chooses to focus its growth efforts on one or two of the four cells in the matrix. The matrix suggests that companies can develop a growth strategy around current customers or new customers and can focus on current offerings or new service offerings. For example, for quite some time Kentucky

FIGURE 8.2
New Service Strategy Matrix for Identifying Growth Opportunities

Source: Adapted from H. I. Ansoff, *Corporate Strategy* (New York: McGraw-Hill, 1965).

Offerings	Markets	
	Current customers	**New customers**
Existing services	Share building	Market development
New services	Service development	Diversification

Strategy Insight Strategic Growth through Services

Firms in many industries are discovering the value of strategically focusing on service innovations to provide value for their customers as well as profits and growth for the firm. By adding services to their traditional offerings, firms can differentiate themselves from their competitors and frequently earn higher profit margins on the new services compared with traditional manufactured or retail product offerings. IBM Global Services is the oldest and best known example of this type of service solutions strategy. Like IBM, many companies are poised to "grow through services" in business-to-consumer as well as business-to-business markets. As they move in this direction, they quickly recognize the great opportunities as well as the complex challenges of introducing new services. Here we highlight three firms from very diverse industries and their growth-through-services strategies.

PROCTER & GAMBLE

Procter & Gamble is one of the world's largest and most admired consumer products companies. So it may come as a surprise that some of their latest ventures are taking the company into innovative services. Through its Agile Pursuits Franchising subsidiary, P&G is extending well-established and respected brands into the realm of service. Tide Dry Cleaners, and Mr. Clean Car Wash, and The Art of Shaving stores are examples. In each case, P&G looked for fragmented industries in which customer expectations are not particularly high and where P&G brand names could enhance value through proprietary technologies and an improved customer experience. For example, Tide Dry Cleaners feature bright, cheerful, bold-colored signage and interiors, drive-through lanes, and lockers accessible for after-hours pickup. The experience and the cleaning quality itself are intended to contrast sharply with consumers' experiences with typical dingy, dark, and sometimes

© Ed Zurga/Bloomberg/Getty Images

Tide Dry Cleaners—a service strategy for Procter & Gamble.

inconvenient dry cleaners. However, P&G's expansion into services must be very deliberate and done with great care so as not to risk harming the parent brand.

ERICSSON

Headquartered in Sweden, Ericsson is a leading global provider of telecommunications equipment and related services and solutions. Since the mid-1990s, it has pursued a growth strategy focused on customers, services, and solutions that add value to its sophisticated technology products. Ericsson employs about 64,000 service professionals and operates in over 180 countries. Ericsson Global Services focuses on providing services for telecommunication operators around the world, so that these companies can focus on their core business of supporting customers and building revenues. For example, through its managed services contracts, Ericsson works with operators to upgrade their systems and consults with them on network planning, design, and deployment. Beyond the basics of operational efficiency and

Fried Chicken (KFC) has grown through providing its service outside the United States, a form of market development (existing service, new customers). After over two decades of expansion in China, the company has now set its sights on Africa as its new market, with over 1,000 KFC outlets on the African continent (most in South Africa) in 2015.[33] The PetSmart services in our opening vignette, on the other hand, are examples of service development (new services, current customers). Procter & Gamble's venture into services through its Tide Dry Cleaners and Mr. Clean Car Washes are examples of yet another type of growth strategy through diversification (new services, new customers). Like Procter & Gamble and PetSmart, many companies are looking to grow strategically through service innovation (see the Strategy Insight).

reliability of systems, Ericsson also focuses on the experience of its customers' customers. They have innovated the managed services offering to include customer experience design and delivery metrics as well as operational metrics in their performance assessments. In addition to operators, Ericsson works directly with government and private business entities.

As Ericsson continues to move away from its traditional base in manufacturing, the company is reorienting its entire organization toward providing integrated solutions for customers.

VWR INTERNATIONAL

VWR International's tagline is "we enable science." VWR "is the leading, global, independent provider of products, services, and solutions to laboratory and production facilities for customers in the pharmaceutical, biotechnology, industrial, education, government and healthcare industries." This 160-year-old company serves scientific laboratories across industries in helping them to be more effective and efficient at what they do. VWR started as a product distribution company that supplied all types of scientific products (for example, beakers, pipettes, measurement scales, and so on) to labs and production facilities. As they progressed as a company, they realized that the employees of their customers—the people who actually did the science—were spending a lot of their time on non-core activities. To be specific, these highly paid scientists were spending time ordering supplies, cleaning equipment, and configuring combinations of materials they needed to run experiments, among other things, and not doing science. Enter VWRCatalyst, VWR's service company. VWRCatalyst provides services to its customers to allow them to focus on what they do best—science—while VWR manages their inventories of supplies, cleans their

equipment, and customizes packages of materials to efficiently conduct experiments in labs. VWRCatalyst can even send its employees to work alongside the customer's employees—serving as lab techs, supply managers, or in scientific support roles. VWRCatalyst supports more than 120,000 customers and employs more than 9,300 associates around the world, providing innovative services that help its customers to be more productive, efficient, and effective.

For each of these companies, the move to services represented a significant strategic choice that initially took them into uncharted waters. For P&G it meant learning how to run a service business, including designing the customer experience and hiring and training employees to deliver service on the front line. For Ericsson it meant moving away from a manufacturing and technology mind-set to one that focuses on customers and solutions. For VWR, it meant interacting with and serving their scientific laboratory customers in entirely new ways, and becoming much more intimate with their customers' businesses. Yet the potential rewards are great and customer demands for services and solutions are real. These rewards and demands are what compel more and more firms to pursue the strategic service path.

Sources: M. Sawhney, S. Balasubramanian, and V. V. Krishnan, "Creating Growth with Services," *Sloan Management Review* 45 (Winter 2004), pp. 34–43; L. Coleman-Lochner and M. Clothier, "P&G Looks to Franchise Tide Dry Cleaning," *Bloomberg Business Week*, September 2, 2010; B. Brown and S. D. Anthony, "How P&G Tripled Its Innovation Success Rate," *Harvard Business Review* 89 (June 2011), pp. 64–72; L. A. Bettencourt, *Service Innovation* (New York: McGraw-Hill, 2010), https://www.ericsson.com/portfolio/services-and-solutions, accessed July 25, 2016; https://www.vwr.com/vwrcatalyst _laboratory_services.htm, accessed July 25, 2016; V. A. Zeithaml, S. W. Brown, M. J. Bitner, and J. Salas, *Profiting from Services and Solutions: What Product-Centric Firms Need to Know*, (Business Expert Press, New York 2014).

Idea Generation

The next step in the process is the generation of new ideas that can be passed through the new service strategy screen described in the preceding step. Formal brainstorming, solicitation of ideas from employees and customers, lead user research, and learning about competitors' offerings are some of the most common approaches. Some companies are even collaborating with outsiders (e.g., competitors, vendors, alliance partners) or developing licensing agreements and joint ventures in an effort to exploit all possible sources of new ideas.[34]

Observing customers and how they use the firm's products and services can also generate creative ideas for new innovations. Sometimes referred to as *empathic design,* observation is particularly effective in situations in which customers may not be able to recognize or verbalize their needs.[35] In service businesses, contact personnel, who actually deliver the services and interact directly with consumers, can be particularly good sources of ideas for complementary services and ways to improve current offerings.[36] Some organizations have found that internal networks of employees, across functions and disciplines, can be great sources of innovative ideas; thus, organizational practices that encourage networking and make collaboration easy are also ways to encourage new ideas.[37]

Whether the source of a new idea is inside or outside the organization, some established mechanism should exist for ensuring an ongoing stream of new service possibilities. This mechanism might include a formal service innovation or service R&D department or function with responsibility for generating new ideas, online repositories where customers and/or employees can submit ideas for new services, new service development teams that meet regularly, surveys and focus groups with customers and employees, or formal competitive analysis to identify new services.

Service Concept Development and Evaluation

Once an idea surfaces that is regarded as a good fit with both the business and the new service strategies, it is ready for initial development. The inherent characteristics of services place complex demands on this phase of the process. Drawing pictures and describing an intangible service in concrete terms are difficult, particularly when the service is not standardized and may be cocreated in real time with customers. It is therefore important that agreement be reached at this stage on exactly what the concept is and what customer need it is filling. By involving multiple parties in sharpening the concept definition, it often becomes apparent that individual views of the concept are not the same. For example, in one documented case, the design and development of a new discount brokerage service was initially described by the bank as a way "to buy and sell stocks for customers at low prices."[38] Through the initial concept development phase it became clear that not everyone in the organization had the same idea about how this description would translate into an actual service and that there were a variety of ways the concept could be developed. Only through multiple iterations of the service—and the raising of hundreds of issues, large and small—was an agreement finally reached on the discount brokerage concept.

After clear definition of the concept, it is important to produce a description of the service that represents its specific characteristics and then determine initial customer and employee responses to the concept. The service design document should describe the problem addressed by the service, discuss the reasons for offering the new service, explain the service process and its benefits, and provide a rationale for purchasing the service.[39] The roles of customers and employees in the delivery and/or cocreation process are also described. It may also be very useful to create a concept-level blueprint at this point in the service innovation process. The service concept is then evaluated by asking employees and customers whether they understand the idea of the proposed service, whether they are favorable to the concept, and whether they feel it satisfies an unmet need.

Business Analysis

Assuming that the service concept is favorably evaluated by customers and employees at the concept development stage, the next step is to estimate its economic feasibility and potential profit implications. Demand analysis, revenue projections, cost analyses, and operational feasibility are assessed at this stage. Because the development of service concepts is so closely tied to the operational system of the organization, this stage will involve preliminary assumptions about the costs of personnel hiring and training, delivery system enhancements, new technology or online enhancements, facility changes, and any other projected operations costs. The organization will pass the results of the business analysis through its profitability and feasibility screen to determine whether the new service idea meets the minimum requirements.

Implementation

Once the new service concept has passed all the front-end planning hurdles, it is ready for the implementation stages of the process.

Service Prototype Development and Testing

In the development of new tangible products, the development and testing stage involves the construction of product prototypes and testing for consumer acceptance. Again, because services are intangible and simultaneously produced, consumed, and frequently cocreated, this step presents unique challenges. To address these challenges, this stage of service development should involve all who have a stake in the new service: customers and contact employees as well as functional representatives from marketing, operations, and human resources. During this phase, the concept is refined to the point at which a detailed service blueprint illustrating the customer experience and the implementation plan for the service can be produced. The blueprint is likely to evolve over a series of iterations on the basis of input from all involved parties.

In its service innovation practice, the internationally known design firm IDEO makes extensive use of full-scale prototypes and mock-ups to experiment with service concepts, testing both customer reactions and operational aspects of the service. In its work with Marriott's extended stay hotel chain, TownePlace suites, IDEO's Smart Space researchers first spent several weeks living in and talking with TownePlace guests to observe and learn how they used the space and what their unmet needs were.[40] The result was a completely redesigned lobby area, including a map wall with notations about local shopping, restaurants, parks, and recreation areas that can be annotated by guests. Another change was a redesigned bedroom that provides the flexibility to be turned into a workspace. To test the design concepts, IDEO built a life-sized lobby and suite out of white foam core and invited Marriott executives, hotel managers, and guests to provide feedback on the prototype. Similar service innovation prototyping and testing projects have been undertaken by IDEO for many other service organizations, including Walgreens's designing the pharmacy experience for the 21st century, Lufthansa's reimagining the first-class flying experience, and Holiday Inn Express Europe's revamping the brand in Europe by redesigning everything from public places to food and beverage, to guest room and digital experiences.[41] Exhibit 8.2 illustrates how Mayo Clinic's Center for Innovation tests new patient experience concepts and health delivery services.

Market Testing

At the market testing stage of the development process, a tangible product might be test marketed in a limited number of trading areas to determine marketplace acceptance of the product as well as other marketing mix variables such as promotion, pricing, and distribution systems. Because new service offerings are often intertwined with the delivery system for existing services, it is difficult to test new services in isolation. And in some cases, it may not be possible to introduce the service

Exhibit 8.2 Service Innovation at the Mayo Clinic

The Mayo Clinic in the United States is more than 100 years old and one of the most respected names in health care globally. It is consistently listed among the top hospitals in the United States and is known for its collaborative health care model, high levels of service, and position in the forefront of medicine. Following its innovative traditions, Mayo established its Center for Innovation (formerly the SPARC Innovation Lab) to focus on innovating and "transforming the experience of health and healthcare." While medical and technological advances have changed the face of health care dramatically over the past 50 years, the same is not necessarily true of the way health care is delivered to patients. Everything from patient exam rooms to the patient's waiting experience has changed relatively little in comparison to scientific advances in medicine. Mayo recognized this and determined it should again be in the forefront of innovation—this time in the processes and practices of health care delivery.

The Center for Innovation has become a testing ground for all types of service and delivery innovations at Mayo—innovations that are intended to enhance the patient's experience and that have potential health benefits. Working with the design firm IDEO, Mayo designed an experimental lab and innovation center at its Rochester, Minnesota, facility, where service innovations can be tested with real patients and real Mayo doctors and staff

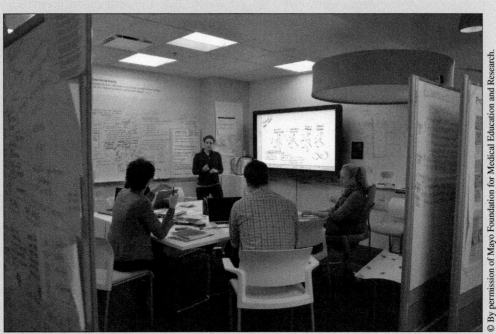

Center for Innovaton at Mayo Clinic, Rochester.

to an isolated market area because the organization has only one point of delivery. There are alternative ways of testing the response to marketing mix variables, however. The new service might be offered to employees of the organization and their families for a time to assess their responses to variations in the marketing mix.

It is also extremely important at this stage in the development process to do a pilot run of the service to be sure that the operational details are functioning smoothly. Frequently this step is overlooked, and the actual market introduction may be the first test of whether the service system functions as planned. By this point, mistakes in design are harder to correct. As one noted service expert says, "There is simply no substitute for a proper rehearsal" when introducing a new service.[42]

before they are introduced into the clinics. The lab is set up as an actual clinic within the Mayo facility, and experiments are conducted with doctors and patients (of course, with their prior knowledge and consent). The space is highly flexible, so that exam rooms, common spaces, walls, furniture, and computers can be moved around to test different configurations and services. Sometimes researchers take their questions and experiments into the clinics themselves, working directly with doctors and patients on site.

Within the Center for Innovation, researchers focus on complex and important issues for the health care industry in general, with the overarching principle of "patient-centered design." For example, here are some of the topics they have explored and "re-imagined"—the term they use for service improvement and futuristic innovation:

- What would integrated health care look like from the patient's perspective?
- What is the relationship among communication, understanding, and satisfaction for the patient?
- How could exam rooms be reconfigured for a better patient experience and to improve patient–doctor communication?
- How can the on-site check-in process for appointments be improved?
- How can space within the health care facility be optimized to serve patients and staff?
- What are the unmet educational needs of patients, and how can a service be designed to meet those needs?

While innovation in health care delivery practices such as those listed is rare, Mayo's practices within the Center for Innovation are unique—combining principles from service, design, and health care. For example, the patient check-in process at Mayo Rochester was viewed as particularly problematic for patients, with long lines and frustration at having to stand and wait when all they wanted

to do was sit down. The multidisciplinary team began by observing and listening to both patients and staff to start the process of identifying innovative solutions to this challenge. Through this human-centered, participatory approach, they developed ideas by conveying narratives that morphed into innovations, which were tested with prototypes in the lab. In the case of the patient check-in process, the basic innovation idea was to develop an automated self-check-in process. Initial prototypes of the self-service check-in kiosk were quite unsophisticated. For example, the first version was a piece of paper representing a computer screen. Later versions of the prototype evolved to inactive computer screens to actual touch screens displayed on a kiosk. At each version of the prototype, the team collected feedback from both patients and staff. The results of this experiment led Mayo to invest resources in investigating a roll-out of this innovative solution.

In another case, an innovation studied in the lab led to innovative ways to communicate treatment options to diabetic patients who were considering taking statin drugs. A number of patient–doctor communication prototypes were tested to help patients understand their options by conveying information on medical evidence, risk factors, and treatment options via different formats. The prototypes ranged from online information to a one-page decision aid, and each was tested to determine what was most effective for patient participation, preferences, and adherence to the treatment choice. In this case, not only did the innovation improve the patient's experience in the interaction with the physician, but it also resulted in increased likelihood of the patient following through on the treatment plan—ultimately affecting the health outcome itself.

Mayo's commitment to innovation in health care is also seen in its annual "Transform" conferences, which bring together speakers and the latest in thinking related to design and innovation in health care.

Sources: http://www.mayo.edu/center-for-innovation, 2016; C. Salter, "A Prescription for Innovation," *Fast Company* (April 2006), p. 83.

Commercialization

During the commercialization stage, the service goes live and is introduced to the marketplace. This stage has two primary objectives. The first is to build and maintain acceptance of the new service among large numbers of the service delivery personnel who will be responsible day-to-day for service quality. This task is made easier if acceptance has been built by involving service delivery personnel as one of the key groups in the design and development process all along. The second objective is to monitor all aspects of the service during introduction and through the complete service cycle. If the customer needs six months to experience the entire service, then careful monitoring must be maintained through at least six months. Every detail of the service should be assessed—phone calls, face-to-face transactions, billing, complaints, and delivery problems. Operating efficiency and costs should also be tracked.

Postintroduction Evaluation

At this point, the information gathered during commercialization of the service can be reviewed and changes made to the delivery process, staffing, or marketing mix variables on the basis of actual market response to the offering. No service will ever stay the same. Whether deliberate or unplanned, changes will always occur. Therefore, formalizing the review process to make those changes that enhance service quality from the customer's point of view is critical.

SERVICE BLUEPRINTING: A TECHNIQUE FOR SERVICE INNOVATION AND DESIGN

A stumbling block in service innovation, design, and development is the difficulty of describing and depicting the service at the concept development, service development, and market test stages. One of the keys to matching service specifications to customer expectations is the ability to describe critical service process characteristics objectively and to depict them so that employees, customers, and managers alike know what the service is, can see their roles, and can understand all the steps and flows involved in the service process. In this section, we look in depth at service blueprinting, a useful technique for designing and specifying intangible service processes.[43]

What Is a Service Blueprint?

A *service blueprint* is a picture or map that portrays the customer experience and the service system, so that the different people involved in providing the service can understand it objectively, regardless of their roles or their individual points of view. Blueprints are particularly useful at the design stage of service development. A service blueprint visually displays the service by simultaneously depicting the process of service delivery, the points of customer contact, the roles of customers and employees, and the visible elements of the service (see Figure 8.3). It provides a way to break a service down into its logical components and to depict the steps or tasks in the process, the means by which the tasks are executed, and the evidence of service as the customer experiences it. Blueprinting has its origins in a variety of fields and techniques, including logistics, industrial engineering, decision theory, computer systems analysis, and software engineering—all of which deal with the definition and explanation of processes.[44] Because services are "experiences" rather than objects or technologies, blueprinting is a particularly useful technique for describing them.

FIGURE 8.3 **Service Blueprinting**

Service blueprinting
A technique for simultaneously depicting the service process, the points of customer contact, and the evidence of service from the customer's point of view.

Blueprint Components

The key components of service blueprints are shown in Figure 8.4.[45] They are customer actions, onstage/visible contact employee actions, backstage/invisible contact employee actions, and support processes. The conventions for drawing service blueprints are not rigidly defined, and thus the particular symbols used, the number of horizontal lines in the blueprint, and the labels for each part of the blueprint may vary somewhat depending on the complexity of the blueprint being described. These variations are not a problem, as long as you keep in mind the purpose of the blueprint and view it as a useful technique rather than as a set of rigid rules for designing services. In fact, its flexibility—when compared with other process mapping approaches—is one of service blueprinting's major strengths.

The *customer actions* area encompasses the steps, choices, activities, and interactions that the customer performs in the process of purchasing, experiencing, and evaluating the service. The total customer experience is apparent in this area of the blueprint. In a legal services example, the customer actions might include a decision to contact an attorney, phone calls to the attorney, face-to-face meetings, receipt of documents, and receipt of a bill.

Paralleling the customer actions are two areas of contact employee actions. The activities that the contact employee performs that are visible to the customer are the *onstage/visible contact employee actions.* In the legal services setting, the actions of the attorney (the contact employee) visible to the client are, for example, the initial interview, intermediate meetings, and final face-to-face delivery of legal documents.

Those contact employee actions that occur behind the scenes to support the onstage activities are the *backstage/invisible contact employee actions.* In the example, anything

FIGURE 8.4
Service Blueprint Components

the attorney does behind the scenes to prepare for the meetings or to prepare the final documents will appear in this section of the blueprint, together with phone call contacts the customer has with the attorney or other frontline staff in the firm. All *nonvisible* contact employee actions are shown in this area of the blueprint.

The *support processes* section of the blueprint covers the internal services, steps, and interactions that take place to support the contact employees in delivering the service. Again, in our legal example, any service support activities such as legal research by staff, preparation of documents, and secretarial support to set up meetings will be shown in the support processes area of the blueprint.

At the very top of the blueprint you see the *physical evidence* of the service. Typically, above each point of contact the actual physical evidence of the service is listed. In the legal example, the physical evidence of the face-to-face meeting with the attorney would be such items as office decor, written documents, lawyer's clothing, and so forth.

The four key action areas are separated by three horizontal lines. First is the *line of interaction,* representing direct interactions between the customer and the organization. Anytime a vertical line crosses the horizontal line of interaction, a direct contact between the customer and the organization, or a service encounter, has occurred. The next horizontal line is the critically important *line of visibility.* This line separates all service activities visible to the customer from those not visible. In reading blueprints, it is immediately obvious whether the consumer is provided with much visible evidence of the service simply by analyzing how much of the service occurs above the line of visibility versus the activities carried out below the line. This line also separates what the contact employees do onstage from what they do backstage. For example, in a medical examination situation, the doctor would perform the actual exam and answer the patient's questions above the line of visibility, or onstage, whereas she might read the patient's chart in advance and dictate notes following the exam below the line of visibility, or backstage. The third line is the *line of internal interaction,* which separates customer-contact employee activities from those of other service support activities and people. Vertical lines cutting across the line of internal interaction represent internal service encounters.

One of the most significant differences between service blueprints and other process flow diagrams is the primary focus on customers and their experience with the service process. In fact, in designing effective service blueprints it is recommended that the diagramming start with the customer's experience and then work into the delivery system. The boxes shown within each action area depict steps performed or experienced by the actors at that level.

Service Blueprint Examples

Figures 8.5 and 8.6 show service blueprints for two interpersonal services: express mail delivery and an overnight hotel stay.[46] These blueprints are deliberately kept very simple, showing only the most basic steps in the services. Complex diagrams could be developed for each step, and the internal processes could be much more fully developed. In addition to the four action areas separated by the three horizontal lines, these blueprints also show the physical evidence of the service from the customer's point of view at each step of the process.

Examine the express mail delivery blueprint in Figure 8.5. It is clear that from the customer's point of view there are only three steps in the service process: the

FIGURE 8.5 **Blueprint for Express Mail Delivery Service**

Source: E. E. Scheuing and W. F. Christopher, *Service Quality Handbook*, 1993, AM MGMT ASSN/AMACOM(B).

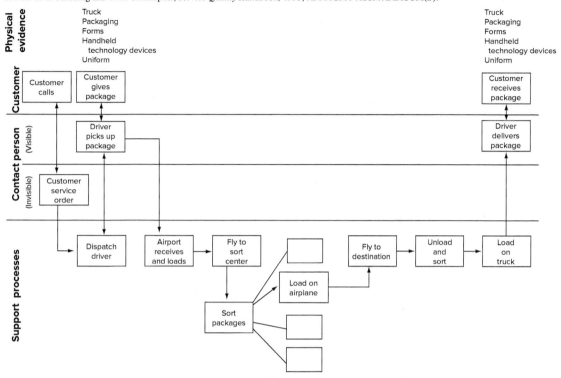

phone call, the package pickup, and the package delivery. The process is relatively standardized; the people who perform the service are the phone order-taker and the delivery person; and the physical evidence includes the document package, the transmittal forms, the truck, and the handheld technology device. In some cases the customer may also engage the online or phone-based package tracking system, although it is not depicted here. Although critical for the firm's success, the complex process that occurs behind the line of visibility is of little interest or concern to the customer. However, for the three visible-to-the-customer steps to proceed effectively, invisible internal services are needed. What these steps are and the fact that they support the delivery of the service to the external customer are apparent from the blueprint. Any of the steps in the blueprint could be exploded into a detailed blueprint, if needed for a particular purpose. For example, if the delivery company learned that the "unload and sort" step was taking too long and causing unacceptable delays in delivery, that step could be blueprinted in much greater detail to isolate the problems.

In the case of the overnight hotel stay depicted in Figure 8.6, the customer obviously is more actively involved in the service than he or she is in the express mail service. The guest first checks in, then goes to the hotel room, where a variety of steps take place (receiving bags, sleeping, showering, eating breakfast, and so on), and finally checks out. Imagine how much more complex this process could be and how

FIGURE 8.6   **Blueprint for Overnight Hotel Stay Service**

Source: E. E. Scheuing and W. F. Christopher, *Service Quality Handbook,* 1993, AM MGMT ASSN/AMACOM(B).

many more interactions could occur if the service blueprint depicted a week-long vacation at the hotel, or even a three-day business conference. The service blueprint also makes clear (by reading across the line of interaction) those employees who directly interact with the customer. Each step in the customer action area is also associated with various forms of physical evidence, from the hotel parking area and hotel exterior and interior to the forms used at guest registration, the lobby, the room, and the food. In the hotel case, the process is relatively complex (although again somewhat standardized), the people providing the service are a variety of frontline employees, and the physical evidence includes everything from the guest registration form to the lobby and room decor, to the uniforms worn by frontline employees.

Blueprints for Technology-Delivered Self-Service

To this point our discussion of service blueprints has related to services delivered in person, that is services in which employees interact directly with customers at some point in the process. But what about technology-delivered services including self-service websites and interactive kiosks? Can service blueprinting be used effectively to design these types of services? Certainly it can, but the lines of demarcation will change, and some blueprint labels may need to be adapted.

If no employees are involved in the service (except when there is a problem or the service does not function as planned), the contact person areas of the blueprint are not needed. Instead, the area above the line of visibility can be used to illustrate the interface

FIGURE 8.7 Blueprint for DVD Rental Kiosk

between the customer and the website or the physical interaction with the kiosk. This area can be relabeled *onstage/visible technology*. The backstage contact person actions area is irrelevant in this case.

Many services have both interpersonal and technology-delivered elements. Consider the airline check-in process. The actual check-in may be done through an electronic kiosk, while baggage, security screening, and handling of tickets while boarding are all done by people. In such a case, the blueprint would include all three contact rows: one for technology, one for the onstage contact person (visible), and one for the backstage contact person (invisible). Figure 8.7 is a blueprint for a DVD rental kiosk, showing the technology interactions in the added "onstage technology" area of the blueprint. This blueprint also illustrates what the customer experiences if the DVD is scratched. When that happens, the customer calls customer service, a "backstage contact person (invisible)" activity.

Reading and Using Service Blueprints

A service blueprint can be read in a variety of ways, depending on the purpose. If the purpose is to understand the customer's view of the process or the customer experience, the blueprint can be read from left to right, tracking the events in the customer action area. Questions that might be asked include these: How is the service initiated by the customer? What choices does the customer make? Is the customer highly involved in cocreating the service, or are few actions

Exhibit 8.3 Blueprinting in Action at ARAMARK Parks and Destinations

ARAMARK is a global leader in professional services, operating as an outsourcer for food, hospitality, facility management, and uniform services. ARAMARK's customers include large businesses, universities, health care organizations, parks and resorts, convention centers, and other groups. It was ranked first in its industry among *Fortune's* Most Admired companies in 2007, 2009, 2010, and 2011. The company has approximately 255,000 employees serving clients in 22 countries. One of its divisions is ARAMARK Parks and Destinations, a group that provides services for 17 major park destinations within the United States, including Denali National Park in Alaska, Shenandoah National Park in Virginia, and Lake Powell Destinations and Marinas in the Glen Canyon National Recreation Area of Arizona. Each of the parks has at least three or four service businesses within it that ARAMARK operates on an outsourcing contract.

GOAL: SERVICE IMPROVEMENT AND CUSTOMER RETENTION

A number of years ago, Renee Ryan, then marketing director for ARAMARK Parks, confronted a challenge. It was clear that repeat business at ARAMARK's parks was declining overall. This was particularly the case at Lake Powell Resorts and Marinas in Arizona, where the company operated houseboat rentals, a resort, campgrounds, boat tours, and food service operations. Research revealed that many people were not returning to Lake Powell because

their first experience there did not match what they had expected or were accustomed to based on visits to other resort destinations. Ryan employed both traditional and visual (photos, video) blueprints to help convince the organization that changes were in order and specifically what should be done. The results benefited customers through improvements in service and the company through increased repeat business.

First, Ryan developed a blueprint of a typical, quality hotel/resort experience from a typical customer's point of view. Then she blueprinted the Lake Powell resort experience. The comparison of the two blueprints was revealing in terms of differences in basic services, standards, and processes. This comparison process resulted in the development of new services, facilities upgrades, and modernization of key service elements. Through the visual blueprint in particular, showing all aspects of the service through photos and videos, the need for service upgrades became apparent.

Another revelation also jumped out of the blueprint. By visually tracking the customer's experience, it was clear that customers were being asked to work extremely hard for their vacations! To experience the luxurious and not-inexpensive houseboat experience they had purchased, customers first had to create extensive grocery lists, shop in crowded stores near the resort, carry all of their food and belongings down a steep embankment, and haul them out to the boat. Once the trip started, more hard labor was required.

case illustrated in Exhibit 8.3. Managers and others who are not on the front lines may be quite surprised when they view the actual service experience through their customers' eyes.

Step 4: Map Contact Employee Actions and/or Technology Actions

First the lines of interaction and visibility are drawn, and then the process from the customer contact person's point of view is mapped, distinguishing visible onstage activities from invisible backstage activities. For existing services, this step involves questioning or observing frontline operation employees to learn what they do and which activities are performed in full view of the customer versus which activities are carried out behind the scenes.

For technology-delivered services or those that combine technology and human delivery, the required actions of the technology interface are mapped above the line of visibility as well. If no employees are involved in the service, the area can be relabeled "onstage technology actions." If both human and technology interactions are involved, an additional horizontal line can separate "visible contact employee actions" from "visible technology actions." Using the additional line facilitates reading and interpretation of the service blueprint.

Houseboat Vacation on Lake Powell.

Anchoring a large houseboat each night is not a trivial matter, and cooking onboard can be arduous and time consuming. Navigating the houseboat can also be stressful, especially for inexperienced captains. The run-down resort facilities on land, the arduous work required to get on the water, and the stress of navigation all combined to discourage customers from returning after surviving their first Lake Powell vacation.

The blueprinting exercise made all of this extremely vivid for top management and resulted in a suite of new services, renovations of existing facilities, training of staff to perform to new service standards, and new measurement and reward systems. Some of the new services introduced included various levels of concierge services that started with the basic service of taking guests' things to the boat for them and later transporting guests in a cart to the boat dock. Service packages were extended at the high end to include buying groceries for guests and providing executive chefs, who would travel with the party and cook on board. Trained captains could also be hired to lessen the stress of navigation. A variety of services in between were also available a la carte.

RESULTS FOR ARAMARK

The result for Lake Powell of all of these service quality improvements and innovative new services was 50 percent fewer complaints. Repeat business increased by 12 percent, and customer satisfaction also increased dramatically. The blueprints in this case were extremely valuable in that they allowed managers to see the service in ways they had never seen it before. The blueprints also provided a focal point for conversations, leading to change and ultimately to new service standards and measures. Using the blueprinting technique helped people within the parks division develop a true customer focus.

Sources: M. J. Bitner, A. L. Ostrom, and F. N. Morgan, "Service Blueprinting: A Practical Technique for Service Innovation," *California Management Review 50* (Spring 2008), pp. 66–94.; Interview with Renee Ryan; www.lakepowell.com, accessed May 2016.

Step 5: Link Contact Activities to Needed Support Functions

The line of internal interaction can then be drawn and linkages from contact activities to internal support functions can be identified. In this process, the direct and indirect impact of internal actions on customers becomes apparent. Internal service processes take on added importance when viewed in connection with their link to the customer. Alternatively, certain steps in the process may be viewed as unnecessary if there is no clear link to the customer's experience or to an essential internal support service.

Step 6: Add Evidence of Service at Each Customer Action Step

Finally, the evidence of service can be added to the blueprint to illustrate what the customer sees and experiences as tangible evidence of the service at each step in the process. A photographic blueprint, including photos, slides, or video of the process, can be very useful at this stage to aid in analyzing the impact of tangible evidence and its consistency with the overall strategy and service positioning.

Exhibit 8.4 provides answers to frequently asked questions about service blueprinting.

What process should be blueprinted?

What process to map depends on the team or organization's objectives. If these are not clearly defined, then identifying the process can present a challenge. Questions to ask: Why are we blueprinting the service? What is our objective? Where does the service process begin and end? Are we focusing on the entire service, a component of the service, or a period of time?

Can multiple market segments be included on one blueprint?

Generally the answer to this question is no. Assuming that market segments require different service processes or attributes, the blueprint for one segment may look very different from the blueprint for another. Only at a very high level (sometimes called a *concept blueprint*) might it be relevant to map multiple segments simultaneously.

Who should "draw" the blueprint?

A blueprint is a team effort. It should not be assigned as an individual task, certainly not in the developmental stages. All relevant parties should be involved or represented in the effort. The task might include employees across multiple functions in the organization (marketing, operations, human resources, facilities design), as well as customers in some cases.

Should the actual or desired service process be blueprinted?

If a new service is being designed, then clearly it is important to start with the desired service process. However, in cases of service improvement or service redesign, it is very important to map (at least at a conceptual level) the actual service process first. Once the group knows how the service is actually functioning, then the blueprint can be modified or used as a base for changes and improvements.

Should exceptions or recovery processes be incorporated in the blueprint?

It may be possible to map relatively simple, commonly occurring recovery processes onto a blueprint, assuming there are not a lot of these. However, this process can quickly become complex and cause the blueprint to be confusing or unreadable. Often a better strategy is to indicate common fail points on the blueprint and, if needed, develop separate blueprints for the service recovery processes.

What is the appropriate level of detail?

The answer to this question depends on the purpose for doing the blueprint in the first place. If it is to be used primarily to communicate the general nature of the service, then a concept blueprint with few details is best. If it is being used to focus on diagnosing and improving the service process, then more detail is needed. Because some people are more detail oriented than others, this question will always arise and needs to be resolved in any team blueprinting effort.

What symbols should be used?

There is not a lexicon of blueprinting symbols that is required to be used. What is most important is that the symbols be defined, kept relatively simple, and used consistently by the team and across the organization if blueprints are being shared internally.

Should time or dollar costs be included on the blueprint?

Blueprints are very versatile. If reducing the time taken for various parts of the service process is an objective of the blueprinting effort, then time can be included. The same is true for dollar costs or anything else that is relevant as an objective. However, it is not advisable to put such information on the blueprint unless it is of central concern.

Summary

Service providers must effectively match customer expectations to new service innovations and actual service process designs. However, because of the very nature of services—specifically, their intangibility, variability, and cocreation elements—the design and development of service offerings are complex and challenging. Many services are only vaguely defined before their introduction to the marketplace. This chapter outlines some of the challenges involved in innovating and designing services and strategies for effectively overcoming the challenges. The chapter also describes a variety of types of service innovation, including service offering innovation, innovating around customer roles, innovation through service solutions, and innovation through interconnected products.

Through adaptations of the new product development process that is commonplace in goods production and manufacturing companies, service providers can not only make their offerings and service solutions more explicit but also avoid failures. The service development process presented in the chapter includes nine stages, beginning with the development of a business and new service strategy and ending with postintroduction evaluation of the new service. Between these initial and ending stages are a number of steps and checkpoints designed to maximize the likelihood of innovation success. Carrying out the stages requires the inclusion of customers, contact employees, business partners, and anyone else who will affect or be affected by the new service.

Service blueprinting, a particularly useful technique for service innovation and design, is described in detail in this chapter. A blueprint can make a complex service concrete through its visual depiction of all the steps, actors, processes, and physical evidence of the service. The key feature of service blueprints is the focus on the customer—the customer's experience is documented first and is kept fully in view as the other features of the blueprint are developed.

Discussion Questions

1. Why is it challenging to innovate, design, and develop services?
2. Why is service innovation so critical for firms and countries?
3. What are the risks of attempting to describe services in words alone?
4. Find and discuss your own examples of the different types of service innovations presented in the "Types of Service Innovation" section in this chapter.
5. Compare and contrast the blueprints in Figures 8.5, 8.6, and 8.7.
6. How might a service blueprint be used for marketing, human resource, and operations decisions? Focus on one of the blueprint examples shown in the text as a context for your answer.
7. Assume that you are a multiproduct service company that wants to grow through adding new services. Describe a logical process you might use to introduce a new service to the marketplace. What steps in the process might be most difficult and why? How might you incorporate service blueprinting into the process?
8. Discuss Figure 8.2 in terms of the four types of opportunities for growth represented there. Choose a company or service, and explain how it could grow by developing new services in each of the four cells.

Exercises

1. Think of a new service you would like to develop if you were an entrepreneur. How would you go about it? Describe what you would do and where you would get your information.
2. Find a new and interesting service in your local area or a service offered on your campus. Document the service process via a service blueprint. To do this exercise, you will probably need to interview one of the service employees and experience the service yourself, if possible. After you have documented the existing service, use blueprinting concepts to redesign the service or change it in some way.
3. Choose a service you are familiar with and document the customer action steps through a photographic or video blueprint. What is the "evidence of service" from your point of view as a customer?
4. Develop a service blueprint for a technology-delivered service such as streaming a movie on your TV or laptop, or renting a DVD from a RedBox kiosk). Compare and contrast this blueprint to one for the same service delivered via a traditional channel (such as watching a movie in a theater).

5. Compare two services on the Internet. Discuss the design of each in terms of whether it meets your expectations. How could the design or the service process be changed? Which one is most effective, and why?

Notes

1. www.petsmart.com, 2016; C. Dalton, "A Passion for Pets: An Interview with Philip L. Francis, Chairperson and CEO of PetSmart, Inc.," *Business Horizons* 48 (November–December 2005), pp. 469–475; D. Brady and C. Palmeri, "The Pet Economy," *BusinessWeek,* August 6, 2007, p. 44; M. Jarman, "PetSmart Quarterly Income Up 33%," *Arizona Republic,* May 19, 2011, p. D1; R. Dezember, "PetSmart to Get New Leadership in Buyout," *LBO Wire,* March 11, 2015.

2. D. H. Henard and D. M. Szymanski, "Why Some New Products Are More Successful Than Others," *Journal of Marketing Research* 38 (August 2001), pp. 362–375.

3. R. G. Cooper, *Winning at New Products,* 3rd ed. (Cambridge, MA: Perseus, 2001); R. G. Cooper and S. J. Edgett, *Product Development for the Service Sector* (Cambridge, MA: Perseus Books, 1999); and C. M. Froehle, A. V. Roth, R. B. Chase, and C. A. Voss, "Antecedents of New Service Development Effectiveness," *Journal of Service Research* 3 (August 2000), pp. 3–17; R. G. Cooper, "Effective Gating: Make Product Innovation More Productive by Using Gates with Teeth," *Marketing Management* 18 (March–April 2009), pp. 12–17.

4. M. J. Bitner and S. W. Brown, "The Service Imperative," *Business Horizons 50th Anniversary Issue* 51 (January–February 2008), pp. 39–46.

5. G. L. Shostack, "Understanding Services through Blueprinting," in *Advances in Services Marketing and Management,* vol. 1, ed. T. A. Swartz, D. E. Bowen, and S. W. Brown (Greenwich, CT: JAI Press, 1992), pp. 75–90.

6. Ibid., p. 76.

7. See: S. S. Tax, D. McCutcheon, and I. F. Wilkinson, "The Service Delivery Network (SDN): A Customer-Centric Perspective of the Customer Journey," *Journal of Service Research* 16 (November 2013), pp. 454–470; J. D. Chandler and R. F. Lusch, "Service Systems: A Broadened Framework and Research Agenda on Value Propositions, Engagement, and Service Experience," *Journal of Service Research* 18 (February 2015), pp. 6–22.

8. For coverage of issues in new services development and service innovation, see *Journal of Operations Management* 20 (2002), Special Issue on New Issues and Opportunities in Service Design Research; A. Johne and C. Story, "New Service Development: A Review of the Literature and Annotated Bibliography," *European Journal of Marketing* 32 (1998), pp. 184–251; B. Edvardsson, A. Gustafsson, M. D. Johnson, and B. Sanden, *New Service Development and Innovation in the New Economy* (Lund, Sweden: Studentlitteratur AB, 2000); and B. Edvardsson, A. Gustafsson, P. Kristensson, P. Magnusson, and J. Matthing, *Involving Customers in New Service Development* (London: Imperial College Press, 2006); A. Gustafsson, P. Kristensson, G. Schirr, and L. Witell, *Service Innovation* (Business Expert Press, Gustafsson 2016); L. Patricio, R. Fisk, and A. Gustafsson (guest editors), *Journal of Service Research,* Special Issue on Service Design and Innovation, forthcoming 2017.

9. Gustafsson, Kristensson, Schirr, and Witell, *Service Innovation.*

10. A. Ordanini and A. Parasuraman, "Service Innovation Viewed through a Service-Dominant Logic Lens: A Conceptual Framework and Empirical Analysis," *Journal of Service Research* 14 (February 2011), pp. 3–23.

11. B. Schneider and D. E. Bowen, "New Services Design, Development and Implementation and the Employee," in *Developing New Services,* ed. W. R. George and C. Marshall (Chicago: American Marketing Association, 1984), pp. 82–101.

12. S.Thomke, "R&D Comes to Services: Bank of America's Pathbreaking Experiments," *Harvard Business Review* 81 (April 2003), pp. 70–79.

13. See: A. L. Ostrom, M. J. Bitner, S. W. Brown, K. A. Burkhard, M. Goul, V. Smith-Daniels, H. Demirkan, and E. Rabinovich, "Moving Forward and Making a Difference: Research Priorities for the Science of Service," *Journal of Service Research* 13 (February 2010), pp. 4–36; and A. L. Ostrom, A. Parasuraman, D. E. Bowen, L. Patricio and C. Voss, "Service Research Priorities in a Rapidly Changing Context," *Journal of Service Research* 18 (May 2015), pp. 127–159.

14. B. Mager on Service Design Network, www.service-design-network.org, accessed August 2011.

15. A. L. Ostrom, M. J. Bitner, S. W. Brown, K. A. Burkhard, M. Goul, V. Smith-Daniels, H. Demirkan, and E. Rabinovich, "Moving Forward and Making a Difference: Research Priorities for the Science of Service," *Journal of Service Research* 13 (February 2010), pp. 4–36.

16. M. Stickdorn and J. Schneider, *This Is Service Design Thinking,* Wiley (Amsterdam, 2010), pp. 34–35.

17. B. Mager on Service Design Network, www.service-design-network.org, accessed August 2011.

18. For additional detail and background on service design and service design thinking see: S. Dasu and R. B. Chase, "Designing the Soft Side of Customer Service," *Sloan Management Review* 52 (Fall 2010), pp. 33–39; L. G. Zomerdijk and C. A. Voss, "Service Design for Experience-Centric Services," *Journal of Service Research* 13 (February 2010), pp. 67–82; L. Patricio, R. P. Fisk, J. Falcao e Cunha, and L. Constantine, "Multilevel Service Design: From Customer Value Constellation to Service Experience Blueprinting," *Journal of Service Research* 14 (May 2011), pp. 180–200; Stickdorn and Schneider, *This Is Service Design Thinking*; Service Design Network, www.service-design-network.org.

19. L. L. Berry, V. Shankar, J. T. Parish, S. Cadwallader, and T. Dotzel, "Creating New Markets through Service Innovation," *Sloan Management Review* 47 (Winter 2006), pp. 56–63.

20. S. Michel, S. W. Brown and A. S. Gallan, "An Expanded and Strategic View of Discontinuous Innovations: Deploying a Service Dominant Logic," *Journal of the Academy of Marketing Science* 36, no. 1 (March 2008), pp. 54–66.

21. K. R. Tuli, A. K Kohli, and S. G. Bharadwaj, "Rethinking Customer Solutions: From Product Bundles to Relational Processes," *Journal of Marketing* 71 (July 2007), pp. 1–17.

22. L. A. Bettencourt, *Service Innovation*, New York: McGraw-Hill, 2010; L. A. Bettencourt and A. W. Ulwick, "The Customer-Centered Innovation Map," *Harvard Business Review* 86 (May 2008), pp. 109–114.

23. M. Sawhney, S. Balasubramanian, and V. V. Krishnan, "Creating Growth with Services," *MIT Sloan Management Review* 45, no. 2 (Winter 2004), pp. 34–43.

24. See: C. Gronroos and P. Helle, "Adopting a Service Logic in Manufacturing," *Journal of Service Management* 21 (2010), 564–590; H. Gebauer, A. Gustafsson, and L. Witell, "Competitive Advantage Through Service Differentiation by Manufacturing Companies," *Journal of Business Research*, 64: 12 (2011), pp. 1270–1280;

W. Ulaga and W. J. Reinartz, "Hybrid Offerings: How Manufacturing Firms Combine Goods and Services Successfully," *Journal of Marketing* forthcoming, 2011; V. A. Zeithaml, S. W. Brown, M. J. Bitner, and J. Salas, *Profiting from Services and Solutions: What Product-Centric Firms Need to Know*, Business Expert Press, 2014.

25. A. M. Epp and L. L. Price, "Designing Solutions Around Customer Network Identity Goals," *Journal of Marketing* 75 (March, 2011), pp. 36–54.

26. "Gartner Says 6.4 Billion Connected 'Things' Will Be in Use in 2016, Up 30 Percent from 2015," Stamford, CT, Gartner Press Release, November 10, 2015, http://www.gartner.com/newsroom/id/3165317.

27. See M. E. Porter and J. E. Heppelmann, "How Smart Connected Products are Transforming Competition," *Harvard Business Review* 92 (2014), pp. 64–88; M. E. Porter and J. E. Heppelmann, "How Smart, Connected Products Are Transforming Companies," *Harvard Business Review* 93 (2015), pp. 53–71.

28. For a discussion of these adaptations and related research issues, see I. Stuart, "Designing and Executing Memorable Service Experiences: Lights, Camera, Experiment, Integrate, Action!" *Business Horizons* 49 (2006), pp. 149–159; M. V. Tatikonda and V. A. Zeithaml, "Managing the New Service Development Process: Synthesis of Multidisciplinary Literature and Directions for Future Research," in *New Directions in Supply Chain Management: Technology, Strategy, and Implementation,* ed. T. Boone and R. Ganeshan (New York: AMACOM, 2002), pp. 200–236; and Edvardsson, Gustafsson, Johnson, and Sanden, *New Service Development and Innovation in the New Economy.*

29. See M. J. Bowers, "An Exploration into New Service Development: Organization, Process, and Structure," Doctoral dissertation, Texas A&M University, 1985; A. Khurana and S. R. Rosenthal, "Integrating the Fuzzy Front End of New Product Development," *Sloan Management Review* 38 (Winter 1997), pp. 103–120; and R. G. Cooper, *Winning at New Products,* 3rd ed. (Cambridge, MA: Perseus Publishing, 2001). J. Hauser, G. J. Tellis, and A. Griffin, "Research on Innovation: A Review and Agenda for Marketing Science," *Marketing Science* 25 (November–December 2006), pp. 687–717.

30. See A. Griffin, "PDMA Research on New Product Development Practices: Updating Trends and Benchmarking Best Practices," *Journal of Product Innovation Management* 14 (1997), pp. 429–458; Thomke, "R&D Comes to Services"; Organization for Economic Cooperation and Development, "Promoting Innovation in Services," 2005.

31. R. G. Cooper, "Stage Gate Systems for New Product Success," *Marketing Management* 1 (1992), pp. 20–29; J. Hawser, G. J. Tellis and A. Griffin, "Research on Innovations. A Review and Agenda for Marketing Science," *Marketing Science* 25 (2006) pp. 687–717; Cooper, "Effective Gating."

32. A. Khurana and S. R. Rosenthal, "Integrating the Fuzzy Front End of New Product Development," *Sloan Management Review* 38 (Winter 1997), pp. 103–120.

33. J. Jargon, "KFC Savors Potential in Africa," *The Wall Street Journal*, December 8, 2010, p. B1; E. Nurse, "KFC's Secret Recipe for Africa," *CNN*, January 15, 2016, http://www.cnn.com/2016/01/15/africa/kfc-africa-expansion-mpa/

34. D. Rigby and C. Zook, "Open-Market Innovation," *Harvard Business Review* 80 (October 2002), pp. 80–89.

35. D. Leonard and J. F. Rayport, "Spark Innovation through Empathic Design," *Harvard Business Review* 75 (November–December 1997), pp. 103–113; also

see P. Underhill, *Why We Buy: The Science of Shopping* (New York: Simon and Schuster, 2007).

36. See Ordanini and Parasuraman, "Service Innovation Viewed through a Service-Dominant Logic Lens"; H. L. Melton and M. D. Hartline, "Customer and Frontline Employee Influence on New Service Development Performance," *Journal of Service Research* 13 (November 2011), pp. 411–425; L. McCreary, "Kaiser Permanente's Innovation on the Front Lines," *Harvard Business Review* 88 (September 2010), pp. 92–97.

37. R. Cross, A. Hargadon, S. Parise, and R. J. Thomas, "Together We Innovate," *The Wall Street Journal,* September 15–16, 2007, p. R6; J. C. Spender and B. Strong, "Who Has Innovative Ideas? Employees." *Wall Street Journal*, August 23, 2010, p. R5.

38. G. L. Shostack, "Service Design in the Operating Environment," in *Developing New Services,* ed. W. R. George and C. Marshall (Chicago: American Marketing Association, 1984), pp. 27–43.

39. E. E. Scheuing and E. M. Johnson, "A Proposed Model for New Service Development," *Journal of Services Marketing* 3 (1989), pp. 25–34.

40. L. Chamberlain, "Going Off the Beaten Path for New Design Ideas," *New York Times,* March 12, 2006, Sunday Business Section.

41. See IDEO's website for many examples of their current work, https://www.ideo.com/work/, accessed May 30, 2016.

42. Shostack, "Service Design in the Operating Environment," p. 35.

43. The service blueprinting section of the chapter draws from pioneering as well as current works in this area: G. L. Shostack, "Designing Services That Deliver," *Harvard Business Review* 62 (January–February 1984), pp. 133–139; G. L. Shostack, "Service Positioning through Structural Change," *Journal of Marketing* 51 (January 1987), pp. 34–43; and J. Kingman-Brundage, "The ABC's of Service System Blueprinting," in *Designing a Winning Service Strategy,* ed. M. J. Bitner and L. A. Crosby (Chicago: American Marketing Association, 1989), pp. 30–33; M. J. Bitner, A. L. Ostrom, and F. N. Morgan, "Service Blueprinting: A Practical Technique for Service Innovation," *California Management Review* 50 (Spring 2008), pp. 66–94.

44. Shostack, "Understanding Services through Blueprinting."

45. These key components are drawn from Kingman-Brundage, "The ABC's."

46. The text explaining Figures 8.5 and 8.6 relies on M. J. Bitner, "Managing the Evidence of Service," in *The Service Quality Handbook,* ed. E. E. Scheuing and W. F. Christopher (New York: American Management Association, 1993), pp. 358–370.

47. S. Fliess and M. Kleinaltenkamp, "Blueprinting the Service Company: Managing Service Processes Efficiently," *Journal of Business Research* 57 (2004), pp. 392–404.

48. Sources: For coverage of the practical benefits of blueprinting see E. Gummesson and J. Kingman-Brundage, "Service Design and Quality: Applying Service Blueprinting and Service Mapping to Railroad Services," in *Quality Management in Services,* ed. P. Kunst and J. Lemmink (Assen/Maastricht, Netherlands: Van Gorcum, 1991); and M. J. Bitner, A. L. Ostrom, and F. N. Morgan, "Service Blueprinting: A Practical Technique for Service Innovation," *California Management Review* 50 (Spring 2008), pp. 66–94.

49. A. R. Hubbert, A. Garcia Sehorn, and S. W. Brown, "Service Expectations: The Consumer vs. the Provider," *International Journal of Service Industry Management* 6 (1995), pp. 6–21.

Chapter Nine

Customer-Defined Service Standards

This chapter's objectives are to

1. Distinguish between company-defined and customer-defined service standards.
2. Differentiate among "hard" and "soft" customer-defined service standards and one-time fixes.
3. Explain the critical role of the service encounter sequence in developing customer-defined standards.
4. Illustrate how to translate customer expectations into behaviors and actions that are definable, repeatable, and actionable.
5. Explain the process of developing customer-defined service standards.

FedEx Sets Standards through SQI

Marketing research data are not the only numbers that FedEx tracks to run its business. The company drives its operations with the aid of one of the most comprehensive, customer-defined indices of service standards and measures in the world. The FedEx service quality indicator (SQI) was designed from the start to be an "unforgiving internal performance measurement" to ensure that the company delivered its goal of "100 percent customer satisfaction after every interaction and transaction and 100 percent service performance on every package handled."[1] The development and implementation of SQI has helped FedEx stay focused on its customers in becoming one of the world's most admired brands.

What makes this service index different from those of other companies is its foundation in customer feedback. Since the 1980s, FedEx has documented customer complaints and used the information to improve internal processes. The initial composite listing of the 12 most common customer complaints, originally called the "Hierarchy of Horrors," included wrong day

© Jb Reed/Bloomberg via Getty Images

The entire FedEx organization is driven by customer-defined service standards.

deliveries, right day late deliveries, pickups not made, lost packages, customers misinformed by FedEx, billing and paperwork mistakes, employee performance failures, and damaged packages. Although this list was useful, it fell short of giving management the ability to anticipate and eliminate customer complaints before they occurred.

In 1988 the company developed a 12-item statistical SQI to be a more "comprehensive, pro-active, customer-oriented measure of customer satisfaction and service quality."[2] The items included in SQI have changed slightly over time, as have the weights assigned to each of the items. Recent versions of SQI for FedEx Express have included the following components and weighting (based on relative importance of each component to customers):[3]

Indicator	Weight
Lost packages	50
Damaged packages	30
Failed (call-in) pickup	20
Wrong day/late delivery	15
Failed (regularly scheduled) pickup	10
Missing packages	10
Right day/late delivery	5

Sources: E-mail communication from David Spear, manager of global service and quality assurance, *FedEx Express,* June 14, 2016.

Another distinguishing feature of the SQI is its reporting in terms of *numbers* of errors rather than percentages. Management of the company strongly believes that percentages distance the company from the consumer: to report 1 percent of packages late diminishes the reality of 110,000 unhappy customers (1 percent of the more than 11 million packages shipped a day, including 4.1 million for FedEx Express and 6.9 million for FedEx Ground). The SQI report is disseminated weekly to everyone in the company. On receipt of the report, root causes of recurring service failures are investigated. With a senior officer assigned to each component, and with bonuses for everyone in the company tied to performance on the SQI, the company continuously strives to meet its goal of 100 percent satisfaction with every transaction. In addition to FedEx Express using these items in its SQI, similar SQI metrics are used by other divisions of FedEx, including FedEx Ground, FedEx Freight, FedEx Office, and FedEx Services.[4]

As we saw in Chapters 5, 6, and 7, understanding customer requirements is the first step in delivering high service quality. Once managers of service businesses accurately understand what customers expect, they face a second critical challenge: using this knowledge to set service quality standards and goals for the organization. Service companies often experience difficulty in setting standards to match or exceed customer expectations, partly because doing so requires that the marketing and operations departments within a company work together. In most service companies, integrating the work of the marketing function and the operations function (appropriately called *functional integration*) is not a typical approach; more frequently these two functions operate separately—setting and achieving their own internal goals—rather than pursuing a joint goal of developing operations standards that best meet customer expectations.

Creating service standards that address customer expectations is not a common practice in most firms. Doing so often requires altering the very process by which work is accomplished, which is ingrained in tradition in many companies. Often change requires new equipment or technology. Change also necessitates aligning executives from different parts of the firm to understand collectively the comprehensive view of service quality from the customer's perspective. And almost always, change requires a willingness to be open to different ways of structuring, calibrating, and monitoring the way service is provided.

FACTORS NECESSARY FOR APPROPRIATE SERVICE STANDARDS

Standardization of Service Behaviors and Actions

The translation of customer expectations into specific service quality standards depends on the degree to which tasks and behaviors to be performed can be standardized or routinized. *Standardization* usually implies a nonvarying sequential process—similar to the mass production of goods—in which each step is laid out in order and all outcomes are uniform, whereas *customization* usually refers to some level of adaptation or tailoring of the process to the individual customer.[5] The goal of standardization is for the service firm to produce a consistent service product from one transaction to the next. The goal of customization for the service firm is to develop a service that meets each customer's individual needs. Some executives and managers believe that services cannot be standardized—that customization is essential for providing high-quality service. Managers also may feel that standardizing tasks is inconsistent with employee empowerment—that employees will feel controlled by the company if tasks are standardized. Further, they feel that services are too intangible to be measured. This view leads to vague and loose standard setting with little or no measurement or feedback.

In reality, many service tasks are routine (such as those needed for opening checking accounts or spraying lawns for weeds), and for these, specific rules and standards can be fairly easily established and effectively executed. Employees may welcome knowing how to perform actions most efficiently: it frees them to use their ingenuity in the more personal and individual aspects of their jobs.

Standardization of service can take three forms: (1) substitution of technology for personal contact and human effort, (2) improvement in work methods, and (3) combinations of these two methods. Examples of technology substitution include websites and mobile applications for ordering take-out, airport check-in kiosks, advanced soft-drink vending machines that allow for elaborate customization, and smart office equipment that can summon a repairman on its own. Improvements in work methods are illustrated by home cleaning methods by maid services such as Molly Maid or The Maids, as well as routinized tax and accounting services developed by firms such as H&R Block.

Technology and work improvement methods facilitate the standardization of service necessary to provide consistent delivery to customers. By breaking tasks down and providing them efficiently, technology also allows the firm to calibrate service standards such as the length of time a transaction takes, the accuracy with which operations are performed, and the number of problems that occur. In developing work improvements, the firm comes to understand completely the process by which the service is delivered. With this understanding, the firm more easily establishes appropriate service standards.

Standardization, whether accomplished by technology or by improvements in work processes, reduces gap 2. Customer-defined standardization ensures that the most critical elements of a service are performed as expected by customers, not just that every action in a service is executed in a uniform manner. Using customer-defined standardization can, in fact, allow for and be compatible with employee empowerment—a topic discussed in more detail in Chapter 11. One example of this compatibility involves the time limits many companies establish for customer service calls. If their customers' highest priorities involve feeling good about the call or resolving problems, then setting a time limit for calls would be company defined and not in customers' best interests. Companies such as American Express, L.L. Bean, and Zappos.com, in using customer priorities rather than company priorities, have no set standard for the amount of time an employee spends on the telephone with a customer. Instead, they have standards that focus on making the customer satisfied and comfortable, allowing telephone representatives to use their own judgment about the time limits. As these companies have found, standardization of service is not appropriate in all situations. See the Strategy Insight for examples of these situations.

Formal Service Targets and Goals

Companies that have been successful in delivering consistently high service quality are noted for establishing formal standards to guide employees in providing service. These companies have an accurate sense of how well they are performing service that is critical to their customers—how long it takes to conduct transactions, how frequently service fails, how quickly they settle customer complaints—and strive to improve by defining goals that lead them to meet or exceed customer expectations.

One type of formal goal setting that is relevant in service businesses involves specific targets for individual behaviors or actions. As an example, consider the behavior "calls the customer back quickly," an action that signals responsiveness in contact employees. If the service goal for employee behavior is stated in such a general term as "call the customer back quickly," the standard provides little direction for service employees. Different employees will interpret this vague objective in their own ways, leading to inconsistent service: some may call the customer back in 10 minutes, whereas others may wait two to four days. And the firm itself will not be able to determine when or if individual employees meet the goal because its expression is not measurable—virtually any amount of time could be justified as "quickly." On the other hand, if the individual employee's service goal is to call each customer back within four hours, employees have a specific, unambiguous guideline about how quickly they should execute the action (four hours). Whether the goal is met is also unequivocal: if the call occurs within four hours, the company meets the goal; otherwise it does not.

Another type of formal goal setting involves the overall department or company target, most frequently expressed as a percentage, across all executions of the behavior or action. A department might set as its overall goal "to call the customer back within four hours 97 percent of the time" and collect data over a month's or year's time to evaluate the extent to which it meets the target. To illustrate, Puget Sound Energy—a utility company that serves customers in Washington State—has as part of its SQI a goal of answering 75 percent of customer calls with a "live" person within 30 seconds.[6]

Service firms that produce consistently excellent service—firms such as Walt Disney, FedEx, and Singapore Airlines—have very specific, quantified, measurable service goals. Disney calibrates employee performance on myriad behaviors and

Strategy Insight   Using Big Data to Define Service Standards and Improve Customer Experience

With the proliferation of mobile phones, social media, and online shopping, firms have access to more customer data than they ever have before. The data that can now be collected includes detailed demographic and psychographic information, purchase history, location data, and social network connections. With this incredibly granular data, service providers can gain better insight into the wants, needs, and habits of their customers. This level of data can help service providers to develop appropriate service standards to improve the aspects of the offering that are most important to customers.

Many retailers—such as Amazon, Overstock.com, and Walmart—use the data to make product suggestions to customers based on real-time data that includes factors such as age, gender, location, recent and historical online activity, and even the responses of other customers to the same suggestions.

However, in addition to using big data in crafting product recommendations, service providers can use information to improve the service offering itself. For example, does the firm have any unhappy customers? If so, what do they all have in common? What separates them from the happy customers? Can this difference be addressed by implementing a service standard?

Beyond survey data asking customers what they do not like about the company, big data allows for the examination of actual behavior. For example, a customer might tell a firm, "I'm on hold too long." But how long is too long? The collection and analysis of call data can tell a firm that the average customer will hold for 13 minutes before hanging up; such information can suggest to the firm's management to set a hard service standard that customers should not be placed on hold for more than 10 minutes.

Firms are beginning to recognize the value of moment-by-moment customer data, and are even taking strides to actively collect more data and to design the customer experience around real-time access to this data. For example, Disney Parks now provide customers with the opportunity to wear a MagicBand, which uses radio frequency identification (RFID) technology to track a guest's every movement throughout the park. The data collected from these bands allows Disney to craft an experience for customers that maximizes the "magic". For example, the bands can tell employees in character (such as Mickey Mouse or Snow White) about the children they are meeting, allowing them to greet the children by name and even wish them a happy birthday. Conveniently, the MagicBand also tracks purchase behavior, which could allow Disney to know which "magic" works to maximize revenue. Hypothetically, Disney could determine whether families whose children were greeted by name spent more money in the park or returned more often than families who were not. If the data shows that personal greetings increase customer spending, then a soft standard to cheerfully greet a child by name could conceivably follow.

Additionally, the data allows managers to streamline the entire experience for customers. For example, movement data lets Disney know which areas of the park are most susceptible to crowding, allowing managers to plan activities and other events in other areas of the park to help disperse the crowds. Standards relating to crowd density and wait times, such as a hard standard that no wait should be more than two hours, could be implemented and tracked, quantifying the improvements to the customer experience.

Big data is an amazing tool that allows for detailed customer insights that were never before possible, creating, tracking, and managing the customer experience right down to the moment or click. The information is also invaluable in learning which aspects of the experience are most important to patrons, allowing service providers to create both hard and soft service standards that ensure customers gets the experience they are looking for every time.

Sources: T. H. Davenport, L. Dalle Mule, and J. Lucker, "Know What Your Customers Want Before They Do," *Harvard Business Review* 89 (December 2011), pp. 84–92; D. Sweeney, "4 Benefits That MagicBands Bring to the Wonderful World of Disney Parks," *Forbes,* January 9, 2013, http://www.forbes.com /sites/deborahsweeney/2013/01/09/4-benefits-that-magicbands -bring-to-the-wonderful-world-of-disney-parks/#3a9a02c9396c; A. Carr, "The Messy Business of Reinventing Happiness," *Fast Company,* April 15, 2015, http://www.fastcompany .com/3044283/the-messy-business-of-reinventing-happiness.

actions that contribute to guest perceptions of high service quality. Whether they are set and monitored using audits (such as timed actions) or customer perceptions (such as opinions about courtesy), service standards provide a means for formal goal setting.

Customer-, Not *Company-*, Defined Standards

Virtually all companies possess service standards and measures that are *company defined*—they are established to reach internal company goals for productivity, efficiency, cost, or technical quality. One company-defined standard that often does not meet customer expectations is the common practice of voice-activated telephone support systems that do not allow customers to speak to humans. Because these systems save companies money (and actually provide faster service to some customers), many organizations have switched from the labor-intensive practice of having customer representatives to using these "automated" systems. However, to close gap 2, standards set by companies must be based on customer requirements and expectations rather than just on internal company goals. In this chapter we make the case that company-defined standards are not typically successful in driving behaviors that close provider gap 2. Instead, a company must set *customer-defined standards*: operational standards based on pivotal customer requirements identified by customers. These standards are deliberately chosen to match customer expectations and to be calibrated the way the customer views and expresses them. Because these goals are essential to the provision of excellent service, the rest of this chapter focuses on customer-defined standards.

Knowing customer requirements, priorities, and expectation levels can be both effective and efficient. Anchoring service standards on customers can save money by identifying what the customer values, thus eliminating activities and features that the customer either does not notice or will not pay for. One of the key desires of customers visiting a Department of Transportation office is to not have to wait a long time. In Oregon a few years ago, government officials made it a top priority to improve service at all of the state's Driver and Motor Vehicle (DMV) offices and get wait-times down—and the results were impressive. The goal was to have customers wait no more than 20 minutes when visiting any DMV office in the state—a decision based on customer surveys indicating people generally expected to wait no more than 20 minutes for service. In less than three years' time, the percentage of customers who were served in under 20 minutes increased from 52 percent to about 70 percent. To increase this percentage the DMV encouraged the use of alternative channels—such as online services or the mail—for simple transactions such as vehicle registration renewals, address changes, and notice of vehicle sales, reducing the number of people who needed to visit a DMV office. The DMV pursued other strategies to reduce wait time, including adding express counters and information kiosks; they also scheduled relief help between offices and developed alternative work schedules to make DMV staff more readily available when demand was high.[7] The Oregon DMV identified what was important to its customers and then implemented processes, reassigned staff, and trained employees to deliver service accordingly. Puget Sound Energy (PSE) has used customer-defined standards for nearly two decades. Its customers have identified missed appointments, frequency and duration of power outages, and the amount of time it takes the company to field its calls as among the most important issues. Figure 9.1 displays how PSE did in nine customer-defined standards in three key areas.

Although customer-defined standards need not conflict with productivity and efficiency, they do not originate with these company concerns. Rather, they are anchored in and steered by customer perceptual measures of service quality or satisfaction. The service standards that evolve from a customer perspective are likely to be different from company-defined service standards.

requirements into hard standards and measures. Many of the FedEx standards relate to on-time delivery and not making mistakes, and for good reason. As we stressed in Chapter 3, customer expectations of reliability—fulfillment of service promises—are high. Studies across numerous industries have found that the most frequent customer complaints are associated with service mistakes or problems (32 percent of all complaints) or poor product performance (30 percent of all complaints).[9]

To address the need for reliability, companies can institute a "do it right the first time" and an "honor your promises" value system by establishing reliability standards. An example of a generic reliability standard that is relevant to virtually any service company is "right the first time," which means the service performed is done correctly the first time according to the customer's assessment. If the service involves delivery of physical products, "right the first time" to the customer might mean the shipment is accurate— that it contains all that the customer ordered and nothing that the customer did not order. If the service involves installation of equipment, "right the first time" likely means that the equipment was installed correctly and was able to be used immediately by the customer. Another example of a reliability standard is "right on time," which means that the service is performed at the scheduled time. The company representative arrives when promised or the delivery is made at the time the customer expects it. In more complex services, such as disaster recovery or systems integration in computer service, "right on time" would likely mean that the service was completed by the promised date.

Reliability is often the most important concern of service customers. In electronic retailing, on-time and accurate fulfillment of orders is one of the most important aspects of reliability. One of the best examples of customer-defined hard standards in the Internet context is the single summary metric used by Dell Technologies for fulfillment. This metric is the Perfect Order Metric, which Dell developed in response to a declining Net Promoter Score.[10] The Net Promoter Score is determined based on customers' response to a single question: "How likely is it that you would recommend our company/product/ service to a friend or colleague?" After talking to many customers, Dell learned that customers simply wanted Dell to deliver what the customer ordered when Dell said they would. Based on this feedback, the Perfect Order Metric is calculated as follows: (% of on-time deliveries) × (% of complete orders) × (% of orders delivered damage-free) × (% of orders delivered with accurate documentation). Dell tracks its performance on this reliability metric and rewards employees based on how well they do, ensuring employees are working toward goals that are most important to the customer.

Hard service standards for responsiveness are set to ensure the speed or promptness with which companies deliver products (within two working days), handle complaints (by sundown each day), answer questions (within two hours), answer the telephone and arrive for repair calls (within 30 minutes of the estimated time). In addition to setting standards that specify levels of response, companies must have well-staffed customer service departments. Responsiveness perceptions diminish when customers wait to get through to the company by telephone, are put on hold, or are dumped into a telephone voice mail system.

When it comes to providing service across cultures and continents, service providers need to recognize that customer-defined service standards often need to be adapted. Our Global Feature provides examples of companies with worldwide brands that have found ways to achieve universally high service quality while allowing for local differences in service standards.

Soft Customer-Defined Standards

Not all customer priorities can be counted, timed, or observed through audits. As Albert Einstein said, "Not everything that counts can be counted, and not everything that can be counted, counts." For example, "understanding and knowing the customer" is a customer priority that cannot be adequately captured by a standard that counts, times, or observes employees. In contrast to hard measures, soft measures must be documented using perceptual data. We call the second category of customer-defined standards *soft standards and measures* because they are opinion-based measures and cannot be directly observed. They must be collected by talking to customers, employees, or others. Soft standards provide direction, guidance, and feedback to employees in ways to achieve customer satisfaction and can be examined by measuring customer perceptions and beliefs.

Soft standards are especially important for person-to-person interactions such as the selling process and the delivery process for professional services. Exhibit 9.2 displays several examples of soft customer-defined standards. A casino that one of us has worked with has identified five soft service standards to encourage its employees to provide an appropriate level of attention and respect to its guests—two issues that its customers have indicated are important to them. Two of these standards are for employees to "display a demeanor that could be described as friendly, polite, cheerful, or upbeat" and to "offer an appropriate verbal greeting" when interacting with customers. Unlike the hard service standards described earlier, such soft standards are not easily quantifiable, but a firm's performance on these standards can be assessed via surveys and other means that capture customer perceptions of how the firm is doing on the standards.

Many firms have both hard and soft customer-defined standards. The differences between hard and soft standards are illustrated in Exhibit 9.3 using the customer care standards developed at Ford Motor Company.

One-Time Fixes

When customer research is undertaken to find out what aspects of service need to be changed, requirements can sometimes be met using one-time fixes. *One-time fixes* are technology, policy, or procedure changes that, when instituted, address customer requirements. We further define one-time fixes as company standards that can be met by an outlet (e.g., a franchisee) making a one-time change that does not involve employees and therefore does not require motivation and monitoring to ensure compliance. We include one-time fixes in our discussion of standards because organizations with multiple outlets often must clearly define these standards to ensure consistency. As an example, Hampton Inns' "Make It Hampton" program required that all inns institute 60 new product and service standards, many of which were one-time fixes. The fixes implemented in the first phase of the program included lap desks in rooms, outdoor planter gardens to hide trash containers, red carpet welcome mats, and new lobby artwork and music.[11] The second phase of the program, labeled the "Cloud Nine Bed Experience," included raising all of its 150,000 hotel beds at the time to a standard of 28–31 inches off the floor—in line with most home bedrooms today, upgrading pillows to jumbo size, and adding comforters, sheets with a greater thread count, and fitted bottom sheets. Performance standards do not typically need to be developed for such fixes because the one-time change in technology, equipment, furnishings, policies, or procedures accomplishes the desired change.

Two other examples of successful one-time fixes include Hertz's rental car express check-in and Granite Rock's 24-hour express service. In both of these examples, customers expressed a desire to be served in ways different from the past. Hertz's customers had clearly indicated their frustration at waiting in long lines. Granite Rock, an innovative company in California that sells a "commodity" product, had customers who desired 24-hour availability of ground rock from its quarry.

Whereas most companies in these industries decided for various reasons not to address these customer requirements, Hertz and Granite Rock each responded with one-time fixes that virtually revolutionized the service quality delivered by their

How do companies adjust for cultural or local differences in service standards if they recognize that these geographic differences are related to varying customer expectations? Companies with worldwide brands have much to lose if their service standards vary too much across countries, and therefore they must find ways to achieve universally high quality while still allowing for local differences.

SERVICE STANDARDS AT FOUR SEASONS: GLOBAL AND LOCAL NORMS

As the world's leading luxury hospitality company, Four Seasons Hotels and Resorts successfully manages nearly 100 properties in more than 40 countries by balancing universal service standards with standards that vary by country. The company, consistently ranked among the world's best hotels and most prestigious brands in reader polls, traveler reviews, and industry awards, owes much of its success to its service standards expected of *all* staff *all* over the world at *all* times. Four Seasons regularly revisits their standards and thinking on service, and generally do not share the standards publicly. However, one known set of seven standards used in the early 2000s formed the acrostic SERVICE:

1. **Smile:** employees will actively greet guests, smile, and speak clearly in a friendly manner.
2. **Eye:** employees will make eye contact, even in passing, with an acknowledgment.
3. **Recognition:** all staff will create a sense of recognition by using the guest's name, when known, in a natural and discreet manner.
4. **Voice:** staff will speak to guests in an attentive, natural, and courteous manner, avoiding pretension and in a clear voice.
5. **Informed:** all guest contact staff will be well informed about their hotel, will take ownership of simple requests, and will not refer guests elsewhere.
6. **Clean:** staff will always appear clean, crisp, well groomed, and well-fitted.
7. **Everyone:** everyone, everywhere, all the time, will show care for our guests.

Global service standards at Four Seasons are adapted, when necessary, to local cultures.

In addition to these standards, the hotel identified other core standards that applied to different aspects of service provision (such as "the staff will be aware of arriving vehicles and will move toward them, opening doors within 30 seconds" and "unanswered guest room phones will be picked up within 5 rings, or 20 seconds"). Exceptions to these other standards were allowed if they made local or cultural sense. For example, in the United States, coffee pots were left on tables at breakfast; in many parts of Europe, including France, customers perceived this practice as a lack of service, so servers were encouraged to personally refill coffee cups as needed. Standards for uniforms and decor differed across cultures, but minimum expectations were to be met everywhere.

SERVICE STANDARDS AT TOYOTA IN JAPAN

In 2005 Toyota began selling its luxury car, Lexus, in Japan. Although Lexus was already the best-selling luxury brand in the United States, in Japan it had very little name recognition. The company wanted a way to set Lexus apart from the Toyota brand and decided to focus on emphasizing customer service. Japan has a long history of unique customs and Toyota thought that perhaps they could bring that to the Lexus brand. So Toyota approached an etiquette school—the Ogasawara Ryu Reihou Institute in Tokyo—that

companies. Hertz used technology to create Express Checkout, a one-time fix that also resulted in productivity improvements and cost reductions. The company also pioneered a similar one-time fix for hotel Express Check-In, again in response to customers' expressed desires. Granite Rock created an ATM-like system for 24-hour customer access to rock ground to the 14 most popular consistencies. The company created its own Granite Xpress Card that allowed customers to enter, select, and receive their supplies at any time of the day or night.

specializes in teaching the art of daily behavior, including the correct way to bow, hold chopsticks, and sit on a tatami mat floor, to help develop techniques that they could apply to selling cars.

Although typical clients of the school are well-bred families who want their children to learn good table manners and posture, the institute spent several months studying Lexus and its employees' interactions with customers. The result was the development of new service standards, several patterned after samurai behaviors. For example, salespersons are instructed to:

- Assume the samurai warrior's "waiting position" by leaning 5 to 10 degrees forward when a customer is looking at a car.
- Bow more deeply to a customer who has purchased a car than to a casual window shopper.
- Display the "Lexus Face," a closed-mouth smile intended to put customers at ease.
- Stand with left hand over right, fingers together and thumbs interlocked, as the samurais did to show they were not about to draw their swords.
- Stand about two arms' lengths from customers when they are looking at a car and come in closer when closing a deal.
- Point with all five fingers to a car door's handle, right hand followed by left, then gracefully open the door with both hands.
- When serving coffee or tea, kneel on the floor with both feet together and both knees on the ground.

Toyota understands that these standards would not work well in many of their markets, particularly the United States, but felt the standards were necessary for the Lexus brand to compete with the two luxury car market leaders—BMW and Mercedes Benz—in Japan.

SERVICE STANDARDS IN PAKISTAN

Research on service quality in Western countries generally finds reliability to be the most important dimension. Western customers expect firms to be dependable and accurate and to do what they have promised. Research in Pakistan, however, suggests that customers have different standards of service quality:

- Reliability has been conceptualized as the ability to perform the promised service dependably and accurately. Although Pakistani customers seem to concur with this conceptualization, they do not expect service delivery to be executed in absolute terms. "Promises are mostly kept" is how reliability would be described. They can apparently tolerate service failure with the content or timing of service as long as an acceptable substitute is provided within an appropriate time frame. It is generally important for them to maintain a long-term relationship with the service provider.
- Pakistani customers seem to include accessibility as a part of their evaluation of a service provider's reliability. This is especially important in case of health care and other public services. Availability of a service at the time when it is needed is of extreme importance in Pakistan.
- Physical safety is also an important factor when Pakistani customers evaluate service offerings. In a society that frequently has law-and-order problems, a customer's physical safety becomes important when doing business with a service provider.

Such findings suggest that service firms from Western cultures doing business in Pakistan can probably succeed with service standards that do not call for perfectly reliable service, emphasize service recovery, focus on delivering service when promised and across a wide range of times, or address issues of personal safety.

Sources: R. Hallowell, D. Bowen, and C. Knoop, "Four Seasons Goes to Paris," *Academy of Management Executive* 16 (2002), pp. 7–24; A. Chozick, "The Samurai Sell: Lexus Dealers Bow to Move Swank Cars," *The Wall Street Journal,* July 9, 2007, p. A1; and N. Raajpoot, "Reconceptualizing Service Encounter Quality in a Non-Western Context," *Journal of Service Research* 7 (November 2004), pp. 181–201.

One-time fixes are often accomplished by technology. Technology can simplify and improve customer service, particularly when it frees company personnel by handling routine, repetitive tasks and transactions. Customer service employees can then spend more time on the personal and possibly more essential portions of the job. In recent years some hospital emergency rooms have added check-in kiosks so that patients who are not experiencing a true "emergency" can enter personal information, thus reducing time spent waiting in line to register and explain symptoms.[12]

Exhibit 9.2 Examples of Soft Customer-Defined Standards

Company	Customer Priorities	Customer-Defined Standards
American Express	Resolution of problems	• Resolve problem at first contact (no transfers, other calls, or multiple contacts) • Communicate and give adequate instructions • Take all the time necessary
	Treatment	• Listen • Do everything possible to help • Be appropriately reassuring (open and honest)
	Courtesy of representative	• Put card member at ease • Be patient in explaining billing process • Display sincere interest in helping card member • Listen attentively • Address card member by name • Thank card member at end of call
General Electric	Interpersonal skills of operators:	• Take ownership of the call • Follow through with promises made • Be courteous and knowledgeable • Understand the customer's question or request
L.L. Bean	Calming human voice; minimal customer anxiety	• Use appropriate tone of voice • Do not engage in other tasks (e.g., arranging gift boxes) while on the telephone with customers
Mayo Clinic	Getting well	• Compliance with processes known to enhance care
	Feeling well taken care of	• Each patient is treated with respect, kindness, and dignity by every member of the (Mayo) team
Nationwide Insurance	Responsiveness	• Provide a human voice on the line when customers report problems
Peninsula Regional Medical Center	Respect	• Keep patient information confidential • Never discuss patients and their care in public areas • Listen to patients with empathy • Be courteous and do not use jargon • Keep noise to a minimum • Never "talk over" a patient
Ritz-Carlton	Being treated with respect	• React quickly to solve any problems immediately • Use proper telephone etiquette • Do not screen calls • Eliminate call transfers when possible

DEVELOPMENT OF CUSTOMER-DEFINED SERVICE STANDARDS

Turning Customer Requirements into Specific Behaviors and Actions

How have firms such as FedEx, Puget Sound Energy, and Zappos.com been able to develop commendable customer-defined service standards? Figure 9.2 shows the general process for setting customer-defined service standards.

In this chapter we discuss two types of customer-defined service standards. "Hard" standards and measures are operational measures that can be counted, timed, or observed through audits. The other category, "soft" standards, makes use of opinion-based measures that cannot be obtained by counting or timing but instead must be asked of the customer. Ford Motor Company provides an example that illustrates the difference between hard and soft standards. Several years ago Ford was looking to develop Customer Care standards for service at their many dealerships. Marketing research involving 2,400 customers asked them about specific expectations for automobile sales and service; Ford used this input to help identify the level of service that dealerships would need to provide to receive "Blue Oval Certified" status. The following seven specific service standards were established as most critical to customers in the service department of dealerships.

1. Appointment available within one day of customer's requested service day.
2. Write-up begins within four minutes or less of customer arrival.
3. Service needs are courteously identified, accurately recorded on repair order, and verified with customer.
4. Vehicle serviced right on the first visit.
5. Service status provided within one minute of inquiry.
6. Vehicle ready at agreed-upon time.
7. Thorough explanation given of work done, coverage, and charges.

HARD STANDARDS AND MEASURES

Several of the standards Ford identified fall into the category of hard standards—they can be counted, timed, or observed through audits. Standards 2 and 5, for example, could be timed by an employee in the service establishment. The hard measure could be either the frequency or percentage of times that the standard's time periods are met or the average times themselves (e.g., average time that write-ups begin). Other standards could be counted or audited, such as standards 1, 4, and 6. The service clerk who answers the telephone could record the number of times that appointments were available within one day of the customer's request. The number of repeat visits could be counted to measure standard 4, and the number of vehicles ready at the agreed-upon time could be tallied as customers came in to pick up their cars.

SOFT STANDARDS AND MEASURES

Consider standards 3 and 7 and note how they differ from the ones we have just discussed. These standards represent desired behaviors that are soft and therefore cannot be counted or timed. For example, the courteous behavior included in standard 3 cannot be counted. Likewise, standard 7 requires a different type of measure—the customer's perception or opinion about whether this behavior was performed appropriately. It is not that soft standards cannot be measured; instead, they must be measured in different ways.

Soft standards provide direction, guidance, and feedback to employees in ways to achieve customer satisfaction and can be quantified by measuring customer perceptions and beliefs. Soft standards are especially important for person-to-person interactions such as the selling process and the delivery process for professional services. To be effective, companies must provide feedback to employees about customer perceptions of their performance.

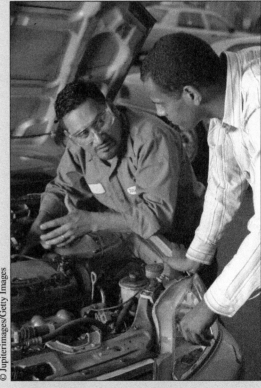

© Jupiterimages/Getty Images

Ford Motor Company Customer Care has a variety of both hard and soft service standards.

FIGURE 9.2
Process for Setting Customer-Defined Standards

1. Identify existing or desired service encounter sequence.

2. Translate customer expectations into behaviors/actions.

3. Determine appropriate standards.

Measure by audits or operating data ← Hard standards ← 4. Develop measurements for standards. → Soft standards → Measure by transaction-based surveys

5. Establish target levels for standards.

6. Track measures against standards.

7. Provide feedback about performance to employees.

8. Update target levels and measures.

Step 1: Identify Existing or Desired Service Encounter Sequence

A customer's overall service quality evaluation is the accumulation of evaluations of multiple service experiences. Service encounters are the component pieces needed to establish service standards in a company. In establishing standards firms are concerned with service encounter quality and thus want to understand the specific requirements and priorities of the customer for each service encounter. Therefore, the first step in establishing customer-defined standards is to delineate the *service encounter sequence*. Identifying the sequence can be done by listing the sequential steps and activities that the customer experiences in receiving the service. Alternatively, service blueprints (see Chapter 8) can be used to identify the sequence by noting customer activities across the top of the blueprint. Vertical lines from customer activities into the lower levels of the blueprint signal the points at which service encounters take place. Standards that meet customer expectations for each interaction can then be identified. Ideally, the company would be open to discovering customers' desired service encounter sequences, exploring the ways customers want to do business with the firm.

A firm might also consider which of its service encounters have the greatest impact on customers. Marriott, for example, has found that encounters in the first 10 minutes of a hotel stay are the most critical, leading to a focus on customers' front-desk experiences (such as express check-in). Some research indicates that a strong finish in the final event of the service encounter sequence has a greater impact on overall satisfaction.[13] As

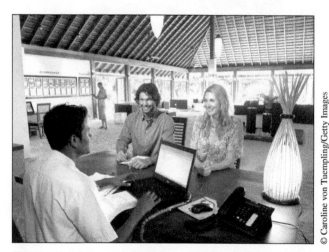

First encounters, such as for a hotel stay, are critical and have a significant impact on customers in most service settings.

© Caroline von Tuempling/Getty Images

a result, other hotels have chosen to focus on the "back end" of the hotel experience—checkout, parking, bellperson services—to leave a strong final impression. To be safe, the Ritz-Carlton assumes both the first and last encounters are important and therefore includes as two of the three "Steps of Service" (part of its famous "Gold Standards") instructions for employees to provide guests with "a warm and sincere greeting" and "a fond farewell [with] a warm good-bye" while using the guests' names.[14]

Step 2: Translate Customer Expectations into Specific Behaviors and Actions

Setting a standard in broad conceptual terms, such as "improve skills in the company," is ineffective because the standard is difficult to interpret, measure, and achieve. When a company collects data, it often captures customer requirements in very abstract terms. In general, customer-contact personnel often find such data are not diagnostic but rather too broad and general. Such research neither tells them specifically what is wrong and right in their customer relationships nor helps them understand what activities can be eliminated, so that the most important actions can be accomplished. In most cases, frontline employees need help translating the data into specific actions to deliver better customer service.

Figure 9.3 shows different levels of abstraction/concreteness for standards in a service firm, arrayed from top (most abstract) to bottom (most concrete and specific). At the very abstract level are customer requirements too general to be useful to employees: customers want satisfaction, value, and relationships. The next level under these very general requirements includes abstract dimensions of service quality already discussed in this text: reliability, responsiveness, empathy, assurance, and tangibles. One level further are attributes which are more specific in describing requirements.[15] If we dig still deeper beneath the attribute level, we get to specific behaviors and actions at the appropriate level of specificity for setting standards. Thus, in step 2, abstract customer requirements and expectations must be translated into concrete, specific

FIGURE 9.3   **What Customers Expect: Getting to Actionable Steps**

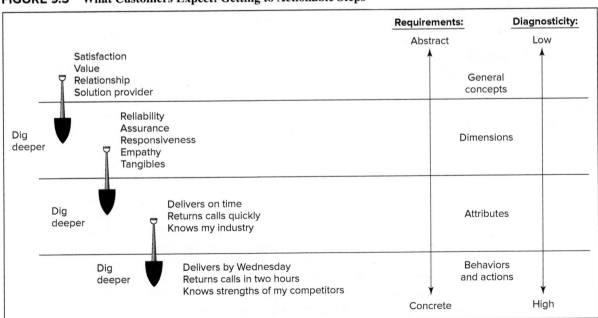

John Robert's Spa has developed a reputation for extraordinary service as a hair salon in northeast Ohio. Part of its success stems from its understanding and careful management of the sequence of service encounters customers are subjected to, which it labels the "Customer Experience Cycle." In identifying the seven most typical service encounters that form the basis of its service process, John Robert's has specified precisely what every client should experience when receiving a haircut at John Robert's. The following service standards are expected of employees across these seven encounters.

Preexperience: provided by guest care personnel

- Answer the phone enthusiastically, saying, "Thank you for calling John Robert's Mayfield (salon location). This is Kelly. How can I help you?"
- Allow plenty of time to answer all of the client's questions concerning services, the designers' credentials, availability, and so on.
- Give each client an opportunity to book appointments for additional services.
- Use the client's name at least four times during the call.
- Offer directions to the salon.
- Confirm the service, operator, time, and date.
- As the last thing before hanging up, ask, "Is there anything else I can do for you?"
- Make a confirmation call to the client 24 hours before the appointment.

Start of the experience: provided by hostess

- Greet the client enthusiastically within 8–10 seconds.
- Confirm the client's appointment.
- Ask the client to fill out the information card.
- Immediately notify the operator of the client's arrival.
- Offer to hang up the client's coat and to provide a refreshment.
- Inform the client of any delays.

- Offer a tour of the entire facility.
- Show the client where the changing rooms are.
- Monitor the client's wait, and notify the operator again if the client is not taken within 10 minutes of the scheduled appointment.
- Use the client's name at least four times during the check-in.

Preservice: provided by designer

- Provide consultation every time with every client.
- Show portfolio, analyze client's needs, and discuss client's expectations.
- Provide stress-relieving scalp massage.
- For men, provide a minifacial.
- Provide shampoo and conditioner.
- Use a white cape for new clients.

Service: provided by designer

- Give an excellent haircut.
- Massage hands and arms.
- Clean client's jewelry during massage.
- Keep the conversation on a professional level.
- Give lesson on blow-dry styling.
- Explain products used.

Postservice: provided by designer

- Touch-up makeup for all female clients.
- Make client aware of additional services that salon/spa offers:
  - Give complimentary bang trim.
  - Inform client of complimentary blow-dry lesson in the future, to help the client duplicate it on her own.
  - Offer men complimentary neck and sideburn trimmings between visits.
  - Offer referral incentives: $5 gift certificate for every referral and contest with prizes for the clients who refer the most new clients during the year.

---

behaviors and actions associated with each service encounter. Abstract requirements (like reliability) can call for a different behavior or action in each service encounter.

Information on behaviors and actions should be gathered and interpreted by an objective source such as a research firm or an inside department with no stake in the ultimate decisions. If the information is filtered through company managers or frontline people with an internal bias, the outcome can easily result in company-defined, rather than customer-defined, standards. Research techniques discussed in Chapter 5 that are relevant for eliciting behaviors and actions include in-depth interviewing of

Conclusion of experience: provided by various staff

- Assistant, operator, and receptionist: give client a friendly and enthusiastic send-off.
- Designer and receptionist: give an opportunity to purchase products used.
- Main operator: give client a business card.
- Receptionist: give client opportunity to schedule next appointment.
- Receptionist: for new clients, give client a new-client package that includes a menu of services, newsletter, business card, magnet, and five-question form. Inform client of 10 percent off next visit if she returns the completed form within six weeks.
- Receptionist: during check-out use client's name at least four times.
- Operator: input personal information (such as name of spouse, children) in computer under client's name for use on future visits.

Postexperience: provided by support staff

- Client receives an enthusiastic phone call within 24 hours.
- Client receives a thank-you postcard within 48 hours.
- Client receives a quarterly newsletter.
- Client receives a birthday card.
- If client has a challenge, handle it immediately on the spot. Make it right. Fill out customer challenge sheet and have management follow up.
- If client is not retained after four months: send out a reminder card that client is due for an appointment.
- If a client is not retained after eight months: send out an incentive to return (such as 25 percent off for next visit).
- If a client is not retained after 12 months: survey with a letter or phone call to find out why.

Source: J. R. DiJulius, *Secret Service: Hidden Systems That Deliver Unforgettable Customer Value* (New York: American Management Association, 2001), pp. 8–11.

© Courtesy John Robert's Spa

John Robert's Spa has identified service standards expected of employees across the seven most typical service encounters.

customers, focus group interviews, and other forms of research such as partnering. Using such research, John Robert's Spa, a salon in northeast Ohio, identified seven typical service encounters that the average customer experiences when coming to the spa, including the initial phone call to schedule a visit, arrival at the spa, consultation with an employee prior to receiving any treatment, delivery of the spa service itself, wrap-up of the treatment, paying and exiting the spa, and postexperience contact. For each encounter, specific employee behaviors were identified (see Exhibit 9.4). For example, when the client first enters the spa, the hostess is expected to greet the customer enthusiastically within 10 seconds, confirm the appointment, offer to hang up the customer's coat, offer a tour of the facility (if a new customer), and use the customer's name at least four times during the check-in.

A real-world example of the difference in requirements across the four levels depicted in Figure 9.3 illustrate their practical significance. In a traditional measurement system for a major company's training division, only one aspect of the instructor was included in its class evaluation: ability of instructor. During qualitative research relating to the attributes that satisfy students, three somewhat more specific requirements were elicited: (1) instructor's style, (2) instructor's expertise, and (3) instructor's management of class. Although the articulation of the three attributes was more helpful to instructors than the broad "ability of instructor," management found that the attributes were still too broad to help instructors wanting to improve their course delivery. When the company invested in a customer-defined standards project, the resulting measurement system was far more useful in diagnosing student requirements because the research focused on *specific behaviors and actions* of instructors that met student requirements. Instead of a single broad requirement or three general attributes, the requirements of students were articulated in 14 specific behaviors that related to the instructor and 11 specific actions that related to the course content. These behaviors and actions were clearly more diagnostic for communicating what was good and bad in the courses. An additional benefit of this approach was that feedback on behaviors and actions was perceived as less personal than feedback on traits or personal characteristics. It was also easier for employees of the company to make changes that related to behaviors rather than to personality traits.

Step 3: Determine Appropriate Standards

The next step involves determining whether hard or soft standards should be used to capture a given behavior and action. Recall that hard standards consist of quantifiable measures of employee behaviors and actions; soft standards are often concerned with more abstract requirements or issues, are not as easily quantifiable, and are often much more subjective. One of the biggest mistakes companies make in this step is to hastily choose a hard standard. Companies are accustomed to operational (and often easily quantifiable) measures and often have a bias toward them. However, unless the hard standard adequately captures the expected behavior and action, it is not customer defined. The best way to decide whether a hard standard is appropriate is to first establish a soft standard by means of trailer calls and then determine over time which operational aspect most correlates to this soft measure. Figure 9.4 shows the linkage between speed of complaint handling (a hard measure) and satisfaction (a soft measure); the figure illustrates that satisfaction strongly depends on the number of hours it takes to resolve a complaint.

Prioritizing the behaviors and actions—of which there will be many—into those for which customer-defined standards will be established is also crucial in determining standards. The following are the most important criteria for creation of appropriate service standards.

1. The standards are based on behaviors and actions that are very important to customers.
2. The standards cover performance that needs to be improved or maintained.
3. The standards cover behaviors and actions employees have control over and can improve.
4. The standards are understood and accepted by employees.

FIGURE 9.4
Linkage between Hard and Soft Measures for Speed of Complaint Handling

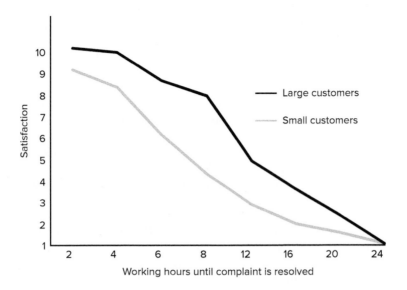

5. The standards are predictive rather than reactive—based on current and future customer expectations rather than past complaints.
6. The standards are challenging but realistic.

Step 4: Develop Measurements for Standards

Once companies have determined whether hard or soft standards are appropriate and which specific standards best capture customer requirements, they must develop feedback measures that adequately capture the standards. Two types of measures are hard measurements and soft measurements.

Hard measurements typically involve mechanical counts or technology-enabled measurement of time or errors. What distinguishes these measurements from soft measurements is that they can be measured continuously and operationally without asking the customer's opinion of them. To demonstrate, here are some of the actual measurements of hard standards of the FedEx Express SQI:

- *Missing packages:* the number of packages that do not have a final disposition scan or have no package status scans for two consecutive business days after commit date.
- *Damaged packages:* the number of claims filed by customers for cost of contents for packages with visible or concealed damage.
- *Wrong day, late deliveries:* the number of packages delivered after the commitment date.[16]

In these and other hard measurements, assessment involves a count of the number and type of actions or behaviors that are correct or incorrect. Somewhere in the operation system these actions and behaviors are tabulated, frequently through information technology. Other gauges of hard standards include service guarantee lapses (the number of times a service guarantee is invoked because the service did not meet the promise), amounts of time (as in the number of hours or days to respond to a question or complaint or minutes waited in line), and frequencies associated with relevant standards (such as the number of visits made to customers or the number of abandoned telephone inquiries). L.L. Bean earned its reputation for outstanding customer service using continually updated data (i.e., hard measures) on models, colors, and sizes of products in stock. This system allows the company to set and achieve high standards of customer service—and it enables L.L. Bean to regularly receive awards for superior customer service and order fulfillment.[17]

The appropriate hard measure to deliver to customer requirements is not always intuitive or obvious, and the potential for counting or tracking an irrelevant aspect of operations is high. For this reason, it is often desirable to link operational performance measures with soft measures (gathered via surveys or trailer calls) to be sure that they are strongly correlated.

Soft measurements are based on customer perceptions that often cannot be directly observed. Two research methods described in Chapter 5 can document customers' opinions about whether performance has met the standards established: relationship surveys and posttransaction surveys. Relationship and SERVQUAL surveys cover all aspects of the customer's relationship with the company, are typically expressed in attributes, and are usually completed once per year. Posttransaction surveys are associated with specific service encounters, are short (approximately six or seven questions), and are administered as close in time to a specific service encounter as possible. For requirements that are longer term and at a higher level of abstraction (such as at the attribute level), annual relationship surveys can document customer perceptions on a periodic basis. Posttransaction surveys can be administered continuously, whenever customers experience a service encounter of the type being considered, to provide data on a continuous basis.

Step 5: Establish Target Levels for the Standards

The next step requires that companies establish target levels for the standards. Without this step the company lacks a way to quantify whether the standards are being met. Figure 9.4 provides a good example of an approach that can be used to set standards for timeliness in responding to complaints in a service company. In this illustration, each time a complaint is made to the company, and each time one is resolved, employees can record the times. They can also ask each customer his or her satisfaction with the performance in resolving the complaint. The company can then plot the information from each complaint to determine how well the company is performing and where the company would like to be in the future. This technique is but one of several for determining the target level for service standards.

Another technique is a simple perception–action correlation study. When the service consists of repetitive processes, companies can relate levels of customer satisfaction with actual performance of a behavior or task. Consider, for example, a study to determine the standard for customers' wait-time in a line. The information gathered should include both customer perceptions of their wait in line (soft perceptual measure) and the amount of time they actually stand in line (hard operations measure). The joint collection of these data over many transactions provides evidence of the sensitivity of customers to different wait-times.

One airline conducted precisely such a study by having a flight attendant intercept customers as they approached the ticket counter. As each customer entered the line, the attendant stamped the entry time on a ticket (using a machine like those in parking lots) and handed the customer the stamped ticket. As the customer exited the line at the end of the transaction, the flight attendant restamped the ticket with the exit time and asked the customer three or four questions about perceptions of the wait in line and satisfaction with the transaction. Aggregating the individual customer data provided a graph that allowed the company to evaluate the impact on perceptions of various levels of line waits.

Step 6: Track Measures against Standards

Roger Milliken, former head of Milliken Industries, is reported to have said, "In God we trust, all others bring data." Successful service businesses, such as FedEx and Disney, have careful and comprehensive fact-based systems that provide information about their operations—allowing them to continually examine how the company is performing in comparison to its service standards. One company that lives and thrives through management by fact is Granite Rock, the family-run business in Watsonville, California (mentioned earlier in the chapter) that provides concrete, asphalt, and crushed stone products. Granite Rock has systems in place to gather, analyze, and act on information. Statistical process control and other types of charts are everywhere, tracking a wide range of issues—from characteristics of its concrete and crushed stone to processes such as the time it takes customers to fill their trucks. Customer complaints are also tracked through what the company calls "product-service discrepancy reports" and root-cause analysis, and updates are distributed to all plants. The reports show how long it takes to resolve complaints and provide detailed quarterly analyses of trends. Plants can track their trends for four years running. When it comes to product quality and customer service, Granite Rock leaves nothing to chance.

Step 7: Provide Feedback about Performance to Employees

Once companies have determined appropriate standards, developed specific measures that best capture customer requirements, and set appropriate target levels for the standards, they must develop mechanisms to provide feedback on employee actions and behaviors. One example of such feedback is employee monitoring—in firms with customer service departments, this involves the practice of supervisors listening in on employee telephone interactions with customers. You may have experienced this practice when you have called customer service numbers for many organizations and noticed that the voice prompts tell you that calls may be monitored for quality purposes. The purpose of such monitoring is often to provide feedback on employee performance to the service standards set by the organization. One critical aspect of developing feedback mechanisms is ensuring that performance captures the process from the customer's view rather than the company's perspective. A supervisor monitoring an employee's handling of a customer service call, for example, should focus not so much on how quickly the employee gets the customer off the telephone but on how adequately she handles the customer's request.

FedEx communicates the performance on its service quality indicator (SQI) weekly, so that everyone in the company knows how the company is performing. When problems occur, they can be identified and corrected. The SQI measurement gives everyone in the company immediate feedback on activity that is strongly related to customer perceptions. In a general sense, data and facts need to be analyzed and distributed to support evaluation and decision making at multiple levels within the company. The data also must be deployed quickly enough that the people who need it to make decisions about service or processes can do so. Responsibility for meeting service requirements must also be communicated throughout

Developing Service Performance Indexes

One outcome of following the process for developing customer-defined standards is a service performance index. *Service performance indexes* are comprehensive composites of the most critical performance standards. Development of an index begins by identifying the set of customer-defined standards that the company will use to drive behavior. Not all service performance indexes contain customer-defined standards, but the best ones, like the FedEx SQI or Singapore Airline's SPI, are based on them. Most companies build these indexes by understanding the most important requirements of the customer, linking these requirements to tangible and measurable aspects of service provision, and using the feedback from these indexes to identify and improve service problems. The most progressive companies also use the feedback for reward and recognition systems within the company.

Summary

This chapter discussed the discrepancy between company perceptions of customer expectations and the standards set to deliver to these expectations. Among the major causes of provider gap 2 are inadequate standardization of service behaviors and actions, absence of formal processes for setting service quality goals, and lack of customer-defined standards. These problems were discussed and detailed, along with strategies to close the gap. To close the service design and standards gap, standards set by companies must be based on customer requirements and expectations rather than just on internal company goals. That is, company-defined standards are typically not successful in driving behaviors that close provider gap 2 and a company must set *customer*-defined standards based on key customer requirements visible to and measured by customers.

In this chapter we described two types of service standards: hard standards, those that can be counted, timed, or observed through audits, and soft standards, customer perceptions that cannot be directly observed. Customer-defined standards are at the heart of service delivery that customers expect: they are the link between customers' expressed expectations and company actions to deliver to those expectations. Creating customer-defined service standards is not a common practice in U.S. firms. Doing so requires that companies' marketing and operations departments work together by using the customer research as input for operations. Unless the operations standards are defined by customer priorities, they are not likely to have an impact on customer perceptions of service.

Discussion Questions

1. How does the service measurement described in this chapter differ from the service measurement in Chapter 5? Which of the two types do you think is most important? Why?

2. In what types of service industries are standards most difficult to develop? Why? Recommend three standards that might be developed in one of the firms from the industries you specify. How would employees react to these standards? How could you gain buy-in for them?

3. Given the need for customer-defined service standards, do firms need company-defined standards at all? Could all standards in a company be customer defined?

Why or why not? What functional departments in a firm would object to having all standards be customer defined?

4. What is the difference between hard and soft standards? Which do you think would be more readily accepted by employees? By management? Why?

5. Consider the university or school you currently attend. What are examples of hard standards, soft standards, and one-time fixes that would address student requirements? Does the school currently use such standards for delivery of service to students? Why or why not? Do you think your reasons would apply to private-sector companies as well? To public or nonprofit companies?

6. Think about a service that you currently use; then map out the service encounter sequence for that service. What is your most important requirement in each interaction? Document these requirements, and make certain that they are expressed at the concrete level of behaviors and actions.

Exercises

1. Select a local service firm. Visit the firm and ascertain the service measurements that the company tracks. What hard measures does it monitor? Soft measures? On the basis of what you find, develop a service performance index.

2. Choose one of the peripheral services (such as computer, library, placement) provided by your school. What hard standards would be useful to track to meet student expectations? What soft standards would be appropriate? What one-time fixes would improve service?

3. Think about a service company you have worked for or know about. Using Figure 9.3, write in customer requirements at each of the levels. How far down in the chart can you describe requirements? Is that far enough?

4. Look at three websites from which you can order products (such as amazon.com, llbean.com, and zappos.com). What are the companies' delivery promises? What types of standards might they set for these promises? Are these customer- or company-defined standards?

Notes

1. "Taking the Measure of Quality," *Service Savvy,* March 1992, p. 3.
2. Ibid.
3. E-mail communication from David Spear, manager of global service and quality assurance, *FedEx Express,* June 14, 2016.
4. 2015 FedEx Annual Report, http://s1.q4cdn.com/714383399/files/doc_financials /annual/FedEx_2015_Annual_Report.pdf, accessed July 6, 2016.
5. G. L. Shostack, "Breaking Free from Product Marketing," *Journal of Marketing* 41 (April 1977), pp. 73–80.
6. Puget Sound Energy, "2015 Service Quality Report Card," http://pse.com /accountsandservices/NewToPSE/Documents/2774_SQI_Report_Card_2015 _wb.pdf, accessed May 21, 2016.
7. Oregon Department of Transportation website, www.oregon.gov/ODOT/CS /PERFORMANCE/OnePagers/DMV Field Office Wait Time One pager.pdf, accessed July 13, 2016.
8. For a good discussion of creating service standards, see M. Solomon, "A Ritz-Carlton Caliber Experience Requires Employee Empowerment and Customer Service Standards," *Forbes,* September 18, 2013, http://www.forbes.com/sites

/micahsolomon/2013/09/18/empowered-employees-vs-brand-standards-the
-customer-experience-needs-both/.

9. 2015 Customer Rage Study conducted by Customer Care Measurement and
Consulting in collaboration with the Center for Services Leadership at Arizona
State University's W. P. Carey School of Business.

10. S. Banker, "A Leading Computer Manufacturer's Perfect Order Journey," *Forbes,*
February 3, 2016, www.forbes.com/sites/stevebanker/2016/02/03/a-leading
-computer-manufacturers-perfect-order-journey/print/.

11. J. Weinstein, "Redesigning the Box," *Hotels* 38 (2004), p. 7.

12. J. Stengle, "ER Kiosks Let Patients Avoid Long Lines," *Associated Press,*
September 13, 2007.

13. See D. E. Hansen and P. J. Danaher, "Inconsistent Performance during the Service Encounter: What's a Good Start Worth?" *Journal of Service Research* 1
(February 1999), pp. 227–235; and V. Dalakas, "The Importance of a Good Ending in a Service Encounter," *Services Marketing Quarterly* 28 (2006), pp. 35–53.

14. These are two of the "three Steps of Service" included in Ritz-Carlton's Gold
Standards, which can be found on the company website at http://www.ritzcarlton
.com/en/about/gold-standards, accessed May 22, 2016.

15. For a comprehensive list of service attributes found to be important across a variety of services, see M. Paul, T. Hennig-Thurau, D. D. Gremler, K. P. Gwinner,
and C. Wiertz, "Toward a Theory of Repeated Purchase Drivers for Consumer
Services," *Journal of the Academy of Marketing Science* 37 (Summer 2009),
pp. 215–237.

16. Based on e-mail communication with David Spear, manager of global service and
quality assurance, *FedEx Express*, June 16, 2016.

17. "L.L. Bean Rated #1 in Customer Satisfaction," *Trailmix* (blog) *L.L. Bean,* January 21, 2014, blog.llbean.com/2014/01/l-l-bean-rated-1-in-customer-satisfaction.

Chapter Ten

Physical Evidence and the Servicescape

This chapter's objectives are to

1. Explain the impact of physical evidence, particularly the servicescape, on customer perceptions and experiences.
2. Illustrate differences in types of servicescapes, the roles played by the servicescape, and the implications for strategy.
3. Explain *why* the servicescape affects customer and employee behavior, using a framework based in marketing, organizational behavior, and environmental psychology.
4. Present elements of an effective physical evidence strategy.

Marriott Creates Uniquely Branded Experiences with Distinctive Servicescapes[1]

Marriott International Inc., the world's largest hotel company, has a brand for every price point, every occasion, and every type of customer. The company is consistently ranked as the most admired company in the hotel industry and one of the best places to work by *Fortune* magazine. Operating in 87 countries and territories, Marriott employs approximately 127,500 people. From its high-end Ritz-Carlton and J. W. Marriott Hotels to its more budget-oriented Fairfield Inns, the company has been successful at clearly positioning its many brands, distinguishing them from each other, and attracting well-defined market segments for each. According to branding and strategy executives at Marriott, building these distinctive hotel brands involves a complex strategy that meshes hotel design, employee training and selection to match the brand strategy, careful customer segmentation, and specific operational brand standards.

From the customer's perspective, the most visible aspect of Marriott's distinctive brand strategies is the "servicescape," or the physical environment where the service is delivered—the hotel design itself. The luxury design of the Ritz-Carlton brand fits well with its position as the hotel where the long-standing motto, "ladies and gentlemen serving ladies and gentlemen" guides employee attitudes and behaviors. The Ritz-Carlton enjoys a global reputation for "setting the gold standards" through the underlying values and philosophies by which it operates. Its vision is to "inspire life's most meaningful journeys." The physical

This Marriott Courtyard lobby design promotes working and socializing among guests.

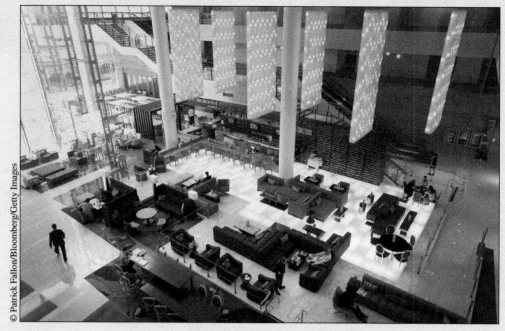

© Patrick Fallon/Bloomberg/Getty Images

servicescape of every Ritz-Carlton reinforces its high-end luxury positioning, from the lobby areas to the acclaimed restaurants, elegant spas, and upscale retail opportunities. In contrast, the physical presence of a Marriott Courtyard, while still expressing personal comfort and style, is much more efficient and business-like in its design. The lobby area is open and flexible, inviting guests to socialize, relax, and enjoy casual food options in a comfortable, yet upscale environment. In the lobby there are efficient spaces for working, connecting to the Internet for free, and conducting meetings (see photo). The space is designed to promote collaboration, productivity, and social interaction. Guest rooms are designed similarly with moveable workspaces, plenty of electrical outlets, the latest in technology connections, and refreshing colors to recharge business guests after a long day.

Marriott's most recent hotel brand introduction is "Edition," a boutique hotel that marries unique, destination-inspired hotel design with sophisticated service. This concept, a partnership with Ian Schrager, a well-known pioneer in the modern boutique-hotel industry, provided the foundation for Marriott to enter an entirely new market for the company. The Edition-branded hotels are generally smaller, upscale properties that emphasize exclusive and unique styles for each location. The specific design elements of this new boutique hotel are critical to the positioning of the concept. There are currently four uniquely designed Edition hotels in London, Miami Beach, New York, and Istanbul, with twelve more planned in the coming years. Each existing and planned hotel reflects the local character, as well as the geographic and cultural uniqueness of the area through its distinctive and high-end servicescape design.

We have highlighted only three of Marriott's 18 brands. What is noteworthy is that each of the 18 brands has a distinctive servicescape design, reinforcing its positioning along the continuum from midscale to luxury hotels. Along with the servicescape, Marriott also reinforces each brand with employee training, dress codes, and internal processes that are consistent with the brand.

In this chapter we explore the importance of physical evidence for communicating service quality attributes, setting customer expectations, and creating the service experience. In Chapter 1, when we introduced the expanded marketing mix for services, we defined physical evidence as *the environment in which the service is delivered and in which the firm and the customer interact, and any tangible commodities that facilitate performance or communication of the service.* The first part of this definition encompasses the actual physical facility in which the service is performed, delivered, and consumed; throughout this chapter the physical facility is referred to as the *servicescape.*[2] Physical evidence is particularly important for communicating about credence services (such as auto repair and health care), and it is important for services such as hotels, hospitals, and theme parks that are dominated by experience attributes, as described in our opening vignette on Marriott International.

PHYSICAL EVIDENCE

What Is Physical Evidence?

Customers often rely on tangible cues, or physical evidence, to evaluate the service before its purchase and to assess their satisfaction with the service during and after the experience. Effective design of physical, tangible evidence is important for closing provider gap 2. General elements of physical evidence are shown in Table 10.1. They include all aspects of the organization's physical facility (the servicescape) as well as other forms of tangible communication. Elements of the physical servicescape that affect customers include both exterior attributes (such as signage, parking, and the landscape) and interior attributes (such as design, layout, equipment, and decor). Web pages and virtual servicescapes shown online are forms of physical evidence that companies use to communicate about the service experience, making services more tangible for customers both before and after purchase (see the Technology Spotlight).

TABLE 10.1
Elements of Physical Evidence

Servicescape	Other Tangibles
Facility exterior	Business cards
Exterior design	Stationery
Signage	Billing statements
Parking	Reports
Landscape	Employee dress
Surrounding environment	Uniforms
Facility interior	Brochures
Interior design	Web pages
Equipment	Virtual servicescape
Signage	
Layout	
Air quality/temperature	
Sound/music/scent/lighting	

Technology Spotlight Virtual Servicescapes: Experiencing Services through the Internet

Web pages and virtual service tours allow customers to preview service experiences through the Internet and see tangible evidence of the service without actually being there. This medium allows firms to communicate experiential aspects of their services in ways that were previously very difficult, if not impossible. Here we present several examples, across different industries.

TRAVEL

Travelers can now preview destinations, view hotels and their rooms, tour natural environments, and "experience" entertainment venues before booking their trips or even deciding where to travel. Before booking a trip to Great Britain, travelers can preview websites that show hotels, bed and breakfast inns, and other lodging all over the country. The exterior of the facilities as well as actual rooms can be examined in selecting accommodations. In planning a trip to visit the national parks of the United States, travelers can view full-length videos of the parks and various tours within the parks. For example, at the Yellowstone site (www.yellowstone.net/) potential visitors can watch a video that shows many of the star attractions of the park. Detailed maps are also included, allowing a traveler to plan a route and choose among the many possible sights prior to even arriving at the park. Additionally, their website features live webcam feeds,

allowing visitors to see up-to-the-moment views from several points around the park.

SPORTS AND LEISURE

Through sports and leisure websites and live feeds to technology devices, fans can now view much of the action and preview upcoming sports experiences online. A great example is NASCAR, whose race enthusiasts are among the most loyal sports fans anywhere. And there are a lot of these fans—75 million currently! For those fans who experience a race first-hand, the atmosphere is charged with excitement, the food is plentiful, and a kaleidoscope of paraphernalia is available for sale. And, the race itself is highly involving, with its thundering noise, blurring visuals of cars, and edge-of-the chair anticipation for the eventual winners. As if this live experience were not enough, NASCAR provides many opportunities for fans to experience the servicescape and more through technology. Live video feeds from inside several of the vehicles allow spectators to listen to radio chatter among drivers and crews via smart phones, laptops, or tablets; to see the view from the cockpit of these cars; and even to observe mishaps and accidents close up via video. In addition, NASCAR has an online service that provides real-time race information, driver statistics, and a live leaderboard that fans can access for a monthly fee.

Physical evidence examples from different service contexts are given in Table 10.2. It is apparent that some services (such as hospitals, resorts, and child care) rely heavily on physical evidence to communicate and create customer experiences. Others (insurance, express mail) provide limited physical evidence for customers. All the elements of evidence listed for each service communicate something about the service, facilitate performance of the service, and/or add to the customer's total experience. Although we focus in this chapter primarily on the servicescape and its effects, keep in mind that what is said applies to the other forms of evidence as well.

How Does Physical Evidence Affect the Customer Experience?

Physical evidence, particularly the servicescape, can have a profound effect on the customer experience. This is true whether the experience is mundane (e.g., a bus or

UNIQUE RETAIL EXPERIENCES

Many of today's unique retail experiences can be conveyed effectively via the Internet to give customers a preview of what they can expect. A great example is Build-A-Bear Workshop®, where children "from 3 to 103" can create their own teddy bears and other furry friends during their visit to the store. Build-A-Bear Workshop operates approximately 400 stores worldwide, including company-owned stores in the United States, Puerto Rico, Canada, the United Kingdom, Ireland, and France, and franchise stores in Europe, Asia, Australia, Africa, and the Middle East. The interactive retail entertainment experience itself is memorable and fun, and the highly visual teddy-bear-themed environment throughout the stores is a big part of the fantasy of this special place. For a preview of how it works and what the stores look like, the website of Build-A-Bear Workshop (www.buildabear.com) includes a tour that shows each of the steps involved in creating a bear and a "Workshop Wall" that shows potential customers pictures of a wide array of creations that can be made at a Build-A-Bear store. Additionally, the website includes a "Play" area that features activities, games, and videos that allow children and parents to get to know the different creations and characters that can be brought home from a store. These colorful pictures and videos give a sense of the store environment and the emotions of its patrons.

HIGHER EDUCATION

One of the most significant decisions that young people and their families make is what university to attend. For students fortunate enough to have the means and abilities, the choices can be endless. The physical environment of the university—the campus itself as well as specific facilities—can play a major role in students' choices as well as their actual experiences. Many universities offer virtual tours of their campuses online allowing students to preview the physical environment in advance. The University of Oregon in the United States offers a virtual tour (http://www.youvisit.com/tour/60299/80256/) that allows students to click on different areas of the campus to view that particular spot and listen to narration that gives specific details on various aspects of campus life. Within each view, the prospective students and family members can see 360-degree views and videos, as well as read information related to that particular place on campus. In exploring university environments this way, students who are unable to visit, or who wish to narrow their visit choices, are much better informed.

Internet technology clearly provides tremendous opportunities for firms to communicate about their services. Images on the Internet create expectations for customers that set standards for service delivery, and it is critical that the actual services live up to these expectations. Images and virtual service tours presented on the Internet also need to support the positioning of the service brand and be consistent with other marketing messages.

---

subway ride), personally meaningful (e.g., a destination wedding experience, or a birthing room at a hospital), or spectacular (e.g., a week-long travel adventure). In all cases, the physical evidence of the service will influence the flow of the experience, the meaning customers attach to it, their satisfaction, their emotional connections with the company delivering the experience, and their social and personal interactions with others experiencing the service.

As marketers and corporate strategists pay more attention to customer experiences, they have recognized the impact of physical space and tangibles in creating those experiences. Lewis Carbone, a leading consultant on experience management, has developed an entire lexicon and management process around the basic idea of "experience engineering" through "clue management."[3] *Clue management* refers to the process of clearly identifying and managing *all* the various clues that customers

TABLE 10.2
Examples of Physical Evidence from the Customer's Point of View

| | Physical Evidence | |
Service	Servicescape	Other Tangibles
Insurance	Not applicable	Policy itself Billing statements Periodic updates Company brochure Letters/cards Claims forms Website
Hospital	Building exterior Parking Signs Waiting areas Admissions office Patient care room Medical equipment Recovery room	Uniforms Reports/stationery Billing statements Website
Airline	Airline gate area Airplane exterior Airplane interior (decor, seats, air quality) Check-in kiosks Security screening area Baggage return area	Onboard technology Food Uniforms Website
Express mail	Free-standing stores Package drop boxes	Packaging Trucks Uniforms Handheld devices Website
Sporting event	Parking Stadium exterior Ticketing area Entrance Seating Restrooms Concession areas Playing field Scoreboard	Tickets Employee uniforms Programs Team mascot Website

use to form their impressions and feelings about the company. Included in this set of clues are what Carbone refers to as *mechanics clues,* or the physical and tangible clues that we focus on in this chapter. Other writers and consultants who focus on managing customer experiences also zero in on the importance of tangible evidence and physical facilities in shaping those experiences.[4] Throughout this chapter are numerous examples of how physical evidence communicates with customers and shapes their experiences.

TYPES OF SERVICESCAPES

This chapter relies heavily on ideas and concepts from environmental psychology, a field that encompasses the study of human beings and their relationships with built (human-made), natural, and social environments.[5] The physical setting may be more or less important in achieving the organization's marketing and other goals, depending on certain factors. Table 10.3 is a framework for categorizing service organizations on two dimensions that capture some of the key differences that will affect the management of the servicescape. Organizations that share a cell in the table tend to face similar issues and decisions regarding their physical spaces.

Servicescape Usage

First, organizations differ in terms of *whom* the servicescape will affect. That is, who actually comes into the service facility and thus is potentially influenced by its design—customers, employees, or both groups? The first column of Table 10.3 suggests three types of service organizations that differ on this dimension. At one extreme is the *self-service* environment, in which the customer performs most of the activities and few if any employees are involved. Examples of self-service environments include ATMs, movie theaters, check-in kiosks at airports, self-service entertainment such as golf and theme parks, and online services. In these primarily self-service environments, the organization can plan the servicescape to focus exclusively on marketing goals such as attracting the right market segment, making the facility pleasing and easy to use, and creating the desired service experience for the customer.

TABLE 10.3
Typology of Service Organizations Based on Variations in Form and Use of the Servicescape

Source: From M. J. Bitner, "Servicescapes: The Impact of Physical Surroundings on Customers and Employees," *Journal of Marketing* 56 (April 1992), pp. 57–71.

Servicescape Usage	Complexity of the Servicescape	
	Elaborate	Lean
Self-service (customer only)	Water park eBay	ATM Car wash Simple Internet services Express mail drop box
Interpersonal services (both customer and employee)	Hotel Restaurant Health clinic Hospital Bank Airline School	Dry cleaner Retail cart Hair salon
Remote service (employee only)	Telecommunications Insurance company Utility Many professional services	Telephone mail-order desk Automated voice-messaging services

At the other extreme of the use dimension is the *remote service,* which has little or no customer involvement with the servicescape. Telecommunications, utilities, financial consultants, editorial, and mail-order services are examples of services that can be provided without the customer ever seeing the service facility. In fact, the facility may be in a different state or a different country (see the Global Feature in Chapter 1). In remote services, the facility can be set up to keep employees motivated and to facilitate productivity, teamwork, operational efficiency, or whatever organizational behavior goal is desired without any consideration of customers because they will never see or visit the servicescape. This is the case with SAS, a data analytics and software company that was number one in *Fortune* magazine's Best Places to Work in both 2010 and 2011 and which consistently appears among the top ten companies in that list through 2016. The company provides health care and high-quality child care on site, along with car cleaning, a beauty salon, and a state-of-the-art fitness center for its over 13,500 employees. Since most of its customers never visit the SAS campus, the facilities can be designed entirely with employee well-being and productivity in mind.[6]

In Table 10.3, *interpersonal services* are placed between the two extremes and represent situations in which both the customer and the employee are present and active in the servicescape. Examples abound, such as hotels, restaurants, hospitals, educational settings, and banks. In these situations, the servicescape must be designed to attract, satisfy, and facilitate the activities of both customers and employees simultaneously. Special attention must also be given to how the servicescape affects the nature and quality of the social interactions between and among customers and employees. A cruise ship provides a good example of a setting in which the servicescape must support customers and the employees who work there, as well as facilitate interactions between and within the two groups.

Servicescape Complexity

Table 10.3 suggests another factor that will influence servicescape management, the complexity of the servicescape. Some service environments are very simple, with few elements, few spaces, and few pieces of equipment. Such environments are termed *lean.* Shopping mall information kiosks and FedEx drop-off kiosks are considered lean environments because both provide service from one simple structure. For lean servicescapes, design decisions are relatively straightforward, especially in self-service or remote service situations in which there is no interaction among employees and customers.

Other servicescapes are very complicated, with many elements and many forms. They are termed *elaborate* environments. An example is a hospital with its many floors and rooms, sophisticated equipment, and complex variability in functions performed within the physical facility. In such an elaborate environment, the full range of marketing and organizational objectives theoretically can be approached through careful management of the servicescape. For example, a patient's hospital room can be designed to enhance patient comfort and satisfaction while facilitating employee productivity. Firms such as hospitals that are located in the elaborate interpersonal service cell face the most complex servicescape decisions. To illustrate, when the Mayo Clinic opened its hospital in Scottsdale, Arizona, the organization painstakingly considered the interrelated goals, needs, and feelings of its employees, doctors, patients, and visitors in designing its distinctive servicescape (see Exhibit 10.3 later in this chapter).

STRATEGIC ROLES OF THE SERVICESCAPE

Within the cells of the typology, the servicescape can play many strategic roles simultaneously. An examination of the variety of roles and how they interact makes clear how strategically important it is to provide appropriate physical evidence of the service. In fact, the servicescape is frequently one of *the* most important elements used in positioning a service organization (see the Strategy Insight).

Package

Similar to a tangible product's package, the servicescape and other elements of physical evidence essentially "wrap" the service and convey to consumers an external image of what is "inside." Product packages are designed to portray a particular image as well as to evoke a particular sensory or emotional reaction. The physical setting of a service does the same thing through the interaction of many complex stimuli. The servicescape is the outward appearance of the organization and thus can be critical in forming initial impressions or setting up customer expectations—it is a visual metaphor for the intangible service. This packaging role is particularly important in creating expectations for new customers and for newly established service organizations trying to build a particular image. The physical surroundings offer an organization the opportunity to convey an image in a way not unlike the way an individual chooses to "dress for success." The packaging role extends to the appearance of contact personnel through their uniforms or dress and other elements of their outward appearance.[7]

Interestingly, the same care and resource expenditures given to package design in product marketing are often not provided for services, even though the service package serves a variety of important roles. There are many exceptions to this generality, however. Smart companies like Apple Stores (see the Strategy Insight), Starbucks, FedEx, and Marriott spend a lot of time and money relating their servicescape design to their brand, providing their customers with strong visual metaphors and "service packaging" that conveys the brand positioning. Recognizing the power of retail environment design, Starbucks is on a path to create unique environments for its 23,000 stores so that they don't all have the look and feel of a store straight out of Seattle. The goal behind this sophisticated approach to design is to have every store feel not like a "mass produced" replica, but rather like a local coffee shop.[8]

Facilitator

The servicescape can also serve as a facilitator in aiding the performances of persons in the environment. How the setting is designed can enhance or inhibit the efficient flow of activities in the service setting, making it easier or harder for customers and employees to accomplish their goals. A well-designed, functional facility can make the service a pleasure to experience from the customer's point of view and a pleasure to perform from the employee's. On the other hand, poor and inefficient design may frustrate both customers and employees. For example, an international air traveler who finds himself in a poorly designed airport with few signs, poor ventilation, and few places to sit or eat will find the experience quite dissatisfying, and employees who work there will probably be unmotivated as well. In reality, many airports today are designed for passengers, inviting them to spend time shopping in a variety of

Strategy Insight   Strategic Positioning through Architectural Design

BusinessWeek and *Architectural Record,* both McGraw-Hill publications, together sponsor an annual international competition to identify the best use of architecture that solves strategic business challenges. Company winners clearly demonstrate the impact of design on people—customers, employees, the general public, or all three. Here we present award winners from several years to illustrate the ways that architecture and servicescapes execute or reinforce strategic decisions and marketing positioning.

APPLE STORES, NEW YORK

In designing its store in New York's Soho district, Apple Computers brought together architects, graphic designers, product developers, merchandising people, and its late CEO Steve Jobs to create a retail space that would both convey the company's philosophy and sell computers. The result is a clean, open, and spacious store that displays only a few computers to create the ambience of a museum. The company establishes a modern feel using a central glass staircase, white walls, and a large skylight. A second-floor area encourages children to play with software and offers a large conference room for Apple product demonstrations. As one judge put it, "the store, like Apple, is all about information, interaction, and access." Apple's 5th Avenue store in New York City, its highest volume store, was also an award winner in a later competition. This cube-shaped store is free of structural steel and it relies on a taut glass skin and glass beams to create a sense of a free-floating structure that sits above the actual retail space. Similar to the Soho store, the "cube" is highly effective at drawing customers in, and its cleanly designed interior provides an inviting atmosphere to experiment with innovative and futuristic Apple products. The store has very high sales per square foot and the space is beautiful, functional, and very profitable (award winners in 2003 and 2006).

EVERSHEDS LAW OFFICES, LONDON, ENGLAND

Eversheds is a global law firm that seeks to attract the best young talent to its employee ranks. When it relocated its London headquarters, it recognized an opportunity to attract talent through its workplace design. In seeking to build a law office for the future, the designers conducted extensive research, along with a nine-month prototype trial of the new design at its existing facility. It involved employees in the process from start to finish. The result was a radical shift away from traditional law firm design, including modular furniture that can be moved as needed to foster collaboration and communication among lawyers and staff. There are also added amenities, including lounges, dining venues, showers, bicycle storage, and sleeping accommodations. Sustainability was also at the core of the design. For example, through centralizing much of its information and documents, the firm was able to

Apple Store, Soho, NY.

© Mario Tama/Getty Images

stores, eating in good restaurants, and working in areas set up with connection stations and Wi-Fi.

The same international traveler will appreciate seats on the airplane conducive to work and sleep. The seating itself, part of the physical surroundings of the service, reduce the number of filed documents by 57 percent and the number of printers by 63 percent. The project had outstanding results as well, with 96 percent of the staff being more motivated to work due to the design of the new workplace (award winner in 2009).

ST. PAUL SAINTS BALLPARK

The St. Paul Saints, the much beloved minor league baseball team of St. Paul, Minnesota, needed a new ballpark. Their old one was outdated and in need of replacement. Because the team was known for its community involvement, family orientation, and even its sense of humor, the new design needed to be in keeping with that low-key and approachable vibe. After many community meetings to gain input and assure people about the design, a friendly new ballpark was built. From the colors and materials to the openness of the design, everything speaks loudly to the goal of being community-oriented and approachable. Passersby on the street can look through open, glass-enclosed concourses to the field. Fan seating is below the street level, which reinforces the informal and non-imposing feel. The low physical structure and street-level design connects the neighboring buildings and the ballpark, reinforcing a sense of harmony and togetherness. During off-hours the park is a true community asset, open to the public free of charge for exercising on a walking track, bringing dogs to the dog park north of the field, or for events. The team was always a community treasure, and the new ballpark was designed and built on that foundation. Between 2014 and 2015 the new 7,000-seat stadium increased the team's revenue by 100 percent, with 400,000 visitors (award winner 2016).

SAN FRANCISCO JAZZ (SFJAZZ) CENTER

Jazz clubs and concert halls do not have a lot in common, yet those are the two design extremes that the San Francisco Jazz Center aimed to bridge when it created the first permanent home for SFJAZZ in its 35-year history. The jazz group wanted a permanent and well-designed, modern facility; they also wanted the intimacy and character of a jazz club. To address the second goal, a new 700-seat concert venue was created and arranged with steep seating around the stage so that no one is more than 45 feet from the stage. The theater is set up so the audience can be with the performers in close proximity. Glass walls with views into the ground-floor lobby connect those passing by on the street with SFJAZZ and reinforce the goal of being inviting. The building itself features a rhythmic-themed façade that is in keeping with the jazz genre. In the first two years following the opening of the new building, membership went up from 3,000 to 10,000 and the number of performance events tripled (award winner 2015).

SWEDBANK HEADQUARTERS, STOCKHOLM

Swedbank had occupied the same office building, located in the heart of Stockholm, for four decades. The building was very traditional, with long hallways and individual offices; it was dark and crowded. In moving its headquarters from the center of the city to the suburbs, the company wanted to match its vision of the future of banking with a new building and completely new design. They wanted the new space to be flexible and to foster collaboration and creativity for its 2,700 employees. The result is a dramatic and modern facility, made of steel and concrete, designed with a zigzagging pattern that forms "folds" in the building. Within the folds are five atriums with skylights that allow visual connections among the working groups. There are almost no private offices and employees are not tied to a specific desk. They instead select their work locations daily from areas featuring cubicles, upholstered chairs, niches with tables, and glass-enclosed conference rooms. Although the total floor space is less than the old building, there are many more opportunities for meeting spaces and flexible work arrangements. The new building fits the bank's image of the future and is also efficient in its use of space and energy (award winner 2015).

Source: "The *BusinessWeek/Architectural Record* Awards," Special Report, *BusinessWeek,* November 3, 2003, pp. 57–64; and http://archrecord.construction.com/features/bwarAwards/, accessed July 2011; "Good Design is Good Business," *Architectural Record,* http://www.architecturalrecord.com/topics/148 -good-design-is-good-business, accessed August 9, 2016.

has been improved over the years to better facilitate airline travelers' needs to sleep. In fact, the competition for better seat and aircraft interior design continues as a major point of contention among the international airline carriers, and the results have translated into greater customer satisfaction for business travelers.[9] Some of the

Exhibit 10.1 Servicescapes and Well-Being in Health Care

There is solid and growing evidence from the field of "evidence-based design" that the design of health care environments can profoundly influence patient, family, and employee well-being. Notably, researchers have shown that outcomes such as stress reduction, shorter hospital stays, improved health, increased patient satisfaction, and improved safety are all affected by the design of the physical facilities. Here are a few examples of what has been learned.

SOUNDS, MUSIC, AND NOISE REDUCTION

A number of studies have shown that reducing noise and introducing more pleasing sounds such as water falling or music can positively affect patients and staff in hospitals. Minimizing noise, which is a constant challenge in hospitals and other health care settings, can help reduce sleep disturbance and stress and lower blood pressure, among other outcomes. Noise can also distract doctors and nurses, resulting in greater stress, interrupted communication, and errors, so noise reductions have benefits for employees as well.

NATURE AND VISUAL DISTRACTION

Research has shown that positive visual distractions divert patient attention from pain and negative feelings, improving their psychological and emotional well-being. In particular, nature distractions, including such things as gardens, indoor plants, and window views to outdoor nature scenes, have been shown to reduce stress, reduce pain, reduce pain medication usage, and speed recovery. Natural daylight is also very beneficial and has been linked to improved patient outcomes and higher staff productivity.

SINGLE-BED ROOM DESIGN

Many studies have shown the benefits of single-bed rooms for patients instead of multi-bed rooms. The benefits include reduced stress, better sleep, reduction in infection rates, increased patient satisfaction, and shorter hospital stays. A number of these benefits are also experienced by family and other support members who spend time with the patient. Giving the patient control over elements of the room design is also positive—for example, providing them with the ability to control the lighting and temperature in their rooms.

PATIENT SAFETY

The design of the physical facility can have a huge impact on safety issues that are paramount in health care settings. For example, avoiding patient falls and infections is a major safety issue that can be influenced by physical design. One hospital located all of its patient bathrooms on the side of the room where the head of the bed was located. This simple design feature avoided the patient having to cross the room to use the bathroom, which reduced falls. Flexible room designs that allow equipment to be moved into a patient's room temporarily help avoid transferring patients to different locations during their stay. In other words, the equipment goes to the patient rather than vice versa. Research shows that transferring patients from room to room increases medication errors, patient falls, and the rate of infections.

DESIGN FOR WELL-BEING

Hospital administrators, designers, and architects are paying attention to these and other research results. Many new hospitals are designed with only single-bed rooms, natural lighting where possible, music and gardens, hands-free personal technology-based communicators (think *Star Trek* communicators), centralized nursing stations, and adaptable rooms to avoid patient transfers. Family lounges and eating areas and overnight sleeping accommodations for them are also provided to improve patient and family well-being and satisfaction. Exhibit 10.3 later in this chapter describes how the Mayo Clinic Hospital in Scottsdale, Arizona, was designed with many of these evidence-based principles in mind.

Sources: R. S. Ulrich, L. L Berry, X. Quan, and J. T. Parish, "A Conceptual Framework for the Domain of Evidence-Based Design," *Health Environments Research and Design Journal* 4 (Fall 2010), pp. 95–114; R. S. Ulrich, C. M. Zimring, X. Zhu, J. DuBose, H. Seo, Y. Choi, and A. Joseph, "A Review of the Research Literature on Evidence-Based Healthcare Design," *Health Environments Research and Design Journal* 1 pp. 6–125; "Good Healthcare by Design," *The Hastings Center Report* 41 (January–February 2011).

business, the current focus on the customer experience has also drawn attention to the effects of physical spaces and design on customer behavior.[11] As an example, one recent study explores the effects of a servicescape redesign in a fast-food industry context, looking at both short- and long-term effects on customer perceptions, as well as spending patterns and the store image. The research found that the remodeling positively increased customer perceptions, store image, and the amount of money customers spent in the restaurant, particularly in the short term. After about six months, the effects of the remodeling lost some strength as the

FIGURE 10.1   A Framework for Understanding Physical Environment–User Relationships in Service Organizations

Source: Adapted from M. J. Bitner, "Servicescapes: The Impact of Physical Surroundings on Customers and Employees," *Journal of Marketing* 56 (April 1992), pp. 57–71.

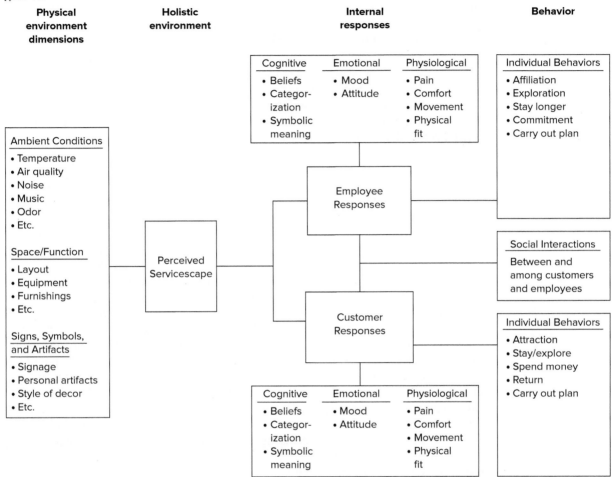

remodeled restaurant became the new frame of reference for customers.[12] Another study found these same types of effects, only they found that sales after a remodel were higher for new customers than for existing customers and that this difference persists for about a year.[13]

Individual Behaviors

Environmental psychologists suggest that individuals react to places with two general, and opposite, forms of behavior: approach and avoidance. *Approach behaviors* include all positive behaviors that might be directed at a particular place, such as a desire to stay, explore, work, and affiliate.[14] *Avoidance behaviors* reflect the opposite—a desire not to stay, to explore, to work, or to affiliate. Over many decades, consumer research in retail contexts has found that approach behaviors (including shopping enjoyment, returning, attraction and friendliness toward others, spending money, time spent browsing the exploration of the store) are influenced by perceptions of the environment.[15] At one 7-Eleven store, the owners played "elevator music" to drive away the youthful market segment that was detracting from the store's image.

And our cookie cart example is reminiscent of cinnamon roll bakeries in malls that attract patrons through the power of smell.

In addition to attracting or deterring entry, the servicescape can actually influence the degree of success that consumers and employees experience in executing their plans once inside. Each individual goes to a particular service organization with a goal or purpose that may be aided or hindered by the setting. NBA basketball fans are aided in their enjoyment of the game by adequate, easy-access parking; clear signage directing them to their seats; efficient food service; and clean restrooms. The ability of employees to do their jobs effectively is also influenced by the servicescape. Adequate space, proper equipment, and comfortable temperature and air quality all contribute to an employee's comfort and job satisfaction, causing him or her to be more productive, stay longer, and affiliate positively with coworkers.

Social Interactions

In addition to its effects on their individual behaviors, the servicescape influences the nature and quality of customer and employee interactions, most directly in interpersonal services. It has been stated that "all social interaction is affected by the physical container in which it occurs."[16] The "physical container" can affect the nature of social interaction in terms of the duration of interaction and the actual progression of events. In many service situations, a firm may want to ensure a particular progression of events (a "standard script") and limit the duration of the service. Environmental variables such as physical proximity, seating arrangements, size, and flexibility can define the possibilities and limits of social episodes such as those occurring between customers and employees, or customers and other customers. The Holland America Cruise Line photo shown here illustrates how the design of the servicescape can help define the social rules, conventions, and expectations in force in a given setting, thus defining the nature of social interaction.[17] The close physical proximity of passengers on the sunbathing deck will in and of itself prescribe certain patterns of behavior. This vacation is not designed for a social recluse! Some researchers have implied that recurring social behavior patterns are associated with particular physical settings and that when people encounter typical settings, their social behaviors can be predicted.[18]

Examples of how environments shape social interactions—and how these interactions in turn influence the environment—are abundant.[19] Even casual observation of the retail phenomenon "Nike Town" shows how this form of "entertainment retail" shapes the behaviors of consumers but at the same time allows them to interpret and create their own realities and experiences.[20] In a river-rafting trip, the "wilderness servicescape" profoundly influences the behaviors, interactions, and total experiences of rafting consumers and their guides. In this case the natural, and for the most part uncontrollable, environment is the setting for the service.[21] In some cases, important social bonds and connections are forged within a service place, resulting its becoming a "third place" for the individuals who frequent it (see Exhibit 10.2).[22]

© Meunierd/Shutterstock.com

Social interactions are defined partially by the configuration of the servicescape.

Exhibit 10.2   Social Support in "Third Places"

The social interactions and attachments among customers and between customers and employees in "third places" can provide companionship and emotional support that results in strong attachments and loyalty to the place itself. A third place is a public or commercial place where people gather regularly and voluntarily outside of work (or school) and home, which are viewed as the first two places in people's lives. Often third places are diners, coffee shops, taverns, pubs, or clubs, but a fitness club, a civic center, or other public gathering place could also be a third place. The neighborhood bar on the classic television show *Cheers* epitomized a third place. Think about what types of places might qualify as a third place for you. Do you have a third place?

A study by Mark Rosenbaum and colleagues showed that people can grow attached to a third place to the point where they depend on it above all other alternatives, they are committed to the place and care about it, they personally identify with it, and they structure their lifestyle around it. This type of attachment happens because of the companionship and emotional support they receive from the other customers and employees in the place, not simply because they like the service or feel comfortable in the physical surroundings. These emotional attachments and interactions are particularly strong for people who are lonely or in need of contact with others. The researchers observed and conducted depth interviews with patrons of Sammy's, a casual dining restaurant in the suburbs of a major U.S. metropolitan area that was clearly a third place for many regulars who frequented the restaurant. Through the interviews, they established that patrons who were lonely or who had lost an established form of social support through death, divorce, or illness, found significant companionship and emotional support at Sammy's. The regular patrons who had lost a spouse through death, divorce, or separation had a full 58 percent of their social supportive relationships with people (customers and employees) at Sammy's. These patrons were also extremely attached and loyal to Sammy's.

The research reinforces the idea that servicescapes, while they are defined by their physical elements, can take on a third place character when they become the source of social interactions, bonds, and support for the people who frequent them. The benefits of this type of support go far beyond the benefits intended by the core service. The regulars at Sammy's receive far more than a good meal in pleasant surroundings. Through their interactions with others, their daily lives are enhanced and they are emotionally better off. As the problems associated with loneliness grow in our modern-day society (e.g., the population is aging, more and more people are caring for chronically ill family members or friends, divorce is prevalent, and work hours are increasing, resulting in less time for friendships), the importance of third places as a form of social support may grow as well. While consumer support networks do not require a physical presence—for example, online communities can provide social support—physical places are often more accessible and more preferable for nurturing companionship and emotional connections among people.

© Travel Images/Universal Images Group/Getty Images

The *Cheers* bar epitomized a third place in the classic television show.

Sources: M. S. Rosenbaum, "Exploring the Social Supportive Role of Third Places in Consumers' Lives," *Journal of Service Research* 9 (August 2006), pp. 59–72; A. Tombs and J. R. McColl-Kennedy, "Social-Servicescape Conceptual Model," *Marketing Theory* 3 (2003), pp 447–475; M. S. Rosenbaum, J. Ward, B. A. Walker, and A. L. Ostrom, "A Cup of Coffee with a Dash of Love: An Investigation of Commercial Social Support and Third-Place Attachment," *Journal of Service Research* 10 (August 2007), pp. 43–59; and M. S. Rosenbaum, J. C. Sweeney, and C. Windhorst, "The Restorative Qualities of an Activity-Based, Third Place Cafe for Seniors," *Seniors Housing and Care Journal* 17 (2009), pp. 75–90; E. D. Brocato, J. Baker, and C. M. Voorhees, "Creating Consumer Attachment to Retail Service Firms Through Sense of Place," *Journal of the Academy of Marketing Science* 43 (2015), pp. 200–220.

Internal Responses to the Servicescape

Employees and customers respond to dimensions of their physical surroundings cognitively, emotionally, and physiologically, and those responses are what influence their behaviors in the environment (as shown in the middle portion of Figure 10.1). In other words, the perceived servicescape does not directly *cause* people to behave in certain ways. Although the internal responses are discussed independently here, they are clearly interdependent: a person's beliefs about a place, a cognitive response, may well influence the person's emotional response, and vice versa. For example, patients who go into a dentist's office designed to calm and soothe their anxieties (emotional responses) may believe as a result that the dentist is caring and competent (cognitive responses).

Environment and Cognition

The perceived servicescape can have an effect on people's beliefs about a place and their beliefs about the people and products found in that place. In a sense, the servicescape can be viewed as a form of nonverbal communication, imparting meaning through what is called "object language."[23] For example, particular environmental cues such as the type of office furniture and decor and the apparel worn by the lawyer may influence a potential client's beliefs about whether the lawyer is successful, expensive, and trustworthy. In a consumer study, variations in descriptions of store atmospheres were found to alter beliefs about a product (perfume) sold in the store.[24] Another study showed that a travel agent's office decor affected customer attributions and beliefs about the travel agent's behavior.[25] Travel agents whose facilities were more organized and professional were viewed more positively than were those whose facilities were disorganized and unprofessional.

In other cases, perceptions of the servicescape may simply help people distinguish a firm by influencing how it is categorized. The overall perception of the servicescape enables the consumer or employee to categorize the firm mentally. Research shows that in the restaurant industry a particular configuration of environmental cues suggests "fast food," whereas another configuration suggests "elegant sit-down restaurant."[26] In such situations, environmental cues serve as a shortcut device that enables customers to categorize and distinguish among types of restaurants.

Environment and Emotion

In addition to influencing beliefs, the perceived servicescape can directly elicit emotional responses that, in turn, influence behaviors. Just being in a particular place can make a person feel happy, lighthearted, and relaxed, whereas being in another place may make that person feel sad, depressed, and gloomy. The colors, decor, music, and other elements of the atmosphere can have an unexplainable and sometimes very subconsciousness effect on the moods of people in the place. For some people, certain environmental stimuli (noises, smells) common in a dental office can bring on immediate feelings of fear and anxiety. In very different contexts, the marble interior and grandeur of the Supreme Court buildings in Washington, D.C., call up feelings of pride and awe and respect; lively music and bright decor in a local night spot may cause people to feel excited and happy. In all these examples, the response from the consumer probably does not involve thinking but, rather, is just an unexplained emotional feeling.

REI (Recreational Equipment Inc.) provides another example of emotional connection facilitated through architectural design and the servicescape. At its flagship store in Seattle, the company has created an experience for consumers that includes a climbing mountain, a bicycle track, and walking trails. And, its store in Bloomington, Indiana has a mountain biking trail around it. REI, through its servicescape design, is simulating the experiences and emotions that customers associate with its products, reinforcing a strong approach response to its stores.

Environmental psychologists have researched people's emotional responses to physical settings.[27] They have concluded that any environment, whether natural or engineered, will elicit emotions that can be captured by two basic dimensions: (1) pleasure/displeasure and (2) degree of arousal (amount of stimulation or excitement). Servicescapes that are both pleasant and arousing would be termed *exciting,* whereas those that are pleasant and nonarousing, or sleepy, would be termed *relaxing.* Unpleasant servicescapes that are arousing would be called *distressing,* whereas unpleasant, sleepy servicescapes would be *gloomy.* These basic emotional responses to environments can be used to begin predicting the expected behaviors of consumers and employees who find themselves in a particular type of place.

Environment and Physiology

The perceived servicescape may also affect people in purely physiological ways. Noise that is too loud may cause physical discomfort, the temperature of a room may cause people to shiver or perspire, the air quality may make it difficult to breathe, and the glare of lighting may decrease ability to see and cause physical pain. All these physical responses may, in turn, directly influence whether people stay in and enjoy a particular environment. It is well known that the comfort of seating in a restaurant influences how long people stay. The hard seats historically found in a fast-food restaurant cause most people to leave within a predictable period of time, whereas the soft, cozy chairs in some Starbucks coffee shops have the opposite effect, encouraging people to stay. Similarly, environmental design and related physiological responses affect whether employees can perform their job functions well.

A vast amount of research in engineering and design has addressed human physiological responses to ambient conditions as well as physiological responses to equipment design.[28] Such research fits under the rubric of *human factors design* or *ergonomics.* Human factors research systematically applies relevant information about human capabilities and limitations to the design of items and procedures that people use. As populations around the world age (with accompanying physical limitations), and as individuals with a variety of physical disabilities are entering the mainstream of society, laws and practices are being introduced to accommodate their physical limitations. Service organizations and others are responding by adopting "universal design standards and principles," which simply means designing all products, buildings, and spaces to be usable by all people to the greatest extent possible.[29] For example, many hotel rooms are designed to accommodate people with disabilities. Wall switches have lights so they can be found at night. To help people with arthritis, doors have lever handles instead of knobs so that every door and every drawer in the room can be opened with a fist rather than requiring hand and wrist dexterity.

Variations in Individual Responses

In general, people respond to the environment in the ways just described—cognitively, emotionally, physiologically—and their responses influence how they behave in the environment. However, the response will not be the same for every individual, every time. Personality differences as well as temporary conditions such as moods or the purpose for being there can cause variations in how people respond to the servicescape.[30]

One personality trait that has been shown to affect how people respond to environments is *arousal seeking.* Arousal seekers enjoy and look for high levels of stimulation, whereas arousal avoiders prefer lower levels of stimulation. Thus, an arousal avoider in a loud, bright dance club with flashing lights might show strong dislike for the environment, whereas an arousal seeker would be very happy. In a related vein, it has been suggested that some people are better *screeners* of environmental stimuli than others.[31] Screeners of stimuli would be able to experience a high level of stimulation but not be affected by it. Nonscreeners would be highly affected and might exhibit extreme responses even to low levels of stimulation.

The particular purpose for being in a servicescape can also affect a person's response to it. A person who is on an airplane for a one-hour flight will likely be less affected by the atmosphere on the plane than will the traveler who is embarking on a 14-hour flight from Los Angeles to Shanghai. Similarly, a day-surgery hospital patient will likely be less sensitive and demanding of the hospital environment than would a patient who is spending two weeks in the hospital. And a person who is staying at a resort hotel for a business meeting will respond differently to the environment than will a couple on their honeymoon. Temporary mood states can also cause people to respond differently to environmental stimuli. A person who is feeling frustrated and fatigued after a long day at work is likely to be affected differently by a highly arousing restaurant than the same person would be after a relaxing three-day weekend.

Cultural differences also influence preferences for environmental features and responses to servicescape design. For example, there is a strong cultural preference for the color red in China, whereas Westerners would not share this attraction. And, while Americans and Europeans may prefer to shop in orderly and quiet supermarkets, many Indian shoppers prefer a more jumbled, chaotic environment.[32] This is what India's largest retailer, Pantaloon Retail Ltd, learned when it introduced Western-style supermarkets in India. At first, customers just walked through the wide, pristine aisles and left the store without buying. By studying Indian consumer behavior and focusing on the preferences of Indian shoppers (often the maids, cooks, nannies, and farmers of India, not the elite), Pantaloon redesigned its supermarkets to make them messier, noisier, and more cramped, re-creating in some sense the atmosphere of a public market. This design was appealing to the target market and sales increased far above where they were with the original design.

Environmental Dimensions of the Servicescape

The preceding sections have described customer and employee behaviors in the servicescape and the three primary responses—cognitive, emotional, and physiological—that lead to those behaviors. In this section, we turn to the complex mix of environmental features that influence these responses and behaviors (the left portion of Figure 10.1 on p. 295 shown earlier in the chapter). Specifically, environmental dimensions of the physical surroundings can include all the objective physical factors that can be controlled by the firm to enhance (or constrain) employee and customer actions. There is an endless list of possibilities: lighting, color, signage, textures, quality of materials, style of furnishings, layout, wall decor, temperature, and so on. In Figure 10.1 and in the discussion that follows, the hundreds of potential elements have been categorized into three composite dimensions: *ambient conditions; spatial layout and functionality;* and *signs, symbols, and artifacts.* Exhibit 10.3 illustrates how the Mayo Clinic took into consideration all these dimensions in designing its hospital to accommodate patients, doctors, employees, and visitors.

Although we discuss the three dimensions separately, environmental psychology explains that people respond to their environments holistically. That is, although individuals perceive discrete stimuli (e.g., they can perceive noise level, color, and decor as distinct elements), it is the total configuration of stimuli that determines their reactions to a place. Hence, although the dimensions of the environment are defined independently in the following sections, it is important to recognize that they are perceived by employees and customers as a holistic pattern of interdependent stimuli. The holistic response is shown in Figure 10.1 as the "perceived servicescape."

Ambient Conditions

Ambient conditions include background characteristics of the environment such as temperature, lighting, noise, music, scent, and color. As a general rule, ambient conditions affect the five senses. Sometimes such dimensions are totally imperceptible (gases, chemicals, infrasound) yet have profound effects, particularly on employees who spend long hours in the environment.

All these factors can affect how people feel, think, and respond to a service establishment. For example, a number of studies have documented the effects of music on consumers' perceptions of products, their perceptions of how long they have waited for service, and the amount of money they spend.[33] When there is music, shoppers tend to perceive that they spend less time shopping and in line than when there is no music. Slower music tempos at lower volumes tend to make people shop more leisurely, and in some cases, they spend more. In the Mayo Hospital lobby, piano music serves to reduce stress (see Exhibit 10.3). Shoppers also spend more time when the music "fits" the product or matches their musical tastes. Other studies have similarly shown the effects of scent on consumer responses.[34] Scent in bakeries, coffee shops, and tobacco shops, for example, can be used to draw people in, and pleasant scents can increase lingering time. The presence of a scent can reduce perceptions of time spent and improve store evaluations. The effects of ambient conditions are especially noticeable when they are extreme. For example, people attending a symphony in a hall in which the air conditioning has failed and the air is hot and stuffy will be uncomfortable, and their discomfort will be reflected in how they feel about the concert. If the temperature and air quality were within a comfort tolerance zone, these ambient factors would probably go unnoticed.

Spatial Layout and Functionality

Because service environments generally exist to fulfill specific purposes or needs of customers, spatial layout and functionality of the physical surroundings are particularly important. *Spatial layout* refers to the ways in which machinery, equipment, and furnishings are arranged; the size and shape of those items; and the spatial relationships among them. *Functionality* refers to the ability of the same items to facilitate the accomplishment of customer and employee goals. Previous examples in this chapter illustrate the layout and functionality dimensions of the servicescape (e.g., the cruise ship photo earlier and the design of the Mayo Hospital in Exhibit 10.3).

The spatial layout and functionality of the environment are particularly important for customers in self-service environments, where they must perform the service on their own and cannot rely on employees to assist them. Thus, the functionality of an ATM machine and of self-serve restaurants, gasoline pumps, and Internet shopping are critical to success and customer satisfaction.

The importance of facility layout is particularly apparent in retail, hospitality, and leisure settings, where research shows it can influence customer satisfaction, store performance, and consumer search behavior.[35]

Exhibit 10.3 Designing the Mayo Clinic Hospital

Mayo Clinic is the best known health care brand in the United States. More than 100 years old, Mayo operates three clinics across the country. Its original and best-known facility is in Rochester, Minnesota, and the two other clinics are in Jacksonville, Florida, and Scottsdale, Arizona. In 1998 Mayo opened the Mayo Clinic Hospital in Arizona, the first hospital planned, designed, and built by Mayo Clinic. Located on a 210-acre site, the hospital houses 268 licensed hospital beds on seven floors. The hospital supports inpatient care for a wide range of medical and surgical specialties. It has 21 operating rooms and a full emergency department, with emergency room services available 24 hours a day.

What is unique about this hospital facility is the tremendous care that was taken in its design to serve the needs of patients, doctors, staff, and visitors. The hospital is designed as a "healing environment" focused on patient needs. Focus groups were held with all constituents to determine how the hospital should be designed to facilitate this overall goal. A quotation from the Mayo brothers (founders of the clinic) captures the underlying belief that supported the design of the hospital: "The best interest of the patient is the only interest to be considered." This statement lies at the foundation of all Mayo does, even today, more than 100 years after the Mayo brothers began their practice of medicine. To focus on the best interests of the patient also requires acknowledgment of the needs of the care providers and the patient's family and friend support system. All these interests were clearly considered in the design of the hospital.

A FIVE-STORY ATRIUM LOW-STRESS ENTRY

As patients and others enter the Mayo Hospital, they encounter a five-story enclosed atrium, reminiscent of a luxury hotel lobby. A grand piano sits in the lobby, and volunteers play beautiful, relaxing music throughout the day. An abundance of plants and glass gives the lobby a natural feel and provides a welcoming atmosphere. On entering, visitors see the elevator bank directly in front of them across the atrium, so there is no stress in figuring out where to go.

ALL PATIENT AND VISITOR SERVICES ARE TOGETHER

All services needed by patients and their families (information desk, cafeteria, chapel, patient admissions, gift shop) are located around the atrium, easily visible and accessible. A sense of peace and quiet permeates the lobby—all by deliberate design to reduce stress and promote caring and wellness. There is no confusion here and very little of the atmosphere of a typical hospital entry.

ROOMS ARE DESIGNED AROUND PATIENT NEEDS AND FEELINGS

On disembarking the elevators to go to patient rooms, people again sense relaxation and peace in the environment. As the doors open, patients and guests face a five-story wall of paned glass with views out to the desert and mountains that surround the hospital site. As people progress left or right down well-marked corridors to the patient rooms, the atmosphere becomes even quieter. Rooms (all of them private) are arranged in 12-bed pods surrounding a nursing station. Nurses are within 20 steps of any patient room. Nurses and other attendants use cell phones—there is no paging system with constant announcements, as in many hospitals.

The rooms themselves have interesting features, some designed by patients. For example, rooms contain a multishelf display area on which patients can put cards, flowers, and other personal items. Fold-out, cushioned bedchairs are

Signs, Symbols, and Artifacts

Many items in the physical environment serve as explicit or implicit signals that communicate about the place to its users. *Signs* displayed on the exterior and interior of a structure are examples of explicit communicators. They can be used as labels (name of company, name of department, and so on), for directional purposes (entrances, exits), and to communicate rules of behavior (no smoking, children must be accompanied by an adult). Adequate signs have even been shown to reduce perceived crowding and stress.

Other environmental *symbols* and *artifacts* may communicate less directly than signs, giving implicit cues to users about the meaning of the place and norms and expectations for behavior in the place. Quality construction materials, artwork, certificates and photographs, floor coverings, and personal objects displayed in the environment can all communicate symbolic meaning and create an overall aesthetic in each room so family members can nap or even spend the night with their loved ones. Visitors are never told they must leave. The rooms are arranged with consideration to what patients see from the beds, where they spend the most time. For example, special attention is paid to the ceilings, which patients view while flat on their backs; all rooms have windows; and a white board on the wall at the foot of each bed displays important information that patients want to know (like the name of the nurse on duty, the date, the room phone number, and other information).

DEPARTMENTS THAT WORK TOGETHER ARE ADJACENT

Another interesting design feature in this hospital is that departments that work together are housed very close to each other to facilitate communication and to reduce walking time between areas. This important feature allows caregivers to spend more time with patients and lessens employee fatigue.

MAXIMIZE NURSES' TIME WITH PATIENTS

A critical element in the recovery of patients is the quality of care they are given by nurses. Many of the Mayo Clinic Hospital design features facilitate the quality of nursing care. The pod design puts nurses close to their patients; the white boards in the rooms allow easy communication; the accessible placement of supplies and relevant departments helps maximize the time nurses spend with patients.

It is clear that the design of the Mayo Hospital takes into account the critical importance of the servicescape in facilitating Mayo's primary goal: patient healing. All parties' voices were heard, and the place itself provides an environment that promotes well-being for patients, visitors, doctors, nurses, and other staff.

© Mayo Foundation for Medical Education and Research

Mayo Hospital Lobby.

Sources: *Teamwork at Mayo: An Experiment in Cooperative Individualism* (Rochester, MN: Mayo Press, 1998); http://www.mayo.edu; author's personal tour of the Mayo Clinic Hospital in Scottsdale; L. L. Berry and K. D. Seltman, "Building a Strong Services Brand: Lessons from Mayo Clinic," *Business Horizons* 50 (2007), pp. 199–209; and L. L. Berry and K. D. Seltman, *Management Lessons from the Mayo Clinic* (New York: McGraw-Hill, 2008).

impression. The meanings attached to environmental symbols and artifacts are culturally embedded, as illustrated in this chapter's Global Feature.

Signs, symbols, and artifacts are particularly important in forming first impressions and for communicating service concepts. When customers are unfamiliar with a particular service establishment, they look for environmental cues to help them categorize the place and form their expectations. A study of dentists' offices found that consumers use the environment, in particular its style of decoration and level of quality, as a cue to the competence and manner of the service provider.[36] Another interesting study explored the roles of ethnicity and sexual orientation on consumers' interpretation of symbols within consumption environments. Specifically, the study found that people of Jewish descent observe particular symbols in places that encourage them to feel at home and approach those places.[37] The same study found that homosexuals were also drawn to environments that included particular symbols and artifacts that they

People's reactions to elements of the physical environment and design are shaped to a large degree by culture and expectations they have formed through their life experiences, dominated by where they live. Just think of one design element—color—and the variety of uses it has across cultures. Other cultural differences—personal space requirements, social distance preferences, sensitivity to crowding—can affect how consumers experience servicescapes around the world.

McDonald's Corporation recognizes these culturally defined expectations in allowing its franchisees around the world tremendous freedom in designing their servicescapes. In most McDonald's franchises, a large percentage of the ownership is retained locally. Employees are nationals, and marketing strategies reflect local consumers' buying and preference patterns. In all cases, the restaurant is a "community institution," involved in social causes as well as local events. McDonald's strategy is to have its restaurants worldwide reflect the cultures and communities in which they are found—to mirror the communities they serve.

Not only are the servicescapes different, but the delivery options are also different around the globe. In the United States, drive-through windows are prevalent, reflecting the country's automobile culture and relative lack of space constraints. In contrast, many people in cities around the world can now have McDonald's food delivered to them via cars, motor scooters, and bicycles. The delivery model works well and is profitable in cities where there is plenty of labor, congested traffic, and little space for stand-alone restaurants, such as Taipei, Taiwan. At the same time that it allows this creative energy to flourish in design, delivery, and marketing strategies, McDonald's is extremely tight on its operating procedures and menu standards.

Although the golden arches are always present, a brief tour around the globe shows the wide variation in McDonald's face to the community:

- Bologna, Italy: In Bologna, known as the "City of Arches" for hundreds of years, McDonald's took on the weathered, crafted look of the neighboring historic arches. Even the floor in the restaurant was done by hand, using old-world techniques. The restaurant used local architects and artists to bring the local architectural feel to the golden arches.

- Paris, France: Near the Sorbonne in Paris, the local McDonald's reflects its studious neighbor. The servicescape there has the look of a leather-bound library with books, statues, and heavy wood furniture.

- Salen, Sweden: On the slopes of Lindvallen Resort in Salen, you can find the world's first "ski-thru" restaurant, named McSki, located next to the main ski lift. The building is different from any other McDonald's restaurant, built in a typical mountain style with wood panels and natural stone from the surroundings. Skiers can simply glide to the counter without taking off their skis, or they can be seated indoors or out.

- Beijing, China: McDonald's restaurants here have become a "place to hang out," very different from the truly "fast-food" role they have historically played in the United States. They are part of the community, serving young and old, families and couples. Customers can be seen lingering for long periods of time, relaxing, chatting, reading, enjoying the music, or celebrating birthdays. Teenagers and young couples even find the restaurants to be very romantic environments. The emphasis on a Chinese-style family atmosphere is apparent from the interior walls of local restaurants, which are covered by posters emphasizing family values.

- Tokyo, Japan: Although some McDonald's restaurants in Japan are located in prime real-estate districts such as the Ginza in Tokyo, many others are situated near major train stations or other high-traffic locations. The emphasis at these locations is on convenience and speed, not on comfort or socializing. Many of these locations have little frontage space and limited seating. Customers frequently stand while eating, or they may sit on stools at narrow counters. Even the elite Ginza location has few seats. Some locations have a small ordering and service area on the first floor, with limited seating (still primarily stools rather than tables and chairs) on the second floor.

identified with. In the presence of other symbols, these groups felt unwelcome or even discriminated against.

GUIDELINES FOR PHYSICAL EVIDENCE STRATEGY

To this point in the chapter we have presented ideas, frameworks, and psychological models for understanding the effects of physical evidence and most specifically the effects of the physical facility or servicescape. In this section, we suggest some general guidelines for an effective physical evidence strategy.[38]

Interestingly, while the trend in the United States is to sell healthier menu items, Japanese guests are showing strong preference for big burgers with high calorie counts.

- Taupo, New Zealand: The McDonald's here is a unique site, as the restaurant has incorporated a decommissioned DC3 plane as part of the dining area. The plane has been adorned with the familiar red paint and golden arches that McDonald's is famous for. Customers can eat at seats inside the plane, and patrons are also welcome to explore the cockpit and experience a piece of New Zealand history.

McDonald's has begun an extensive makeover aimed at modernizing the entire chain's overall look. Many existing restaurants have already invested in extensive upgrades that feature a cleaner and simpler overall design; less plastic; warmer, muted colors (terra cotta instead of bright red);

Wi-fi access; and different types of seating sections, including bar stools for customers who eat alone and family areas with booths and fabric-covered seating. Of course, the golden arches (being replaced by the "eyebrow" in some current remodels) still play a role in the modernized design.

Sources: *Golden Arches East: McDonald's in East Asia,* ed. J. L. Watson (Stanford, CA: Stanford University Press, 1997); "A Unique Peak," *Franchise Times* 3 (1997), p. 46; P. Gogoi, "Mickey D's McMakeover," *BusinessWeek,* May 15, 2006, pp. 42–43; M. Arndt, "Knock Knock, It's Your Big Mac; From Sao Paulo to Shanghai, McDonald's Is Boosting Growth with Speedy Delivery," *Business-Week,* July 23, 2007, p. 36; M. Sanchanta and Y. Koh, "McDonald's in Japan Gives New Meaning to Supersize," *The Wall Street Journal,* January 12, 2011, p. 1; L. R. Brett, "Join the Mile Fry Club! McDonald's Opens 20-Seat Restaurant on a Vintage Luxury Plane," *Mail Online,* August 12, 2014, http://www.dailymail.co.uk/travel/travel_news /article-2722653/Join-mile-fry-club-McDonald-s-opens-20-seat -restaurant-vintage-luxury-PLANE-cabin-crew-not-included.html.

McDonalds restaurant in China.

© Michael Lassman/Bloomberg/Getty Images

Recognize the Strategic Impact of Physical Evidence

Physical evidence can play a prominent role in determining service quality expectations and perceptions. For some organizations, just acknowledging the impact of physical evidence is a major first step. After this step, they can take advantage of the potential of physical evidence and plan strategically.

For physical evidence strategy to be effective, it must be linked clearly to the organization's overall goals and vision. Thus, planners must know what those goals are and then determine how the physical evidence strategy can support them. At a minimum, the basic service concept must be defined, the target markets (both internal and external) identified, and the firm's broad vision of its future known. Because many evidence decisions are relatively permanent and costly (particularly servicescape decisions), they must be planned and executed deliberately.

Blueprint the Physical Evidence of Service

The next step is to blueprint the service. Everyone in the organization should be able to see the service process and the existing elements of physical evidence. An effective way to depict service evidence is through the service blueprint. (Service blueprinting was presented in detail in Chapter 8.) Although service blueprints clearly have multiple purposes, they can be particularly useful in visually capturing physical evidence opportunities. People, processes, and physical evidence can all be seen in the blueprint. The actions involved in service delivery are visible, as are the complexity of the process, the points of human interaction that provide evidence opportunities, and the tangible representations present at each step. To make the blueprint even more useful, photographs or videos of the process can be added to develop a photographic blueprint that provides a vivid picture of physical evidence from the customer's point of view.

Clarify Strategic Roles of the Servicescape

Early in the chapter we discussed the varying roles played by the servicescape and how firms could locate themselves in the typology shown in Table 10.3 to begin to identify their roles. For example, a day care center would locate itself in the "elaborate, interpersonal" cell of the table and quickly see that its servicescape decisions would be relatively complex and that the servicescape strategy may have to consider the needs of both the children and the service providers and could impact marketing, organizational behavior, and consumer satisfaction goals.

Sometimes the servicescape has no role in service delivery or marketing from the customer's point of view, such as in telecommunications services or utilities (although in these cases other forms of physical evidence would still be important). Clarifying the roles played by the servicescape in a particular situation will aid in identifying opportunities and deciding who needs to be consulted in making facility design decisions. Clarifying the strategic role of the servicescape also forces recognition of the importance of the servicescape in creating customer experiences.

Assess and Identify Physical Evidence Opportunities

Once the current forms of evidence and the roles of the servicescape are understood, possible changes and improvements can be identified. One question to ask is, are there missed opportunities to provide service evidence? The service blueprint of an insurance or utility service may show that little if any evidence of service is ever provided to the customer. A strategy might then be developed to provide more evidence of service to show customers exactly what they are paying for. This was the case for a large technology services company that provided a "remote repair service" for its customers. Remote service (sometimes referred to as "smart service") means they were able to anticipate and repair certain technology equipment from afar without the customer actually being aware anything had been done. A blueprint of the service revealed that no physical evidence of the service existed at all. Thus, customers did not appreciate the service they had received nor were they anxious to pay for it. Realizing this, the company developed ways to communicate and provide evidence of the service for customers.

Or it may be discovered that the evidence provided is sending messages that do not enhance the firm's image or goals or that do not match customer expectations. For example, a restaurant might find that its high-price menu cues are not consistent with the design of the restaurant, which suggests "family dining" to its intended market segment. Either the pricing or the facility design would need to be changed, depending on the restaurant's overall strategy.

Another set of questions addresses whether the current physical evidence of service suits the needs and preferences of the target market. To begin answering such questions, the framework for understanding environment–user relationships (Figure 10.1) and the research approaches suggested in this chapter could be employed. And finally, does the evidence strategy take into account the needs (sometimes incompatible) of both customers and employees? This question is particularly relevant in making decisions regarding the servicescape.

Update and Modernize the Evidence

Some aspects of the evidence, particularly the servicescape, require frequent or at least periodic updating and modernizing.[39] Even if the vision, goals, and objectives of the company do not change, time itself takes a toll on physical evidence, necessitating change and modernization. Clearly, an element of fashion is involved, and over time different colors, designs, and styles may come to communicate different messages. Organizations obviously understand this concept when it comes to advertising strategy, but sometimes they overlook the many elements of physical evidence discussed in this chapter.

Work Cross-Functionally

In presenting itself to the consumer, a service firm is concerned with communicating a desired image, with sending consistent and compatible messages through all forms of evidence, and with providing the type of service evidence the target customers want and can understand. Frequently, however, physical evidence decisions are made over time and by various functions within the organization. For example, decisions regarding employee uniforms may be made by the human resources area, servicescape design decisions may be made by the facilities management group, process design decisions are most frequently made by operations managers, and advertising and pricing decisions may be made by the marketing department. Thus, it is not surprising that the physical evidence of service may at times be less than consistent. A multifunction team approach to physical evidence strategy is often necessary, particularly for making decisions about the servicescape.

Summary

In this chapter we explored the roles of physical evidence in forming customer and employee perceptions and shaping customer experiences. Because services are intangible and often produced and consumed at the same time, they can be difficult to comprehend or evaluate before their purchase. The physical evidence of the service thus serves as a primary cue for setting customer expectations before purchase. These tangible cues, particularly the servicescape, also influence customers' responses as they experience the service. Because customers and employees often interact in the servicescape, the physical surroundings also influence employees and the nature of employee–customer interactions.

The chapter focused primarily on the physical servicescape—the physical surroundings or the facility where the service is produced, delivered, and consumed.

Service employees directly impact customers' satisfaction.

© John A. Rizzo/Getty Images

after his tweet he turned off his phone as the plane prepared for departure. To his disbelief, when he landed he was met at the airport by one of Morton's staff, who had driven 23 miles to the airport to deliver to him a full meal.[3]

- In a Panera Bread parking lot a couple of years ago one woman attempted to catch another customer (who suffered from multiple sclerosis) as she lost her balance. Both customers ended up falling on the pavement, and the one who caught the other broke her right arm. Before the woman was taken by ambulance to an emergency room for treatment, a Panera employee gave her his card and told her to call him if she needed anything. A couple of hours later she called and asked if she could get a ride back to the restaurant to get her car. Once there, she realized that she could not drive the car—it had a manual transmission and she could not shift gears with a broken arm. While she was attempting to contact family to get a ride home, the Panera employee provided her with a free meal. After not being able to find someone to drive her home, she asked the employee for another favor—to give her a ride home. He did—to a town that was nearly an hour's drive away. The woman was ecstatic and could not believe a "restaurant employee" would do all of this for her.[4]

These stories illustrate the important roles played by service employees in creating satisfied customers and in building customer relationships. The frontline service providers in each example are enormously important to the success of the organizations they represent. They are responsible for understanding customer needs and for interpreting customer requirements in real time (as suggested by the accompanying photo). Leonard Berry has documented that, in case after case, companies that achieve sustained service success all recognize the critical importance of their employees.[5]

In this chapter we focus on service employees and human resource practices that facilitate delivery of quality services. Even when customer expectations are well understood (gap 1) and services have been designed and specified to conform to those expectations (gap 2), there may still be discontinuities in service quality when the service is not delivered as specified. These discontinuities are labeled gap 3—the *service performance gap*—in the service quality framework. Because employees frequently deliver or perform the service, human resource issues are a major cause of this gap. By focusing on the critical role of service employees and by developing strategies that lead to effective customer-oriented service, organizations can begin to close the service performance gap.

SERVICE CULTURE

Before addressing the role of the employee in service delivery, we should look at the bigger picture. The behavior of employees in an organization will be heavily influenced by the culture of that organization or the pervasive norms and values that shape individual and group behavior. *Corporate culture* has been defined as "the pattern of shared values and beliefs that give the members of an organization meaning, and provide them with the rules for behavior in the organization."[6] *Culture* has been defined more informally as "the way we do things around here."

To understand at a personal level what corporate culture is, think of different places you have worked or organizations you have been a member of, such as churches, fraternities, schools, or associations. Your behavior and the behaviors of others were no doubt influenced by the underlying values, norms, and culture of the organization. Even when you first interview for a new job, you can begin to get a sense of the firm's culture through talking to a number of employees and observing behavior. Once you are on the job, your formal training and informal observation of behavior will work together to give you a better picture of the organization's culture.

Experts have suggested that a customer-oriented, service-oriented organization will have at its heart a *service culture,* defined as "a culture where an appreciation for good service exists, and where giving good service to internal as well as ultimate, external customers is considered a natural way of life and one of the most important norms by everyone."[7] This very rich definition has many implications for employee behaviors. First, a service culture exists if there is an "appreciation for good service." This phrase does not mean that the company has an advertising campaign that stresses the importance of service, but people know that good service is appreciated and valued. A second important point in this definition is that good service is given to internal as well as external customers.[8] It is not enough to promise excellent service to final customers; all people within the organization deserve the same kind of service. Finally, in a service culture good service is "a way of life" and it comes naturally because it is an important norm of the organization. Service culture is critical to the creation of a customer-focused organization and has been identified as a source of competitive advantage in companies.[9]

Exhibiting Service Leadership

A strong service culture begins with leaders in the organization who demonstrate a passion for service excellence. Leonard Berry suggests that leaders of successful service firms tend to have similar core values, such as integrity, joy, and respect, and they "infuse those values into the fabric of the organization."[10] Leadership does not consist of bestowing a set of commands from a thick rulebook but, rather, the regular and consistent demonstration of one's values. Employees are more likely to embrace a service culture when they see management living out these values. Espoused values—what managers *say* the values are—tend to have less impact on employees than enacted values—what employees believe the values to be because of what they observe management actually *doing.*[11] That is, culture is driven by what employees perceive that management *really* believes, and employees gain an understanding of what is important in the organization through the daily experiences they have with those people in key roles throughout the organization.

Developing a Service Culture

A service culture cannot be developed overnight, and there is no easy way to sustain a service culture. The human resource and internal marketing practices discussed later in the chapter can help develop a service culture over time. If, however, an organization has a culture rooted in product-, operations-, or government regulation–oriented traditions, no single strategy will change it into a service culture. Hundreds of little (but significant) factors, not just one or two big factors, are required to build and sustain a service culture.[12] When companies shift from an engineering, sales, or

Although international markets offer tremendous opportunities for growth, many companies find significant challenges when they attempt to transport their services to other countries. Services depend on people, are often delivered by people, and involve the interaction between employees and customers. Differences in values, norms of behavior, language, and even the definition of service become evident quickly and have implications for training, hiring, and incentives that can ultimately affect the success of the international expansion. Companies with strong service cultures are faced with the question of whether to try to replicate their culture and values in other countries or to adapt significantly. A few examples illustrate different approaches.

McDONALD'S APPROACH

McDonald's has been very successful in its international expansion. In some ways it has remained very "American" in everything it does—people around the world want an American experience when they go to McDonald's. However, the company is sensitive to cultural differences as well. This subtle blending of the "McDonald's" way with adaptations to cultural nuances has resulted in great success. One way that McDonald's maintains its standards is through its Hamburger University (HU), which is required training for *all* McDonald's employees worldwide before they can become managers. Each year approximately 7,500 employees from more than 100 countries attend the Advanced Operations Course at HU, located in Oak Brook, Illinois. The curriculum is 80 percent devoted to communications and human relations skills. Because of the

international scope of McDonald's, translators and electronic equipment enable instructors to teach and communicate in 28 languages at one time. The result is that all managers in all countries have the same "ketchup in their veins," and the restaurant's basic human resources and operating philosophies remain fairly stable from operation to operation. Certain adaptations in decor, menu, and other areas of cultural differences are then allowed (see the Global Feature in Chapter 10 for some specific examples).

UPS'S EXPERIENCE

UPS has a strong culture built on employee productivity, highly standardized service delivery processes, and structured training. Its brown trucks and uniforms are instantly recognizable in the United States. However, as it expanded into countries across Europe, UPS was surprised by some of the challenges of managing a global workforce. Here are some of the surprises: indignation in France, when drivers were told they could not have wine with lunch; protests in Britain, when drivers' dogs were banned from delivery trucks; and dismay in Spain, when it was found that brown UPS trucks resembled the local hearses.

DISNEY IN EUROPE

When Disney first expanded into Europe by opening Disneyland Paris, it also faced challenges and surprises. The highly structured, scripted, and customer-oriented approach that Disney used in the United States was not easily duplicated with European employees. In particular, the smiling, friendly, always customer-focused behaviors

operations culture to a service culture, they find that it can take years of consistent, concerted effort to build a service culture and to shift an organization from its old patterns to new ways of doing business. Even for companies such as FedEx, Charles Schwab, Disney, Southwest Airlines, Zappos, and the Ritz-Carlton, which started with a strong service and customer focus, sustaining their established service cultures still takes constant attention to hundreds of details.

Transporting a Service Culture

Transporting a service culture through international business expansion is also very challenging. Attempting to "export" a corporate culture to another country creates additional issues. For instance, will the organization's service culture clash with a different *national* culture? If there is a clash, is it over *what* the actual values are or over *how* they are to be enacted? If the issue is over what the values are, and they are core values critical to the firm's competitive advantage, then perhaps the company cannot be successful in that setting. If the issue is over how the values are enacted, then perhaps some service practices can be modified in the new setting. To illustrate, as discussed in Chapter 9, Four Seasons Hotels created seven globally uniform "SERVICE" of Disney's U.S. workforce did not suit the experience and values of young French employees. In attempting to transport the Disney culture and experience to Europe, the company confronted clashing values and norms of behavior in the workplace that made the expansion difficult. Customers also needed to be "trained" in the Disney way—not all cultures are comfortable with waiting in long lines, for example. And not all cultures treat their children the same. For example, in the United States, families will spend lots of money at Disneyland on food, toys, and other things that their children "must" have. Some European cultures view this behavior as highly indulgent, so families will visit the park without buying much beyond the ticket for admission.

DELIVERING THE APPLE STORE'S "STEPS OF SERVICE" GLOBALLY

Perhaps no company has been better at connecting with its customers than Apple. The company carefully considers the experience its customers have at every touch-point. As part of the training Apple uses an acronym (the company's name) to describe the "steps of service" expected of every Apple Store employee:

- **A**pproach customers with a personalized warm welcome.
- **P**robe politely to understand all the customer's needs.
- **P**resent a solution for the customer to take home today.
- **L**isten for and resolve any issues or concerns.
- **E**nd with a fond farewell and an invitation to return.

These steps of service, adapted from the Ritz-Carlton, provide a framework for what Apple Store employees are to do in service encounters. "APPLE" is intended to help create great customer experiences in each country Apple Stores are present.

As Apple looks to expand its retail presence globally, it will be challenging to consistently deliver service in this manner. In China, for example, retail chief Angela Ahrendts believes Apple Store's biggest challenge will be to keep up with the demand for Apple products while providing the same level of customer service outlined in the "steps of service." Apple will face similar challenges in transferring its service culture as it continues its expansion in such countries as India, Hong Kong, Brazil, and the United Arab Emirates. Employees in these countries will need to learn how to appropriately interact with customers, how to phrase communications in a positive rather than a negative way, and what to say when customers react emotionally, with the ultimate goal to help customers solve problems rather than to sell products.

Sources: www.mcdonalds.com, accessed July 19, 2016; D. Milbank, "Can Europe Deliver?" *The Wall Street Journal,* September 30, 1994, pp. R15, R23; C. Gallo, "How the Apple Store Creates Irresistible Customer Experiences," *Forbes* April 10, 2015, http://www.forbes.com/sites/carminegallo/2015/04/10 /how-the-apple-store-creates-irresistible-customer-experiences; "Apple Retail Chief Angela Ahrendts Talks Expansion in China Amid Five New Store Openings," *Mac Rumors* (blog), http://www.macrumors.com/2015/01/15/ahrendts-china-expansion/, January 15, 2015.

standards that it expects of all its employees throughout the world. The company has also identified several core values that it believes transcend national culture. One such value is to anticipate guests' needs. This value has been enacted in the United States by leaving a coffeepot on the table in the hotel restaurant, so that guests can help themselves whenever they like. However, when Four Seasons opened a hotel in Paris, it decided to never leave a coffeepot on restaurant tables; doing so would not be received favorably by French customers, who generally believe one should not have to pour coffee oneself. Four Seasons did not alter other practices; it continued, for example, its employee-of-the-month program as a way to provide recognition for exceptional service, even though such programs are not generally offered in France.[13] These standards and values reflect Four Seasons's attempt to transport its service culture across national borders, but management is keenly aware that they need to carefully consider how these values are enacted in each hotel.

Although tremendous opportunities exist in the global marketplace, the many legal, cultural, and language barriers become particularly evident for services that depend on human interaction. Our Global Feature highlights the issues and experiences of several companies as they attempt to transport their service cultures.

THE CRITICAL ROLE OF SERVICE EMPLOYEES

An often-heard quotation about service organizations goes like this: "In a service organization, if you're not serving the customer, you'd better be serving someone who is."[14] People—frontline employees and those supporting them from behind the scenes—are critical to the success of any service organization. The importance of people in the marketing of services is captured in the *people* element of the service marketing mix, which we described in Chapter 1 as *all the human actors who play a part in service delivery and thus influence the buyer's perceptions: namely, the firm's personnel, the customer, and other customers in the service environment.*

The key focus in this chapter is on customer-contact service employees because:

- They *are* the service.
- They *are* the organization in the customer's eyes.
- They *are* the brand.
- They *are* marketers.

In many cases, the contact employee *is the service*—there is nothing else. For example, in most personal and professional services (like haircutting, personal trainers, child care, limousine services, counseling, and legal services) the contact employee provides the entire service singlehandedly. The offering *is* the employee. Thus, investing in the employee to improve the service parallels making a direct investment in the improvement of a manufactured product.

Even if the contact employee does not perform the service entirely, he or she may still *personify the firm in the customer's eyes.* All the employees of a law firm or health clinic—from the professionals who provide the service to the receptionists and office staff—represent the firm to the client, and everything these individuals do or say can influence perceptions of the organization. Even off-duty employees, such as flight attendants or restaurant employees on a break, reflect the organizations they represent. If they are unprofessional or make rude remarks about or to customers, customers' perceptions of the organization will suffer, even though the employee is not on duty. The Disney Corporation insists that its employees maintain "onstage" attitudes and behaviors whenever they are in front of the public; employees may relax these behaviors only when they are truly behind the scenes or "backstage" in underground tunnels where guests cannot see them in their off-duty times.

Service employees *are the brand.* An Edward Jones financial advisor, a Nordstrom sales associate, a Southwest Airlines flight attendant, an Abercrombie & Fitch retail employee—in each case, the primary image that a customer has of the firm is formed by the interactions the customer has with the employees of that firm. A customer sees Edward Jones as a good provider of financial services if the employees she interacts with are knowledgeable, understanding, and concerned about her financial situation and goals. Similarly, a customer sees Nordstrom as a professional and empathetic company because of interactions he has with its sales associates. Southwest Airlines seeks employees who are outgoing and fun-loving and Abercrombie & Fitch looks to hire people who have a certain "look." Online shoe retailer Zappos makes the hiring process a primary focus of its branding strategy and evaluates potential employees on their ability to serve as brand ambassadors.[15] These companies understand that the brand image is not just built and maintained by the products sold and the advertising: it is a function of the people who work for them. Strategies that recognize the power of employees to create the brand have been referred to as "branded customer service."[16] For firms using such strategies, employees truly "are the brand" and epitomize the company image that each is attempting to create in the minds of its customers.

Because contact employees represent the organization and can directly influence customer satisfaction, they *perform the role of marketers.* They physically embody the product and are walking billboards from a promotional standpoint. Some service employees may also perform more traditional selling roles. For example, bank tellers are often called on to cross-sell bank products, a departure from the traditional teller role of focusing on operational functions only. In this chapter we examine frameworks, tools, and strategies for ensuring that service employees perform their marketing and service functions well.

The Service Triangle

Service marketing is about promises—promises made and promises kept to customers. A strategic framework known as the *service triangle* (illustrated in Figure 11.1) visually reinforces the importance of people in the ability of firms to keep their promises and succeed in building customer relationships.[17] The triangle shows the three interlinked groups that work together to develop, promote, and deliver services. These key players are labeled on the points of the triangle: the *company* (SBU, department, or "management"), the *customers,* and the *providers.* Providers can be the firm's employees, subcontractors, or outsourced entities who actually deliver the company's services. Between these three points on the triangle, three types of marketing must be successfully carried out for a service to succeed: external marketing, interactive marketing, and internal marketing.

On the right side of the triangle are the *external marketing* efforts that the firm engages in to develop its customers' expectations and make promises to customers regarding what is to be delivered. Anyone or anything that communicates to the customer before service delivery can be viewed as part of this external marketing function. But external marketing is just the beginning for service marketers: promises made must be kept. On the bottom of the triangle is what has been termed *interactive marketing* or *real-time marketing.* Here is where promises are kept or broken by the firm's employees, subcontractors, or agents. Those people representing the organization are critical at this juncture. If promises are not kept, customers become dissatisfied and

FIGURE 11.1
The Service Marketing Triangle

Sources: Adapted from M. J. Bitner, "Building Service Relationships: It's All about Promises," *Journal of the Academy of Marketing Science* 23 (Fall 1995), pp. 246–251; P. T. Kotler and K. L. Keller, *Marketing Management,* 15th ed. (Upper Saddle River, NJ: Pearson Prentice Hall, 2016), p. 410.

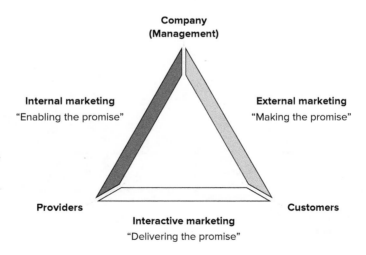

Company (Management)

Internal marketing
"Enabling the promise"

External marketing
"Making the promise"

Providers

Customers

Interactive marketing
"Delivering the promise"

eventually leave. The left side of the triangle suggests the critical role played by *internal marketing*. Management engages in these activities to help the providers deliver on the service promise: recruiting, training, motivating, rewarding, and providing equipment and technology. Unless service employees are able and willing to deliver on the promises made, the firm will not be successful.

All three sides of the triangle are essential, and the sides of the triangle should be aligned. That is, what is promised through external marketing should be the same as what is delivered; and the enabling activities inside the organization should be aligned with what is expected of service providers. Strategies for aligning the triangle, particularly the strategies associated with internal marketing, are the subject of this chapter.

Employee Satisfaction, Customer Satisfaction, and Profits

Satisfied employees make for satisfied customers (and satisfied customers can, in turn, reinforce employees' sense of satisfaction in their jobs). Some researchers have even gone so far as to suggest that, unless service employees are happy in their jobs, customer satisfaction will be difficult to achieve.[18]

Through their research with customers and employees in bank branches, Benjamin Schneider and David Bowen have shown that both a *climate for service* and a *climate for employee well-being* are highly correlated with overall customer perceptions of service quality.[19] That is, both service climate and human resource management experiences that *employees* have within their organizations are reflected in how *customers* experience the service. Similar research suggests that employees who feel they are treated fairly by their organizations will treat customers better, resulting in greater customer satisfaction.[20]

The underlying logic connecting employee satisfaction and loyalty to customer satisfaction and loyalty and ultimately profits is illustrated by the *service profit chain* shown in Figure 11.2.[21] In earlier chapters we focused on customer satisfaction and retention; here we focus on employee issues. The service profit chain suggests that there are critical linkages among internal service quality, employee satisfaction/ productivity, the value of services provided to the customer, and ultimately customer satisfaction, retention, and profits.

Service profit chain researchers are careful to point out that the model does not suggest causality. That is, employee satisfaction does not *cause* customer satisfaction; rather the two are interrelated and feed off each other.[22] The model does imply that

FIGURE 11.2   **The Service Profit Chain**

Source: Adapted from J. L. Heskett, T. O. Jones, G. W. Loveman, W. E. Sasser Jr., and L. A. Schlesinger, "Putting the Service-Profit Chain to Work," *Harvard Business Review* 72 (March–April 1994), pp. 164–174.

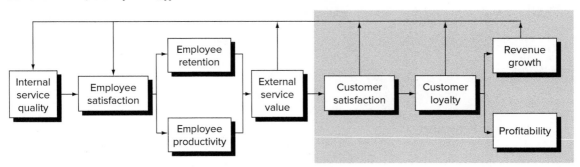

companies that exhibit high levels of success on the elements of the model will be more successful and profitable than those that do not.

The Effect of Employee Behaviors on Service Quality Dimensions

Customers' perceptions of service quality are affected by the customer-oriented behaviors of employees.[23] In fact, all five dimensions of service quality (reliability, responsiveness, assurance, empathy, and tangibles) can be influenced directly by service employees.

Delivering the service as promised—*reliability*—is often totally within the control of frontline employees. Even in the case of services delivered primarily through technology (such as airline or hotel check-in kiosks, banking apps on smart phones, or self-checkout in retail stores), behind-the-scenes employees are critical for making sure all the systems are working properly. When services fail or errors are made, employees are essential for setting things right and using their judgment to determine the best course of action for service recovery.

Frontline employees directly influence customer perceptions of *responsiveness* through their personal willingness to help and their promptness in serving customers. Consider the range of responses you receive from different retail store clerks when you need help finding a particular item of clothing. One employee may ignore your presence, whereas another offers to help you search and calls other stores to locate the item. One may help you immediately and efficiently, whereas another may move slowly in accommodating even the simplest request.

The *assurance* dimension of service quality is highly dependent on employees' ability to communicate their credibility and to inspire the customer's trust and confidence in the firm. The reputation of the organization will help, but in the end, individual employees with whom the customer interacts confirm and build trust in the organization or detract from its reputation and ultimately destroy trust. For startup or relatively unknown organizations, credibility, trust, and confidence will be tied totally to employee actions.

It is difficult to imagine how an organization would deliver "caring, individualized attention" to customers independent of its employees. *Empathy* implies that employees will pay attention, listen, adapt, and be flexible in delivering what individual customers need.[24] For example, research documents that when employees are customer oriented, have good rapport with customers, display emotional competence, and exhibit perceptive and attentive listening skills, customers will evaluate the service more highly and are more likely to return.[25] Employee appearance and dress are important aspects of the *tangibles* dimension of quality, along with many other factors that are independent of service employees (the service facility, decor, brochures, signage, and so on).

BOUNDARY-SPANNING ROLES

Our focus in this chapter is on frontline service employees who interact directly with customers, although much of what is described and recommended can be applied to internal service employees as well. Frontline service employees are referred to as *boundary spanners* because they operate at the organization's boundary. As indicated in Figure 11.3, boundary spanners provide a link between the external customer and environment and the internal operations of the organization. They serve a critical function in understanding, filtering, and interpreting information and resources to and from the organization and its external constituencies.

Strategy Insight   Strategies for Managing Emotional Labor

Customer contact employees in service positions are often required to display (or, conversely, to withhold display of) a variety of emotions. Such employees are increasingly being required to invest personal identity and expression into their work in many situations. The following description suggests how the experience of the service employee, even in the most routine of occupations, is markedly different from that of the traditional manufacturing worker:

> The assembly-line worker could openly hate his job, despise his supervisor, and even dislike his coworkers, and while this might be an unpleasant state of affairs, if he [completes] his assigned tasks efficiently, his attitude [is] his own problem. For the service worker, inhabiting the job means, at the very least, pretending to like it, and, at most, actually bringing his whole self into the job, liking it, and genuinely caring about the people with whom he interacts.*

Emotional labor occurs more often when the job requires frequent contact and long durations of voice contact or face-to-face contact with customers. These employees often need emotional management to deal with such situations. Later in this chapter we suggest many strategies for organizations to create an environment that helps employees deal with the realities of emotional labor on the job. Here we present specific strategies some firms use to more directly support employee efforts to manage their emotions in the face of demanding, obnoxious, or unruly customers.

SCREENING FOR EMOTIONAL LABOR ABILITIES

Many firms look to hire employees who are well suited to meet the emotional labor requirements of the job. Dungarvin, an organization that provides a variety of services to people who have mental and physical disabilities, displays a realistic job preview on its website to indicate to prospective employees the emotional labor requirements. In doing so, Dungarvin's intent is to identify applicants who are comfortable with the emotional demands required of employees who must regularly interact with clients with special needs. Call centers often provide job candidates with a realistic job preview, in part, to allow a prospective employee to gauge if he or she is well suited to exert the emotional labor required to interact with customers—often frustrated and unhappy ones—on a continual basis. These simulated customer contact exercises also allow the company to assess the level of friendliness and warmth prospective candidates naturally communicate. Such practices help in identifying employees whose values, background, personality, and emotional competence abilities match the job's emotional labor requirements.

TEACHING EMOTIONAL MANAGEMENT SKILLS AND APPROPRIATE BEHAVIORS

Most customer contact employees are taught that they need to be courteous to customers. However, customers have no obligation to return empathy or courtesy. In situations in which customers exercise the privilege of "the customer is always right," employees face challenges in suppressing their true feelings. Seldom do firms provide much training to assist employees in facing these challenges. Arlie Hochschild identifies two forms of emotional labor: *surface acting,* in which employees pretend to feel emotions that are not really present and, in doing so, could involve both suppression of felt emotions and faking of unfelt emotions; and *deep acting,* in which employees attempt to experience the real feelings they are expected (or required) to express to the customer, including the active invocation of thoughts, images, and memories to induce the associated emotion. Retail store clerks and airline flight attendants are often encouraged to engage in deep-acting strategies such as imagining that the client is a friend or that the passenger is a frightened little child flying for the first time. Companies may also train employees in how to avoid absorbing a customer's bad mood, perhaps by having employees spend hours role-playing to suppress their natural reaction to return negative customer emotions with their own negative emotions.

is greatest when the employee believes the organization is wrong in its policies and must decide whether to accommodate the client and risk losing a job or to follow the policies. These conflicts are especially severe when service employees depend directly on the customer for income. For example, employees who depend on tips or commissions are likely to face greater levels of organization/client conflict because they have even greater incentives to identify with the customer.

CAREFULLY FASHIONING THE PHYSICAL WORK ENVIRONMENT

As we discussed in Chapter 10, the environment in which the service is delivered can have an impact on employee behaviors and emotions. MedAire, a company that provides telephone consultation to airlines when medical emergencies arise on flights, regularly has employees in the midst of life-threatening situations. To reduce the stress that MedAire employees face on a daily basis, the company designed its Tempe, Arizona, office with an open floor plan so that all employees are able to look through windows to see trees, grass, and cars driving by. Taking this idea one step further, JetBlue Airways allows its reservation agents to work from home rather than requiring them to sit all day in an office call center.

ALLOWING EMPLOYEES TO VENT

Employees who must exert emotional labor often need to have an outlet to let off steam. Allowing employees to vent lets them get rid of their frustrations. If such venting is done in a group setting, it provides emotional support and encouragement, allows employees to see that others are experiencing the same problems, and delivers a message to employees that the company is aware of and acknowledges the emotional contribution they make. Ritz-Carlton, Walmart, and other companies regularly set aside time for such venting. In addition to the cathartic benefit this experience can provide, other employees may reveal coping strategies that they have found useful.

GIVING EMPLOYEES A BREAK

In situations in which employees have extended voice or face-to-face contact with customers, a particularly helpful strategy is to allow them a short break to regroup. Many companies with toll-free call centers rotate employees into different positions throughout the day so that they do not spend the entire time on the telephone with customers. Customer contact employees can be reenergized and refreshed after spending a little time away from demanding or difficult situations, even if they take only a few minutes to finish paperwork or complete some other job responsibility. One call center in Australia has a pool table near the employee work area and plays movies while employees work at their desk to reduce the stress of interacting with customers.

HANDING OFF DEMANDING CUSTOMERS TO MANAGERS

Some customers may be too much for an employee to handle. In such situations, to alleviate pressure on the customer contact employee, firms may shift responsibility for the interaction to managers. Wing Zone, a restaurant chain specializing in chicken wings, understands the stress that angry customers can cause employees, many of whom are college students. A majority of the company's orders are taken over the phone, and employees—particularly those with little experience—are trained to simply hand off demanding customers to the nearest manager. And a manager who is unsuccessful in handling the situation is encouraged to direct such customers to the corporate office via a toll-free number.

*Quoted from C. L. Macdonald and C. Sirianni, *Working in the Service Society.* (Philadelphia: Temple University Press, 1996), p. 4.

Sources: A. Hochschild, *The Managed Heart: Commercialization of Human Feeling* (Berkeley: University of California Press, 1983); B. F. Ashforth and R. H. Humphrey, "Emotional Labor in Service Roles: The Influence of Identity," *Academy of Management Review* 18 (1993), pp. 88–115; www.dungarvin.com, accessed July 20, 2016; S. D. Pugh, "Service with a Smile: Emotional Contagion in the Service Encounter," *Academy of Management Journal* 44 (2001), pp. 1018–1027; A. A. Grandey, "When 'The Show Must Go On': Surface Acting and Deep Acting as Determinants of Emotional Exhaustion and Peer-Rated Service Delivery," *Academy of Management Journal* 46 (2003), pp. 86–96; and T. Hennig-Thurau, M. Groth, M. Paul, and D. D. Gremler, "Are All Smiles Created Equal? How Employee-Customer Emotional Contagion and Emotional Labor Impact Service Relationships," *Journal of Marketing* 70 (July 2006), pp. 58–73.

Interclient Conflict

Sometimes conflict occurs for boundary spanners when incompatible expectations and requirements arise from two or more customers. This situation occurs most often when the service provider is serving customers in turn (a bank teller, a ticketing agent, a doctor) or is serving many customers simultaneously (teachers, entertainers).

When serving customers in turn, the provider may satisfy one customer by spending additional time, customizing the service, and being very flexible in meeting the customer's needs. Meanwhile, waiting customers may become dissatisfied because their needs are not being met in a timely way. Beyond the timing issue, different clients may prefer different modes of service delivery; one client may prefer personal recognition and a degree of familiarity while another client may be "all business" and prefer little interpersonal interaction.

When serving many customers at the same time, employees often find it difficult or impossible to serve the full range of needs of a group of heterogeneous customers. This type of conflict is readily apparent in any college classroom in which the instructor must meet a multitude of student expectations and different preferences for formats and style. It is also apparent in an entertainment venue or any type of group training service.

Quality/Productivity Trade-Offs

Frontline service workers are asked to be both effective and efficient: they are expected to deliver satisfying service to customers and at the same time to be cost-effective and productive in what they do. A physician in an HMO, for example, is expected to deliver caring, quality, individualized service to her patients but at the same time to serve a certain number of patients within a specified time frame. A checker at a grocery store is expected to know his customers and to be polite and courteous, yet also process the groceries accurately and move people through the line quickly.[34] These essential trade-offs between quality and quantity and between maximum effectiveness and efficiency place real-time demands and pressures on service employees. Technology is being used to an ever-greater degree to balance the quality/quantity trade-off to increase the productivity of service workers and free them to provide higher-quality service for the customer (see the Technology Spotlight).

A vivid example of the quality/productivity trade-off occurred with Verizon employees in Florida. They were frustrated by the firm's requirement that a service call to a customer not go beyond a certain amount of time, regardless of whether the issue was resolved. That is, employees felt the firm's customer service priorities revolved around efficiencies, not solving a customer's problems. They eventually went on strike to get management to reconsider their service processes, and customers subsequently communicated their appreciation.[35]

STRATEGIES FOR DELIVERING SERVICE QUALITY THROUGH PEOPLE

A complex combination of strategies is needed to ensure that service employees are willing and able to deliver quality services and that they stay motivated to perform in customer-oriented, service-minded ways. These strategies for enabling service promises are often referred to as *internal marketing,* as shown on the left side of Figure 11.1.[36] By approaching human resource decisions and strategies with the primary goal to motivate and enable employees to deliver customer-oriented promises successfully, an organization will move toward delivering service quality through its people. The strategies presented here are organized around four basic themes. To build a customer-oriented, service-minded workforce, an organization must (1) hire the right people, (2) develop people to deliver service quality, (3) provide the needed support systems, and (4) retain the best people. Within each

FIGURE 11.4
Human Resource Strategies for Delivering Service Quality through People

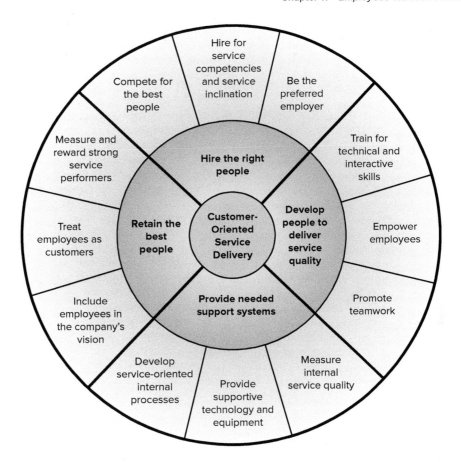

of these basic strategies are a number of specific substrategies for accomplishing the goal, as shown in Figure 11.4.

Hire the Right People

To effectively deliver service quality, considerable attention should be focused on recruiting and hiring service personnel. Such attention is contrary to traditional practices in many service industries, where service personnel are the lowest on the corporate ladder and work for minimum wage. At the other end of the spectrum, in professional services, the most important recruiting criteria are typically technical training, certifications, and expertise. However, successful service organizations generally look beyond the technical qualifications of applicants to assess their customer and service orientation as well. Figure 11.4 shows a number of ways to go about hiring the right people.

Compete for the Best People

To get the best people, an organization needs to identify them and compete with other organizations to hire them. Leonard Berry and A. Parasuraman refer to this approach as "competing for talent market share."[37] They suggest that firms act as marketers in their pursuit of the best employees, just as they use their marketing expertise to compete for customers. Firms that think of recruiting as a marketing activity will address issues of market (employee) segmentation, product (job) design, and promotion of

Technology Spotlight How Technology Is Helping Employees Serve Customers More Effectively and Efficiently

OPTIMIZATION TECHNOLOGY HELPS UPS DRIVERS' RELIABILITY EFFORTS

UPS delivers more than 18 million packages every day. Historically, UPS drivers worked off maps, 3 × 5 note cards, and their own memory to figure out the best way to navigate their routes. However, to more efficiently determine the best routes, UPS implemented a route optimization system; each evening, it maps out the next day's schedule for the majority of its more than 100,000 drivers. This software designs each route to minimize the number of left turns, thus reducing the time and gas that drivers waste idling at stoplights. It also reduced a day or more in transit time in nearly 3 million zip code pairings. UPS's technology allowed it to capture institutional knowledge about its customers. Before, when employees retired or quit, the knowledge of package loading techniques or route tips they had accumulated over the years usually went with them. This knowledge was captured in a centralized system that shortened the training time for new drivers, lessening the chances of a lapse in customer service. This technology enabled UPS to run its routes more efficiently, resulting in quicker and more reliable deliveries for its customers.

BLACKBOARD ASSISTS UNIVERSITY INSTRUCTORS

Universities both within and outside the United States use the Internet and other technologies to create a networked learning environment on their campuses. One tool universities use, called Blackboard, provides an infrastructure that increases instructor effectiveness and efficiency. To illustrate, Blackboard helps instructors organize nearly all teaching-related materials. Among the course management capabilities are electronic storage and controlled access of materials (readings, syllabi, assignments, discussion questions), management of class discussion boards, collection of student assignments, administration of online quizzes and exams, administration of group projects, provision of an online gradebook, and many other capabilities. In effect, most course administration tasks required of instructors can be handled by Blackboard. Students also benefit from having one source for accessing course materials, receiving updated course information, and submitting course assignments—without having to bother instructors with such administrative issues.

Blackboard provides instructors with the ability to manage many sections of a course. Instead of having to create material for each section, instructors can create a learning object (e.g., a handout or reading supplement), store it once, and link it to all course sections. Thus, Blackboard makes more effective usage of the instructor's time—providing the instructor with more time to be accessible to students outside of the classroom. Blackboard also provides instructors with an organized way to track and evaluate student learning. For example, Blackboard's e-portfolio option provides an online repository for storing student work—making it easy for both faculty *and* students to assess a student's progress in a given course or program of study. And, in response to the

job availability in ways that attract potentially long-term employees. Intuit, Harrah's, Yahoo!, Marriott, and other firms have changed the title of the head recruiting person to "vice president of talent acquisition." Doing so recognizes the importance of the function and helps elevate the role to the strategic importance it deserves.

Hire for Service Competencies and Service Inclination

Once potential employees have been identified, organizations need to be conscientious in interviewing and screening to identify the best people from the pool of candidates. Service employees need two complementary capacities: service competencies and service inclination.[38]

Service competencies are the skills and knowledge necessary to do the job. In many cases, employees demonstrate competencies by achieving particular degrees and certifications, such as attaining a doctor of law (JD) degree and passing the relevant state bar examination for lawyers. Similar rites of passage are required of doctors,

ELECTRONIC MEDICAL RECORDS SUPPORT MAYO CLINIC STAFF

Mayo Clinic has been described as one of the most powerful services brands in the world and is arguably the leading health care brand in the United States. Although there are many reasons for this (as noted in other places in this text), technology plays a key role in its ability to deliver high-quality care for patients with serious medical needs such as cancer treatment, heart surgery, or neurosurgery. At its Jacksonville, Florida, location Mayo Clinic invested $18 million during the past decade in computer system technology, with a large portion of the emphasis on electronic medical records. Like most hospitals, Mayo's inpatient system is very complex and requires that patient care efforts be coordinated across departments and specialists. The many systems required for patient care, including pharmacy systems, laboratory systems, and monitoring systems, need to be interconnected and to function 24/7 without fail.

Mayo Clinic's order-entry system enables hospital physicians to order tests, treatments, and medications. When an entry is made, it automatically launches a series of activities associated with the patient's care. For example, consider a person being admitted to the oncology department for a cancer treatment. A physician might place an order for the patient to receive an anti-nausea medicine 30 minutes before chemotherapy, then receive three different chemical agents at specific times and in a particular sequence—and it might specify that the treatment be repeated every 12 hours. Mayo's order-entry system automatically notifies physicians, pharmacists, and others in the hospital when a particular treatment needs to be performed and monitors dosage amounts and method of administration (e.g., orally or through a vein).

In addition to a savings of nearly $7 million to its Jacksonville clinic, the automated system makes Mayo medical staff more effective and improves patient care. For example, when new test results are reported in a patient's file, they are highlighted, so that a nurse or doctor sees them immediately. Thus, the medical staff spends less time waiting or looking for patient files. By transitioning to electronic medical records, Mayo has found staff workflow to be better coordinated in the care of patients suffering from chronic diseases. Thus, electronic medical records have enabled Mayo Clinic staff to be even more efficient and effective in delivering quality health care.

Sources: D. Foust, "How Technology Delivers for UPS," *BusinessWeek* (March 5, 2007), p. 60; 2015 UPS Annual Report; L. L. Berry and K. D. Seltman, "Building a Strong Services Brand: Lessons from Mayo Clinic," *Business Horizons* 50 (May–June 2007), pp. 199–209; and A. M. Virzi, "A Complex Operation," *Baseline* (October 2006), pp. 56–59.

---

airline pilots, university professors, teachers, and many other job seekers before they are ever interviewed for service jobs in their fields. In other cases, service competencies may not be degree-related but may instead relate to basic intelligence or physical requirements. A retail clerk, for example, must possess basic math skills and the potential to operate a cash register. Recent research suggests that many frontline employees may also need to have a sufficient level of emotional competence—defined as the ability to perceive, understand, and regulate a customer's emotions—in order to do their jobs well.[39]

Given the multidimensional nature of service quality, service employees should be screened for more than their service competencies. They should also be screened for *service inclination*—their interest in doing service-related work—which is reflected in their attitudes toward service[40] and orientation toward serving customers and fellow employees. Self-selection suggests that most service jobs will draw applicants with some level of service inclination and that most employees in service organizations are inclined toward service. However, some employees clearly have a greater service

Exhibit 11.1   Google Quickly Becomes a Preferred Employer in Its Industry

In 1996 Google's founders, Larry Page and Sergey Brin, developed a new approach to online search that took root in a Stanford University dorm room and quickly spread to information seekers around the globe. They continued to refine their search approaches and in 1998 formed Google—the world's largest search engine—an easy-to-use, free service that usually returns results in a fraction of a second.

In its short history Google has become a preferred employer and has been ranked number 1 in *Fortune's* list of the 100 best companies to work for seven times between 2007 and 2016. One study reported that one in four young professionals wants to work at Google. Google has used a variety of approaches to become an employer of choice for over 60,000 employees worldwide, including:

- *The Googleplex*—The Google world headquarters building is located in Mountain View, California, and helps to attract and retain "Googlers" (employees). Some of the essential elements of the facility, which are presented on its company website, include a lobby with piano, lava lamps, and live projection of current search queries from around the world. In the hallways there are bicycles, large rubber exercise balls are on the floors, and press clippings from around the world are posted on bulletin boards everywhere. A three-dimensional rotating image

© Google and the Google logo are registered trademarks of Google Inc., used with permission.

Google employees working together in the company's atrium.

of the world toggles between displaying points of light representing real-time searches rising from the surface of the globe toward space, color-coded by language and viewing traffic patterns for the entire Internet.

inclination than others. Research has shown that service effectiveness is correlated with service-oriented personality characteristics such as helpfulness, thoughtfulness, and sociability[41] and that the best service companies put a greater emphasis on hiring those with positive attitudes rather than a specific skill set.[42] An ideal selection process for service employees assesses both service competencies and service inclination, resulting in employee hires who are high on both dimensions.

In addition to traditional employment interviews, many firms use innovative approaches to assessing service inclination and other personal characteristics that fit the organization's needs. Southwest Airlines looks for people who are compassionate and who have common sense, a sense of humor, a "can do" attitude, and an egalitarian sense of themselves (they think in terms of "we" rather than "me"). One way the company assesses these service inclinations is by interviewing potential flight attendants in groups to see how they interact with each other. Pilots are also interviewed in groups to assess their teamwork skills, a critical factor above and beyond the essential technical skills they are required to possess.[43]

Be the Preferred Employer

One way to attract the best people is to be known as the preferred employer in a particular industry or location. UPS regularly conducts a survey among its employees to create an "Employer of Choice Index" and sets annual goals to remain a preferred

- *Recreation facilities*—Google provides a workout room with weights and rowing machines, locker rooms, washers and dryers, a massage room, assorted video games, Foosball, a baby grand piano, a pool table, and Ping-Pong. Twice a week roller hockey is played in the parking lot.

- *Dining facilities*—Google runs 11 free gourmet cafeterias at its headquarters and offers free meals to all its employees. Its food stations include "Charlie's Grill," "Back to Albuquerque," "East Meets West," and "Vegheads." Snack rooms contain bins packed with various cereals, gummy treats, M&Ms, toffee, licorice, cashew nuts, yogurt, carrots, fresh fruit, and other snacks, as well as dozens of different drinks, including fresh juice, soda, and make-your-own cappuccino.

- *Services for employees*—A wide variety of services are provided to Googlers. For example, on-site car washes and oil changes are among the numerous perks Google offers to all its workers. Haircuts are provided on-site. Employees can attend subsidized exercise classes; get a massage; study Mandarin, Japanese, Spanish, or French; and ask a personal concierge to arrange dinner reservations. Other services available to employees include child care, on-site notaries, and five on-site doctors available for employee checkups, all free of charge. And, when traveling to and from the office, Google operates free, Wi-Fi–enabled shuttle buses from five Bay Area locations for its employees.

- *Other benefits*—Several other benefits are also provided to Google employees. Those who buy a hybrid car receive $5,000. A weekly TGIF party takes place, usually with a live band playing, and a "pajama day" is a frequent occurrence. Lactation rooms, complete with breast pumps (so that nursing mothers do not have to haul equipment to work), are provided. Googlers are free to bring their pets to work. And, Google's 80/20 rule allows employees to dedicate 80 percent of time to their primary job and 20 percent working on passion projects that they believe will help the company—Gmail, Google News, and the Google Finance site all resulted from such activity.

It is no surprise that Google receives about 3,000 résumés per day. And if these benefits are not enough to encourage employees to talk up the company, Google provides a $2,000 reward for each person hired as a result of a referral.

Sources: A. Lashinsky, "Search and Enjoy," *Fortune*, January 29, 2007, pp. 70–82; J. Light, "Google Is No. 1 on List of Desired Employers," *The Wall Street Journal*, March 21, 2011, p. B8; J. D'Onfro, "An Insider Look at Google's Best Employee Perks," *Inc.*, September 21, 2015, www.inc.com/business-insider/best-google -benefits.html; and www.google.com, accessed July 21, 2016.

employer.[44] Google, the online search service provider used daily by customers around the world, also enjoys a reputation as a preferred employer. Google states on its website that it "puts employees first when it comes to daily life" in all of its offices.[45] Exhibit 11.1 provides some insight into why Google has been chosen by *Fortune* as the "Best Company to Work For" seven times in the past decade and is the preferred employer in its industry.

Other strategies that support a goal of being the preferred employer include extensive training, career and advancement opportunities, excellent internal support, attractive incentives, and quality goods and services with which employees are proud to be associated. SAS Institute, a regular in the top five of *Fortune*'s annual "Best Company to Work For" list, has long been a preferred employer in the statistical software industry. Employees who work for SAS are, for the most part, professional or technical and well paid. A quote from the company's website captures SAS's philosophy about its people: "if you treat employees as if they make a difference to the company, they will make a difference to the company." The company invests heavily in its people: every employee has a private office, a 35-hour schedule is promoted, flexible hours are available, the company provides top-quality day care centers with very reasonable prices on-site, on-site health care, and a free 66,000-square-foot fitness center. For these reasons, the best performers at SAS seldom leave to work for competitors.[46]

In a very different industry, dominated by lower-paid workers, Marriott International has a stated company goal of being the "preferred employer" in its industry. Marriott's philosophy concerning its employees, which sounds very similar to that of SAS, has been stated by Bill Marriott: "if the employees are well taken care of, they'll take care of the customer and the customer will come back . . . that's basically the core value of the company."[47] Marriott uses flexible workplace options (including flex time, telework, compressed work weeks, shift swapping, part-time work, and job sharing), tuition reimbursement, child and elder care discounts, job and life skills training, and companywide health and wellness programs to be the preferred employer in the highly competitive hospitality industry. The company even offers global language learning programs—with 30 languages to choose from. Marriott International, like Google and SAS, is consistently rated among *Fortune*'s list of the top 100 companies to work for.

Develop People to Deliver Service Quality

To grow and maintain a workforce that is customer oriented and focused on delivering quality, an organization must develop its employees to deliver service quality. That is, once it has hired the right employees, the organization must train and work with these individuals to ensure service performance.

Train for Technical and Interactive Skills

To provide quality service, employees need ongoing training in the necessary technical and interactive skills. Examples of *technical skills* are working with accounting systems in hotels, cash machine procedures in a retail store, underwriting procedures in an insurance company, and any operational rules the company has for running its business. Most service organizations are quite conscious of and relatively effective at training employees in technical skills. These skills may be taught through formal education, as is the case at McDonald's Hamburger University, which trains McDonald's managers from all over the world. Additionally, technical skills are often taught through on-the-job training, as when call center service trainees listen in on the conversations of experienced employees. Companies frequently use information technology to train employees in the technical skills and knowledge needed on the job.

Service employees also need training in *interactive skills* that allow them to provide courteous, caring, responsive, and empathetic service. Research suggests firms can teach employees how to develop rapport with customers—one type of interactive skill—by teaching them how to engage in pleasant conversation, ask questions, or use humor as they interact with customers.[48] Employees can be taught conversation prompts to help them identify commonalities with their customers. Several firms, such as Starbucks and the Elysian Hotel in Chicago, even teach customer-contact employees improvisation to improve their communication and listening skills, read customers' body language, and establish an immediate rapport with them.[49]

Outback Steakhouse coaches waiters and waitresses to squat next to or even sit at a customer's table and spend a couple of minutes interacting; such action allows them to establish better eye contact with customers and provides opportunities for engaging interactions. Starbucks created a board game, *Inside Out,* to be used in training sessions to help its baristas to connect with customers.[50] As part of the game, a barista is presented with a specific scenario—say, a sighing customer doing last-minute Christmas shopping has stopped by for a pick-me-up drink—and is challenged to figure out how to cheer up the customer.

Successful companies invest heavily in training and make sure that the training fits their business goals and strategies. For example, at the Ritz-Carlton, all employees go through extensive initial training and are given pocket-sized, laminated credo cards to carry in their wallets. In addition to the credo, the card specifies the three steps of service and Ritz-Carlton's well-known motto "We are Ladies and Gentlemen Serving Ladies and Gentlemen." Further, employees in every hotel attend a brief standing staff meeting each day to review Ritz-Carlton's "Gold Standards" and employee service values, so as to continually reinforce earlier training.

Empower Employees

Many organizations have discovered that, to be truly responsive to customer needs, frontline providers need to be empowered to accommodate customer requests and to recover on the spot when things go wrong. *Empowerment* means giving employees the authority, skills, tools, and desire to determine how to best serve the customer. Although the key to empowerment is giving employees authority to make decisions on the customer's behalf, authority alone is not enough. Employees need the knowledge and tools to be able to make these decisions, and they need incentives that encourage them to make the right ones. Organizations do not succeed in empowering their employees if they simply tell them, "You now have the authority to do whatever it takes to satisfy the customer." First, employees often do not believe this statement, particularly if the organization has functioned hierarchically or bureaucratically in the past. Second, employees often do not know what it means to "do whatever it takes" if they have not received training, guidelines, and the tools needed to make such decisions. Third, not all employees have a desire to be empowered by the firm.[51]

Research suggests that some of the benefits of empowering frontline service workers include a reduction in job-related stress, improved job satisfaction, greater adaptability, more creative ideas, and better outcomes for customers.[52] But such success does not come easily. In fact, some experts have concluded that few organizations have truly taken advantage of, or properly implemented, successful empowerment strategies.[53] Nor is empowerment the answer for all organizations. Exhibit 11.2 enumerates both the costs and the benefits of empowerment.

Promote Teamwork

The nature of many service jobs suggests that customer satisfaction will be enhanced when employees work as teams. Because service jobs are frequently frustrating, demanding, and challenging, a teamwork environment will help alleviate some of the stresses and strains. Employees who feel supported and feel that they have a team backing them up will be better able to maintain their enthusiasm and provide quality service.[54] Such teamwork is the driving force behind the service philosophy at the Mayo Clinic. One of Mayo's core principles encourages all of those in the organization to practice medicine as "an integrated team of compassionate, multidisciplinary physicians, scientists and allied health professionals who are focused on the needs of patients."[55] By promoting teamwork, an organization can enhance the employees' *abilities* to deliver excellent service, while the camaraderie and support enhance their *inclination* to be excellent service providers.

One way of promoting teamwork is to encourage the attitude that "everyone has a customer." That is, even when employees are not directly responsible for or do not directly interact with the final customer, they need to know whom they serve directly and how the role they play in the total service picture is essential to the final delivery of quality service. If each employee can see how he or she is somehow integral in

Exhibit 11.2 Potential Benefits and Costs of Empowerment

BENEFITS

- *Quicker responses to customer needs during service delivery.* Employees who are allowed to make decisions on behalf of the customer can make decisions more quickly, bypassing what in the past might have meant a long chain of command or at least a discussion with an immediate supervisor.

- *Quicker responses to dissatisfied customers during service recovery.* When failures occur in the delivery system, customers hope for an immediate recovery effort on the part of the organization. Empowered employees can recover on the spot, and a dissatisfied customer can be turned into a satisfied, even loyal one.

- *Employees feel better about their jobs and themselves.* Giving employees control and authority to make decisions makes them feel responsible and gives them ownership of the customer's satisfaction. Decades of job design research suggest that, when employees have a sense of control and of doing meaningful work, they are more satisfied. The results are lower turnover and less absenteeism.

- *Employees will interact with customers with more warmth and enthusiasm.* Employees feel better about themselves and their work, and these attitudes will spill over into their feelings about customers and will be reflected in their interactions.

- *Empowered employees are a great source of service ideas.* When employees are empowered, they feel responsible for the service outcome and they will be excellent sources of ideas about new services or how to improve current offerings.

- *Great word-of-mouth advertising from customers.* Empowered employees do special and unique things that customers will remember and tell their friends, family, and associates about.

COSTS

- *A potentially greater dollar investment in selection and training.* To find employees who will work well in an empowered environment requires creative, potentially more costly selection procedures. Training will also be more expensive in general because employees need more knowledge about the company, its products, and how to work in flexible ways with customers.

- *Higher labor costs.* The organization may not be able to use as many part-time or seasonal employees, and it may need to pay more for asking employees to assume responsibility.

- *Potentially slower or inconsistent service delivery.* If empowered employees spend more time with all, or even some, customers, then service overall may take longer and may annoy customers who are waiting. Empowerment also means that customers will get what they need or request. When decisions regarding customer satisfaction are left to the discretion of employees, there may be inconsistency in the level of service delivered.

- *May violate customers' perceptions of fair play.* Customers may perceive that sticking to procedures with every customer is fair. Thus, if they see that customers are receiving different levels of service or that employees are cutting special deals with some customers, they may believe that the organization is not fair.

- *Employees may "give away the store" or make bad decisions.* Many people fear that empowered employees will make costly decisions that the organization cannot afford. Although this situation can happen, good training and appropriate guidelines will help.

Source: Adapted from "The Empowerment of Service Workers: What, Why, How, and When," by D. E. Bowen and E. E. Lawler, Sloan *Management Review* 33 (Spring 1992), pp. 31–39.

---

delivering quality to the final customer and if each employee knows whom to support to make service quality a reality, teamwork will be enhanced. Service blueprints, described in Chapter 8, can serve as useful tools to illustrate for employees their integral roles in delivering service quality to the ultimate customer.

Team goals and rewards also promote teamwork. Harrah's Entertainment is one company that provides incentives and compensation focused on teamwork. The casino hotel company's incentive program is weighted toward team results and a relatively small percentage of compensation (often less than 40 percent) is based on individual goals. Everyone in the organization, from meeting planners to blackjack dealers, are rewarded based on customer service scores. When a firm rewards teams of individuals rather than basing all rewards on individual achievements and performance, team efforts and team spirit are encouraged.

Provide Needed Support Systems

To be efficient and effective in their jobs, service workers require internal support systems that are aligned with their need to be customer focused. This point cannot be overemphasized. In fact, without customer-focused internal support and customer-oriented systems, it is nearly impossible for employees to deliver quality service, no matter how much they want to. For example, a bank teller who is rewarded for customer satisfaction as well as for accuracy in bank transactions needs easy access to up-to-date customer records, a well-staffed branch (so that he or she is not constantly facing v long line of impatient customers), and supportive customer-oriented supervisors and back-office staff. In examining customer service outcomes in Australian call centers, researchers found that internal support from supervisors, teammates, and other departments as well as evaluations of technology used on the job were all strongly related to employee satisfaction and ability to serve customers.[56] The following sections suggest strategies for ensuring customer-oriented internal support.

Measure Internal Service Quality

One way to encourage supportive internal service relationships is to measure and reward internal service. By first acknowledging that everyone in the organization has a customer and then measuring customer perceptions of internal service quality, an organization can begin to develop a strong internal quality culture.[57] In its quest to provide the best possible service to patients, the Mayo Clinic formally measures internal service quality between departments annually. An internal customer service audit is one tool that can be used to implement a culture of internal service quality. Through the audit, internal organizations identify their customers, determine their needs, measure how well they are doing, and make improvements. The process parallels market research practices used for external customers.

One risk of measuring and focusing on internal service quality and internal customers is that employees can sometimes get so wrapped up in meeting the needs of internal customers that they forget they are in business to serve the ultimate, external customers.[58] In measuring internal service quality, therefore, it is important to constantly draw the linkages between what is being delivered internally and how it supports the delivery of the final service to customers. Service blueprinting, introduced in Chapter 8, can help illustrate these critical linkages.

Provide Supportive Technology and Equipment

When employees do not have the right equipment or their equipment fails them, they can be easily frustrated in their desire to deliver quality service. To do their jobs effectively and efficiently, service employees need the right equipment and technology. Our Technology Spotlight earlier in this chapter highlights the role of technology in providing support for employees.

Having the right technology and equipment can extend into strategies regarding workplace and workstation design. For example, Zappos provides its customer service representatives with computer systems that provide comprehensive information concerning product inventory in their warehouses—allowing them to provide customers with up-to-date information and options. Hallways in the company's facilities are covered with murals and cartoons, rooms are filled with props, and workspaces are filled with personalized clutter—all designed to create an environment where employees feel like part of a team and are comfortable serving customers. In fact, the atmosphere that Zappos has created in the work environment has become so well known that tours through the cubicles at company headquarters are given almost daily to outsiders.

Develop Service-Oriented Internal Processes

To best support service personnel in their delivery of quality service on the front line, an organization's internal processes should be designed with customer value and customer satisfaction in mind. In other words, internal procedures must support quality service performance. In many companies, internal processes are driven by bureaucratic rules, tradition, cost efficiencies, or the needs of employees. Providing service- and customer-oriented internal processes can therefore imply a need for total redesign of systems. This kind of redesign of systems and processes is known as "process reengineering." Although developing service-oriented internal processes through reengineering sounds sensible, it is probably one of the most difficult strategies to implement, especially in organizations steeped in tradition.

Retain the Best People

An organization that hires the right people, trains and develops them to deliver service quality, and provides the needed support must also work to retain them. Employee turnover, especially when the best service employees are the ones leaving, can be very detrimental to customer satisfaction, employee morale, and overall service quality. And, just as they do with customers, some firms spend a lot of time attracting employees but then tend to take them for granted (or even worse), causing these good employees to search for job alternatives. Although all the strategies depicted earlier in Figure 11.4 will support the retention of the best employees, here we will focus on some strategies that are particularly aimed at this goal.

Include Employees in the Company's Vision

For employees to remain motivated and interested in sticking with the organization and supporting its goals, they need to share an understanding of the organization's vision. People who deliver service day in and day out need to understand how their work fits into the big picture of the organization and its goals. They will be motivated to some extent by their paychecks and other benefits, but the best employees will be attracted away to other opportunities if they are not committed to the vision of the organization. And they cannot be committed to the vision if that vision is kept secret from them. What this strategy means in practice is that the vision is communicated to employees frequently and that it is communicated by top managers, often by the CEO.[59] Respected CEOs such as Howard Schulz of Starbucks, Fred Smith of FedEx, Jeff Bezos of Amazon, and Tony Hsieh of Zappos are known for communicating their visions clearly and often to employees.

At Sherwin-Williams, management has communicated throughout the organization that its goal is to deliver "Trademark Service." To include all of its customer-contact employees in the company's vision of providing such service, for the past 10 years the company has developed an extensive internal campaign to "treat every customer like a GUEST." The "GUEST" acronym translates as G—Greet every customer, U—Use the customer's name, E—Evaluate and fulfill needs, S—Smile with face and voice, and T—Thank and invite them back. These actions are expected of all those in the organization who interact with customers.[60] This approach sends a strong message to employees, reinforcing the company vision. When the vision and direction are clear and motivating, employees are more likely to remain with the company through the inevitable rough spots along the path to the vision.

Treat Employees as Customers

If employees feel valued and their needs are taken care of, they are more likely to stay with the organization. For example, Tom Siebel, founder of Siebel Systems (now part of Oracle), saw the CEO's primary job as cultivating a corporate culture that benefits all employees and customers. "If you build a company and a product or service that delivers high levels of customer satisfaction, and if you spend responsibly and manage your human capital assets well, the other external manifestations of success, like market valuation and revenue growth, will follow."[61]

Many companies have adopted the idea that employees are also customers of the organization and that basic marketing strategies can be directed at them.[62] The products that the organization has to offer its employees are a job (with assorted benefits) and quality of work life. To determine whether the job and work-life needs of employees are being met, organizations conduct periodic internal marketing research to assess employee satisfaction and needs. For example, as illustrated in Exhibit 11.1, Google has launched a number of initiatives that could be considered treating employees as customers. In addition to the benefits listed in the exhibit, other benefits include free haircuts, swim-in-place swimming pools, video games, dry cleaning, health care, and massages—all provided on-campus at the Googleplex.[63] What Google and many other companies have found is that, to ensure employee satisfaction, productivity, and retention, companies must get involved in the private lives and family support of their workers. Employees appreciate such efforts; Google is regularly at the top of *Fortune*'s list of "Top 100 Companies to Work For"!

Measure and Reward Strong Service Performers

If a company wants the strongest service performers to stay with the organization, it must reward and promote them. This strategy may seem obvious, but often the reward systems in organizations are not set up to reward service excellence. Reward systems may value productivity, sales, or some other dimension that can work *against* providing good service. Even those service workers who are intrinsically motivated to deliver high-quality service will become discouraged at some point and start looking elsewhere if their efforts in providing good service are not recognized and rewarded.

Reward systems need to be linked to the organization's vision and to outcomes that are truly important. For instance, if customer satisfaction and retention are viewed as critical outcomes, service behaviors that increase those outcomes need to be recognized and rewarded. In years past, a portion of employee compensation at Harrah's Casinos and Hotels was linked to customer satisfaction scores as a "Performance Payout," so employees would have an investment in achieving excellent service levels. Employees also had a vested interest in the performance of the entire team in serving customers exceptionally well. Beyond monetary incentives, outstanding employees were recognized with special Chairman Awards and their names published in Harrah's annual report. Management was also awarded incentives based on the positive improvement in customer service, as 25 percent of a manager's annual bonus was tied to achieving customer service goals.[64] Similarly, Enterprise Rent-a-Car branch managers wishing to move up in the organization can do so only if the customer satisfaction scores from pyramid" in its employee training materials. A statement by Michel Bon, former CEO of France Telecom, succinctly summarizes the philosophy behind such an approach:

> If you sincerely believe that "the customer is king," the second most important person in this kingdom must be the one who has a direct interaction on a daily basis with the one who is king.[68]

By flipping the service marketing triangle, the two groups that are the most important people to the organization—customers and those who interact with customers—are placed in a position of prominence.

Summary

Because many services are delivered by people in real time, closing the service performance gap is heavily dependent on human resource strategies. The successful execution of such strategies begins with the development and nurturing of a true service culture throughout the organization.

Often, service employees *are* the service, and they represent the organization in customers' eyes. They affect service quality perceptions to a large degree through their influence on the five dimensions of service quality: reliability, responsiveness, empathy, assurance, and tangibles. It is essential to match what the customer wants and needs with service employees' abilities to deliver.

In this chapter we focused on service employees to provide you with an understanding of the critical nature of their roles and appreciation of the inherent stresses and conflicts they face. You learned that frontline service jobs demand significant investments of emotional labor and that employees confront a variety of on-the-job conflicts.

Grounded in this understanding of the importance of service employees and the nature of their roles in the organization, you learned strategies for integrating appropriate human resource practices into service firms. The strategies are aimed at allowing employees to effectively satisfy customers as well as be efficient and productive in their jobs. The strategies are organized around four major human resource goals in service organizations: hire the right people, develop people to deliver service quality, provide needed support systems, and retain the best people. A company that works toward implementing these strategies is well on its way to delivering service quality through its people, thereby diminishing gap 3—the service performance gap.

Discussion Questions

1. Define *service culture*. Why is service culture so important? Can a manufacturing firm have a service culture? Why or why not?

2. Why are service employees critical to the success of any service organization? Why do we include an entire chapter on service employees in a marketing course?

3. What is *emotional labor*? How is it different from physical or mental labor?

4. Reflect on your own role as a frontline service provider, whether in a current job or in any full- or part-time service job you have had in the past. Did you experience the kinds of conflicts described in the boundary-spanning roles section of the chapter? Be prepared with some concrete examples for class discussion.

5. Select a service provider (your dentist, doctor, lawyer, hair stylist) with whom you are familiar, and discuss ways this person could positively influence the five dimensions of service quality in the context of delivering his or her services. Do the same for yourself (if you are currently a service provider).

6. Describe the four basic human resource strategy themes and why each plays an important role in building a customer-oriented organization.
7. What is the difference between technical and interactive service skills? Provide examples (preferably from your own work context or from another context with which you are familiar). Why do service employees need training in both?
8. Is empowerment always the best approach for effective service delivery? Why is employee empowerment so controversial?

Exercises

1. Visit the websites of companies with known world-class service cultures (such as Ritz-Carlton, FedEx, Starbucks, or Zappos). How does the information conveyed on the website reinforce the company's service culture?
2. Review the section of the chapter on boundary-spanning roles. Interview at least two frontline service personnel regarding the stresses they experience in their jobs. How do the examples they provide relate to the sources of conflict and trade-offs described in the text?
3. Assume that you are the manager of a crew of frontline customer-service employees in a credit card company. Assume that these employees work over the phone and that they deal primarily with customer requests, questions, and complaints. In this specific context,
   a. Define what is meant by *boundary-spanning roles,* and discuss the basic purposes or functions of participants in these roles.
   b. Discuss two of the potential conflicts that your employees may face on the basis of their roles as boundary spanners.
   c. Discuss how you, as their supervisor, might deal with these conflicts based on what you have learned.
4. Choose one or more of the human resource strategy themes (hire the right people, develop people to deliver service quality, provide needed support systems, retain the best people). Interview a manager in a service organization of your choice regarding his or her current practices within the theme you have chosen. Describe the current practices, and recommend any appropriate changes for improving them.

Notes

1. L. L. Berry, *Discovering the Soul of Service* (New York: The Free Press, 1999).
2. Interview with Singapore Airlines senior vice president of marketing services, included in "How May I Help You?" *Fast Company* (March 2000), pp. 93–126.
3. G. Ciotti, "10 Stories of Unforgettable Customer Service," www.helpscout.net/10 -customer-service-stories/, accessed July 19, 2016; P. Shankman, "The Greatest Customer Service Story Ever Told, Starring Morton's Steakhouse," http:// shankman.com/the-best-customer-service-story-ever-told-starring-mortons -steakhouse/, accessed July 19, 2016.
4. Chris Shelley, Panera Bread manager, Personal Interview, December 30, 2010.
5. Berry, *Discovering the Soul of Service.*
6. S. M. Davis, *Managing Corporate Culture* (Cambridge, MA: Ballinger, 1985).
7. C. Grönroos, *Service Management and Marketing: Customer Management in Service Competition,* 3rd ed. (West Sussex, UK: John Wiley and Sons, 2007), p. 418.

8. See K. N. Kennedy, F. G. Lassk, and J. R. Goolsby, "Customer Mind-Set of Employees throughout the Organization," *Journal of the Academy of Marketing Science* 30 (Spring 2002), pp. 159–171.

9. R. Hallowell, D. Bowen, and C. Knoop, "Four Seasons Goes to Paris," *Academy of Management Executive* 16 (2002), pp. 7–24; J. L. Heskett, L. A. Schlesinger, and E. W. Sasser Jr., *The Service Profit Chain* (New York: The Free Press, 1997); B. Schneider and D. E. Bowen, *Winning the Service Game* (Boston: Harvard Business School Press, 1995); and D. E. Bowen and S. D. Pugh, "Linking Human Resource Management Practices and Customer Outcomes" in *The Routledge Companion to Strategic Human Resource Management,* ed. J. Storey, P. Wright, and D. Ulrich (Abingdon, Oxon: Routledge 2008), pp. 509–518; B. Schneider and D. E. Bowen, "Winning the Service Game; Revisiting the Rules by Which People Co-Create Value," in *Handbook of Service Science,* ed. P. P. Maglio, C. A. Kieliszewski, and J. C. Spohrer (New York: Springer, 2010), pp. 31–59.

10. Berry, *Discovering the Soul of Service*, p. 40.

11. Hallowell, Bowen, and Knoop, "Four Seasons Goes to Paris."

12. For an excellent discussion of the complexities involved in creating and sustaining a service culture, see Schneider and Bowen, *Winning the Service Game,* chap. 9. See also Michael D. Hartline, James G. Maxham III, and Daryl O. McKee, "Corridors of Influence in the Dissemination of Customer-Oriented Strategy to Customer-Contact Service Employees," *Journal of Marketing* 64 (April 2000), pp. 35–50.

13. This discussion is based on Hallowell, Bowen, and Knoop, "Four Seasons Goes to Paris."

14. This quote is most frequently attributed to J. Carlzon, former chief executive officer of Scandinavian Airline Systems.

15. P. Andruss, "Your Employees Are Your Brand," *Marketing News,* October 30, 2010, pp. 22–23.

16. J. Barlow and P. Stewart, *Branded Customer Service* (San Francisco: Barett-Koehler, 2004). For an discussion of branded service encounters, see N. J. Sirianni, M. J. Bitner, S. W. Brown, and N. Mandel, "Branded Service Encounters: Strategically Aligning Employee Behavior with the Brand Positioning," *Journal of Marketing* 77 (November 2013), pp. 108–123.

17. The conceptualization of the service triangle presented in Figure 11.1 and the related text discussion are based on M. J. Bitner, "Building Service Relationships: It's All about Promises," *Journal of the Academy of Marketing Science* 23 (Fall 1995), pp. 246–251; P. T. Kotler and K. L. Keller, *Marketing Management,* 15th ed. (Upper Saddle River, NJ: Pearson Prentice Hall, 2016); and Grönroos, *Service Management and Marketing.*

18. See, L. A. Schlesinger and J. L. Heskett, "The Service-Driven Service Company," *Harvard Business Review* 69 (September–October 1991), pp. 71–81; and B. Schneider, M. Ehrhart, D. Mayer, J. Saltz, and K. Niles-Jolley, "Understanding Organization-Customer Links in Service Settings," *Academy of Management Journal* 48 (December 2005), pp. 1017–1032; A. Zablah, B. D. Carlson, D. T. Donavan, J. G. Maxham, and T. J. Brown, "A Cross-Lagged Test of the Association Between Customer Satisfaction and Employee Job Satisfaction in a Relational Context," *Journal of Applied Psychology* 101 (May 2016), pp. 743–755.

19. B. Schneider and D. E. Bowen, "The Service Organization: Human Resources Management Is Crucial," *Organizational Dynamics* 21 (Spring 1993), pp. 39–52.

20. D. E. Bowen, S. W. Gilliland, and R. Folger, "How Being Fair with Employees Spills Over to Customers," *Organizational Dynamics* 27 (Winter 1999), pp. 7–23; S. Masterson, "The Trickle-Down Model of Organizational Justice: Relating Employees' and Customers' Perceptions of and Reactions to Fairness," *Journal of Applied Psychology* 86 (August 2001), pp. 594–604; J. G. Maxham III and R. G. Netemeyer, "Firms Reap What They Sow: The Effects of Shared Values and Perceived Organizational Justice on Customers' Evaluations of Complaint Handling," *Journal of Marketing* 67 (January 2003), pp. 46–62.

21. See J. L. Heskett, T. O. Jones, G. W. Loveman, W. E. Sasser Jr., and L. A. Schlesinger, "Putting the Service–Profit Chain to Work," *Harvard Business Review* 72 (March–April 1994), pp. 164–174; G. W. Loveman, "Employee Satisfaction, Customer Loyalty, and Financial Performance," *Journal of Service Research* 1 (August 1998), pp. 18–31; A. Rucci, S. P. Kirn, and R. T. Quinn, "The Employee–Customer Profit Chain at Sears," *Harvard Business Review* 76 (January–February 1998), pp. 82–97; R. Hallowell and L. L. Schlesinger, "The Service–Profit Chain," in *The Handbook for Services Marketing and Management,* ed. T. A. Swartz and D. Iacobucci (Thousand Oaks, CA: Sage, 2000), pp. 203–222; and J. Hogreve, A. Iseke, K. Derfuss, and T. Eller, "The Service–Profit Chain: A Meta-Analytic Test of a Comprehensive Theoretical Framework," *Journal of Marketing* (forthcoming 2017).

22. For additional research on the service-profit chain, see J. L. Heskett, W. E. Sasser Jr., and L. A. Schlesinger, *The Value Profit Chain: Treat Employees Like Customers and Customers Like Employees* (New York: The Free Press, 2003); G. A. Geladel and S. Young, "Test of a Service Profit Chain Model in the Retail Banking Sector," *Journal of Occupational and Organizational Psychology* 78 (March 2005), pp. 1–22; R. D. Anderson, R. D. Mackoy, V. B. Thompson, and G. Harrell, "A Bayesian Network Estimation of the Service-Profit Chain for Transport Service Satisfaction," *Decision Sciences* 35 (Fall 2004), pp. 665–689; W. A. Kamakura, V. Mittal, F. de Rosa, and J. A. Mazzon, "Assessing the Service-Profit Chain," *Marketing Science* 21 (Summer 2002), pp. 294–317; Zablah, Carlson, Donavan, Maxham, and Brown. "A Cross-Lagged Test of the Association between Customer Satisfaction and Employee Job Satisfaction in a Relational Context"; and Schneider, Ehrhart, Mayer, Saltz, and Niles-Jolley, "Understanding Organization-Customer Links in Service Firms."

23. M. K. Brady and J. J. Cronin Jr., "Customer Orientation: Effects on Customer Service Perceptions and Outcome Behaviors," *Journal of Service Research* 3 (February 2001), pp. 241–251.

24. L. A. Bettencourt and K. Gwinner, "Customization of the Service Experience: The Role of the Frontline Employee," *International Journal of Service Industry Management* 7 (1996), pp. 3–20.

25. For research on the influence of frontline employee behaviors on customers, see D. D. Gremler and K. P. Gwinner, "Customer–Employee Rapport in Service Relationships," *Journal of Service Research* 3 (August 2000), pp. 82–104; and T. J. Brown, J. C. Mowen, D. T. Donavan, and J. W. Licata, "The Customer Orientation of Service Workers: Personality Trait Effects of Self and Supervisor Performance Ratings," *Journal of Marketing Research* 39 (February 2002), pp. 110–119; C. Delcourt, D. Gremler, A. C. R. van Riel, and M. J. H. van Birgelen, "Employee Emotional Competence: Construct Conceptualization and Validation of a Customer-Based Measure," *Journal of Service Research* 19 (February 2016), pp. 73–87.

55. Mayo Clinic website, www.mayo.edu/pmts/mc4200-mc4299/mc4270.pdf, accessed July 21, 2016.

56. A. Sergeant and S. Frenkel, "When Do Customer-Contact Employees Satisfy Customers?" *Journal of Service Research* 3 (August 2000), pp. 18–34.

57. J. Reynoso and B. Moores, "Operationalising the Quality on Internal Support Operations in Service Organisations," in *Advances in Services Marketing and Management,* vol. 6, ed. T. A. Swartz, D. E. Bowen, and S. W. Brown (Greenwich, CT: JAI Press, 1997), pp. 147–170.

58. Schneider and Bowen, *Winning the Service Game,* pp. 230–234.

59. O. Gadiesh and J. L. Gilbert, "Transforming Corner-Office Strategy into Frontline Action," *Harvard Business Review* 79 (May 2001), pp. 73–79.

60. Telephone Interview with Guy Papa, Training Manager, The Sherwin-Williams Company, January 6, 2011.

61. B. Fryer, "High Tech the Old Fashioned Way," *Harvard Business Review* 79 (March 2001), pp. 119–125.

62. L. L. Berry, "The Employee as Customer," *Journal of Retail Banking* 3 (March 1981), pp. 33–40; R. L. Cardy, "Employees as Customers?" *Marketing Management* 10 (2001), pp. 12–13; M. R. Bowers and C. L. Martin, "Trading Places Redux: Employees as Customers, Customers as Employees," *Journal of Services Marketing* 21 (2007), pp. 88–98.

63. computer.howstuffworks.com/googleplex.com, accessed July 21, 2016.

64. J. Mackey, "Putting the Service Profit Chain to Work: How to Earn Your Customer's Loyalty," http://www.franchising.com/articles/how_to_earn_your_customers_loyalty.html, accessed July 21, 2016.

65. N. Bendapudi and R. P. Leone, "Managing Business-to-Business Customer Relationships Following Key Contact Employee Turnover in a Vendor Firm," *Journal of Marketing* 66 (April 2002), pp. 83–101; S. Wang and L. Davis, "Stemming the Tide: Dealing with the Imbalance of Customer Relationship Quality with the Key Contact Employee versus with the Firm," *Journal of Services Marketing* 22 (2008), pp. 533–549.

66. Bendapudi and Leone, "Managing Business-to-Business Customer Relationships"; T. Jones, S. F. Taylor, and H. S. Bansal, "Commitment to a Friend, a Service Provider, and a Service Company—Are They Distinctions Worth Making?" *Journal of the Academy of Marketing Science* 36 (Winter 2008), pp. 473–487.

67. J. R. Katzenbach and J. A. Santamaria, "Firing Up the Front Line," *Harvard Business Review* 77 (May–June 1999), pp. 107–117.

68. Quoted in D. Stauffer, "The Art of Delivering Great Customer Service," *Harvard Management Update* 4 (September 1999), pp. 1–3.

Chapter **Twelve**

Customers' Roles in Service

This chapter's objectives are to

1. Illustrate the importance of customers in successful service delivery, creation, and cocreation of service experiences.
2. Discuss the variety of roles that service customers play: productive resources for the organization, contributors to and cocreators of value, and competitors.
3. Explain strategies for involving service customers effectively to increase satisfaction, quality, value, and productivity.

Customers as Creators and Cocreators of Service Value[1]

In today's economy, customers play increasingly active roles in service value creation and cocreation—more than they ever have before. They create service value for themselves through active involvement and customization and they enjoy value-in-use of the service over time through their own continued engagement and actions. Value-in-use refers to the value that customers get as they use products and services for various purposes in their own lives, most often independent of the provider. Rather than "delivering value," companies are often simply providing platforms for customers to create value for themselves. Customers also cocreate value together with service providers through direct interactions online, over the phone, or in person. Through these types of interactions, customers and service providers bring their resources together to cocreate unique value.

These expanded customer roles are probably most apparent in the world of Internet-based services and apps, where customers play active roles in producing service value for themselves with little or no personal interaction with the service provider. The service provider provides the platform and facilitates the customer's ability to create value for him or herself, sometimes including (but not always) direct interactions with the company as well. Services like Facebook, Uber, Airbnb, MyFitnessPal, and Amazon are just a few names of successful, Internet-reliant services where customers create value for themselves and also cocreate value with the provider and other customers. Value-in-use comes about for customers as they enjoy and continue to create and cocreate different forms of value—for example: social and communication value (e.g., Facebook), product usage value from the things they purchase (e.g., Amazon), greater fitness and health (MyFitnessPal), convenient transportation to where they need to be (Uber), and reasonably priced accommodations in places they desire to travel (Airbnb). Customers create their own unique value-in-use for each of these services, drawing on their own resources and those of the company.

Global retailer IKEA is a company that has built its strategy around expanded customer roles since the company opened its doors in the 1950s. Headquartered in Sweden, IKEA is today the world's largest home furnishings retailer, operating in 28 countries with over 300 physical stores and a major online presence including products and services. Known for its "do-it-yourself" or "DIY" business model, IKEA engages customers in tasks that are not typical for a furniture retailer. At IKEA, customers create their own value by finding and picking the products they want from IKEA's warehouse shelves, loading them and transporting them to their own homes, assembling the furniture, and then using these purchases to support their lifestyles. The customer is a clear creator of value in this context and value-in-use comes when the furniture is assembled and used in the customer's personal space. IKEA also provides extensive online catalogs, tools for creating personalized designs, and in-store assistance from designers if desired. Thus, IKEA is a cocreator of value through the resources it makes available to customers and the interactions it has with them. (For more on IKEA, see the Global Features in this chapter and in Chapter 2).

Terms like collaboration, coproduction, cocreation, and value-in-use are becoming increasingly common across industries in strategic discussions and in new business models. While definitions of these terms are still evolving, it is clear that innovative services have emerged as companies begin to think about their customers as "value creators" and "value cocreators" rather than "value recipients." IKEA understands this and has built its highly successful business model on this kind of thinking. Companies are also recognizing that the customer is engaged in a larger ecosystem of services, products, and people that revolve around the products and services they purchase from any one company. In the IKEA example, the ecosystem for an individual customer might include services related to finding a home or apartment, professional design services, home products from other providers, services from other home trades (e.g., painting, tile work, or electrical), and family and friends who are involved in home furnishing decisions and use. As companies expand their view of what it means to serve the customer and recognize the varied and essential roles that customers play in value creation, opportunities for innovation and new business models abound. As they look outside their immediate sphere of influence into the customer's broader ecosystem, even more opportunities reveal themselves.

In this chapter we examine the unique and varied roles played by customers in creating and cocreating service value. In some cases, service customers are present in the "factory" (the place the service is produced and/or consumed), interacting with employees and other customers. For example, in a classroom or training situation, students (the customers) are sitting in the factory (the classroom), interacting with the instructor and other students as they cocreate educational services. Because they are present during service production, customers can contribute to or detract from the successful cocreation and to their own satisfaction. In contrast, in a manufacturing context, rarely does the production facility contend with customer presence on the factory floor, nor does it rely on the customer's immediate, real-time input to manufacture the product. As our opening vignette illustrates, service customers can actually create and cocreate services themselves and to some extent are responsible for their own satisfaction.

Because customers are participants in service production and value creation, they can contribute to the widening of gap 3, the service performance gap. That is, customers themselves can influence whether the service meets customer-defined specifications. Sometimes customers contribute to gap 3 because they lack understanding of their roles and exactly what they can or should do in a given situation, particularly if the customer is confronting a service concept for the first time. In other situations customers may understand their roles but be unwilling or unable to perform. In a health club context, members may understand that to get into good physical shape they must follow the workout guidelines set up by the trainers. If work schedule, illness, or lack of motivation keeps members from living up to their part of the guidelines, the service will not be successful because of customer inaction. In a different service situation, customers may choose not to perform the roles defined for them because they are not rewarded in any way for contributing their effort. For example, many grocery store customers choose not to use the automated self-checkout because they see no benefit in terms of speed or convenience. When service customers are enticed through price reductions, greater convenience, or some other tangible benefit, they are more likely to perform their roles willingly.

Finally, the service performance gap may be widened not through actions or inactions on the part of the customer but because of what *other* customers do. Other customers who are in the service factory either receiving the service simultaneously (passengers on an airplane flight or students in a classroom) or waiting their turn to receive the service sequentially (bank customers waiting in line or Disneyland customers waiting for one of the rides) can influence whether the service is delivered effectively and efficiently.

THE IMPORTANCE OF CUSTOMERS IN SERVICE COCREATION

Customer participation at some level is inevitable in all service situations. Services are actions or performances, often produced and consumed simultaneously. In many situations employees, customers, and even others in the service environment interact to produce the ultimate service outcome. Because they participate, customers are indispensable to the production process of service organizations, and in many situations they can control or contribute significantly to their own dis/satisfaction.[2] This view of participatory customers is consistent with new logics in marketing that promote the idea that customers are always creators and cocreators of value.[3] Our Strategy Insight illustrates this broadened view and how it can lead to innovative service strategies and offerings. Recognition of the role of customers is also reflected in the definition of the *people* element of the service marketing mix given in Chapter 1: *all human actors who play a part in service delivery and thus influence the buyer's perceptions; namely, the firm's personnel, the customer, and other customers in the service environment.* Chapter 11 examined the role of the firm's employees in delivering service quality. In this chapter we focus on the customer who is receiving or cocreating the service and on fellow customers in the service environment.

Customers Themselves

Because the customer participates in the delivery process, he or she can contribute to narrowing or widening gap 3 through behaviors that are appropriate or inappropriate, effective or ineffective, productive or unproductive. The level of customer participation—low, medium, or high—varies across services, as shown in Table 12.1. In some cases, all that is required is the customer's physical presence (*low level of*

Strategy Insight Customer Cocreation of Value: An Important Strategy Frontier

Consultants, researchers, and strategists are urging companies to think about their customers in new ways. Instead of viewing customers as passive targets and recipients of predesigned goods and services, they encourage a view of customers as *active* cocreators of value. This perspective goes beyond focusing on customer involvement in generating ideas for new products, and it is more than customer participation in service delivery. Instead, this view suggests that the value customers receive is a *cocreated experience* they build for themselves through interactions with service providers and other customers, as well as by choosing and combining elements of the company's offerings to create their own "total experience." In creating value for themselves within a particular problem solution domain, customers often combine, reconfigure, and join services from a network of providers to get the total value they are seeking. For example, to solve the problem of getting a college degree, students (customers of higher education) combine services from universities, financial loan providers, study support groups, and housing entities, among others.

The following examples from very different contexts help make the cocreation idea more concrete and the strategic possibilities apparent. Our chapter opener on IKEA is another example of a company that has strategically engaged with customers to create and cocreate value.

JOHN DEERE

John Deere is a 175-year-old global firm that serves the knowledge- and capital-intensive farming industry with sophisticated equipment, services, information, and online support for its farm manager customers. The company is geared toward making the farmer's life easier and more productive. The "experience environment"

John Deere services connect equipment, owners, operators, and agricultural consultants.

for its innovations is broadly defined to include anything that will help achieve the farmer's professional objectives. For example, new technologies available through Deere, branded and trademarked as "FarmSight," can help the farmer monitor equipment remotely to assess the location of the equipment and engine condition, maximize machine operations, and provide agricultural decision support. These remote monitoring and support capabilities are uniquely set up for each farmer and require the farmer's active involvement with the system to fully take advantage of its value. Another service that Deere offers is sensor technologies on its equipment that can precisely map soil conditions and thereby prescribe the application of seeds and fertilizers based on the soil conditions in an area. Depending on the farmer's land conditions and the specific crops he grows, the information provided by the sensors can be customized to the situation and used to better control that farmer's crop yields. Deere also provides educational opportunities for farmers through John Deere

participation), with the employees of the firm doing all the service production work, as in the example of a symphony concert. Symphony-goers must be present to receive the entertainment service, but little else is required once they are seated. In other situations, consumer inputs are required to aid the service organization in creating the service (*moderate level of participation*). Inputs can include *information, effort,* or *physical possessions.* For example, all three of these are required for a certified public accountant (CPA) to prepare a client's tax return effectively: information in the form of tax history, marital status, and number of dependents; effort in putting the information together in a useful fashion; and physical possessions such as receipts and past tax returns. In some situations, customers are truly cocreators of the service (*high level of*

University courses and online learning, as well as books and publications. It is up to each farmer to determine how much to participate in the various services, how to use the information provided, and whether to take advantage of other educational opportunities. Deere's strategy and suite of offerings are customer-centric, with the resulting experience being uniquely cocreated with each farmer. Deere has shifted its strategic innovation paradigm to one where value is cocreated through services, solutions, and experiences rather than exclusively through product or technology innovation.

SHUTTERFLY, INC

Shutterfly, Inc. began as a company that helped people print photos from their digital cameras. Today it is an innovative, online, and cloud-based company whose vision is "to make the world a better place by helping people share life's joy" and whose mission is "to deepen your personal connections with the people who matter most with unique, personalized photo products." The company is a leader in the digital world of creative memory sharing through photos, and it has grown over the years to include a suite of related brands: Shutterfly, Tiny Prints, Wedding Paper Divas, BorrowLenses, MyPublisher, and Groovebook. Through its family of brands, Shutterfly has expanded its products and services to include photo and video storage, award-winning photo books, gifts, home decor, premium cards, invitations, stationery, and more. Its focus is to stay on the forefront of innovation, introducing new technology and expanding product and service offerings that make it easier for customers to share life's joys.

For example, customers can create lasting memories by integrating their own photos into high-quality photo books, customized stationery, event announcements, and photo gifts like jewelry, ceramic tiles, and calendars, just to name a few. Personalized birth and wedding announcements, along with related stationery items, can also be designed by customers through Shutterfly. Through customized photo books, customers can become the authors of their own stories, creating permanent ways to save and express their memories of special events or trips.

While Shutterfly can offer and provide access to a wide repertoire of memory-sharing products and services, customers must configure them and combine them with their own photos and ideas to create unique memories and ways of sharing for themselves. While there are standardized products that Shutterfly offers in a traditional sense (e.g., photo calendars, coffee mugs with photos, photo printing services), each customer will put these traditional products together with innovative services (e.g., photo books, trip logs, personal websites, and photo sharing and storage platforms) to create distinctive value for themselves. Strategically, Shutterfly has moved from a "photo printing" service to a resource that includes a suite of products, services, and solutions to share memories and joy. Customers create value for themselves and also cocreate value with Shutterfly. The value to the customer is recognized through the process of creating and also through "value-in-use" as they share their memories in various ways with others.

Sources: C. Gronroos and P. Voima, "Critical Service Logic: Making Sense of Value Creation and Co-Creation," *Journal of the Academy of Marketing Science* 41 (March 2013), pp. 133–150. S. L. Vargo and R. F. Lusch, "Evolving to a New Dominant Logic for Marketing," *Journal of Marketing* 68 (January 2004), pp. 1–17; C. K. Prahalad and V. Ramaswamy, *The Future of Competition: Co-Creating Unique Value with Customers* (Boston, MA: Harvard Business School Press, 2004); M. Sawhney, S. Balasubramanian, and V. V. Krishnan, "Creating Growth with Services," *Sloan Management Review* 45 (Winter 2004), pp. 34–43; www.johndeere.com, accessed August 2016; www.shutterfly.com, accessed August 2016.

participation). For these services, customers have important participation roles that affect the nature of the service outcome. For example, in a weight reduction program, the customer, working with a counselor, may actively cocreate a personalized nutritional and exercise program. Then, it is largely up to the customer to carry out the plan and/or enhance it, resulting in value that is unique to that person. Similarly, in a complex or long-term business-to-business consulting engagement, the client can be involved in activities such as identification of issues, shared problem solving, ongoing communication, provision of equipment and work space, and implementation of solutions.[4] Facilitating this type of positive customer participation can help ensure a successful outcome, as described in Exhibit 12.1. Table 12.1 provides several examples

TABLE 12.1 Levels, Characteristics, and Examples of Customer Participation across Different Services

Source: Adapted from A. R. Hubbert, "Customer Co-Creation of Service Outcomes: Effects of Locus of Causality Attributions," Doctoral dissertation, Arizona State University, Tempe, AZ, 1995.

Low: Customer Presence Required during Service Production	Moderate: Customer Inputs Required for Service Creation	High: Customer Cocreates the Service
Service is standardized.	Client inputs (information, materials) help customize a standard service.	Active client participation guides the customized service.
Service is provided regardless of any individual purchase.	Provision of service requires customer purchase.	Service cannot be created apart from the customer's purchase and active participation.
Payment may be the only required customer input.	Customer inputs are necessary for an adequate outcome, but the service firm provides the service.	Customer inputs, choices, and actions cocreate the outcome.
Consumer Examples		
Airline travel	Haircut	Marriage counseling
Motel stay	Annual physical exam	Personal training
Fast-food restaurant	Full-service restaurant	Weight reduction program
Business-to-Business Customer Examples		
Uniform cleaning service	Agency-created advertising campaign	Management consulting
Pest control	Payroll service	Executive management seminar
Interior greenery maintenance service	Freight transportation	Installation of computer network

of each level of participation for both consumer and business-to-business services. The effectiveness of customer involvement at all the levels will affect organizational productivity and, ultimately, service quality and customer satisfaction.

Fellow Customers

In many service contexts, customers receive and/or cocreate the service simultaneously with other customers or must wait their turn while other customers are being served. In both cases, "fellow customers" are present in the service environment and can affect the nature of the service outcome or process. Fellow customers can *enhance* or *detract from* customer satisfaction and perceptions of quality.[5]

Some of the ways fellow customers can negatively affect the service experience are by exhibiting disruptive behaviors, causing delays, excessively crowding, and manifesting incompatible needs. In restaurants, hotels, airplanes, and other environments in which customers are cheek to jowl as they receive the service, crying babies, smoking patrons, and loud, unruly groups can be disruptive and detract from the experiences of their fellow customers. In college classrooms and other types of education and training environments, customers often complain when fellow customers interrupt and/or detract from the experience of others by using their laptops or texting on their phones in distracting ways. In other cases, overly demanding customers (even customers with legitimate problems) can cause a delay for others while their needs are met. This occurrence is common in banks, post offices, and customer service counters in retail stores. Excessive crowding or overuse of a service can also affect the nature of the customer's experience. Visiting Sea World in San Diego on a U.S. national holiday such as the Fourth of July is a very different experience from visiting the same park midweek in February.

Finally, customers who are being served simultaneously but who have incompatible needs can negatively affect each other. This situation can occur in restaurants, college classrooms, hospitals, and any service establishment in which multiple segments are served simultaneously. In a study of critical service encounters in tourist attractions across central Florida, researchers found that customers negatively affected each other when they failed to follow either explicit or implicit "rules of conduct." Customers reported such negative behaviors as pushing, shoving, smoking, drinking alcohol, being verbally abusive, and cutting in line. Other times, dissatisfaction resulted when other customers were impersonal, rude, unfriendly, or even spiteful.[6] Research has suggested that it is possible that the misbehavior of other customers may even be contagious, causing other customers to act inappropriately as well.[7]

There are just as many examples of customers enhancing satisfaction and quality for their fellow customers as detracting from them. Sometimes the mere presence of other customers enhances the experience, for example, at sporting events, in movie theaters, and in other entertainment venues. In other situations, fellow customers provide a positive social dimension to the service experience, as suggested in the photo on page 356. In some situations, customers may help each other achieve service goals and outcomes. The success of the Weight Watchers organization, for example, depends significantly on the camaraderie and support that group members provide each other. And health providers have long recognized the importance of family members (often viewed as customers in this context) in aiding hospital patients in their care and full recovery. Some hospitals have even started encouraging family members to stay and assist with their loved ones who are being cared for in intensive care units (ICUs), turning family members into active members of the health care team.[8]

Academic research also supports the power of other customers to influence service outcomes. In a study done with a franchise of Gold's Gym, it was found that customers who received support from other members of the gym were more likely to participate in positive ways like keeping the gym clean, cooperating with personnel, showing empathy toward other members, and encourageing others to join the gym.[9] The study of central Florida tourist attractions mentioned earlier found that customers increased the satisfaction of others by having friendly conversations while waiting in line, by taking photos, by assisting with children, and by returning dropped or lost items.[10] And an ethnographic study that observed hundreds of hours of customer interactions among travelers on the U.K. rail system found that customers often helped each other by (1) providing important service-related information (e.g., schedules, interesting features en route) that can reduce trip-related anxiety; (2) engaging in enjoyable conversation, thus making the trip more pleasant; and (3) serving as someone to complain to when mishaps and service failures occurred.[11]

The influence of fellow customers in helping others is even more apparent in some online service environments such as Facebook, LinkedIn, eBay, Amazon.com, and Craigslist, where customers literally cocreate services together. Customers helping each other is not limited to consumer services, as illustrated by networking giant Cisco. By giving business customers open access to its information and systems through its online self-service, Cisco enables customers to engage in a dialogue with timing of their demands and the uncontrollability of their attitudes and actions. The logical conclusion is that any service activities that do not require customer contact or involvement should be performed away from customers: the less direct contact there is between the customer and the service production system, the greater the potential for the system to operate at peak efficiency.[15] Other experts believe that services can be delivered most efficiently if customers are truly viewed as partial employees and their coproduction roles are designed to maximize their contributions to the service creation process. The logic behind this view is that organizational productivity can be increased if customers are educated to perform service-related activities they currently are not doing or to perform more effectively the tasks they are doing.[16] For example, the introduction of many automated airline services such as baggage check-in and self-ticketing is intended to speed up the process for customers while freeing employees for other tasks.[17] Organizational productivity is increased by using customers as a resource to perform tasks previously completed by employees.

There are many examples of organizations seeking to increase productivity through transferring tasks to customers. Although organizations derive obvious cost benefits by involving them as coproducers, customers do not always like or accept their new roles, especially when they perceive the purpose to be bottom-line cost savings for the company. If customers see no clear benefit to being involved in coproduction (e.g., lower prices, quicker access, or a better-quality outcome), then they are likely to resent and resist their coproduction roles, particularly if they feel their own productivity or efficiency is suffering to benefit the company.[18] Similarly, employees can sometimes be frustrated by customer participation, as was discovered in research conducted in a professional banking context that explored the effects of customer participation on both customers and employees. While the research found that customer participation in general enhanced the experience and value for the customer, it created stress for employees, presumably due to disruptions in the employees' standard work procedures.[19]

Customers as Contributors to Quality, Satisfaction, and Value

Another role customers can play is that of contributor to their own satisfaction and the ultimate quality and value of the services they experience. In this sense, customers are creators and cocreators of value, as discussed in the chapter opener. Customers may care little that they have increased the productivity of the organization through their participation, but they likely care a great deal about whether their needs are fulfilled. Effective customer participation can increase the likelihood that needs are met and that the benefits the customer seeks are actually attained, especially for services such as health care, education, personal fitness, and weight loss, in which the service outcome is highly dependent on customer participation.

Research in education has shown that active participation by students—as opposed to passive listening—increases learning (a desired service outcome) significantly.[20] The same is true in health care; patient compliance, in terms of taking prescribed medications or changing diet or other habits, can be critical to whether patients regain their health (the desired service outcome).[21] Other research in financial and medical service settings has shown that effective participation and cocreation by customers leads to higher perceptions of service quality, improved well being, and greater loyalty to the service provider.[22] Effective customer participation and cocreation can be just as important in business-to-business contexts. For example, companies in the trucking and shipping industries have found that in many situations customers cause their own

For each scenario, ask, "Which customer (A or B) will be most satisfied and receive the greatest quality and value, and why?"

SCENARIO 1: A MAJOR INTERNATIONAL HOTEL

Guest A called the desk right after check-in to report that his TV was not working and that the light over the bed was burned out; both problems were fixed immediately. The hotel staff exchanged his TV for one that worked and fixed the lightbulb. Later they took him a fruit plate to make up for the inconvenience. Guest B did not communicate to management until checkout time that his TV did not work and he could not read in bed. His complaints were overheard by guests checking in, who wondered whether they had chosen the right place to stay.

SCENARIO 2: OFFICE OF A PROFESSIONAL TAX PREPARER

Client A has organized into categories the information necessary to do her taxes and has provided all documents requested by the accountant. Client B has a box full of papers and receipts, many of which are not relevant to her taxes but which she brought along "just in case."

SCENARIO 3: AN AIRLINE FLIGHT FROM LONDON TO NEW YORK

Passenger A arrives for the flight with a device preloaded with movies and reading material and wearing several layers of clothing; passenger A also ordered a special meal in advance. Passenger B, who arrives empty-handed, becomes annoyed when the crew runs out of blankets, complains about the magazine selection and the meal, and starts fidgeting when he is disappointed by the inflight movie selection.

SCENARIO 4: ARCHITECTURAL CONSULTATION FOR REMODELING AN OFFICE BUILDING

Client A has invited the architects to meet with its remodeling and design committee made up of managers, staff, and customers to lay the groundwork for a major remodeling job that will affect everyone who works in the building, as well as customers. The committee has already formulated initial ideas and surveyed staff and customers for input. Client B has invited architects in following a decision the previous week to remodel the building; the design committee is two managers who are preoccupied with other, more immediate tasks and have little idea what they need or what customers and staff would prefer in terms of a redesign of the office space.

dissatisfaction with the service by failing to pack shipments appropriately, resulting in breakage or delays while items are repacked. A more complex example of business-to-business cocreation in the context of "knowledge intensive service businesses" is discussed in Exhibit 12.1.

Research suggests that customers who believe they have done their part to be effective in service interactions are more satisfied with the service. In a study of the banking industry, bank customers were asked to rate themselves on questions related to their contributions to service delivery in terms of what they did (e.g., cooperated with the bank employee and gave proper information) and how they did it (e.g., being friendly and courteous to the bank employee). Results of the study indicated that those customers who responded more positively to the questions about their own participation were also more satisfied with the bank.[23] Research in another context showed that customers' perceptions of service quality increased with greater levels of participation. Specifically, members of a YMCA who participated more in the club gave the club higher ratings on aspects of service quality than did those who participated less.[24]

Customers contribute to quality service delivery when they ask questions, take responsibility for their own satisfaction, and complain when there is a service failure. Consider the service scenarios shown in Exhibit 12.2.[25] The four scenarios illustrate the wide variations in customer participation that can result in equally wide variations in service quality and customer satisfaction. Customers who take responsibility and providers who encourage their customers to become their partners in identifying

IKEA of Sweden has managed to transform itself from a small, mail-order furniture company in the 1950s into the world's largest retailer of home furnishings. In 2015 more than 300 stores in 28 countries generated more than 31 billion euros in sales. The company sells simple, functional, yet well-designed furnishings, charging significantly less than its competitors.

THE "DO-IT-YOURSELF" (DIY) CONCEPT

A key to IKEA's success is the company's relationship with its customers. IKEA has drawn the customer into its production system: "if customers agree to take on certain key tasks traditionally done by manufacturers and retailers—the assembly of products and their delivery to customers' homes—then IKEA promises to deliver well-designed products at substantially lower prices." In effect, IKEA's customers become essential contributors to value—they create value for themselves through participating in the selection, transportation, and assembly processes.

IKEA has made being part of the value creation process an easy, fun, and pleasant experience for customers. The company's stores are a pleasure to shop in. The stores are set up with "inspirational displays," including realistic room settings and real-life homes that allow customers to get comfortable with the furnishings, try them out, and visualize the possibilities in their own homes. To make shopping easy, free strollers and supervised child care are provided, as are wheelchairs for those who need them.

When customers enter the store they are given store maps, tape measures, pens, and notepaper to use as they shop, allowing them to perform functions commonly done by sales and service staff. Once customers have made their selections, they find the boxed furniture in the IKEA warehouse and load it onto carts. After payment, customers take their purchases to their cars; if necessary, they can rent or buy a roof rack to transport larger purchases. Thus, customers also provide furniture loading and delivery services for themselves. At home, IKEA customers take on the role of manufacturer in assembling the new furnishings following carefully written, simple, and direct instructions. To accommodate customer needs, IKEA does have a fee-based delivery, assembly, and installation service for products over a certain price.

GLOBAL ADAPTATIONS

IKEA prints catalogs and provides detailed websites in many languages, making its products and instructions for their use accessible worldwide. In addition to tailoring its catalogs and websites, another key to IKEA's successful global expansion has been the company's policy of allowing each store to tailor its mix according to the local market needs and budgets. For example, when the Swedish retailer first expanded to the United States, executives quickly learned that Americans prefer larger drinking glasses, bigger beds, and more closet space.

On the other side of the world, Chinese customers save a high percentage of their income and are extremely price sensitive, so the prices there were initially the lowest in the world to lure the Chinese customers into the stores;

and satisfying their own needs together produce higher levels of service quality. Our Global Feature shows how Sweden's IKEA, has creatively engaged its customers in a new role: "IKEA wants its customers to understand that their role is not to *consume* value but to *create* it."[26]

In addition to contributing to their own satisfaction by enhancing the quality of service delivered to them, some customers simply enjoy participating in service value creation. These customers find the act of participating to be intrinsically attractive.[27] They enjoy using the Internet to purchase airline tickets, doing all their banking via ATMs and online, or shopping at IKEA. Often customers who like self-service in one setting are predisposed to serving themselves in other settings as well.

Interestingly, because service customers must participate in service creation and cocreation, they frequently blame themselves (at least partially) when things go wrong. Why did it take so long to reach an accurate diagnosis of my health problem? Why was the service contract for our company's cafeteria food full of errors? Why was the room we reserved for our meeting unavailable when we arrived? If

$1 placemats and 12¢ ice cream cones are examples. And some furniture items were 50–60 percent less than similar items in the United States. Amidst the price changes, IKEA learned that its "furniture for the masses" positioning was confusing consumers. What IKEA had not realized was that in China, IKEA was seen as an aspirational brand by many consumers. IKEA subsequently altered its targeting strategy to focus on younger middle-class consumers to help maintain its aspirational brand status. The response has been extremely positive, with 21 IKEA stores now open in China. The Beijing store that opened in 2006 is the largest IKEA store in the world outside of the flagship store in Sweden.

In addition to price variations, the store layout in Chinese stores was also adapted to reflect the design of many Chinese apartments. Because many of the apartments have balconies, the stores have a selection of balcony furnishings and displays. And because Chinese kitchens are generally small, relatively few kitchen items and furnishings are shown. Even IKEA's famous DIY assembly concept has been adapted to some extent in China. Because fewer people have cars and therefore use public transportation, IKEA has more extensive delivery service in China than in most countries. And because labor is cheaper in China, many customers choose to have their furniture assembled for them rather than doing it themselves. Another interesting adaptation to Chinese culture is IKEA's acceptance of extensive browsing by customers, in some cases even allowing customers and their children to nap in the display bed areas.

IKEA'S SUCCESS

IKEA's success is attributable in part to recognizing that customers can be part of the business system, performing roles they have not performed before. The company's flexible implementation of this idea through clearly defining customers' new roles and making it fun to perform these roles is the genius of its strategy. Through the process, customers around the globe cocreate their own experiences and contribute to their own satisfaction. And IKEA continues to experience financial success and acceptance globally with its strategy. In 2015 sales increased by 11.2 percent to 31.9 billion euros over the previous year. The number of visits to their stores increased to 1.9 billion visits, up 21 percent from 2014.

Sources: http://www.ikea.com, August, 2011; B. Edvardsson and B. Enquist, "The IKEA Saga: How Service Culture Drives Service Strategy," *The Service Industries Journal* 22 (October 2002), pp. 153–186; P. M. Miller, "IKEA with Chinese Characteristics," *The China Business Review* (July/August 2004), pp. 36–38; M. Fong, "IKEA Hits Home in China," *The Wall Street Journal*, March 3, 2006, pp. B1; M. Wei, "In IKEA's China Stores, Loitering is Encouraged," *Bloomberg Businessweek*, October 28, 2010; Anonymous, "Business: The Secret of IKEA's Success," *The Economist*, February 26, 2011, pp. 67–68. V. Chu, "Couching Tiger Tames the Dragon," *Business Today*, July 21, 2013, www.businesstoday.in/story/how-ikea-adapted-its-strategies-to-expand-in-china/1/196322/.html; R. Milne, "Ikea Faces Cultural Challenge as Flat-Pack Empire Expands," *Financial Times*, November 28, 2013, www.ft.com/content/83389238-5819-11e3-82fc-00144feabdc0.

customers believe they are partially (or totally) to blame when failures such as these occur they may be less dissatisfied with the service provider than when they believe the provider is responsible.[28] A series of studies suggests the existence of this "self-serving bias." That is, when services go better than expected, customers who have participated tend to take credit for the outcome and are less satisfied with the firm than are those customers who have not participated. However, when the outcome is worse than expected, customers who have chosen to participate in service production are less dissatisfied with the service than are those who choose not to participate—presumably because the participating customers have taken on some of the blame.[29]

Customers as Competitors

A third role played by service customers is that of potential competitor. If self-service customers can be viewed as resources of the firm, or as "partial employees," they can also partially or entirely perform the service for themselves and not need the provider at all. Thus, customers in a sense are competitors of the companies that supply the service. Whether to produce a service for themselves (*internal exchange*)—for example, child care, home maintenance, or car repair— or have someone else provide the service for them (*external exchange*) is a common dilemma for consumers.[30] Similar internal versus external exchange decisions are made by organizations. Firms frequently choose to outsource service activities such as payroll, data processing, research, accounting, maintenance, and facilities management. They find it advantageous to focus on their core businesses and leave these support services to others with greater expertise. Alternatively, a firm may decide to stop purchasing services externally and bring the service production process in-house.

Whether a household or a firm chooses to produce a particular service for itself or contract externally for the service depends on a variety of factors. A proposed model of internal/external exchange suggests that such decisions depend on the following:[31]

- *Expertise capacity.* The likelihood of producing the service internally is increased if the household or firm possesses the specific skills and knowledge needed to produce it. Having the expertise will not necessarily result in internal service production, however, because other factors (available resources and time) will also influence the decision. (For firms, making the decision to outsource is often based on recognizing that, although they may have the expertise, someone else can do it better.)

- *Resource capacity.* To decide to produce a service internally, the household or firm must have the needed resources, including people, space, money, equipment, and materials. If the resources are not available internally, external exchange is more likely.

- *Time capacity.* Time is a critical factor in internal/external exchange decisions. Households and firms with adequate time capacity are more likely to produce services internally than are groups with time constraints.

- *Economic rewards.* The economic advantages or disadvantages of a particular exchange decision will be influential in choosing between internal and external options. The actual monetary costs of the two options will sway the decision.

- *Psychic rewards.* Rewards of a noneconomic nature have a potentially strong influence on exchange decisions. Psychic rewards include the degree of satisfaction, enjoyment, gratification, or happiness associated with the external or internal exchange.

- *Trust.* In this context, trust means the degree of confidence or certainty the household or firm has in the various exchange options. The decision will depend to some extent on the level of self-trust in producing the service versus trust of others.

- *Control.* The household or firm's desire for control over the process and outcome of the exchange will also influence the internal/external choice. Entities that desire and can implement a high degree of control over the task are more likely to engage in internal exchange.

The important thing to remember from this section is that, in many service scenarios, customers can and often do choose to fully or partially produce the service themselves. Thus, in addition to recognizing that customers can be productive resources and cocreators of quality and value, organizations also need to recognize the customer's role as a potential competitor.

SELF-SERVICE TECHNOLOGIES—THE ULTIMATE IN CUSTOMER PARTICIPATION

Self-service technologies (SSTs) are services produced entirely by the customer without any direct involvement or interaction with the firm's employees. As such, SSTs represent the ultimate form of customer participation along a continuum from services produced entirely by the firm to those produced entirely by the customer. This continuum is depicted in Figure 12.1, using the example of H&R Block tax preparation services to illustrate the various ways the same service could be created and cocreated along all points on the continuum. At the far right end of the continuum, the tax advisor does everything from preparing the tax return to filing it. On the other end of the spectrum, the customer does everything; in between are various forms and levels of customer participation. Many service delivery options, across industries, could be laid out on this type of continuum from total customer production through total firm production. Christian Gronroos and colleagues refer to this continuum and the various ways of creating value as "value creation spheres" where providers produce potential value in the provider sphere, customers create their own value independently in the customer sphere, and the two jointly produce cocreated value in the joint sphere.[32]

A Proliferation of New SSTs

Advances in technology, particularly the Internet, have allowed the introduction of a wide range of self-service technologies that occupy the far left end of the customer participation continuum in Figure 12.1. These technologies have proliferated as companies see the potential cost savings and efficiencies that can be achieved, potential sales growth, increased customer satisfaction, and competitive advantage. The following is a partial list of some of the self-service technologies available to consumers.

- ATMs.
- Pay at the pump.
- Airline check-in.
- Hotel check-in and checkout.
- Automated car rental.
- Automated filing of legal claims.
- Online driver's license testing.
- Automated betting machines.
- Electronic blood pressure machines.
- Various vending services.
- Tax preparation software.
- Self-scanning at retail stores.
- Online banking.
- Vehicle registration online.
- Online auctions.
- Home and car buying online.
- Automated investment transactions.
- Insurance online.
- Package tracking
- Internet shopping.
- Interactive voice response phone systems.
- Online training and education.

The proliferation of SSTs has occurred for several reasons.[33] Many times firms are tempted by the cost savings that they anticipate by shifting customers to technology-based, automated systems and away from expensive personal service. If cost savings are the only reason for introducing an SST and if customers see no apparent benefits, the SST is likely to fail. Customers quickly see through this strategy and are not likely to adopt the SST if they have alternative options for service. Other times, firms introduce SSTs based on customer demand. For example, customers expect to find information, services, and delivery options online. When they do not find what they want from a particular firm online, they are likely to choose a competitor. Thus, customer

FIGURE 12.1
Service Production
Continuum[34]

Customer production		Joint production			Firm production
1	2	3	4	5	6

H&R Block Tax Preparation Example

1. Customer consults H&R Block website for tips and help, then prepares and files own tax return.
2. Customer consults H&R Block website for tips and help, purchases H&R Block software, and uses the software to file taxes online.
3. Customer partially prepares own return and meets with H&R Block advisor to check it over before finishing it and filing it online.
4. H&R Block tax advisor meets with customer, provides guidance and advice, and then customer prepares and files own tax return using H&R Block software.
5. H&R Block tax advisor meets with customer, helps customer prepare tax return in the office, provides direction for completing the process, and customer files it.
6. H&R Block tax advisor meets with the customer, prepares the tax return for her, files it for the customer, and provides her with copies of the return.

demand in some industries is forcing firms to develop and offer their services via technology. Other companies are developing SSTs to open up geographic, socioeconomic, and lifestyle markets that were not available through traditional channels.

Customer Usage of SSTs

Some of the SSTs listed earlier—ATMs, online ordering, and airline check-in—have been very successful, embraced by customers for the benefits they provide in terms of convenience, accessibility, and ease of use.[35] Benefits to firms, including cost savings and revenue growth, can also result for SSTs that succeed. Others—airline ticketing kiosks, grocery self-scanning—have been less quickly embraced by customers. With grocery self-scanning systems (as illustrated in the accompanying photo) the early reluctance of customers to adopt them reflected many factors, including fear of the technology, looking incompetent in front of other customers, desire for human interaction, and a sense that "scanning and bagging groceries is the store's job, not mine."

SST failures result when customers see little personal benefit in the new technology or when they do not have the ability to use it or know what they are supposed to do. Often, adopting a new SST requires customers to change their traditional behaviors significantly, and many are reluctant to make those changes, at least initially. Research looking at customer adoption of SSTs found that "customer readiness" is a major factor in determining whether customers will even try a new self-service option.[36] Customer readiness results from a combination of personal motivation (What is in it for me?), ability (Do I have the ability to use this SST?), and role clarity (Do I understand what I am supposed to do?). In other cases, customers see no value in using the technology when compared to the alternative interpersonal mode of delivery, or the SSTs may be so poorly designed that customers may prefer not to use them.[37] Research shows that customers

Customers help produce the service for themselves through scanning their own groceries.

© B.O'Kane/Alamy Stock Photo

also react negatively when they are forced to use an SST, with no alternative service channel offered. Any choice at all will improve customer perceptions, and having an employee available to assist or provide backup support can help.[38] Many studies have been done to try to understand why customers choose to adopt self-service technologies or not. One piece of research compared the results of 96 previous studies, concluding that demographics (e.g., age, education) are <u>not</u> good predictors of SST adoption and that ease of use and usefulness of the SST are key determining factors, influenced themselves by a number of factors including the ones just discussed. They also found that the factors that predict SST acceptance vary depending on the type of SST and country culture.[39]

Success with SSTs

Throughout the text we have highlighted some of the most successful self-service technologies in the marketplace: Amazon.com (Chapter 4), Cisco Systems (Chapter 7), and others. These companies have been successful because they offer clear benefits to customers, the benefits are well understood and appreciated compared to the alternative delivery modes, and the technology is user-friendly and reliable. In addition, customers understand their roles and have the capability to use the technology.

From a strategic perspective, research suggests that, as firms continue to move to SSTs as a mode of delivery, these questions are important to ask:[40]

- What is our strategy? What do we hope to achieve through the SST (cost savings, revenue growth, competitive advantage)?
- What are the benefits to customers of producing the service on their own through the SST? Do they know and understand these benefits?
- How can customers be motivated to try the SST? Do they understand their role? Do they have the capability to perform this role?
- How "technology ready" are our customers?[41] Are some segments of customers more ready to use the technology than others?
- How can customers be involved in the design of the service technology system and processes, so that they will be more likely to adopt and use the SST?
- What forms of customer education will be needed to encourage adoption? Will other incentives be needed?
- How will inevitable SST failures be handled to regain customer confidence?

STRATEGIES FOR ENHANCING CUSTOMER PARTICIPATION

The level and the nature of customer participation in the service process are strategic decisions that can impact an organization's productivity, its positioning relative to competitors, its service quality, and its customers' satisfaction. In the following sections we will examine the strategies captured in Figure 12.2 for involving customers effectively in the service production and cocreation process. The overall goals of a customer participation strategy will typically be to increase organizational productivity and customer satisfaction while decreasing uncertainty due to unpredictable customer actions.

Define Customers' Roles

In developing strategies for addressing customer involvement in service cocreation and delivery, the organization first determines what type of participation is desirable from customers, what the customer is capable of doing, and how the customer wishes

FIGURE 12.2
Strategies for Enhancing Customer Participation

Source: Adapted from M. L. Meuter and M. J. Bitner, "Self Service Technologies: Extending Service Frameworks and Identifying Issues for Research," in *Marketing Theory and Applications,* ed. D. Grewal and C. Pechmann (American Marketing Association Winter Educators' Conference, 1998), pp. 12–19.

Define Customers' Roles
• Clarify level of participation
• Identify specific jobs and tasks
• Understand implications for productivity, quality, and satisfaction

Recruit, Educate, and Reward Customers
• Identify and recruit appropriate segment(s)
• Educate customers for their roles
• Provide reasons to participate
• Reward customer performance

Manage the Customer Mix
• Assess compatibility of segments
• Isolate incompatible segments
• Enhance segment compatibility

Effective Customer Participation

to participate. Identifying the current level of customer participation can serve as a starting point.[42] Customers' roles may be partially predetermined by the nature of the service, as suggested in Table 12.1. The service may require only the customer's presence (a concert, airline travel), or it may require moderate levels of input from the customer in the form of effort or information (a haircut, tax preparation), or it may require the customer to cocreate the service outcome (fitness training, consulting, self-service offerings). In some cases, the service may be dependent on customers cocreating the service with and for each other, as in the case of eBay, Facebook, and many of the other social networking services available through the Internet.

The organization may decide that it is satisfied with the existing level of participation it requires from customers but wants to make the participation more effective. For example, Charles Schwab has always positioned itself as a company whose customers are highly involved in their personal investment decisions and it has communicated this role clearly to customers. The company's positioning around high customer involvement and self-service has been consistent over time, yet the actual role of the customer has changed. Technological advances, for example, have greatly facilitated the self-service role of Charles Schwab customers.

Alternatively, the organization may choose to increase the level of customer participation, which may reposition the service in the customers' eyes. Experts have suggested that higher levels of customer participation are strategically advisable when service production and delivery are inseparable; marketing benefits (cross-selling, building loyalty) can be enhanced by on-site contact with the customer; and customers can substitute for the labor and information provided by employees.[43] Higher levels of customer participation may also be advisable when increased participation is desired by customers and when it can enhance their satisfaction and service outcomes. For example, in health care, researchers and providers are working on ways to gain more active customer participation in treatment decisions. The Internet and other technological advances have helped propel customers into this role in taking responsibility for their own health and well-being, as illustrated in our Technology Spotlight.

Once the desired level of participation (from both the customer and firm perspectives) is clear, the organization can define more specifically what the customer's role and tasks entail. The range of possible roles and tasks are described next.

Helping Oneself

In many cases the organization may decide to increase the level of customer involvement in service delivery through active participation. In such situations, the customer becomes a productive resource, performing aspects of the service previously performed by employees or others. Many of the examples presented in this chapter are illustrations of customers "helping themselves" (IKEA of Sweden, Charles Schwab, and those in the Technology Spotlight). The result may be increased productivity for the firm and/or increased value, quality, and satisfaction for the customer.

Helping Others

Sometimes the customer is called on to help others who are experiencing the service. A child at a day care center might be appointed "buddy of the day" to help a new child acclimate to the environment. Long-time residents of retirement communities often assume comparable roles to welcome new residents. Many universities have established mentoring programs in which experienced students with similar backgrounds help newcomers adjust to and learn the system. Many membership organizations (like health clubs, churches, and social organizations) also rely heavily, although often informally, on current members to help orient new members and make them feel welcome. In a different context, social media and online game sites rely on customers to help each other and enhance each other's experiences. In engaging in these types of roles, customers are performing productive functions for the organization, increasing customer satisfaction and retention. Acting as a mentor or facilitator can have very positive effects on the person performing the role and is likely to increase his or her loyalty.

Promoting the Company

In some cases the customer's job includes a sales or promotional element. Service customers rely heavily on word-of-mouth endorsements in deciding which providers to try. They are more comfortable getting a recommendation from someone who has experienced the service than from advertising or other forms of nonpersonal communication. A positive recommendation from a friend, relative, colleague, or even an acquaintance can pave the way for a positive service experience. Many service organizations are imaginative in getting their current customers to work as promoters or salespeople. For example, a dental practice encourages referrals by sending flowers, candy, or tickets to a local sports event to its patients whose names appear frequently in its "who referred you?" database. Online reviews, Facebook posts, endorsements via Twitter, and other social media are common ways for customers to promote specific service providers.

Individual Differences: Not Everyone Wants to Participate

In defining customers' roles it is important to remember that not everyone will want to participate.[44] Some customers enjoy self-service, whereas others prefer to have the service performed entirely for them. Companies that provide education and training services to organizations know that some customers want to be involved in designing

Technology Spotlight Technology Facilitates Customer Participation in Health Care

Customer participation is facilitated by technology in many industries. For example, in education, technology allows students to interact with each other and their professors via e-mail, discussion boards, group chat sessions, and course materials provided online. In real estate, technology allows buyers to preview homes and develop lists of places they would like to visit without having to rely totally on a real estate agent to find all available properties. And in high-technology industries, business customers often interact with each other on the Web, helping each other solve problems, answering each other's questions, and so forth. All these examples show how technology—particularly the Internet—has facilitated customer participation and increased customer satisfaction.

Increased participation is particularly apparent in health care. There is probably no greater, high-participation service context than health care, where the customer must participate and where the provider and customer clearly cocreate the service. Patient participation is required at multiple levels. To achieve optimal health outcomes, patients must

- Provide accurate information about symptoms and health background.
- Answer detailed questions.
- Help decide on a course of treatment.
- Carry out the prescribed regimen leading to recovery and/or prevention.

Technology is clearly influencing how customers perform these roles and shifting in some senses the power of information into the hands of consumers. Annual studies by the Pew Internet and American Life Project, funded by the Pew Charitable Trusts, illuminate the trends in online health care. This research showed that, as of 2012, 72 percent of U.S. Internet users, or approximately 87 percent of all adults in the United States, had gone online in search of health information. These percentages are similar to the number of users who are paying bills online, reading blogs, or using the Internet to look up an address or a phone number on any given day. They seek information about specific diseases, mental health, nutrition and fitness, drugs and drug interactions, and specific doctors and hospitals. While many seek information for themselves and their own medical conditions, half of these online health information seekers search for information on behalf of a friend or family member. People like getting health information this way because of the convenience, the wealth of information that is available, and the fact that research can be done anonymously. In the United States, people are even beginning to use their cell phones to look up health information. In 2012, 31 percent of cell phone owners used their phones in this way.

Thousands of Internet sites provide some type of health-related information. Some belong to health care providers like Mayo Clinic (www.mayo.edu) or pharmacy benefits providers like CVSCaremark (www.caremark.com). Others are operated totally online—like WebMD (www.webmd.com) or Everyday Health (www.everydayhealth.com)—without affiliation to a specific health care provider. Some respected sites are sponsored by governmental entities such as the U.S. Department of Health and Human Services (www.healthfinder.gov) and the National Library of Medicine and National Institutes of Health (www.medlineplus.gov). Yet other sites provide information for specific health conditions such as AIDS, depression, diabetes, and breast cancer. Still others such as Hospital Compare (www.medicare.gov/hospitalcompare) can help patients determine the best hospitals to go to based on various quality and health outcome criteria.

All this readily available medical information is changing the role of the health care consumer to one of active participant in diagnosing illnesses, assessing treatment options, and determining overall well-being. Armed with information, patients gain confidence in asking questions and seeking appropriate diagnoses. In some cases they

the training and perhaps in delivering it to their employees. Other companies want to hand over the entire training design and delivery to the consulting organization, staying at arms length with little of their own time and energy invested in the service. In health care, it is clear that some patients want lots of information and want to be involved in their own diagnosis and treatment decisions. Others simply want the doctor to tell them what to do. Despite all the customer service and purchase options now can e-mail questions to their doctors or other providers or find support in chat groups, bulletin boards, and e-mail lists on the Internet. They are also comforted (or at times frightened) by what they find online and often make decisions or change their overall approach to maintaining their health based on what they find. Still, it is important to note that, while they play a growing role, online sources are still supplemental to health professionals, family, and friends as sources of health information.

Sources: "Health Fact Sheet," The Pew Internet Project, September 2012, www.pewinternet.org, accessed August 2016; https://medlineplus.gov, accessed August 2016.

available via the Internet, many customers still prefer human, high-contact service delivery rather than self-service.[45] Research has shown, for example, that customers with a high "need for human interaction" are less likely to try new self-service options offered via the Internet and automated phone systems.[46] Because of these differences in preferences, most companies find they need to provide service delivery choices for different market segments.

Recruit, Educate, and Reward Customers

Once the customer's role is clearly defined, the organization can think in terms of facilitating that role. In a sense, the customer becomes a partial employee of the organization, and strategies for facilitating customer behavior in service cocreation and delivery can mimic to some degree the efforts aimed at service employees discussed in Chapter 11. As with employees, customer participation in service cocreation and delivery will be facilitated when (1) customers understand their roles and how they are expected to perform, (2) customers are able to perform as expected, and (3) customers receive valued rewards for performing as expected.[47] Through these means, the organization will also reduce the inherent uncertainty associated with the unpredictable quality and timing of customer participation.

In some cases, customers may feel overwhelmed or react negatively to what is required of them to produce or cocreate the service. For example, this can be the case for prolonged negative services such as the treatment of chronic illnesses.[48] In other cases, customers perceive their roles to be overly intense in requiring too much effort, as with some do-it-yourself services. In this case, research has shown that communication strategies that focus on highlighting the value of the customer's efforts and providing supplemental strategies for them to reduce their effort can compensate for the negative effects of asking so much from them.[49] Exhibit 12.3 illustrates how the utility industry is innovating new services that engage customers as partial employees while rewarding them for their efforts. These initiatives also serve the larger common good by protecting the environment and preserving natural resources.

Recruit the Right Customers

Before the company begins the process of educating and socializing customers for their roles, it must attract the right customers to fill those roles. The expected roles and responsibilities of customers should be clearly communicated in advertising, personal selling, and other company messages. By previewing their roles and what is required of them in the service process, customers can self-select into (or out of) the relationship. Self-selection should result in enhanced perceptions of service quality from the customer's point of view and reduced uncertainty for the organization.

To illustrate, a child care center that requires parent participation on the site at least one-half day per week needs to communicate that expectation before it enrolls any child in its program. For some families, this level of participation will not be possible or desirable, thus precluding them from enrolling in the center. The expected level of participation needs to be communicated clearly to attract customers who are ready and willing to perform their roles.[50]

Educate and Train Customers to Perform Effectively

Customers need to be educated, or in essence "socialized," so that they can perform their roles effectively. Through the socialization process, service customers gain an appreciation of specific organizational values, develop the abilities necessary to function within a specific context, understand what is expected of them, and acquire the skills and knowledge to interact with employees and other customers.[51] Customer education programs can take the form of formal orientation programs, written literature provided to customers, directional cues and signage in the service environment, and information obtained from employees and other customers.

New technologies are allowing utility companies to communicate directly with customers and provide them with innovative tools and information that are shaping energy consumption behavior. The result should benefit all parties by cutting greenhouse emissions from power plants, slowing down rising electricity costs, and saving customers money as well. Surveys suggest that U.S. consumers are becoming increasingly open and willing to make the adjustments needed to reduce energy consumption overall and to begin addressing climate change predictions and fears. The new energy saving tools include such things as online calculators, high-tech meters in homes, visible in-home displays that show energy consumption at different times of day, smart phone apps, remote control devices, prepaid electricity, and innovative pricing.

Utilities across the United States are experimenting with different approaches. For example, in northern California, Pacific Gas & Electric has an online tool that shows customers how their personal energy consumption is tied to greenhouse gas emissions. This tool can help individual customers see how changes in their behavior can have significant energy and pollution-reducing results. In southern California, customers are volunteering to be part of a plan that allows the utility to turn their air-conditioning units off at predetermined times to save peak demand. One company, Southern California Edison, has a program called "Save Power Days," whereby residents are notified in advance when there is a "save power day." If those enrolled in the program reduce their energy consumption on those 12 to 15 days per year, they can save up to $100. And Florida Power & Light has a program for small-business owners that calculates how much energy different pieces of equipment use and when energy usage is most costly.

Another new technology is a "home electricity monitor," which helps customers determine their energy usage and what it is costing them in real time. The device, which connects to a customer's electronic breaker box, can transmit information to a display unit, which tells the customer what various power-using devices are costing. One early adopter of the technology discovered that her energy consumption rose significantly when she turned on her electric oven to heat up a pizza. By purchasing a toaster oven and using it and her microwave oven more often, she was able to reduce her energy consumption and her power bill. Finally, DTE Energy developed a smart phone app, called Insight, that offers to help customers track their home energy usage for free. It tracks usage in real time and gives users a daily summary. The app works with electric and gas customers, allowing them to identify consumption patterns and make adjustments as needed.

All of these innovative programs depend on customer acceptance, participation, and significant changes in behavior. To be successful, these innovative programs require investments in consumer education and incentives that will encourage them to change their behavior. Through this process, utility customers become "partial employees" of the utility companies by monitoring their own energy consumption and taking actions to reduce it. The result is reduced costs for the energy company, reduced prices for customers, less energy consumption overall, and better air quality in the short and long term.

Sources: R. Smith, "Letting the Power Company Control Your AC," *The Wall Street Journal,* July 10, 2007, p. D1+; R. Smith, "New Ways to Monitor Your Energy Use," *The Wall Street Journal,* July 19, 2007, p. D1+; R. Gold, "The Power of Knowledge: With New Monitors, Homeowners Can Keep Track of Their Electricity Use In Real Time," *The Wall Street Journal,* February 28, 2011, p. R7; www .sce.com, 2011; F. Witsil, "DTE App Gives Customers Insight into Power Usage," *Detroit Free Press,* October 24, 2015, http://www .freep.com/story/money/business/michigan/2015/10/24/dte -energy-app-insight/73932382/.

Many services offer "customer orientation" programs to assist customers in understanding their roles and what to expect from the process before experiencing it. When customers begin the Weight Watchers in-person program, for example, the company website and their first group meeting include a thorough orientation to the program and their responsibilities, as described in Exhibit 12.4.

Customer education can also be partially accomplished through written literature, online resources, and customer "handbooks." Many hospitals have developed patient materials, very similar in appearance to employee handbooks, to describe what the patient should do in preparation for arrival at the hospital, what will happen when he or she arrives, and policies regarding visiting hours and billing procedures. The

TABLE 12.2 **Characteristics of Service That Increase the Importance of Compatible Segments**

Source: Adapted from C. L. Martin, Dr C. A. Pranter, "Compatibility Management: Customer-to-Customer Relationships in Service Environments," *Journal of Services Marketing* 3 (Summer 1989), pp. 5–15.

Characteristic	Explanation	Examples
Customers are in close physical proximity to each other.	Customers will more often notice each other and be influenced by each other's behavior when they are in close physical proximity.	Airplane flights Entertainment events Sports events
Verbal interaction takes place among customers.	Conversation (or lack thereof) can be a component of both satisfying and dissatisfying encounters with fellow patrons.	Full-service restaurants Cocktail lounges Educational settings
Customers are engaged in numerous and varied activities.	When a service facility supports varied activities all going on at the same time, the activities themselves may not be compatible.	Universities Health clubs Resort hotels
The service environment attracts a heterogeneous customer mix.	Many service environments, particularly those open to the public, will attract a variety of customer segments.	Public parks Public transportation Open-enrollment colleges
The core service is compatibility.	The core service is to arrange and nurture compatible relationships between customers.	Big Brothers/Big Sisters Weight loss group programs Mental health support groups
Customers must occasionally wait for the service.	Waiting in line for service can be monotonous or anxiety producing. The boredom or stress can be magnified or lessened by other customers, depending on their compatibility.	Medical clinics Tourist attractions Restaurants
Customers are expected to share time, space, or service utensils with each other.	The need to share space, time, and other service factors is common in many services but may become a problem if segments are not comfortable with sharing with each other or if the need to share is intensified because of capacity constraints.	Golf courses Hospitals Retirement communities Airplanes

as to enhance satisfying encounters and minimize dissatisfying encounters."[57] Compatibility management is critical for some businesses (such as health clubs, public transportation, and hospitals) but less important for others. Table 12.2 lists seven interrelated characteristics that increase the importance of compatibility management for service businesses.

To manage multiple (and sometimes conflicting) segments, organizations rely on a variety of strategies. Attracting maximally homogeneous groups of customers through careful positioning and segmentation strategies is one approach. This strategy is used by the Ritz-Carlton Hotel, for which upscale travelers are the primary target segment. The Ritz-Carlton is positioned to communicate that message to the marketplace, and customers self-select into the hotel. However, even in that context there are potential conflicts—for example, when the hotel is simultaneously hosting a business convention, an NBA basketball team, and individual leisure travelers. Another strategy is often used in such cases. Compatible custers are grouped together physically, so that the segments are less likely to interact directly with each other. The Ritz-Carlton keeps meetings and large-group events separated from the areas of the hotel used by individual businesspeople. Many amusement parks that face similar issues offer a special fee for those who attend after 6:00 p.m. Their target for this special fee is typically price-sensitive teenagers and/or college students. Families with small children tend to go at the beginning of the day and are likely to have exited the park by early evening; thus, the pricing strategy keeps these incompatible segments separated in time.

Other strategies for enhancing customer compatibility include customer "codes of conduct," such as the regulation of smoking behavior and dress codes. Clearly such codes of conduct vary from one service establishment to another. Finally, training employees to observe customer-to-customer interactions and to be sensitive to potential conflicts is another strategy for increasing compatibility among segments. Employees can also be trained to recognize opportunities to foster positive encounters among customers in certain types of service environments.

Summary

This chapter focused on the role of customers in delivery, creation, and cocreation of service value. The customer him or herself and fellow customers in the service environment can all cause a widening of gap 3. Customers may widen the service performance gap for a number of reasons: customers lack understanding of their roles, customers are unwilling or unable to perform their roles, customers are not rewarded for good performance, other customers interfere, or market segments are incompatible.

Managing and facilitating customers in the process of service value cocreation is a critical challenge for service firms. Whereas manufacturers are not concerned with customer participation in the manufacturing process, service managers constantly face this issue because their customers are often present and active partners in service production and cocreation. As participants in service cocreation, production, and delivery, customers can perform three primary roles: *productive resources* for the organization; *contributors* to quality, satisfaction, and value; and *competitors* in performing the service for themselves.

Through understanding the importance of customers in service creation and cocreation and identifying the roles played by the customer in a particular context, managers can develop strategies to enhance customer participation. Strategies include defining the customers' roles and jobs, recruiting customers who match the customer profile in terms of desired level of participation, educating customers so they can perform their roles effectively, rewarding customers for their contributions, and managing the customer mix to enhance the experiences of all segments. By implementing these strategies, organizations should see a reduction in the service performance gap due to effective and efficient customer contributions to service value.

Discussion Questions

1. Using your own personal examples, discuss the general importance of customers in the successful creation and delivery of service experiences.

2. Why might customer actions and attitudes cause the service performance gap to occur? Use your own examples to illustrate your understanding.

3. Using Table 12.1, think of specific services you have experienced that fall within each of the three levels of customer participation: low, medium, and high. Describe specifically what you did as a customer in each case. How did your involvement vary across the three types of service situations?

4. Describe a time when your satisfaction in a particular situation was *increased* because of something another customer did. Could (or does) the organization do anything to ensure that this experience happens routinely? What does it do? Should it try to make this situation a routine occurrence?

5. Describe a time when your satisfaction in a particular situation was *decreased* because of something another customer did. Could the organization have done anything to manage this situation more effectively? What could it have done?

6. Discuss the customer's role as a *productive resource* for the firm. Describe a time when you played this role. What did you do and how did you feel? Did the firm help you perform your role effectively? If so, how?

7. Discuss the customer's role as a *contributor to service quality and satisfaction.* Describe a time when you played this role. What did you do and how did you feel? Did the firm help you perform your role effectively? If so, how?

8. Discuss the customer's role as a potential *competitor.* Describe a time when you chose to provide a service for yourself rather than pay someone to provide the service for you. Why did you decide to perform the service yourself? What could have changed your mind, causing you to contract with someone else to provide the service?

Exercises

1. Visit a service establishment where customers can influence each other (such as a theme park, an entertainment establishment, a resort, a shopping mall, a restaurant, an airline, a school, or a hospital). Observe (or interview) customers and record cases of positive and negative customer influence. Discuss how you would manage the situation to increase overall customer satisfaction.

2. Interview someone regarding his or her decision to outsource a service—for example, legal services, payroll, or maintenance in a company or cleaning, child care, or pet care in a household. Use the criteria for internal versus external exchange described in the text to analyze the decision to outsource.

3. Think of a service in which a high level of customer participation is necessary for the service to be successful (health club, weight loss, educational setting, health care, golf lessons, online social media, or the like). Interview a service provider in such an organization to find out what strategies the provider uses to encourage effective customer participation.

4. Visit a service setting in which multiple types of customer segments use the service at the same time (such as a theater, golf course, resort, or theme park). Observe (or interview the manager about) the organization's strategies to manage these segments effectively. Would you do anything differently if you were in charge?

5. Visit the website of an online printing service such as iPrint (www.iPrint .com). Compare its printing service process to similar brick-and-mortar services offered by FedEx Kinko's. Compare and contrast the customer's role in each situation.

Notes

1. For more on value creation and cocreation see: C. Gronroos and P. Voima, "Critical Service Logic: Make Sense of Value Creation and Co-Creation," *Journal of the Academy of Marketing Science* 41 (March 2013), pp. 133–150; H. Saarijari, P. K. Kannan, and H. Kuusela, "Value Co-Creation: Theoretical Approaches and Practical Implications," *European Business Review* 25 (January 2013), pp. 6–19.

2. See B. Schneider and D. E. Bowen, *Winning the Service Game* (Boston: Harvard Business School Press, 1995), chap. 4; L. A. Bettencourt, "Customer Voluntary Performance: Customers as Partners in Service Delivery, *Journal of Retailing* 73 (Fall 1997), pp. 383–406; P. K. Mills and J. H. Morris, "Clients as 'Partial' Employees: Role Development in Client Participation," *Academy of Management Review* 11 (1986), pp. 726–735; C. H. Lovelock and R. F. Young, "Look to Customers to Increase Productivity," *Harvard Business Review* 57 (Summer 1979), pp. 9–20; A. R. Rodie and S. S. Kleine, "Customer Participation in Services Production and Delivery," in *Handbook of Services Marketing and Management,* ed. T. A. Swartz and D. Iacobucci (Thousand Oaks, CA: Sage, 2000), pp. 111–126; C. K. Prahalad and V. Ramaswamy, "Co-opting Customer Competence," *Harvard Business Review* 78 (January–February 2000), p. 7; and N. Bendapudi and R. P. Leone, "Psychological Implications of Customer Participation in Co-Production," *Journal of Marketing* 67 (January 2003), pp. 14–28; A. S. Gallan, C. B. Jarvis, S. W. Brown, and M. J. Bitner, "Customer Positivity and Participation in Services: An Empirical Test in a Health Care Context," *Journal of the Academy of Marketing Science* 41 (May 2013), pp. 338–356.

3. S. L. Vargo, and R. F. Lusch, "Evolving to a New Dominant Logic for Marketing," *Journal of Marketing* 68 (January 2004), pp. 1–17; R. F. Lusch, S. L. Vargo, and M O'Brien, "Competing through Service: Insights from Service-Dominant Logic," *Journal of Retailing* 83 (2007), pp. 5–18; Gronroos and Voima, "Critical Service Logic: Making Sense of Value Creation and Co-Creation"; S. L. Vargo and R. F. Lusch, "Institutions and Axioms: An Extension and Update of Service-Dominant Logic," *Journal of the Academy of Marketing Science* 44 (January 2016), pp. 5–23.

4. L. A. Bettencourt, S. W. Brown, A. L. Ostrom, and R. I. Roundtree, "Client Co-Production in Knowledge-Intensive Business Services," *California Management Review* 44 (Summer 2002), pp. 100–128.

5. See S. J. Grove and R. P. Fisk, "The Impact of Other Customers on Service Experiences: A Critical Incident Examination of 'Getting Along'," *Journal of Retailing* 73 (Spring 1997), pp. 63–85; C. I. Martin and C. A. Pranter, "Compatibility Management: Customer-to-Customer Relationships in Service Environments," *Journal of Services Marketing* 3 (Summer 1989), pp. 5–15; and R. Nicholls, "New Directions for Customer-to-Customer Interaction Research," *Journal of Services Marketing* 24 (2010), pp. 87–97.

6. Grove and Fisk, "The Impact of Other Customers on Service Experiences."

7. T. Schaefers, K. Wittkowski, S. Benoit, and R. Ferraro, "Contagious Effects of Customer Misbehavior in Access-Based Services," *Journal of Service Research* 19 (February 2016), pp 3–21.

8. L. Landro, "ICUs' New Message: Welcome, Families," *The Wall Street Journal,* July 12, 2007, pp. Al+.

9. M. S. Rosenbaum and C. A. Massiah, "When Customers Receive Support from Other Customers," *Journal of Service Research* 9 (February 2007), pp. 257–270.

10. Grove and Fisk, "The Impact of Other Customers on Service Experiences."

11. K. Harris and S. Baron, "Consumer-to-Consumer Conversations in Service Settings," *Journal of Service Research* 6 (February 2004), pp. 287–303.

12. See P. K. Mills, R. B. Chase, and N. Margulies, "Motivating the Client/Employee System as a Service Production Strategy," *Academy of Management Review* 8

37. M. L. Meuter, A. L. Ostrom, R. I. Roundtree, and M. J. Bitner, "Self-Service Technologies: Understanding Customer Satisfaction with Technology-Based Service Encounters," *Journal of Marketing* 64 (July 2000), pp. 50–64.

38. M. J. Reinders, P. A. Dabholkar, and R. T. Frambach, "Consequences of Forcing Consumers to Use Technology-Based Self-Service," *Journal of Service Research* 11 (November 2008), pp. 107–123.

39. M. Blut, C. Wang, and K. Schoefer, "Factors Influencing the Acceptance of Self-Service Technologies: A Meta-Analysis," *Journal of Service Research* 19 (November 2016), pp. 396–416.

40. Meuter, Bitner, Ostrom, and Brown, "Choosing Among Alternative Service Delivery Modes"; see also Y. Moon and F. X. Frei, "Exploding the Self-Service Myth," *Harvard Business Review* 78 (May–June 2000), pp. 26–27; and Bitner, Ostrom, and Meuter, "Implementing Successful Self-Service Technologies."

41. A. Parasuraman and C. L. Colby, *Techno-Ready Marketing: How and Why Your Customers Adopt Technology* (New York: The Free Press, 2001); A. Parasuraman and C. L. Colby, "An Updated and Streamlined Technology Readiness Index TRI 2.0," *Journal of Service Research* 18 (February 2015), pp. 59–74.

42. R. C. Ford and J. R. McColl-Kennedy, "Organizational Strategies for Filling the Customer Can-Do/Must-Do Gap," *Business Horizons* 58 (August 2015), pp. 459–468.

43. Bowen, "Managing Customers as Human Resources."

44. Bateson, "The Self-Service Customer."

45. J. Light, "With Customer Service, Real Person Trumps Text," *The Wall Street Journal,* April 25, 2011, p. B7.

46. Meuter, Bitner, Ostrom, and Brown, "Choosing among Alternative Service Delivery Modes."

47. Bowen, "Managing Customers as Human Resources"; Schneider and Bowen, *Winning the Service Game,* chap. 4; Meuter, Bitner, Ostrom, and Brown, "Choosing Among Alternative Service Delivery Modes"; Dellande, Gilly, and Graham, "Gaining Compliance and Losing Weight"; Ford and McColl-Kennedy, "Organizational Strategies for Filling the Customer Can-Do/Must-Do Gap."

48. J. Spanjol, A. S. Cui, C. Nakata, L. K. Sharp, S. Y. Crawford, Y. Xiao, and M. B. Watson-Manheim," Co-Production of Prolonged, Complex, and Negative Services: An Examination of Medication Adherence in Chronically Ill Individuals," *Journal of Service Research* 18 (August 2015), pp. 284–302.

49. T. Haumann, P. Gunturkun, L. M. Schons, and J. Wieseke, "Engaging Customers in Coproduction Processes: How Value-Enhancing and Intensity-Reducing Communication Strategies Mitigate the Negative Effects of Coproduction Intensity," *Journal of Marketing* 79 (November 2015), pp. 17–33.

50. S. Moeller, R. Ciuchita, D. Mahr, G. Odekerken-Schroder, and M. Fassnacht, "Uncovering Collaborative Value Creation Patterns and Establishing Corresponding Customer Roles," *Journal of Service Research* 16 (November 2013), pp. 471–487.

51. S. W. Kelley, J. H. Donnelly Jr., and S. J. Skinner, "Customer Participation in Service Production and Delivery," *Journal of Retailing* 66 (Fall 1990), pp. 315–335; Schneider and Bowen, *Winning the Service Game,* chap. 4; L. Guo, E. J. Arnould, T. W. Gruen, and C. Tang, "Socializing to Co-Produce: Pathways to Consumers' Financial Well-Being," *Journal of Service Research* 16 (November 2013),

pp. 549–563; B. Dong, K. Sivakumar, K. R. Evans, and S. Zou, "Effect of Customer Participation on Service Outcomes: The Moderating Role of Participation Readiness," *Journal of Service Research* 18 (May 2015), pp. 160–176; Mende, Scott, Bitner, and Ostrom, "Activating Consumers for Better Service Coproduction Outcomes Through Eustress."

52. L. Landro, "When a Doctor Isn't Enough," *The Wall Street Journal,* August 16, 2011, p. D1; T. Salge, C. Breidbach, and D. Antons, "Seamless Service? On the Role and Impact of Service Orchestrators," *Journal of Service Research* 19 (November 2016), pp. 458–476.

53. Bowen, "Managing Customers as Human Resources."

54. H. Hudson, "Eva Restaurant Cellphone Discount Gives Los Angeles Patrons 5 Percent Off For Surrendering Phone," *Huffington Post,* January 3, 2013, http://www.huffingtonpost.com/2013/01/03/eva-restaurant-cellphone-_n_2399274.html, accessed August 6, 2016.

55. Ibid.; see also L. C. Harris and K. L. Reynolds, "The Consequences of Dysfunctional Customer Behavior," *Journal of Service Research* 6 (November 2003), pp. 144–161.

56. E. Yu, "Shanghai Issues Etiquette Guide for Disneyland Visitors," *CNN,* May 25, 2016, http://www.cnn.com/2016/05/25/travel/shanghai-disneyland-etiquette-guide/.

57. Martina and Pranter, "Compatibility Management."

Chapter **Thirteen**

Managing Demand and Capacity

This chapter's objectives are to

1. Explain the underlying issue for capacity-constrained services: lack of inventory capability.
2. Present the implications of time, labor, equipment, and facilities constraints combined with variations in demand patterns.
3. Lay out strategies for matching supply and demand through (a) shifting demand to match capacity or (b) adjusting capacity to meet demand.
4. Demonstrate the benefits and risks of yield management strategies in forging a balance among capacity utilization, pricing, market segmentation, and financial return.
5. Provide strategies for managing waiting lines for times when capacity and demand cannot be aligned.

How to Fill Over 600 Rooms 365 Days of the Year

The Phoenician Hotel in Scottsdale, Arizona, is an upscale hotel in the center of a metropolitan area of approximately 4.5 million people, the twelfth largest metropolitan area in the United States. The hotel is frequently cited for its service and has been given the Five Star Award by Forbes Travel four times. It has just over 600 luxury rooms, three restaurants, seven beautiful pools, and spacious meeting and conference facilities.[1] These restaurants and meeting facilities are available to guests 365 days and nights of the year. Yet natural demand for them varies tremendously. During the tourist season from November through mid-April, demand for rooms is high, often exceeding available space. From mid-May through September, however, when temperatures regularly exceed 100 degrees Fahrenheit, the demand for rooms drops considerably. Because the hotel caters to business travelers and business meetings, demand has a weekly cycle in addition to the seasonal fluctuations. Business travelers do not stay over weekends. Thus, demand for rooms from the hotel's primary market segment drops on Friday and Saturday nights.

To smooth the peaks and valleys of demand for its facilities, the Phoenician has employed a number of strategies. Group business (primarily business conferences) is pursued throughout the year to fill the lower demand periods. A variety of special event, sports, wedding, and getaway packages are offered year-round to increase weekend demand for rooms. During the hot summer months, the hotel encourages local Phoenix metro and nearby Tucson residents to experience the luxury of the hotel. One creative package used in the past included an attractively priced hotel stay combined with a "culinary countdown," which gives patrons the option to enjoy a three-course meal, afternoon tea, and burgers and dessert at the on-site restaurants. The hotel also advertises spa specials and deals to entice these "stay-cationers." By encouraging local people to use the hotel, the hotel increases its occupancy during slow demand times, while residents of the community get a chance to enjoy an experience they may not be able to afford during the high season.

Most downtown hotels in urban areas face the same weekly demand fluctuations that the Phoenician deals with, and many have found a partial solution by catering to families and children on the weekends. For many dual-career couples, weekend getaways are a primary form of relaxation and vacation. The downtown hotels cater to these couples and families by offering discounted room rates, child-oriented activities and amenities, and an environment in which families feel comfortable. For example, the Lotte New York Palace Hotel—the closest hotel to American Girl Place—attempts to increase weekend stays by offering an "American Girl Place Package" to families with young daughters. The package, targeted for nonbusiness customers, comes with a complimentary American Girl doll-sized travel bed for an American Girl doll that girls can take home with them and includes turndown service for their dolls.

For the Phoenician Hotel in Scottsdale and many other hotels, managing demand and utilizing the hotel's fixed capacity of rooms, restaurants, and meeting facilities can be a seasonal, weekly, and even daily challenge. Although the hotel industry epitomizes the challenges of demand and capacity management, many service providers face similar problems. For example, tax accountants and air-conditioning maintenance services face seasonal demand fluctuations, whereas services such as commuter trains and restaurants face daily and even hourly variations in customer demand. For some businesses, demand is predictable, as for a tax accountant. For others, such as management or technology consultants, demand may be less predictable, fluctuating based on customer needs and business cycles. Sometimes firms experience too much demand for the existing capacity and sometimes capacity sits idle.

Overuse or underuse of a service can directly contribute to gap 3: failure to deliver what was designed and specified. For example, when demand for services exceeds maximum capacity, the quality of service may drop because staff and facilities are overtaxed. And some customers may be turned away, not receiving the service at all. During periods of slow demand it may be necessary to reduce prices or cut service amenities; however, when firms change the nature of the service and, perhaps, the makeup of the clientele, they run the risk of not delivering what customers expect. For example, older travelers or business groups who are in a hotel on a weekend may resent the invasion of families and children because it changes the nature of the service they expected. At the pool, for example, collisions can occur between adults trying to swim laps and children playing water games.

In this chapter we focus on the challenges of matching supply and demand in capacity-constrained services. The service performance gap can occur when organizations fail to smooth the peaks and valleys of demand, overuse their capacities, attract an inappropriate customer mix in their efforts to build demand, or rely too much on price in smoothing demand. The chapter examines these issues and suggests strategies for addressing them. The effective use of capacity is frequently a key success factor for service organizations.

THE UNDERLYING ISSUE: LACK OF INVENTORY CAPABILITY

The fundamental issue underlying supply and demand management in services is the lack of inventory capability. Unlike manufacturing firms, service firms cannot build up inventories during periods of slow demand to use later when demand increases. This lack of inventory capability is due to the perishability of services and their simultaneous production and consumption. An airline seat not sold on a given flight cannot be left in inventory and resold the following day. The productive capacity of that seat on that flight has perished. Similarly, an hour of a lawyer's billable time cannot be saved from one day to the next. Services also cannot be transported from one place to another or transferred from person to person. Thus, the Scottsdale Phoenician's services cannot be moved to an alternative location in the summer months—say, to the Pacific coast, where summers are ideal for tourists and demand for hotel rooms is high.

The lack of inventory capability combined with fluctuating demand leads to a variety of potential outcomes, as illustrated in Figure 13.1.[2] The horizontal lines in Figure 13.1 indicate service capacity, and the curved line indicates customer demand for the service. In many services, capacity is fixed; thus, capacity can be designated by a flat horizontal line over a certain time period. Demand for service frequently fluctuates, however, as indicated by the curved line. The topmost horizontal line in Figure 13.1 represents maximum capacity. For example, in our opening vignette, the horizontal line would represent the Scottsdale Phoenician's over 600 rooms, or it could

FIGURE 13.1   **Variations in Demand Relative to Capacity**

J. Wirtz and C. H. Lovelock, Services Marketing, 8th Edition, 2016, p. 334., World Scientific Publishing Co (Hackensack, NJ).

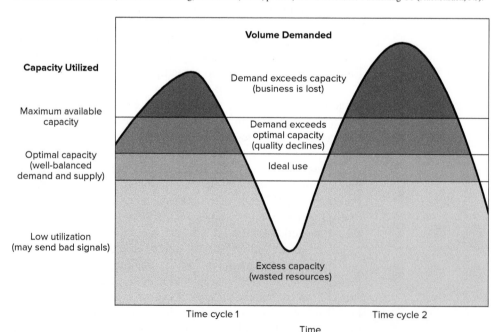

represent 70,000 seats in a large university football stadium. The rooms and the seats remain constant, but demand for them fluctuates. The band between the second and third horizontal lines represents optimal capacity—the best use of the capacity from the perspective of both customers and the company (the difference between optimal and maximum capacity utilization is discussed later in the chapter). The areas in the middle of Figure 13.1 are labeled to represent four basic scenarios that can result from different combinations of capacity and demand:

1. *Excess demand.* The level of demand exceeds maximum capacity. In this situation some customers will be turned away, resulting in lost business opportunities. For the customers who do receive the service, its quality may not match what was promised because of crowding or overtaxing of staff and facilities.

2. *Demand exceeds optimum capacity.* No one is being turned away, but the quality of service may still suffer because of overuse, crowding, or staff being pushed beyond their abilities to deliver consistent quality.

3. *Demand and supply are balanced at the level of optimal capacity.* Staff and facilities are occupied at an ideal level. No one is overworked, facilities can be maintained, and customers are receiving quality service without undesirable delays.

4. *Excess capacity.* Demand is below optimal capacity. Productive resources in the form of labor, equipment, and facilities are underutilized, resulting in low productivity and lower profits. Customers may receive excellent quality on an individual level because they have the full use of the facilities, no waiting, and complete attention from the staff. If, however, service quality depends on the presence of other customers, customers may be disappointed or may worry that they have chosen an inferior service provider.

Not all firms will be challenged equally in terms of managing supply and demand. The seriousness of the problem will depend on the *extent of demand fluctuations over time* and the *extent to which supply is constrained* (Table 13.1).[3] Organizations in some service industries will experience wide fluctuations in demand (hospitals,

TABLE 13.1
Demand and Capacity for Service Providers

Extent to Which Supply Is Constrained	Extent of Demand Fluctuations over Time	
	Wide	**Narrow**
	1	2
Peak demand can usually be met without a major delay.	Electricity Natural gas Police and fire emergencies Internet services	Insurance Legal services Banking Laundry and dry cleaning Hair salon
	4	3
Peak demand regularly exceeds capacity.	Accounting and tax preparation Passenger transportation Hotels Restaurants Hospital emergency rooms	Services similar to those in cell 2 that have insufficient capacity for their base level of business

Source: Adapted from C. H. Lovelock, "Classifying Services to Gain Strategic Marketing Insights," *Journal of Marketing* 47 (Summer 1983), p. 17.

transportation, restaurants), whereas others will have narrower fluctuations (insurance, laundry, banking). For some, peak demand can usually be met even when demand fluctuates (electricity, natural gas, Internet services), but for others peak demand may frequently exceed capacity (hospital emergency rooms, restaurants near football stadiums, hotels next to universities). Those firms with wide variations in demand (cells 1 and 4 in Table 13.1), and particularly those with wide fluctuations in demand that regularly exceed capacity (cell 4), will find the issues and strategies in this chapter particularly important to their success. Those firms that find themselves in cell 3 may decide a "one-time-fix" (as discussed in Chapter 9) to expand their capacity to match regular patterns of excessive demand will sufficiently address the situation. The industries in Table 13.1 are provided to illustrate where *most* firms in those industries would likely be classified. In reality, an individual firm from any industry could find itself in any of the four cells, depending on its immediate circumstances.

To identify effective strategies for managing supply and demand fluctuations, an organization needs a clear understanding of the constraints on its capacity and the underlying demand patterns.

CAPACITY CONSTRAINTS

For many firms, service capacity is fixed. As indicated in Table 13.2, critical fixed-capacity factors can be—depending on the type of service—time, labor, equipment, facilities, or (in many cases) a combination of these.

TABLE 13.2
Constraints on Capacity

Nature of the Constraint	Type of Service*
Time	Legal
	Consulting
	Accounting
	Medical
Labor	Law firm
	Accounting firm
	Consulting firm
	Health clinic
Equipment	Delivery services
	Telecommunications
	Network services
	Utilities
	Health clubs
Facilities	Hotels
	Restaurants
	Hospitals
	Airlines
	Schools
	Theaters
	Churches

*The examples illustrate the most common capacity constraint for each type of service. In reality, any of the service organizations listed can be operating under multiple constraints. For example, a law firm may be operating under constrained labor capacity (too few attorneys) and facilities constraints (not enough office space) at the same time.

Time, Labor, Equipment, and Facilities

For some service businesses, the primary constraint on service production is *time*. For example, a lawyer, a consultant, a hairdresser, a plumber, and a psychological counselor all primarily sell their time. In such contexts, if the service worker is not available or if his or her time is not used productively, profits are lost. If there is excess demand at a specific time, additional time cannot be created to satisfy it. From the point of view of the service provider, time is the constraint.

From the point of view of a firm that employs a large number of service providers, *labor* or staffing levels can be the primary capacity constraint. A law firm, a university department, a consulting firm, a tax accounting firm, and a repair and maintenance contractor may all face the reality that at certain times demand for their organization's services cannot be met because the staff is already operating at peak capacity. However, it does not always make sense (nor may it be possible in a competitive labor market) to hire additional service providers if low demand is a reality a large percentage of the time.

In other cases, *equipment* may be the critical constraint. For trucking or air-freight delivery services, the trucks or airplanes needed to service demand may be the capacity limitation. During the Christmas holidays, UPS, FedEx, and other delivery service providers face this issue. Health clubs also deal with this limitation, particularly at certain times of the day (before work, during lunch hours, after work) and in certain months of the year. For network service providers, bandwidth, servers, and switches represent their capacity constraints.

Finally, many firms face restrictions brought about by their limited *facilities*. Hotels have only a certain number of rooms to sell, airlines are limited by the number of seats on their aircraft, educational institutions are constrained by the number of rooms and the number of seats in each classroom, and restaurant capacity is restricted to the number of tables and seats available.

Understanding the primary capacity constraint, or the combination of factors that restricts capacity, is a first step in designing strategies to deal with supply and demand issues.

Optimal versus Maximum Use of Capacity

To fully understand capacity issues, it is important to know the difference between *optimal* and *maximum* use of capacity. As suggested in Figure 13.1, optimal and maximum capacity may not be the same. Using capacity at an optimal level means that resources are fully employed but not overused and that customers are receiving quality service in a timely manner. Maximum capacity, on the other hand, represents the absolute limit of service availability. In the case of a sporting event, optimal and maximum capacity may be the same. The entertainment value of the game is enhanced for customers when every seat is filled, and obviously the profitability for the home team is greatest under these circumstances (see accompanying photo on the next page). On the other hand, in a university classroom it is usually not desirable for students or faculty to have every seat filled. In this case, optimal use of capacity is less than the maximum. In some cases, maximum use of capacity may result in excessive waiting by customers, as in a popular restaurant. From the perspective of customer satisfaction, optimal use of the restaurant's capacity will be less than maximum use.

In the case of equipment or facilities constraints, the maximum capacity at any given time is obvious. There are only a certain number of weight machines in the health club, a certain number of seats in the airplane, and a limited amount of space in a cargo carrier. In the case of a bottling plant, when maximum capacity on the assembly line is exceeded, bottles begin to break and the system shuts down. Thus, it is relatively easy to observe the effects of exceeding maximum equipment capacity in many manufacturing situations.

FIGURE 13.2 **Strategies for Shifting Demand to Match Capacity**

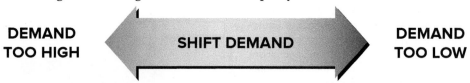

DEMAND TOO HIGH

SHIFT DEMAND

DEMAND TOO LOW

(*Reduce Demand during Peak Times*)

- Communicate busy days and times to customers.
- Modify timing and location of service delivery.
- Offer incentives for nonpeak usage.
- Set priorities by talking care of loyal or high-need customers first.
- Charge full price for the service—no discounts.

(*Increase Demand to Match Capacity*)

- Educate customers about peak times and benefits of nonpeak use.
- Vary how the facility is used.
- Vary the service offering.
- Differentiate on price.

Reduce Demand during Peak Times

One strategic approach to matching capacity and demand for a service provider focuses on *reducing demand* during times when customer demand is at its peak for the service.

Communicate with Customers One approach for shifting demand is to communicate with customers, letting them know the times of peak demand to persuade them to use the service at alternative times and avoid crowding or delays. For example, signs in banks and post offices that let customers know their busiest hours and busiest days of the week can serve as a warning, encouraging customers to shift their demand to another time if possible. Forewarning customers about busy times and possible waits can have added benefits. Many customer service call centers provide a similar warning by informing waiting customers about approximately how long it will be until they are served. Those who do not want to wait may choose to call back later when the customer service department is less busy, leave a call back number, or visit the company's website for faster service.

Modify Timing and Location of Service Delivery Some firms adjust their hours and days of service delivery to more directly reflect customer demand. Historically, U.S. banks were open only during "bankers' hours" from 10:00 a.m. to 3:00 p.m. every weekday—creating a heavy demand for their services during those hours. However, these hours did not necessarily match the times when most people preferred to do their personal banking. Now U.S. banks open early, stay open until 6:00 p.m. many days, and are open on Saturdays, better reflecting customer preferences and smoothing demand patterns. Many banks now have branches in hypermarkets such as Walmart and Meijer, and supermarkets such as Albertson's and Kroger, providing customers with multiple choices of both where and when to do their banking. Online banking has also shifted demand from branches to "anytime, anywhere" websites. Movie theaters often augment their primary viewing schedules by offering additional matinees on weekends and holidays to try to shift demand for their service.

Offer Incentives for Nonpeak Usage In an attempt to shift demand away from peak times, some firms will offer incentives to encourage customers to shift their use of the service to other times. In northern Midwest states, swimming pool contractors offer additional amenities (e.g., free diving board, free heater, larger pool) to customers who are willing to postpone the purchase/use of their services until the end of the swimming season (say, September or October). Fitness centers that offer Pilates classes during times of lower demand often tout the advantages of smaller classes and increased instructor interaction with clients and frequently extend the class time by 25 percent or more.

Set Priorities   When demand for the service is high and there is limited capacity, service providers can prioritize who is served by taking care of loyal or high-need customers first. A tax firm might decide to serve its best customers rather than first-time walk-ins just prior to income tax due dates, and emergency medical centers move the most severe cases to the top of the priority list.

Charge Full Price   Firms generally charge full price for service during those periods of time that they know their services are historically in high demand; no discounts are allowed during such times. One of the busiest periods of the year for airlines are those days just before and just after the Thanksgiving holiday; for this reason, most airlines give priority for seating to those paying full fares and prohibit the use of frequent flyer miles for free seats on those days. Because demand is so high, customers looking for discounted or free tickets find that the days around this holiday have been "blacked out"; to travel on those days, they must purchase tickets at regular fares.

Increase Demand to Match Capacity

Other approaches service providers may consider in matching capacity and demand focus on *increasing demand* for service during times when the service is operating at less than full capacity.

Educate Customers   Although a firm may know well and be able to anticipate times of increased demand, customers may not be aware of these times. Advertising and sales messages can be used to inform customers about times when demand is low. Electric utility companies often publicize periods of the day when demand for electricity is lower and urge customers to use washing machines or other equipment that consume large amounts of energy during those times. Promotional campaigns can also emphasize different service benefits to customers during peak and slow periods. For example, air-conditioning firms often promote their preventive maintenance services in early spring, before temperatures get too high, encouraging customers to use their services before demand is high and pointing out the quick availability of their service people and the reduced anxiety from not waiting "until it is too late" by calling early.

Vary How the Facility Is Used   Another approach to increasing demand to change how the service facility is used, depending on the season of the year, day of the week, or time of day. For example, Whistler Mountain, a ski resort in Vancouver, Canada, offers its slopes to mountain bikers and its facilities for executive development and training programs during the summer, when snow skiing

© Steve Bly/Getty Images

In summer months many ski resorts switch from targeting snow skiers to mountain bikers.

is not possible. A hospital in the Los Angeles area rents its facilities to film production crews who need realistic hospital settings for movies or television shows. Movie theaters are sometimes rented during weekdays by business groups and on Sunday mornings by church groups who have no building of their own. All of these are examples of how varying the use of the service facility can occur during a period of low demand.

Vary the Service Offering A similar approach entails changing the nature of the service offering. Accounting firms, for example, focus on tax preparation late in the year and until April 15, when federal taxes are due in the United States. During other times of the year, they can focus on audits and general tax consulting activities. During professional basketball games, the demand for food at concession stands increases dramatically during the breaks between quarters—so much so that many customers decide not to make purchases for fear they will miss seeing the game because of long lines. In response to this situation, concessions at many sport stadiums are now offered through menu orders taken by staff roaming through the aisles, and food is delivered right to customers' seats while the game is going on. In larger cities across the globe, McDonald's offers food delivery as a way to increase demand for its service.[6] In these examples, the service offering and associated benefits are changed to smooth customer demand for the organization's resources.

Care should be exercised in implementing strategies to change the service offering because such changes may imply and require alterations in other marketing mix variables—such as promotion, pricing, and staffing—to match the new offering. Unless these additional mix variables are altered effectively to support the offering, the strategy may not work. Even when done well, the downside of such changes can be confusion about the organization's image from the customers' perspective or a loss of strategic focus for the organization and its employees.

Differentiate on Price A common response during periods of slow demand is to discount the price of the service. This strategy relies on basic economics of supply and demand. To be effective, however, a price differentiation strategy depends on solid understanding of customer price sensitivity and demand curves. For example, business travelers are far less price sensitive than are families traveling for pleasure. For the Phoenician in Scottsdale (our opening vignette), lowering prices during the slow summer months is not likely to increase bookings from business travelers dramatically. However, the lower summer prices attract considerable numbers of families and local guests who want an opportunity to experience a luxury hotel but are not able to afford the rooms during peak season.

Heavy use of price differentiation to smooth demand can be a risky strategy. Customers may grow accustomed to the lower price and expect to get the same deal the next time they use the service. If communication with customers is unclear, customers may not understand the reasons for the discounts and will expect to pay the same during peak demand periods. Overuse or exclusive use of price as a strategy for smoothing demand is also risky because of the potential impact on the organization's image, the potential for attracting undesired market segments, and the possibility that those customers paying higher prices may feel they have been treated unfairly.

Adjusting Capacity to Meet Demand

A second strategic approach to matching supply and demand focuses on *adjusting capacity*. The fundamental idea here is to adjust, stretch, and align capacity to match customer demand (rather than working on shifting demand to match capacity, as just described). During periods of peak demand the organization seeks to stretch or expand its capacity as much as possible. During periods of slow demand it tries to shrink capacity so as not to waste resources. General strategies for adjusting the four primary service

FIGURE 13.3   **Strategies for Adjusting Capacity to Match Demand**

| DEMAND TOO HIGH | ADJUST CAPACITY | DEMAND TOO LOW |

(Increase Capacity Temporarily)

- Stretch people, facilities, and equipment temporarily.
- Use part-time employees.
- Cross-train employees.
- Outsource activities.
- Rent or share facilities and equipment.

(Adjust Use of Resources)

- Schedule downtime during periods of low demand.
- Perform maintenance and renovations.
- Schedule vacations and employee training strategically.
- Modify or move facilities and equipment.

resources (time, people, equipment, and facilities) are discussed throughout the rest of this section. In Figure 13.3, we summarize specific ideas for adjusting capacity during periods of peak and slow demand. Often, a number of different strategies are used simultaneously.

Increase Capacity Temporarily

Existing capacity can often be expanded temporarily to match demand. In such cases, no new resources are added; rather, the people, facilities, and equipment are asked to work harder and longer to meet demand.

Stretch People, Facilities, and Equipment Temporarily   It may be possible to extend the hours of service temporarily to accommodate demand. A health clinic might stay open longer during flu season, retailers are open longer hours during the holiday shopping season, and accountants have extended appointment hours (evenings and Saturdays) in the weeks just before tax deadlines. Indeed, in many service organizations, employees are asked to work longer and harder during periods of peak demand. For example, consulting organizations face extensive peaks and valleys with respect to demand for their services. During peak demand, associates are asked to take on additional projects and work longer hours. And frontline service personnel in banks, tourist attractions, restaurants, and telecommunications companies are asked to serve more customers per hour during busy times than during "normal" hours or days.

Facilities such as theaters, restaurants, meeting facilities, and classrooms can sometimes be expanded temporarily by the addition of tables, chairs, or other equipment needed by customers. Or, as in the case of a commuter train, a car that holds a fixed number of people seated comfortably can "expand" by accommodating standing passengers. Similarly, computers, power lines, tour buses, and maintenance equipment can often be stretched beyond what would be considered the maximum capacity for short periods to accommodate peak demand.

In using these types of "stretch" strategies, the organization needs to recognize the wear and tear on resources and the potential for inferior quality of service that may go with extended usage of such strategies. These strategies should thus be used for relatively short periods to allow for refreshment of the people who are asked to exceed their usual capacity and for maintenance of the facilities and equipment. Sometimes it is difficult to know in advance, particularly in the case of human resources, when capacity has been stretched too far.

Use Part-Time Employees   In this situation the organization's labor resources are being aligned with demand. Retailers hire part-time employees during the holiday rush; tax accountants engage temporary help during tax season; tourist resorts bring in extra workers during peak season. To address the increased demand for package delivery at the end of the year, UPS has been known to hire more than 90,000 temporary employees to work between Thanksgiving and Christmas to handle the holiday rush.[7] Restaurants often ask employees to work split shifts (work the lunch shift, leave for a few hours, and come back for the dinner rush) during peak mealtime hours.

Cross-Train Employees   If employees are cross-trained, they can shift among tasks, filling in where they are most needed. Cross-training increases the efficiency of the whole system and avoids underutilizing employees in some areas while others are being overtaxed. Many airlines cross-train their employees to move from ticketing to working the gate counter to assisting with baggage if needed. In some fast-food restaurants, employees specialize in one task (like making french fries) during busy hours, and the team of specialists may number 10 people. During slow hours the team may shrink to 3, with each of the remaining persons performing a variety of other functions. Grocery stores also use this strategy, with most employees able to move as needed from cashiering to stocking shelves to bagging groceries.

Outsource Activities   Firms that find they have a temporary peak in demand for internal services may choose to outsource the service. For example, in recent years, many firms have found they do not have the capacity to fulfill their own needs for technology support, web design, and software-related services. Hospitals in Arizona often use health care staffing agencies to temporarily hire registered nurses for three months during the winter to handle the influx of winter visitors and the onset of the flu season. Rather than try to hire and train additional employees, these companies look to firms that specialize in outsourcing these types of functions as a temporary (or sometimes long-term) solution.

Rent or Share Facilities and Equipment   For some organizations it is best to rent additional equipment or facilities during periods of peak demand. For example, express mail delivery services rent or lease trucks during the peak holiday delivery season. It would not make sense to buy trucks that would sit idle during the rest of the year. Sometimes organizations with complementary demand patterns can share facilities. An example is a church that shares its facilities during the week with a Montessori preschool. The school needs the facilities Monday through Friday during the day; the church needs the facilities in the evenings and on the weekend. Some businesses have been created to satisfy other businesses' fluctuating demand. For example, a firm may offer temporary office suites and clerical support to individuals who do not need such facilities and support on a continuous basis.

Adjust Use of Resources

This basic strategy is sometimes known as a "chase demand" strategy. By adjusting service resources creatively, organizations can, in effect, chase the demand curves to match capacity with customer demand patterns. People, facilities, and equipment are again the focus, this time with an eye toward adjusting the basic mix and use of these resources. Specific actions might include the following.[8]

Schedule Downtime during Periods of Low Demand If people, equipment, and facilities are being used at maximum capacity during peak periods, then it is imperative to schedule downtime during off-peak periods. Online banking services, for example, often schedule software upgrades on early Sunday morning (4:00–6:00 a.m.) to keep those affected by the disruption of their service to a minimum.

Perform Maintenance and Renovations For almost all services, facilities and equipment need to be repaired and maintained periodically. Such scheduling should take place during periods of slow demand, as should renovations. Universities, for example, frequently arrange for the painting of classrooms or restriping of parking lots to be done when students are on a break.

Schedule Vacations and Employee Training Strategically To ensure that employees are available when most needed, employee vacations and training should take place during periods of slow demand. Some firms adjust capacity by laying employees off when they know demand will be low. Hotels in popular tourist destinations routinely lay employees off during the off season. In fact, some employees know this well in advance and look forward to working in ski resort hotels in the winter months and coastal resort hotels in the summer months. Throughout all of these strategies, such scheduling attempts to ensure that a provider's resources are in top condition and available when they are most needed.

Modify or Move Facilities and Equipment Sometimes it is possible to adjust, move, or creatively modify existing capacity to meet demand fluctuations. Hotels utilize this strategy by reconfiguring rooms—two rooms with a locked door between can be rented to two different parties in high demand times or turned into a suite during slow demand. The airline industry offers another example of this strategy. Using an approach known as "demand-driven dispatch," airlines often assign airplanes to flight schedules on the basis of fluctuating market needs.[9] The method depends on accurate knowledge of demand and the ability to quickly move airplanes with different seating capacities to flight assignments that match their capacity. The Boeing 787 aircraft is so flexible that it can be reconfigured in less than an hour to vary the number of seats allocated to one, two, or three classes.[10] The plane can thus be quickly modified to match demand from different market segments, essentially molding capacity to fit demand. Another strategy may involve moving the service to a new location to meet customer demand or even bringing the service to customers. Mobile training facilities, pet grooming vans, and flu shot and blood donation facilities are examples of services that physically follow customers.

Combining Demand and Capacity Strategies

Many firms use multiple strategies, combining marketing-driven demand management approaches with operations-driven capacity management strategies. Figuring out which is the best set of strategies for maximizing capacity utilization, customer satisfaction, and profitability can be challenging, particularly when the service represents a constellation of offerings within one service setting. Examples of such services include theme parks with rides, restaurants, and shopping; hotel vacation villages with hotels, shopping, spas, pools, and restaurants; and ski resorts with ski slopes, spas, restaurants, and entertainment. Firms face complex problems in trying to balance demand across all the different offerings with an eye to quality and profitability. Our Strategy Insight describes a ski resort simulation that was created to use operations and marketing variables to determine the optimal combination of demand and capacity management strategies across the resort's various offerings and activities.

is the ratio of actual revenue to potential revenue for a particular measurement period:

$$\text{Yield} = \frac{\text{Actual revenue}}{\text{Potential revenue}}$$

where

Actual revenue = Actual capacity used × Average actual price
Potential revenue = Total capacity × Maximum price

The equations indicate that yield is a function of price and capacity used. Recall that capacity constraints can be in the form of time, labor, equipment, or facilities. Yield is essentially a measure of the extent to which an organization's resources (or capacities) are achieving their full revenue-generating potential. Assuming that total capacity and maximum price cannot be changed, yield approaches a value of 1 as actual capacity utilization increases or when a higher actual price can be charged for a given capacity used. For example, in an airline context, a manager could focus on increasing yield by finding ways to bring in more passengers to fill the capacity or by finding higher-paying passengers to fill a more limited capacity. In reality, expert yield managers work on capacity and pricing issues simultaneously to maximize revenue across different customer segments. Exhibit 13.1 shows simple yield calculations and the inherent trade-offs for two types of services: hotel and legal.

Implementing a Yield Management System

Our Technology Spotlight illustrates several examples of how information technology supports effective yield management applications. To implement a yield management system, an organization needs detailed data on past demand patterns by market segment as well as methods of projecting current market demand. The data can be combined through mathematical programming models, threshold analysis, or expert systems to project the best allocation of limited capacity at a particular point in time.[12] Allocations of capacity for specific market segments can then be communicated to sales representatives or reservations staff as targets for selling rooms, seats, time, or other limited resources. Sometimes the allocations, once determined, remain fixed. At other times allocations change weekly, or even daily or hourly, in response to new information.

Research indicates that traditional yield management approaches are most appropriate for service firms when:

1. They have relatively fixed capacity.
2. They have perishable inventory.
3. They have different market segments or customers, who arrive or make their reservations at different times.
4. They have low marginal sales costs and high marginal capacity change costs.
5. The product is sold in advance.
6. There is fluctuating demand.
7. Customers who arrive or reserve early are more price sensitive than those who arrive or reserve late.[13]

When these conditions are present, yield management approaches can generally be employed to identify the best mix of service offerings to produce and sell in the period, and at what prices, to generate the highest expected revenue. These criteria exactly fit the situation for airlines, car rental agencies, and many hotels—industries that have

Basic yield calculations can be done for any capacity-constrained service, assuming the actual capacity, average price charged for different market segments, and maximum price that could be charged are known. Ideally, yield will approach the number 1, or 100 percent, where

Yield = Actual revenue / Potential revenue

In this box we describe yield calculations for two simple examples—a 200-room hotel and a lawyer with a 40-hour work week—under different assumed pricing and usage situations. Although companies use much more complex mathematical models to determine yield, the underlying ideas are the same. The goal is to maximize the revenue-generating capability of the organization's capacity.

200-ROOM HOTEL WITH MAXIMUM ROOM RATE OF $200 PER ROOM PER NIGHT

Potential revenue = $200 × 200 rooms
= $40,000 per night

1. Assume: the hotel rents all its rooms at a discounted rate of $100 per night.

    Yield = ($100 × 200 rooms) / $40,000 = 50%

    At this rate, the hotel is maximizing capacity utilization but not getting a very good price.

2. Assume: the hotel charges its full rate but can only rent 40 percent of its rooms at that price, due to price sensitivity.

    Yield = ($200 × 80 rooms) / $40,000 = 40%

    In this situation the hotel has maximized the per-room price, but the yield is even lower than in the first situation because so few rooms are rented at that relatively high rate.

3. Assume: the hotel charges its full rate of $200 for 40 percent of its rooms and then gives a discount of $100 for the remaining 120 rooms.

Yield = [($200 × 80) + ($100 × 120)] / $40,000
= $28,000 / $40,000 = 70%

Clearly, the final alternative, which takes into account price sensitivity and charges different prices for different rooms or market segments, results in the highest yield among these three alternatives.

40 HOURS OF A LAWYER'S TIME ACROSS A TYPICAL WORK WEEK AT $200 PER HOUR MAXIMUM (PRIVATE CLIENT RATE)

Potential revenue = 40 hours × $200 per hour
= $8,000 per week

1. Assume: the lawyer is able to bill out 30 percent of her billable time at $200 per hour.

    Yield = ($200 × 12 hours) / $8,000 = 30%

    In this case the lawyer has maximized her hourly rate but has only enough work to occupy 12 billable hours.

2. Assume: the lawyer decides to charge $100 for non-profit or government clients and is able to bill out all 40 hours at this rate for these types of clients.

    Yield = ($100 × 40 hours) / $8,000 = 50%

    In this case, although she has worked a full week, yield is still not very good, given the relatively low rate per hour.

3. Assume: the lawyer uses a combined strategy in which she works 12 hours for private clients and fills the rest of her time with nonprofit clients at $100 per hour.

    Yield = [($200 × 12) + ($100 × 28)] / $8,000
    = $5,200 / $8,000 = 65%

    Again, catering to two different market segments with different price sensitivities is the best overall strategy in terms of maximizing revenue-generating capacity of the lawyer's time.

effectively and extensively used yield management techniques to allocate capacity. In other services (entertainment, sports, fashion), those customers willing to pay the higher prices are the ones who buy early rather than late. People who really want to see a particular performance reserve their seats at the earliest possible moment. Discounting for early purchases would reduce profits. In these situations, the price generally starts out high and is reduced later to fill capacity if needed.

Interestingly, some airlines use both these strategies effectively. They start with discounted seats for customers who are willing to buy early, usually leisure and discretionary travelers. They charge a higher fare for those who want a seat at the last minute, typically the less-price-sensitive business travelers whose destinations

Technology Spotlight Information and Technology Drive Yield Management Systems

Yield management is not a new concept. In fact, the basic idea behind yield management—achieving maximum profits through the most effective use of capacity—has been around forever. It is easy to find examples of capacity-constrained businesses using price to shift demand: theaters that charge different prices for matinees versus evening performances, intercity trains with different prices on weekdays than on weekends, ski resorts with cheaper prices for night skiing, and restaurants with "twilight" dinner specials. All these strategies illustrate attempts to smooth the peaks and valleys of demand using price as the primary motivator.

The difference in these basic pricing strategies and more sophisticated yield management approaches currently in use by airlines, car rental companies, hotels, shippers, and others is the reliance of these latter strategies on massive databases, sophisticated mathematical algorithms, and complex analyses. These forms of yield management consider not only price but also market segments, price sensitivity among segments, timing of demand, and potential profitability of customer segments—all simultaneously. What makes new forms of yield management possible are the technology and systems underlying them. Here are a few examples of what some companies and industries have done.

AMERICAN AIRLINES

American Airlines is the original pioneer and still the king of yield management. Beginning with Super Saver Fares in the mid-1970s, American has depended on systems developed by Sabre (the oldest and leading provider of technology for the travel industry) to support an exceedingly complex system of fares. Using a system of models containing algorithms that optimize prices, manage wait lists, and handle traffic management, American uses Sabre to allocate seats on every one of its flights. The number of seats sold on each of American's flights is continuously compared with a sales forecast for that flight. Blocks of seats are moved from higher to lower fares if sales are below projections. If sales are at or above the forecast, no changes are made. American's stated objective has historically been to "sell the right seats to the right customers at the right price."

AIR BERLIN

Air Berlin, one of Europe's leading airllines, provides relatively low-cost services worldwide to more than 130 destinations and uses yield management in an effort to maximize passenger revenue. Its yield management process begins six to nine months prior to a flight's scheduled departure date. Air Berlin often sells initial blocks of seats at what it terms "headline prices" to price-sensitive customers and tour operators; any seats

and schedules are inflexible. However, in some cases a bargain fare can be found at the last minute as well, commonly via Internet sales, to fill seats that would otherwise go unoccupied. Online auctions and services offered by companies like Priceline.com, Expedia.com, or Booking.com serve a purpose in filling capacity at the last minute, often charging much lower fares. (See the Technology Spotlight in Chapter 15 for examples of dynamic pricing via the Internet.)

Challenges and Risks in Using Yield Management

Yield management programs can significantly improve revenues. However, although yield management may appear to be an ideal solution to the problem of matching supply and demand, it is not without risks. By becoming focused on maximizing financial returns through differential capacity allocation and pricing, an organization may encounter these problems:[14]

- *Loss of competitive focus.* Yield management may cause a firm to overfocus on profit maximization and inadvertently neglect aspects of the service that provide long-term competitive success.

not initially sold are then managed through Air Berlin's yield management technology. Its yield management system requires massive amounts of data that take into account the season when the flight takes place, general popularity of the route, local holiday schedules and upcoming events, and exact time of departure. Similar to other airlines, Air Berlin adjusts its fares frequently, sometimes several times a day as the flight's departure date nears, to reflect customer demand and the time remaining until the departure date. However, because Air Berlin's focus is on relatively short routes, it offers only a single class of service on all of its flights and each flight is available on a one-way ticket basis. This practice means that each flight is subject to its own price management, enabling Air Berlin to charge passengers different fares on outbound flights and return flights. By developing profiles for each flight, Air Berlin's yield management technology helps it maximize passenger revenue by flight and by regions while maintaining high passenger load factors.

MARRIOTT HOTELS

The hotel industry has also embraced the concepts of yield management, and Marriott Hotels has been a leader. The systems at Marriott, for example, maximize profits for a hotel across full weeks rather than by day. In its hotels that target business travelers, Marriott has peak days during the middle of the week. Rather than simply sell the hotel out on those nights on a first-come, first-served basis with no discounts, the revenue management system (which is reviewed and revised daily) projects guest demand both by price and by length of stay, providing discounts in some cases to guests who will stay longer, even on a peak demand night. One early test of the system was at the Munich Marriott during Oktoberfest. Typically, no discounts would be offered during this peak period. However, the yield management system recommended that the hotel offer some rooms at a discount, but only for those guests who stayed an extended period before or after the peak days. Although the average daily rate went down 11.7 percent for the period, occupancy went up more than 20 percent and overall revenues went up 12.3 percent. Using yield management practices, Marriott Hotels estimates it generates an additional $400 million per year in revenue.

Sources: The primary source for the American Airlines and Marriott discussions is R. G. Cross, *Revenue Management* (New York: Broadway Books, 1997). Other sources include "Dynamic Pricing at American Airlines," *Business Quarterly* 61 (Autumn 1996), p. 45; Air Berlin's website (www.airberlin.com), accessed June 28, 2016; and N. Templin, "Your Room Costs $250 . . . No! $200 . . . No," *The Wall Street Journal,* May 5, 1999, p. B1.

- *Customer alienation.* If customers learn that they are paying a higher price for service than someone else, they may perceive the pricing as unfair, particularly if they do not understand the reasons. However, a study done in the restaurant industry found that, when customers were informed of different prices being charged by time of day, week, or table location, they generally felt the practice was fair, particularly if the price difference was framed as a discount for less desirable times rather than a premium for peak times or table locations.[15] Customer education is thus essential in an effective yield management program.

- *Overbooking.* Customers can be further alienated if they fall victim (and are not compensated adequately) to the overbooking practices often necessary to make yield management systems work effectively. Research suggests that customers who experience negative consequences of revenue management (i.e., denied service or downgrades), particularly high-value customers, subsequently reduce their number of transactions with the firm.[16]

- *Incompatible incentive and reward systems.* Employees may resent yield management systems that do not match incentive structures. For example, many managers are rewarded on the basis of capacity utilization *or* average rate charged, whereas yield management balances the two factors.

- *Inappropriate organization of the yield management function.* To be most effective with yield management, an organization must have centralized reservations. Although airlines and some large hotel chains and shipping companies do have such centralization, smaller organizations may have decentralized reservations systems and thus find it difficult to operate a yield management system effectively.

WAITING LINE STRATEGIES: WHEN DEMAND AND CAPACITY CANNOT BE MATCHED

Sometimes it is not possible to manage capacity to precisely match demand, or vice versa. It may be too costly—for example, most health clinics would not find it economically feasible to add facilities or physicians to handle peaks in demand during the winter flu season; patients usually simply have to wait to be seen. Or demand may be very unpredictable and the service capacity very inflexible (it cannot be easily stretched to match unpredictable peaks in demand). Sometimes waits occur when demand backs up because of the variability in length of time for service. For example, even though patients are scheduled by appointments in a physician's office, frequently there is a wait because some patients take longer to serve than the time allotted to them. The misalignment in capacity and demand is particularly troublesome in emergency health care, as is described in Exhibit 13.2.

For most service organizations, waiting customers are a fact of life at some point. Waiting can occur on the telephone (customers put on hold when they call in to ask for information, order something, or make a complaint) and in person (customers waiting in line at the bank, the post office, Disneyland, or a physician's office). Waiting can occur even with service transactions through the mail—delays in mail-order delivery—or backlogs of correspondence on a manager's desk.

In today's fast-paced society, waiting is not something most people tolerate well. As people work longer hours, as individuals have less leisure time, and as families have fewer hours together, the pressure on people's time is greater than ever. In this environment, customers are looking for efficient, quick service with no wait. Organizations that make customers wait may lose business or at the very least create dissatisfied customers.[17] Research suggests that waiting time satisfaction is nearly as important as service delivery satisfaction with respect to customer loyalty.[18] To deal effectively with the inevitability of waits, organizations can utilize a variety of strategies; four general strategies are described next.

Customer satisfaction is heavily dependent on the amount of time customers spend waiting for a service.

© Ryan McVay/Getty Images

Employ Operational Logic

If customer waits are common, a first step is to analyze the operational processes to remove any inefficiencies. It may be possible to redesign the system to move customers along more quickly. In introducing its express check-in, Marriott Hotels

Nowhere is there a more vivid example of demand and capacity issues than in the more than 5,000 emergency departments (EDs) in hospitals across the United States (*emergency department* is the preferred term within the medical community for what has traditionally been called the ER). In a typical ED, rooms are filled, the corridors may be clogged with waiting patients, wait time may be anywhere from 15 minutes to 8 or 10 hours, and ambulances are routinely turned away to seek other hospitals on what is called "reroute" or "diversion." Many experts have referred to these issues as a national crisis in health care. The emergency department is the front door of hospitals and is the treatment of last resort for many. Why has this overcrowding issue reached national proportions? Many factors come into play, including increased demand and severe capacity constraints.

© Ryan McVay/Getty Images

INCREASED DEMAND FOR SERVICES

Emergency departments are to some extent victims of their own success. Decades of public health campaigns urging people to call 911 in case of medical emergency have been successful in educating people to do just that—and they end up in the ED. Many do indeed have life-threatening emergencies that belong in the ED. Others waiting in the ED are uninsured; as of 2015, more than 36 million people in the United States were uninsured. The ED is their only option, and legally the ED must care for them. But it is not only the uninsured and those with life-threatening emergencies who crowd the ED. It is also insured patients who cannot get appointments with their doctors in a timely manner or who learn that it may be their fastest entry into a hospital bed. Patients and their doctors are becoming aware that they can get sophisticated care in the ED relatively quickly. Thus, the demand for ED services has increased.

CAPACITY CONSTRAINTS

It is not just an increase in demand that is causing the overcrowding. It is also a shrinkage or unavailability of critical capacity at the same time. Doctors are overbooked in private practices, so patients who do not want to wait turn to the ED. Also, a shortage of specialists who are willing to take patients on call from the ED results in increased waiting times because these patients waiting for specialized care occupy beds in the ED longer than necessary. Another very critical capacity constraint is the number of beds in hospitals. Over the years, many hospitals across the country have closed for financial reasons, reducing the number of beds available. So ED patients often cannot get beds right away even if they need one, increasing waiting time for themselves and

others. There is a critical shortage of nurses as well, and a hospital bed requires a nurse to attend it before it can be occupied. In the 1990s enrollment in nursing programs slumped as people turned to more lucrative careers, and as of 2015 the average age of a registered nurse was nearly 45. Many hospitals have 20 percent of their nursing slots empty. Staffing shortages in housekeeping also play a role. A bed may be empty, but until it is cleaned and remade, it is not available for a waiting patient. In some communities, patients may find that ED facilities are simply not available. Some hospitals have actually closed their emergency departments after determining that it is unprofitable to run them because of poor reimbursement rates. In other areas, population growth is outpacing hospital and ED construction.

HOSPITALS' RESPONSES

To address this complex set of issues, a few changes have been made.

Technology

A partial solution has been to turn to technology to smooth the process of admitting patients into the ED and to track the availability of hospital beds. Some web-based systems are used to reroute ambulances to hospitals that have capacity. Other systems help EDs track the availability of rooms in their own hospitals in terms of knowing exactly when a bed is vacant and when it has been cleaned and is available—similar to what hotels have done for decades. Wireless systems for registering patients at bedside and "radar screens" that track everything going on in the ED are other partial solutions. These screens can track patients,

(continued)

Exhibit 13.2 (concluded)

staff, carts, and equipment, making the service delivery process more efficient and quicker.

Systems Improvements

Other hospitals have segmented their patients and have developed parallel "fast track" processes for dealing with minor emergency patients that can account for 30–50 percent of total visits. This process can be separated from the major-emergency situations that may require more time and special equipment. Quicker admitting processes are also being implemented. Kiosks have been installed in some hospitals to allow emergency patients to check themselves in and describe their symptoms to help speed up the admission process. Patients who are not experiencing true emergencies (true emergencies being gunshot victims or car accident victims with serious injuries) use touch screens to enter their name, age, and other personal information. Such kiosks display a list of ailments to choose from, like "pain" or "fever and/or chills," and a list of body parts to indicate where the discomfort is occurring. Once a patient's problem is entered into the system, it pops up on a screen accessible to nurses; those with chest pains, stroke symptoms, or other potentially serious issues take priority.

Yet another innovation is to have staff administer routine tests while the patient is waiting, so that the doctor who finally sees the patient has information at hand. This solution also satisfies the patient's need for "something to happen" during the waiting time. Giving patients pagers so they can do something else while waiting is another way that EDs are helping patients cope with the long waits.

Increasing Capacity

Another set of partial solutions relates directly to hospital and staff capacity issues. Some hospitals have added rooms and other facilities. More urgent care centers are being built to take some of the pressure off EDs. For patients who need to be admitted to the hospital, however, increasing capacity is not a total solution. The nursing shortage, one of the most critical problems, is very difficult to solve. Individual hospital systems have gotten creative in their efforts to steal nurses away from other hospitals, even recruiting heavily overseas. However, in the long term the solution rests more in making the occupation attractive in salaries and working conditions, thus increasing the number of people entering nursing programs.

It is obvious that this classic dilemma of matching supply and demand in a service context such as emergency care has multiple, deeply rooted causes. The solutions to the issues are also multifaceted—some can be undertaken by individual hospitals, whereas others need to be addressed by the entire health care industry.

Sources: L. Landro, "ERs Now Turn to Technology to Help Deal with Overcapacity," *The Wall Street Journal*, July 13, 2001, p. B1; J. Snyder, "Curing the ER," *The Arizona Republic*, December 9, 2001, pp. D1+; N. Shute and M. B. Marcus, CODE BLUE "Crisis in the ER," *US News & World Report*, September 10, 2001, pp. 54–61; U.S. Census Bureau, @ 2008 Nursing Shortage Fact Sheet, @ http://www.aacn.nche.edu/media/pdf/NrsgShortageFS.pdf, accessed December 27, 2010; J. Stengle, "ER Kiosks Let Patients Avoid Long Lines," *Associated Press*, September 13, 2007, http://www.gallup.com/poll/186047/uninsured-rate-third-quarter.aspx, accessed July 12, 2016.

used an operations-based modification to eliminate much of the waiting previously experienced by its guests. Guests who use a credit card and preregister can avoid waiting in line at the hotel front desk altogether. The guest can make it from the curb outside the hotel to his or her room in as little as three minutes when escorted by a "guest service associate," who checks the guest into the hotel, picks up keys and paperwork from a rack in the lobby, and then escorts the guest directly to the room.[19] The U.S. Department of Transportation Security Administration (TSA) offers similar preferential treatment for selected frequent travelers through its "TSA Pre✓®" program.[20] Only U.S. citizens and permanent legal residents who meet certain flying criteria may apply. After registering with the system and clearing an extensive background check, travelers who qualify for this program are allowed to bypass the usual security checkpoint in their designated airport and instead be screened through a security system that reads either their fingerprints or the irises in their eyes. They must still go through a metal detector and their bags are still passed through an X-ray scanner, but they get their own special line and are not randomly selected for additional screening.

When queues are inevitable, the organization faces the operational decision of what kind of queuing system to use or how to configure the queue. *Queue configuration* refers to the number of queues, their locations, their spatial requirement, and their effect on customer behavior.[21] Several possibilities exist, as shown in Figure 13.4. In the multiple-queue

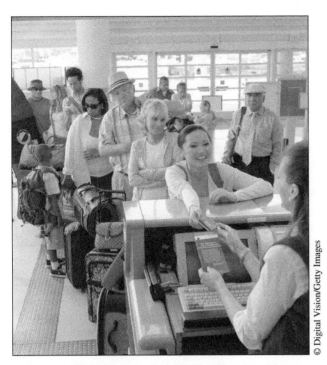

Waiting is common in many service industries.

alternative, the customer arrives at the service facility and must decide which queue to join and whether to switch later if the wait appears to be shorter in another line. In the single-queue alternative, fairness of waiting time is ensured in that the first-come, first-served rule applies to everyone; the system can also reduce the average time customers spend waiting overall. However, customers may leave if they perceive that the line is too long or if they have no opportunity to select a particular service provider. The last option shown in Figure 13.4 is the take-a-number option, in which arriving customers take a number to indicate line position. Advantages are similar to the single-queue alternative with the additional benefit that customers are able to mill about, browse, and talk to each other. The disadvantage is that customers must be on the alert to hear their numbers when they are called. Research suggests that length of the queue and perceived cost of waiting are not the only influences on customers' likelihood of staying in line. In a series of experiments and field tests, researchers showed that, the larger the number of customers waiting in line *behind* a consumer, the more likely that consumer is to stay in line and wait for the service.[22]

Establish a Reservation Process

When waiting cannot be avoided, a reservation system can help to spread demand. Restaurants, transportation companies, theaters, physicians, and many other service providers use reservation systems to alleviate long waits. The California Department of Motor Vehicles allows customers to make appointments via the Internet to help reduce the time they must spend waiting at its offices. The idea behind a reservation system is to guarantee the service will be available when the customer arrives. Beyond simply reducing waiting time, a reservation system has the added benefit of potentially shifting demand to less

FIGURE 13.4
Waiting Line Configurations

J. A. Fitzsimmons, M. J. Fitzsimmons, and S. K. Bordoloi, Service Management: Operations, Strategy, Information Technology, 8th ed. (New York: McGraw-Hill/Irwin, 2014), ch. 12, p. 345.

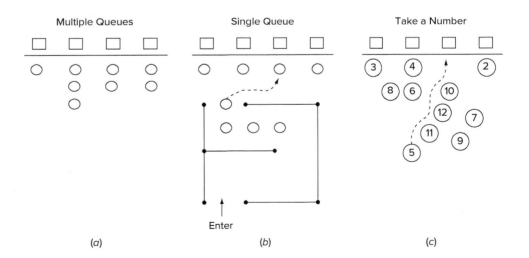

desirable time periods. A challenge inherent in reservation systems, however, is what to do about "no shows." Inevitably there will be customers who reserve a time but do not show up. Some organizations deal with this problem by overbooking their service capacity on the basis of past records of no-show percentages. If the predictions are accurate, overbooking is a good solution. When predictions are inaccurate, however, customers may still have to wait and sometimes may not be served at all, as when airlines overbook the number of seats available on a flight. Victims of overbooking may be compensated for their inconvenience in such cases. To minimize the no-show problem, some organizations (such as hotels, airlines, conferences/training programs, and theaters) charge customers who fail to show up or to cancel their reservations within a certain time frame.

Differentiate Waiting Customers

Not all customers need to wait the same length of time for service. On the basis of need or customer priority, some organizations differentiate among customers, allowing some to experience shorter waits for service than others. Known as "queue discipline," such differentiation reflects management policies regarding whom to select next for service.[23] The most popular discipline is first-come, first-served. However, other rules may apply. Differentiation can be based on factors such as these:[24]

- *Importance of the customer.* Frequent customers or customers who spend large amounts with the organization can be given priority in service by providing them with a special waiting area or segregated lines.

- *Urgency of the job.* Those customers with the most urgent need may be served first. This strategy is used in emergency health care. It is also used by maintenance services such as air-conditioning repair that give priority to customers whose air conditioning is not functioning over those who call for routine maintenance.

- *Duration of the service transaction.* In many situations, shorter service jobs get priority through "express lanes." At other times, when a service provider sees that a transaction is going to require extra time, the customer is referred to a designated provider who deals only with these special-needs customers.

- *Payment of a premium price.* Customers who pay extra (e.g., first class on an airline) are often given priority via separate check-in lines or express systems. At several Six Flags amusement parks, groups of up to six customers can purchase a Flashpass for about $45 per person (in addition to park entrance fees). Doing so allows them to use a palm-sized device, which is inserted at signs near the popular rides throughout the park, to keep their place in line virtually. The device sends a signal 10 minutes before it is time to come back and get on the ride (through a separate entrance), allowing customers to visit other attractions in the park without having to spend as much time in line. A "Gold" Flashpass can also be purchased, for about $25 more, to move customers up in a queue so that they experience very little or even no wait, and for $70 more a "Platinum" pass can be purchased that allows customers to ride a ride twice consecutively.[25] In recent years a variation of this service, Qsmart, allows mobile phone users to reserve their place in a virtual queue and notifies them once their virtual queue time has elapsed. To use this service customers pay an additional fee to avoid standing in a queue at amusement parks.[26]

Make Waiting More Pleasurable

Even when they have to wait, customers can still be satisfied, depending on how the wait is handled by the organization. Of course, the actual length of the wait will affect how customers feel about their service experience. But it is not just the actual time spent waiting that has an impact on customer satisfaction—it is how customers feel about the wait and their perceptions during it. The type of wait (e.g., a standard queue versus a wait due to a delay of service) can also influence how customers will react.[27] In a classic article entitled "The Psychology of Waiting Lines," David Maister proposes several principles about waiting, each of which has implications for how organizations can make waiting more pleasurable.[28]

Unoccupied Time Feels Longer Than Occupied Time

When customers are unoccupied they will likely be bored and will notice the passage of time more than when they have something to do. Providing something for waiting customers to do, particularly if the activity offers a benefit in and of itself or is related in some way to the service, can improve the customer's experience and may benefit the organization as well.[29] Examples include giving customers menus to look at while waiting in a restaurant, providing interesting information to read or watch on a monitor in a dentist's office, and playing entertaining programs over the phone while customers are on hold.

Preprocess Waits Feel Longer Than In-Process Waits

If wait time is occupied with activities that relate to the upcoming service, customers may perceive that the service has started and that they are no longer actually waiting. This in-process activity will make the length of the wait seem shorter and will benefit the service provider by making the customer better prepared when the service actually does begin. Filling out medical information while waiting to see the physician, reading a menu while waiting to be seated in a restaurant, and watching a videotape of the upcoming service event are all activities that can both educate the customer and reduce perceptions of waiting.

Research in a restaurant context has found that customers react more negatively to preprocess waits than to either in-process or postprocess waits; that is, preprocess waits are relatively more important in determining customers' overall satisfaction.[30] Other researchers have found that, if a wait is due to routine slowness of the process, then preprocess waits produce the most negative impact. However, if the wait is due to a service failure, then the in-process wait is viewed more negatively than the preprocess wait.[31] Thus, how customers perceive preprocess, in-process, and postprocess waits may depend to some extent on the cause of the wait.

Anxiety Makes Waits Seem Longer

When customers fear that they have been forgotten or do not know how long they will have to wait, they become anxious, and this anxiety can increase the negative impact of waiting. Anxiety also results when customers are forced to choose in a multiple-line situation and they discover they have chosen the "wrong" line. To combat waiting line anxiety, organizations can provide information on the length of the wait. At its theme parks, Disney uses signs at intervals along the line that let customers know how long the wait will be from that point on. Using a single line also alleviates customer anxiety over having chosen the wrong line. Explanations and reassurances that no one has forgotten them alleviate customer anxiety by taking away their cause for worry.

Uncertain Waits Are Longer Than Known, Finite Waits

Anxiety is intensified when customers do not know how long they will have to wait. Health care providers combat this problem by letting customers know when they check in how far behind the physician is that day. Some patients resolve this uncertainty themselves by calling ahead to ask. Maister provides an interesting example of the role of uncertainty, which he terms the "appointment syndrome."[32] Customers who arrive early for an appointment will wait patiently until the scheduled time, even if they arrive very early. However, once the expected appointment time has passed, customers grow increasingly anxious. Before the appointment time the wait time is known; after that, the length of the wait is not known.

Research in an airline context has suggested that, as uncertainty about a wait increases, customers become angrier, and their anger results in greater dissatisfaction.[33] Research also shows that giving customers information on the length of the anticipated wait and/or their relative position in the queue can result in more positive feelings and acceptance of the wait and ultimately more positive evaluation of the service.[34]

Unexplained Waits Are Longer Than Explained Waits

When people understand the causes for waiting, they frequently have greater patience and are less anxious, particularly when the wait is justifiable. An explanation can reduce customer uncertainty and may help customers estimate how long they will be delayed. One of us, when waiting once with our children to see a pediatrician, was told that the doctor was delayed because another child had arrived with possible life-threatening injuries and he chose to focus his attention on that child. As a parent who would want the same treatment for our children, the amount of extra wait time was acceptable—much more so than if there had been no explanation at all and we were left to think that perhaps the doctor had not yet arrived from his early morning trip to the golf course. Customers who do not know the reason for a wait begin to feel powerless and irritated.

Unfair Waits Are Longer Than Equitable Waits

When customers perceive that they are waiting while others who arrived after them have already been served, the apparent inequity will make the wait seem even longer. This situation can easily occur when there is no apparent order in the waiting area and many customers are trying to be served. Queuing systems that work on a first-come, first-served rule are best at combating perceived unfairness. However, other approaches may be required to determine who will be served next. For example, in an emergency medical care situation, the most seriously ill or injured patients would be seen first. When customers understand the priorities and the rules are clearly communicated and enforced, they will tend to see the wait as fair and the negative effects of having to wait will tend to be significantly dampened.[35]

The More Valuable the Service, the Longer the Customer Will Wait

Customers who have substantial purchases or who are waiting for a high-value service will be more tolerant of long wait times and may even expect to wait longer. For example, customers waiting to see a lawyer might consider a 15-minute wait to be acceptable, whereas the same wait at a convenience store might be considered completely unacceptable. In a supermarket, customers who have a full cart of groceries will generally wait longer than customers who have only a few items. And diners expect to wait longer for service in an expensive restaurant than they do when eating at a "greasy spoon."

Solo Waits Feel Longer Than Group Waits

People are more accepting of a longer wait when they are in a group than when they are alone because of the distractions provided by other members of the group. People also feel comfort in waiting with a group rather than alone.[36] In some group waiting situations, such as at Disneyland or when patrons are waiting in long lines to purchase concert tickets, customers who are strangers begin to talk to each other and the waiting experience can become a fun part of the total service experience.

Summary

Because service organizations lack the ability to inventory their products, the effective use of capacity can be critical to success. Idle capacity in the form of unused time, labor, facilities, or equipment represents a direct drain on bottom-line profitability. When the capacity represents a major investment (e.g., airplanes, expensive medical imaging equipment, or lawyers and physicians paid on a salary), the losses associated with underuse of capacity are even more accentuated. Overused capacity can also be a problem. People, facilities, and equipment can become worn out over time when used beyond optimal capacity. People can quit, facilities can become run down, and equipment can break. From the customer's perspective, service quality also deteriorates. Organizations focused on delivering quality service, therefore, have a natural drive to balance capacity utilization and demand at an optimal level in order to meet customer expectations.

Based on grounding in the fundamental issues, the chapter presented a variety of strategies for matching supply and demand. The basic strategies fall under two headings: *demand strategies* (shifting demand to match capacity) and *capacity strategies* (adjusting capacity to meet demand). Demand strategies seek to flatten the peaks and valleys of demand to match the flat capacity constraint, whereas capacity strategies seek to align, flex, or stretch capacity to match the peaks and valleys of demand. Organizations frequently employ several strategies simultaneously to solve the complex problem of balancing supply and demand.

Yield management is a sophisticated form of supply and demand management that balances capacity utilization, pricing, market segmentation, and financial return. This strategy is used by airline, hotel, shipping, car rental, and other capacity-constrained industries in which bookings are made in advance. Essentially, yield management allows organizations to decide on a monthly, weekly, daily, or even hourly basis to whom they want to sell their service capacity at what price.

In the last section of the chapter, we discussed situations in which it is not possible to align supply and demand. In these unresolved capacity utilization situations, the inevitable result is customer waiting. We described strategies for effectively managing waiting lines, such as employing operational logic, establishing a reservation process, differentiating waiting customers, and making waiting more pleasurable, or at least tolerable.

Discussion Questions

1. Why do service organizations lack the capability to inventory their services? Compare a car repair and maintenance service with an automobile manufacturer/dealer in terms of inventory capability.

2. Discuss the four scenarios illustrated in Figure 13.1 and presented in the text (excess demand, demand exceeds optimal capacity, demand and supply are balanced, excess capacity) in the context of a professional basketball team selling seats for its games. What are the challenges for management under each scenario?

3. Discuss the four common types of constraints (time, labor, equipment, facilities) facing service businesses, and give an example of each (real or hypothetical).

4. How does optimal capacity utilization differ from maximum capacity utilization? Give an example of a situation in which the two might be the same and one in which they are different.

5. Choose a local restaurant or some other type of service with fluctuating demand. What is the likely underlying pattern of demand? What causes the pattern? Is it predictable or random?

6. Describe the two basic strategies for matching supply and demand, and give at least two specific examples of each.

7. What is yield management? Discuss the risks in adopting a yield management strategy.

8. How might yield management apply in the management of the following: a Broadway theater? A consulting firm? A commuter train?

9. Describe the four basic waiting line strategies, and give an example of each one, preferably based on your own experiences as a consumer.

Exercises

1. Choose a local service organization that is challenged by fixed capacity and fluctuating demand. Interview the marketing manager (or other knowledgeable person) to learn (a) in what ways capacity is constrained, (b) the basic patterns of demand, and (c) strategies the organization has used to align supply and demand. Write up the answers to these questions, and make your own recommendations regarding other strategies the organization might use.

2. Assume you manage a winter ski resort in Colorado or Banff, Canada. (a) Explain the underlying pattern of demand fluctuation likely to occur at your resort and the challenges it would present to you as a manager. Is the pattern of demand predictable or random? (b) Explain and give examples of how you might use both demand-oriented and capacity-oriented strategies to smooth the peaks and valleys of demand during peak and slow periods.

3. Choose a local organization in which people have to wait in line for service. Design a waiting line strategy for the organization.

4. Visit the website of Wells Fargo Bank (www.wellsfargo.com), a leader in online banking. What online services does the bank currently offer? How do these online services help Wells Fargo manage the peaks and valleys of customer demand? How do its strategies to use more ATMs, in-store bank branches, and other alternative delivery strategies complement the online strategies?

Notes

1. The Phoenician website, www.thephoenician.com/, accessed July 12, 2016; The Lotte NY Palace website, www.lottenypalace.com/, accessed July 12, 2016.

2. C. Lovelock, "Getting the Most Out of Your Productive Capacity," in *Product Plus* (New York: McGraw-Hill, 1994), chap. 16.

3. C. H. Lovelock, "Classifying Services to Gain Strategic Marketing Insights," *Journal of Marketing* 47 (Summer 1983), pp. 9–20.

4. Portions of this section are based on C. H. Lovelock, "Strategies for Managing Capacity-Constrained Service Organizations," in *Managing Services: Marketing, Operations, and Human Resources,* 2nd ed. (Englewood Cliffs, NJ: Prentice Hall, 1992), pp. 154–168.

5. www.unhcr.org/517a5d589.html, accessed July 12, 2016.

6. M. Arndt, "Knock Knock, It's Your Big Mac," *BusinessWeek,* July 23, 2007, p. 36.

7. UPS Press Release from September 15, 2015, pressroom.ups.com/pressroom /ContentDetailsViewer.page?ConceptType=PressReleases&id=1442320318917-170, accessed June 28, 2016.

8. Lovelock, "Getting the Most Out of Your Productive Capacity."

9. J. M. Feldman, "Matching Planes to Demand," *Air Transport World* 39 (December 2002), pp. 31–33; J. M. Feldman, "IT Systems Start to Converge," *Air Transport World* 37 (September 2000), pp. 78–81.

10. Boeing website, http://www.boeing.com, accessed July 12, 2016.

11. See J. A. Fitzsimmons, M. J. Fitzsimmons, and S. K. Bordoloi, *Service Management: Operations, Strategy, Information Technology,* 8th ed. (New York: McGraw-Hill/Irwin, 2014), pp. 314–320; S. E. Kimes, "Yield Management: A Tool for Capacity-Constrained Service Firms," *Journal of Operations Management* 8 (October 1989), pp. 348–363; S. E. Kimes and R. B. Chase, "The Strategic Levers of Yield Management," *Journal of Service Research* 1 (November 1998), pp. 156–166; and S. E. Kimes, "Revenue Management: A Retrospective," *Cornell Hotel and Restaurant Administration Quarterly* 44 (2003), pp. 131–138.

12. Kimes, "Yield Management."

13. R. Desiraji and S. M. Shugan, "Strategic Service Pricing and Yield Management," *Journal of Marketing* 63 (January 1999), pp. 44–56; Fitzsimmons, Fitzsimmons, and Bordoloi, *Service Management,* chap. 12, p. 345.

14. Kimes, "Yield Management."

15. S. E. Kimes and J. Wirtz, "Has Revenue Management Become Acceptable? Findings from an International Study on the Perceived Fairness of Rate Fences," *Journal of Service Research* 6 (November 2003), pp. 125–135.

16. F. v. Wangenheim and T. Bayón, "Behavioral Consequences of Overbooking Service Capacity," *Journal of Marketing* 71 (October 2007), pp. 36–47.

17. For research supporting the relationship between longer waits and decreased satisfaction, quality evaluations, and patronage intentions, see S. Taylor, "Waiting for Service: The Relationship between Delays and Evaluations of Service," *Journal of Marketing* 58 (April 1994), pp. 56–69; K. L. Katz, B. M. Larson, and R. C. Larson, "Prescription for the Waiting-in-Line Blues: Entertain, Enlighten, and Engage," *Sloan Management Review* 33 (Winter 1991), pp. 44–53; S. Taylor and J. D. Claxton, "Delays and the Dynamics of Service Evaluations," *Journal of the Academy of Marketing Science* 22 (Summer 1994), pp. 254–264; and D. Grewal, J. Baker, M. Levy, and G. B. Voss, "The Effects of Wait Expectations and Store Atmosphere on Patronage Intentions in Service-Intensive Retail Stores," *Journal of Retailing* 79 (Winter 2003), pp. 259–268; E. G. Miller, B. E. Kahn, and M. F. Luce, "Consumer Wait Management Strategies for Negative Service Events: A Coping Approach," *Journal of Consumer Research* 34 (February 2008), pp. 635–648.

18. F. Bielen and N. Demoulin, "Waiting Time Influence on the Satisfaction-Loyalty Relationship in Services," *Managing Service Quality* 17 (2007), pp. 174–193.

19. R. Henkoff, "Finding, Training, and Keeping the Best Service Workers," *Fortune,* October 3, 1994, pp. 110–122.

20. TSA website, www.tsa.gov/tsa-precheck, accessed on June 29, 2016.

21. Fitzsimmons, Fitzsimmons, and Bordoloi, *Service Management,* chap. 12.

22. R. Zhou and D. Soman, "Looking Back: Exploring the Psychology of Queuing and the Effect of the Number of People Behind," *Journal of Consumer Research* 29 (March 2003), pp. 517–530.

23. Fitzsimmons, Fitzsimmons, and Bordoloi, *Service Management,* chap. 12.

24. Lovelock, "Getting the Most Out of Your Productive Capacity."

service marketing organization's external and interactive communications channels. The chapter describes why this communication is necessary and how companies can do it well. Successful company communications are the responsibility of both marketing and operations: marketing must accurately but beguilingly reflect what happens in actual service encounters, and operations must deliver what is promised in marketing communication. If communications set up unrealistic expectations for customers, the actual encounter will disappoint the customer.

Chapter 15 deals with another issue related to managing promises, the pricing of services. In packaged goods (and even in durable goods), many customers possess enough price knowledge before purchase to be able to judge whether a price is fair or in line with competition. With services, customers often have no internal reference point for prices before purchase and consumption. Techniques for developing prices for services are more complicated than those for pricing tangible goods, and all the approaches for setting prices must be adapted for the special characteristics of services.

In summary, external communications—whether from marketing communications or pricing—can create a larger customer gap by raising expectations about service delivery. In addition to improving service delivery, companies must also manage all communications to customers, so that inflated promises do not lead to higher expectations. Companies must also manage the messages conveyed by pricing, so that customer expectations are in line with what they perceive that they receive.

Chapter **Fourteen**

Integrated Service Marketing Communications

This chapter's objectives are to

1. Discuss the key service communication challenges.
2. Introduce the concept of integrated service marketing communications.
3. Discuss ways to integrate marketing communications in service organizations.
4. Present specific strategies for addressing service intangibility, managing promises, managing customer expectations, educating customers, and managing internal communications.

Three Successful Cross-Channel Integrated Service Marketing Campaigns

In this chapter, we will discuss integrated marketing communications, which has been a staple of company advertising campaigns for more than thirty years. The foundational idea of integrated marketing communication (IMC) was to assure that all creative, media, television, radio, and print were cohesive and communicated the same message. When digital and social marketing came on the scene, integrated marketing communication became more complex because advertisers had to combine the controllable aspects of traditional media with an entire host of new media, some of it controlled by the consumer rather than the company. According to Tony Wright of Wright IMC, an industry expert, cross-channel, cross-device targeting remains the most powerful differentiator for profitable marketing strategies. In his view, two services campaigns were notable integrated campaigns that were extremely successful in 2015: Southwest Airlines Transfarency and Nike RE2PECT, a campaign to celebrate the legendary baseball player Derek Jeter's retirement. Another expert cites the Domino's emoji campaign as one of the best.

Southwest Airlines Transfarency

Southwest Airlines, long known for its low fares, faced more competition in recent years, making their value promise more difficult to communicate. To emphasize its position as the best value in the skies, Southwest launched a Transfarency campaign using both traditional (television, radio, print) and digital media. The campaign also featured a microsite that revealed hidden airline fees charged by competitors such as Spirit Airlines and Delta. Interactive components to the site allowed visitors to take a quiz called "fee or fake" where the site featured fees charged by their competitors, highlighted by a dancing Southwest Airlines pilot.

The site also featured an approach where users chose pre-selected words to send a letter to Southwest to complain about how the customer had been treated on other airlines. The final characteristic of the site was a "fee hacker" that helped customers minimize fees when flying an airline other than Southwest. One of the best aspects of the campaign was that it created buzz on social media sites such as Twitter and Facebook, where some customers adopted the Southwest Twitter hashtag and promoted the airline on their own.[1]

1. Nike RE2PECT

When the former New York Yankees shortstop Derek Jeter, a true sports legend, announced his plans to retire from baseball at the end of the 2015 season, Nike's advertising agency created the most memorable digital effort honoring a sports hero that had ever been developed. With the hashtag #RE2PECT, the campaign began with an inspirational video depicting famous New Yorkers of all stripes tipping their hats to Jeter for his accomplishments with the Yankees. As with most integrated campaigns, it used television, print, outdoor, and—best of all—digital media to praise Jeter in his final season of Major League Baseball.

The campaign reached more than 44 million unique individuals online and was trending on most social media networks, including Facebook, Instagram, and Twitter. According to Wright, the video "inspired hundreds of fan-created videos that were put on various social media platforms, thus pushing the campaign to true viral status."[2]

2. Domino's #EasyOrder Pizza Emojis

Domino's created a campaign that encouraged consumers to order pizza with a simple emoji tweet, allowing them to capitalize on emojis before most companies. The campaign was consistent with its past campaigns, with a solid focus on simplification of the ordering process. All customers needed to do was opt in to the service by adding their mobile numbers to their Pizza Profiles on Dominos.com. After that, they could order their pre-programmed "Easy Order" just by texting a pizza emoji. With #EasyOrder emojis, the brand positioned itself among the first in the fast food delivery industry to effectively use digital media. As Pat Hong, an editor at LinkDex, commented, "If these little symbols represent the zeitgeist of our times, then Domino's has placed an invaluable stake on what could one day become valuable emoji real estate, and even if not, they showed they are a brand that is ready to capitalize on digital opportunities when and if they arrive."[3]

Each of these examples demonstrate creative use of integrated marketing communications. The proliferation of digital media added to traditional communications media makes the clear and uniform message across all channels more important than ever before. And as you will learn in this chapter, integrated *services* marketing communications is more complicated than IMC alone, for it also involves employees, the servicescape, and other "real time" interactional communications that need to match the advertising and promotional communication that is emphasized in media alone.

A major cause of poorly perceived service is the difference between what a firm promises about a service and what it actually delivers. Customer expectations are shaped by both uncontrollable and company-controlled factors. Word-of-mouth communication, social media, publicity, customer-generated media, customer experiences with other service providers, and customer needs are key factors that influence customer expectations and are rarely controllable by the firm. Controllable factors such as company advertising, personal selling, and promises made by service personnel also influence customer expectations. In this chapter, we discuss both types of communication but focus more heavily on the controllable factors because these factors can be influenced by the company. Accurate, coordinated, and appropriate company communication—advertising, personal selling, and online and other messages that do not overpromise or misrepresent—is essential to delivering services that customers perceive as high in quality.

Because company communications about services promise what *people* do and because people's behavior cannot be standardized, as can physical goods produced by machines, the potential for a mismatch between what is communicated and perceptions of actual service delivery (provider gap 4, the communications gap) is high. By coordinating communication within and outside the organization, companies can minimize the size of this gap.

THE NEED FOR COORDINATION IN MARKETING COMMUNICATION

Marketing communication is more complex today than it used to be. In the past, customers received marketing information about goods and services from a limited number of sources, usually mass communication sources such as network television and newspapers. With a limited number of sources, marketers could easily convey a uniform brand image and coordinate promises. However, today's consumers of both goods and services receive communications from a far richer variety of marketing vehicles—websites, social media, mobile advertising, blogs, virtual communities, direct mail, movie theater advertising, e-mail solicitation, targeted magazines, and a host of sales promotions. Service consumers receive additional communication from servicescapes, customer service departments, and everyday service encounters with employees. These service interactions add to the variety, volume, and complexity of information that a customer receives. A company cannot control outside sources, but even ensuring that messages from all company sources are consistent is a major challenge for service marketers.

Any company that disseminates information through multiple channels needs to be certain that customers receive unified messages and promises. These channels include not only marketing communication messages that flow directly from the company but also personal messages that employees send to customers. Figure 14.1 shows an enhanced version of the service marketing triangle that we presented in Chapter 11, emphasizing that the service customer is the target of two types of communication. First, external marketing communication includes traditional channels such as sales promotion, advertising, and public relations. Second, interactive marketing communication involves the messages that employees give to customers through such channels as personal selling, customer service interactions, service encounter interactions, social media, and servicescapes (discussed in Chapter 10). A service company must be sure that these interactive messages are consistent both among themselves and with those sent through external communications. To do so, the third side of the triangle, internal marketing communications, must be managed so that information from the

- *Abstractness.* Service benefits such as financial security, fun, and health do not correspond directly with objects, making them difficult to visualize and understand. When businesses need consulting, for example, they often do not know where to begin because the concept is so vague that they do not understand the specific goals, processes, or deliverables they are seeking.
- *Generality.* *Generality* refers to a class of things, persons, events, or properties whereas *specificity* refers to particular objects, people, or events. Many services and service promises are described in generalities (wonderful experience, superior education, completely satisfied customers), making them difficult to differentiate from those of competitors.
- *Nonsearchability.* Because service is a performance, it often cannot be previewed, or inspected in advance of purchase. If we are interested in finding a doctor, an air-conditioning repair firm, a personal trainer, or virtually any service, we cannot search with certainty the options as easily as we can search the shelves in a grocery store. Considerably more effort must be expended, and what we find may not be useful. For example, if a customer needs a plumber, the information contained in a source such as the Internet may not adequately discriminate among the choices.
- *Mental impalpability.* Services are often complex, multidimensional, and difficult to grasp mentally. When customers have not had prior exposure, familiarity, or knowledge, services are difficult to interpret. You may have experienced this when buying automobile insurance for the first time.

These five aspects of service intangibility make customers feel more uncertain about their purchases, and evidence indicates that, the greater the risk that customers perceive in purchasing services, the more actively they will seek and rely on word-of-mouth communications to guide their choices.[7] Word of mouth can be a very convincing source of information about services for consumers, but it is not under the control of the service provider.

Management of Service Promises

A serious problem occurs when companies fail to manage service marketing communications—the vows made by salespeople, advertising, and service personnel—and service falls short of what is promised. This sometimes occurs because the part of the company making the promise lacks the information necessary to make accurate statements. For example, business-to-business salespeople often sell services, particularly new business services, before their actual availability and without having an exact date of when they will be ready for market. Demand and supply variations make service provision possible at some times, improbable at others, and difficult to predict. The traditional functional structure in many companies (often called silos) also makes communication about promises and delivery difficult internally.

Management of Customer Expectations

Appropriate and accurate communication about services is the responsibility of both marketing and operations. Marketing must accurately (and compellingly) reflect what happens in actual service encounters; operations must deliver what is promised in communications. For example, when a management consulting firm introduces a new offering, the marketing and sales departments must make the offering appealing enough to be viewed as superior to competing service offerings. In promoting and differentiating the service, however, the company cannot afford to raise expectations above the level at which its consultants can consistently perform. If advertising, personal selling, or any other external communication sets up unrealistic expectations, actual encounters will disappoint customers.

Many product and service companies also find themselves in the position of having to actively manage customer expectations downward—to tell customers that service previously provided will be discontinued or available only at a higher price. Airlines cancel flights that are not full and charge for food. Credit card companies that offer multiple value-added services when interest rates are high withdraw these services when interest rates drop. Health care insurers cut back on service while raising prices, and hospital patients experience far shorter stays and fewer diagnostic procedures than in the past. In these situations—perhaps more than any others—the need to manage customer expectations is critical.

Customer Education

Service companies must educate their customers. If customers are unclear about how service will be provided, what their role in delivery involves, and how to evaluate services they have never used before, they will be disappointed. When disappointed, they will often hold the service company, not themselves, responsible. These errors or problems in service—even when they are "caused" by the customer—still lead customers to defect. For this reason the firm must assume responsibility for educating customers.

For services high in credence properties—expert services that are difficult for customers to evaluate even after they have received the services—many customers do not know the criteria by which they should judge the service. For high-involvement services, such as long-term medical treatment or purchase of a first home, customers are also unlikely to comprehend and anticipate the service process. First-time home buyers rarely understand the complex set of services (inspection, title services, insurance) and processes (securing a mortgage, offers and counteroffers, escrow) that will be involved in their purchases. Professionals and other providers of high-involvement services often forget that customers who are novices must be educated about each step in the process. They assume that an overview at the beginning of the service, or a manual or set of instructions, will equip the customer. Unfortunately, these steps are rarely sufficient, and customers defect because they can neither understand the process nor appreciate the value received from the service.

A final condition under which customer education can be beneficial involves services in which demand and supply are not synchronized, as discussed in Chapter 13. If the customer is not informed about peaks and valleys in demand, service overloads and failures, as well as underutilized capacity, are likely to result.

Internal Marketing Communication

Multiple functions in the organization, such as marketing and operations, must be coordinated to achieve the goal of quality service provision. Because service advertising and personal selling promise what *people* do, frequent and effective communication across functions—horizontal communication—is critical. If internal communication is poor, perceived service quality is at risk. If company marketing communication and other promises are developed without input from operations, contact personnel may not be able to deliver service that matches the image portrayed in marketing efforts.

Not all service organizations advertise, but all need coordination or integration across departments or functions to deliver quality service. All need internal communication between the sales force and service providers. Horizontal communication also must occur between the human resource and marketing departments. To deliver excellent customer service, firms must be certain to inform and motivate employees to deliver what their customers expect. If marketing and sales personnel who understand customer expectations do not communicate this information to contact employees, the lack of knowledge for these employees will affect the quality of service that they deliver.

A final form of internal coordination central to providing service excellence is consistency in policies and procedures across departments and branches. If a service organization operates many outlets under the same name, whether franchised or company owned, customers expect similar performance across those outlets. If managers of individual branches or outlets have significant autonomy in procedures and policies, customers may not receive the same level of service quality across the branches.

FIVE CATEGORIES OF STRATEGIES TO MATCH SERVICE PROMISES WITH DELIVERY

Figure 14.2 shows the major approaches to overcome the service communication challenges that we just described. The goal is to deliver service that is greater than or equal to promises made, and all three sides of the triangle must be addressed to do so.

Address Service Intangibility

Approaches to address service intangibility are (1) advertising and other communication strategies that clearly communicate service attributes and benefits to consumers and (2) strategies designed to encourage word-of-mouth communication.

If service companies recognize the challenges they face due to intangibility, they can use selected strategies to compensate. In one way or another, each of the individual strategies we discuss here focuses on ways to make the message dramatic and memorable.

Use Narrative to Demonstrate the Service Experience   Many services are experiential, and a uniquely effective approach to communicating them involves story-based appeals.

FIGURE 14.2
Five Major Approaches to Overcome Service Communication Channels

Showing consumers having realistic and positive experiences with services is generally more effective than describing service attributes, particularly because the attributes themselves are often intangible. Research has concluded that consumers with relatively low familiarity with a service category prefer appeals based on stories to appeals based on lists of service attributes. An example of this is a State Farm campaign in which someone experiencing a situation in which a State Farm agent is needed simply calls out, "Like a good neighbor, State Farm is there," and an agent instantly appears to take care of the situation.

Present Vivid Information Effective service marketing communication creates a strong or clear impression on the senses and produces a distinct mental picture. One way to use vivid information is to evoke a strong emotion such as fear. Using vivid information cues is particularly desirable when services are highly intangible and complex. A print example of vividness is shown in an ad for the United Negro College Fund. The abstract themes of "limitless potential" and "chance to achieve" are made vivid by a photograph of a mind filled with books.

Use Interactive Imagery One type of vividness involves what is called *interactive imagery*.[8] Imagery (defined as a mental event that involves the visualization of a concept or relationship) can enhance recall of names and facts about service. Interactive imagery integrates two or more items in some mutual action, resulting in improved recall. Some service companies effectively integrate their logos or symbols with an expression of what they do, such as the Prudential rock—the rock symbolizes strength and stability. The accompanying photo shows an advertisement for The Travelers Companies Inc., a provider of property casualty insurance, that demonstrates interactive imagery. The umbrella symbolizes protection and reassurance, an appropriate symbol to identify an insurance company. An umbrella is believed to have first appeared in a Travelers ad in 1870 and the red umbrella became the official company trademark in 1959. The advertisement shown in the photo refers to the reacquisition in 2007 of the trademark from Citigroup, which also used the umbrella as part of its logo.

Focus on the Tangibles Another way that advertisers can increase the effectiveness of service communications is to feature the tangibles associated with the service, such as showing a bank's marble columns or gold credit card.[9] Showing the tangibles provides clues about the nature and quality of the service. The photo on page 424, which is an advertisement for the Sierra Club, features the tangible benefits of the club of protecting consumers, particularly babies, from the harm from mercury pollution.

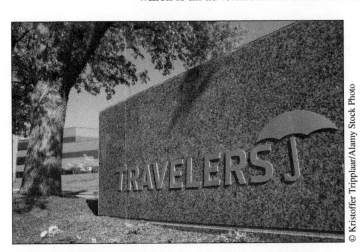

© Kristoffer Tripplaar/Alamy Stock Photo

Interactive imagery is demonstrated by the Travelers umbrella.

Use Brand Icons to Make the Service Tangible How does an advertiser of services gain in competitive differentiation and strong brand awareness in a highly competitive market? In the fast-food and insurance industries, one answer is to create a recognizable brand icon that represents the company and generates brand visibility. One of the most enduring service brand icons is Ronald McDonald, the red-and-yellow clown that represents McDonald's and its children's charity, the Ronald McDonald House. Advertising icons are even more critical in industries

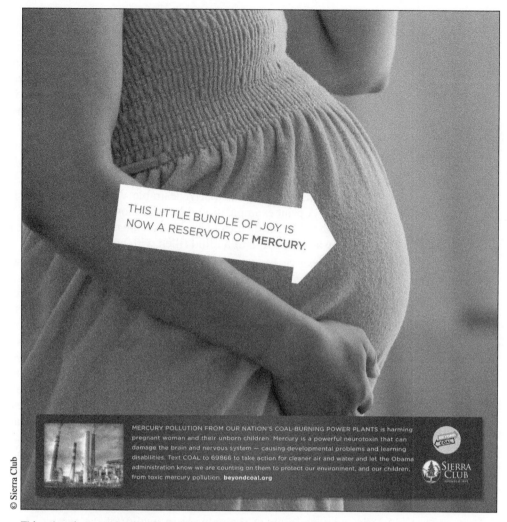

THIS LITTLE BUNDLE OF JOY IS NOW A RESERVOIR OF **MERCURY**.

MERCURY POLLUTION FROM OUR NATION'S COAL-BURNING POWER PLANTS is harming pregnant woman and their unborn children. Mercury is a powerful neurotoxin that can damage the brain and nervous system — causing developmental problems and learning disabilities. Text COAL to 69866 to take action for cleaner air and water and let the Obama administration know we are counting on them to protect our environment, and our children, from toxic mercury pollution. **beyondcoal.org**

© Sierra Club

This advertisement for the Sierra Club demonstrates in a tangible way the dangers of mercury pollution from coal-burning plants. Focusing on the unborn baby is a vivid way for the Sierra Club to communicate its message.

in which the service is complex and difficult to understand. Insurance is an example. American Family Life Insurance Company, or Aflac, a company that sells supplemental insurance on a voluntary basis in U.S. and Japanese worksites, faced a difficult challenge: getting potential customers to ask for its service by name. Enter the Aflac duck, an insistent and vocal character who screams, "Aflac!" in commercials in which actors are trying to solve their insurance problems. The duck, introduced in 2000, has generated such visibility that he has been featured on CNBC, *The Tonight Show with Jay Leno,* and *Saturday Night Live.* GEICO has TV ads such as the one shown in the image on this page, featuring the Cockney-speaking Gecko lizard. The GEICO Gecko reinforces the company's brand image with natural tenacity, constantly good cheer and an insatiable need to help people save money on car insurance. The GEICO Gecko has become a force to be reckoned with in the advertising world and has been voted America's favorite advertising icon.

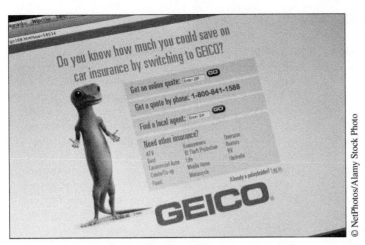

The GEICO gecko is an advertising icon.

© NetPhotos/Alamy Stock Photo

Use Association, Physical Representation, Documentation, and Visualization

Leonard Berry and Terry Clark propose four strategies of tangibilization: association, physical representation, documentation, and visualization.[10] *Association* means linking the service to a tangible person, place, or object. *Physical representation* means showing tangibles that are directly or indirectly part of the service, such as employees, buildings, or equipment. *Documentation* means featuring objective data and factual information. *Visualization* is a vivid mental picture of a service's benefits or qualities, such as showing people on vacation having fun. Our Strategy Insight shows how marketing communication icons can be used as tangibles.

Feature Service Employees in Communication

Customer contact personnel are tangible representations of the service and are an important second audience for service advertising.[11] Featuring actual employees doing their jobs or explaining their services in advertising is effective for both the primary audience (customers) and the secondary audience (employees) because it communicates to employees that they are important. Furthermore, when employees who perform a service well are featured in marketing communication, they become standards for other employees' behaviors.

Earlier in this chapter, we discussed five aspects of intangibility that make service marketing communication challenging. In Exhibit 14.1, Mittal describes strategies that can be used in service advertising to overcome these properties. Through careful planning and execution, the abstract can be made concrete, the general can be made specific, the non-searchable can be made searchable, and the mentally impalpable can be made palpable.

Recommendations and opinions from other customers are virtually always more credible than firm communications. In situations in which consumers have little information prior to purchase—something that occurs far more often in services than in goods because services are high in experience and credence properties—people turn to others for information rather than to traditional marketing channels. Service advertising and types of promotion can generate word-of-mouth communication that extends the investment in paid communication and improves the credibility of the messages.

Use Buzz, or Viral, Marketing

Buzz marketing, also called viral marketing, involves the use of real consumers to spread the word about products without (or without the appearance of) being paid by the company. Sometimes buzz marketing occurs simply because customers are avid fans of the service, and sometimes the company seeds customers with services or products. Chipotle Mexican Grill, a Denver-based company with nearly 600 outlets, avoids advertising and instead depends almost completely on the word-of-mouth communication its customers spread about its unique and tasty food. Chipotle's founder, M. Steven Ells, makes giving away samples of its food (as well as satisfying customers) the basis for its strategy. For example, when the chain opened a midtown Manhattan outlet in 2006, it gave burritos away to 6,000 people. Even though this cost the company $35,000, the strategy created 6,000 satisfied spokespeople.[12]

A Wharton researcher points our four distinctive characteristics of a mobile device: (1) it is uniquely tied to one user; (2) it is almost always a given that consumers carry it everywhere; (3) it allows for immediate consumption because it is a channel of distribution with a payment system; and (4) it is highly interactive because it allows for geotracking and picture and video taking. The proliferation of smart phones has benefits such as the advent of apps, the ability to boost loyalty programs, and the facility of sending promotions at the right time and right place for peak usage.

These characteristics make mobile advertising the most powerful communications medium of the future. Further, mobile advertising is growing at a faster rate than any other Internet approach. Projections indicate that spending will rise to more than $65 billion by 2019 and that mobile will account for almost three-quarters of all digital advertising. However, as you will see in the Technology Spotlight later in this chapter, companies are not keeping up with the potential strategic impact because they are neither spending enough on the medium nor optimizing the effectiveness of their ads. These two facts—lack of adequate investment and embryonic knowledge about the best approaches to create successful advertising—must be overcome to make mobile advertising realize its promise.

As a researcher at Texas A&M University recently delineated, the following questions need to be answered about mobile advertising to maximize its effectiveness:

- What are the types and functions of mobile promotions?
- Which mobile promotions work and which do not?
- How do consumers use mobile promotions in their shopping journey?
- How should managers use mobile promotions to influence shoppers along and beyond their purchasing journey?

Some of what has been developed to answer these questions deals with the design of mobile advertising. Because these ads are much smaller than others, simple, clear, and clean sites obviously work best. Company experts claim that mobile copy should only occupy 50 percent of the screen, that ads should have only the offer and the tagline, that brands should place their logo in the corner of the mobile ad frame, and that ads should use at least one bright color but no more than two.

Marketing researchers have also studied different aspects of mobile advertising and have contributed to what we know about what works best. In terms of redemption rates, studies conducted by researchers have found that mobile restaurant coupon redemptions are high for users who pre-specify when they want coupons delivered; that framing a product as either utilitarian or hedonic (characterized by pleasure) generates substantial differences depending on when the ad appears; distance to store,

time of delivery, and expiration date matter particularly for snack foods; and messages are effective if the mobile ad content fits the consumer mindset in two locations.

Findings on other topics are limited and scattered across different topics. For example, one study found that commuters in crowded subway trains are twice as likely to make a purchase on mobile devices than those on non-crowded trains. Another study found that mobile display advertising is more effective for high involvement and utilitarian products. Another study found that a mix of web and mobile display advertising triggers more clicks and purchases compared with either web ads only or mobile ads only. Still another discovered that SMS advertising generates awareness, stronger brand attitudes, and direct behavioral responses.

It is important to note that this research only begins to address the questions that need to be answered to understand what, where, and how mobile advertising works. Each of these studies is only a brick in the edifice of knowledge that will be developed in the next decade to allow mobile advertising to reach its projected $65 billion spending by 2019. After all, companies will only use mobile advertising if it works. As the newest channel in digital advertising, there remains much to be learned about how consumers respond and what companies can do to best communicate.

Sources: P. Chamikuttyl, "Wharton Professor David Bell on Brand Building in the Offline and Online World," *Your Story,* September 3, 2013; "Mobile Will Account for 72% of U.S. Digital Ad Spend by 2019," *eMarketer,* March 24, 2015, http://www .emarketer.com/Article/Mobile-Will-Account-72-of-US-Digital-Ad-Spend-by2019/1012258; V. Shankar, "Mobile Marketing: The Way Forward," *Journal of Interactive Marketing* 34 (2016); P. Levy, "Set Your Sites on Mobile," *Marketing News,* April 30, 2010; C. Heine, "Agencies and Cannes Judges Say Less is More for Mobile," *Ad Week,* June 17, 2013; M. Andrews, X. Luo, F. Zheng, and A. Ghose, "Mobile Ad Effectiveness: Hypercontextual Targeting with Crowdedness," *Marketing Science*, April 16, 2015; B. Baker, Z. Fang, and X. Luo, "Hour-by-Hour Sales Impact of Mobile Advertising," accessed at SSRN 2439396; P. Danaher, M. Smith, K. Ranasinghe, and T. Danaher, "Where, When and How Long: Factors that Influence the Redemption of Mobile Phone Coupons," *Journal of Marketing Research* 52 (October, 2015); X. Luo, M. Andrews, F. Zheng, and C. Phang, "Mobile Targeting," *Management Science,* 2014; D. Grewal, Y. Bart, M. Spann, and P. Zubcsek, "Mobile Advertising: A Framework and Research Agenda," *Journal of Interactive Marketing* 34 (2016); M. Andrews, X. Luo, F. Zheng, and A. Ghose, "Mobile Ad Effectiveness: Hypercontextual Targeting with Crowdedness," *Marketing Science,* April 16, 2015; Y. Bart, A. Stephen, and M. Sarvary, "Which Products are Best Suited to Mobile Advertising? A Field Study of Mobile Display Advertising Effects on Consumer Attitudes and Intentions," *Journal of Marketing Research* 51 (2014); A. Ghose, S. Han, and H. Park, "Analyzing the Interdependence between Web and Mobile Advertising: A Randomized Field Experiment," working paper, New York University: Leonard N. Stern School of Business; P. Barsie and C. Strong, "Permission-Based Mobile Advertising," *Journal of Interactive Marketing* (2002).

Property of Intangibility	Advertising Strategy	Description
Incorporeal existence	Physical representation	Show physical components of service that are unique, indicate high quality, and create the right association.
Abstractness	Service consumption episode	Capture and display typical customers benefiting from the service, evoking particular incidents.
Generality	System documentation	Objectively document physical system capacity by showing facts and figures.
	Performance documentation	Document and cite past positive performance statistics.
	Service performance episode	Present a vivid story of an actual service delivery incident that relates to an important service attribute.
Nonsearchability	Performance documentation	Cite independently audited performance.
	Consumption documentation	Obtain and present customer testimonials.
Mental impalpability	Service process episode	Present a vivid documentary on the step-by-step service process.
	Case history episode	Present an actual case history of what the firm did for a specific client

Source: Adapted from B. Mittal, "The Advertising of Services: Meeting the Challenge of Intangibility," *Journal of Service Research* 2 (August 1999), pp. 98–116.

Leverage Social Media   Social media—interactive communication among customers on the Internet through such sites as Twitter, YouTube, and Facebook—are becoming avenues for consumers to exchange information. The growth of social media is affecting many aspects of consumer purchase behavior. In a comScore survey, almost 28 percent of consumers reported that social media influenced their decisions about holiday purchasing in 2009.[13] Another study showed that 61 percent of consumers rely on online ratings and reviews before making a purchase. And 26 percent of consumers post online ratings and reviews.[14] According to a Nielsen study, a full 90 percent of consumers trust recommendations from other consumers versus 56 percent who trust brand advertising.[15] While social media are not controllable by the firm, the company can monitor the media and understand what consumers are saying and recommending. Formal methods and sophisticated technologies are being developed to track, monitor, and analyze online communication for brands. Nielsen BuzzMetrics, the innovator of this approach, gathers brand information online by trolling millions of lines of Internet communication to find out how customers feel about brands, how many are talking online, what issues they are discussing, how marketing is being viewed, and how efforts to affect word-of-mouth communications are being received. The service provides industry norms and benchmarks to the companies who buy their service as well as real-time alerts about issues.[16]

Aim Messages to Influencers   Improved technologies are now allowing companies to identify online influencers—those individuals with more connections than others and therefore more ability to influence others about services. Both researchers and research companies are developing technologies similar to the BuzzMetric approach described earlier that can identify those people in a viral community who are most critical to receive brand messages. When identified, these individuals can be "seeded"—given information about the service, invited to participate in special events, and otherwise encouraged to know and communicate about a service.

Create Advertising That Generates Talk Because It Is Humorous, Compelling, or Unique Humorous advertisements are memorable and vivid. Over the years, GEICO has developed many of the most humorous service commercials. Many of the ads focus on the brand's gecko, but other campaigns are humorous in different ways. A current campaign emphasizes different content points, each with settings and characters that are funny. For example, to emphasize the fact that GEICO has been growing rapidly, the company generated a television ad called "Life Forms" in a laboratory setting. An initially contained green blob in a small plastic box grows huge enough to engulf one of the scientists in the lab. To communicate GEICO's 24/7 availability, another television commercial called "More, More, More" shows two clowns blowing up balloons at a child's birthday party while discussing the 24/7 availability of GEICO. The TV network HBO created a humorous commercial for its streaming service entitled, "Awkward Family Viewing." The advertisement features two teenagers watching *Game of Thrones* with their parents; Mom and Dad can't stop asking questions during an episode of the complicated show. The ad ends with the suggestion that getting the app for HBO Go allows you to watch the program on your own, without all the pesky questions from your parents.

Feature Satisfied Customers in the Communication Advertising testimonials featuring actual service customers simulate personal communications between people and are thereby a credible way to communicate the benefits of service.

In 2010, Xerox created a series of testimonial commercials with its business customers that were highly believable and successful. You can see them on YouTube by searching "Xerox commercials 2010."

Generate Word of Mouth through Employee Relationships Research shows that customer satisfaction with a service experience alone is not sufficient to stimulate word-of-mouth activity. However, when customers gain trust in a specific employee, positive word of mouth results. In this research, trust was shown to be a consequence of three aspects of the employee–customer relationship: a personal connection between employees and customers, care displayed by employees, and employee familiarity with customers.[17] Companies can strengthen the interpersonal bonds that lead to trust using strategies that focus on service design, support systems, employees, and customers.[18] Examples include designing the service environment so that opportunities for interactions between customers and employees are plentiful, using support systems (such as customer relationship management software) to help employees remember customer characteristics, and empowering employees to correct problems fully and quickly.

Manage Service Promises

In manufacturing physical goods, the departments that make promises and those that deliver them can operate independently. Goods can be fully designed and produced and then turned over to marketing for promotion and sale. In services, however, the sales and marketing departments make promises about what other employees in the organization will fulfill. Because what employees do cannot be standardized, greater coordination and management of promises are required. This coordination can be accomplished by creating a strong service brand and by coordinating all of the company's marketing communications.

Create a Strong Service Brand

Leonard Berry, an expert in *service branding,* emphasizes that branding plays a special role in service companies:

> Strong brands enable customers to better visualize and understand intangible products. They reduce customers' perceived monetary, social, or safety risk in buying services, which are difficult to evaluate prior to purchase. Strong brands are the surrogates when the company offers no fabric to touch, no trousers to try on, no watermelons or apples to scrutinize, no automobile to test drive.[19]

In contrast to branding in goods situations, where each product has its own brand, the primary brand in service is the company itself. The focus of brand creation is on awareness, meaning, and equity of the company. For example, companies like FedEx, Disney World, Starbucks, and Facebook all focus communication and information on their companies rather than individual services that the company offers. Therefore, the brand becomes the company's method of integrating marketing communication.

Figure 14.3 is a service branding model developed by Berry that shows the relationships among the main elements in creating a strong service brand.[20] The *presented brand* is the part of the brand image that the company controls and disseminates through all personal and impersonal channels. Advertising, the brand name itself, websites, employees, facilities, and all other types of information dissemination must be coordinated and controlled. These messages lead to *brand awareness,* the customer's recall and recognition of the brand. The higher and more positive the brand awareness, the stronger the brand image and the more differentiation—or *brand equity*—the service company has. *Customer experience with the company*—the actual interactions with company employees and other firm manifestations—is another element that shapes the brand and is likely to be more powerful than any marketing messages. No matter how effective and unified advertising is for a service, actual experiences disproportionately provide meaning to customers.

The Mayo Clinic, one of the strongest service brands in the world, carefully cultivates its brand through patient experience rather than media promotion, which it avoids. Strong core values, teamwork, physician responsibility, patient care, high-quality staff, and facilities all contribute to the Mayo Clinic Model of Care, which ensures that patient experience is strong enough to perpetuate the clinic's brand strength. Notably, the brand awareness of the Mayo Clinic is strong even though it

FIGURE 14.3
A Service Branding Model

Source: L. L. Berry, "Cultivating Service Brand Equity," *Journal of the Academy of Marketing Science* 28 (Winter 2000), pp. 128–137.

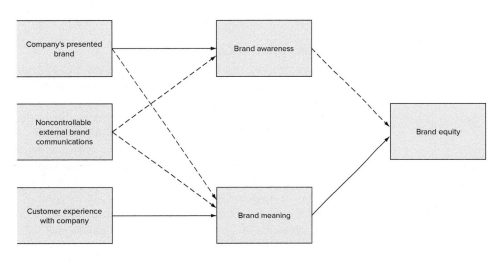

does not use media promotion. In a study in which primary decision makers in the United States were asked what health care institutions in the United States they would choose if they could go anywhere for a serious medical problem, almost 27 percent of respondents named Mayo Clinic, far more than the second choice, which was named about 9 percent of the time.[21] Other research indicates that 95 percent of Mayo clinic patients voluntarily say positive things about the clinic to others, a testament to the Mayo brand and to the positive experiences they have there.[22]

Figure 14.3 shows two other factors that shape the service brand. First, *noncontrollable external brand communications* involve information—such as word-of-mouth communication and publicity—that the company does not have in its power. These sources of communication are potent because they are perceived by customers to be credible and unbiased but can have either positive or negative effects on the service brand. In another section of this chapter, we describe ways to influence word-of-mouth communication in positive ways. Second, *brand meaning* is the collection of customers' associations with the brand. Brand meaning largely emanates from customer experience but is also shaped by the company's presented brand and external communications.

An example of a successful service brand based firmly in brand meaning is the Boston Red Sox baseball team. The team, which until 2004 had not won a World Series since 1918, has built a fan base with messianic loyalty through deliberate management and marketing strategies that have been highly successful.[23] Virtually all elements of the strategy involve giving fans a meaningful personal and community experience. First, owners created a community of fans around the team by deliberately building the stadium right in the middle of the city's neighborhoods and taverns. They knew that locating the field in the center of the city would encourage fans to come to multiple games. Second, rather than focus on superstar players, they emphasized Fenway Park itself, avoiding the loss of allegiance when star players left. As part of this approach, the builders created the "Green Monster," the unique left-field wall that became part of the Boston region's folklore. Third, owners and managers promised a competitive team but not a winning team, credibly managing fan expectations while delivering strong teams. Fourth, owners vowed to make the park "Friendly Fenway," partly by staging fun and entertaining events at games and partly by instilling in all vendors a strong fan-oriented culture. Finally, the team shows respect for its fans' desires for tradition: its uniforms, logo, and focus on the game itself have remained the same for more than half a century. The success of these strategies is evident every game. As of May 22, 2011, the Red Sox have sold out 657 consecutive games, an all time record for major league baseball and 200 games better than the next streak.

Coordinate External Communication

For any organization, one of the most important yet challenging aspects of managing brand image involves coordinating all the external communication vehicles that send information to customers. This task has become far more challenging in recent years because a notable trend is the proliferation of new media. Not only are traditional communication vehicles such as advertising, company websites, sales promotion, public relations, direct marketing, and personal selling proliferating, but many forms of new media are now available to marketers. Social media, digital signage, blogs, mobile advertising, many forms of Internet advertising, and increasing usage of product placement in movies and television all complicate the goal of coordinating messages. Our Global Feature shows an international campaign for Virgin Atlantic Airways that uses many elements of the *marketing communication mix.*

A brand name that is known internationally for innovation, quality and a sense of fun—this is what we have always aspired to with Virgin.

Richard Branson

Richard Branson, first known for Virgin Records, the legendary record label that signed the Rolling Stones, Janet Jackson, and The Human League, surprised the world when he launched an upstart airline called Virgin Atlantic Airways. His vision was to create a high-quality, value-for-money airline to challenge the United Kingdom's market leader, British Airways. Thirty years later, Virgin Atlantic includes destinations in the United States, Caribbean, Far East, India, China, Hong Kong, and Africa. From those early days the airline has become stronger and stronger. Now based at Gatwick, Heathrow, and Manchester airports, it operates long-haul services from Heathrow to New York (Newark and JFK), Los Angeles, San Francisco, Washington, Boston, Miami, Tokyo, Hong Kong, Johannesburg, Cape Town, Shanghai, Delhi, Lagos, Dubai, Vancouver, Mumbai, and Chicago.

© Chris Parypa Photography/Shutterstock.com

Parent company Virgin Group, with combined sales exceeding $20 billion, is known worldwide as an innovative global brand with megastore music retailing, book and software publishing, film and video editing facilities, clubs, trains, and financial advising through more than 200 branded companies in 29 countries. Virgin Atlantic Airways' brand and marketing campaign epitomizes successful global communication, with universal marketing components that are integrated in theme and design across the world as well as individual advertisements that adapt to geographies. Virgin Atlantic Airways' common global marketing elements include its brand values, logo, and distinctive airplanes. The airline's brand values—"caring, honest, value, fun, innovative"— are executed in all communications and strategies. Virgin focuses on customer service and low cost while also being the first to offer up unique services. For example, Virgin was the first airline to install television screens in every seat, offer massages and beauty services in first class, and mount a gambling casino right in the plane! The red and white logo, in the shape of an airline tail fin, appears in all worldwide marketing communication media including television, press, magazines, price promotions, outdoor posters, and taxi sides. Another common image is the company's Flying Lady, a Vargas painting of a red-headed, scantily dressed woman holding a scarf. Distinctive airplanes feature the Flying Lady on the fuselage and Union Jacks on their wings in three core colors of red, purple, and silver metallic. Even the paint technology—based on mica, a hard mineral that produces a pearl-like shine—is unique. When the iridescent gleam combines with the plane's vibrant colors, the aircraft stirs up memories of the 1930s, when flying was glamorous and romantic. As shown in the accompanying international advertisement, Virgin Atlantic Airways manages to translate its brand themes in culturally specific ways while retaining its global image. The Caribbean ad draws in readers with its bananas. Although the text and appeal change to suit the culture, all international advertisements contain the same Virgin Atlantic Airways logo and the same company colors.

The airline's communication campaigns have led to many awards over the years. In recent years, the airline has won the following awards:

- Data Storytelling Award, for the best real-time data (2015)
- Europe's leading airline to North America (2015)
- Silver Award in the Best Airline for Groups (2015)
- Wearable Technology Show (2014)
- Future Travel Experience Awards (2014)
- Travolution Award—best airline website as voted by consumers (2014)
- Winner of the coveted ORA Prix d'OR (top accolade) (2013)
- Best Leisure & Travel Website (2013)
- Commendation in BIMA Award for best website user experience (2013)
- Bronze Medal for best use of digital in the travel and leisure sector (2013)
- Travel Brand of the Year (2012)
- Campaign of the Year (2012)
- Best TV Commercial (2012)
- Best Press Campaign (Upper Class) (2012)
- Best Website (VSFlyinghub for global trade website) (2012)
- Best Brochure—Little Red Book—interactive online Flying Club brochure (2012)

Their mission statement provides a simple, yet effective foundation for everything they do at Virgin Atlantic Airways: . . . **to embrace the human spirit and let it fly.**

Source: www.virgin-atlantic.com

Advertising is any paid form of nonpersonal presentation and promotion of a company's offerings by an identified sponsor. Dominant advertising vehicles include television, radio, newspapers, magazines, outdoor signage, and the Internet. Because advertising is paid, marketers control the creative appeals, placement, and timing. Internet advertising has become a large portion of companies' advertising budgets (see the Technology Spotlight) and should be synchronized with traditional advertising vehicles. MasterCard's highly successful "Priceless" advertising campaign listed three or four tangible items and their prices followed by a key customer benefit that was "priceless." The campaign was an example of strong integration because it was flexible and carried a brand message that was relevant and also adapted well to different media, payment channels, and markets." The campaign, seen in 96 countries and 47 languages, generated strong brand recall and received the advertising industry's prestigious Gold Effie, Addy, and Cresta awards.[24]

Sales promotion includes short-term incentives such as coupons, premiums, discounts, and other activities that stimulate customer purchases and stretch media spending. The fast-food industry, including McDonald's, Burger King, and Wendy's, offers premiums such as action figures that link the chains' offerings to current movies and television shows. A particularly successful version of joint promotions between service advertisers and entertainment was created by CKE Restaurants' Carl's Jr. The restaurant incorporated footage of television season premieres, finales, and other television shows into the company's advertising, "[deliver]ing upwards of 30 percent of an increase in the impact of media spending."[25]

Public relations includes activities that build a favorable company image with a firm's publics through publicity, relations with the news media, and community events. Richard Branson, founder of Virgin Atlantic Airways (see the Global Feature) is a master at obtaining publicity for his airline. When launching the airline, he claimed, "I knew that the only way of competing with British Airways and the others was to get out there and use myself to promote it."[26] In the years since the airline's launch, his publicity-winning stunts included recording the fastest time across the Atlantic Ocean in a speedboat, flying a hot-air balloon across the Atlantic Ocean and from Japan to Canada, dressing up in everything from a stewardess's uniform to a bikini on Virgin flights, and being photographed in his bath.

Direct marketing includes the use of mail, telephone, fax, e-mail, and other tools to communicate directly with specific consumers to obtain a direct response. American Express is a service company that uses direct marketing extensively and ensures that it integrates well with all other messages, including interactive messages from employees. As the executive vice president of global advertising at American Express clearly states,

> Service brands are not created solely in advertising. In fact, much of a brand's equity stems from the direct consumer experiences with the brand. We partner with [a relationship marketing company] to help us manage consumer experiences with our brand across all products and services—Card, Travel, Financial Services, and Relationship Services—via all direct channels, including phone, Internet, and mail.[27]

Personal selling is face-to-face presentation by a representative from the firm to make sales and build customer relationships. One way that personal selling and advertising are integrated in business-to-business companies is through the development of advertising materials that salespeople distribute to customers. This approach not only creates an integrated message to customers but also keeps salespeople fully informed of the promises the company is making.

Technology Spotlight   Internet Expert Mary Meeker Predicts What Companies Most Need to Know

Widely respected Internet analyst Mary Meeker, a partner at Kleiner Perkins Caufield & Byers (KPCB), a Silicon Valley venture capital firm, has published Internet trends annually since 1995. She is known for many accurate forecasts, including the emergence of mobile video and messaging apps. Meeker's current-year predictions were unveiled on June 1, 2016 in a 213-slide presentation given at a California conference.

One of the most sought-after statistics every year is the overall growth of U.S.-based Internet advertising; she reported that Internet advertising increased by one-fifth between 2014 and 2015. Most of that rise is due to just two companies, Facebook and Google, which, when combined, claim a 76 percent share of U.S. Internet ad growth. The ability to provide advertisers with highly specific user data for targeting purposes is a pivotal advantage for any platform—seeking advertisers, and that is what those two platforms provide better than any others.

While Meeker covered many topics and presented myriad statistics in her 213-slide presentation, her most compelling comments this year concerned mobile, voice, and image.

MOBILE ADVERTISING

Mobile ads grew by an incredible 66 percent in 2015 over 2014, while desktop grew only 5 percent. Meeker claims that spending on mobile advertising is far too low compared to spending on legacy media such as newspapers and television. Consumers now expend only 4 percent of their time reading print media versus 25 percent of their time on their mobile devices and another 22 percent of their time browsing the Internet. However, U.S. companies spend 16 percent of their budgets on print advertising and just 12 percent on mobile, creating a $22 billion gap between mobile consumption rates and mobile ad spending.

Another fascinating aspect of Meeker's predictions is that messaging apps could overtake the home screen on mobile devices. A full 80 percent of users' mobile time is spent on three apps—Facebook, WhatsApp, and Chrome—and the average global mobile user accesses just 12 apps daily. As messaging shifts from being simple social interaction to increasingly expressive over time, having the messaging apps on the home screen makes sense.

IMAGE SEARCH

One of Meeker's predictions is that searching by text is fading and that in five years, at least half of all searches will be made through images or speech. The importance of images is due largely to users' increasing use of smart phones for "storytelling, sharing, messaging and creative expression." She predicts that Generation Z (people currently aged 1–20) will be known for their use of images and video. She confirms what you likely already know: among current social network users, Facebook, Snapchat, and Instagram are the leading platforms for engaging millennials. Facebook continues to be most dominant, with users between 18 and 34 years old averaging more than 1,000 minutes per month on the platform. Instagram and Snapchat were the next most popular networks.

More than 10 billion short videos are viewed online every day, with viral videos having an effect on consumer behavior more than ever before. Meeker cited the "Chewbacca mom" video that drew more than 150 million view and made Kohl's the most downloaded app in the U.S. iOS App store, even though Kohl's was mentioned just twice in the video. As the Chewbacca video indicates, users will drive the landscape. Because so many devices exist and memory, computing power, and cloud storage are increasing exponentially, users will be able to seamlessly combine live video with contextual information, then annotate and distribute it on many platforms.

VOICE SEARCH

Voice searches currently account for one-fifth of all queries on Google and Android, partially because Google's voice recognition software now possesses a word accuracy rate of over 90 percent after being calibrated at below 80 percent as recently as 2013. Meeker said voice possesses a major benefit because it is hands- and vision-free. Humans can speak 150 words per minute, for instance, but can type only 40 words per minute. According to *Forbes* writer Kathleen Chaykowski, "the conversational aspect of the medium lends itself to personalized experiences with computers understanding context from previous questions the user has asked and the user's location."

Meeker predicts that when speech recognition reaches 99 percent accuracy, people will go from barely using the tool to using it constantly. As further evidence, while sales of iPhones peaked in 2015, she predicts that voice-based devices—such as the Amazon Echo—could be just about to take off.

Sources: Z. Brooke, "Meeker's 2016 Internet Trends Report Describes a Maturing Digital Industry," *American Marketing Association Report*, June 2, 2016; K. Chaykowski, "Five Highlights from Mary Meeker's 2016 Internet Trends Report," *Forbes*, June 1, 2016, http://www.forbes.com/sites/kathleen-chaykowski/2016/06/01/five-highlights-from-mary-meekers-2016-internet-trends-report/#36e318097dac; M. Meeker, "2016 Internet Trends," accessed at www.kpcb.com /InternetTrends.

advance. Upon arrival at the airport to return home, the seat had been given to another customer who had conformed to the airline's request for confirmation. Depending on the perspective taken, you could argue that either the company or the customer was right in this situation. Whose responsibility is it to make sure that customers perform their roles properly?

Companies can avoid such situations by preparing customers for the service process. And companies may need to prepare the customer often, even every step of the way, for the subsequent actions the customer needs to take. A business-to-business example will help illustrate this strategy.

Customers of management consulting services purchase intangible benefits: marketing effectiveness, motivated workforces, and culture change. The very fact that companies purchase these services usually indicates that they do not know how to perform them alone. Many clients will also not know what to look for along the way to judge progress. In management consulting and other complex service situations, the effective provider prepares the customer for the service process and creates structure for the customer. At the beginning of the engagement, the management consulting firm establishes checkpoints throughout the process, at which times progress will be evaluated, and leads the customer to establish objectives for project completion. Because customers do not know what that progress will look like, the consulting firm takes the lead in setting goals or criteria to be examined at those times.

Confirm Performance to Standards and Expectations

Service providers sometimes provide service, even explicitly requested service, yet fail to communicate to the customer what has been accomplished. These providers stop short of getting credit for their actions when they do not reinforce actions with communication about their fulfillment of the request. This situation may happen under one or more of the following conditions:

- The customer cannot evaluate the effectiveness of a service.
- The decision maker in the service purchase is a person different from the users of the service.
- The service is performed out of sight of the customer.

When customers cannot evaluate service effectiveness, usually because they are inexperienced or the service is technical, the provider may fail to communicate specific actions that address client concerns because the actions seem too complex for the customer to comprehend. In this situation, the service provider can improve perceptions by translating the actions into customer-friendly terms. A personal injury lawyer who aids a client with the medical and financial implications of an accident needs to be able to tell the client in language the client can understand that the lawyer has performed the necessary actions.

When the decision maker in service purchases is different from the users of the service, a wide discrepancy in satisfaction may exist between decision makers and users. An example is in the purchase of information technology products and services in a company. The decision maker—the manager of information technology or someone in a similar position—makes the purchase decisions and understands the service promises. If users are not involved in the purchase process, they may not know what has been promised and may be dissatisfied.

Customers are not always aware of everything done behind the scenes to serve them well. Most services have invisible support processes. For instance, physicians frequently request diagnostic tests to rule out possible causes for illness. When these tests come back negative, doctors may neglect to inform patients. Many hairstyling firms have guarantees that ensure customer satisfaction with haircuts, permanents, and color treatments. However, only a few of them actively communicate these guarantees in marketing communication because they assume customers know about them. The firm that explicitly communicates the guarantee may be selected over others by a customer who is uncertain about the quality of the service. Making customers aware of standards or efforts to improve service that are not readily apparent can improve service quality perceptions.

Clarify Expectations after the Sale

When service involves a hand-off between sales and operations, clarifying expectations with customers helps the operations arm of the company align delivery with customer expectations. Salespeople are motivated and compensated to raise customer expectations—at least to the point of making the sale—rather than to communicate realistically what the company can provide. In these situations, service providers can avoid future disappointment by clarifying to customers what was promised as soon as the hand-off is made from sales to operations.

Manage Internal Marketing Communication

The fifth major category of strategies necessary to match service delivery with promises is managing internal marketing communications. Internal marketing communications can be both vertical and horizontal. *Vertical communications* are either downward, from management to employees, or upward, from employees to management. *Horizontal communications* are those across functional boundaries in an organization. A third strategy is *internal branding,* which consists of various strategies to sell the brand inside the company. Other strategies, discussed in the following paragraphs, include *creating effective upward communication, aligning back-office and support personnel with external customers,* and *creating cross-functional teams.*

Create Effective Vertical Communications

Companies that give customer-contact employees adequate information, tools, and skills allow them to perform successful interactive marketing. Some of these skills come through the training and other human resource efforts discussed in Chapter 11, but some are provided through *downward communications.* Among the most important forms of downward communications are company newsletters and magazines, corporate television networks, e-mail, briefings, videos and internal promotional campaigns, and recognition programs. One of the keys to successful downward communications is keeping employees informed of everything that is being conveyed to customers through external marketing. Employees should see company marketing communication before it is aired or published and should be familiar with the website, mailings, and direct-selling approaches used. If these vertical communications are not present, both customers and employees suffer—customers will not receive the same messages from employees that they hear in company external marketing, and employees will feel uninformed and not be aware of what their company is doing. Customers go to them, asking for services that have been marketed externally but not internally, making the employees feel uninformed, left out, and helpless.[29]

Create Effective Horizontal Communications

Horizontal Communications—communication across functional boundaries in an organization—facilitate coordinated efforts for service delivery. This task is difficult because functions typically differ in goals, philosophies, outlooks, and views of the customer—but the payoff is high. Coordination between marketing and operations can result in communication that accurately reflects service delivery, thus reducing the gap between customer expectations and actual service delivery. Integration of effort between marketing and human resources can improve the ability of each employee to become a better marketer. Coordination between finance and marketing can create prices that accurately reflect the customer's evaluation of a service. In service firms, all these functions need to be integrated to produce consistent messages and to narrow the service gaps.

One important strategy for effective horizontal communications is to open channels of communication between the marketing department and operations personnel. For example, when a company creates advertising that depicts the service encounter, it is essential that the advertising accurately reflect what customers will experience in actual service encounters. Puffery or exaggeration puts service quality perceptions at risk, especially when the firm is consistently unable to deliver to the level of service portrayed in the marketing communication. Coordination and communication between advertising and service providers are pivotal in delivering service that meets expectations.

Featuring actual employees doing their jobs or explaining the services they provide, a strategy mentioned earlier in this chapter, is one way to coordinate advertising portrayals and the reality of the service encounter. To create this type of advertising, the advertising department or agency interacts directly with service employees, facilitating horizontal communications. Similar benefits can be achieved if employees are included in the advertising process in other ways, such as by being shown advertising in its pretest forms.

Another important strategy for horizontal communications involves opening channels of communication between sales and operations. Mechanisms for achieving this goal can be formal or informal and can include annual planning meetings, retreats, team meetings, or workshops in which departments clarify service issues. In these sessions, the departments can interact to understand the goals, capabilities, and constraints of the other. Some companies hold "gap workshops" at which employees from both functions meet for a day or two to try to understand the difficulties in matching promises made through selling with delivery accomplished by operations personnel.[30]

Involving the operations staff in face-to-face meetings with external customers is also a strategy that allows operations personnel to more readily understand the salesperson's role and the needs and desires of customers. Rather than filtering customers' needs through the sales force, operations employees can witness firsthand the pressures and demands of customers. A frequent and desirable result is better service to the internal customer—the salesperson—from the operations staff as they become aware of their own roles in satisfying both external and internal customers.

Sell the Brand inside the Company

Having knowledge about what the company is doing in marketing communications is one aspect of internal marketing communication, but it is not enough. Consultant Colin Mitchell emphasizes, the importance of marketing the company's brand and brand message to employees, so that they can make powerful connections with customers.[31] He recommends three principles for bringing the brand alive: choosing the right moment to teach and inspire employees, linking internal and external marketing, and bringing the brand alive for employees. Choosing the right moment is essential because employees are not capable of or willing to accept too many change initiatives, and therefore the company has to be selective in identifying opportunities when it can create enthusiasm for the brand.

Linking internal and external marketing means that employees need to hear the same thing from management that customers hear. If customers hear that serving them is most important and employees are told that cost savings matter more, employees will be confused and unable to live the message. One of the best ways to link the two types of communication is to create advertising that targets both customers and employees. When IBM launched its highly successful e-business campaign, it took out a large advertisement in *The Wall Street Journal* to show its intent to both target audiences, then followed up with support for both audiences throughout the campaign.

Bringing the brand alive to employees involves creating a strong emotional connection between employees and the company. Employees at Southwest Airlines are encouraged to live the Southwest brand by dressing informally (although still in uniform), ad-libbing when giving instructions both on the ground and in the plane, and decorating the check-in counters on holidays. Singapore Airlines, on the other hand, connects with its employees through the company's emphasis on grace, formal dress, quiet tone, and Asian food.

Create Effective Upward Communication

Upward Communications is also necessary in closing the gap between service promises and service delivery. Employees are at the front line of service, and they know—more than anyone else in the organization—what can and cannot be delivered. They know when service breakdowns are occurring and, very often, why they are happening. Having open communication channels from employees to management can prevent service problems before they occur and minimize them when they do take place.

Align Back-Office and Support Personnel with External Customers through Interaction or Measurement

As companies become increasingly customer focused, frontline personnel develop improved skills in discerning what customers require. As they become more knowledgeable about and empathetic toward external customers, they also experience intrinsic rewards for satisfying customers. Back-office and support personnel, who typically do not interact directly with external customers, miss out on this bonding and, as a consequence, fail to gain the skills and rewards associated with it.

Companies can create ways to facilitate the interaction between back-office and support personnel and external customers. Weyerhaeuser, for example, sends hourly employees to customers' plants to better understand their needs. When actual interaction is difficult or impossible, some companies videotape customers in their service facilities during the purchase and consumption process to vividly portray the needs and requirements of customers and to show personnel the support that frontline people need to deliver to those expectations.

When company measurement systems are established, employees are sometimes judged on the basis of how they perform for the next internal customer in the chain. Although this approach provides feedback in terms of how well the employees are serving the internal customer, it lacks the motivation and reward that come from seeing their efforts affect the end customer. FedEx has aligned internal personnel with the external customer using measurement. FedEx's service quality indicator (SQI) computes daily the number of companywide service failures. To clearly communicate customer fail points to internal employees, the company created linking measures to trace the causes to each internal department. For example, the company's information

4. P. G. Lindell, "You Need Integrated Attitude to Develop IMC," *Marketing News,* May 26, 1997, p. 5.

5. D. Legg and J. Baker, "Advertising Strategies for Service Firms," in *Add Value to Your Service,* ed. C. Suprenant (Chicago: American Marketing Association, 1987), pp. 163–168.

6. B. Mittal, "The Advertising of Services: Meeting the Challenge of Intangibility," *Journal of Service Research* 2 (August 1999), pp. 98–116.

7. H. S. Bansal and P. A. Voyer, "Word-of-Mouth Processes within a Services Purchase Decision Context," *Journal of Service Research* 3 (November 2000), pp. 166–177.

8. K. L. Alesandri, "Strategies That Influence Memory for Advertising Communications," in *Information Processing Research in Advertising,* ed. R. J. Harris (Hillsdale, NJ: Erlbaum, 1983).

9. L. L. Berry and T. Clark, "Four Ways to Make Services More Tangible," *Business,* October–December 1986, pp. 53–54.

10. www.geico.com; www.Aflac.com; "Who's Your Favorite Advertising Icon?" advertising insert, *New York Times,* September 20, 2004, p. 6.

11. Berry and Clark, "Four Ways to Make Services More Tangible."

12. W. R. George and L. L. Berry, "Guidelines for the Advertising of Services," *Business Horizons,* May–June 1981, pp. 52–56.

13. M. Arndt, "Burrito Buzz—and So Few Ads," *BusinessWeek,* March 12, 2007, pp. 84–85.

14. G. Fulgoni, "No Time to Lose for Online Retailers," comScore Inc. blog, accessed December 7, 2009.

15. "The 90/10 Split," www.emarketer.com, accessed May 28, 2011.

16. Cited in S. Gupta, K. Armstrong and Z. Clayton, "Social Media," *Harvard Business School,* February 15, 2011, from a study by The Nielsen Company, "Trust, Value, and Engagement in Advertising," July 2009, http://blog.nielsen.com/nielsenwire/wp-content/uploads/2009/07/trustinadvertising0709.pdf, accessed January 2010.

17. "VNU Brings Together BuzzMetrics, Intelliseek to Create Nielsen BuzzMetrics Service," www.prnewswire.com, September 25, 2006.

18. D. D. Gremler, K. P. Gwinner, and S. W. Brown, "Generating Positive Word-of-Mouth Communications through Customer-Employee Relationships," *International Journal of Service Industry Management* (January 2001), pp. 44–59.

19. Ibid, pp. 54–56.

20. L. L. Berry, "Cultivating Service Brand Equity," *Journal of the Academy of Marketing Science* 28 (Winter 2000), pp. 128–137.

21. The figure and definitions contained in this section are all from Berry, "Cultivating Service Brand Equity."

22. L. L. Berry and K. D. Seltman, "Building a Strong Brand: Lessons from Mayo Clinic," *Business Horizons* 50 (2007), pp.199–209.

23. Ibid., p. 201.

24. G. Rifkin, "How the Red Sox Touch All the Branding Bases," strategy + business .com, accessed April 2007.

25. www.mastercardinternational.com2011.

26. Alice Z. Cuneo, "Sue Johenning," *Advertising Age,* September 27, 2004.

27. P. Denoyelle and J. Larreche, "Virgin Atlantic Airways—Ten Years Later," INSEAD Case, 1995.

28. D. E. Bell and D. M. Leavitt, "Bronner Slosberg Humphrey," *Harvard Business School Case 9-598-136,* 1998, p. 5.

29. L. L. Berry, V. A. Zeithaml, and A. Parasuraman, "Quality Counts in Services, Too," *Business Horizons,* May–June 1985, pp. 44–52.

30. V. A. Zeithaml, A. Parasuraman, and L. L. Berry, *Delivering Quality Service: Balancing Customer Perceptions and Expectations* (New York: The Free Press, 1990), p. 120.

31. C. Mitchell, "Selling the Brand Inside," *Harvard Business Review* 80 (January 2002), pp. 5–11.

Chapter **Fifteen**

Pricing of Services

This chapter's objectives are to

1. Discuss three major ways that service prices are perceived differently from goods prices by customers.
2. Articulate the key ways that pricing of services differs from pricing of goods from a company's perspective.
3. Demonstrate what value means to customers and the role that price plays in value.
4. Describe strategies that companies use to price services.
5. Give examples of pricing strategy in action.

Airlines Make Huge Profits but Baffle Customers with Fees

The year 2015 was the most profitable year in decades for U.S. airlines, with $25.6 billion after taxes—due in part to low fuel prices and reduced competition, but largely because of the restructured fees they charge passengers. In 2013, the major airlines combined made about $31.5 billion in income just from extra passenger fees. In the good old days of traditional airline ticketing, customers could easily assess the cost of a ticket and compare the price of flights on competing airlines. A flight had a basic cost plus taxes, making the final price easy to determine. Not so today. With separate and different fees charged for myriad services such as ticket changes, seat selection, premium seats, early boarding, and in-flight food and drinks (to mention just a few), passengers can be easily overwhelmed by the cost of a ticket.

To make matters worse, airlines charge extra fees for different services—or charge a different amount for the services that are the same—so comparisons across companies are difficult to make. As shown in "The Ultimate Guide to Airline Fees" referred to later in this chapter, fees vary across airlines for nine different services: bags (carry-on, first or second checked, additional, overweight, and oversized); ticket change; booking (on phone, in person); unaccompanied minors; pets; seat selection; premium seats, in-flight food/beverages; and blanket/pillows. Unless a potential customer happens upon the "Ultimate Guide," which is continually updated, it would take hours to find and compare actual fees, many of which are not known until they check in or are actually on the flight. As an example, premium seat selection is available for widely different fees and customers can purchase extra miles on many flights for yet more money. Some airlines charge for location (e.g., front of the plane preferred), while others offer and charge for seats configured with extra legroom. And if you want to board early, charges vary widely to board right after first and business class. Fees for pets and in-flight food and beverages have so many diverging prices that customers are completely puzzled unless they know how to find these prices, which most customers do not.

The one airline that distinguishes itself because it *does not* charge for bags is Southwest Airlines, where the slogan is "Bags Fly Free." This price differentiator supports Southwest's low-cost airline positioning and generates goodwill from passengers. On the other hand, Spirit Airlines, also a low-fare carrier, negatively stands out because it was the first U.S. airline to charge passengers for bringing carry-on bags aboard. Frontier and Allegiant also charge for carry-on bags and collectively have the most complicated pricing approaches. Each has a low basic price for a flight, designed to capture customers who are looking for the cheapest flight, but figuring out what each flight ultimately costs with variations in *every* service takes a calculator. In fact, Spirit has its own "Bag-o-Tron" on its website to allow passengers to calculate in advance the bag prices for a trip.

Charging for individual services is a relatively new strategy for airlines in the United States, but it has been a common practice for Ryanair, Dublin's discount airline. The company prices its "extra" services—such as baggage and online check-in—far from cheaply. Depending on your perspective, it could be called penny-pinching (water costs almost as much as beer on U.S. flights) or pay-for-service (even making reservations online requires payment). While the fares are low, everything else costs money. In fact, at one time the airline charged $34 for the use of a wheelchair! Customers are not the only ones who have to pay: staff buy their own uniforms and provide their own pens. The CEO of Ryanair's holding company clearly states his philosophy: "You want luxury? Go somewhere else."[1]

According to one of the leading experts on pricing, most service organizations use a "naive and unsophisticated approach to pricing without regard to underlying shifts in demand, the rate that supply can be expanded, prices of available substitutes, consideration of the price–volume relationship, or the availability of future substitutes."[2] What makes the pricing of services more difficult than pricing of goods? What approaches work well in the context of services?

This chapter builds on three key differences between customer evaluation of pricing services and goods:

1. Customers often have inaccurate or limited reference prices for services.
2. Monetary price is not the only price relevant to service customers.
3. Price is a key signal of quality in services.

These three differences can have profound impact on the strategies companies use to set and administer prices for services.

The chapter also discusses common pricing structures, including (1) cost-based, (2) competition-based, and (3) demand-based pricing. One of the most important aspects of demand-based pricing is perceived value, which service providers must understand, so that they price in line with offerings and customer expectations. For that reason, we also describe how customers define value and discuss pricing strategies in the context of value.

THREE KEY WAYS THAT SERVICE PRICES ARE DIFFERENT FOR CUSTOMERS

What role does price play in customer decisions about services? How important is price to potential buyers compared with other factors and service features? Service companies must understand how pricing works, but first they must understand how customers perceive prices and price changes. The three sections that follow describe ways that customers perceive services, and each is central to effective pricing.

Customer Knowledge of Service Prices

To what extent do customers use price as a criterion in selecting services? How much do they know about the costs of services? Before you answer these questions, take the services pricing quiz in Exhibit 15.1. Were you able to fill in a price for each of the services listed? If you were able to answer the questions on the basis of memory, you have internal *reference prices* for the services. A reference price is *a price point in memory for a good or a service* and can consist of the price last paid, the price most frequently paid, or the average of all prices customers have paid for similar offerings.[3]

To see how accurate your reference prices for services are, you can compare them with the actual price of these services from the providers in your hometown. If you are like many consumers, you feel quite uncertain about your knowledge of the prices of services, and the reference prices you hold in memory for services are not generally as accurate as those you hold for goods. There are many reasons for this difference.

Service Variability Limits Knowledge

Because services are not created on a factory assembly line, service firms have great flexibility in the configurations of services they offer. Firms can conceivably offer an infinite variety of combinations and permutations, leading to complex and complicated pricing structures. As an example, consider how difficult it is to get comparable price quotes when buying life insurance. With the multitude of types (such as whole life versus term), features (different deductibles), and variations associated with customers (age, health risk, smoking or nonsmoking), few insurance companies offer exactly the same features and the same prices. Only an expert customer, one who knows enough about insurance to completely specify the options across providers, is likely to find prices that are directly comparable. Some insurance companies— such as Progressive—base their strategy on giving customers competitive prices for insurance.

How did you answer the questions about prices for a medical checkup? If you are like most consumers, you probably wanted more information before you offered a reference price. You probably wanted to know what type of checkup the physician is providing. Does it include X-rays and other diagnostic tests? What types of tests? How long does the checkup take? What is its purpose? If the checkup is undertaken simply to get a signature on a health form or a marriage certificate, the doctor may take a brief medical history, listen for a heartbeat, and measure blood pressure. If, however, the checkup is to monitor a chronic ailment such as diabetes or high blood pressure, the doctor may be more thorough. The point is that a high degree of variability exists across providers of services. Not every physician defines a checkup the same way.

Exhibit 15.1   What Do You Know about the Prices of Services?

1. What do the following services cost in your hometown?

   Dental checkup _____

   General medical checkup _____

   Legal help with a DWI (driving while
   intoxicated) charge _____

   Dental braces _____

   One hour of housecleaning _____

   Room at the Marriott _____

   Haircut _____

   Oil change and lube _____

2. Which of the following would you select if you needed
   a filling replaced in a tooth?

   a. Dentist A—cost is $75, located 15 miles from your
      home, wait is three weeks for an appointment and
      1.5 hours in waiting room

   b. Dentist B—cost is $100, located 15 miles from your
      home, wait is one week for appointment and
      0.5 hour in waiting room

   c. Dentist C—cost is $150, located three miles from
      your job, wait is one week for appointment and no
      time in waiting room

   d. Dentist D—cost is $225, located three miles from
      your job, wait is one week for appointment and
      no time in waiting room; nitrous oxide used, so no
      pain is involved

Providers Are Unwilling to Estimate Prices

Another reason customers lack accurate reference prices for services is that many providers are unable or unwilling to estimate price in advance. For example, legal and hospital service providers are rarely willing—or even able—to estimate a price in advance. The fundamental reason is that they do not know themselves what the services will involve until they have fully examined the patient or the client's situation or until the process of service delivery (such as an operation in a hospital or a trial) unfolds. Most hospitals contend that their fee schedules, called chargemasters, should not be made available to patients beforehand and have fought to keep them private.[4] In a business-to-business context, companies obtain bids or estimates for complex services such as consulting or construction, but this type of price estimation is typically not undertaken with end-consumers; therefore, they often buy without advance knowledge about the final price of the service.

Individual Customer Needs Vary

Another factor that results in the inaccuracy of reference prices is that individual customer needs vary. Some hairstylists' service prices vary across customers on the basis of length of hair, type of haircut, and whether a conditioning treatment and style are included. Therefore, if you ask a friend what a haircut costs from a particular stylist, chances are that your haircut from the same stylist will be a different price. In a similar vein, a service as simple as a hotel room will have prices that vary greatly: by size of room, time of year, type of room availability, and individual versus group rate. These two examples are for very simple services. Now consider a service purchase as idiosyncratic as braces from a dentist or help from a lawyer. In these and many other services, the fact that customers have different requirements will play a strong role in the price of the service.

Collection of Price Information Is Overwhelming in Services

Still another reason customers lack accurate reference prices for services is that customers feel overwhelmed with the information they need to gather. With most goods, retail stores display the products by category to allow customers to compare and contrast the prices of different brands and sizes. Rarely is there a similar display of services in a single outlet. If customers want to compare prices (such as for dry cleaning), they must drive to or call individual outlets or search on the Internet in situations where prices are available. This can be an overwhelming task for consumers, even for the most basic services, as illustrated in Exhibit 15.1.

When services are more specialized, finding out what they cost is even more difficult, see if you have reference prices for these providers: wedding planner, executive coach, and home security system. Your reference prices, if you can even come up with them, are probably even more uncertain and less accurate than for the services in the price quiz in Exhibit 15.1. After considerable searching, we have found that these are starting points for these services. Full-service wedding planners will cost $2,000–$3,000 in the South and $3,500–$10,000 in metro areas. The Association of Bridal Consultants cites the average consultant costs $3,636 in the Northeast and $2,635 in the South, for a national average of $3,262. Sherpa Executive Coaching, the most widely recognized association in the field, regularly surveys members about compensation rates. The organization reports that fees vary widely from between $200 to $3,500 per hour, depending on the level of executive and type of skills being trained, as well as costs for high-level skills and executive groups between $500 and $725 per hour. A recent survey by Sherpa of 500 behavioral and leadership coaches in the United States and Canada found that the majority of rates for all levels and skills fall between $220 and $340 per hour. As for home security systems, so many variables enter the purchase—size of home, installation versus monitoring fees, cameras, window alarms, CO_2 alarms, type of provider—that even Angie's List concluded that there is no one estimate.[5]

The fact that consumers often possess inaccurate reference prices for services has several important managerial implications. Promotional pricing (as in couponing or special pricing) may be less meaningful for services, for which price anchors typically do not exist. Perhaps that is why price is not featured in service advertising as much as it is featured in advertising for goods. Promotional pricing may also create problems if the promotional price (such as a $50 permanent wave special from a salon) is the only one customers see in advertising: it could become the customer's anchor price, making the regular price of $75 for a future purchase seem high by comparison.

The absence of accurate reference prices also suggests that advertising actual prices for services the customer is not used to purchasing may reduce uncertainty and overcome a customer's inflated price expectations for some services. For example, a marketing research firm's advertisements citing the price for a simple study (such as $10,000) would be informative to business customers who were not familiar with the costs of research studies and therefore would be guessing at the cost. By featuring price in advertising, the company overcomes the fear of high cost by giving readers a price anchor.

Prices Are Not Visible

One requirement for the existence of customer reference prices is *price visibility*—the price cannot be hidden or implicit. In many services, particularly financial services, most customers know about only the rate of return and not the costs they pay in the form of fund and insurance fees. In securities and term life insurance, customers are made aware of fees. However, price is invisible in certificates, whole-life insurance, and annuities (which have rear-load charges), and customers rarely know how they are charged or what they pay. Credit card fees are assessed on the basis of what consumers spend, and while customers may know their interest rates they are often shocked at what they are spending in fees to the financial institutions. Compounding and other financial practices—such as compressed periods to pay and dramatic increases in interest rates due to late payments—do not affect their costs until after they have made purchases.

For all the reasons discussed here, many customers do not see the price at all until *after* they receive certain services. Of course, in situations of urgency, such as in accident or illness, customers must make the decision to purchase without respect to cost. And if cost is not known to the customer before purchase, it cannot be used as a key criterion for purchase, as it often is for goods.

The Role of Nonmonetary Costs

Economists have long recognized that monetary price is not the only sacrifice consumers make to obtain products and services. Demand, therefore, is not just a function of monetary price but is influenced by other costs as well. Nonmonetary costs represent other sources of sacrifice perceived by consumers when buying and using a service. Time costs, search costs, and psychological costs often enter into the evaluation of whether to purchase or repurchase a service and may at times be more important concerns than monetary price. Customers will trade money for these other costs.

Time Costs

Most services require customers' direct participation and thus consume real time: time waiting as well as time when the customer interacts with the service provider. Consider the investment you make to exercise, see a physician, or get through the crowds to watch a concert or baseball game. Not only are you paying money to receive these services, but you are also expending time. Time becomes a sacrifice made to receive service in multiple ways. First, because service providers cannot completely control the number of customers or the length of time it will take for each customer to be served, customers are likely to expend time waiting to receive the service. The average waiting time in physicians' offices is 24 minutes, according to the American Medical Association.[6] Waiting time for a service is frequently longer and less predictable than waiting time to buy goods. Second, customers often wait for an available appointment from a service provider (in the price quiz, dentist A required a three-week wait, whereas dentist D required only one week). Virtually everyone has expended waiting time to receive services.

Search Costs

Search costs—the effort invested to identify and select from among services you desire—are often higher for services than for physical goods. Prices for services are rarely displayed on shelves of service establishments for customers to examine as they shop, so these prices are often known only when a customer has decided to experience the service. As an example, how well did you estimate the costs of an hour of housecleaning in the price quiz? As a student, it is unlikely that you regularly purchase housecleaning, and you probably have not seen the price of an hour of cleaning displayed in any retail store. Another factor that increases search costs is that each service establishment typically offers only one "brand" of a service (with the exception of brokers in insurance or financial services), so a customer must initiate contact with several

FIGURE 15.1
Three Basic Marketing Price Structures and Challenges Associated with Their Use for Services

Challenges:
1. Small firms may charge too little to be viable.
2. Heterogeneity of services limits comparability.
3. Prices may not reflect customer value.

Challenges:
1. Costs are difficult to trace.
2. Labor is more difficult to price than materials.
3. Costs may not equal the value that customers perceive the services are worth.

Challenges:
1. Monetary price must be adjusted to reflect the value of nonmonetary costs.
2. Information on service costs is less available to customers; hence, price may not be a central factor.

Special Challenges in Cost-Based Pricing for Services

What is unique about services when using cost-based approaches to pricing? First, costs are difficult to trace or calculate in service businesses, particularly where multiple services are provided by the firm.[9] Consider how difficult it must be for a bank to allocate teller time or ATM costs accurately across its checking, savings, and money market accounts to decide what to charge for the services. Second, a major component of cost is employee time rather than materials, and the value of people's time, particularly non-professional time, is not easy to calculate or estimate. One of the major difficulties in cost-based pricing involves defining the units in which a service is purchased. Thus, the *price per unit*—a well-understood concept in the pricing of manufactured goods—is a vague entity. For this reason many services are sold in terms of input units rather than units of measured output. For example, most professional services (such as consulting, engineering, architecture, psychotherapy, and tutoring) are sold by the hour.

An added difficulty is that actual service costs may underrepresent the value of the service to the customer. A local tailor in one of the authors' hometowns charges $10 for taking in a seam on a $350 ladies' suit jacket and an equal $10 for taking in a seam on a pair of $14 sweat shorts. The tailor's rationale is that both jobs require the same amount of time. What she neglects to see is that the customer would pay a higher price—and might even be happier about the alterations—for the expensive suit jacket and that $10 is too high a price for the sweat shorts.

Examples of Cost-Based Pricing Strategies Used in Services

Cost-plus pricing is a commonly used approach in which component costs are calculated and a markup added. In product pricing, this approach is quite simple; in service industries, however, it is complicated because the tracking and identification of costs are difficult. The approach is typically used in industries in which cost must be estimated in advance, such as construction and engineering. In construction or engineering, bids are solicited by clients on the basis of the description of the service desired. Using their knowledge of the costs of the components of the service (including the raw materials such as masonry and lumber), labor (including both professional and unskilled), and margin, the company estimates and presents to the client a price for the finished service. A contingency amount—to cover the possibility that costs may be higher than estimated—is also stated because, in large projects, specifications can change as the service is provided.

Fee for service is the pricing strategy used by professionals; it represents the cost of the time involved in providing the service. Consultants, psychologists, accountants, and lawyers, among other professionals, charge for their services on an hourly basis. Virtually all psychologists and social workers have a set hourly rate they charge to their clients, and most structure their time in increments of an hour.

In the early 1900s, lawyers typically billed clients a certain fee for services rendered regardless of the amount of time they spent delivering them. Then in the 1970s, law firms began to bill on an hourly rate, in part because this approach offered accountability to clients and an internal budgeting system for the firm. One of the most difficult aspects of this approach is that recordkeeping is tedious for professionals. Lawyers and accountants must keep track of the time they spend for a given client, often down to 10-minute increments. For this reason the method has been criticized because it does not promote efficiency and sometimes ignores the expertise of the lawyers (those who are very experienced can accomplish much more than novices in a given time period, yet billings do not always reflect this). Clients also feared padding of their legal bills and began to audit them. Despite these concerns, the hourly bill dominates the industry, with the majority of revenues billed this way.[10]

Competition-Based Pricing

The competition-based pricing approach focuses on the prices charged by other firms in the same industry or market. Competition-based pricing does not always imply charging the identical rate others charge but rather using others' prices as an anchor for the firm's price. This approach is used predominantly in two situations: (1) when services are standard across providers, such as in the dry cleaning industry, and (2) in oligopolies with a few large service providers, such as in the rental car industry. Difficulties involved in provision of services sometimes make competition-based pricing less simple than it is in goods industries.

Special Challenges in Competition-Based Pricing for Services

Competition-based pricing, commonly practiced in goods firms, can be difficult for service firms. Small firms may find it difficult to charge the same prices that larger service firms charge and make margins high enough to remain in business. Many local service establishments—dry cleaning, retail, and tax accounting, among others—cannot deliver services at the low prices charged by chain operations.

Further, the heterogeneity of services across and within providers makes this approach complicated. As an example, banks offer many types of accounts and services. To try to determine how a competitive bank prices for individual accounts and may differ in features and costs—and whether those prices give sufficient margins and profits—can be difficult. Only in very standardized services that a bank provides, such as ATM surcharges, can banks benefit from competitive prices. In 2007, Bank of America made

Strategy Insight Pricing Variation in Airlines Offers Strategic Opportunities

Our chapter opener described the phenomenon of price variability among airlines—the fact that airlines no longer charge a base price plus tax but instead use differences in the fees for multiple services to compete with each other. This price variation allows them to make larger revenues and profits while positioning themselves among their competitors. For example, please refer to www.smartertravel.com/blogs/today-in-travel/airline-fees-the-ultimate-guide.html?id=2623262 which presents the different fees for most airlines. As you can see in the two guides (which are updated constantly), airlines like Allegiant, Frontier, and Spirit can claim the best-price position in the market by having the lowest base prices. However, because they charge extra fees for virtually everything including water (Spirit) and call center reservations (Allegiant), they are able to make money based on passengers' sensitivity to weight of bags, priority seating, early check-in and a myriad of other services. On the other hand, Southwest distinguishes itself as the only U.S. airline that does not charge for carry-on, first, or second bags, a strategy that makes them stand out among competitors. Larger airlines like American, Delta, and United have frequent flyer programs that reward regular flyers with early red-carpet boarding and in-airport clubs.

Look carefully over these two charts and see if you can determine what the strategy is that five of the airlines (other than those mentioned above) are using. Are the airlines focusing on low price, high service, loyalty, or some other approach? You will need to look carefully at the prices to distinguish the positioning. While other marketing variables such as advertising and routes play a role in the positioning of airlines, you can see that pricing may very well be the most important variable in competitive standing in the industry.

Source: Smarter Travel accessed and continually updated at www.smartertravel.com/blogs/today-in-travel/airline-fees-the-ultimate-guide.html?id=2623262.

headlines by raising ATM withdrawal charges for noncustomers to $3 per withdrawal. Other banks like Citi, Chase, Wachovia, and Wells Fargo did not immediately match the increase but did comment that they review what their competitors do in setting prices.[11]

Examples of Competition-Based Pricing in Service Industries

Price signaling occurs in markets with a high concentration of sellers. In this type of market, any price offered by one company will be matched by competitors to avoid giving a low-cost seller a distinct advantage. The airline industry exemplifies price signaling in services. When any competitor drops the price of routes, others match the lowered price almost immediately.

Going-rate pricing involves charging the most prevalent price in the market. Rental car pricing is an illustration of this technique (and an illustration of price signaling, because the rental car market is dominated by a small number of large companies). For years, the prices set by one company (Hertz) have been followed by the other companies. When Hertz instituted a new pricing plan that involved "no mileage charges, ever," other rental car companies imitated the policy. They then had to raise other factors such as base rates, size and type of car, daily or weekly rates, and drop-off charges to continue to make profits. Prices in different geographic markets, even cities, depend on the going rate in that location, and customers often pay different rates in contiguous cities in the same state. The Global Feature in this chapter illustrates some of the practices in pricing that differ across countries.

Demand-Based Pricing

The two approaches to pricing just described are based on the company and its competitors rather than on customers. Neither approach takes into consideration that customers may lack reference prices, may be sensitive to nonmonetary prices, and may judge quality on the basis of price. All these factors can be accounted for in

TIPPING

A classic Cornell University study revealed an interesting fact about tipping: the custom of tipping is more prevalent in countries where citizens value status and prestige than in countries where they do not. Michael Lynn found that the number of service professionals tipped is relatively small in countries where citizens value recognition and esteem less. "Tipping is really a form of conspicuous consumption. We tip more people in this country because we value status. Americans value recognition and esteem, and we receive that when we tip these service professionals."

One measure of the differences in tipping is the number of service professionals who are given tips in different countries. The United States leads the list with about 35 different professions. Other countries that place a high value on recognition and esteem also tip a large number of professionals. These include Spain (29), Canada (25), India (25), and Italy (24). In contrast, in Denmark and Sweden, the number of tipped professionals is under 10, reflecting the lower value placed on recognition and esteem in these countries.

Tipping is not practiced at all in many countries, including Malaysia, Japan, Oman, New Zealand, Samoa, Singapore, South Korea, Thailand, United Arab Emirates, and Vietnam.

Magellan's, a company that sells travel supplies from retail stores and a website, provides the following general regional tipping "tips" in a guide:

- In *Asia and the Pacific,* tipping could be considered insulting.
- In *Europe,* many hotels and restaurants add a service charge to the bill, making an additional tip unnecessary.
- In the *Middle East and Africa,* tips will not be seen as insulting but are unnecessary.
- In *Central and South America,* most restaurants and hotels add a service charge, making an additional tip unnecessary.

TIPPING BY COUNTRY

In 2015, the Condé Nast Traveler, a well-known travel company, published the following specific tipping advice for virtually all countries. Here are some examples:

Country	Food Server	Guides	Drivers
Egypt	Tip included in bill, add 5–10% above that	$20 per person per day	10–15%
Morocco	10%, but check that it isn't included in bill	$20 per day	Round up to the next dirham note
Brazil	None required	$20–50 for full day	Round up
Canada	15–20%	$10–15 per day	10–15%
Mexico	10–15% cash	100–200 pesos per day	200–300 pesos per day
China	10%	400–500 rupees per day	Usually combined with guides
Spain	7–13%	30 euros per person per day	15 euros

PRICELESS

A London restaurant called Just Around the Corner, which has since closed after a lengthy successful run, had an extraordinary demand-oriented pricing policy: it let customers pay whatever they thought the meal was worth. The policy had been extremely successful since it was started in 1986, with most customers paying more for their meals than the restaurant would charge if it set the prices. According to the founder, it was the first French restaurant in the world without prices—you paid what you thought the meal was worth. His belief was that diners would appreciate his extremely high standards of cooking and presentation and he was shown to be right. Michael Vasos, the founder and owner, claimed, "I make more money from this restaurant than from any of my other [four] establishments." He thought his customers' generosity accounted for the success of the restaurant and its pricing policies, although others stated that the fear of embarrassment common to the English prevents patrons from paying too little.

Other restaurants in Germany (Perlin • Forum), Austria (Der Wiener Deewan), Ireland (Seva Café), India (Indus Valley and Lentil as Anything), and Japan (Annalakshmi) follow the same "pay as you prefer" practices. Virtually all of them ask diners to pay what they can or help either in the kitchen or in the dining room.

Other interesting pricing practices exist internationally. At Tsiferblat Restaurant in Russia and Ukraine, diners pay only for the time they are in the restaurant, not the amount they consume. Even more unique are two restaurants in Austria called Japan Grillhaus and Wafu, where customers pay a fine if they do not finish their plates. At El Tintero II in Spain, entrées are auctioned off rather than having a set price.

Sources: Tim Murphy and Condé Nast Traveler editors, "Etiquette 101: Your Guide to Tipping around the World," http://www.cntraveler.com/stories/2008-11-11/etiquette-101-tipping-guide; "Study Examines Tipping," Hotel and Motel Management, March 17, 1997, p. 14; "Just Around the Corner," accessed June 19, 2016 at http://www.whichtable.com/JustAroundtheCorner-restaurant.asp; "Unusual International Restaurant Practices," accessed June 19, 2016 at http://restoran.us/trivia/unusual.htm.

a company's pricing decisions. The third major approach to pricing, *demand-based pricing,* involves setting prices consistent with customer perceptions of value: prices are based on what customers will pay for the services provided.

Special Challenges in Demand-Based Pricing for Services

One of the major ways that pricing of services differs from pricing of goods in demand-based pricing is that nonmonetary costs and benefits must be factored into the calculation of perceived value to the customer. When services require time, inconvenience, and psychological and search costs, the monetary price must be adjusted to compensate. And when services save time and search costs, the customer is willing to pay a higher monetary price. The challenge is to determine the value to customers of each of the nonmonetary aspects involved.

Another way services and goods differ with respect to this form of pricing is that information on service costs may be less available to customers, making monetary price not as salient a factor in initial service selection as it is in goods purchasing.

Four Meanings of Perceived Value

One of the most appropriate ways that companies price their services is basing the price on the perceived value of the service to customers. Among the questions a service marketer needs to ask are the following: What do consumers mean by *value*? How can we quantify perceived value in dollars, so that we can set appropriate prices for our services? Is the meaning of value similar across consumers and services? How can value perceptions be influenced? To understand demand-based pricing approaches, we must fully understand what value means to customers.

This is not a simple task. When consumers discuss value, they use the term in many different ways and talk about myriad attributes or components. What constitutes value, even in a single service category, appears to be highly personal and idiosyncratic. As depicted in Figure 15.2, customers define value in four ways:

1. Value is low price.
2. Value is whatever I want in a product or service.
3. Value is the quality I get for the price I pay.
4. Value is what I get for what I give.[12]

Let us take a look at each of these definitions more carefully.

FIGURE 15.2
Four Customer Definitions of Value

Value Is Low Price Some consumers equate value with low price, indicating that what they have to give up in terms of money is most salient in their perceptions of value, as typified in these representative comments from customers:

For dry cleaning: "Value means the lowest price."

For carpet steam cleaning: "Value is price—which one is on sale."

For a fast-food restaurant: "When I can use coupons, I feel that the service is a value."

For airline travel: "Value is when airline tickets are discounted."[13]

Value Is Whatever I Want in a Product or Service Rather than focusing on the money given up, some consumers emphasize the benefits they receive from a service or product as the most important component of value. In this value definition, price is far less important than the quality or features that match what the consumer wants. In the telecommunications industry, for example, business customers strongly value the reliability of the systems and are willing to pay for the safety and confidentiality of the connections. Service customers describe this definition of value as follows:

For an MBA degree: "Value is the very best education I can get."

For medical services: "Value is high quality."

For a social club: "Value is what makes me look good to my friends and family."

For a rock or country music concert: "Value is the best performance."

For a hotel room for a honeymoon: "Value is a luxurious room with a hot tub."

Value Is the Quality I Get for the Price I Pay Other consumers see value as a trade-off between the money they give up and the quality they receive.

For a hotel for vacation: "Value is price first and quality second."

For a hotel for business travel: "Value is the lowest price for a quality brand."

For a computer services contract: "Value is the same as quality. No—value is affordable quality."

Value Is What I Get for What I Give Finally, some consumers consider all the benefits they receive as well as all sacrifice components (money, time, effort) when describing value.

For a housekeeping service: "Value is how many rooms I can get cleaned for what the price is."

For a hairstylist: "Value is what I pay in cost and time for the look I get."

For executive education: "Value is getting a good educational experience in the shortest time possible."

The four consumer expressions of value can be captured in one overall definition consistent with the concept of utility in economics: *perceived value is the consumer's overall assessment of the utility of a service based on perceptions of what is received and what is given.* Although what is received varies across consumers (some may want volume, others high quality, still others convenience), as does what is given (some are concerned only with money expended, others with time and effort), value represents a trade-off of the give-and-get components. Customers will make a purchase decision on the basis of perceived value, not solely to minimize the price paid. These definitions are the first step in identifying the elements that must be quantified in setting prices for services.

Technology Spotlight Dynamic Pricing on the Internet Allows Price Adjustments Based on Supply and Demand

When shopping for an airline ticket on the Internet, have you ever found a low-priced ticket that you did not purchase immediately, then returned four hours later to find the same ticket had increased $100 in price? This experience is dynamic pricing in action—the buying and selling of services in markets in which prices move quickly in response to supply and demand fluctuations. In the case of your airline ticket, chances are that other travelers had purchased tickets at the original low price, reducing the airlines' inventory and allowing the airline to gamble on getting customers to buy the remaining seats at higher prices.

Also called real-time pricing, dynamic pricing is an approach to setting the cost for a product or service that is highly flexible. The goal is to allow a company that sells goods or services over the Internet to adjust prices in response to various factors that affect market demand. Changes are controlled by pricing bots, which are software agents that gather data and use algorithms to adjust pricing according to rules involving the customer's location, the time of day, the day of the week, the level of demand, and competitors' pricing.

The approach—often incorporating auctions and other forms of online bidding—is typically used at the end of the supply chain to eliminate surplus inventory or perishable service capacity, as with airline seats. Dynamic pricing has allowed companies to generate significant revenue from excess supply or discontinued products, which they used to turn over to intermediaries.

AUCTIONS: EBAY AND 1,500 RIVALS

Online auctions represent dynamic pricing because customers pay what they are willing and they compete with each other on the goods they desire. In 1995, eBay pioneered the Internet auction, but more than 1,500 websites now offer person-to-person online trading. Market leader eBay offers thousands of new items for auction each day and reported revenue for the quarter ending December 31, 2015, at $23.5 billion. Whereas eBay focuses on consumer-to-consumer transactions, uBid.com acts as a consignment house for manufacturers selling directly to customers. Founded in 1997, uBid offers leading manufacturers' merchandise to consumers and businesses at prices lower than wholesale. Most uBid auctions begin at $1 and allow market dynamics to set the price.

REVERSE AUCTIONS

Reverse auctions are used on the buy-side, allowing buyers to see the lowest bid, but not identify the buyer or the seller. The brand or identity of the seller is revealed only if the seller decides to accept the bid offered by the buyer. An advantage for buyers is that they do not need to guess at the price and can receive the same products and services offered elsewhere with static prices at significant discounts. One disadvantage is that, although buyers see a rating of the seller, they cannot be sure who the seller is and what the service outcome will be. For example, with Priceline, the buyers do not always

Incorporating Perceived Value into Service Pricing

The buyer's perception of total value prompts the willingness to pay a particular price for a service. To translate the customer's value perceptions into an appropriate price for a specific service offering, the marketer must answer a number of questions: What benefits does the service provide? How important is each of these benefits? How much is it worth to the customer to receive a particular benefit from a service? At what price will the service be economically acceptable to potential buyers? In what context is the customer purchasing the service?

The most important thing a company must do—and often a difficult thing—is to estimate the value to customers of the company's services.[14] Value may be perceived differently by consumers because of idiosyncratic tastes, knowledge about the service, buying power, and ability to pay. In this type of pricing, what the consumers value—not what they pay—forms the basis for pricing. Therefore, its effectiveness rests solely on accurately determining what the market perceives the service to be worth.

When the services are for the retail consumers, service providers can rarely afford to give each individual exactly the bundle of attributes valued. They will, however, get their desired flight days and times. Furthermore, the buyer has to sacrifice control over some aspects of the service being consumed.

GROUP BUYING: RAKUTEN

Group buying sites aggregate demand for sellers. The sites offer group rates on long distance and cell phone service, automobile and term life insurance, and mortgages. The concept behind this form of dynamic pricing is that the greater the number of people who want to buy products, the lower the price will be for everyone. Sellers generally bucket the prices of the product being sold based on the number of buyers. For example, for 0–10 buyers, the price for each buyer is $100; for 10–20 buyers, the price for each buyer is $95, and so on. Word-of-mouth communication is critical, because interested buyers are encouraged to enlist their friends and relatives to get a cheaper price for the whole group. Sellers motivate this action by placing an "Invite Your Friend" icon right next to the service or price information. Advantages of this form of dynamic pricing are that the price decreases as a greater number of people bid and the exact service and its specifications are known to buyers when bidding.

DINING WITH DYNAMIC PRICING

Flexible, or dynamic, pricing in the restaurant industry involves changing menu prices by the hour or time of day to attract diners during nonpeak hours, such as afternoons between 2:00 and 6:00 p.m. or late evenings. Restaurants may use discounts, such as 15–30 percent off the total check, to build traffic during off-hours. Typically the restaurants use a "dining aggregator," a site that collects and coordinates information about all restaurants in an area that want to offer dynamic pricing. One of these sites is Upromise.com by Sallie Mae, which offers up to 8 percent rewards on over 10,000 restaurants and has a searchable database of restaurants that shows the average entrée price, which days the rewards are available, and the type of restaurant. Others include Restaurant.com (offering 2-for-1 deals or a percentage off specials at 18,000 restaurants) and DealGator, a website that includes Groupon, LivingSocial, and hundreds of other discount companies and provides search-by-location and by-keyword capabilities.

Sources: https://finance.yahoo.com/quote/ebay/financials?ltr=1; M. Rouse, "Dynamic Pricing," 2015, accessed at http://whatis.techtarget.com/definition/dynamic-pricing; A. Sekar, "Five Websites that Save 10% or More on Dining Out," *NerdWallet*, September 16, 2013, https://www.nerdwallet.com/blog/shopping/restaurant-deals-5-websites-save-10-dining/; S. Toto, "Buy.com Gets Acquired By Japanese E-Commerce Giant Rakuten For $250 Million," *TechCrunch*, May 20, 2010, https://techcrunch.com/2010/05/20/buy-com-gets-acquired-by-japanese-e-commerce-giant-rakuten-for-250-million; T. Demos, "Exactly What is a Dutch Auction?" *Wall Street Journal*, July 21, 2012.

attempt to find one or more bundles that address segments of the market. When individual customers are large (e.g., business-to-business customers or very large and profitable retail customers), the company may find it worthwhile to provide individual bundles to each customer. An interesting manifestation of demand-oriented pricing is shown in the Technology Spotlight.

One of the most complex and difficult tasks of service marketers is setting prices internationally. If service marketers price on the basis of perceived value and if perceived value and willingness to pay differ across countries (which they often do), then service firms may provide essentially the same service but charge different prices in different countries.

PRICING STRATEGIES THAT LINK TO THE FOUR VALUE DEFINITIONS

In this section we describe the approaches to service pricing that are particularly suited to each of the four value definitions. Exhibit 15.2 presents research approaches to setting prices.

One of the reasons that pricing of services is more difficult than pricing of goods is that service units are more variable and difficult to identify than units of goods. Units of goods—automobiles, jeans, gallons of milk, and microwave ovens—are easy to define. Units of service are more difficult in part because they are sold by a variety of components. Information services, for example, are sold by the minute, the web page, the file (as in buying online music), or the search (as in finding and purchasing magazine articles). The services of your doctor are sold by the length and type of the visit, the test performed, the shot given, and the X-rays taken. Cable television is sold by the month (basic fees, premium charges for HBO and Showtime), by the type of equipment leased (digital video recorders, remote controls, digital cable boxes), and by the unit (pay-per-view movies). One approach to dealing with the complexity of pricing services is to develop modular service bundles.

As described in this chapter, pricing a service in line with what customers perceive it is worth is often difficult. Two approaches that have gained favor in recent years are modular service pricing and service tiering.

MODULAR SERVICE PRICING

Modular service pricing involves first identifying the basic and value-added services of a provider as components or building blocks for pricing. To create modules, the company first defines the full range of services that could meet customer needs and for which customers will pay. To create modular pricing, firms need the following:

1. Available prices for each different service.
2. The ability to combine prices and services using easy rules.
3. Minimum overlap among the service elements, so that customers do not pay twice for the same service.

One context in which modular pricing is being developed is publications (e.g., *The Wall Street Journal, Sports Illustrated, The New York Times*) that are bundling their digital, print, and mobile subscriptions. Publications are attempting to determine the customer-perceived value of digital, online, tablet, and mobile formats. The pricing models represent a major change from the past few years, when publications charged for print and gave away digital content. Publishers now recognize that today's consumer values digital content more than print, and they are pricing in line with this revised perception of value. The change illustrates a broader effort by publishers to change from print-only to print-plus-digital

combinations. However, media companies are still trying to maintain their print subscribers because advertisers pay much more for print ads than for digital ones.

Ideally, each component in a modular pricing framework has a price that is in line with customers' perceptions of the worth of that service, and customers can select the components individually and combine them in bundles. A difficulty in the current evolution to modular publication pricing is that each publication has a different approach, making choices confusing to customers.

SERVICE TIERING

Sometimes even good modular pricing can become too complex, and simpler ways to present the company's prices are needed. *Service tiering,* usually called versioning when applied to the pricing of goods, involves creating prices that correspond to the price points and value bundles of different customer segments. For example, cable companies offer service tiers that correspond to service components that are typically desired together. When customers buy the bundles, they receive discounts from what the services would cost individually.

In general, service tiers allow customers to quickly and simply match their desires and the price they are willing to pay with an offering from the company. The customer perceives a benefit in choosing one of the tiers because each tier provides a discount over individual services. The company enjoys a benefit because customers typically buy more services when they are sold in tiers than when they are offered individually. In the context of cable offerings, basic cable is an example of a low tier with a low price, whereas extended cable includes the addition of premium channels such as HBO, Showtime, and the Golf Channel for a higher price. The highest tier, for the highest price, might include all cable channels plus DVRs.

Modular pricing and service tiering allow the company to maximize sales from all parts of a service that the customer desires without having to create unique service bundles for each customer.

Sources: Elizabeth Wasserman, "How to Price Business Services," *Inc.* Magazine, accessed online at www.inc.com/guides/price-your-services.html, June 15, 2016. R. Docters, M. Reopel, J. Sun, and S. Tanny, "Capturing the Unique Value of Services: Why Pricing of Services Is Different," *Journal of Business Strategy* 25, no. 2 (2004), pp. 23–28; R. Adams, "Many Formats, One Price: More Publications Begin Bundling Their Digital, Print, and Mobile Subscriptions," *The Wall Street Journal,* May 16, 2011, p. B4.

Pricing Strategies When the Customer Means "Value Is Low Price"

When monetary price is the most important determinant of value to a customer, the company focuses mainly on price. This focus does not mean that the quality level and intrinsic attributes are always irrelevant, just that monetary price dominates in importance. To establish a service price in this definition of value, the marketer must understand to what extent customers know the objective prices of services in this category, how they interpret various prices, and how much is too much of a perceived sacrifice. These factors are best understood when the service provider also knows the relative dollar size of the purchase, the frequency of past price changes, and the range of acceptable prices for the service. Some of the specific pricing approaches appropriate when customers define value as low price include discounting, odd pricing, synchro-pricing, and penetration pricing (Figure 15.3).

Discounting

Service providers offer discounts to communicate to price-sensitive buyers that they are receiving value. Among the most prevalent discounting approaches are those from online companies such as Groupon, Living Social, Angie's List, and an ever-increasing number of competitors. These Web companies, of which Groupon was the first, offer daily discounts to consumers through e-mail, Facebook, and Twitter feeds. The discounts are all for local companies, most of which are services such as restaurants, cleaning services, massages, plumbing, home inspections, and hotels. Consumers request the deals and can bid for them until they are sold out. Online companies are paid sometimes as much as 50 percent of the revenue from purchased coupons.

Odd Pricing

Odd pricing is the practice of pricing services just below the exact dollar amount to make buyers perceive that they are getting a lower price. Dry cleaners charge $2.98 for a shirt rather than $3.00, health clubs have dues priced at $33.90 per month rather than $34, and haircuts are $9.50 rather than $10.00. Odd prices suggest discounting and bargains and are appealing to customers for whom value means low price.

Synchro-Pricing

Synchro-pricing is the use of price to manage demand for a service by capitalizing on customer sensitivity to prices. Certain services, such as tax preparation, passenger transportation, hotels, and theaters, have demand that fluctuates over time as well as constrained supply at peak times. For companies in these and other industries, setting a price that provides a profit over time can be difficult. Pricing can, however, play a role

FIGURE 15.3
Pricing Strategies When the Customer Defines Value as Low Price

Value is low price.
- Discounting
- Odd pricing
- Synchro-pricing
- Penetration pricing

in smoothing demand and synchronizing demand and supply. Time, place, quantity, and incentive differentials have all been used effectively by service firms, as discussed in Chapter 13.

Place differentials are used for services in which customers have a sensitivity to location. The front row at concerts, the 50-yard line in football, center court in tennis or basketball, ocean-side rooms in resort hotels—all these represent place differentials that are meaningful to customers and that therefore command higher prices.

Time differentials involve price variations that depend on when the service is consumed. Telephone service after 11:00 p.m., hospital rooms on weekends, and health spas in the off-season are time differentials that reflect slow periods of service. By offering lower prices for underused time periods, a service company can smooth demand and gain incremental revenue.

Quantity differentials are usually price decreases given for volume purchasing. This pricing structure allows a service company to predict future demand for its services. Customers who buy a booklet of coupons for a tanning salon or facial, a quantity of tokens for public bridges, or packages of advertising spots on radio or television are all responding to price incentives achieved by committing to future services. Corporate discounts for airlines, hotels, and rental cars exemplify quantity discounts in the business context; by offering lower prices, the service provider locks in future business.

Differentials as incentives are lower prices for new or existing clients in the hope of encouraging them to be regular users or more frequent users. Some professionals—lawyers, dentists, electrologists, and even some physicians—offer free consultations at the front end, usually to overcome fear and uncertainty about high service prices. Other companies stimulate use by offering regular customers discounts or premiums during slow periods. Sports teams are now using differential prices as incentives to attract customers who would otherwise not be able to afford the high cost of attending sports events. The Phoenix Suns, in claiming that "you should have pricing for every pocketbook," revamped its ticket pricing by raising premium seats by 26 percent, decreasing arena seats by 31 percent, and adding 500 $10 tickets. The net result was a 6 percent increase in the average ticket price (paid for by the premium seat holders) but more attendance at the games because more fans in different segments could afford the seats.[15]

Penetration Pricing

Penetration pricing is a strategy in which new services are introduced at low prices to stimulate trial and widespread use. The strategy is appropriate when (1) sales volume of the service is very sensitive to price, even in the early stages of introduction; (2) it is possible to achieve economies in unit costs by operating at large volumes; (3) a service faces threats of strong potential competition very soon after introduction; and (4) there is no class of buyers willing to pay a higher price to obtain the service.[16] Penetration pricing can lead to problems when companies then select a "regular" increased price. Care must be taken not to penetrate with so low a price that customers feel the regular price is outside the range of acceptable prices.

Pricing Strategies When the Customer Means "Value Is Everything I Want in a Service"

When the customer is concerned principally with the "get" components of a service, monetary price is not of primary concern. The more desirable intrinsic attributes a

FIGURE 15.4
Pricing Strategies When the Customer Defines Value as Everything Wanted in a Service

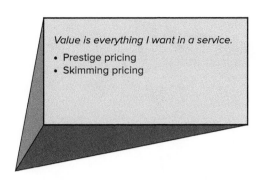

Value is everything I want in a service.
- Prestige pricing
- Skimming pricing

given service possesses, the more highly valued the service is likely to be and the higher the price the marketer can set. Figure 15.4 shows appropriate pricing strategies.

Prestige Pricing

Prestige pricing is a special form of demand-based pricing by service marketers who offer high-quality or status services. For certain services—restaurants, health clubs, airlines, and hotels—a higher price is charged for the luxury end of the business. For example, for hotel guests who crave pampering, many chains offer club floors that add high-end amenities into their offerings for large price increases. Some Ritz-Carltons offer free lunch foods such as sandwiches and salads with these high-priced rooms.[17] Some customers of service companies that use this approach may actually value the high price because it represents prestige or a quality image. Others prefer purchasing at the high end because they are given preference in seating or accommodations and are entitled to other special benefits. In prestige pricing, demand may actually increase as price increases because the costlier service has more value in reflecting quality or prestige.

Skimming Pricing

Skimming, a strategy in which new services are introduced at high prices, is an effective approach when services are major improvements over past services. In this situation, customers are more concerned about obtaining the service than about the cost of the service, allowing service providers to skim the customers most willing to pay the highest prices. Services related to anti-aging, such as Botox injections and laser liposuction, often are introduced at high prices, thereby attracting customers who are willing to pay more to obtain the services in the short term rather than wait until a later time, when the prices might be reduced.

Pricing Strategies When the Customer Means "Value Is the Quality I Get for the Price I Pay"

Some customers primarily consider both quality and monetary price. The task of the marketer is to understand what *quality* means to the customer (or segments of customers) and then to match quality level with price level. Specific strategies are shown in Figure 15.5.

Value Pricing

The widely used term *value pricing* has come to mean "giving more for less." In current usage, it involves assembling a bundle of services desirable to a wide group of customers and then pricing them lower than they would cost alone. Taco Bell pioneered value pricing with a $0.59 Value Menu. After sales at the chain rose 50 percent in two years to $2.4 billion, McDonald's and Burger King adopted the value pricing

FIGURE 15.5
Pricing Strategies
When the Customer
Defines Value as
Quality for the
Price Paid

Value is the quality I get for the price I pay.
- Value pricing
- Market segmentation pricing

practice. The menu at Taco Bell has since been reconfigured to emphasize plain tacos and burritos (which are easier and faster for the chain to make) for less than a dollar. As mentioned in the chapter opener, Southwest Airlines also offers value pricing in its airline service: a low cost for a bundle of desirable service attributes such as frequent departures, friendly and funny employees, and on-time arrival. The airline offers consistently low fares with bare-bones service.

Market Segmentation Pricing

With *market segmentation pricing,* a service marketer charges different prices to groups of customers for what are perceived to be different quality levels of service, even though there may not be corresponding differences in the costs of providing the service to each of these groups. This form of pricing is based on the premise that segments show different price elasticities of demand and desire different quality levels.

Service marketers often price by *client category,* based on the recognition that some groups find it difficult to pay a recommended price. Health clubs located in college communities typically offer student memberships, recognizing that this segment of customers has limited ability to pay full price. In addition to the lower price, student memberships may also carry with them reduced hours of use, particularly in peak times. The same line of reasoning leads to memberships for "seniors," who are less able to pay full price but are willing to patronize the clubs during daytime hours, when most full-price members are working.

Companies also use market segmentation by *service version,* recognizing that not all segments want the basic level of service at the lowest price. When they can identify a bundle of attributes that are desirable enough for another segment of customers, they can charge a higher price for that bundle. Companies can configure service bundles that reflect price and service points appealing to different groups in the market. Hotels, for example, offer standard rooms at a basic rate but then combine amenities and tangibles related to the room to attract customers willing to pay more for the concierge level, jacuzzi, Wi-Fi, additional beds, and sitting areas.

Pricing Strategies When the Customer Means "Value Is All That I Get for All That I Give"

Some customers define value as including not just the benefits they receive but also the time, money, and effort they put into a service. Figure 15.6 illustrates the pricing strategies described in this definition of value.

FIGURE 15.6
**Pricing Strategies
When the Customer
Defines Value as All
That Is Received for
All That Is Given**

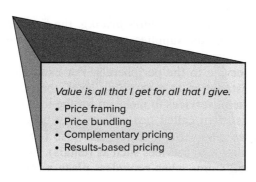

Value is all that I get for all that I give.
- Price framing
- Price bundling
- Complementary pricing
- Results-based pricing

Price Framing

Because many customers do not possess accurate reference prices for services, service marketers are more likely than goods marketers to organize price information for customers so they know how to view it. Customers naturally look for price anchors as well as familiar services against which to judge focal services. If they accept the anchors, they view the price and service package favorably. Groupon, Living Social, and other online couponing sites let customers know the actual values of the offers being made as well as the discounted costs in the offer. As mentioned earlier in the chapter, customers often do not have a reference price for services—particularly household services such as plumbing, gutter cleaning, and pressure washing. Framing the offers by providing actual prices allows customers to recognize the value they will receive if they purchase the Groupon.

Price Bundling

Some services are consumed more effectively in conjunction with other services; other services accompany the products they support (such as extended service warranties, training, and expedited delivery). When customers find value in a package of interrelated services, price bundling is an appropriate strategy. Bundling, which means pricing and selling services as a group rather than individually, has benefits to both customers and service companies. Customers find that bundling simplifies their purchase and payment, and companies find that the approach stimulates demand for the firm's service line, thereby achieving cost economies for the operations as a whole while increasing net contributions.[18] Bundling also allows the customer to pay less than when purchasing each of the services individually, which contributes to perceptions of value.

The effectiveness of price bundling depends on how well the service firm understands the bundles of value that customers or segments perceive and on the complementarity of demand for these services. Effectiveness also depends on the right choice of services from the firm's point of view. Because the firm's objective is to increase overall sales, the services selected for bundling should be those with a relatively small sales volume without the bundling to minimize revenue loss from discounting a service that already has a high sales volume.

Complementary Pricing

Services that are highly interrelated can be leveraged by using *complementary pricing*. This pricing includes three related strategies—captive pricing, two-part

Virtually all companies hunger for evidence and tools to ascertain and monitor the payoff and payback of new investments in service. Many managers still see service and service quality as costs rather than as contributors to profits, partly because of the difficulty involved in tracing the link between service and financial returns. Determining the financial impact of service parallels the age-old search for the connection between advertising and sales. Service quality's results—like advertising's results—are cumulative, and therefore evidence of the link may not come immediately or even quickly after investments. And like advertising, service quality is one of many variables—among them pricing, advertising, efficiency, and image—that simultaneously influence profits. Furthermore, spending on service per se does not guarantee results because strategy and execution must both be considered.

In recent years, however, researchers and company executives have sought to understand the relationship between service and profits and have found strong evidence to support the relationship. For example, one study examined the comparative benefits of revenue expansion and cost reduction on return on quality. The research addressed a common strategic dilemma faced by executives: whether to reduce costs through the use of programs that focus on efficiencies and cost cutting or to build revenues through improvements to customer service, customer satisfaction, and customer retention.[3] Using managers' reports as well as secondary data on firm profitability and stock returns, the study investigated whether the highest return on quality was generated from cost cutting, revenue expansion, or a combination of the two approaches. The results suggest that firms that adopt primarily a revenue expansion emphasis perform better and have higher return on quality than firms that emphasize either cost reduction or both revenue expansion and cost reduction together.[4]

Executives are also realizing that the link between service and profits is neither straightforward nor simple. Service quality affects many economic factors in a company, some of them leading to profits through variables not traditionally in the domain of marketing. For example, some approaches express the financial impact of service quality in lowered costs or increased productivity. These relationships involve operational issues that concern marketing only in the sense that marketing research is used to identify service improvements that customers notice and value.

More recently, other types of evidence have become available with which to examine the relationship between service and profitability. The overall goal of this chapter is to synthesize that evidence and to identify relationships between service and profits. In each section we assess the evidence and identify what is currently known about the topics. The chapter is organized using a conceptual framework linking all the variables in these topics.

SERVICE AND PROFITABILITY: THE DIRECT RELATIONSHIP

Figure 16.1 shows the underlying question at the heart of this chapter: how does service affect profits? Managers were first interested in this question in the late 1980s, when service quality emerged as a pivotal competitive strategy. The executives of leading service companies such as FedEx and Disney were willing to trust their intuition that better service would lead to improved financial success. Without formal documentation of the financial payoff, they committed resources to improving service and were richly rewarded for their leaps of faith. In the 1990s, the strategy of using service for competitive advantage and profits was embraced by forward-thinking manufacturing

FIGURE 16.1
The Direct Relationship between Service and Profits

and information technology companies such as General Electric and IBM. However, executives in other companies withheld judgment about investing in service, waiting for solid evidence of its financial soundness.

Early evidence came from the U.S. General Accounting Office (GAO), which sought grounds for belief in the financial impact of quality in companies that had been finalists or winners of the Malcolm Baldrige National Quality Award. The GAO found that these elite quality firms had benefited in terms of market share, sales per employee, return on sales, and return on assets. Based on responses from 22 companies that won or were finalists, the GAO found that 34–40 financial variables showed positive performance improvements, while only 6 measurements were negative or neutral.[5] In subsequent years, evidence from more rigorous quantitative research showed the positive impact of service. One study showed the favorable financial impact of complaint recovery systems.[6] Another found a significant and positive relationship between patient satisfaction and hospital profitability.[7] Extending the definition of financial performance to include stock returns, another study found a significant positive link between changes in customer quality perceptions and stock return while holding constant the effects of advertising expenditures and return on investment. Many more studies have shown links between customer satisfaction and financial returns. Exhibit 16.1 reviews the studies that have examined links among customer satisfaction, service quality, and financial performance. This information is enlightening, for it validates that improving customer satisfaction and service quality generates financial returns.

As is indicated in the exhibit, more than two decades of research have demonstrated that customer satisfaction drives corporate earnings, stock prices, shareholder value, and market value added. Many studies that correlate customer satisfaction and financial performance have been conducted through the American Customer Satisfaction Index (ACSI), a joint undertaking of the University of Michigan and The American Society for Quality. The ACSI is an economic indicator that measures the satisfaction of consumers across the U.S. economy (www .theacsi.org) on a 0–100 point scale.[8] Researchers have studied the relationship between ACSI findings and firm financial performance and have consistently shown that improvement in customer satisfaction has a significant and positive impact on firms' financial performance. For example, one comprehensive study using 200 of the *Fortune* 500 firms across 40 industries showed that a 1 percent change in ACSI is associated with 1.016 percent change in shareholder value as measured by Tobin's q (the ratio of market value of a firm to the replacement cost of its tangible assets). This means that a 1 percent improvement in satisfaction for these firms will lead to an increase in firm value of approximately $275 million.[9] Supporting this finding, a similar study found that a 1-point increase in ACSI results in an increase of $55 million in a firm's net operational cash the following year and a decrease of 4 percent in cash flow variability.[10] Also supporting this finding is a study showing that a unit increase in ACSI leads to a $240 million

Exhibit 16.1 Customer Satisfaction, Service Quality, and Firm Performance

A review of two decades of studies examining the links among customer satisfaction, service quality, and firm performance resulted in several important recurring findings across studies. Some studies explicitly consider the impact of service quality on financial performance, while others subsume service quality as a driver of customer satisfaction and therefore focus on the impact of overall customer satisfaction on financial performance. As discussed in Chapter 4, customer satisfaction is a broader concept than service quality, but service quality is almost always an important driver of customer satisfaction across all types of industries. Therefore, the results of the review of both concepts are relevant in this chapter. Because so many studies were examined in the review, only a subset is mentioned in this exhibit, but the complete list of sources can be found in the published review listed as the first reference in this exhibit.

Studies that were reviewed used a variety of metrics for financial performance: profit, stock price, Tobin's q (ratio of market value of a firm to the replacement cost of its tangible assets), return on assets (ROA), return on investment (ROI), abnormal earnings, and cash flows. The following is what the authors concluded.

Generalization 1: Improvements in customer satisfaction have a significant and positive impact on firms' financial performance.

Many studies have shown a strong link between customer satisfaction and firm profitability. For example, one comprehensive study by Anderson, Fornell, and Mazvancheryl using 200 of the *Fortune* 500 firms across 40 industries showed that a 1 percent change in ACSI (as measured by the American Customer Satisfaction Index on a 0–100 scale) is associated with 1.016 percent change in shareholder value as measured by Tobin's q. This implies that a 1 percent improvement in satisfaction for these firms will lead to an increase in the firm's value of approximately $275 million. Supporting this finding, a similar study by Gruca and Rego found that a 1-point increase in ACSI results in an increase of $55 million in a firm's net operational cash flow next year and a decrease of 4 percent in cash flow variability.

In a service-industry study using data from almost 8,000 customers of a national hotel chain, researchers found that return on investment in service quality (e.g.,

cleanliness) was almost 45 percent. Another study showed that a 1-point improvement in satisfaction (on a 7-point scale) increased ROA by 0.59 percent. With data from 106 firms in 68 industries during the period 1981–1991, still another study found that news reports about increases in customer service led to average cumulative abnormal earnings of about 0.46 percent, or $17 million in market value.

Collectively, these studies show a strong and positive impact of customer satisfaction on firm performance. They further provide a rough benchmark about the size of the impact: a 1 percent change in ACSI can lead to a $240 to $275 million improvement in firm value. In sum, these results provide a strong guideline to firms about how much they should spend on improving customer satisfaction.

Generalization 2: The link between satisfaction and firm performance is asymmetric.

An *asymmetric relationship* means that increases in customer satisfaction do not always have the same impact on firm performance as decreases in customer satisfaction. For example, a study by Anderson and Mittal found that a 1 percent increase in satisfaction led to a 2.37 percent increase in ROI, whereas a 1 percent drop in satisfaction reduced ROI by 5.08 percent (see the accompanying figure). Another study by Nayyar found that positive news about customer service led to an increase in compounded annualized rate (CAR) of about 0.46 percent, whereas reports of reductions in customer service were met with declines in CAR of about 0.22 percent. Still another study by Anderson and Mittal found that a drop in satisfaction produced twice the impact on ROI than an increase in satisfaction. In contrast, the Nayyar study found negative news of customer service had only half the impact on CAR than the positive news.

Generalization 3: The strength of the satisfaction–profitability link varies across industries as well as across firms within an industry.

The strength of the relationships among customer satisfaction, service quality, and profitability are not consistent across industries. In a study by Ittner and Larcker, the impact was found to be stronger in service industries than in durable and nondurable manufacturing firms. In that study, the ACSI had a positive but insignificant impact on market value of durable and nondurable manufacturing firms and a positive and

increase in market value.[11] In a service–industry study using data from almost 8,000 customers of a national hotel chain, researchers found that return on investment in service quality was 44.6 percent.[12] Collectively, these studies show a significant and positive impact of customer satisfaction on firm performance. However, as the chapter opener mentioned, the statistically significant relationships in these studies do not always translate into meaningful *practical* relationships as the correlations

The Asymmetric Relationship between Satisfaction and ROI (Based on 125 Swedish Firms)

Source: E. Anderson and V. Mittal, "Strengthening the Satisfaction-Profit Chain," *Journal of Service Research* 3 (2000), pp. 107–120.

significant impact on the market value of transportation, utility, and communication firms. The effect was strongly negative for retailers. Another study by Anderson found that trade-offs between customer satisfaction and productivity (e.g., labor productivity) were more likely for services than for goods. Specifically, a simultaneous 1 percent increase in both customer satisfaction and productivity is likely to increase ROI by 0.365 percent for goods, but only 0.22 percent for services.

In addition to the differences found in the studies cited, Anderson et al.'s study found that, while a 1 percent change in satisfaction had an *average* impact of 1.016 percent on shareholder value (Tobin's q), the impact ranged from 2.8 percent for department stores to −0.3 percent for discount stores. Anderson and Mittal's study found that industry characteristics explain 35 percent of the variance in cash flow growth and 54 percent of the variance in cash flow variability. They also found that the influence of customer satisfaction on cash flow growth is greatest for low-involvement, routinized, and frequently purchased products (e.g., beer and fast food).

While this summary represents a considerable improvement over what we knew in the past, companies are very eager to learn more. This general information about the relationships among customer satisfaction, service quality, and financial performance will help them understand that investing in customer satisfaction and service quality is beneficial. Thus, indications are that the investments are worthwhile and that not investing can be harmful to firms. Later in the chapter, we will describe other, more specific information that firms want to understand about these relationships.

Sources: S. Gupta and V. Zeithaml, "Customer Metrics and Their Impact on Financial Performance," *Marketing Science* 25 (November–December 2006), pp. 718–739; E. Anderson, C. Fornell, and S. Mazvancheryl, "Customer Satisfaction and Shareholder Value," *Journal of Marketing* 68 (2004), pp. 172–185; C. Ittner and D. Larcker, "Are Non-Financial Measures Leading Indicators of Financial Performance? An Analysis of Customer Satisfaction," *Journal of Accounting Research* 36, no. 3, (1998), pp. 1–35; R. Rust, A. Zahorik, and T. Keiningham, "Return on Quality (ROQ): Making Service Quality Financially Accountable," *Journal of Marketing* 59 (1995) pp. 58–70; T. S. Gruca and L. L. Rego, "Customer Satisfaction, Cash Flow and Shareholder Value," *Journal of Marketing* 69 (2005), pp. 115–130; E. Anderson and V. Mittal, "Strengthening the Satisfaction-Profit Chain," *Journal of Service Research* 3 (2000), pp. 107–120; P. Nayyar, "Stock Market Reactions to Customer Service Changes," *Strategic Management Journal* 16, no. 1 (1995), pp. 39–53.

are sometimes weak even though statistically related. For this reason, while the general question about the broad linkage between service quality and profits has been established, it is also—and perhaps more—meaningful to focus on questions about particular elements of the relationship. For example, what role does service quality have in getting customers? How does service quality contribute to keeping the customers a firm already has?

OFFENSIVE MARKETING EFFECTS OF SERVICE: ATTRACTING MORE AND BETTER CUSTOMERS

Service quality can help companies attract more and better customers to the business through *offensive marketing*.[13] Offensive effects (shown in Figure 16.2) involve market share, reputation, and price premiums. When service is good, a company gains a positive reputation and through that reputation a higher market share and the ability to charge more than its competitors for services. These benefits were documented in a classic multiyear, multicompany study called PIMS (profit impact of marketing strategy). The PIMS research shows that companies offering superior service achieve higher-than-normal market share growth and that service quality influences profits through increased market share and premium prices, as well as lowered costs and less rework.[14] The study found that businesses rated in the top fifth of competitors on relative service quality average an 8 percent price premium over their competitors.[15]

To document the impact of service on market share, a group of researchers described their version of the path between quality and market share, claiming that satisfied customers spread positive word of mouth, which leads to the attraction of new customers and then to higher market share. They claim that advertising service excellence without sufficient quality to back up the communications will not increase market share.[16]

DEFENSIVE MARKETING EFFECTS OF SERVICE: CUSTOMER RETENTION

When it comes to keeping the customers a firm already has—an approach called *defensive marketing*[17]—researchers and consulting firms have in the past 20 years documented and quantified the financial impact of existing customers. Customer defection is costly to companies because new customers must replace lost customers, and replacement comes at a high cost. Getting new customers is expensive; it involves advertising, promotion, and sales costs, as well as start-up operating expenses. New customers are often unprofitable for a period of time after acquisition. In the insurance industry, for example, the insurer does not typically recover selling costs until the third or fourth year of the relationship. Capturing customers from other companies is also an expensive proposition.

FIGURE 16.2
Offensive Marketing Effects of Service on Profits

In general, the longer a customer remains with a company, the more profitable the relationship is for the organization:

> Served correctly, customers generate increasingly more profits each year they stay with a company. Across a wide range of businesses, the pattern is the same: the longer a company keeps a customer, the more money it stands to make.[18]

For example, one study examined this question using a financial services company's internal records. Researchers tested the service–profit chain framework (described earlier in Chapter 11) and examined the links among customer satisfaction, service quality, and share-of-wallet measures to data on customer retention and customer profitability. Most notably, the study found that different levels of share of wallet generated different levels of customer profitability and that the relationship between share of wallet and profitability varies over time. This more complicated answer to the relationship between service quality and profitability hints at what we are going to describe later in this chapter: that the relationship sometimes is not direct or straightforward.

Research on the topic of lost customers has examined the defensive marketing effects of service. In contrast to studies done in the past, one study indicated that traditional ways of examining defensive effects may be inappropriate for markets involving new services because they fail to account for the social effects (e.g., word of mouth and imitation) that can influence future customer acquisitions. They show how the impact of a lost customer on the profitability of the firm depends on (a) whether the customer defects to a competing firm or stops using the service altogether and (b) when the customer stops using the service—distinctions are often overlooked in conventional studies. Their results demonstrate how the value of a lost customer changes throughout the product life cycle, showing that the loss of an early adopter costs the firm much more than the loss of a later adopter.[19]

The money a company makes from retention comes from four sources (shown in Figure 16.3): costs, volume of purchases, price premium, and word-of-mouth communication. This section provides research evidence for many of the sources.

Lower Costs

Attracting a new customer is five times as costly as retaining an existing one. Consultants who have focused on these relationships assert that customer defections have a stronger effect on a company's profits than market share, scale, unit costs, and

FIGURE 16.3
Defensive Marketing Effects of Service on Profits

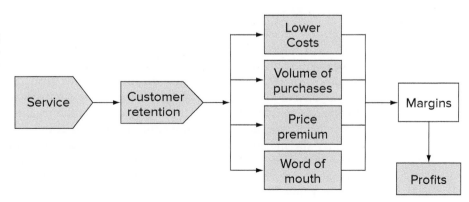

many other factors usually associated with competitive advantage.[20] They also claim that, depending on the industry, companies can increase profits from 25 to 85 percent by retaining just 5 percent more of their customers.

Consider the following facts about the role of service quality in lowering costs:

- "Our highest quality day was our lowest cost of operations day" (Fred Smith, founder and chairman of FedEx).
- "Our costs of not doing things right the first time were from 25 to 30 percent of our revenue" (David F. Colicchio, Hewlett-Packard Company).[21]
- Bain and Company, a consulting organization specializing in retention research, estimates that, in the life insurance business, a 5 percent annual increase in customer retention lowers a company's costs per policy by 18 percent.

Research studies also confirm the lower costs that relate to higher service quality. For example, one study looked at the relationship between three years of service quality and operational performance data from 1,135 franchised Holiday Inn hotels. The purpose was to determine the relationship between service quality, operational performance, and costs. Hotels with defects—at least one quality defect in the exterior, the guest room, and the guest bath—had a revenue per available room per day (RevPAR) of approximately $2.80 less than hotels that did not have defects in each of the areas. This implies that hotels can be more successful and reduce costs by maintaining high quality standards in areas that have the greatest impact on financial return.

Volume of Purchases

Customers who are satisfied with a company's services are likely to increase the amount of money they spend with that company or the types of services offered. A customer satisfied with a broker's services, for example, will likely invest more money when it becomes available. Similarly, a customer satisfied with a bank's checking services is likely to open a savings account with the same bank and to use the bank's loan services.

Price Premium

Most of the service quality leaders in industry command higher prices than their competitors: FedEx collects more for overnight delivery than the U.S. Postal Service, Hertz rental cars cost more than Avis cars, and staying at the Ritz-Carlton is a more expensive undertaking than staying at the Hyatt. Therefore, offering high service quality often pays for itself in price increases.

Word-of-Mouth Communication

Because word-of-mouth communication is considered more credible than other sources of information, the best type of promotion for a service may come from other customers who advocate the services provided by the company. Word-of-mouth communication brings new customers to the firm, and the financial value of this form of advocacy can be calibrated by the company in terms of the promotional costs it saves as well as the streams of revenue from new customers. In fact, researchers have developed models of customer lifetime value, in which they can quantify the monetary worth of word-of-mouth communications, called *referral values,* for different segments of consumers.[22] As discussed in Exhibit 16.2, many companies are now using the extent of word of mouth as their main measure of customer loyalty.

Many different methods of customer measurement—customer satisfaction, service quality, loyalty, and retention for example—have been used to predict a firm's financial performance. One metric that has become popular yet controversial in recent years is called the *Net Promoter Score* (NPS). The score, developed by loyalty expert Frederick Reichheld, is based on the idea that word of mouth communication, rather than any of the other metrics, is the best predictor of growth and therefore financial performance.

The score itself is based on just one survey question: Would you recommend us to a friend or colleague? To get the NPS, a company asks consumers about the likelihood (out of 10) that they would recommend the company, and then subtracts the proportion of "detractors" (who rate the company lower than 6) from the proportion of "promoters" (who rate the company at 9 or 10).

Executives of many of the world's most prestigious firms agree with Frederick Reichheld that the NPS is the "single most reliable indicator of a company's ability to grow." General Electric, American Express, Microsoft, Intuit, and The Progressive Corporation are but a few companies that have adopted the approach. The popularity of the Net Promoter Score comes in large part because the approach is simple. To top management, long confused by the growing complexity of customer measurement and how to apply it, the idea of having just one number on which to focus is very appealing. And the measure is intuitive—if customers like the firm or its service enough to talk about it to others, that signals a stronger bond than merely being satisfied. The Net Promoter Score became, in essence, a "magic number" for companies.

HOW DO COMPANIES MEASURE UP ON THE NET PROMOTER SCORE?

In many firms promoters barely outnumber detractors, giving them NPS scores of only 5 to 10 percent. Worse yet, many firms and industries have negative Net Promoter Scores, which means that they are constantly creating detractors. Some firms shine, however, and the following chart indicates some of the stars.

CONTROVERSY: IS THE NET PROMOTER INDEX SUPERIOR, APPROPRIATE, OR COMPLETE?

While executives are embracing the Net Promoter Score, researchers and many loyalty experts question the superiority, appropriateness, and completeness of the metric. For example, one researcher questioned, convincingly, whether word of mouth would be a better driver of growth than other factors like reducing customer loss or increasing current customers' volume through cross-sales and

NPS® Scores by Industry

Source: Satmetrix 2015 Net Promoter Study of US Consumers

Industry	Company	NPS
Brokerage and Investments	Vanguard	59%
Banking	USAA	75%
Credit Cards	Discover and American Express	52%
Insurance	USAA	75%
Grocery	Trader Joe's	62%
Department Stores	Costco	72%
Online Shopping	Amazon	71%
Online Travel	Trip Advisor (Airbnb)	50% (38%)
Airlines	JetBlue	75%
Software and Applications	TurboTax	52%
Shared Driving	Uber	37%
Television Entertainment	Netflix	50%

share of category purchase. More dramatically, would actions driven to increase word of mouth create stronger growth than actions to acquire profitable new customers?

Another key concern is the extent to which word of mouth is a relevant goal for all products and services in all contexts. Consumers feel strongly about some products and services and these feelings drive word of mouth. Services (such as restaurants, vacations, and entertainment), fashions, and new electronic products are referral-worthy products. However, the majority of products and services are unlikely to be interesting enough for customers to talk about them. From a practical standpoint, while using a single number alone provides a sign of health, as a thermometer would do in signaling body temperature, it neither diagnoses firm problems nor describes how to treat them. To be actionable, companies must follow up with metrics that also contain other questions (such as those we described in Chapter 5 of this textbook) to identify what customers expect and perceive about the company. In the past two years, Satmetrix (the company that administers NPS) has added a small number of additional questions such as "value for the money" to its questions. However, this and other very general questions are not diagnostic.

Reichheld's findings have been put to the test by other researchers. One team of loyalty experts matched the way

(continued)

FIGURE 16.5
The Effects of Service on Behavioral Intentions and Behavior

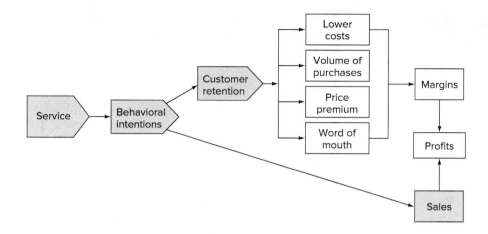

found that intent to repurchase a Toyota automobile increased from a base of 37 to 45 percent with a positive sales experience, from 37 to 79 percent with a positive service experience, and from 37 to 91 percent with both positive sales and service experiences.[30]

THE KEY DRIVERS OF SERVICE QUALITY, CUSTOMER RETENTION, AND PROFITS

Understanding the relationship between overall service quality and profitability is important, but it is perhaps more useful to managers to identify specific drivers of service quality that most relate to profitability (shown in Figure 16.6). Doing so will help firms understand what aspects of service quality to change to influence the relationship and, therefore, where to invest resources.

Most evidence for this issue has come from examining the effects of specific aspects of service (e.g., responsiveness, reliability, assurance, and tangibles) on overall service quality, customer satisfaction, and purchase intentions rather than on financial outcomes such as retention or profitability. As you have discovered in this text, service is multifaceted, consisting of a wide variety of customer-perceived dimensions and resulting from innumerable company strategies such as technology and process

FIGURE 16.6
The Key Drivers of Service Quality, Customer Retention, and Profits

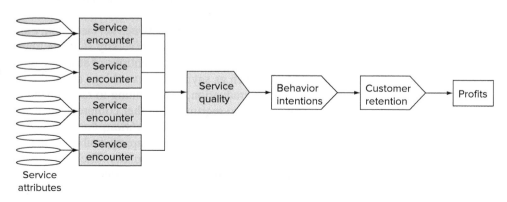

improvement. In research exploring the relative importance of service dimensions on overall service quality or customer satisfaction, the bulk of the support confirms that reliability is most critical; but other research has demonstrated the importance of customization and other factors. Because the dimensions and attributes are delivered in many cases with totally different internal strategies, resources must be allocated where they are most needed.[31]

Some companies and researchers have viewed the effect of specific service encounters on overall service quality or customer satisfaction and the effect of specific behaviors within service encounters. Marriott Hotels conducted extensive customer research to determine what service elements contribute most to customer loyalty. They found that four of the top five factors came into play in the first 10 minutes of the guest's stay—those that involved the early encounters of arriving, checking in, and entering the hotel rooms. Other companies have found that mistakes or problems that occur in early service encounters are particularly critical, because a failure at early points results in greater risk for dissatisfaction in each ensuing encounter. IBM found that the sales encounter was the most critical of all, in large part because interactions with salespeople establish customer expectations for the remaining service encounters.

Another way of looking at the problem, based largely in the operations and management literature, involves investigating the effect of service programs and managerial approaches within an organization on financial measures such as profitability. A customer-focused approach to metrics is described in the Strategy Insight.

Effective Nonfinancial Performance Measurements

According to field research conducted in 60 companies and survey responses from 297 senior executives, many companies do not identify and act on the correct non-financial measures.[32] One example involves a bank that only surveyed the satisfaction of customers who physically entered the branches (rather than all customers, including those who banked by phone or ATM), a policy that caused some branch managers to offer free food and drinks in order to increase their scores. According to the authors of the study, companies make four major mistakes:

1. Not linking measures to strategy. Companies can easily identify hundreds of nonfinancial measures to track, but they also need to use analysis that identifies the most important drivers of their strategy. Successful organizations use value driver maps, tools that lay out the cause-and-effect relationships between drivers and strategic success. Figure 16.7 shows the causal model developed by a successful fast-food chain to understand the key drivers of shareholder value. The factors on the right were identified as most important in leading to the concepts on the left, and the sequence of concepts from top to bottom shows the relationships among company strategies (such as selection and staffing) and intermediate results (such as employee and customer satisfaction) that result in financial results (such as sustained profitability and shareholder value). The study found that fewer than 30 percent of the firms surveyed used this causal modeling approach.

2. *Not validating the links.* Only 21 percent of companies in the study verify that the nonfinancial measures lead to financial performance. Instead, many firms decide what they are going to measure in each category and never link the categories. Many managers believed that the relationships were self-evident instead of conducting analysis to validate the linkages. This chapter's Strategy Insight showed

Strategy Insight Customer Equity and Return on Marketing: Metrics to Match a Strategic Customer-Centered View of the Firm

Although the marketing concept has articulated a customer-centered viewpoint since the 1960s, marketing theory and practice have become incrementally customer-centered. For example, marketing has only recently decreased its emphasis on short-term transactions and increased its focus on long-term customer relationships. Much of this refocus stems from the changing nature of the world's leading economies, which have undergone a century-long shift from the goods sector to the service sector.

Because service tends to be more relationship based, this structural shift in the economy has resulted in more attention to relationships and therefore more attention to customers. This customer-centered viewpoint is now reflected in the concepts and metrics that drive marketing management, including such metrics as customer value and voice of the customer. For example, the concept of brand equity, a fundamentally product-centered concept, is now being challenged by the customer-centered concept of *customer equity,* defined as the total of the discounted lifetime values summed over all the firm's customers.

In other words, customer equity is obtained by summing up the customer lifetime values of the firm's customers. In fast-moving industries that involve customer relationships, products come and go but customers remain. Customers and customer equity may be more central to many firms than brands and brand equity, although current management practices and metrics do not yet fully reflect this shift. The shift from product-centered thinking to customer-centered thinking implies the need for an accompanying shift from product-based metrics to customer-based metrics.

USING CUSTOMER EQUITY IN A STRATEGIC FRAMEWORK

Consider the issues facing a typical marketing manager or marketing-oriented CEO: How do I manage my brand? How will my customers react to changes in service and service quality? Should I raise prices? What is the best way to enhance the relationships with my current customers? Where should I focus my efforts? Determining customer lifetime value, or customer equity, is the first step, but the more important step is to evaluate and test ideas and strategies using lifetime value as the measuring stick. At a very basic level, strategies for building customer relationships can affect five basic factors: retention rate, referrals, sales, direct costs, and marketing costs.

Researchers Roland Rust, Valarie Zeithaml, and Kay Lemon have developed an approach based on customer equity that can help business executives answer their questions. The model that represents this approach is shown in the accompanying figure. In this context, customer equity is an approach to marketing and corporate strategy that finally puts the customer—and, more importantly, strategies that grow the value of the customer—at the heart of the organization. The researchers identify the drivers of customer equity—value equity, brand equity, and relationship equity—and explain how these drivers work, independently and together, to grow customer equity. Service strategies are prominent in both value equity and relationship equity. Within each of these drivers are specific actions ("levers") that the firm can take to enhance the firm's overall customer equity.

WHY IS CUSTOMER EQUITY IMPORTANT?

For most firms, customer equity—the total of the discounted lifetime values of all the firm's customers—is certain to be the most important determinant of the long-term value of the firm. Although customer equity will not be responsible for the entire value of the firm (e.g., physical assets, intellectual property, research and development competencies), the firm's current customers provide the most reliable source of future revenues and profits—and provide a focal point for marketing strategy.

one way that companies can create this type of linkage. In general, it is critical that companies pull together all their data and examine the relationships among the categories.

3. *Not setting the right performance targets.* Companies sometimes aim too high in setting improvement targets. Trying to make all customers 100 percent satisfied might

The Customer Equity Model

Although it may seem obvious that customer equity is key to long-term success, understanding how to grow and manage customer equity is much more complex. Growing customer equity is of utmost importance, and doing it well can lead to significant competitive advantage.

CALCULATING RETURN ON MARKETING USING CUSTOMER EQUITY

At the beginning of this chapter, we told you about an approach called return on quality that was developed to help companies understand where they could get the greatest impact from quality investments. A more general form of that approach is called *return on marketing,* which enables companies to look at all competing marketing strategy options and trade them off on the basis of projected financial return. This approach allows companies to not just examine the impact of service on financial return but also compare the impact of service with the impact of branding, price changes, and all other marketing strategies. Using the customer equity model, firms can analyze the drivers that have the greatest impact, compare the drivers' performance with that of competitors' drivers, and project return on investment from improvements in the drivers. The framework enables what-if evaluation of marketing return on investment, which can include such criteria as return on quality, return on advertising, return on loyalty programs, and even return on corporate citizenship, given a particular shift in customer perceptions. This approach enables firms to focus marketing efforts on strategic initiatives that generate the greatest return.

Sources: R. Rust, K. Lemon, and V. Zeithaml, "Return on Marketing: Using Customer Equity to Focus Marketing Strategy," *Journal of Marketing* 68 (January 2004), p. 109; R. Rust, V. Zeithaml, and K. Lemon, *Driving Customer Equity* (New York: The Free Press, 2000).

seem to be a desirable goal, but many companies expend far too many resources to gain too little improvement in satisfaction. The study's authors found that a telecommunications company aiming for customers who were completely satisfied was wasting resources because these customers spent no more money than those who were 80 percent satisfied.[33]

FIGURE 16.7
The Measures That Matter Most:
A causal model for a fast-food company shows the critical drivers of performance and the concepts that lead to shareholder value.

Source: Christopher D. Ittner and David F. Larcker, "Coming Up Short on Nonfinancial Performance Measurement," *Harvard Business Review* 81 (November 2003), pp. 88–95.

4. *Measuring incorrectly.* Companies need to use metrics with statistical validity and reliability. Organizations cannot measure complex phenomenon with one or two simple measures, nor can they use inconsistent methodologies to measure the same concept, such as customer satisfaction. Another problem that companies may encounter is trying to use quantitative metrics to capture qualitative results for important factors such as leadership and innovation.

Creating a balanced scorecard in and of itself does not improve performance. Companies will not reap the benefits of techniques such as the balanced scorecard unless they address these four issues.

Technology Spotlight   Cost-Effective Service Excellence through Technology

In addition to affecting the top line by increasing revenues, companies across the globe are taking a hard look at what they can to do make bottom-line improvements by enhancing productivity, making processes more efficient, and innovating systems. Among the approaches that are effective in bottom-line improvement are reducing waste in the service system, standardizing service behaviors and actions, shifting the service boundary by having customers perform more of the service, and substituting technology for personal contact and human effort. We have discussed technology throughout this textbook, and in this spotlight we feature several ways that technology has been used to make service more efficient and therefore more profitable.

ROBOT-POWERED YOGURT KIOSKS

Delivering frozen yogurt from a traditional retail store is a very expensive endeavor with a great deal of overhead to cover. The next stage, developed to save money and allow customization, were yogurt stores where you decide how much yogurt to buy and how you want to decorate it. However, you may not yet be aware of the latest in automated yogurt: the robot-powered kiosk. Allan Jones, the CEO of the frozen yogurt kiosk concept Robofusion, claims that the business potential for the automated yogurt market was the reason he quit his job at a chemical company to pursue a venture in robotically served yogurt.

Robofusion's kiosks dispense yogurt and ice cream with the help of a robotic arm that fills the cup, adds the toppings, and delivers the treat to the customer through a revolving platform. A touchscreen user interface allows the customer to select and customize the product, which sells for between $3 and $6, depending on the size.

While the company only had 37 Robofusion kiosks deployed globally at the time of this writing, they are currently in Singapore, Brazil, Turkey, Australia, Dubai, and the United Arab Emirates, and there are plans to ship kiosks to Saudi Arabia and Mexico.

A competitor to Robofusion is Reis & Irvy's automated frozen yogurt kiosk, which allows consumers to create completely personalized creations. It can be installed in convenience stores, airports, schools, and even corporate offices. To use the machine, consumers simply choose their size and style of frozen yogurt. They can then choose from nine different flavor options and a wide variety of toppings. The machine will then create the custom order while the consumers pays. The process is hassle-free and energy efficient, using 90 percent less energy than a traditional frozen yogurt shop.

LOUISE THE TECHNOLOGY NURSE

One of the highest costs in hospitals comes from preventable 30-day re-admissions, which can be as high as 4.4 million per year. Re-admissions are largely due to patient noncompliance with hospital instructions about medication and home care. The highest rates are for heart attacks (19.9 percent), heart failure (24.7 percent), pneumonia (18.3 percent), and circulatory system disorders (10.4 percent). One of the newest strategies to assure that patients understand posthospital instructions is a virtual nurse—patient advocate"—named Louise. Developed by Boston University Medical Center, Louise is an animated character that explains medical instructions to patients on a computer screen, thereby carefully and fully communicating home care. On a laptop, Louise is wheeled to the patient's bedside and reviews the discharge packet while also looking at a paper copy. Patients can ask and re-ask questions using a touchscreen. Louise helped cut re-admissions by 30 percent in a 2008 study. Further, the virtual discharge system automates 30 minutes of time, for a savings in time for human nurses.

Sources: L. Landro, "Don't Come Back, Hospitals Say," *The Wall Street Journal*, June 7, 2011; Agency for Healthcare Research and Quality 2011, hospitalcompare.gov, accessed August 2011; N. Gagliordi, "Robot-Powered Kiosks Seek Yogurt Domination," *Kiosk Marketplace*, February 26, 2014, http://www.kioskmarketplace.com/articles/robot-powered-kiosks-seek-frozen-yogurt-domination/; K. Pendrell, "This Machine Creates Custom Yogurt Creations on Demand," *Trend Hunter*, March 11, 2016, http://www.trendhunter.com/trends/automated-frozen-yogurt.

3. R. T. Rust, C. Moorman, and P. R. Dickson, "Getting Return on Quality: Revenue Expansion, Cost Reduction, or Both?" *Journal of Marketing* 66 (October 2002), pp. 7–24.

4. Ibid.

5. *Management Practice, U.S. Companies Improve Performance through Quality Efforts,* Report No. GAO/NSIAD-91-190 (Washington, DC: U.S. General Accounting Office, 1992).

6. R. Rust, B. Subramanian, and M. Wells, "Making Complaints a Management Tool," *Marketing Management* 3 (1993), pp. 40–45. R. Rust, Roland, C. Moorman, and G. Bhalla, "Rethinking Marketing," *Harvard Business Review,* January-February 2010; R. Rust, V. Zeithaml, and K. Lemon, "Customer-Centered Brand Management," *Harvard Business Review,* September 2004; S. Gupta and D. Lehmann, *Managing Customers as Investments,* Wharton School Publishing, 2005.

7. E. Nelson, R. T. Rust, A. Zahorik, R. L. Rose, P. Batalden, and B. Siemanski, "Do Patient Perceptions of Quality Relate to Hospital Financial Performance?" *Journal of Healthcare Marketing* 12 (December 1992), pp. 1–13.

8. www.theacsi.org, website for the American Customer Satisfaction Index, University of Michigan, Ann Arbor, Michigan.

9. E. Anderson, C. Fornell, and S. Mazvancheryl, "Customer Satisfaction and Shareholder Value," *Journal of Marketing* 68 (October 2004), pp. 172–185.

10. T. S. Gruca and L. L. Rego, "Customer Satisfaction, Cash Flow and Shareholder Value," *Journal of Marketing* 69 (July 2005), pp. 115–130.

11. C. Ittner and D. Larcker, "Are Non-Financial Measures Leading Indicators of Financial Performance? An Analysis of Customer Satisfaction," *Journal of Accounting Research* 36 (1998), pp. 1–35.

12. R. Rust, A. Zahorik, and T. Keiningham, "Return on Quality (ROQ): Making Service Quality Financially Accountable," *Journal of Marketing* 59 (April 1995), pp. 58–70.

13. C. Fornell and B. Wernerfelt, "Defensive Marketing Strategy by Customer Complaint Management: A Theoretical Analysis," *Journal of Marketing Research* 24 (November 1987), pp. 337–346; see also C. Fornell and B. Wernerfelt, "A Model for Customer Complaint Management," *Marketing Science* 7 (Summer 1988), pp. 271–286.

14. B. Gale, "Monitoring Customer Satisfaction and Market-Perceived Quality," *American Marketing Association Worth Repeating Series,* no. 922CS01 (Chicago: American Marketing Association, 1992).

15. Ibid.

16. R. E. Kordupleski, R. T. Rust, and A. J. Zahorik, "Why Improving Quality Doesn't Improve Quality (or Whatever Happened to Marketing?)," *California Management Review* 35 (Spring 1993), pp. 82–95.

17. Fornell and Wernerfelt, "Defensive Marketing Strategy by Customer Complaint Management"; Fornell and Wernerfelt, "A Model for Customer Complaint Management."

18. F. Reichheld and E. Sasser, "Zero Defections: Quality Comes to Services," *Harvard Business Review* 68 (September–October 1990), p. 106.

19. J. Hogan, K. Lemon, and B. Libai, "What Is the True Value of a Lost Customer?" *Journal of Service Research* 5, 2003.

20. Ibid., p. 105.

21. D. F. Colicchio, regional quality manager, Hewlett-Packard Company, personal communication.

22. V. Kumar, J. A. Petersen, and R. P. Leone, "How Valuable Is Word of Mouth?" *Harvard Business Review* 85 (October 2007), pp. 139–146.

23. V. Kumar, J. A. Petersen, and R. P. Leone, "Driving Profitability by Encouraging Customer Referrals: Who, When, and How," *Journal of Marketing,* September 2010.

24. R. Hallowell, "Word-of-Mouth Referral," *Harvard Business School Module Note,* 2002.

25. J. L. Heskett, W. E. Sasser Jr., and L. A. Schlesinger, *The Service Profit Chain* (New York: The Free Press, 1997).

26. Information provided by TARP Worldwide Inc., August 2007.

27. E. W. Anderson and M. Sullivan, "The Antecedents and Consequences of Customer Satisfaction for Firms," *Marketing Science* 12 (Spring 1992), pp. 125–143.

28. W. Boulding, R. Staelin, A. Kalra, and V. A. Zeithaml, "Conceptualizing and Testing a Dynamic Process Model of Service Quality," report no. 92–121, Marketing Science Institute, 1992.

29. V. A. Zeithaml, L. L. Berry, and A. Parasuraman, "The Behavioral Consequences of Service Quality," *Journal of Marketing* 60 (April 1996), pp. 31–46.

30. J. P. McLaughlin, "Ensuring Customer Satisfaction Is a Strategic Issue, Not Just an Operational One," presentation at the AIC Customer Satisfaction Measurement Conference, Chicago, December 6–7, 1993.

31. Paul, Michael, Thorsten Hennig-Thurau, Dwayne D. Gremler, Kevin P. Gwinner, and Caroline Wiertz (2009), "Toward a Theory of Repeated Purchase Drivers for Consumer Services," *Journal of the Academy of Marketing Science,* 37 (2), 215–237.

32. The material in this section comes from C. D. Ittner and D. F. Larcker, "Coming Up Short on Nonfinancial Performance Measurement," *Harvard Business Review* 81 (November 2003), pp. 88–95.

33. Ibid., p. 92.

Index

Abercrombie & Fitch, 320
Abstractness, 422
Accenture, 5, 356
Accountability, 190
Achrol, R., 303
Active cocreators of value, 352
Activists, 187
Adams, M., 358
Adaptability, 99
Adelman, M. B., 152
Adequate service expectations, 53, 60–63, 71
Adequate signs, 302
Adjusting capacity, 394–397
Advertising, 434
    customer education management, 437–439
    customer expectation management, 436–437
    humor in, 430
    internal marketing communication management, 439–442
    mobile, 428, 435
    service intangibility, 424–430
    service promises, 44, 63, 430–435
    strategies, 429
Aesthetic impression, 302, 303
Aflac, 426
Agents, 41, 90, 138, 298, 468
Ahuvia, A., 152
Air Berlin, 402, 403
Åkerlund, H., 170
Aksoy, L., 83, 86, 474, 475, 484
Al-Natour, S., 364
Albertson, 392
Alesandri, K. L., 425
Ali, S., 17
Allegiant, 447, 456
Allen, C. T., 99, 184
Allstate, 90
Altman, I., 287
Amazon.com, 13, 14, 78, 100, 138, 355, 365
Amazon Echo, 13
Amazon Prime, 452
Ambient conditions, 300, 301
American Airlines, 4, 158, 402
American Customer Satisfaction Index (ACSI), 83–85, 477, 494
American Express, 257, 268, 399, 434, 437, 483

American Family Life Insurance Company, 426
American Life Project, 368
Andersen, A., 166, 478
Anderson, E., 163, 477, 479
Anderson, E. W., 12, 83, 86, 487
Anderson, R. D., 322
Andreassen, T., 484
Andreassen, T. W., 199
Andrews, M., 428
Ansoff, H. I., 231
Anthony, S. D., 233
Antonides, 81, 97
Antons, D., 372
Apple Computers, 3, 290
    Apple store's delivering "steps of service" globally, 319
Approach behaviors, 295
ARAMARK, 246
Architectural design, 290, 298
Argyris, C., 335
Armstrong, K., 429
Arndt, M., 394, 427
Arnould, E., 80
Arnould, E. J., 81, 152, 296, 370
Arousal seekers, 300
Artifacts, 300, 302–304
Ashforth, B. F., 327
Asmus, C., 287
Association, 426
Assurance, 87, 90–91
    dimension, 323
Asymmetric relationship, 478
Attributions for service, 82
Audit, 45, 46–47
Auh, S., 358
Automated teller machines (ATMs), 14, 59
Avoidance behaviors, 295

"Bag-o-Tron", 447
"Bags Fly Free", 447
Bakec, J., 301
Baker, B., 428
Baker, J., 297, 301, 404, 410, 421
Balasubramanian, S., 9, 227, 233, 353
Banker, S., 262
Bank of America, 222
Bansal, H. S., 161, 207, 340, 422
Barker, R. G., 296
Barlow, J., 289, 321
Barnes, D. C., 69

Barnes, J., 298
Baron, S., 355
Barry, T. E., 64
Barsie, P., 428
Bart, Y., 428
Baruch, J. J., 4
Batalden, P., 477
Bateson, J. E. G., 360, 367
Bayón, T., 403
Bean, L. L., 275
Beatty, S. E., 91, 99, 160, 198
Beauchamp, M. B., 69
Behavioral intentions, 121, 488
Behaviors, 293
    effects of service on, 488
    in servicescape, 293–296
Bell, D. E., 434
Bellman, E., 300
Bell, P. A., 287
Bell, S. J., 358
Benavent, C., 162
Benbasat, I., 364
Bendapudi, N., 147, 152, 162, 285, 332, 340, 351, 361
Bendapudi, V., 332
Bennett, D. J., 296
Bennett, J. D., 296
Bennett, P., 181
Benoit, S., 355
Berman, B., 203, 205
Berry, L., 11
Berry, L. L., 19, 20, 35, 51, 57, 59, 64, 66, 67, 70, 79, 81, 87, 89, 117, 128, 141, 144, 146, 147, 169, 170, 184, 202, 207, 226, 285, 294, 294, 303, 315, 328, 331, 339, 360, 425, 427, 431, 432, 439, 440, 487
Bettencourt, L. A., 162, 227, 323, 325, 351, 353, 357
Bezos, Jeff, 100–101
Bhalla, G., 477
Bharadwaj, S. G., 184, 227
Biased interpretation, 221
Bielen, F., 404
Big Data, 258
Bijmolt, T. H. A., 64
Bitner, M. J., 9, 16, 17, 26, 43, 59, 79, 82, 87, 91, 99, 101, 102, 124, 152, 180, 220, 223, 224, 228, 233, 238, 240, 244, 247, 283, 295, 298, 321, 351, 358, 361, 363, 364, 365, 366, 369, 370, 420

Bloch, T. M., 124
Blocker, C. P., 162
Block, L. G., 301
Blodgett, J. G., 301
Blueprint, 306
Blueprinting service, 238–248
    building, 244–248
    components, 239–240
    examples, 240–242
    reading and using, 243–244
    self-service, 242–243
    service encounter sequence, 267,
        268, 270
Blut, M., 365
Bobbitt, L. M., 364
Boeck, G., 464
Bolton, R. N., 159, 180, 181, 184, 195
Bone, S. A., 335
Bon, Michel, 342
Booms, B. H., 26, 99, 101, 124, 180
Boone, T., 229
Bordoloi, S. K., 399, 406, 408
Bottom-line effectiveness, 11
Boulding, W., 487
Boundary spanners, 323 324
Boundary-spanning roles, 323–328
    critical roles of boundary
        spanners, 324
    emotional labor, 324–325
    quality/productivity trade-offs, 328
    sources of conflict, 325–328
Bourdeau, B. L., 410
Bove, L. L., 152
Bowen, D., 267, 317
Bowen, D. E., 79, 82, 220, 221, 223, 289,
    317, 319, 322, 332, 336, 337, 351,
    357, 366, 370, 372
Bowen, J., 325
Bowers, M. J., 229
Bowers, M. R., 339
Bradley, G., 191
Brady, D., 12, 158, 218–219, 292
Brady, M. K., 79, 87, 89, 180, 181, 183,
    186, 197, 198, 323
Brand awareness, 431
Branded customer service, 321
Brand equity, 431, 490
Branding, 281, 431
Brand meaning, 432
Brandyberry, G., 38
Branson, Richard, 433
Brax, S., 9
Brazil, customer research in, 134
Breidbach, C., 372
Brett, L. R., 305
Bristol-Myers, 11
Brocato, E. D., 297, 410
Brooker, K., 28
Brooke, Z., 435
Brooks, R., 157

Brown, 358, 365, 369, 370
Brown, B., 233
Brown, S. W., 9, 16, 59, 79, 82, 153, 163,
    180, 181, 193, 194, 201, 201, 220,
    223, 224, 227, 228, 233, 245, 289,
    321, 325, 330, 337, 351, 353, 357,
    362, 364, 430
Brown, T. J., 64, 322, 323
Brüggen, E. C., 295, 301, 307
Bruhn, M., 83
Brunswick, G. J., 362
Bryant, B. E., 83
Brynjolfsson, E., 133
Bucket theory of marketing, 146
Buckley, J., 125
Bucklin, R. E., 64
Bundling, 467
Buoye, A., 475
Burkhard, K. A., 223, 224
Burnham, T. A., 160
Burton, J., 208
Busby, P. L., 287
Busch, C. M., 332
Bush, R., 453
Business-to-Business services, client
    cocreation of value in, 356, 357
Business-to-business situations, 436
Business-to-consumer (B2C), 43
Business-to business (B2B), 43
Business analysis, 234–235
Businesses, service, 2
    Apple, 3
    GE, 3
    Marriott, 3
    Uber, 3
Business strategy development, 231
Buttle, F., 208
Buzz marketing, 427
BuzzMetric approach, 430

CAD computer model, 136
Cadotte, E. R., 53
Cadwallader, S., 226
California Department of Motor
    Vehicles, 407
Cameron, M., 410
Capacity and demand management,
    382–410
    adjusting capacity, 394–397
    capacity constraints, 386–388
    Cemex creatively manages chaotic
        demand for services, 391
    combining demand and capacity
        strategies, 397–398, 399
    demand patterns, 388–390
    lack of inventory capability, 384–386
    optimal vs. maximum use of capacity,
        387–388
    Phoenician hotel in Scottsdale,
        382–383

    shifting demand to match capacity,
        390, 392–394
    strategies for matching, 390–398
    time, labor, equipment, and facilities,
        387
    waiting line strategies, 404–410
    yield management, 398–404
Capacity-constrained businesses, 402
Capacity-constrained services, 383
Capacity constraints, 386–388, 405
    optimal vs. maximum use of capacity,
        387–388
    time, labor, equipment, and
        facilities, 387
Capacity expansion, 398
Capacity upgrades, 398
Capella, L. M., 301
Capitol Services Inc. (CSI), 169
Captive pricing, 468
Carbone, L. P., 286, 294
Cardy, R. L., 339
Carey, J., 125
Carey, W. P., 13
Carlson, B. D., 322
Carlzon, J., 320
Carroll, Dave, 182–183
Caterpillar, 15, 199
Caterpillar Corporation, 162
Cemex creatively manages chaotic
    demand for services, 391
Centers for Disease Control (CDC), 133
Certified public accountant (CPA), 352
Cha, J., 83
Chamberlain, L., 235
Chamikuttyl, P., 428
Chandler, J. D., 220
Chandrashekaran, M., 180
Chan, K. W., 162, 358
Chaotic demand, 390
Chargemasters, 449
Charles Schwab, 4, 15, 33, 315, 318,
    366, 367
"Chase demand" strategy, 396
Chase, R. B., 202, 220, 225, 357,
    358, 399
Chebat, J., 301
Chebat, J. C., 301, 335
Check-out kiosk technology, 58, 59
Chen, H., 133
Chiang, R. H. L., 133
Chief executive officer (CEO), 76
Childers, Terry L., 160
China
    customer research in, 135
    innovation in, 222
    migration of jobs to, 18
Chipotle Mexican Grill, 427
Chitturi, R., 69
Choi, Y., 294
Chozick, A., 267

Global marketplace
  adjusting service standards for, 266
  service innovations in, 222–223
Global positioning system (GPS), 391
Global Reach of Services, extending,
  16–17
Gloomy, 299
Goals, 257–258
  team, 336
Going-rate pricing, 456
Gold tier, 157
Golledge, R. G., 298
Goods-focused businesses, service as
  business imperative in, 9
Goodstein, R. C., 206
Goodwin, C., 152, 359
Google, 42, 133, 332–333, 339, 435
Google/Alphabet, 14
Googleplex, 332
Goolsby, J. R., 317, 325
Goul, M., 223, 224
Graham, J., 370
Graham, J. L., 358
Grandey, A., 325
Grandey, A. A., 167, 327
Grayson, K. A., 79
Gregoire, Y., 198
Greguras, G. J., 325
Gremler, D., 99, 323, 334
Gremler, D. D., 43, 82, 124, 152, 153,
  163, 186, 203, 271, 295, 301, 307,
  323, 324, 327, 331, 430, 489
Grewal, D., 104, 162, 206, 301, 364, 366,
  404, 428
Griffin, A., 229, 230
Grisaffe, D., 484
Groening, C., 86
Gronroos, C., 53, 87, 146, 228, 317, 328,
  349, 351, 353, 363
Gross domestic product (GDP), 7
Gross, T. S., 68
Groth, M., 82, 324, 327
Group buying, 461
Grove, S., 167
Grove, S. J., 154, 355
Growth, 474
Gruber, T., 191
Gruca, T. S., 477, 478, 479
Gruen, T. W., 370
Grund, M. A., 83
Guarantees for service, 202–207
  service attribute guarantees, 203
  unconditional satisfaction
    guarantees, 203
Guiltinan, J. G., 64
Guiltinan, J. P., 160
Gummesson, E., 146, 330
Gunst, R. F., 64
Gunther, M., 334
Gunturkun, P., 370

Guo, L., 370
Gupta, S., 153, 477, 479
Gustafsson, A., 9, 221, 228
Gustavsson, B., 330
Gwinner, K., 323, 334
Gwinner, K. P., 152, 153, 185, 186, 271,
  323, 430, 489

Haenlein, M., 170
Hainline, David, 169
Halinen, A., 170
Hallmark, 42
Hallowell, R., 17, 267, 317, 319, 322, 484
Hamburger University (HU), 318
Hamilton, J. O. C., 19
Hampton Inn Hotels, 199, 204, 263–264
Handrich, M., 361
Han, S., 428
Hansen, D. E., 270
Hansen, H., 163
Hansen, J. D., 162
Harari, O., 201
Hard customer-defined standards,
  260–262
Hard measurements, 275
Hard standards
  for Ford Motor Company, 269
  for speed of complaint handling, 274
Hargadon, A., 234
Harker, P. T., 358
Harrah's Casinos and Hotels, 339
Harrah's Entertainment, 336
Harrell, G., 322
Harris, K., 355
Harris, L. C., 167, 170, 372
Harrison, M. P., 99
Hart, C. W., 184
Hart, C. W. L., 203, 205
Hartline, M. D., 234, 317, 325
Harvey, Tim, 151
Haumann, T., 370
Hauser, J., 229
Hawser, J., 230
Healing environment, 302
Health care, technology facilitates
  customer participation in, 368, 369
Heidenreich, S., 361
Heine, C., 428
Helle, P., 228
Helm, S. V., 154
Hempel, J., 334
Henard, D. H., 220
Henderson, P. W., 301
Henkoff, R., 406
Hennig-Thurau, T., 82, 153, 186, 271,
  324, 327
Henrique, J. L., 184
Hensley, R. L., 409
Heppelmann, J. E., 15, 228
Herrington, J. D., 301

Herrman, A., 160
Hertz, 263–264, 452, 456
Heskett, J. L., 12, 85, 156, 184, 317,
  322, 487
Hess, R. L., Jr., 66, 198, 207
Heterogeneity, 21
Hetter, K., 189
Hewlett-Packard, 9, 13
Hilton Garden Inn, 150–151
Hilton Hotels, 149, 150, 163
Hilton's OnQ system, 150–151
Hindo, B., 86
Hinterhuber, H. H., 156
Hiring, 38, 219, 318, 340
Hochschild, A., 324, 327
Hofstede, G., 89
Hogan, J., 332, 481
Hogan, R., 332
Hogreve, J., 322
Holiday Inns Inc., 11, 146, 235, 482
Holistic service, 224
Holland America Cruise Line, 296
Holloway, B. B., 91, 99, 198
Homburg, C., 153, 157
Home electricity monitor, 371
Honeycutt, E. D., Jr., 184
Hong, P., 418
Horizontal communication, 423, 439–440,
  442. See also Communication
Horowitz, D. M., 180, 181, 183
Houston, M. B., 162
Hoyer, W. D., 153
Huang, M-H., 14
Hubbert, A. R., 79, 82, 245
Huber, F., 160
Hudson, H., 372
Hui, M. K., 301, 409, 410
Hulland, J., 104
Hult, G. T. M., 79
"Human Cloud", 18
Human factors design, 299
Human factors research, 299
Human resource
  management benefits of relationship
    marketing, 154
  strategies for delivering service
    quality through people, 329
Humorous advertisements, 430
Humphrey, R. H., 327
Hunt, S. D., 147, 453
Hu, T. L., 160
Hutt, M. D., 159
Hyatt Hotels, 164, 482
Iacobucci, D., 19, 79, 81, 205, 207, 283,
  322, 351, 409

IBM, 13, 37, 199
IBM Global Services, 78, 232
IBM's Smarter Planet, 226
Idea generation, 233–234

IDEO, 130, 235
IKEA, 38, 350, 360
Image search, 435
Implicit service promises, 64
Importance/performance matrices, 136
Incompleteness, 220
Incorporeal existence, 421
Indexes, for customer satisfaction, 83–85
India
    customer research in, 135
    largest retailer, 300
Individual behaviors, 295–296
Individual customer, 449
Information and technology drive yield
        management systems, 402, 403
Inks, L. W., 359
Innovation, in service, 226
    blueprinting, 238–248
    challenges, 220–221
    considerations for, 221–225
    customer and employee involvement,
        221–222
    and customer roles, 227
    front-end planning, 231–235
    globally, 222–223
    implementation, 235–238
    through interconnected products,
        228–229
    at Mayo Clinic, 236–137
    PetSmart, 218–220
    service design, 222–225
    service offering innovation, 226
    through service solutions, 227–228
    stages in, 229
    strategic growth through, 232
    types, 225–229
Intangibility, 6, 20–21
Integrated marketing communication
        (IMC), 417, 421
Integrated service marketing
        communications (ISMC), 421
    address service intangibility, 424–430
    categories of strategies to match
            service promises with delivery,
            424–442
    communication challenges, 421–424
    coordination in marketing
            communication, 419–421
    cross-channel integrated service
            marketing campaigns, 417–418
    manage service promises, 430–435
Intensive care units (ICUs), 355
Interactional fairness, 193, 197–199
Interactive imagery, 425
Interactive marketing, 44, 321, 419
Interclient conflict, 327–328
Intermediaries, 41
Intermediate customers, 138
Internal branding, 439
Internal communication, 423

Internal customers, 139
Internal exchange, 362
Internal marketing communication, 322,
        423–424, 439–442
Internal responses, 298
Internal service quality, measuring, 337
International Retailer Puts Customers in
        Wish Mode, 38
Internet, 363
    internet-reliant services, 349
    service, 17
    technology, 285
Internet expert Mary Meeker
        predicts, 435
Internet of Things (IOT), 15, 17, 228
Interpersonal services, 288
Intimacy, customer, 163
Intuit Corporation, 155
Inventory capability, 384–386
iPrint, 376
Irates, 187
Iron tier, 158
Irving, P. G., 161
Iseke, A., 322
Ittner, C., 478, 479
Ittner, C. D., 489

Jansen, B., 447
Jap, S. D., 162
Jargon, J., 232
Jarman, M., 218–219
Jarvis, C. B., 351, 358
J. D. Power and Associates, 70, 151,
        168, 178
Jenkins, R. L., 53
JetBlue Airways, 178–179
John Deere, 15, 199
Johne, A., 221
John Robert's Spa, 272
Johnson, 80, 82
Johnson, D. W., 358
Johnson, E. M., 234
Johnson, L. W., 152
Johnson, M. D., 83, 146, 148, 160, 221
Johnson, R. T., 358
Johnson Smith & Knisely, 11
Jones, Allan, 493
Jones, M. A., 160
Jones, T., 340
Jones, T. O., 12, 322
Jones, W. H., 64
Joseph, A., 294
J. W. Marriott Hotels, 281

Kahn, B. E., 301, 404
Kaiser, S., 191
Kallenberg, R., 9
Kalra, A., 487
Kaltcheva, V., 299
Kamakura, W. A., 322

Kannan, P. K., 349
Kaplan, A. M., 170
Karmarkar, U., 18
Karni, E., 23
Katzenbach, J. R., 340
Katz, K. L., 404
Keaveney, S. M., 180, 207, 208
Keeffe, D. A., 167
Keh, H. T., 22, 162
Keiningham, T., 69, 474, 475, 478, 479, 484
Keiningham, T. L., 83, 86, 475
Kelleher, H., 28
Keller, K. L., 321
Kelley, S. W., 359, 370
Kennedy, K. N., 317
Kentucky Fried Chicken (KFC), 232
Khermouch, G., 130
Khurana, A., 229, 230
Kieliszewski, C. A., 317
Kimes, S. E., 103, 399, 400, 402,
        403, 409
Kim, J. J., 161
Kingman-Brundage, J., 239
Kirn, S. P., 322
Kleinaltenkamp, M., 244
Kleiner Perkins Caufield & Byers
        (KPCB), 435
Kleine, S. S., 351
Klein, N. M., 66, 198, 207
Knasko, S. C., 301
Knisely, G., 11, 146
Knoop, C., 267, 317, 319
Knowledge-intensive business services
        (KIBS), 356
Knox, G., 184
Kodak, 10
Koepp, S., 139
Kohli, A. K, 227
Koh, Y., 305
Kollias, P., 335
Kooge, E., 133
Kordupleski, R. E., 480
Kornfeld, L., 183
Koschate, N., 153
Kotler, P., 321
Kowitt, B., 34
Krishnan, M. S., 12, 85
Krishnan, V. V., 9, 227, 233, 353
Kristensson, P., 132, 221
Kroger, 392
Kumar, P., 79
Kumar, V., 156, 482, 484
Kum, D., 206
Kunst, P., 244
Kuo, Y. F., 160
Kuusela, H., 349

Labich, K., 28
Labor, 387
Lacey, R., 162

Perceived service. *See also* Customer(s)
alternatives, 61
quality, 79
Perceived value, 458–459, 460–461
Perceptions, 79–80, 82–83
Perfect Order Metric, 262
Perishability, 22–23
Perot Systems, 9
"Personal banker", 91
Personal consumer services, offshoring of, 54, 55
Personality differences, 299
Personal needs, 57–58
Personal selling, 434
Personal service philosophy, 59–60
Personal situational factors, 61–62
Personas, 225
Person/role conflict, 325
Peterson, J. A., 104, 482, 484
"Pet parents", 13
PetSmart, 9, 13, 218–220
Petzinger, T., Jr., 391
Pew Charitable Trusts, 368
Pew Internet, 368
Pew organization, 15
Phang, C., 428
"Photo printing" service, 353
"Physical container", 296
Physical evidence, 26, 28, 40, 283–287.
See also Servicescapes
affecting customer experience, 284–287
assessing and identifying opportunities, 306–307
blueprint, 306
guidelines for strategy, 304
strategic impact of, 305–306
strategic roles of servicescape, 306
updating and modernizing evidence, 307
work cross-functionally, 307
Physical representation, 426
Physical work environment, fashioning, 327
Pick, D., 161
Pieters, R., 181
Pillsbury, 11
Pine, B. J., 286
"Ping-ponging", 188
Pizza Hut, 205
Pizzi, G., 81
Place differentials, 464
Place orientation, 372
Plant, R., 14
Platinum tier, 157
Poka yokes, 202
Porter, M. E., 15, 228
Positive behavioral intentions, 121
Positive emotions, 81

Postintroduction evaluation, 238
Posttransaction surveys, 128–129
Powder Valley (PV), 398
Prahalad, C. K., 351, 353
Pranter, C. A., 354, 374
Pratt, G., 299
Predictable cycles, 389
Predicted service, 62–63
Prestige pricing, 465
Price, 25
bundling, 467
framing, 467
information collection, 449–450
per unit, 454
premium, 482
signaling, 456
visibility, 450–451
Price, L., 80
Price, L. L., 81, 83, 152, 228, 296
PricewaterhouseCoopers, 9
Pricing of services
airlines, 446–447
approaches to, 453–461
competition-based pricing, 455–456
complementary pricing, 467–468
cost-based pricing, 453–455
customer knowledge of, 448–451
demand-based pricing, 456–461
differences between customer evaluation of pricing services and goods, 447
different for customers, 448
discounting, 463
marketing price structures and challenges, 454
market segmentation pricing, 466
nonmonetary costs, 451–453
odd pricing, 463
penetration pricing, 464
prestige pricing, 465
price as indicator of service quality, 453
price bundling, 467
price framing, 467
priceless, 457
pricing around world, 457
pricing for customer-perceived value with modular service pricing and service tiering, 462
pricing strategies, 461–469
results-based pricing, 468–469
skimming pricing, 465
synchro-pricing, 463–464
tipping, 457
tipping by country, 457
value, 463–469
value pricing, 465–466
variability in airlines, 456
Priluck, R., 184, 207

ProAdvisor program, 155
Procedural fairness, 193, 195–197
Process, 26
checkpoint evaluations, 130
reengineering, 338
service delivery, 28
Procter & Gamble, 9, 10, 11, 232
Product, 25
Productive resources, customers as, 356–358
Product packages, 289
Profitability, 476, 488
customer satisfaction, service quality, and firm performance, 478–479
direct relationship between service and profits, 477
key drivers of, 488–494
nonfinancial performance measurements, 489–494
Profitability tiers, 157–159
customer pyramid, 157–158
customer's view of, 158
making business decisions using, 158–159
Profit impact of marketing strategy (PIMS), 480
Promotion, 25
Prospero, M. A., 140
Provider gap, 36–45
communication gap, 44–45
listening gap, 36–37
service design and standards gap, 37, 39–40
service performance gap, 40–41, 44
Providers, 449
Psychic rewards, 362
Psychological costs, 452
Public relations, 434
Puget Sound Energy (PSE), 259
Pugh, S. D., 317, 327, 332
Pulido, A., 114
Pullman, M., 409
Pullman, M. E., 399

Qualitative research, 116–117
Quality/productivity trade-offs, 328
Quality products, 485
Quantitative research, 116–117
Quantitative techniques, 124–125
Quantity differentials, 464
Quan, X., 294
Queue configuration, 406
Queue discipline, 408
Quinn, J. B., 4
Quinn, R. T., 322

Raajpoot, N., 89, 267
Rabinovich, E., 223, 224

Radio frequency identification technology (RFID technology), 258
Rafaeli, A., 289, 325
Raghunathan, R., 69
Ramaswamy, V., 351, 353
Ramirez, R., 360
Ranasinghe, K., 428
Random demand fluctuations, 389–390
Rapoport, A., 298
Ravid, S., 325
Rayport, J. F., 234
Real-time marketing, 321
Real-time pricing. *See* Dynamic pricing
Recreational Equipment Inc (REI), 298–299
Recruiting and hiring, 329–334
Reference price, 448
Referral intentions, 487
Referral values, 482
Rego, L. L., 477, 478, 479, 484
Reichheld, F., 157, 481, 483, 484
Reichheld, F. F., 86, 144, 153, 156, 200
Reinartz, W., 9
Reinartz, W. J., 156, 228
Reinders, M. J., 365
Relationship marketing/management, 36, 146–154. *See also* Customer relationships management
  benefits, 150–154
  bonds, 161–166
  challenges, 166–171
  development strategies, 159–166
  ending business, 170–171
  goal of, 149–150
  value of customers, 154–156
Relationship surveys, 125–128
Reliability, 87, 89–90, 323
Remote encounters, 98
Remote repair service, 306
Remote service, 288, 306
Repurchase intentions, 487
Requirements research, 124–125
Research
  analyzing and interpreting, 132–136
  big data, 133
  complaint solicitation (*See* Complaints)
  cost of, 120
  criteria for effective, 116–121
  customer experiences, 113–114
  customer panels, 131–132
  customer research on web, 122, 123
  in emerging markets, 134, 135
  future expectations, 132
  importance/performance matrices, 136
  lost customer, 132
  market-oriented ethnography, 130–131
  using marketing research information, 137
  mystery shopping, 131

objectives for, 115–116
process checkpoint evaluations, 130
qualitative and quantitative, 116–117
requirements, 124–125
service expectation meetings and reviews, 129
statistical validity, 120
using surveys, 125–129
upward communication, 137–141
Research and development (R&D), 220
Reservation process, 407–410
  differentiate waiting customers, 408
  waiting more pleasurable, 408–410
Resource capacity, 362
Responsiveness, 87, 90, 323
Results-based pricing, 468–469
Return on assets (ROA), 477, 478
Return on marketing, 490–491
Return on quality, 491
Return on sales, 477
Revenue management. *See* Yield management
Revenue per available room per day (RevPAR), 482
Revenue(s), 474
  revenue-producing services, 13
Reverse auctions, 460
Reward customers for contributions, 373
Reward systems, 339
Reynolds, K. E., 160
Reynolds, K. L., 167, 170, 372
Reynoso, J., 337
Rhoads, G. K., 325
Rifkin, G., 432
Rigby, D., 233
Ritz-Carlton, 189, 199, 281–282, 374, 375, 482
Robot-powered yogurt kiosks, 493
Rock, Granite, 264–265
Rodie, A. R., 351
Roggeveen, A. L., 206
Roland, 477
Roland T., 14
Roos, I., 208
Rosario, A. B., 64
Roschk, H., 191
Rosenbaum, M. S., 154, 163, 296, 297, 303, 355
Rosenblum, D., 159
Rosenthal, S. R., 229, 230
Rose, R. L., 477
Rossi, C. A. V., 184
Rossiter, J., 295
Roth, A. V., 220
Roundtree, R. I., 17, 91, 102, 353, 357, 364
Rucci, A., 322
Russell-Bennett, R., 167
Russell, J. A., 295, 299

Russia, customer research in, 134, 135
Rust, R., 477, 478, 479, 490, 491
Rust, R. T., 11, 14, 68, 69, 79, 87, 157, 475, 476, 477, 480

Saarijari, H., 349
Sabol, B., 149
Saegert S., 287
Sagan, M., 208
Salas, J., 9, 228, 233
Sales per employee, 477
Sales promotion, 434
Salge, T., 372
Salopek, J. J., 334
Saltz, J., 322
Salvendy, G., 299
Sanchanta, M., 305
Sanden, B., 221
Sanders, M. S., 299
Sandvik, K., 163
San Francisco JAZZ center (SFJAZZ center), 291
Santamaria, J. A., 340
Santana, K., 450
Sarvary, M., 428
Sasser, E., 481
Sasser, E. W., Jr., 317
Sasser, W. E., Jr., 12, 85, 153, 156, 184, 322, 487
Satisfiers, 68
Sauter, M. B., 2
"Save Power Days", 371
Sawhney, M., 9, 227, 233, 353
Sawhney, R., 183
Schaefers, T., 355
Schechter, D., 330
Schefter, P., 156
Schepers, J. J. L., 335
Scheuing, E. E., 234, 240, 304
Schirr, G., 221
Schlesinger, L. A., 12, 85, 156, 317, 322, 487
Schlesinger, L. L., 322
Schmitt, B. H., 286
Schneider, B., 82, 221, 317, 322, 330, 351, 370
Schneider, J., 224
Schoefer, K., 365
Schons, L. M., 370
Schorr, James L., 146
Schulz, Howard, 338
Schwab, Charles, 366
Scott, L., 159
Scott, M. L., 358
Screeners of stimuli, 300
Seaney, R., 447
Search costs, 451–452
Search qualities, 23–24
Seasonality, 388

Sehorn, A. Garcia, 245
Seiders, K., 169, 170
Self-service environment, 287
Self-service innovations, 226
Self-service technologies (SSTs), 363–365
  customer usage, 364–365
  proliferation, 363–364
  success with, 365
"Self-serving bias", 361
Selnes, F., 146, 148, 160, 163
Seltman, K. D., 303, 331, 432
Sensors track drug, 229
Seo, H., 294
Sequencing service, 224
Serbin, J., 86
Sergeant, A., 337
Service attribute guarantees, 203
Service blueprinting, 238–248
  building, 244–248
  components, 239–240
  examples, 240–242
  reading and using, 243–244
  self-service, 242–243
  service encounter sequence, 267,
    268, 270
Service branding, 431–432
Service cocreation
  client cocreation of value in Business-
    to-Business services, 356, 357
  customer cocreation of value, 352, 353
  customer participates in delivery
    process, 351
  customers in, 351–356
  fellow customers, 354–355, 356
  levels, characteristics, and examples of
    customer participation, 354
Service competencies, 330–331
Service concept, 305–306
  development and evaluation, 234
Service culture, 13, 316–319. *See also*
    Culture
  company's service culture travelling,
    318, 319
  developing, 317, 318
  exhibiting service leadership, 317
  transporting, 318, 319
Service delivery
  customer-oriented, 340–342
  process, 28
Service design, 37, 39–40
Service development
  and design, 39
  implementation, 235–238
  process, 229–231
Service employees
  boundary-spanning roles, 323–328
  in communication, 427
  in company's vision, 338–339
  critical role of, 320
  critical roles of boundary spanners, 324

developing people to delivering
    service quality, 334
developing service-oriented internal
    processes, 338
emotional labor, 324–325
effect of employee behaviors on
    service quality dimensions, 323
employee satisfaction, customer
    satisfaction, and profits, 322–323
empowerment, 335
job satisfaction, 335
measuring internal service quality, 337
measuring rewarding, 339–340
providing supportive technology and
    equipment, 337–338
quality/productivity trade-offs, 328
recruiting and hiring, 329–334
retention of, 338–340
service marketing triangle, 321–322
sources of conflict, 325–328
strategies for delivering service
    quality through people, 328–340
support systems, 337–338
teamwork, 335–337
training for technical and interactive
    skills, 334–335
treating as customers, 339
Service encounters
  customer satisfaction, 94–95
  explanation of, 93–96
  importance of, 96–97
  sequence, 267, 268, 270
  service behaviors, 102
  sources of pleasure and displeasure in,
    98–102
  technology-based service encounters,
    102–104
  types, 98
Service expectations, 52–57. *See also*
    Customer expectations
Service failure. *See also* Service recovery
  customers respond to, 181–187
  impact of, 179–180
  reports of, 200
Service inclination, 330–332
Service industries and companies, 4
Service innovation. *See* Innovation, in
    service
Service intangibility, 421–422, 424–430
  advertisement for Sierra Club
    demonstrates, 426
  BuzzMetric approach, 430
  GEICO gecko is advertising icon, 427
  interactive imagery is demonstrated by
    travelers umbrella, 425
  mobile advertising, 428
  service advertising strategies
    matched with properties of
    intangibility, 429
Service-line extensions, 226

Service marketers, 24, 419
Service marketing, 8–14, 35
  competing strategically through
    service, 13
  deregulated industries and
    professional service needs, 10
  marketing and managing services, 10
  principal of consulting firm, 11
  service-based economies, 8
  service as business imperative in
    goods-focused businesses, 9
  service equals profits, 10–12
  service stinks, 12, 14
  triangle, 321–322
Service marketing mix, 24–27
  expanded mix for services, 26–27
  traditional marketing mix, 25
Service marketing research program, 121
  CIT, 124
  complaint solicitation, 121–124
  customer panels, 131–132
  future expectations research, 132
  lost customer research, 132
  market-oriented ethnography, 130–131
  mystery shopping, 131
  process checkpoint evaluations, 130
  relationship surveys, 125–128
  requirements research, 124–125
  service expectation meetings and
    reviews, 129
  SERVQUAL surveys, 125–128
  trailer calls, 128–129
Service packaging, 289
Service performance
  gap, 40–41, 44, 316
  indexes, 278
Service production, 365
  continuum, 364
  process, 11
Service profit chain, 322
Service promises, 63–64
  address service intangibility, 424–430
  customer education management,.
    437–439
  customer expectations management,
    436–437
  internal marketing communication
    management, 439–442
  management, 422, 430–435
Service prototypes, 225, 235
Service quality, 87, 201, 423, 476, 477,
    478–479, 486
  cultures, 88–89
  customer perceptions of service
    quality and purchase intentions,
    484, 486–488
  dimensions, 87–91, 92
  dimensions, employee behaviors effect
    on, 323
  e-service quality, 91–93

gaps audit, 45, 46–47
  key drivers of, 488–494
  outcome, interaction, and physical
      environment quality, 87
  price as indicator of, 453
Service quality indicator (SQI), 254
Service recovery, 37, 99. *See also* Service
    failure
  and cultures, 196
  effects, 180–181
  fairness, 194–196
  fixing customer, 187–198
  fixing problem, 198–202
  impact of, 179–180
  paradox, 180, 184
  provider gap and, 37
  service guarantees, 202–207
  strategies, 187–202
  switching *vs.* staying following,
      207–208
  United Breaks Guitars, 182–183
Service research program
  appropriate frequency, 120–121
  behavior, 121
  behavioral intentions, 121
  cost of research, 120
  criteria for effective, 116, 117
  measures of loyalty, 121
  measuring priorities, 120
  perceptions and expectations of,
      117–119
  qualitative and quantitative, 116–117
  statistical validity, 120
  value of information, 120
Service(s), 4, 476
  advertising strategies, 429
  behaviors, 102
  businesses, 2–3
  challenges and questions for service
      marketers, 24
  characteristics of, 19–24
  comparing Goods and Services, 20
  contributions of service industries to
      U. S. GDP, 5
  customer, 27, 350
  customer perceptions of service
      quality and purchase intentions,
      484, 486–488
  customer research program for,
      118–119
  customer service, 4–6
  defensive marketing effects of service,
      480–484, 485, 486
  derived service, 4–6
  economic importance, 8
  expectation meetings and reviews, 129
  financial and economic impact of, 474
  globalization, 14, 18
  heterogeneity, 21
  increased demand for, 405

industries, 4–6
  innovation, 9
  intangibility, 20–21
  key drivers of service quality,
      customer retention, and profits,
      488–494
  migration of service jobs, 18
  new delivery methods, 15
  offensive marketing effects of
      service, 480
  organizations, 351
  perishability, 22–23
  as product, 4–6
  as product, 5
  and profitability, 476–479
  search, experience, and credence
      qualities, 23–24
  service-based economies, 8
  service-oriented internal processes
      developing, 338
  service marketing mix, 24–27
  service–profit chain, 12, 481
  simultaneous production and
      consumption, 21–22
  as strategic differentiator, 76
  tangibility spectrum, 6
  and technology, 14–19
  trends in service sector, 6
  value, customers as creators and
      cocreators of, 349–350
  variability limiting knowledge,
      448–449
  version, 466
  wallet allocation rule, 475
Servicescapes, 38, 40, 281–307
  behaviors in, 293–296
  complexity, 288–289
  design decisions, 307
  differentiator, 292
  environmental dimensions of,
      300–304
  facilitator, 289, 291–292
  framework for understanding, 293
  internal responses to, 298–300
  Marriott International Inc., 281–282
  Mayo Clinic hospital, 302, 303
  McDonald's adaptation, 304, 305
  package, 289
  socializer, 292
  strategic positioning through
      architectural design, 290, 291
  strategic roles of, 306
  third places, 297
  types of, 287
  underlying framework, 293
  usage, 287–288
  virtual, 284, 285
  and well-being in health care, 294
Service science, management and
    engineering (SSME), 223

Service sector, trends in, 6
Service standards. *See* Customer-defined
    service standards
Service stinks, 12, 14
Service tiering, 462
Service triangle, 321–322
SERVQUAL surveys, 125–128, 276
Sexual orientation on consumers, 303
Shamir, B., 325
Shankar, V., 226, 428
Shankman, P., 316
Share of wallet, 474, 485
Sharpe, M. E., 6
Sharp, L. K., 370
Shaw-Ching Liu, B., 89
Shepherd, C. D., 79
Sherry, J. F., Jr., 283, 296
Sheth, J., 181
Sheth, J. N., 146
Shih, E., 358
Shin, J., 171
Short-term effects, 294
Shostack, G. L., 98, 220, 234, 236, 238,
    256, 360
Shostack, L. G., 6
Shrinkage, 405
Shugan, S. M., 400
Shute, N., 406
Shutterfly, Inc, 353
Siebel, Tom, 339
Siemanski, B., 477
Siemens, 13
Signs, symbols, and artifacts, 300, 302–304
Sincronizacion Dinamica de
    Operaciones, 391
Singapore Airlines, 26, 278
Singer, M., 114
Singh, J., 149, 181, 186, 325
Sin, H. P., 167
Siomkos, G., 298
Siredeshmukh, D., 149
Sirianni, N. J., 321
Situational factors, 61–62
Sivakumar, K., 97, 370
Skålén, P., 205
Skimming pricing, 465
Skinner, S. J., 359, 370
"Smart service". *See* Remote service
Smart Service systems, 223
Smith-Daniels, V., 223, 224
Smith, A. K., 180, 181, 184, 186, 195
Smith, J., 125
Smith, K. A., 358
Smith, M., 428
Smith, R., 371
Smith, T., 160
Snodgrass, J., 299
Snyder, J., 406
Social benefits of relationship
    marketing, 152

Social bonds, 162–163
Social interactions, 296
Socializer, 292
Social media, 186, 187
Soft customer-defined standards, 263, 268
Soft measurements, 276
Soft standards
  for Ford Motor Company, 269
  for speed of complaint handling, 274
Solomon, M., 201, 260
Solomon, M. R., 289, 409
Soman, D., 407
Sotgiu, F., 64
Southwest Airlines, 13, 26, 28,
  320, 417
Spangenberg, E. R., 301
Spanjol, J., 370
Spann, M., 428
Sparks, B., 191
Sparks, B. A., 190
Spatial layout and functionality, 300, 301
Special treatment benefits of relationship
  marketing, 153
Spirit Airlines and Delta, 418
Spohrer, J. C., 317
Spontaneity, 99
Sprint/Nextel, 168
Srivastava, S., 169
Staelin, R., 487
Stahl, H. K., 156
Standardization, 256–257
Standard script, 296
Standards gap, 37, 39–40
Stanley, B., 291
Starbucks, 289, 292
State-of-the-art imaging system, 70
Stauffer, D., 342
Stebbins, S., 2
Steiner, D. D., 325
Steinmatz, K., 15
Stellin, S., 167
Stengle, J., 265, 406
Stephen, A., 428
Stephens, N., 185
Stevens, A., 455
Stewart, D. M., 202
Stewart, P., 289, 321
Stickdorn, M. 224
Stimulus–organism–response theory, 293
Stokols, D., 287
Stone, G., 296
Storey, V. C., 133
Story, C., 221
Streukens, S., 199
Strong, C., 428
Structural bonds, 163–166
Stuart, I., 229
Subjectivity, 221
Subramanian, B., 477
Sudharshan, D., 89

Sudhir, K., 171
Sulek, J., 409
Sulek, J. M., 301
Sullivan, M., 487
Sundstrom, E., 287
Surachartkumtonkun, J., 186
Surface acting, 326
Surprenant, C. F., 364, 409
Swanson, S. R., 208
Swartz, T., 205
Swartz, T. A., 79, 82, 220, 283, 289, 322,
  337, 351, 409
Sweden's IKEA, 360, 361
Swedish Customer Satisfaction Barometer
  (SCSB), 487, 494
Sweeney, J. C., 53, 297, 358
Swiss Index of Customer Satisfaction
  (SWICS), 83
Switching
  barriers, 160–161
  costs, 160–161
  service recovery, 207–208
Symbolic meaning, 302
Symbols, 300, 302–304
Symphony-goers, 352
Synchronize demand and capacity, 41
Synchro-pricing, 463–464
Szymanski, D. M., 220

Tähtinen, J., 170
Tang, C., 370
Tangibility spectrum, 6
Tangibles, 87, 91
Tarsi, C. O., 159
Tatikonda, M. V., 229
Tax, S. S., 154, 180, 181, 193, 194,
  201, 220
Taylor, S., 404, 409
Taylor, S. F., 161, 207, 340, 410
Teamwork, 335–337
Teas, R. K., 53
TechCo's clients, 356
Technology
  changing face of customer service,
    16, 17
  enabling both customers and
    employees, 16
  extending Global Reach of Services,
    16–17
  facilitates customer participation in
    health care, 368, 369
  internet, service, 17
  migration of service jobs, 18
  for one-time fixes, 263–265
  paradoxes and dark side of technology
    and service, 19
  service and, 14–19
  technology-based service offerings,
    14–15
  ways to delivering service, 15

Technology-based service encounters,
  102–104
Technology-mediated encounters, 98
TeleCheck International, 156
Tellis, G. J., 229, 230, 468
Templin, N., 403
Temporary mood states, 300
Tetreault, M. S., 99, 180
Thakor, M. V., 409
Thomas, R. J., 234
Thomke, S., 222
Thompson, G., 399
Thompson, V. B., 322
Thorpe, D. I., 79
Thorsten Hennig-Thurau, 489
"Tide Spin", 9
Tierney, P., 296
Time, 387
Time capacity, 362
Time costs, 451
Time differentials, 464
"Tip of iceberg", 180, 200
Tipping, 457
Titus P. A., 301
Tobin's q., 478
Toman, N., 69, 93
Tombs, A., 296, 297
Tomlinson, D., 159
Tong, V. T. -U., 160, 162, 202
Top-box scores, customer satisfaction, 487
Totzek, D., 157
Touchpoints, 225
Toyota, 488–489
Trader Joe, 189
  Service Quality at, 33–34
Traditional marketing mix, 25
Trailer calls, 128–129, 274
Transactional marketing, 36
Transaction perceptions, 79–80
Transportation Security Administration
  (TSA), 406
Travel agent's office decor, 298
Travelers Companies, 425
Tripp, T. M., 198
Trusov, M., 64
Trust, 362
Tse, D. K., 162, 410
Tsiros, M., 79
Tuli, K. R., 227
Turner Parish, J., 146, 152, 162
Twitter, 264, 265, 463
Two-Buck Chuck, 33
Two-part pricing, 468

Uber, 3
Ulaga, W., 9, 163, 228
Ulrich, D., 317
Ulrich, R. S., 294
"Ultimate Guide", 446
Ulwick, A. W., 227

Unconditional satisfaction guarantees, 203
Uncontrollable situational factors, 61
United Airlines, 182
United Breaks Guitars, 182–183
United Services Automobile Association (USAA), 70, 144–145
Universal design standards and principles, 299
University of Michigan American Customer Satisfaction Index (ACSI), 12
Unnikrishnan, M., 28
Unrealistic customer expectations, 66–68
Upah, G. D., 124, 360
Update and modernize evidence, 307
UPS's experience, 318, 330, 332–333
Upward communication, 36, 137–141, 441
    benefits of, 140–141
    at Cabela's, 140
    elements in effective program of, 138
    objectives for, 137
    research for, 138–140
Upward communication, 36, 46, 137–141, 441
User-centered service, 224
U.S. utility companies, 371
Uttal, B., 70

Vail Resorts, 121–122
Valentini, S., 180
Value, 34, 463
    complementary pricing, 467–468
    "creation spheres", 363
    "creators", 350
    of customers, 154–156
    customers receive, 352
    discounting, 463
    intuit customer, 155
    lifetime, 154
    market segmentation pricing, 466
    odd pricing, 463
    penetration pricing, 464
    prestige pricing, 465
    price bundling, 467
    price framing, 467
    pricing, 465–466
    results-based pricing, 468–469
    skimming pricing, 465
    synchro-pricing, 463–464
    value-added services, 13
    value-in-use, 349
    value pricing, 465–466
Value cocreators, 350
van Birgelen, M. J. H., 323, 331
van der Heijden, G. A. H., 335
van Doorne, J., 358
van Doorn, J., 104
van Kasteren, Y. V., 358
van Oest, R., 184
Van Rensburg, L. R. J., 207

van Riel, A. C. R., 323, 331
Van Vaerenbergh, Y., 82
Vargo, S. L., 2, 6, 20, 351, 353, 358
Vashistha, A., 18
Vavra, T., 69
Verhoef, 81, 97
Verhoef, P., 133
Vermeir, I., 82
Vertical communications, 439
Vietor, R. H. K., 10
Viral marketing. *See* Buzz marketing
Virgin Atlantic Airways, 433
"Virtual nurse—patient advocate", 493
Virtual Servicescapes, 283, 284, 285
Virzi, A. M., 331
Visualization, 426
Vivid information, 425
Voicers, 187
Voice search, 435
Voima, P., 349, 351, 353, 363
Volume of purchases, 482
Voorhees, C. M., 180, 181, 183, 297, 410
Voss, C., 223
Voss, C. A., 220, 223, 225
Voss, G. B., 301, 404
Voyer, P. A., 422
VWR International, 233

Wachovia, 456
Waiting line strategies, 404–410
    ED, 405–406
    employ operational logic, 404, 406–407
    reservation process, 407–410
Wakefield, K. L., 301
Waldorf-Astoria, 150
Walker, B. A., 159, 296, 297
Walk, N., 133
Wall, E. A., 294
"Wallet allocation rule", 475
Wall Street Journal, 55
Walmart, 392
Walsh, G., 186
Walt Disney, 138, 257–258
Walton, Sam, 139
Wang, C., 365
Wangenheim, F., 403
Wang, S., 99, 198, 340
Wang, Y., 208
Ward, J., 296, 297
Ward, J. C., 186, 298, 303
Ward, L. M., 299
Watson-Manheim, M. B., 370
Watson, J. L., 305
Webber, A. E., 146
WebMD, 368
Webster, C., 69
Webster, F. E., Jr., 146
Weed, J., 171
Weight Watchers

educates and orients new members, 372
    in-person program, 371
Weil, Virginia, 134
Wei, M., 361
Weinstein, J., 263
Weitz, B. A., 299
Wells Fargo Bank, 231
Wells, M., 477
Wernerfelt, B., 480
Weyerhaeuser, 441
White, L., 160
Wiertz, C., 271
Wiertz, Caroline, 489
Wieseke, J., 370
"Wilderness Servicescape", 296
Wiles, M. A., 86
Wilkinson, I. F., 220
Willcocks, L. P., 14
Williams, L., 475
Wilmet, J., 81
Wilson-Pessano, S., 124
Wilson M., 289
Windhorst, C., 297
Wing Zone, 327
Winkel, G. H., 287
Wirtz, J., 167, 206, 207, 301, 325, 384, 403
Wisconsin, 494
Wish Mode, International Retailer Puts Customers in, 38
Witell, L., 9, 221, 228
Witsil, F., 371
Wittkowski, K., 355, 361
Woellert, W., 449
Wolfinbarger, M., 91
Woodruff, R. B., 53
Woodside, A., 181
Woodside, A. G., 97
Woods, Rodney, 11
Word-of-mouth (WOM), 43
    communication, 64, 66, 482
    CRV, 484
    and customer measurement, 483–484
Word-of-mouth communication, 35, 43, 54, 64–66, 153–154, 180, 186, 191, 198, 205, 427, 429–430, 432, 482–484
World Intellectual Property Organization (WIPO), 222
Wright, P., 317
Wright, T., 418
Wu, S., 208
Wu, T., 447

Xerox, 9, 228, 430, 484, 486
Xerox Corporation, 86
Xiao, Y., 370
Xue, M., 358

Yadav, M. S., 184, 207
Yahoo!, 330, 468
Yalcin, A., 86
Yanamandram, V., 160
Yang, S. C., 160
Yap, K. B., 53
Yeon, H., 114
Yield management, 398–404
    challenges and risks in, 402, 403, 404
    implementation, 400, 402
    information and technology drive
        yield management systems,
        402, 403
    simple yield calculations, 401
Yim, C. K., 162, 358
Yoo, C., 301
Yoon, D. H., 171

Young, R. F., 351
Young, S., 322
YouTube, 182, 187, 193, 429, 430
Yu, E., 373

Zablah, A., 322
Zahorik, A., 477, 478, 479
Zahorik, A. J., 475, 480
Zaltman Metaphor Elicitation Technique
    (ZMET), 117
Zaltman, Olson, 117
Zammit, A., 81
Zane, Chris, 76–78
Zanes Cycles, 13, 76, 168–169
Zappos, 13
Zappos.com, 257, 261, 264, 265, 266
Zeelenberg, M., 181

Zeithaml, V., 153, 477, 479, 490, 491
Zeithaml, V. A., 9, 19, 20, 35, 43, 51, 57,
    59, 66, 67, 70, 79, 87, 89, 91, 117,
    124, 128, 141, 157, 202, 228, 229,
    233, 439, 440, 453, 458, 485, 487
Zheng, F., 428
Zhou, R., 407
Zhu, X., 294
Zimring, C. M., 294
Zinkhan, G., 80
Zomerdijk, L. G., 225
Zone of tolerance, 54–57
Zook, C., 233
Zou, S., 370
Zubcsek, P., 428
Zuckerberg, Mark, 224–225